# The Closing of the
# Western Mind

# The Closing of the Western Mind

*The Rise of Faith and the Fall of Reason*

## CHARLES FREEMAN

ALFRED A. KNOPF

NEW YORK

2003

Library of Congress Cataloging-in-Publication Data
Freeman, Charles, [date]
The closing of the Western mind : the rise of faith and the fall of reason / Charles
Freeman.— 1st American ed.
p.  cm.
Includes bibliographical references and index.
ISBN 1-4000-4085-X

1. Civilization, Western.  2. Christianity—Influence.  3. Church and state—
Europe—History.  4. Church history—Primitive and early church, ca. 30–600.
5. Church history—Middle Ages, 600–1500.  6. Civilization, Western—Classical
influences.  7. Hellenism.  8. Europe—History—To 476.  9. Europe—
History—476–1492.  10. Europe—Intellectual life.  I. Title.

CB245.F73 2003
940.1'2—dc21      2002044821

Manufactured in the United States of America
First American Edition

For Hilary

Blessed is he who learns how to engage in inquiry, with no impulse to harm his countrymen or to pursue wrongful actions, but perceives the order of immortal and ageless nature, how it is structured.

EURIPIDES, FRAGMENT FROM
AN UNNAMED PLAY, FIFTH CENTURY B.C.

There is another form of temptation, even more fraught with danger. This is the disease of curiosity . . . It is this which drives us to try and discover the secrets of nature, those secrets which are beyond our understanding, which can avail us nothing and which man should not wish to learn.

AUGUSTINE,
LATE FOURTH/EARLY FIFTH CENTURY A.D.

# Contents

# Contents

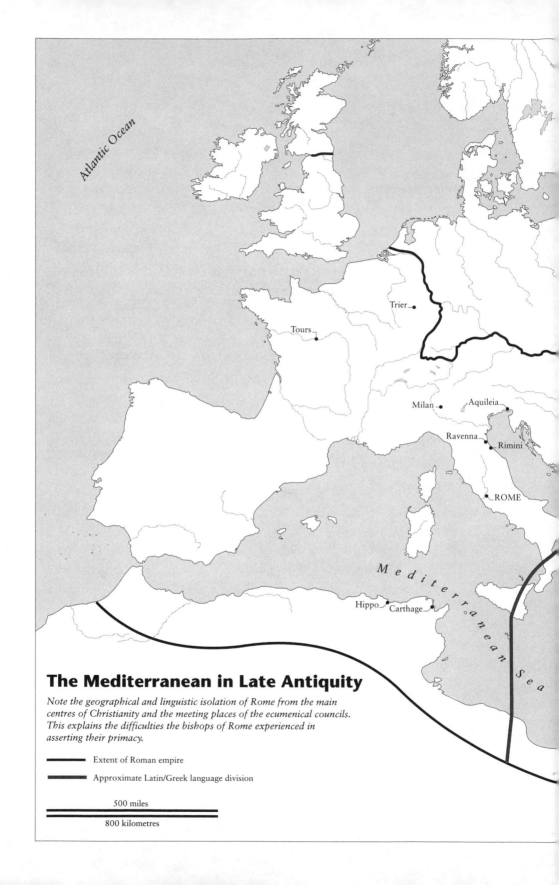

Atlantic Ocean

Trier

Tours

Milan · Aquileia

Ravenna · Rimini

ROME

Mediterranean Sea

Hippo · Carthage

# The Mediterranean in Late Antiquity

*Note the geographical and linguistic isolation of Rome from the main centres of Christianity and the meeting places of the ecumenical councils. This explains the difficulties the bishops of Rome experienced in asserting their primacy.*

——— Extent of Roman empire

━━━ Approximate Latin/Greek language division

500 miles

800 kilometres

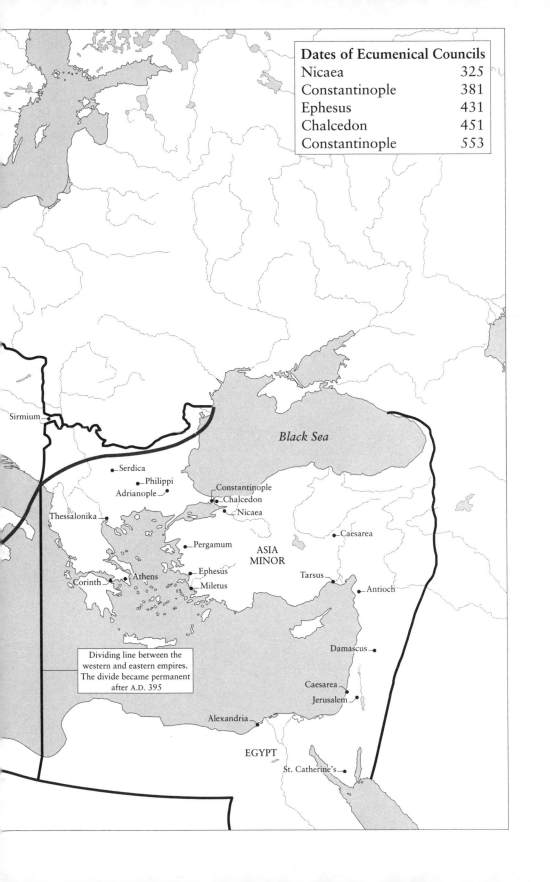

| Dates of Ecumenical Councils | |
|---|---|
| Nicaea | 325 |
| Constantinople | 381 |
| Ephesus | 431 |
| Chalcedon | 451 |
| Constantinople | 553 |

Sirmium

*Black Sea*

Serdica

Philippi

Adrianople

Constantinople

Chalcedon

Nicaea

Thessalonika

Caesarea

Pergamum

ASIA MINOR

Ephesus

Corinth    Athens

Tarsus

Miletus

Antioch

Dividing line between the
western and eastern empires.
The divide became permanent
after A.D. 395

Damascus

Caesarea

Jerusalem

Alexandria

EGYPT

St. Catherine's

# *Introduction*

This book deals with a significant turning point in western cultural and intellectual history, when the tradition of rational thought established by the Greeks was stifled in the fourth and fifth centuries A.D. This "closing of the Western mind" did not extend to the Arab world, where translated Greek texts continued to inspire advances in astronomy, medicine and science, and so its roots must be found in developments in the Greco-Roman world of late antiquity. This book explores those developments.

Before setting out my argument, it is important to define what is meant by a tradition of rational thought. The Greeks were the first to distinguish, assess and use the distinct branch of intellectual activity we know as reasoning. By the fifth century they had grasped the principle of the deductive proof, which enabled them to make complex and irrefutable mathematical proofs. They also set out the principles of inductive reasoning, the formulation of "truths" from empirical evidence. Aristotle (384–322 B.C.) used this method to make significant advances in our understanding of the natural world. These "truths," however, are always provisional. If the sun rises every day of our existence, we might assume that it will always rise, but there is no certainty of this. The Greeks recognized this as well as grasping that theories must always be the servants of facts. Describing what he has observed about the generation of bees, Aristotle notes that "the facts have not been sufficiently ascertained, and if they are ever ascertained, then we must trust perception rather than theories." Implicit in this is the thinking of cause and effect. By the fifth century we find the historian Herodotus attempting to relate what he could observe about the Nile floods with their possible causes, and this approach became rooted in the rational tradition. It was the path to a fuller understanding of the natural world and offered the possibility of effective prediction. Yet one should not idealize. In practice it is impossible to disassociate observation from the influences of the wider world. Women were seen by Greek culture to be inferior to men, and "empirical" observations could all too easily be shaped or interpreted to sustain this, as they certainly were in medicine. The astronomer Ptolemy believed the earth was at the centre of the universe, and all his observations of the planets were interpreted so as not to conflict with this model.

A successful rational tradition needs the support and understanding of the society in which it is based, and in many parts of the Greek world, this is what it received. If truth is to be effectively advanced, any finding must be open to challenge, and this means that even the greatest thinkers must never be made into figures of authority. Aristotle's colleague Theophrastus successfully queried instances of what Aristotle claimed was spontaneous generation by noticing tiny seeds Aristotle had missed. If a tradition of rational thought is to make progress, it is essential that it builds in tolerance. No authority can dictate in advance what can or cannot be believed, or there is no possibility of progress. From the philosophical point of view, it is perhaps as important that it accept the limits of what it can achieve, in those areas of knowledge where there are no basic axioms (as there are in a mathematical model, for instance) or empirical evidence from which rational thought can progress. E. R. Dodds, in his famous study *The Greeks and the Irrational,* notes that "honest distinction between what is knowable and what is not appears again and again in fifth-century [B.C.] thought, and is surely one of its chief glories." In short, one cannot pronounce that a statement is true unless it can be supported by logic or empirical evidence. It followed that nothing of certainty could be said, for instance, about the gods. The problem is too complex and life is too short proclaimed the philosopher Protagoras in the fifth century. Despite these words of caution, Dodds' work reminds us that irrationality flourished in the Greek world; but perhaps one can put up with 999 irrational minds if the thousandth is an Aristotle or an Archimedes (or a Copernicus or a Newton, or, in inductive logic, a Darwin). It takes only one independent and effective rational mind to change the paradigms of understanding for the rest of humankind.

The conventional wisdom is that Greek science and mathematics petered out in the Hellenistic period (323–31 B.C.), but recently scholars have shown greater appreciation of the achievements of such leading figures of the second century A.D. as Galen and Ptolemy. Galen's work on logic is being recognized so that, in the accolade of Geoffrey Lloyd, "Galen is probably unique among practising physicians in any age and culture for his professionalism also as a logician . . . conversely he is also remarkable among practising logicians for his ability in, and experience of, medical practice." The ingenuity of Ptolemy's astronomical calculations (forced on him as they were by his misconception of the universe!) was extraordinary, but one is reminded, by a recent new translation of his *Geography*, that he also tackled the problem of how to represent the globe on a flat surface, introduced "minutes" and "seconds" to divide up degrees and established the notion of grids of coordinates for mapping. So even in the Roman empire we are dealing with a living tradition which is making important and influential scientific advances.

There was an alternative approach to rational thought, that taken by Plato (c. 429–347 B.C.). Plato believed in the reality of a world of Forms, Forms of everything from "the God" to a table, which was eternal and unchanging in contrast to the transient world here below. This world could be grasped, after an arduous intellectual journey of which only a few were capable, by means of reason. So "real" were the Forms that even the observations of the senses must be discarded if they conflicted with a Form as it was eventually discovered. "We shall approach astronomy, as we do geometry, by way of problems, and ignore what is in the sky, if we intend to get a real grasp of astronomy," as Plato put it in *The Republic*. This was, of course, a challenge to the principle that facts should prevail over theories. The problem was that it was impossible to find axioms, unassailable first principles, from which one could progress to a Form such as that of Beauty or "the Good," and the Platonic journey, while offering the lure of an ultimate certainty, never seemed, in practice, to be able to present a Form in terms with which all could agree.

The argument of this book is that the Greek intellectual tradition did not simply lose vigour and disappear. (Its survival and continued progress in the Arab world is testimony to that.) Rather, in the fourth and fifth century A.D. it was destroyed by the political and religious forces which made up the highly authoritarian government of the late

Roman empire. There had been premonitions of this destruction in earlier Christian theology. It had been the Apostle Paul who declared war
on the Greek rational tradition through his attacks on "the wisdom of
the wise" and "the empty logic of the philosophers," words which were
to be quoted and requoted in the centuries to come. Then came the
absorption of Platonism by the early Christian theologians. It was
assumed that Christian dogma could be found through the same process
as Plato had advocated, in other words, through reason, and would have
the same certainty as the Forms. However, as with other aspects of Platonism, it proved impossible to find secure axioms from which to start
the rational argument. Scriptural texts conflicted with each other, different theological traditions had taken root in different parts of the empire,
theologians disagreed whether they should discard pagan Greek philosophy or exploit it. The result, inevitably, was doctrinal confusion. Augustine was to note the existence of over eighty heresies (for which read
"alternative ways of dealing with the fundamental issues of Christian
doctrine"). When Constantine gave toleration to the churches in the
early fourth century, he found to his dismay that Christian communities
were torn by dispute. He himself did not help matters by declaring tax
exemptions for Christian clergy and offering the churches immense
patronage, which meant that getting the "right" version of Christian
doctrine gave access not only to heaven but to vast resources on earth.
By the middle of the fourth century, disputes over doctrine had degenerated into bitterness and even violence as rival bishops struggled to earn
the emperor's favour and the most lucrative bishoprics. At a time of
major barbarian attacks, the threat to order was so marked that it
was the emperors who increasingly defined and enforced an orthodoxy,
using hand-picked church councils to give themselves some theological
legitimacy.

So one finds a combination of factors behind "the closing of the
Western mind": the attack on Greek philosophy by Paul, the adoption of
Platonism by Christian theologians and the enforcement of orthodoxy
by emperors desperate to keep good order. The imposition of orthodoxy
went hand in hand with a stifling of any form of independent reasoning.
By the fifth century, not only has rational thought been suppressed, but
there has been a substitution for it of "mystery, magic and authority," a
substitution which drew heavily on irrational elements of pagan society
that had never been extinguished. Pope Gregory the Great warned those
with a rational turn of mind that, by looking for cause and effect in the

natural world, they were ignoring the cause of all things, the will of God. This was a vital shift of perspective, and in effect a denial of the impressive intellectual advances made by the Greek philosophers.

Some who have found this argument too damning have stressed how it was Christians who preserved the great works of the Greek philosophers by copying them from decaying papyri, or parchment. The historian is indeed deeply indebted to the monks, the Byzantine civil servants and the Arab philosophers who preserved ancient texts, but the recording of earlier authorities is not the same as maintaining a tradition of rational thought. This can be done only if these authorities are then used as inspiration for further intellectual progress or as a bulwark against which to react. This happened in the Arab world (where, for instance, even the findings of a giant such as Galen were challenged and improved on) but not in the Byzantine empire or the Christian west. The Athenian philosopher Proclus made the last recorded astronomical observation in the ancient Greek world in A.D. 475. It was not until the sixteenth century that Copernicus—inspired by the surviving works of Ptolemy but aware that they would make more sense, and in fact would be simpler, if the sun was placed at the centre of the universe—set in hand the renewal of the scientific tradition. The struggle between religion and science had now entered a new phase, one which is beyond the scope of this book. What cannot be doubted is how effectively the rational tradition had been eradicated in the fourth and fifth centuries. The "closing of the Western mind" has been ignored for all too long. I hope this book reinvigorates debate on this turning point in European history.

I have acknowledged the many works I have drawn on for this book in the notes. In addition, my agent, Bill Hamilton, has been a consistent support during the writing of this book, and my editor at Heinemann, Ravi Mirchandani, has played a vital role in helping to set its tone and to clarify its central argument. Josine Meijer gathered the pictures together with great efficiency, and the text was meticulously copy-edited by Caroline Knight. I would also like to thank my editor at Knopf, Carol Janeway, for the enthusiasm with which she has taken on this book for the United States market. For the preparation of this book for the United States market, I am especially grateful to Serena Lehman and Ellen Feldman at Knopf, proofreaders Chuck Antony and Patrice Silverstein and indexer Max Franke.

This book is dedicated to my wife, Hilary, with my love. While I have been dealing with the complex and often stressful relationships between Christianity and pagan society in the fourth and fifth centuries, she, in her work as a psychotherapist, has been dealing with similar tensions in the minds of her clients. So our concerns have often overlapped. A tribute from Helmut Koester to his wife that I came across when reading this distinguished Swiss theologian's work seemed particularly appropriate: "It is therefore fitting that I should express here my indebtedness to her for all the patient and helpful listening to the progress of my work and for her indulgence with respect to all sorts of things around the house that I should have done rather than working on this manuscript." With the closing of this book, such duties can be evaded no longer!

Charles Freeman
April 2003

# Terminology and Sources

This book draws heavily on recent research, particularly in "late antiquity." Much of this is to be found in specialist journals and expensive academic books, and the writing of this book without the help of the Cambridge University Library would have been impossible. Once again I record my thanks to its ever helpful and courteous staff.

I have recorded my sources either in the text or in notes. In addition I have used the notes to recommend further reading and to explore some topics where a digression in the text would have disrupted the flow of argument. So in the section on Alexander (chapter 4) I recommend a recent biography that reflects the state of research (note 3), give references to other sources I have used in the text (notes 4, 5, 6), and then provide a digression on the legacy of Alexander with further sources, both ancient and modern (note 7). The aim is to provide a coherent and readable narrative for the reader, with the notes available as supplementary material.

Finding the right terminology in this area is always difficult. Many of the concepts used in this book, "faith" for instance, shifted with time, and I have used the text and notes to indicate the shifts and explore the difficulties. Some terms need further mention here. The word "pagan" as used nowadays is often one of abuse, associated with witches, hedonistic living and minority spiritual ideas. Even the most cursory knowledge of the wide variety of pagan thought and movements in the Roman empire shows that to use the term in a derogatory sense is inappropriate. The word is used in this book to describe the diverse traditions of spirituality that predated and continued to exist alongside Christianity. They included cult worship of the traditional Greek and Roman gods, mystery religions and highly sophisticated philosophical approaches to the divine. It is obvious that this very variety makes any value judgment about paganism as a whole meaningless, but it is worth saying at this stage that pagans were normally tolerant of each other and that a number of distinct spiritual allegiances could be held by an individual without impropriety. So long as public order was not threatened, an individual could follow his, or in many cases her, spiritual instincts wherever they led.

Studies of early Christianity used to stress the uniformity of Christian belief; they now stress its diversity. It is as difficult to generalize about the early Christian communities as it is to generalize about paganism, but I have used the words "church" (small *c*) or "Christian communities" when appropriate. This should not imply any common agreement in doctrine or belief—such an agreement took many centuries to evolve and never became complete between the Christian communities. (In fact, one of the arguments of this book is that the debate by its very nature could not come to much in the way of agreement.) I have used "Church" (capital C) only when I quote directly from another writer who has done so, or in describing the Roman Catholic Church, which could be said to have had some understanding of its distinctiveness as the church of the west from the time of Gregory in the late sixth century. It was at about this time that the word "pope" was first used as a title for the bishop of Rome, and I have avoided using the word for the earlier bishops on the grounds that it was not a title they used themselves. (The question of the primacy of the bishops of Rome, actual or otherwise, over other bishops is, of course, a separate topic that I explore at appropriate points in the text.) When the emperors began to define and enforce Christian doctrine through law, I have described the doctrines they promulgated as "orthodox" (small *o*), although it should be remembered that in this period an imperial definition of orthodoxy did not mean that Christian communities necessarily became "orthodox" (despite enormous financial incentives to do so). The Roman empire, even in its more authoritarian phase in late antiquity, simply did not have the power to enforce uniformity of thought. In fact, the impassioned nature of much Christian preaching may be seen as a recognition of the churches' continuing impotence in the face of Judaism, paganism and rival Christian traditions. "Orthodox" (capital O) is used to refer to the Greek-speaking churches of the east that remained true to their traditions as the popes gradually consolidated an independent western (and Latin-speaking) church in the first millennium.

A particularly difficult concept to define, at least so far as the fourth century is concerned, is "Nicene orthodoxy." The concept that God the Father and Jesus the Son were *homoousios,* "of identical substance," was first proclaimed at the council of eastern (Greek-speaking) bishops meeting at Nicaea under the auspices of the emperor Constantine in 325. Yet, contrary to traditional interpretations of the council, recent research is stressing the difficulties the *homoousios* formula had in being accepted by the church as a whole (as the text will explain). In the eastern church it was only fully accepted as orthodoxy after the Council of Constantinople in 381, and even then there remained much opposition to the concept. However, in the western church there was always greater sympathy for the idea that Father and Son were of equal divinity, even though, as a result of the linguistic and geographical isolation of the western church, there seems to have been little awareness of the actual Nicene formulation before the 350s. I have tended to use the term "Nicene orthodoxy" rather loosely to describe those in the west who saw Father and Son as being of equal grandeur, whether they knew of or used a strictly Nicene formulation or not.

I have acknowledged translators where possible in the notes. Most of the quoted texts from the Old and New Testaments are from the Jerusalem Bible, which I have long found the most congenial modern translation.

# The Closing of the
# Western Mind

# THOMAS AQUINAS AND
# "THE TRIUMPH OF FAITH"

A friar in the black-and-white habit of the Dominicans sits in a niche set within an elaborate columned edifice crowned by a vault. Carved on the panels either side of him are *fasces,* rods bound together, a symbol of authority that reaches back through the history of ancient Rome to the Etruscans. Conventionally, as those who are attuned to the more sinister aspects of modern European history will be all too well aware, an axe is fixed within the bundle, but here it is omitted and the *fasces* are lit. Even in ancient times the presence of the axe was associated with tyrannical authority, so the omission suggests a deliberate attempt to evoke an authority that is benign rather than menacing. A setting in Rome is confirmed by the views behind the imposing structure. On one side there is part of St. John Lateran, the cathedral church of Rome, fronted by an equestrian statue believed in the 1480s, the date of this fresco, to be of the emperor Constantine, its founder.[1] On the other is the Porta Ripa Grande, the port alongside the river Tiber in Rome. The fresco itself is in the Carafa Chapel in Santa Maria Sopra Minerva, a Dominican church in the city.[2] Even if the *fasces* are not menacing, one aspect of the fresco nevertheless is. The friar crushes a scowling old man beneath his feet. The old man is a personification of evil, and he clutches a banner with the Latin inscription "Wisdom conquers evil." The friar himself is none other than the great Dominican theologian Thomas Aquinas (c. 1225–74). Above him in a roundel are the verses from the Book of Proverbs with which he chose to begin one of his finest works, the *Summa contra gentiles,* "a summary of the case against the heretics":

"For my mouth shall speak truth and wickedness is an abomination to my lips." Also above him, on panels held by *putti,* appears a declaration of the importance of the revealed word of God: "The revelation of Thy words gives light; it gives understanding to the simple." The most important text, however, must be that which Thomas has selected to hold in his left hand; it is from the Apostle Paul: SAPIENTIAM SAPIENTUM PERDAM, "I will destroy the wisdom of the wise." As this book will suggest, the phrase, supported by other texts of Paul which condemn the "empty logic of the philosophers," was the opening shot in the enduring war between Christianity and science.[3]

Here Thomas is in a position of authority, defending the revelatory power of God against "the wisdom of the wise." Yet this "wisdom" is allowed some place. Alongside the saint sit four further personifications, in order from the left, those of Philosophy, Theology, Grammar and Dialectic. Philosophy (largely the study of formal logic), grammar and dialectic (the art of disputation) were the first subjects of the traditional medieval curriculum. However, though they may appear at ease alongside Thomas, they are clearly subordinate to the word of God, as preliminaries that had to be mastered before any advanced study in theology, the longest and most challenging course, could begin. Theology's prominence over the others is shown here by her crown and her hand raised to heaven, as well as by her position immediately to the right of Thomas.

Below Thomas and his intellectual companions two groups of men stand back from a clutter of books and manuscripts. A debate has been in progress, and it seems that its settlement has resulted in a disposal of discarded arguments. The reference here is to the fourth and fifth centuries, when the empire, newly if not fully Christianized, was rocked with debate over the nature of Jesus and his relationship with God. The Arians (followers of Arius) claimed that Jesus was a distinct and lower creation, divine perhaps but not fully God. At the opposite extreme, the followers of Sabellius, a Roman cleric, claimed that the Godhead was one and Jesus on earth was only a temporary manifestation of that Godhead, in no way distinct from it. In the fresco Arius stands on the left, a serious and thoughtful man as tradition records, wearing yellow robes. In front of him a book bearing the words of his thesis, "There was a time when the Son was not," lies condemned. Sabellius, shown as an austere Roman in a red robe, gazes down on his work with its own heretical assertion, that the Father is not to be distinguished from the Son, likewise condemned. Other heretics, including the Persian Mani (to the right of Sabellius in a furred hood), to whose sect St. Augustine belonged before his conversion to Christianity, are in the crowd. These heretics had all been subject to specific refutation by Thomas in his works. What Thomas now upholds is the final solution to the issue, the doctrine of the Trinity. God the Father, Jesus the Son and the Holy Spirit are distinct persons within a single Godhead. It is a doctrine, as Thomas himself wrote in his other great work, the *Summa theologiae,* that cannot be upheld by reason, but only through faith.

The "triumph of faith," as depicted here by the Florentine painter Filippino Lippi,[4] reflects the theme of this book. "Faith" is a complex concept, but whether it is trust in what cannot be seen, belief in promises made by God, essentially a declaration of loyalty or a virtue, it involves some kind of acquiescence in what cannot be proved by rational thought. What makes faith a difficult concept to explore is that it has both theological and psychological elements. At a psychological level one could argue that faith must exist in any healthy mind. If we cannot trust anyone, have any optimism that "all will be well," we cannot live full lives. Such faith will include positive responses to individuals, as evinced by those who met and travelled with Jesus. Here we cross a conceptual boundary because faith in Jesus, and in particular in the saving nature of his crucifixion and resurrection as taught by Paul, was of a different order from faith in the general sense that "all will be well." With the elaboration of Christian doctrine, faith came to mean acquiescence in the teachings of the churches—to be seen as a virtue in itself.[5]

In the fourth and fifth centuries A.D., however, faith in this last sense achieved prominence over reason. The principles of empirical observation or logic were overruled in the conviction that all knowledge comes from God and even, in the writings of Augustine, that the human mind, burdened with Adam's original sin, is diminished in its ability to think for itself. For centuries any form of independent scientific thinking was suppressed. Yet, and this is the paradox of the Carafa fresco, it was actually Thomas, through reviving the works of Aristotle, who brought reason back into theology and hence into western thought. Once again it was possible for rational thought and faith to co-exist. We will meet the other Thomas, the Thomas who champions reason alongside faith, in the final chapter of this book.

We begin by returning to ancient Greece and exploring in particular how reason became established as an intellectual force in western culture. Then we can see how Christianity, under the influential banner of

Paul's denunciation of Greek philosophy, began to create the barrier between science—and rational thought in general—and religion that appears to be unique to Christianity. Far from the rise of science challenging the Christian concept of God (as is often assumed by protagonists in the debate), it was Christianity that actively challenged a well-established and sophisticated tradition of scientific thinking.

# 2

## THE QUEST FOR CERTAINTY

The investigation of the truth is in one way hard, in another easy. An indication of this is found in the fact that no one is able to attain the truth adequately, while, on the other hand, no one fails entirely, but everyone says something true about the nature of things, and while individually they contribute little or nothing to the truth, by the union of all a considerable amount is amassed.

ARISTOTLE[1]

On his long journey home from Troy to his wife, Penelope, in Ithaca, Odysseus, the hero of Homer's *Odyssey*, was swept from his ship through the fury of Poseidon, the god of earthquakes and the sea, who had turned against him. Luckily, the goddess Leukothea, who lived in the depths of the sea, took pity on him and offered him a magic scarf that, when bound around him, would protect him, while the goddess Athena calmed the waves so that he could swim towards the shores of the land of the Phaeacians. In this crisis Odysseus still had to make his own decisions, in the short term at what moment he should leave the timbers of his ship and strike for shore. A massive wave sent by Poseidon made the decision for him, and he found himself swimming without any support. The coast came into view, but it was rugged. Is it better,

Odysseus wondered, to land where he can and risk being crushed against the cliffs by a wave, or continue onwards in his exhaustion in the hopes of finding a sandy bay?

Odysseus' ordeal ended happily. He was washed ashore and rescued by the beautiful Nausicaa, daughter of the Phaeacian king. He was saved by two goddesses who successfully challenged another god, Poseidon. So here is a man at the mercy of divine forces who nevertheless retained the power to think rationally and who saw rational thought as a means of bettering his chances. One can hardly say this is a revolutionary step; archaeological evidence from South African caves shows that individuals were able to provide "rational" adaptations to their changing environment (in the sense of adapting their tools) as long as 70,000 years ago. What is important is that Homer distinguishes rational thought, even at this primitive, almost instinctive level, as a mental activity, independent of the whim of the gods.[2]

This is the mental landscape of Greece in the eighth century or earlier—the *Odyssey* took its final form about 725 B.C. from much older oral traditions—but it is a world that is passing. Odysseus is an aristocrat, a king in his land of Ithaca, where he has palaces and cattle. His wife, Penelope, though vulnerable without him, has her own status. When they are finally reunited, they enjoy each other's conversation as equals before they make together for the royal bed. Emerging is the world of the Greek city state, where, from the eighth century, one finds communities making focused settlements, typically with their own sacred spaces and public arenas. There is a shift, probably as a result of population increase, from the "aristocratic" extravagance of cattle farming to more intensive cultivation, of olives, cereals and vines. A peasant economy emerges based on a free citizenry relying on slaves for extra labour. Women are now segregated, the aristocratic palace replaced by the enclosed home, which, unlike Penelope's palace in Ithaca, contains no allotted space in which women can appear before strangers. Fighting is no longer between aristocratic heroes meeting in single combat but between massed phalanxes of hoplites (the word comes from *hoplon*, a shield), made up of the peasantry, who fight side by side with each other and overwhelm their opponents by sheer weight and determination.[3]

Population increase and political infighting encouraged settlement overseas, and the city state, or *polis* as it was known in Greek, proved eminently exportable throughout the Mediterranean. One finds the same structure, domestic areas, public meeting places and a demarcated area, the *temenos,* for temples and sacrificial altars, in most Greek cities. Remarkably, despite the fragmentation and extent of settlement, there remained a common sense of Greek culture, sustained by religious festivals, many of them with games, oracles and centres of pilgrimage, at which Greeks from across the Mediterranean gathered.

The number and frequency of such festivals reflects the intensely spiritual nature of the ancient Greeks. They had a powerful sense of the sacred, often personified in gods and goddesses, elaborated in myth and celebrated at an enormous number of shrines, some natural such as caves and springs, others opulent temple complexes. Their gods remained close to them, traditionally portrayed in human form and displaying behaviour which was often all too human in its fits of jealousy and anger. Among the twelve Olympian gods the full spectrum of human life was represented, from the wild excess of emotion (Dionysus) to the calm exercise of reason (Apollo), from the lustful enjoyment of sex (Aphrodite) to virgin modesty (Artemis). Each god or goddess played a number of roles, accumulated from different traditions both inside and outside Greece. So Zeus, the father of the gods, could act as lord of the skies, as a bringer of victory, a symbol of sexual potency, the upholder of rulers and the god of thunder and lightning. Alongside the Olympian gods there was a mass of lesser deities, such as Pan, the god of shepherds, and local heroes with a range of roles. Ancient Greece vibrated with spiritual presences.[4]

Mediation with the gods took place through prayer and sacrifice. The sacrifice was the central point of almost every ritual. An animal—an ox, sheep, goat or pig—would be presented to the gods and then killed, burnt and eaten by the community. Sacrifices were not an aberrant or cruel activity—they were a sophisticated way of dealing with the necessity of killing animals in order to eat. In fact, the rituals surrounding sacrifice suggest that the Greeks felt some unease about killing animals they had reared themselves. So the illusion was created that an animal went to its death willingly, and before the killing all present threw a handful of barley at it, as if the community as a whole was accepting responsibility for the death. At the moment of the slaughter women would utter impassioned cries, again a recognition of the seriousness of what was being done in taking life. This was a common theme in ritual, also found in Greek tragic drama, an awareness that any transition involved a loss that had to be recognized within the ritual itself. There was also a strong belief that through the maintaining of the round of rituals the city had been protected. As one Athenian citizen put it in a public debate:

> Our ancestors by sacrificing in accordance with the tablets of Solon [laws instituted in the early sixth century] have handed down to us a city superior in greatness and prosperity to any other in Greece so that it behooves us to perform the same sacrifices as they did if for no other reason than that of the success which has resulted from these rites.[5]

So, Greek religion acted as mediator of political and social tensions. Transitions could be effected through the use of ritual and difficult decisions made with the help of oracles. Even so, political life was not easy, and in the seventh and sixth centuries in particular there were continual clashes between the old aristocratic elites and the newly wealthy, who had made their money through trade, and the rising peasant classes, increasingly conscious of their own cohesion and power. At the very worst a city would explode into civil war. Thucydides describes one case in 427 in Corfu, which saw a vicious spiral of terror and counter-terror between the ruling classes and "democrats." In the resultant complete breakdown of order, where, as Thucydides puts it, "fanatical enthusiasm was the mark of a 'real man,' " fathers killed sons, temples were violated by the massacre of those sheltering in them and many committed suicide rather than wait to be killed. "As for the citizens who held moderate views, they were destroyed by both the extreme parties, either for not taking part in the struggle or in envy at the possibility that they might survive."[6] The most sophisticated resolution of conflicts such as these was to be made in fifth-century Athens, where all male citizens came to share in government equally, in the Assembly, as jurors in the law courts and, for those aged over thirty, as administrators. Athenian democracy lasted some 140 years and, despite its exclusion of women and slaves, remains a remarkable political innovation.

It was in this resolution of internal conflicts that a remarkable intellectual development took place. It seems to have been based in an optimistic belief that there were forces that tended to good order.[7] One finds such a feeling in the early sixth century B.C. in the verses of the Athenian statesman Solon, who had been charged with resolving a political crisis caused by the economic and social exploitation of a debt-ridden peasantry by the landed aristocracy. He proved to be a pragmatic statesman—it is human beings themselves, not the gods, who must bring peace and good order (the Greek word used is *eunomie*) to their cities. However, *eunomie* (who is personified as a daughter of Zeus) is seen as a force in her own right, even if one who works alongside mankind. In Solon's own words:

> *Eunomie* makes all things well ordered and fitted
> and often puts chains on the unjust;
> she smooths the rough, puts an end to excess, blinds insolence,
> withers the flowers of unrighteousness,
> straightens crooked judgements and softens deeds of arrogance,
> puts an end to works of faction
> and to the anger of painful strife, under her
> all men's actions are fitting and wise.[8]

In other words, the political world tends towards stability under the auspices of divine forces. The work of the politician lies in shifting the city's affairs into their natural groove of harmony, and he will be sustained by *eunomie* in achieving this ("under her all men's actions are fitting and wise"). However, remarkably and apparently uniquely to the Greek world, a further intellectual leap appears to have taken place; it was appreciated that if the city tended to good order, perhaps the universe, the cosmos, did as well. The natural world was seen to change according to rhythms, of the seasons but also of the movements of the stars, rhythms that appeared to persist in spite of the fragmented and unpredictable nature of everyday life. Only a few years later than Solon, in 585 B.C. in the Ionian city of Miletus on the coast of Asia Minor, the philosopher-scientist Thales is said to have predicted an eclipse of the sun (the eclipse did indeed take place and was independently recorded by the historian Herodotus). For Aristotle, writing some 200 years later, this was truly the moment when Greek philosophy began. An underlying order to the cosmos had been observed, and its movements were assumed to be so regular that future events could be predicted from empirical observations gathered over time.

This single instance was not revolutionary in itself—after all, the Egyptians had been able to work out a calendar based on the regular phases of the moon as early as 2800 B.C. Where Thales and his associates in Miletus went further was to speculate on why the world was as it was. They began to ask major questions. What was the cosmos made of, and why did it move in the way it did? Thales himself suggested that the world may have originated in a single substance, water, and that it rested on a base of water. He was challenged by another Milesian, Anaximander. What then did the water rest on? Anaximander suggested that the apparent stability of the world arose because it was at the centre of equally powerful forces—the Boundless, he called them—that surrounded the world on all sides and from which it had been formed. Just as a city would tend towards harmony, so would the cosmos be held in balance by these surrounding forces. Another Milesian, Anaximenes, suggested that everything came from air. If steam could be condensed into water and water could be frozen into ice, it followed that a single substance could change form dramatically, and perhaps air could be condensed into solid forms. These speculations were bound to be primitive, but they did represent a new way of thinking and, moreover, one in which each thinker was able to use observation and reason to challenge his rivals. So within 150 years of Odysseus' swim to Phaeacia, rational decision-making had been transformed into something much more sophisticated and universal, what we might call science. Thinking about how the predictable rhythms of the natural world related to the observed chaos of the actual world presented, of course, a daunting challenge. But it was faced as early as 500 B.C. The brilliant Heraclitus (from the city of Ephesus, close to Miletus) believed that the underlying order (the word he used was *logos,* which will reappear many times in this book) was sustained by continual tensions between different forces. The harmonious city, said Heraclitus, is not one in which everyone lives in peace but one among whose citizens there is constant activity and debate. "Justice," said Heraclitus, "is strife."[9]

Heraclitus' insight that reasoned thought is born within the tensions of the city state is supported by modern research. Geoffrey Lloyd, who has carried out intensive explorations of the background to Greek scientific thinking, traces the origins of a systematic use of reason (without which empirical observations cannot be related to each other) to the intense political debates that raged within the Greek cities. If two factions wished to find a "just" solution to a problem without tearing apart their own city, then at some point there was likely to be a consideration of what was meant by "justice." There was an incentive to go back to first principles and attempt to define an agreed basis, some kind of axiomatic statement, from which to begin the arguments that could only take place according to rational principles if agreement was to be maintained between the opposing parties. Lloyd argues that this process can be discerned within the fragments of political debate that survive, and, crucially, it was also applied to the study of the natural world. The terminology used supports this. Lloyd shows how a word such as "witness," as used in the law courts, was the root of the word for "evidence" in scientific discourse, and how the term used for cross-examination of witnesses was adopted to describe the testing of an idea or hypothesis. He also argues that within the city the ability to argue persuasively conferred status, and that this status could be transferred into other areas of intellectual activity.[10]

So began the great adventure of the Greek speculative tradition. It was not a coherent process. Martin West writes:

> Early Greek philosophy was not a single vessel which a
> succession of pilots briefly commanded and tried to steer
> towards an agreed destination, one tacking one way, the
> next altering course in the light of its own perceptions. It
> was more like a flotilla of small craft whose navigators
> did not start from the same point or at the same time,
> nor all aim for the same goal; some went in groups,
> some were influenced by the movements of others, some
> travelled out of sight of each other.[11]

One important development was the distinguishing and segregation of the process of reasoning itself. The earliest surviving sustained piece of Greek philosophical reasoning comes from the first half of the fifth century, from one Parmenides from the Greek city of Elea in southern Italy. Parmenides attempts to grasp the nature of the cosmos through the use of rational thought alone (in other words, without any reliance on empirical observation). He realizes that no argument can begin unless some initial assumptions are made. His "It is and it is impossible for it not to be" is the assumption with which he starts. As Parmenides, through a goddess who is given the role of developing the argument, works towards his conclusion that all material is a single undifferentiated and unchanging mass, many controversies arise, not least because of the problems in using verbs such as "to be" in a completely new context, that of philosophical reasoning. But what Parmenides did achieve was to show that once basic assumptions and axioms have been agreed upon, reason can make its independent way to a conclusion. However, his conclusion, that it is rationally impossible to conceive of materials undergoing change, seems absurd, and it raises for the first time the question of what happens when observation and reason contradict each other.

A follower of Parmenides, Zeno (who also came from Elea), high-lighted this issue in his famous paradoxes. An arrow which has been shot cannot move, says Zeno. How can this possibly be? Because, answers Zeno, it is always at a place equal to itself, and if so it must be at rest in that place. So, as it is *always* at a place equal to itself, it must *always* be at rest. In Zeno's most famous paradox, Achilles, the fastest man on foot, will never catch up with a tortoise, because when he has reached the place where the tortoise was, the tortoise will have moved on, and when he has reached the place to which the tortoise has pro-gressed, it will have moved on yet further. While reason can suggest that Achilles will never catch the tortoise, experience tells us that he will and that he will soon outstrip it. Observation and reason may be in conflict, and the result is a conundrum. The fact that the Greeks recognized such problems yet were not daunted by them is a measure of their growing intellectual confidence.

The next step, then, in this parade of intellectual innovation is to try to isolate the circumstances in which rational argument can be used to achieve certainty without being challenged by what is actually observed by our senses. Here the achievement of Aristotle was outstanding. One of Aristotle's many contributions to the definition of certainty was the introduction of the syllogism, a means by which the validity of a logical argument can be assessed.[12] A syllogism is, in Aristotle's own words, "an argument in which certain things being assumed [the premises], some-thing different from the things assumed [the conclusion] follows from necessity by the fact that they hold." What kinds of things can be "assumed"? The famous examples, although not used by Aristotle him-self, are "All men are mortal" and "Socrates is a man." Both premises seem fully tenable. No one has come up with an example of a man who has not died; it is part of the condition of being human. Similarly, anyone who met Socrates would have agreed that he was a man. From these two assumptions could be drawn the conclusion: "Therefore Socrates is mor-tal." Aristotle went further, replacing the subjects of the assumptions with letters, so that it follows if all As are B, and C is an A, then C is B. One can substitute any suitable premises to create a valid conclusion. Aristotle goes on to explore the cases where the logic does not work. "A dog has four feet" and "A cat has four feet" are both reasonable assumptions to make from one's experience of dogs and cats in everyday life, but it does not follow that a cat is a dog, and the student in logic has to work out why this is so. "All fish are silver; a goldfish is a fish; therefore a goldfish is silver" cannot be sustained because the example of a living goldfish would itself show that the premise that "All fish are silver" is not true.

Aristotle's syllogisms can take us only so far; their premises have to be empirically correct and relate to each other in such a way that a conclusion can be drawn from their comparison. They provide the basis for deductive argument, an argument in which a specific piece of knowledge can be drawn from knowledge already given. The development of the use of deductive proof was perhaps the greatest of the Greeks' intellectual achievements. Deductive argument had, in fact, already been used in mathematics by the Greeks before Aristotle systematized it. In an astonishing breach of conventional thinking, the Greeks conceived of abstract geometrical models from which theorems could be drawn. While the Babylonians knew that in any actual right-angled triangle the square of the hypotenuse equals the sum of the squares of the other two sides, Pythagoras' theorem generalizes to show that this must be true in any conceivable right-angled triangle, a major development both mathematically and philosophically. A deductive proof in geometry needs to begin with some incontrovertible statements, or postulates as the mathematician Euclid (writing c. 300 B.C.) named them. Euclid's postulates included the assertion that it is possible to draw a straight line from any point to any other point and that all right angles are equal to each other. His famous fifth postulate stipulated the conditions under which two straight lines will meet at some indefinite point. (It was the only one recognized as unprovable even in his own day and eventually succumbed to the analysis of mathematicians in the nineteenth century.) Euclid also recognized what he termed "common notions," truths that are applicable to all sciences, not merely mathematics, such as "If equals be added to equals, the wholes are equal." These postulates and "common notions" might seem self-evident, but in his *Elements,* one of the outstanding textbooks in history, Euclid was able to draw no less than 467 proofs from ten of them, while a later mathematician, Apollonius of

Perga, was to show 487 in his *Conic Sections*. As Robert Osserman has put it in his *Poetry of the Universe:*

> In a world full of irrational beliefs and shaky specula-
> tions, the statements found in *The Elements* were
> proven true beyond a shadow of a doubt . . . The aston-
> ishing fact is that after two thousand years, nobody has
> ever found an actual "mistake" in *The Elements*—that
> is to say a statement that did not follow logically from
> the given assumptions.[13]

Later mathematicians, such as the great Archimedes (see below, p. 43), were to develop new branches and areas of mathematics from these foundations.

Dealing with the natural world is a much more complex business. It seems to be in a constant state of change—the weather changes, plants grow, wars happen, men die. As Heraclitus had observed, all is in a process of flux. Yet if an underlying order can be assumed and isolated, then some progress can be made. Such progress assumes that the gods do not disturb the workings of the world on pure whim (as they do, for instance, in prescientific thinking—if the gods can intervene to change the course of the stars or the boiling point of water at random, for instance, then nothing is predictable). The next task is to isolate cause and effect, the forces that cause things to happen in a predictable way. One finds an excellent example of this process in the *Histories* of Herodotus (probably written in the 430s B.C.). Herodotus starts his famous survey of Egypt (book 2) with speculation on the causes of the annual Nile floods. He considers three explanations which, he tells us, others have put forward. One is that the summer winds force back the natural flow of the water, and as they die down a larger volume of water is released in compensation. This cannot be true, he notes, because the floods occur even in years when the winds do not blow. Moreover, no other rivers show this phenomenon. The second explanation is that the Nile flows from an ocean that surrounds the earth. This is not a rational explanation, says Herodotus; it can only be legend. Probably Homer or some other poet (he says somewhat scornfully) introduced the idea. The third explanation is that it is melting snows that cause the floods, but surely, says Herodotus, the further south you go the hotter it gets, as the black skins of the "natives" suggest. Snow would never fall in such regions. He goes on to provide an elaborate explanation of his own, based on the sun causing the Nile to evaporate just at a time when rainfall is low, so creating an artificially low volume of water in comparison to which the normal flow is a "flood." He misses the true cause, the heavy summer rains that run down from the mountains of Ethiopia, but even if he reaches the wrong answer, Herodotus is aware of and consciously rejects mythological explanations. He uses observation and reason to discard some explanations and formulate others. Here is the process of "scientific" thinking at work.[14]

One of the most famous early "scientific" texts relates to epilepsy. Epilepsy had traditionally been known as "the sacred disease," because its sudden onset and violent nature suggested an act of the gods, yet in a text attributed to Hippocrates, probably from the early fourth century B.C., the writer states:

> I do not believe that the so-called "Sacred Disease" is any more divine or sacred than any other diseases. It has its own specific nature and cause; but because it is completely different from other diseases men through their inexperience and wonder at its peculiar symptoms have believed it to be of divine origin . . . [yet] it has the same nature as other diseases and a similar cause. It is also no less curable than other diseases unless by long lapse of time it is so ingrained that it is more powerful than the drugs that are applied. Like other diseases it is hereditary . . . The brain is the cause of the condition as it is of other most serious diseases . . .[15]

Here we have not only the specific rejection of the divine as a cause but a sophisticated attempt based on observation to say something about the real nature of epilepsy, its causes and its cures. It should be stressed, however, that the rejection of divine intervention did not mean a rejection of the gods themselves. The famous Hippocratic oath, which probably dates from the beginning of the fourth century, requires the physician to swear by the gods Apollo, Asclepius and Asclepius' two daughters, Hygeia and Panacea. It was rather that the sphere of activity of the gods was diminished and there was greater reluctance, at least among intellectuals, to see natural events as caused by them. Alternatively, they could be seen as the forces that set in motion the regularity with which the natural world operates.

In dealing with the natural world, whether it be the universe, material objects such as earth and water, plants, animals or human beings themselves, the Greeks assumed, as a starting point, that there was an underlying order to all things. Their self-imposed task was to find out what this was for each discipline. In astronomy the Greeks made three assumptions: that the earth was at the centre of the universe, that the stars moved around it in a regular way, and that their movement was circular. In medicine the Greeks admitted that it was difficult to find a fundamental principle behind the working of so complex an organism as the human body, but they nevertheless began from the premise that the body (like the ideal city) tended towards *eunomie*—in this context, good health—and so illness suggested some aberration in the normal working of things. (The greatest physician of all, Galen, did attempt to base medical knowledge on incontrovertible, geometrical-style proofs but understandably ran into philosophical difficulties.)[16] These assumptions were only a starting point. There had then to be the gathering of empirical evidence, observations of the stars or the working of the body, so that explanations could be made. There were immense difficulties in this. Herodotus could never have reached the source of the Nile. In astronomy one had only the naked eye with which to observe the universe and rudimentary methods of preserving accurate recordings over time, although matters were helped when the findings from many centuries of observation by the Babylonians reached the Greek world in the third century B.C. Similarly in medicine, much could not be observed because a living body's internal organs could not be seen functioning.

What is remarkable is how much the Greeks did achieve. In astronomy, for instance, of their three assumptions about the universe, one was false (that the sun revolves around the earth), but they were right in seeing a predictable pattern of behaviour in the stars, which for the planets at least was circular. Observations of the shadow of the earth on the moon convinced the Greeks that it was a sphere,[17] and their assumption that the earth was at the centre of the universe was not based on ignorance or lazy thinking but was established after serious examination of the alternatives. If the earth was moving around the sun (as Aristarchus hypothesized early in the third century B.C.), then surely its relationship with the stars would change more radically over time. (The Greeks could not conceive that the stars were as far from the earth as they really are.) If the earth spun on its axis (as Heracleides of Pontus proposed in the fourth century), why were the clouds, which could be assumed to be stationary in relationship to the moving earth, not seen to be "left behind" as it spun round? Both reason and experience seemed to confirm the Greek view of an earth-centred universe. In time, of course, science would challenge this "common sense" perception of things.

Perhaps the most impressive feature of Greek astronomy is its ingenuity. It was clear that some stars did not appear to follow a regular course. They were termed *planetes,* the wanderers. Sophisticated attempts were made to give them regular movements that comprehended their observed wanderings in line with the assumption that their movement was circular. One hypothesis was that each planet moved around the circumference of a circle whose own centre was moving in a circle around the earth. As more records were made, such hypotheses became more and more elaborate, the most sophisticated being those of Ptolemy in the second century A.D. They were, of course, erroneous because the original assumption that the planets revolve around the earth was wrong. However, had the Greek intellectual tradition survived, it is easy to imagine that someone in ancient times might have taken the mass of observations, applied them to Aristarchus' hypothesis that the sun was the centre of the solar system and the conclusion—that the earth and the planets revolve around the sun—would have fallen elegantly into place, as it did for Copernicus many centuries later. The very elegance of the solution would have, to the Greeks, confirmed that it was likely to be correct. In line with much of Greek thinking, the view that the earth was the centre of the universe remained an assumption, not an article of faith.

Greek astronomy was not confined to the observation of the planets and their motions. It was the combination of these observations with sophisticated mathematical calculation that was truly impressive. One of the most remarkable achievements of Greek astronomy was Hipparchus' definition of the precession of the equinoxes in the second half of the second century B.C. As the earth is not an exact sphere its axes oscillate slightly. This oscillation causes a consistent shift in its position as a viewing platform, but the shift is so slight that it takes nearly 26,000 years, at a rate of roughly a degree every seventy years, for the earth to complete a circuit back to its original position. Using the naked eye, earlier observations from Babylonia and his own instruments for marking the position of the stars, Hipparchus noted the tiny shift, and his calculation of it as a degree every hundred years was remarkably accurate considering the primitive nature of his technology. Aristarchus calculated the relative sizes and distances of the sun and the moon by observing the full and half moons in relation to the sun, and Eratosthenes' calculation of the circumference of the earth was possibly within 200 miles (320 kilometres) of the true figure. In all these cases mathematics, including for the first time trigonometry, was being put to practical use by being combined with meticulous observation.[18]

Astronomy provides only one example of the Greeks' search for "the truth." Their concerns spread to every aspect of knowledge. It is in the nature of man, according to Aristotle, to be curious. Aristotle (384–322 B.C.) arrived in Athens from the northern Aegean (his father had been court physician to the king of Macedon and legend records that he himself was later tutor to Alexander "the Great"). His Macedonian connections made him vulnerable in Athens (for reasons which will become clear in chapter 4), and he travelled widely. He is found probing into every area of intellectual activity, exploring the ultimate nature of things, the ends of human life, the best form of government, the variety of animal life, the importance of tragedy, the nature of rhetoric, the problems of logic. His method was to master what had been said on any subject before, freely criticizing ideas he found inadequate and isolating the questions that needed to be answered. He would move forward himself only after accumulating as much empirical evidence as he could. So his work on zoology included studies of animal life that ranged from the European bison to the mite and from octopuses to oysters. When he was working out his views on the best form of government, he assembled details of 158 Greek constitutions. He speculated more profoundly than anyone before him on the nature of living organisms, exploring their essence, the essential features which made each distinct from other species, and the purpose of each species, which, in Aristotle's philosophy, was central to its identity.[19]

While Aristotle believed that an underlying unity would be found to all knowledge, he accepted that in the present state of knowledge much must remain provisional and unsure. Take, for example, a difficult question in the natural world, how to differentiate between "plants" and "animals." A dogmatic scientist might have drawn up some arbitrary rules and simply classified each organism as one or the other. Aristotle realized that this was to avoid the real issue. He took some examples from the marine world, the sponge, the jellyfish, sea anemones, razor shells. He noted that when a sponge was pulled from a rock to which it was attached, it reacted by clinging to the rock. So perhaps it was some kind of animal. Yet it could not live detached from a rock, as an animal would. Jellyfish, on the other hand, lived as detached organisms but did not, so far as Aristotle could see, have any perception. They are like plants but, unlike other plants, do not stay attached to a base. Should one create a separate category, "plants which are detached," or does one accept that it is possible to be an animal without having perception? Aristotle's genius lay in realizing that these issues had to be worked out undogmatically, that observation had to continue and that sometimes the boundaries between categories would have to be redrawn as a result. In the natural world one could seldom, perhaps never, talk with absolute certainty in the face of the mass of living organisms that had to be categorized. It was this openness to the provisional nature of knowledge that helps make Aristotle one of the truly great philosophers.[20]

Aristotle also firmly believed that knowledge would be cumulative from generation to generation, and this process was supported by the competitive nature of Greek science. Take, for example, the idea of spontaneous generation. Aristotle first posited the concept after he had tried in vain to find out how eels spawned. He could find elvers, young eels, but no sign of what they grew from. The answer was straightforward if remarkable—eels spawned in the Bermudas and the young swam back to Europe—but, of course, this was well beyond any possibility of discovery in the fourth century B.C. The act of spawning was not observed for the first time until the 1920s. So the idea of spontaneous generation, from mud in the case of eels, was one possibility. Aristotle's successor Theophrastus took the matter further. He examined many different cases of apparent spontaneous generation in plants and showed that, in fact, there were often tiny seeds from which plants grew. He noted too that spontaneous generation seemed to take place when earth was warmed. Even though he could not grasp the importance of this as we can today, he still recorded it as part of his investigation. He concluded by leaving the issue open: "More accurate investigation must be made of the subject and the matter in which spontaneous generation takes place be thoroughly inquired into . . . This is why an experienced person is needed to gather it [the evidence], who has the ability to observe the proper season and recognise the seed itself." For Theophrastus it remained a possibility that every form of apparently spontaneous generation would one day be explained, although he insisted that the concept remain in place until it was actually disproved by empirical observation. He was also insistent on the importance of professional expertise, another important development in the history of science.[21]

Crucially, Theophrastus was not prepared to accept the views of even such a great scientist as Aristotle (who also happened to be an associate of his) uncritically. He actively sought out explanations (the tiny seeds) that might undermine Aristotle's suggestion. This was fundamental to the nature of Greek science. It was essentially competitive, with each scientist not only building on earlier observations but seeking to outdo his predecessors. Geoffrey Lloyd sums up its distinctive nature:

> The extant remains of Egyptian and Babylonian medicine, mathematics and astronomy can be combed in vain for a single example of a text where an individual author explicitly distances himself from, and criticises, the received tradition in order to claim originality for himself, whereas our Greek sources repeatedly do that.[22]

Lloyd gives a wide range of examples from medical treatises where an author explains what he believes, the observations on which the belief is based and why it differs from what has been believed before. Anyone, even an Aristotle, could be challenged by anyone who comes after. There can be certainty, in mathematics for instance, but this is based on postulates on which all agree. For the most part, and so far as the natural world is concerned, knowledge is always provisional, not restricted to an elite, and it grows as a result of "democratic" collaboration (see the quotation from Aristotle at the beginning of the chapter) and competition.[23] This was the mainstream of Greek intellectual tradition. One had to distinguish between what could be known for certain and what could not be and develop tests or methods of argument that could be universally accepted. The Greeks had recognized that science is as much concerned with proving things false as with proving them true. Overall, this was a staggering achievement. In isolating and systematizing rational thought, the Greeks had founded science and mathematics in the form they are still followed today without implying that rational thought was the only path to truth. None of this would have been possible without an atmosphere of intellectual tolerance.

When the Greeks wrote about science, mathematics or any kind of systematic enquiry, including history or geography, they called their text a *logos*, or reasoned account. *Logoi* were typically written in prose, and their language reflected the nature of the task.[24] The word *logos* itself, one of the most complex in Greek philosophy, came to take on other meanings, including "reasoned thought" itself. It was to re-emerge in a Christian context as "the Word" of God, although the relationship between God's Word and reason itself was to prove problematic. The Greeks contrasted *logos* with *muthos*, an account in which reason plays no part. An obvious use of *muthos* is in telling a story about the gods (hence "myth") or relating a narrative poem, and, in contrast to *logoi*, myths were normally related in verse. The important point to make is that myths were not devalued by the emergence of *logoi*. The Greeks realized that telling a story has its own uses far beyond entertainment and fulfills important emotional needs. Many cities focused their identity on foundation myths, which they used to foster the pride of their citizens.[25] Myths were also used to underpin rituals at times of individual transition, from virginity to marriage, for instance. Perhaps the most sophisticated way in which the Greeks used myths was through tragic drama. Here a dilemma, based on the story lines of ancient myths, was presented in a play and acted through so that the consequences of the characters choosing one solution rather than another could be assessed by an audience, a truly democratic way of airing ethical issues. In his *Poetics* Aristotle argued that the purpose of tragic drama was to arouse pity and fear in the audience to give them some form of emotional catharsis, an experience which would make them more complete human beings.[26]

Aristotle's support for the use of myth for human ends emphasizes that there is no necessary conflict between *logos* and *muthos*. Each has its value in its own context and neither threatens the other. One should not search for any form of absolute truth, in the sense of a belief whose certainty could be justified, in *muthoi*. Similarly, one should not use the word *logos* of truths that could not be defended by reasoned argument. Such a relaxed attitude to myth meant that the Greeks were tolerant and open about developing new stories about the gods and were able to speculate about their powers and attributes, even their very nature, without any sense of impropriety. Could the nature of the gods be grasped at all, asked Protagoras in the fifth century, in view "of the difficulty of the subject and the brevity of men's lives"? Why should humans give the gods human form? asked the poet and natural philosopher Xenophanes; on this analogy horses would see their gods as horses. It is just as likely, Xenophanes went on, that there were gods, or even a single supreme divine figure, of a totally different nature from humanity. For Aristotle, reason suggested that there is a supreme "unmoved mover." "Since motion must always exist and must not cease, there must necessarily be something eternal, either one thing or many, that first initiates motion, and this first mover must be unmoved." Others suggested there were no gods at all. The world is totally material, argued the Atomists, with all matter being made up of tiny particles, atoms, literally "that which cannot be cut." These more extreme forms of atheism did arouse concern. There remained a residual fear, certainly found among the population of Athens, for instance, that if the gods were rejected outright they might retaliate by withdrawing their patronage of the city. Sometimes this fear would erupt into intolerance, as in the case of Socrates, who was executed in Athens in 399 B.C. For the most part, however, Greek religion was undogmatic, its theology ever in flux. Myths and rituals were so interwoven into everyday life that no need was felt for an institutional hierarchy to defend them.[27] Arguments over the divine were never restrained by doctrinal orthodoxy.

Although the achievement of the Greeks in establishing an atmosphere of tolerance in which considerable intellectual progress proved possible was remarkable, one should not idealize. We have already noted the difficulties in gathering empirical evidence and the way in which this limited what it was possible to know. Interpretation of empirical evidence also takes place within an ideological context. It was easy to rationalize from the observations of the human body that men were the active sex and women the passive, and the Hippocratic texts which concentrate on the diseases of women show how they were classified as "other" and how their organs, their "soft" flesh and their need to menstruate were explored within the context of male superiority. In her *Hippocrates' Woman: Reading the Female Body in Ancient Greece*, Helen King shows how these attitudes persisted in the field of gynaecology (in the sense of a male profession telling women how they should regulate their bodies) well into modern times.[28] Similarly, Aristotle links a hot climate to indolence and goes on to argue that those born in such regions are naturally slaves, available to the more active peoples, such as the Greeks, who have grown up in a relatively temperate environment. And it has to be remembered that even this level of "rational" thought was alien to most Greeks, who, it can be assumed, were oblivious to the sophisticated discussions of their educated peers. Irrationality flourished in the Greek world, much as it does, alongside scientific thinking, in ours.

The expanding use of rational thought can be seen as a symbol of the self-confidence of the Greeks, yet it was also fully accepted that human self-confidence had to be set within limits—no man should pretend he was a god. One reason, argues Herodotus, why the Persian king Xerxes was defeated when he invaded Greece in 480 was that his attempt to build a bridge across the Hellespont and to cut through a peninsula was an arrogant defiance of the natural order. He deserved his humiliation at the hands of the Greeks. Haughty behaviour (*ate*) or the deliberate humiliation of others (*hubris*) were taboo. Such behaviour deserved the greatest humiliation of all, expulsion from the perpetrator's native city, in addition to divine condemnation.

In his play *Antigone,* Sophocles summed it up:

Wonders are many and none more wonderful than man . . .
In the meshes of his woven nets, cunning of mind, ingenious
    man . . .
He snares the lighthearted birds and the tribes of savage beasts,
    and the creatures of the deep seas . . .
He puts the halter round the horse's neck
And rings the nostrils of the angry bull.
He has devised himself a shelter
    against the rigours of frost and the pelting rains.
Speech and science he has taught himself,
    and artfully formed laws for harmonious civic life . . .
Only against death he fights in vain.
But clear intelligence—a force beyond measure—
    moves to work both good and ill . . .
When he obeys the laws and honors justice, the city stands
    proud . . .
But man swerves from side to side, and when the laws are broken,
    and set at naught, he is like a person without a city,
    beyond human boundary, a horror, a pollution to be avoided.[29]

The closing lines of this famous speech are a reminder that the great achievements of the Greeks in the use of rational thought have to be set within the wider context of their views of just government and correct moral behaviour. How the Greek philosophers tackled this problem is the subject of the next chapter.

## 3

## THE QUEST FOR VIRTUE

If men are to be motivated to fight with commitment, they need to be given good reasons for doing so. In Homer, it is a mark of aristocratic status that one is able to persuade others to risk their lives. Yet Homer also highlights the importance of discussion between leaders who meet in common council at the end of the day. The views of one speaker need to be tempered by those of his listeners so that there is a reasoned consensus. By the sixth century, however, speakers found themselves faced by the much more demanding audiences of the citizen assemblies, raucous, volatile and much less ready to defer to aristocratic status. New demands on speakers forced the Greeks to think about the nature of *rhetorike,* rhetoric, itself, and how to exploit it effectively before audiences. Was it even to be seen as a skill that could be taught? Yes, said the rhetorician Gorgias, who arrived in Athens in 427 from his native city, Leontini, in Sicily. Gorgias had learned his skills negotiating property disputes and had come to Athens to plead for the city to support Leontini against its neighbour Syracuse. He was unashamedly a performer—he would stride into the Athenian theatre, call out "Give me a theme" and then declaim on it without hesitation—but he gave younger citizens starting their political careers in the assembly the confidence that the art of good speaking could be learned.[1]

Yet Gorgias' success highlighted the tension which lay at the core of rhetoric. The effectiveness of a speech seemed to depend as much on the emotional power of the speaker, his learned skills and oratorical devices, as on the quality, in rational terms, of its argument. In the activities of the Athenian assembly, for example, during the tense days of the Peloponnesian War between Athens and Sparta (431–404 B.C.), the citizens, swayed by powerful speeches, decided one day in 427 that all the men of the island of Mytilene, captured after a revolt, should be executed. When tempers had cooled the next day, they realized that so harsh a decision might rebound against them and they reversed it.[2] (A trireme sent off hurriedly to communicate the reversed decision arrived in Mytilene just as the executions were beginning.) In 406, the assembly was persuaded by impassioned speakers to order the execution of eight of its generals who were accused of failing to pick up shipwrecked sailors after a battle. After the executions, the assembly regretted its decision and somewhat hypocritically condemned the speakers for "forcing" it to act the way it did. So emotions could be seen to overrule reason. Playwrights and philosophers explored the dangers of rhetoric. Parmenides has the goddess who declaims his ideas tell her listener: "Now I put an end to persuasive *logos* and thought about truth, and from this point do you learn mortal opinions by listening to the deceptive appearance of my words"—words that, when separated from the *logos* of argument, the goddess recognizes, might prove in themselves "deceptive."[3] In his play *Clouds,* Aristophanes sets up a debate between "Just Speech" and "Unjust Speech," in which "Unjust Speech" triumphs through the unscrupulous use of verbal trickery.

These concerns were countered by teachers of rhetoric such as the influential Athenian Isocrates (436–338 B.C.), who looked back to a golden age when, he claimed, the great men of Athens—Solon, Cleisthenes the bringer of equality among citizens, Themistocles the hero of the Persian Wars, and Pericles—had used rhetoric solely for the good of the state. The very success of Athens in earlier times had shown that good speaking could offer a pathway to greatness. What was vital, argued Isocrates, was the moral independence and integrity of the speaker, and training in moral responsibility was an essential part of training in rhetoric. "The stronger a person desires to persuade hearers, the more he will work to be honourable and good and to have a good reputation among the citizens."[4] Isocrates even recognized that at times a "moral" speaker might have to put the needs of the Greek world as a whole before the concerns of his native city. This stress upon the moral qualities of the orator was to be echoed by the Romans, by the orator and statesman Cicero and by Quintilian (c. A.D. 96), in whose *Institutio Oratoria* an upright character and high ideals are presented as the fundamental qualities of a good speaker.

An input of emotion in a speech was not necessarily a bad thing. In his *Rhetoric*, Aristotle listed the components of a good speech, using the word *logos* to describe the speech itself: "There are three kinds of persuasive means furnished by the *logos*: those in the character of the speaker, those in how the hearer is disposed, and those in the *logos* itself, through its demonstrating or seeming to demonstrate."[5] One could not, argues Aristotle, disassociate "the character of the speaker" from the rational elements (its "demonstrations") of the speech itself. They are both essential components of a speech, and the emphasis should not be on trying to eliminate emotion but to make morally responsible use of it.

Yet for one Athenian, Plato (c. 429–347 B.C.), this was not enough. Plato lived through a time of change and disorder. His native Athens was defeated in the Peloponnesian War by Sparta (404 B.C.), its great walls demolished and its empire dismantled. A new "Government of Thirty," to which Plato had some family links, degenerated into tyranny, and after the restoration of Athenian democracy a witch hunt was launched against Plato's mentor, the philosopher Socrates. Socrates had made himself a well-known figure in Athens, not least through his practice of challenging every assumption of anyone he questioned. "The unexamined life is not worth living," he insisted; "the most knowledgeable man is he who knows he knows nothing." His demolition of any conventional belief held without reflection proved intensely irritating, especially at a time of defeat and political turmoil for Athens. Eventually the patience of his fellow citizens was exhausted, and in 399 they put Socrates on trial. "Socrates does wrong," the charge read, "by not acknowledging the gods the city acknowledges and introducing other, new, powers. He also does wrong by corrupting the young." Such vague charges were a familiar part of Athenian political life and could usually be met by counter-accusations against one's opponents. Socrates refused to debase himself and argued instead, and provocatively, that he should be honoured by the city for his work, not denounced. This only outraged his accusers further, and he was found guilty and, in a rare case of Athenian political intolerance against a fellow citizen, sentenced to death.[6]

The lesson Plato drew from Socrates' condemnation was that the emotional and ephemeral impulses of the masses could lead to the commission of evil, in this case, the execution of a "good" man. "Good" and "evil," it appeared, were unstable concepts, relative to the moment. In his work *Gorgias,* Plato uses the example of Gorgias himself to pour scorn on the idea that a speaker can bring truth to his listeners—whether he himself recognizes it or not, his art lies primarily in deception. For him, Isocrates' claim that it was simply a matter of training speakers to be more morally upright failed to reach the heart of the problem; instead what was needed were objective standards by which to judge moral concepts such as "good," "evil" and "justice." Establishing these standards was the task that Plato set himself.[7]

One of the major influences on Plato was Pythagoras. Pythagoras, active at the end of the sixth century B.C., had been dead for a hundred years, but his followers in southern Italy had preserved his teachings, and Plato visited them in 388 B.C. Among these teachings was a belief that numbers underpinned the natural world. Pythagoras had used the example of a string stretched across a sounding box. Pluck it and record the note. Halve the length of the string and pluck it again, the note is precisely one octave higher. So unseen numbers appear to be present at a different and, Plato argued, more significant level than the world appreciated by the senses. Plato developed this idea to suggest that not only numbers but values and even objects existed beyond this world and at a more perfect level of reality. So while a picture may be beautiful, its beauty, which is essentially transient, is only a reflection and a part of a much greater eternal beauty. This Form of Beauty, as Plato called it, comprised all the elements of beauty known on earth but was in itself greater than they were. It was far more valuable to come to know this Form of Beauty than to search without success for transient beauty in the natural world. There could be Forms of many different entities—in his so-called Seventh Letter Plato suggests there might be Forms "of shapes and surfaces, of the good, the beautiful and the just, of all bodies natural and artificial, of fire and water and the like, of every animal, of every quality of character, of all actions and passivities."[8] Furthermore, Plato suggested that the Forms were not all equal, existing alongside each other, but that they could be arranged hierarchically. If the Forms of "Justice" and "Beauty" are "good" in themselves, then they must form part of a superior Form of "the Good," which could be compared to a sun among other lesser sources of light.

The world of Forms could be grasped by the human soul, which Plato believed was immortal and passed from one body to another on death. Plato was fascinated and perplexed, as many Greek philosophers were, by the relationship between reason and emotion. His solution was to see the soul as split into three parts: a reasoning part, another sensual part based on "desire" (hunger, thirst, sex) and a third on "spirit," which encapsulated emotions such as anger and the desire for honour and reputation. To Plato the reasoning part was by the far the most important; he argued that maturity, in effect the ability to act virtuously, came from bringing the "desiring" and "spirited" parts of the soul under the control of reason.[9] The reasoning part of the soul could achieve its own maturity by grasping the nature of the Forms, which, Plato claimed, it had actually always known but had forgotten. He makes the point in his dialogue the *Meno*. Meno is a slave who is led through a mathematical proof that deals with the area of a square (which quadruples when the length of its side is doubled). Plato argues that the knowledge that the proof was true was concealed in Meno's soul and simply had to be "recollected." The proof relating to the area of a square could be said to exist as a truth which would be true in any circumstances at any time. In other words, it exists independently of the material world and continues to exist even if no human soul is aware of it.

A mathematical proof such as that presented to Meno can be proved by and to any whose minds are capable of elementary deductive logic. But Plato goes on to argue that concepts such as justice, beauty and good are similar to mathematical proofs in that they also exist as eternal truths ("Forms"), independent of the material world. He readily acknowledged the difficulty in grasping these Forms. Few had the intellectual and reasoning power required to conquer their "desire" and "spirit" and set out on the arduous intellectual journey required. In the *Phaedo* Plato talks condescendingly of "the lovers of spectacles and lovers of sounds, who delight in fine voices and colours and shapes, and everything that art fashions from that sort of thing . . . but their minds are incapable of seeing and delighting in the nature of the Beautiful itself . . ." In other words, the reasoning part of their souls is incapable of asserting its power over the other parts. Those who had the intellectual ability to understand the Forms should be selected when children and trained over many years in the use of reason. They (and Plato was unusual for his times in including women as well as men) would gradually come to develop an understanding of the Forms, until finally, after many years of intense reflection, their true and eternal nature would be revealed.

Yet when they had grasped the Forms and the eternal truths enshrined in them, the task of the intellectual elite, "the Guardians," as

Plato termed them, was just beginning. It was they who would take on the task of running society according to their knowledge of the nature of justice, good and similar concepts. They were, as Plato put it, like doctors who knew what was best for their patients and were thus justified in overruling the patients' own beliefs about their illnesses. If anyone resisted them, the Guardians were justified in exiling or even, according to Plato's late work the *Laws,* executing them.

The search for an understanding of the Forms, as well as the implementation of them, required absolute dedication, and those selected to undertake it must not let themselves be diverted by emotion or rhetoric. Plato's world was one in which there was little place for spectacle, theatre or the arts (a beautiful object could only be a pale imitation of the Form of Beauty), spontaneity or sexual passion. The *Laws,* in particular, written when his idealism appears to have soured, seems to demand a joyless society. However, for Plato the achievement of knowledge of the Forms was such a satisfying task in itself that it would transcend any knowledge of the world apparent to the senses. He went further; knowledge gained of the Forms was so significant that observations of the actual world should be disregarded if they were in conflict with the reality of the Forms. "We shall approach astronomy, as we do geometry, by way of problems, *and ignore what's in the sky* [my italics], if we intend to get a real grasp of astronomy," as he puts in *The Republic,* his most famous work, on the nature of good government.[10]

This amounted to a direct attack on the mainstream scientific tradition of Greek thought, which relied, as we have seen, on empirical observation. While Plato stressed that the Forms could be grasped only through reason, was it in fact possible to use reason to prove that the Forms, indeed a whole world of unchanging immaterial "objects" beyond this one, actually existed? Even if it were, how was it possible to be sure that anyone had grasped the Form of, say, "the Good" correctly, and how were disputes to be resolved if there were rival interpretations? In practice, Plato's assertion that such conflict was impossible because all those who grasped a Form would agree on its nature seems untenable. The fundamental, and perhaps fatal, weakness of Plato's philosophy lies in the difficulties of finding axiomatic foundations from which the nature of a Form of, for example, Beauty can be deduced. Without axioms proper reasoning was impossible, and in terms of practical politics it needed only a powerful individual, institution or government to claim that it had discovered the Platonic Forms, and with them the right to impose them on others, for a dictatorship to emerge. Among its casu-alties would be the speculative tradition of empirical research, to which Plato appeared to give such little value.[11]

Platonic thought assumes that the material world is not the ideal set-ting for the soul. A more satisfying home exists elsewhere, in the imma-terial world of the Forms. This was a revolutionary concept in the Greek world, where, for example, the afterlife was traditionally seen as a shad-owy and unfulfilling existence, and it created a radical disagreement between those who attempted to live life to the full within the material world, and whose philosophies and ethical systems reflected that, and those who saw the soul as trapped temporarily in this inadequate and transient world before a greater one to come. Platonists also assumed there was a deep gulf between the world of the senses and that of the Forms. Because it was accessible to so few and needed such an arduous training to reach it, the world of the Forms was divine in a very different sense from that of the traditional world of the Greek gods, whose human forms, behaviour and rich mythology of exploits made them comprehensible, even accessible, to all. If a Form, say that of a supreme Good, was equated with an actual God, then he would indeed be an awesome and remote one. Inherent in Plato's thought was a massive realignment of the relationship between human beings and "the divine" that involved, inevitably, the diminution of the place of "the ordinary man" in the scheme of things. The fruits of Platonic reason might not be self-confidence but the opposite—a realization of how insignificant human beings were in the face of the superior, unchanging, hierarchical world of the Forms. Explicit too was the grading of human beings into a minority who could grasp the nature of the immaterial world and the mass who could not and were therefore dependent on the minority for elucidation. Effective reasoning was the preserve of the few, who had to persuade or coerce those who were unable to grasp the nature of the Forms.

Plato's insistence on an other-worldly basis for ethical belief can be contrasted with Aristotle's. In many respects Aristotle's thought is as alien to us as Plato's: he was aristocratic by temperament and supported the subjection of women and the institution of slavery. Only the free mature male, according to Aristotle, is able to think rationally. Yet, unlike Plato, Aristotle was concerned to create an ethical system that was based in the everyday world of human existence. He was much more sensitive to and accepting of the humanity of others than Plato was. "One may observe in one's travels in distant countries," he writes in the *Nicomachean Ethics,* "the feelings of recognition and affiliation that link every human being to every other human being."[12] Virtue (the word used was *arete,* often translated as "excellence," although this risks depriving it of its ethical connotations) is not an abstract principle to be searched for outside the material world. It exists when a human being lives a life in which his nature as a human being is realized at the highest level. By living in this way he will reach *eudaimonia,* a state of well-being or flourishing. This state does not just happen; it has to be worked for through the actual experience of living. First a child must be brought up by its parents to be disposed towards the doing of "good," but he can only become "good" through the active doing of "good" acts. First the right orientation, the desire to do good as a way of living, then the practical experience of doing "good," which somehow fixes "goodness" within the character of the doer. (This concept, important for educationalists among others, has gained new life in modern philosophical debates.) Yet what does it mean to act in a "good" way? In everyday life the individual is faced with a host of situations. Suppose one takes one type of "good" action, for example, behaving courageously. But while courageous behaviour is undoubtedly virtuous, in practice some undoubted acts of courage, for instance, attacking an armed soldier while unarmed, are scarcely rational. The individual has to exercise discrimination based on knowledge of similar situations and on a thinking-through of possible outcomes to distinguish which courageous acts are likely to have some "good" effect. Ethical judgments should not be based on the emotions of the moment—reasoned control of emotions is central to Aristotelian ethics—and so with increasing experience each individual is likely to develop his or her own moral code, general principles by which they act. However, the ability to adapt this code to the demands of a specific situation must never be lost (it would be a degradation of the power of reason if it were). In Aristotelian ethics there are no absolutes that can be used to allow the individual to surrender his duty to accept responsibility for his own actions in a variety of different circumstances. Aristotle goes further, suggesting that the courageous or other "good" act becomes a truly virtuous one only if it is carried out for its own sake, not just as a means to another end.

A person who combines the right disposition with the ability to be able to discriminate in actual situations will, Aristotle argued, eventually achieve a life in which he is at peace with himself. Everything will come together in harmony, *eudaimonia,* a complex state in which success in human affairs, moral goodness and the ability to use rational thought at its highest level seem to co-exist. (It is perhaps too simplistic to group these attributes together. While Aristotle believed that a state of contemplation, which often requires isolation, was the highest state of man, he was also acutely aware that human beings need company if they are to be fully "themselves.")

Every individual has the potential to find his own *eudaimonia,* the natural end of being a fully functioning human. Aristotle is typical of Greek thinkers in having a confident and optimistic view of human nature. He proclaims that it is worthwhile being human, and, unlike Plato and later Christian thinkers, he says little about the possibility of natural desires pulling one away from *eudaimonia* towards some lower state of existence. "Nature always produces the best," he says on several occasions; in the *Nicomachean Ethics* he states that "all the virtues of character seem to belong to us from birth . . . For we are just and moderate and courageous and the rest straight from our birth . . . even children and animals have these natural dispositions, though they evidently prove harmful without rational guidance."[13] In short, becoming virtuous involves using one's power of reasoning to shape virtues that are innate. Aristotle assumes that human beings will want to achieve the pleasure of reaching their full and undoubted potential. As an inherent condition of being human, that is the direction in which they are oriented.

In Raphael's famous Vatican fresco the *School of Athens,* Aristotle and Plato are shown among the assembled philosophers. Plato's hand points upwards to the heavens, Aristotle's down towards the earth. They represent not only themselves but two contrasting approaches in the quest for certainty. For Aristotle certainty has to be found in this world through the painstaking accumulation of empirical evidence and reasoned deduction from it. It is always subject to reason and challenge through the acquisition of new evidence accumulated by the senses. Outside the world of abstract mathematics and logical syllogisms, knowledge is always provisional. Plato, by contrast, rejects the world of the senses altogether. It holds no real value in comparison to the immaterial world of the Forms, where truth alone resides. The way that these two approaches to certainty were developed in the next centuries and woven into the fabric of Christianity will form a major theme of this book.[14]

Meanwhile, the world of the fourth century B.C. in which both great thinkers taught was in the process of being transformed. The political developments of the next 700 years and the survival of the Greek intellectual tradition are the subject of the next section of this book. In both religion and philosophy, in all its branches, including science and mathematics, there were still important achievements to come.

# 4

## CHANGING POLITICAL CONTEXTS
### Alexander and the Coming of the Hellenistic Monarchies

The most significant political development in the Mediterranean world between 350 B.C. and A.D. 100 was the spread of monarchical government. By the beginning of the second century A.D., the entire Mediterranean world and much else besides (southern Britain, France and Spain in the west, Armenia and Mesopotamia in the east) were subject to a single ruler, the Roman emperor. This office was rooted in the Hellenistic monarchies, which had arisen in the east following the rise of Philip II of Macedon and the destruction of the Persian empire by his son Alexander "the Great" between 334 and 323.[1]

The rise of Macedon became possible because by the fourth century the independent Greek city state had come to an evolutionary dead end. The small elites of male citizens who, typically, ran the *polis* either as a democracy or an oligarchy may have provided an excellent cockpit for political debates—which in turn proved highly stimulating to intellectual and cultural life—but their very exclusiveness prevented any *polis* from controlling an area large enough to provide the resources for any lasting political control. In the fifth century Athens had managed to create an empire of Aegean city states, sustained originally by common fear of a Persian revival and later by Athens' clever manipulation of naval power, but the hope of long-term control of a mass of city states scattered across the islands and shores of the Aegean was far-fetched, and the empire disintegrated when Athens was defeated by its rival Sparta in 404. Sparta lost its advantage in turn through political clumsiness—its formidable hoplite phalanxes were eventually destroyed by Thebes at the battle of

Leuctra in 371. Stripped of its land and the helots, or serfs, who worked it, Sparta never revived. Thebes held a temporary hegemony over central Greece, but this too was dissipated after its leading general, Epaminondas, was killed in battle in 362. During these power struggles most of the smaller Greek cities had been debilitated by war, internal political tensions and the squandering or plunder of their limited resources.[2]

Greece was therefore vulnerable to outsiders, and the most successful of these was King Philip II of Macedonia, a kingdom that lay between Greece and the Balkans. He assumed hegemony over Greece after a crushing victory over the combined armies of Thebes and Athens at Chaeronaea in 338. Philip was a brilliant strategist and diplomat with an appreciation of how important it was to secure his conquests before embarking on others. His long-term ambition was to conquer Asia Minor, whose land was so much more fertile than that of Greece, and so his settlement was a moderate one under which the Greek cities agreed to forge a permanent alliance among themselves with Philip as their leader (the League of Corinth). The peace this brought was its own justification. Athens, for instance, retained her democracy and entered a new phase of prosperity during which her navy, docks and public buildings were restored. It has been traditional for historians to lament the end of the independent city state, but there was clearly much to be gained from acquiescence in Philip's control.

However, the stability of the Greek world was soon placed in jeopardy by the adventures of Philip's son Alexander, who succeeded to the throne of Macedonia after his father was assassinated in 336.[3] In contrast to his father, Alexander imposed his rule on Greece brutally. When Thebes, one of the most ancient of Greek cities and legendary birthplace of Heracles, revolted against him, 6,000 Thebans were killed, 30,000 enslaved. There was a marked contrast between Alexander's proclaimed love of Greek culture (he claimed descent from the Greek hero Achilles and steeped himself in Homer) and his treatment of the Greeks themselves. Turning his back on his kingdom except as a source of manpower, he made for the Persian empire with the armies his father had so meticulously trained. Brilliant though his victories were, they achieved little more than the dismantling and rendering into chaos of an empire that had successfully maintained its stability and multicultural identity for 200 years. His brutality, especially as he moved his isolated armies further into Asia, was often staggering. Cleitarchus of Alexandria, one of the few contemporary historians to write from outside the court circles and thus with no need to glorify Alexander's image, reported that in one Indian valley alone some 80,000 people were slaughtered.[4] Alexander did little to replace the power vacuum he created other than to found a few cities of veterans strategically sited to keep order. It was Alexander's successors who were to found the centres of Greek culture in the east such as Ai Khanoum, on the border of modern Afghanistan, with its library, theatre and gymnasium. Alexander had no aptitude for or interest in administration, and when he returned to the heartland of his new empire he preoccupied himself only with plans for renewed conquests.

Alexander's temperament was autocratic, and the Persian model of kingship and the rituals of Persian court life proved highly attractive to him. The vigour with which he hunted down Darius, the defeated Persian monarch, so that he could become "King of Kings" in his place bordered on the obsessional. His commanders, many of them men who had fought with his father, had been used to a spirit of rough camaraderie with their king. As Alexander headed east on his conquests, the relationship soured. No act shows Alexander's lack of respect for and understanding of Greek culture more clearly than his insistence that his Greek and Macedonian commanders adopt the Persian custom known in Greek as *proskynesis,* prostration before a monarch. This had long been seen by the Greeks as a symbol of the servility of the Persian people and contrasted with the dignified behaviour expected of a free man who would never submit to a display of such subservience. In the face of protest and ridicule, Alexander reluctantly gave way. On his return to Persia, however, he assumed the regalia of the Persian monarchy. An ill-judged attempt to integrate the Macedonians into court life by marrying them to Persian noblewomen failed ignominiously. The Macedonians discarded their Persian wives as soon as Alexander had died. Adding to their disquiet was Alexander's appropriation of divine honours. After a visit to the oracle of Zeus Ammon at Siwa in the Libyan desert early in his campaigns, he seems to have begun to believe that he was the actual son of Zeus (the story went that his mother, Olympias, had conceived through a thunderbolt or a snake), and by the end of his reign he was wearing the purple robe and ram's head of the god at banquets. He appears to have asked the Greek cities to offer him cult worship.

Greece benefited little from Alexander's reign and suffered like his other territories from his autocratic ways. His policies were based on short-term opportunism. In 324 Alexander announced, at the Olympic Games of that year, that exiles from Greek cities would be free to return home. The exiles were delighted; many had lost land in the unsettled conditions of the fourth century and some 20,000 of them turned up at Olympia to hear the decree proclaimed. If settled back home, they would provide centres of support for Alexander. However, for the cities themselves the threatened influx of landless former dissidents and political rivals was deeply unsettling. Governments would be destabilized and Philip's careful settlement of Greece undermined. When rumours of Alexander's death first reached Athens in 323, the Athenian politician Demades argued that it could not possibly be true, because if it were the whole world would know because of the stink of the corpse. When the death was confirmed, Athenian resentment against Macedonia exploded in revolt. Aristotle, sensitive to his links with the Macedonian royal family, left Athens for exile, determined, so he said, that Athens would not commit a second crime against philosophy (the first being, of course, the execution of Socrates). He died a year later. Meanwhile, Macedonian troops put down the uprising. In Athens the world's first sustained democracy, which had lasted 140 years and had been respected by Alexander's father, Philip, was crushed.

The cost of Alexander's inability to create a stable administration for his vast conquests, or even to appoint a successor, soon made itself felt. When asked while he was dying who should succeed him, Alexander reputedly answered, "To the strongest." The result was predictable; for the next twenty years his conquests were torn apart. Those who had a claim to legitimacy, Alexander's half-brother Arrhidaeus and his posthumous son Alexander, proved mere puppets through which rival commanders claimed their own legitimacy until both had been disposed of. By 307 all pretence of a regency had vanished, and those commanders who survived the vicious infighting declared that they themselves were kings. Eventually three new dynasties emerged: the Ptolemies in Egypt, the Seleucids in Asia and the Antigonids in Macedonia. Later, in Asia Minor, the Attalids carved themselves out a kingdom round the commanding site of Pergamum. However destructive Alexander's impact had proved in the short term, the new kings found that they had little option but to see him as their model. They had, like him, no other claim of legitimacy than that of conquest, and they were continually tested on the battlefield. One of the most persistent conflicts was between the Ptolemies and the Seleucids over their common border in Syria, but the successors also faced raiding Celts from Europe, frequent upheavals in Asia and finally, eventually and fatally, the growing power of Rome. The

Hellenistic armies were large, up to 80,000 men recruited as mercenaries from the poorer parts of Greece, and so the relationship between monarchy and war that was to be echoed by and underpin Roman imperial rule was set in place.

The successful dynasts emulated Alexander in other ways. Alexander had been adept at using arts as propaganda. Notably in the work of his favoured sculptor, Lysippus, he portrayed himself as a hero/conqueror, naked with a spear, or in a "romantic" pose, beardless (a symbol of youth in the Greek world), with thick curled hair and gazing upwards with what Plutarch was to call "a melting look." In some representations he was given the attributes of Heracles, from whom the Macedonian royal family claimed descent (ironically so in view of Alexander's destruction of Heracles' legendary birthplace, Thebes).[5] Such idealizations were copied by his successors, who often directly adapted Alexander's poses, as did the Romans after them. The most famous image of the Roman general Pompey shows him with an "Alexander haircut," while some 650 years later Constantine was still using the pose of "the melting look"—in, for instance, a coin struck to commemorate his founding of Constantinople in A.D. 330. Art and propaganda were now inextricably linked in the representation of the ruler.

For the first time in the Greek world, the possibility that the king might be divine was also accepted. Greek myth spoke of how gods might father children who lived on earth as mortal heroes—Heracles was one, as were many of the protagonists in Homer's *Iliad*. However, in their reluctance to accept that men might behave like gods, the Greeks had been hesitant in giving formal honours to living human beings, however great their exploits. There is a record of the Spartan commander Lysander being offered some form of cult worship in the early fourth century, but Alexander was the first Greek to claim that he had actually been born the son of a god. He failed to convince the Greeks, but in Egypt the Ptolemies were more successful in assuming divinity. They made use of the tradition that the pharaoh was the son of the god Amun. Ptolemy II Philadelphos proclaimed in 279 that his late father, Ptolemy I, and his third wife were gods, and he later announced that he and his wife were already divine, so providing the earliest known example of a Greek ruler formally claiming godhead while still alive.[6] Even when not claiming divinity for themselves, Alexander's successors widely claimed a special association with the gods. The Attalids of Pergamum chose that traditional protectress of cities, Athena. The Macedonians maintained their support for Heracles, an ideal model for those who wanted to achieve great deeds. The Ptolemies associated themselves with Dionysus and with two Egyptian deities, Serapis, a god to whom the Egyptian Osiris was linked in the Apis bull cult, and Isis, Osiris' sister. Cities responded with their own ruler cults, though many of these appear to have been designed to attract patronage. Athens, for instance, petitioned one monarch as a god who because he was near at hand could actually get things done! The concept that the monarch was either a god himself or was specially favoured by the gods became one of the most important aspects of Hellenistic and Roman imperial rule. It added the threat of the favoured god's displeasure to any who challenged the king or emperor, and, as we shall see, the assimilation of Christianity into the Roman state cannot be understood without it.

When the Greek biographer and philosopher Plutarch considered Alexander, he wrote a famous eulogy:

> Conquering by force of arms those whom he could not bring together by reasoned persuasion, he brought men from everywhere into a unified body mixed together, as if in a loving cup, their lives and characters and marriages and social customs. He commanded them all to think of the inhabited world as their fatherland, of the encamped army as their acropolis and guard . . .

There are still historians who quote this eulogy uncritically as if it represented some kind of historical truth. In fact, it seems to have been a rhetorical statement that conflicts with other assessments Plutarch himself made of Alexander. One can find little evidence of "reasoned persuasion" in Alexander's unprovoked attack on the Persian empire or in the obsessional way he tracked down Darius. The unrestrained massacres in the Far East hardly speak of men united "in a loving cup," and, as has been seen, the attempt to marry his rough commanders to the elegant ladies of the Persian court was a disaster. Homer may have been Alexander's model, but an appreciation of the pity of war, so movingly expressed in the *Iliad* (as, for example, when Priam comes to seek the body of his son Hector from Achilles), seems to have been beyond Alexander's grasp. His commitment to Greek culture was shallow, and in fact his whole life involved an abuse of the values of reasoned argument, planning and respect for the natural order which, as we have seen, were central to Greek intellectual life. He took a historian, Callisthenes, from the city of Olynthos, with him, but after Callisthenes had bravely articulated opposition to *proskynesis* on the grounds that it was impious to offer Alexander divine honours and the practice of *proskynesis* was an insult to the Greek sense of liberty, he was executed for "conspiracy." The Greek world was outraged. It was not only that Alexander bypassed rational thinking; his elevation of himself to monarch and to godhead brought irrationality and absolutism to the core of government. The extinction of Athenian democracy in 322 at the hands of Macedonian troops after his death comes as no surprise in this context. Although the momentum of Greek intellectual life proved considerable, Alexander's model of absolutism represented a threat to it.[7]

That the Greek intellectual tradition survived at this stage was, paradoxically, partly thanks to Alexander's successors. An important feature of the period was the use of patronage by monarchs as a means of boosting their own status and of maintaining the support of their Greek subjects. It could be shown in flamboyant display and opulent festivals, and by the building of great palaces and new temples both in their capitals and in other favoured cities. The Attalids made Pergamum into one of the great showcase cities of the eastern Mediterranean, and one of them, Attalus II, also honoured Athens with a resplendent new stoa (roofed colonnade). The Ptolemies, able to draw on the considerable resources of the Nile valley, made Alexandria the grandest city of the Mediterranean. It was not only the palaces (each ruler building his own when he succeeded to the throne) and the massive temple complex in honour of Serapis that impressed; it was the Ptolemies' investment in preserving and sustaining Greek culture. They can be credited with the famous library, the greatest ever known in the ancient world, with perhaps some 500,000 rolls of papyrus and with the museum (literally "shrine of the Muses") as a centre of academic debate.

Alexandria's most important cultural role in the Hellenistic period was as a centre for science and mathematics, while Athens maintained its preeminence in philosophy. The continuing breadth of the Greek achievement in the Hellenistic centuries provides evidence that intellectual and artistic achievement was not stifled by the demise of the independent city state and that the barriers between what are now seen as distinct academic disciplines were fluid. While Herophilus, working in Alexandria in the first half of the third century, was able to isolate the nerves and show that they ran back to the brain, a major breakthrough in medical history, his fellow Alexandrian Apollonius Rhodios was writing, for the first time, it seems, of the agonies of adolescent love in his epic *Argonautika,* incorporating Herophilus' findings into his text. As the young Medea sets eyes on Jason:

> . . . her virgin heart now beat a
> Tattoo on her ribs, her eyes shed tears of pity, constant
> Anguish ran smouldering through her flesh, hotwired her finespun
> Nerve ends, needles in the skull's base, the deep spinal
> Cord where pain pierces sharpest when the unresting
> Passions inject their agony into the senses . . .[8]

When Eratosthenes attempted to measure the circumference of the earth in the late third century, he was combining the use of geography, astronomy and geometry. Archimedes (c. 287–212 B.C.) laid the foundations of integral calculus, applied mathematics and hydrostatics as well as formulated the means for the calculation of areas and volumes (such as cones) and the computing of very large numbers. His work is characterized by an extraordinary imagination, through which he conceptualized the problems in hand, allied to a technical ingenuity that allowed him to work them out practically. The two came together in his alleged discovery of a way of determining the proportions of gold and silver in a crown while meditating in his bath. His cry of "Eureka" as he rushed through the streets perhaps best symbolizes this age of excited intellectual discovery.[9]

Older cities such as Athens were honoured for their cultural heritage, and Athens remained the most important centre for philosophy throughout the period. Two major new movements, Epicureanism and Stoicism, were born there.[10] What they had in common was to offer a philosophy of life that was open to everyone, not only to an intellectual elite (Plato) or the male citizen (Aristotle)—but here the similarity ended. The Epicureans preached what seemed a heresy to many Greeks, that the individual should withdraw from society and cultivate peace of mind through the avoidance of stress. With the gods no more than models of good behaviour without the power to harm human beings, it was up to the individual to find his own equilibrium. The goal was to maximize pleasure, by which Epicurus, its founder, did not mean any frenzied search for sensual enjoyment but rather the cultivation of more refined pursuits, predominant among them friendship (extended to include the sharing of women among devotees). If involvement in political life proved stressful, then it should be abandoned. Stoicism was altogether more demanding intellectually and more influential. The name Stoicism comes from the Athenian stoa, where its founder, Zeno of Citium (in Cyprus), began teaching in about 311. It was his successor, Chrysippus, who was responsible for developing Stoicism into a coherent and profound philosophy. Chrysippus' teachings can be reconstructed only with difficulty from later commentaries on them, and Stoicism was never a closed system—internal debate was acceptable and often conducted with great intellectual sophistication. In so far as one can generalize, the Stoics saw all matter as having a fundamental unity, as if it was a single web with each part linked to the rest, but this web was never at rest—it was in a continuous cycle of change. Each cycle would come to an end in fire but then restart itself with new matter being born out of the fire. Matter was not only that which could be seen and touched; it was suffused by an invisible rational principle that could not exist independently of it. This principle is what drove the cosmos through its never-ending cycles, and the ubiquitous term *logos* was used to describe it. Here *logos* was seen as an entity in itself, rooted in nature as it were; this was a transition of some importance in the history of the concept.

The problem that taxed the Stoics was how to fit human beings into their cosmos. If Stoicism was taken to its logical conclusion, human beings were simply part of the cosmos and could not act freely outside it or influence its inexorable unfolding. Yet human beings did appear to be able to act freely, make choices, and think through issues rationally for themselves. (The Stoics stressed that it was this ability to think rationally that marked them out from the rest of the natural world.) The Stoics were challenged to settle this contradiction by Carneades, head of Plato's Academy, whose energy was now focused on making sceptical assessments of rival philosophies. The Stoic response was sophisticated and finally led to the acceptance of the view that human beings could and should act freely, even if within a narrow margin, to improve their health, accumulate money for basic needs and even to act morally within this world as it existed. A rational response by an individual to external events could be accommodated within "the web" without breaking it. Stoic morality consisted of controlling one's passions and irrational impulses so that the individual lived a self-sufficient life that was aligned with the unfolding of the cosmos and accepting of its inexorable progress (hence the conventional meaning of the word "stoical" to refer to the impassive acceptance of the fate the world brings one's way). This was the path to virtue, and when the Stoics talked of freedom, they meant freedom from passion or irrational responses to events. In contrast to the Epicureans, the Stoics did not rule out taking an active part in public life, and so Stoics are found in Roman government and doggedly doing their duty as soldiers.

None of these intellectual developments would have been possible if the Hellenistic monarchs had not succeeded (where Alexander had so conspicuously failed) in maintaining stable administrations and finding a secure way of passing on their rule to successors. They drew heavily on old allegiances and existing administrative structures; the Ptolemies effectively used traditional images of the pharaohs to sustain themselves among the Egyptian population, even building temples in the local style. (Among those whose ruins survive to this day are the temple to Horus at Edfu and that to Isis on the Nile island of Philae.) Like the more effective pharaohs they worked hard to maximize their revenue from taxation through the centuries-old Egyptian bureaucracy. The Seleucids appropriated and developed the royal estates left by the Persian kings and adopted the structure of satrapies, through which each region of the empire was given considerable autonomy so long as tax revenue was maintained.[11] Succession was secured by stressing the divine nature of the dynasty and by ensuring that the son of the king had effective power before his father died. Seleucus I, for instance, the founder of the dynasty, made his son Antiochus a provincial governor before his death, the proclamation being made before his assembled army, and he strengthened Antiochus' position by passing on one of his wives to him. Antiochus I ruled for thirty-six years, Seleucus I for twenty-four, and Seleucus II and Antiochus II another thirty-five years between them. The contrast with Alexander's brief rule need hardly be stressed.

Traditionally the Hellenistic age has been seen as showy and vulgar, even decadent, after the glories of classical Greece. This was after all an age where wealth was concentrated in fewer hands and deliberately flaunted as a means of creating and maintaining status. Its literary achievements cannot be compared with those of Aeschylus and Sophocles. But the Hellenistic achievement in science and mathematics was remarkable, and this was also an age of growing, if still very limited, technological achievement. Pergamum, high on its rock, survived only because water from a spring twenty-five metres higher on a neighbouring hill was piped down and then up again into the city through some 240,000 linked lead pipes. Considering the poor foundations on which they built, the dynasties sustained themselves well. A descendant of the first Ptolemy, Cleopatra, was still in place in Egypt nearly 300 years after her ancestor's seizure of power. Many of the political barriers that had isolated the Greek cities from each other had been dissolved, so that after stability had been restored by Alexander's successors, the Greeks could now see themselves as citizens of a wider world. Greeks from over 200 different cities, some of them as far north as the Black Sea, are recorded as having made their home in Egypt during these years, and the old dialects of Greece were dissolved into a shared *koine,* which was to be the standard Greek of the Gospels and the letters of Paul. They could never have spread if the narrow allegiances to a single city state had continued.

5

## ABSORBING THE EAST, ROME AND THE
## INTEGRATION OF GREEK CULTURE

Alexander had expanded the Greek world far beyond its original limits. No one could have imagined that his empire in its turn would be conquered by what was, in the fourth century, still a small city occupying the centre of the Latin plain in central Italy. From its beginnings in the eighth century Rome's survival had depended on the successful defence of its exposed territory from neighbouring peoples of the plains, and from the mountain peoples who could raid downwards and then retreat to their impregnable strongholds.[1] As the city successfully consolidated its territory on the plain, war became integral to the system of Roman government. From 509, when the city became a republic, the prime role of its leading magistrates, the two consuls, was military command, and, although all magistrates were now elected, there was no path to political power without successful military service.

The secret of Rome's resilience lay in a psychology of aggression married to policies that were dedicated to increasing its fighting manpower. The emerging state was always prepared to give citizenship or, failing that, a favoured status (known as Latin rights) to loyal communities. Their manpower became Rome's own, and defeated cities were usually required to become allies so that their men too would be available for Rome's future wars. The Greek cities had never proved able to share citizenship so easily, one reason why none had created a sustainable empire. The Roman armies were also imbued with a gritty determination honed in the tough wars of the fourth and third centuries against the Samnites, the most formidable of the mountain peoples. This meant that when outsiders such as the brilliant Carthaginian general Hannibal invaded Italy across the Alps in 218, Rome hung on and, despite humiliating defeats in the field, wore him down. Rome also learned, through the copying and improvement of captured Carthaginian ships, how to create a navy and use it effectively. By 200 B.C. Italy and the former Carthaginian empire itself, which had included Sicily, north Africa and Spain, had been conquered and made up a Roman empire in the western Mediterranean.

By this time the Romans were already intruding into the eastern Mediterranean. Despite its unique constitution and culture, Rome had never been isolated from the Greek world. Wealthy Greek cities dotted the coastline of southern Italy and Sicily, and there was early trade between Greeks and the city. Rome itself had adopted a foundation myth that linked it, through Aeneas (a refugee from Troy), with the east. Rome's first history was written by a Roman, Fabius Pictor, in Greek— as if it were the Greeks, rather than the neighbouring Latins, who had to be impressed by the city's growing status. As early as 433 B.C., when Athens was at the height of its power, Apollo, the Greek god of reason and deliverer from disease, had been adopted by the city of Rome when plague broke out there. His presence underlined the fact that, like the Greeks, the Romans were at ease with anthropomorphic gods. Indeed, Roman and Greek gods were to prove easily assimilated with each other: Jupiter absorbed Zeus, the father of the gods; Venus, Aphrodite, the goddess of love; and Ceres, Demeter, the goddess of corn. By the time of the poet Ovid in the late first century B.C., the mythologies of the two cultures had become inextricably mingled.[2]

So when in the third century B.C. Rome began to conquer the Greek cities of the peninsula and bring back vast quantities of statuary and other plunder, there was already some appreciation of what was being appropriated. It is hard to know to what extent this early plunder was used as a symbol of Roman victory and to what extent as art appreciated in its own right, but certainly by the middle of the second century the more cultured commanders were using some discrimination in choosing what they took home. After a victory over the Macedonians in 168, Aemilius Paullus brought back the royal library of Macedonia, while, on the final crushing of Macedonia in 148, the victor, Quintus Caecilius Metellus, selected a group of sculptures by Lysippus of Alexander and his companions. They were set up in Rome under a portico designed specially for them by a Greek architect. However, much of the Greek intel-

lectual tradition remained alien to Rome. Romans proved impatient
with philosophy and relatively indifferent to Greek science and mathematics. When the Skeptic Carneades appeared in Rome in 155 as one of
a group of philosophers and argued on one day that justice was an indis-
pensable part of government and the next day that it was not, traditional
Romans (though not the younger generation) were shocked, and the
group was sent back to Athens. The Romans considered the Greek tradition of competing in games naked undignified, and while Greek-style
basilicas and temples were acceptable in Rome, *gymnasia* (literally
"places of nakedness") appear only later, and then as additions to that
quintessential Roman invention, the monumental public bath.[3]

If there was one Greek skill that was adopted by the Romans with
enthusiasm, it was rhetoric. All the magistrates in Rome were elected by
the citizen body, and while military prowess was important, so was the
ability to speak well before the mass of citizenry, which would flock into
the city for the elections. By the first century a career could be built
through public speaking alone, not only at election time but also as an
advocate at the public trials that had become a feature of political life.
Marcus Tullius Cicero was supreme in the art, the first man to achieve
the post of quaestor, the lowest of the senior magistracies, without having served the normal ten years of military service. He had spent two
years in Greece undertaking an intensive study of the art of rhetoric, and
he made his name in 70 B.C. with a devastating opening speech as prose-
cutor in the trial of Gaius Verres, a former governor of Sicily notorious
for having used his position to ransack the province. Verres, who had
himself employed a leading advocate to defend him, went into exile.
Only seven years later, in 63 B.C., Cicero was elected consul.[4]

By the time of Cicero, however, the Roman republic was proving to
be unstable. A century before, the authority of the Senate, the ruling
council of Rome on which senior magistrates served for life after their
term of office, had been unquestioned. The Senate had successfully
maintained the stability of the state at a time of rapid imperial expansion
and had vigorously enforced the convention that no man, however successful he may have been in war, should be able to use his success to
achieve lasting influence in political affairs. But over time its authority
had waned as it proved itself unable to deal creatively with tensions over
landownership in Italy or to maintain control of its commanders while
they were overseas. While earlier consuls had served for a single year of
office, fought those battles that needed to be fought and then retired to

the Senate, now the demands of a growing empire meant that many were retained overseas year after year on campaign. One commander stayed nine years in Spain, another served eight continuous years in the east. It had long been accepted that a commander was free to make what settlements he could while abroad (while also helping himself and his men to plunder) and then have them ratified by the Senate when he returned. However, long periods of service overseas enabled an ambitious commander to accumulate considerable wealth, an army whose loyalty to him had been cemented by their own share of plunder, and the habit of acting like a dictator. So long as a commander was successfully bringing glory to the empire and remained absent from Rome itself, such a role could be tolerated. But the return to the capital of such a figure could pose an obvious threat to the Senate if he were to disregard the convention that a successful commander should retire quietly. The increasing volatility of the large citizen body of Rome and widespread unrest in the Italian countryside only served to increase the potential threat to the stability of the republic.

The events of the last years (63 to 30 B.C.) of the 500-year-old republic can be seen as a bitter struggle among a small group of men of great talent and extraordinary ambition for supreme power. But they can also be seen as the inevitable if tortuous progress towards a more effective form of government for an empire that by the middle of the first century B.C. reached across the whole Mediterranean. The members of the Senate were too deeply embedded in the old order, and with 300 senators the council proved too cumbersome to act swiftly at times of crisis. Rome's field commanders, especially those fighting in the east, were increasingly treated by their subjects as if they were already monarchs.[5]

The collapse of the republic and the resultant shift towards a form of monarchical government that proved able to maintain authority over the empire can be traced through the careers of three men, Pompey the Great, Julius Caesar and Octavian, later revered as Augustus. Pompey was an exceptionally able general. When put in charge of a campaign against pirates in the Mediterranean, he cleared them from the sea in a mere three months when many had expected it would take three years. In 63 B.C. he was responsible for the final defeat of the Seleucid dynasty, and in the ensuing settlement of the east he created three new provinces of the eastern empire that he protected with a ring of client kingdoms. The settlement brought a substantial and steady income in tribute to Rome, but Pompey's successes also created concern that on his return home with his army he would stage a coup. Yet when the opportunity arose Pompey declined to take it. He landed in Italy, disbanded his army and returned to republican politics. While the threat remained, particularly when he threw in his lot with the brilliant younger commander Julius Caesar, Pompey himself never challenged the constitution. When Caesar, who had fought his own successful and lucrative campaign to conquer the vast expanse of Gaul, actively confronted the state by refusing to surrender his command (a confrontation symbolized by his crossing of the Rubicon, a small river in northern Italy that marked the limit of his command, in 49 B.C., taking his army southwards into territory where he had no such authority), Pompey broke with him and threw his weight behind the senate and the republic.

In Caesar, however, the aging Pompey had met his match. Caesar pursued Pompey to Greece, where in 48 B.C. he defeated him and many of his senatorial supporters at the battle of Pharsalus. Pompey fled to Egypt, where he assumed that the king of the last surviving Hellenistic dynasty (Pergamum having been bequeathed to Rome by its last king in 133 B.C.) would shelter him. Instead he was murdered as he stepped ashore. After enjoying a celebrated liaison with the last of the Ptolemies, Cleopatra, Caesar eventually moved on to destroy Pompey's supporters in Asia, north Africa and Spain.[6]

When Caesar finally returned to Rome, the old order seemed dead. The Senate pandered to him and allowed him to take for life the old title of dictator, which had traditionally been granted only in acute emergencies and then only for a short time. Caesar held it alongside both a consulship that was to prove permanent and the post of *pontifex maximus*, the head of the priesthood. Over time the trappings of his power increased. There were great triumphs to celebrate his victories, and he was allowed to sit in a gilded chair as a mark of his elevated authority. Caesar financed the completion of a large basilica and forum with the proceeds of his campaign in Gaul, and his supporters were packed into the Senate. At one festival his fellow consul Mark Antony went so far as to attempt to place a crown on his head. Although Caesar pushed it aside, ancient sensitivities were being aroused. We cannot know whether Caesar would have made the final break with the past and declared himself a king. He may have been too deeply entrenched in traditional Roman values, and it seems likely that he had come to realize that he had trapped himself and was planning to escape from Rome through initiating a new campaign in the east. However, prior to his planned departure from the city in March 44, a group of senators, exploiting the old rallying cry of *libertas* (resistance to dictatorship), assassinated him.

Nothing was solved by Caesar's assassination. The Senate retained little popular support, which diminished further in Rome when it emerged that Caesar had left a sum of money to each citizen. The leading conspirators, Brutus and Cassius, fled the city after Mark Antony rallied the crowds against them. Mark Antony's own position rapidly came under threat, however, with the arrival in Rome of Caesar's heir, his eighteen-year-old grandnephew, Octavian. Using the aura of Caesar's name to raise an army, within a year Octavian had defeated Mark Antony and forced the Senate to give him a consulship. Although he and Mark Antony patched up their differences, defeated Brutus and Cassius and divided the empire, they remained rivals. Mark Antony assumed control of the eastern empire and unwisely became involved with the ever-ambitious Cleopatra, allowing Octavian, always a master of propaganda, to brand him as the plaything of an unscrupulous and decadent woman. When Cleopatra accompanied Mark Antony to Greece in 31 B.C., Octavian pronounced this to be an invasion by a foreigner. He crossed to Greece with a large fleet, defeated the lovers at Actium and forced them to flee to Egypt. Both committed suicide, and the wealthy territory of Egypt, kingdom of the longest-lasting of the Hellenistic dynasties, was appropriated by Octavian as his personal province. The Hellenistic kingdoms of the Antigonids (northern Greece), Seleucids (much of western Asia), Ptolemies (Egypt) and Attalids (Pergamum in western Asia Minor) were all now under Roman control. Rome's empire embraced the entire Mediterranean.

Perhaps the most prominent of the casualties of these debilitating conflicts, after Caesar himself, was Cicero. In his many surviving letters he reveals his agonies over the turmoil he found around him. Cicero was wedded to the old ideals of public service and the republic, whose virtues he idealized in his *De Republica* (54 B.C.), a dialogue set in the more harmonious days of the second century, but as chaos grew, he reluctantly accepted that only a strong man could restore order. At first Cicero backed Pompey, even joining him as a noncombatant at Pharsalus. After Pompey's defeat, he made his peace with Caesar in the hope that the republic would be restored. Inevitably as Caesar's rule grew more dictatorial, Cicero grew disillusioned. There is no evidence to link Cicero with Caesar's assassination (although he rejoiced at the news), but when Octavian arrived in Rome, Cicero believed he could use him against

Mark Antony. His last great speeches (the Philippics)[7] were in support of Octavian against Mark Antony. It proved a fatal miscalculation: when Mark Antony added Cicero to the list of those to be eliminated as enemies of Caesar, Octavian acquiesced. Cicero was hunted down and killed in December 43 B.C. His head was hacked off and mounted—together, at Mark Antony's request, with the hands which had written the Philippics—on the speaker's rostrum in the Roman Forum.

Largely excluded from political life by the 40s, Cicero spent his last years writing. Steeping himself in Greek culture, he built, in effect, an enduring bridge over which Greek philosophy passed into the Latin world. The death of his daughter, Tullia, in 45 B.C. led him to explore the effects of grief in his *Consolatio*. He moved on to overtly philosophical issues, epistemology, moral philosophy, the ultimate aims of existence and the nature of the gods. Sceptical by nature, he was nevertheless broad-minded enough to read widely across the various schools of Greek philosophy and to examine issues from different perspectives. His work was marked by a cultivated humanism; he valued cultural diversity and distrusted dogmatism, and to this extent he can be seen as one of the founders of European liberal humanism and a forerunner of the eighteenth-century Enlightenment. When the Roman empire fragmented some centuries later and Greek became forgotten in the west, Cicero's works survived, even if, as a result of Christian opposition to his scepticism (and, of course, paganism), a full appreciation of his work was delayed until the Renaissance.

One of Cicero's central philosophical interests was the nature of the gods. He was keenly aware of the difficulties of finding any reasoned justification for their existence, while remaining convinced of the importance of belief and ritual in everyday life. The issue had become one of practical politics. In conquering the east, Roman leaders were absorbed into the spiritual traditions of the Greeks and found themselves treated, as successful Hellenistic monarchs had been, as favoured by the gods, perhaps even as divine themselves. While campaigning in the east, Pompey had been addressed as "saviour," a title used by the Ptolemies, and he had had a cult set up in his honour on the island of Delos and a month named after him in the city of Mytilene. Pompey declined to exploit these honours on his return to Italy, but Caesar proved more susceptible to this form of adulation. He too had been acclaimed in the east as if he were divine and acquiesced in similar acclamations in Rome. He was granted the right to have his own priest, his house was adorned by a pediment as if it were a temple and in state processions his image was placed among those of the gods. A month was named after him in the Roman calendar (it survives today as July). All this no doubt contributed to the unease that led to his assassination. Yet in the backlash following his death all the ancient Roman taboos on making a man divine were ignored, and he was proclaimed to have become a god. The resourceful Octavian subsequently claimed that he was the son (even if only by his adoption) of a god, a title he used with great effect.

When Octavian returned to Rome in 29 B.C. with sixty legions under his command and the wealth of Egypt at his disposal, a military dictatorship must have seemed inevitable, the end to which republican politics had been moving. Yet Octavian had the vision and acumen to realize that it was essential to work within the traditional parameters of republican politics, indeed that he needed to refrain from taking on any of the attributes of dictatorship. He defused the Romans' fears by disbanding much of his vast army and using his own wealth to settle his veterans as farmers, thus making them reliable supporters of any new settlement. He then embarked on elaborate negotiations with the Senate, encouraging its members to transfer him powers, the consulship and the right to administer provinces, posts with republican precedents, in return for his acquiescence in their traditional status. It was a consummate piece of political manoeuvring in which the reality, a transfer of a wide range of powers into Octavian's hands, was effectively masked by the deference he showed to the senators and to republican tradition in public. The entire process was smoothed by the near-universal desire among Romans of all classes for peace. In 27 B.C. the Senate's underlying awe for Octavian was marked by the grant of a new title, Augustus, the "revered one," which remains the name by which he is known.[8]

The next forty years (Augustus died in A.D. 14) saw the evolution of what was, in effect, a Hellenistic monarchy. Augustus continued to gather republican offices: he was made a tribune, the traditional representative of the people, and *pontifex maximus*, head of the priesthood; in 2 B.C. he was awarded a new but honorary accolade, *pater patriae*, "Father of the Fatherland." While the pretence that the Senate made decisions was maintained, in practice petitions came to Augustus and he increasingly took responsibility for them. To his eastern subjects, this was, of course, entirely familiar; and the Greek cities honoured him with cult worship, often linking his name to the city of Rome. Augustus remained sensitive enough not to institute any comparable cult worship within Rome itself, and he assiduously carried out the traditional religious rituals on which the safety of the state had always been assumed to depend. The massive building programme he initiated in Rome included the restoration of no less than eighty-two temples. He presented himself as the living image of the ancient Roman virtue of *pietas,* in which respect for the gods mingled with that for the fatherland and one's own family.[9]

One of the most famous representations of Augustus is on the *Ara Pacis,* the Altar of Peace, now reconstructed in Rome, where he is shown among his family and prominent officials, modestly veiled and approaching a sacrifice. The primary purpose of the altar was to celebrate the peace brought by Augustus both at home and abroad, but the altar's iconography also clearly links his success with the past glories of Rome, in, for example, representing Aeneas among others in the reliefs. It was through public images such as this that Augustus made his most sustained assault on power. Almost every image of Augustus reinforced the values of his regime, both applauding its prosperity and stability and presenting it as the culmination of Rome's long and glorious history. In the great new forum built around a temple to Mars Ultor—Mars as a god of revenge (revenge both against the assassins of Caesar and against the Parthians, by this time the most powerful threat in the east)—Augustus built statues of Rome's founders (Aeneas and Romulus), and the statesmen and commanders who had made the Roman empire great paraded along the sides, while there was an imposing statue of Augustus himself in a four-horse chariot in the centre. This was the end to which the gods themselves had brought their favoured city.[10]

With Augustus Rome came of age as a city where the predominant culture, in architecture and literature in particular, was Greek, albeit used towards Roman ends and for the celebration of the glory of Augustus' regime. The procession on the *Ara Pacis* consciously echoed the frieze of the Parthenon in Athens, and it was carved by Greek craftsmen. An entire fifth-century Greek pediment was re-erected in one restored temple to Apollo. (Augustus preferred the restrained serenity of fifth-century Greek art to the more exuberant creations of the Hellenistic period.) Large spaces surrounded by porticos, theatres and basilicas all echoed Greek models (often mediated through examples from the wealthy Greek cities of southern Italy). In every aspect of culture Greek models were copied but transformed, so as to celebrate the new age. The poet Propertius makes his own debt to Greek literature explicit. He wrote:

> I principally claim for my poetry a descent from the ancient lyric and choral poets, especially Sappho and Alcaeus, in spirit and in my verse form; but I write as well in the spirit of Callimachus and his Roman descendants, and in so doing have naturally transformed my original models; further I write with a special purpose, to make thoroughly Italian, in manner and matter, this double Greek inheritance.[11]

Propertius is echoed by his contemporaries. Horace's poetry is steeped in Greek models—Greece, he acknowledges has taken "its captor Rome captive." In his *Aeneid* Virgil draws on Homer's epics—the wanderings of the first part of the Aeneid suggest the *Odyssey,* the battles of the second, the *Iliad.* In Book 6 of his epic Virgil sums up the accommodations that have been made between the two cultures.

> Others [i.e., the Greeks] will cast more tenderly in bronze
> Their breathing figures, I can well believe,
> And bring more lifelike figures out of marble:
> Argue more eloquently, use the pointer
> To trace the paths of heaven accurately
> And accurately foretell the rising stars.
> Roman, remember by your strength to rule
> Earth's people—for your arts are to be these:
> To pacify, to impose the rule of law,
> To spare the conquered, battle down the proud.[12]

Virgil was right to stress the success of the Romans as rulers. Not the least of Augustus' achievements was the creation of a stable system of government for the empire, even though it was often imposed by force. He oversaw a particularly brutal subjugation of Spain and his reign was marked by tough, and on occasions disastrous, campaigns along the northern (German) borders of the empire. However, he recognized the importance of sound governors who would not exploit their position for gain and the advantage for all of the rising tax revenues that a settled empire would bring. Generally the empire prospered during these years.

The pattern of provincial government remained as it had been in republican times. Often, especially in the east, a conquered territory was left in the hands of a client king, who was responsible for its internal government and the maintenance of Rome's interests in the surrounding territory. Over time the tendency was for client kingdoms to become absorbed into the empire, especially if their rulers made any effective show of independence. They then became provinces, directly governed and taxed by Rome. Alternatively, a subdued territory became a province directly, under the authority of a governor, as did Britain and Gaul (divided into three provinces). Augustus had agreed with the Senate that he would be governor for life of the more vulnerable border provinces of the empire. He had the right to appoint deputies (legates) in these provinces, while the more secure provinces such as Achaia (southern Greece) would have governors selected by lot from senior senators. Augustus' legates normally served a term of three years.

In areas where there was no immediate security threat, Roman rule was comparatively light. In Judaea at the time of Pontius Pilate, for instance, there were only 3,000 Roman troops in the whole province, and most of these were based on the coast or in strategically placed forts. The secret of such successful administration in the long term lay in the creation of quiescent local elites that had their own interest in keeping good order. In the Greek cities of the east such elites existed already, in the form of ruling classes and the city assemblies, although it took time for them to appreciate the advantages for their own status in acquiescing to Roman rule. In the west, where city life was relatively undeveloped, new elites had to be created from the Celtic peoples, many of whom had been shattered by the campaigns of Julius Caesar.[13] It helped enormously that the Romans were tolerant of local deities and that these could be absorbed into the Roman pantheon, as the gods and goddesses of Greece had been some centuries earlier. So the local goddess of the hot springs of Bath, Sulis, was equated with Minerva, while the major Celtic deity Lug was linked with the Roman Mercury. Gradually over the next two centuries Romanization, in terms of a shared Greco-Roman culture, mutually supportive spiritual beliefs and the sense of belonging to a common political entity, took place.[14]

Some areas proved more difficult to govern than others. Among

Pompey's conquests in the east in 63 B.C. was Judaea, which had enjoyed a hundred years of independence under the Hasmonaeans, a family of priests and kings. The Romans proved deeply ambivalent towards Judaism. While they always respected antiquity in any spiritual belief ("[Jewish] rites, whatever their origins, are sanctioned by their antiquity," as the historian Tacitus put it),[15] the Romans felt threatened by the exclusivity of monotheism. Roman high-handedness rapidly upset Jewish sensitivities: Pompey could not refrain from displaying Roman dominance by entering the Holy of Holies in the Temple at Jerusalem, and a later emperor, Caligula, caused outrage when he suggested that a statue of himself be placed inside the Temple. However, a way had to be found to rule Judaea. The Romans began by appointing a Hasmonaean, Hyrcanus, as high priest with responsibility to Rome for Judaean good order. Dissensions between Hyrcanus and his relatives rapidly led to the collapse of this arrangement, and the Romans then appointed a king, Herod, a member of a powerful family of Idumaea (southern Judaea) in 37 B.C. Herod wisely married into the Hasmonaean family and sustained himself in power for over thirty years. Although the Jews always distrusted him, he rebuilt the Jerusalem Temple in great splendour, and until the final years of his reign, when he became increasingly brutal, he remained on good terms with the Romans, who were impressed with the skillful way he maintained peace in a difficult territory. When he died in 4 B.C., his territories, which spread far beyond Judaea (into Galilee, for instance), were divided among his three sons. In Galilee Herod Antipas held on to power until A.D. 39 (that is, for the entire period of Jesus' youth and ministry there). His brother Archelaus, who assumed control over Judaea, was less successful and survived only until A.D. 6, when he was deposed by the Romans after petitions of complaint from the Jews. Judaea then became a Roman province, though the governor was at first a prefect subject to Quirinius, the governor of the neighbouring province of Syria. The tax census conducted by Quirinius (subsequently used by Luke the Evangelist as a means of bringing Joseph and Mary to Bethlehem)[16] led to outbreaks of serious unrest. Some respect for Jewish feeling was shown by the decision to base the prefect in the prosperous port of Caesarea while giving day-to-day responsibility for order to the high priest in Jerusalem. It always remained possible for the Romans to depose the high priest if he was unsatisfactory, and this system worked effectively for a number of years. Annas, high priest from A.D. 6, was succeeded by his son-in-law Caiaphas, who lasted from c. 18 to 37, the longest term of office recorded under the empire. Only at times of the major Jewish festivals did the prefect move with accompanying Roman soldiers into Jerusalem. Images of Judaea—and in some cases Galilee—groaning under the weight of Roman rule, presented by some historians, have little or no historical backing. Most Jews would never have seen a Roman soldier, although Judacans, if not the Galileans who paid their tax to Herod Antipas, would have been fully aware that in addition to the dues they paid as Jews to the Temple, their taxes went to Rome.[17]

In A.D. 26, Augustus' successor, Tiberius, appointed a new prefect of Judaea, Pontius Pilate. His was not a successful appointment. In an attempt to impress the emperor and demonstrate Roman power, he marched into Jerusalem with standards bearing the emperor's image. The Jews reacted with outrage. Pilate did not learn from his experience. His attempt to make use of Temple funds for the building of an aqueduct led to riots that he suppressed violently. In another incident he confronted a group of Samaritans who had assembled for religious reasons, which he interpreted as seditious. The Jewish writer Philo of Alexandria wrote of "the briberies, the insults, the robberies, the outrages and wanton injuries, the executions without trial constantly repeated, the ceaseless and supremely grievous cruelty"[18] that marked Pilate's term in office. It seems unlikely that the decision to order the crucifixion of Jesus would have weighed heavily on him. Eventually, in A.D. 36, Tiberius, who, like all the more effective emperors, knew how counterproductive volatile and vindictive governors were, dismissed him.[19]

Augustus was concerned not only with his own position but also with securing imperial rule for his successors. Technically he was no more than "a first citizen"; in practice, however, his authority and influence were such that he was able to control the succession. The problem was in finding a successor. His daughter, Julia, was exploited in the cause with such insensitivity that after her third marriage, to the elderly Tiberius (himself Augustus' stepson), she took refuge in a string of adulteries so scandalous that her father felt it necessary to exile her. Tiberius himself now became the heir designate, and he succeeded to Augustus' powers on the latter's death in A.D. 14. Once a senator reported that Augustus' body had been seen rising from his funeral pyre towards heaven, the Senate confirmed that he had become a god. His divinity, according to the senatorial decree, rested on "the magnificence of his benefactions to the whole world."

Tiberius was a highly capable ruler, and he preserved the stability of the regime, until old age and his promotion of favourites led to increasing disillusionment with his regime. On his death in 37 the youthful Caligula, Tiberius' great-nephew, succeeded, receiving the grant of all the imperial powers from the Senate within a single day. Caligula was to prove profligate, unstable and cruel. There remained, however, no constitutional means through which he could be deposed, and eventually he was assassinated (A.D. 41). By this time the tradition of single ruler was deeply entrenched, and Caligula's uncle, the scholarly Claudius, whose disabilities (probably the result of cerebral palsy) had previously led to him being passed over, was acclaimed by the imperial guard. Claudius proved an unexpectedly successful ruler, even gaining, through his competent generals, an entirely new province, that of Britain, for the empire. The concept of imperial rule was never again challenged during the history of the empire; and when the Ottoman Turks eventually sacked its final capital, Constantinople, in 1453, the last emperor, Constantine, the eleventh of that name, died in its defence.

# 6

# "ALL NATIONS LOOK TO THE MAJESTY OF ROME"

## The Roman Empire at Its Height

We are at a dinner party, perhaps held in Rome sometime after A.D. 75, although the guests are Greek and they speak in Greek. Between them they represent the major schools of philosophy, Platonism, Stoicism and Aristotelianism, but their subject on this occasion is not philosophy as such but the problem of whether the moon has a face. This might seem a recondite—or perhaps a trivial—theme, but it allows the guests to explore the central questions of astronomy in some depth. The diners debate whether the patterns on the moon are a reflection of the earth's oceans, why the moon does not fall into the earth, the relative sizes of the two, the distances between them and the distance between each and the stars. These are not just speculations. Among the speakers are a geometrician, Apollonides, and a mathematician, Menelaus. They discuss how the size of the moon can be measured by timing eclipses and speculate that the moon is maintained in the sky by its own velocity "just as missiles placed in slings are kept from falling by being whirled around in a circle," and that it may act as its own centre of gravity. They are aware of, even if they do not accept, Aristarchus' hypothesis that the sun, not the earth, is the centre of the universe, and in discussing the distance between the earth and the stars they show themselves at home with Archimedes' work *The Sand Reckoner,* which deals with the issues raised by very large numbers. Furthermore, they relate their astronomical views to the philosophies each champions, and when in need of illustrative material they quote from the great poets of previous generations,

Homer, Sophocles, Aeschylus and Pindar. These are highly educated men engaged in sophisticated conversation.[1]

The author of this reconstruction is Plutarch, a Greek from Chaeronaea in central Greece, writing sometime in the late first or early second century A.D. This period has often been derided for its lack of intellectual energy. In the magnificently sardonic words of Edward Gibbon in his *Decline and Fall of the Roman Empire:* "The name of Poet was almost forgotten; that of Orator usurped by the sophists [for whom see below]. A cloud of critics, of compilers, of commentators darkened the face of learning, and the decline of genius was soon followed by the corruption of taste."[2] Yet, as the conversation at Plutarch's dinner party illustrates, the quality of intellectual life remained high, and in recent years scholars have shown increasing respect for the continuing achievements of the Greeks under the Roman empire.

The experience of conquest by the Romans had been crushing, and one finds little evidence of a revival of Greek confidence before the middle of the first century A.D. Then begins the period known as the second sophistic, the first being the period of the sophists—"those who make a profession from being clever and inventive"—of fifth-century Athens. The second sophistic was led by members of the Greek city elites and characterized by a renewed interest in the glories of classical Greece and in the art of rhetoric.[3] It was essentially conservative, even reactionary, in contrast to the radicalism of the thinkers of the first sophistic, but this does not mean that it lacked sophistication. A speech by Dio Chrysostom (Dio the Golden-tongued), made at the Olympic Games of A.D. 97, in which he praises Zeus, the glory of his image in the monumental statue by Pheidias that stood in his temple at Olympia and the greatness of Hellenism, is fully equal to the best formal speeches of the fifth and fourth century B.C.[4] The leaders of the second sophistic openly recognized the contribution of Rome. As Plutarch put it, while Rome ruled the empire, Greece was culturally superior. Greeks should recognize Roman political hegemony but need not abase themselves before Romans. In his influential, and atmospheric, series of *Lives* Plutarch presented selected Greeks and Romans alongside each other as equals.

The movement owed its origins to a visit to Greece in A.D. 66–67 by Nero, the successor to Claudius as emperor. Nero viewed himself in the role of a Hellenistic monarch, familiar with the arts, and as the benevolent patron of his subjects.[5] His visit, judging by the gossipy report of Suetonius, writing some fifty years later, appears to have been a farce.

Nero was determined to take part in a wide range of traditional contests. Suetonius, a typically upper-class Roman, is clearly appalled by Nero's exhibitionism and regales his readers with tales of chariot races in which Nero falls out of his chariot (but is still awarded first prize) and musical contests in which members of the audience pretend to be dead so that they can be carried out while the emperor is playing. Yet, despite Suetonius' mockery, the Greeks themselves seem to have been flattered by the imperial attention to the traditions of their culture.

Nero's imperial initiative reached its climax in Hadrian, emperor from 117 to 138. Hadrian was born in Spain (and spoke Latin with a rustic accent for which he was much mocked), but family connections to the previous emperor, Trajan, and his overall competence as a commander and administrator placed him in an excellent position to take over as emperor himself when Trajan died suddenly in 117.[6] No emperor was to be better travelled or, perhaps, seen by more of his subjects than Hadrian, and his buildings, the Pantheon and his Mausoleum in Rome, his great villa outside Rome at Tivoli and Hadrian's Wall in northern Britain remain outstanding monuments to his name. Yet, despite his achievements, he was clearly a complex and troubled man whom his contemporaries found impossible to fathom. "In one and the same person stern and cheerful, affable and harsh, impetuous and hesitant, mean and generous, hypocritical and straightforward, cruel and merciful, and always in all things changeable," as one observer put it.[7]

Hadrian's love of all things Greek was to become the dominant cultural influence of his life. In 124 he was initiated into the ancient Eleusinian mysteries (Eleusis was a shrine close to Athens) and set about finally completing the massive temple to Zeus in Athens, which had by then stood unfinished for 600 years. A new quarter of the city was created through his patronage. In the 130s he founded a council of ancient Greek cities, the Panhellenion. The representatives of the cities, mostly provincial grandees, met in the precincts of the now completed temple to Zeus and offered cult worship to Hadrian. He was proud of his learning. In the museum at Alexandria he summoned the academics to his presence, asking the most difficult philosophical questions and then providing the answers himself. His patronage of a beautiful Bithynian adolescent, Antinous, was another manifestation of his Greekness, although this seems to have been a far more intense and passionate relationship than would have been approved of in classical Athens. Antinous appears to have cracked under the pressure, and his death in the Nile in 130 may have been suicide. Hadrian mourned his lover hysterically, even declaring that he was a god. A city, Antinoopolis, was founded in Egypt in his memory, and cult statues of the boy are found throughout the Greek world.

There were eastern themes too in the monumental country villa Hadrian built outside Rome at Tivoli; echoes of Hadrian's journeys are to be found throughout the surviving ruins. The temple complex to the Greco-Egyptian god Serapis at Canopus on the Nile (visited by Hadrian in 130) is commemorated by a pool surrounded by statues; the celebrated temple to Aphrodite at Cnidus, which contained the first nude statue of Aphrodite by Praxiteles (an exemplar for female nudity for centuries), was re-created; and a gorge beside the villa was called the Tempe, after the beautiful valley in Thessaly. Other parts of the building were named after the philosophical schools of Athens, the Academy and the Lyceum.

Yet despite the complexities of his personality, Hadrian was a generous and effective ruler. In the twenty-one years of his reign he lavished over 200 benefactions on 130 cities across the empire. Many were effected directly through their leading citizens, enabling Hadrian to cement his ties with members of the elite while in turn reinforcing their own status with their fellow citizens. Hadrian often fostered local pride by restoring or finishing an ancient building, to which would be added a statue of himself or a dedicatory inscription. About a third of his known building projects involved temples, and, while a few were dedicated to the cult of the emperor, the majority honoured Olympian or local gods. So religious toleration, local pride and the beneficence of the emperor were celebrated in unison.[8]

The reign of the emperor Trajan, Hadrian's immediate predecessor (emperor A.D. 98–117), had seen a transformation in the public perception of the emperor, from his role as its "first citizen," so effectively played by Augustus, to that of "parent" of the empire. Trajan had developed schemes by which poor children in Italy were given assistance, and children maltreated by their fathers were aided. He even set up a rescue service for babies who had been exposed to die (so long as they were free-born). He thus established the convention of the "good" emperor, who actively cared for his people. Hadrian himself was once accosted by an old woman who attempted to foist a petition on him. He turned her away, but she courageously persisted, saying that if he would not respond to her, he should cease being emperor. He took the point and paused to read the petition. Hadrian is credited with laws forbidding the castration of slaves and the shackling of agricultural slaves together in prison. His successor, Antoninus Pius, restricted the circumstances under which the torture of slaves could be ordered. A famous relief panel of the emperor Marcus Aurelius, in the Palazzo dei Conservatori in Rome, from the late 170s, represents imperial clemency. Two barbarians kneel in front of the emperor while he raises his right hand in a gesture of forgiveness. These are the images of benevolence that the emperors fostered of themselves and, even though the reforms were arguably minor and presumably difficult to enforce, they contributed to preventing the post of emperor from degenerating into unrestrained dictatorship.

Within the empire the connections between the emperor and the cities rested on his recognition of their elites, the giving of patronage (Hadrian threw games in any city he visited) and, in the last resort, protection from invaders. In the east the greatest threat (until its overthrow by the Sassanids in the early third century) was the Parthian empire; when an emperor secured the frontier, cities showed their appreciation with great monuments of imperial propaganda. One of the finest was the Antonine Altar at Ephesus, whose sculptures survive only in fragments. The subject of the altar is the emperor Lucius Verus (ruled 161–69), who was adopted by Hadrian's chosen successor, Antoninus Pius, as his son alongside the better-known Marcus Aurelius. On Antoninus' death, both became emperor. Lucius led a successful campaign against the Parthians. In 164 he came to Ephesus, one of the most opulent cities of the Greek east, where imperial unity was cemented through his marriage to Marcus Aurelius' daughter. After his death, the city chose to glorify his achievements. The Antonine Altar celebrates the imperial family. Lucius is shown as a baby being held by Antoninus Pius in the presence of Hadrian. He then appears in battle against the Parthians. Next he is shown being received into heaven and finally he is deified among the gods. In other fragments he is placed alongside personifications of cities rejoicing in their deliverance from the Parthian threat.[9] The emperor is portrayed as a soldier protecting the eastern cities of his empire from invasion and earns the favour of the gods as a reward.[10]

Contrary to Gibbon's claim, the intellectual achievements of the period were not only sophisticated but also wide-ranging. Greek rationalism continued to prove fruitful. In mathematics Diophantus (although his precise dates are unknown, he probably lived in the third century A.D.) achieved a breakthrough in algebra by suggesting the use of symbols for unknown numbers. While the geometricians had hitherto used only powers up to three (all that is needed when working in three dimensions), Diophantus postulated greater powers and found ways to express them. Much of his work was in the study of indeterminate equations, and this branch of algebra is still known as Diophantine analysis.[11]

The most significant figure in medicine at this time was Galen (who was born in A.D. 129 and lived at least until the end of the century), a physician from Pergamum. He eventually made his way to Rome, where he served as a doctor in the court of Marcus Aurelius and his successors. Both Galen's versatility and his energy were remarkable—he wove medical knowledge into philosophy (like many of his time a Platonist by temperament, he borrowed Plato's concept of the tripartite soul, linking its rational elements with the brain, its "spirited" aspects with the heart and its grosser [in Platonic terms] desires or appetites with the liver), wrote prodigiously (some 20,000 pages of his works survive; many have still not been properly studied) and carried out hundreds of dissections. It was Galen who finally understood the function of the arteries as vessels for carrying blood, as well as the workings of the bladder. He was particularly interested in the operation of the nerves and would display his understanding by taking a pig and destroying one function of its nervous system after another before an astonished audience. He was also remarkable for his attempts to define the foundations of certainty in medicine. Geoffrey Lloyd writes: "Galen is probably unique among practising physicians in any age or culture for his professionalism also as a logician . . . conversely he is also remarkable among practising logicians for his ability in, and experience of, medical practice." His work dominated his field for the next thousand years, so successfully, however, that many earlier advances in medicine were assumed to be superseded and texts describing them discarded.[12]

It seems appropriate to refer to the work of Ptolemy in astronomy (his period of most intense work in Alexandria took place between A.D. 127 and 141) as marking the apogée of the science. The word "apogée" (the root is in the Greek "from the earth") was coined by him to describe the moment in its orbit when the moon is furthest from the earth. (It was first used in English in its sense of "a climax" in 1600.) Ptolemy drew on earlier astronomical observations but improved them through the use of the armillary astrolabe, which allowed him to identify the position of stars more effectively and quickly than earlier methods. He then set about plotting and predicting the movements of the moon, the sun and the planets. Sharing as he did the conventional wisdom that the sun moved around a stationary earth, he was forced to come up with extraordinarily complicated models of circles whose own centres moved around other circles. While his models were all flawed, in that his basic assumptions were wrong, the intellectual achievement was magnificent: "extraordinary for the rigour of its mathematical arguments, for the range of data encompassed and the comprehensiveness of the results proposed," as Geoffrey Lloyd puts it. Though the Greek original is lost, his major work on astronomy, now known as the *Almagest* (from the Arabic "the greatest"), survived intact in its Arab edition and was eventually translated back into Latin. Like Galen's, Ptolemy's mind ranged widely—he speculated on geography, studied acoustics and carried out experiments with mirrors.

As a recent review of his *Geography* reminds us:

> Ptolemy was the pioneer who established the graticle (a grid of carefully mapped coordinates) as the basis for serious cartography; who introduced "minutes" and "seconds" to facilitate the division of degrees; who argued for the primacy of the simplest hypothesis that did not contradict observations; who demanded that observations calling for precision should be checked and rechecked over a long period; who insisted that maps be drawn to scale; who developed the use of both gnomon and astrolabe for celestial angle-measurements to determine latitude; who, most notably, tackled the perennial problem of how to represent the globe, in whole or in part, on a flat surface.

Despite his achievements as a scientist, Ptolemy remained in awe of the universe.

> I know that I am mortal, ephemeral; yet when I track the
> Clustering spiral orbits of the stars
> My feet touch earth no longer: a heavenly nursling,
> Ambrosia-filled, I company with God.[13]

Ptolemy's words are a reminder that for the Greeks spirituality and rationality, *muthos* and *logos,* could co-exist without conflict. As we have seen, one of the most sophisticated of the Greek intellectual achievements was the distinction between the areas of knowledge in which certainty was possible and those that were not subject to rationalism. A mathematical proof could be sustained by deductive logic and was unarguably true, while a myth was fluid and flexible, open to individual interpretation. To the Greeks, the idea that anyone could insist that others respect the truth of a myth was absurd, yet this did not mean that a myth lacked power. Whether used to explain or justify a ritual or as a means to explore issues in tragic drama, myth was a crucial way of mediating between the real and imagined world. The mature mind, as Aristotle had stressed, was one in which reason and emotion could be sustained in harmony.

Although few Romans achieved the intellectual creativity of the finest Greek minds (we have no evidence of a Roman carrying out original mathematical work, for instance), like the Greeks, Romans appreciated that their own myths, those connected to the founding of their city, for example, were not dogma. They were woven into ritual in the service of tradition and good order but not as absolute and unassailable truths. Cicero makes the point well. In his *On the Nature of the Gods* he was openly sceptical about the existence of the gods, but he nevertheless served as a priest in civic cults. The fulfillment of public duties was an intrinsic part of being Roman; the question of what an individual believed about the gods or myths surrounding those gods was a private matter. It became relevant only if he publicly offended by disrupting a ritual or openly refusing to follow it. Religious practice was closely tied to the public order of the state and with the psychological well-being that comes from the following of ancient rituals. Religious devotion was indistinguishable from one's loyalties to the state, one's city and one's family.[14]

The Romans assumed that other people's gods were as important a part of the fabric of their society as their gods were of theirs, and this provides one reason why they were so easily prepared to tolerate other deities and beliefs. Their respect for gods was inclusive and involved a concern that local deities should not be offended. When Publius Servius conquered the city of Isaura Palaia in southern Galatia in 67, he set up a dedication to "whichever" gods protected the city he had taken. Again, when Roman legions arrived in the Libyan desert in 201, they conciliated the local god Gholia by placing a representation of him alongside the Roman gods in their camp. Often, over time, these local gods would become assimilated with the Roman deities. A local god of thunder might be Zeus, "in disguise" as it were, and the Romans would willingly make the connection by incorporating the local god into their rituals. One of the gods to whom they erected a temple in Libya was Zeus Hammon, Zeus in his role as protector of caravan routes, a role unimaginable in Greece or Italy, but enthusiastically adopted by the Romans as they encountered new types of territory. The Edict of Milan of 313, in which the emperor Constantine declared toleration of all cults including Christianity, marks the culmination of this process.

By the second century A.D. it was increasingly commonplace to see the divine world as subject to one supreme god, with the other gods being either manifestations of his divinity or as lesser divinities. The Egyptian goddess Isis, for instance, spreads across the empire as a mother goddess with many concerns. "I am nature, the universal mother, mistress of all the elements, primordial child of time, sovereign of all things spiritual, queen of the dead, queen also of the immortals, the single manifestation of all gods and goddesses that are. My nod governs the shining heights of heaven, the wholesome sea breezes, the lamentable silence of the gods below," she tells Lucius, the "hero" of Apuleius' novel *The Golden Ass* (c. A.D. 160).[15] In Aphrodisias, a city in southern Asia Minor, a cult statue dedicated to Aphrodite, traditionally goddess of love and sexuality, has panels detailing her powers over the sea (where she was, in mythology, born) and the underworld. New cults emerged. A mass of inscriptions, found throughout the east and Egypt, are dedicated to *theos hypsistos*, "the Most High God," and worshippers of this divinity seem to have modelled their practices on Judaism while remaining distinct from it. They observed a Sabbath but did not insist on circumcision, and they rejected the ceremonies or institutions of the Roman state. While the origin of this cult dates from before Christianity (it is first attested in the second century B.C.), Christ is also found in a later inscription to be attached as "an angel" to the God.[16]

What is central to these cults is their flexibility. The device of allowing different gods to be assimilated into a supreme deity was an effective one. "It makes no difference," wrote the second-century Platonist Celsus, "whether we call Zeus the Most High or Zeus or Adonis or Sabaoth or Amun like the Egyptians, or Papaeus like the Scythians."[17] It is possible even to go so far as to say that a belief in an overriding deity was, by this period, the most widespread belief of pagan religion. While the cult of *theos hypsistos* is known to have attracted the poorer classes, and

Zeus/Jupiter conventional Romans, Aristotelians could speak of the "unmoved mover" and Platonists of "the Good." The Jews had the God of Israel and the Stoics one supreme rational principle that survived the conflagration that ended each cycle of cosmic history, absorbing all other divine forces into it and then allowing them to re-emerge. All these groups accepted that there was at the apex of the hierarchy of divine forces one higher being, even if the form of this being was conceptualized in different ways and addressed by different names in different cultures. As the sophist Maximus of Madaura put it in A.D. 390 (in a letter to the Christian Augustine):

> That the supreme God is one, without beginning, without offspring [a reference here to the Christian belief in the Incarnation, which Platonists, in particular, found unsustainable], as it were the great and august father of nature, what person is there so mad and totally deprived of sense to deny? His powers diffused through the world that is his work we invoke under various names, because we are obviously ignorant of his real name. For the name "God" is common to all religions. The outcome is that while with our various prayers we each honour as it were his limbs separately all together we are seen to be worshipping him in his entirety.

In the fourth century, the orator Themistius, berating the emperor Valens for his intolerance in insisting on the worship of a narrowly defined Christian God, was to claim that there were some 300 ways of describing the Godhead and that God would actually enjoy being worshipped in a diversity of ways. "Pagan monotheism," write Athanassiadi and Frede in summing up their own survey, "was a deeply rooted trend in ancient philosophy which developed under its own momentum, broadening sufficiently to embrace a good part of the population." They go on to argue that Christianity, with its supreme God and his surrounding entourage of divine forces—Jesus, the Holy Spirit, the Virgin Mary, angels, saints and martyrs—should be seen as an integral part of this trend, not as a force outside it.[18] Belief in a supreme God was, of course, only the starting point for fresh debates as to "his" nature, powers and concerns. Discussion centred on whether the supreme deity had existed and would continue to exist eternally, whether all matter appeared with "him" at the beginning of time (as the Platonists assumed) or was a separate creation from nothingness, whether "he" interacted with the world, and if so benevolently, or was indifferent to it (as Aristotle's "unmoved mover" and the Epicurean gods were assumed to be). So long as no ruler attempted to enforce a definition of the supreme deity and his attributes, these fruitful speculations could continue.

While it is difficult to know what spiritual needs drew worshippers towards the adoption of a single deity, this development was accompanied by a renewed interest in mystery cults. The oldest Greek "mystery" shrine, that of Eleusis near Athens, which centred on cults to Demeter, the Greek goddess of corn, and her daughter Persephone, was by now centuries old and so respectable that emperors and other Roman notables would be initiated without embarrassment into its rituals. The new mystery cults, by contrast, were not tied to any fixed centre and thus could spread widely through the empire. The new cults tended to focus on deities from outside the traditional pantheon, from Persia, Egypt, or in the case of Christianity, which shares some of the features of the mystery cults, from Judaism. The initiation rites of Isis (vividly described in *The Golden Ass*) included a ritual bath, the transmission of secrets of the cult and then ten days of fasting before the final ceremony. No wonder Lucius describes the experience as intense and hallucinatory—he reaches "the borders of death," "sees" the sun blazing at midnight and enters into "the world of the gods." Another mystery cult, Mithraism, which originated in the worship of a Persian cattle god, Mithras, was particularly popular among soldiers and men of business. Initiates, exclusively male, met in "caves," enjoyed communal meals and could rise through a hierarchy of grades as their commitment to the cult grew. Mithraism spread far to the west—among the 400 known Mithraic "caves," one is in London. Christianity, through its initiation rites (baptism), communal meals and the promise of a blessed afterlife, had much in common with these cults, not least in the idea that a priestly elite had privileged access to the cult's secrets and the absolute right to interpret them for others.[19]

While certain behaviours could offend the gods to the extent that individuals or the state were vulnerable to their revenge, Roman religion did not in itself provide an ethical system. Those who wanted to develop their own could turn to the schools of philosophy. Both Epicureanism and Stoicism preached "ideal" ways of living, and the Epicureans openly proselytized, although their idea of withdrawal from society did not impress the traditional Roman. Stoicism, with its celebration of public service, resistance to tyranny and stress on emotional restraint and endurance, even to the extent of committing suicide for one's ideals, accorded rather better with traditional Roman values. Seneca, one of Nero's principal advisers, wrote extensively on how one should behave in unsettling circumstances and became an exemplar for all Stoics by committing suicide as Nero's rule became more intolerable. There was also much of the Stoic in the emperor Marcus Aurelius, who, although not trained as a soldier, saw it as his duty to remain on the northern frontier leading the legions against the onslaughts of the barbarians. His famous *Meditations* (which have inspired some and appeared platitudinous to others) were jotted down in Greek in spare moments during his campaigns.

However, it was Platonism that was to become the dominant school of philosophy in these centuries. Not only did Platonism develop in new directions; it also absorbed aspects of other philosophies, especially Stoicism. Plato valued reason above emotion; indeed, he went further in showing an active distaste for sensual pleasure, which he believed diverted the soul from its highest purpose, which was understanding, through reason, the real world of the Forms that existed on a higher plane than the material world "below." We have seen that "the Good" was to Plato a supreme Form in that it could be assumed that Beauty and Justice and other Forms had some "Good" within them that could be represented by an overriding "Good." The most important development of later Platonism was to consider what this "Good" might be, and whether it was something more than a supreme and unchanging entity that just "was." So, echoing the developments discussed above, evolved the possibility that "the Good" might actually be conceived of as some form of supreme "God."

The traditional Platonic view was that "the Good" and the Forms were timeless; in other words, there was no act of creation, they had always been there. Did they, however, have a purpose? An important development in Middle Platonism (the name given by nineteenth-century scholars to developments in Platonic philosophy in the period between the 60s B.C. and A.D. 204, the birthdate of Plotinus, who introduces a new phase of Platonism, Neoplatonism) was the argument that "the Good" was something more than simply an entity to be recognized by the reasoning human soul—it had an active intelligence and the Forms were its "thoughts." The Forms too had an active purpose in that they provided a blueprint for entities in the material world. One view was that the material world had been in chaos until the Forms had acted on it in some way to produce order. To put it crudely, the Form of Table had acted to produce actual usable tables, the Form of Beauty to produce objects with the characteristics of being beautiful.[20]

These ideas were drawn on by a Jewish philosopher, the Greek-speaking Philo of Alexandria (active in the first half of the first century A.D.), to offer a radically new approach to Jewish theology. If Plato was right and the Forms existed eternally, then others living before Plato might have been able to grasp them. Philo went so far as to argue that Moses had been a Platonic philosopher who had understood the Forms in the way Plato had hoped his followers would. Moses' Old Testament God was none other than "the Good" of Plato. (The later Platonist Numenius [second century A.D.] went so far as to claim, "Who is Plato, if not Moses speaking Greek?") For Philo, however, God was eternal and unchanging, outside space and time and free of all passion, but able to act creatively, in bringing into being the material world, the human soul and virtues, from what Philo, like other Platonists, believed to have been an original state of chaos, and in upholding good and punishing evil. The influence of Plato on Philo was so pronounced that, despite his Jewish background, Philo rejected Old Testament portrayals of God which talk of his face, his hands and his emotional power. As an entity who was beyond all human attributes and even beyond human understanding, he could not be classified in such an anthropomorphic way.

The Forms, Philo continued, had come into being at the same time as God but were organized by him through the divine power of reason (once again the word *logos* is used), which somehow acted as a directing force for the Forms, encapsulating them and ordering their work. It is not always clear from Philo's writings whether he believed the *logos* to be an attribute of God employed for a specific purpose, or a separate entity acting under God's control, but the distinction between God's fundamental essence (*ousia*) and his power as manifested in the world was a crucial one. (It is paralleled in other Jewish writings, for example, in the Book of Proverbs 8:22 and 8:31, where it is said that Wisdom was created by God as "the oldest of his works" and "at play everywhere in the world delighting to be with the sons of men.") For Philo the *logos* could actually appear in the world—he gave as an example the voice speaking to Moses from the Burning Bush—and it was the *logos* that organized the creation of the world in line with a blueprint that God had had in his mind from the beginning. (Philo makes an analogy with an architect who has a clear idea of the city he wishes to build before he commences work on it.) The Forms act as the ideals to which each entity in the material world aspires, in other words (as noted), a table in the material world can be judged as an imitation of the Form of Table, even if it is never likely to be so perfect. However, some tables will be closer to the ideal table than others, and the same can be said of men. Philo names some men, Abraham, Isaac and Jacob, for instance, as more "ideal" than others. What marked them out was their commitment to the Forms and God, a commitment implied through their desire for goodness and the avoidance of any emotion and sensuality that would draw them away from God.

Philo knew nothing of Christianity, but he was to prove enormously important in bridging the gap between Judaism and Greek philosophy in representing God of the Old Testament as a Platonic God, thus enabling Greek philosophers to find a home within the Jewish and, later, the Christian tradition. Although no direct connection with Philo has been established, John's use of *logos,* translated into English as "word" in the prologue to his Gospel ("And the Word was made flesh"), uses *logos* as a force which was both "with God in the beginning" and actively involved in the creation, as Philo and earlier writers suggest. Where John innovates is to see the *logos* becoming flesh in Jesus, an idea unique to Christianity and deeply troubling to traditional Platonists.

The Middle Platonists who followed Philo maintained his view that God or "the Good" was a simple unchangeable unity with an intelligence that worked actively in the material world through the Forms. He was to be "reached" by reason rather than emotion and through asceticism rather than sensuality; Philo went so far as to argue that the ideal human being would be asexual. Much debate focused on the act of creation. Plato suggested that the universe had existed eternally but (in the dialogue *Timaeus*) left open the possibility of a divine craftsman intervening to create from an already existing chaos (a possibility that might be reconciled with the account given in Genesis). An alternative strand of thought suggested that God existed before matter. Greek thinkers found it difficult to conceive of the notion of non-existence—some even proposed an entity termed "that which is not" (!)—but one thinker, Basilides, expounded the idea of creation from nothing in the early second century, and it is found adopted by Christians by A.D. 180.

The human race appears, of course, as part of God's creation, although pagan philosophers disagreed as to whether it was created directly by God or through the agency of the Forms. Platonists continued to make a distinction between soul and body, and to place these within a hierarchy of creation. At the top of this was God ("the Good"), then the Forms, below which was the human soul, and finally the material world, including the human body. Here the human soul is the noblest part of the "material" world, but each level of the hierarchy is understood to be less divine and good than the one above it (rather as copies taken of copies gradually lose the quality of the original). Some argued that there would be a level in the hierarchy at which the original goodness of God was so diluted that evil would become part of that level, while others argued that the goodness of "the Good" or God could never, however diluted, become evil. It was human beings acting freely who created evil. Alternatively, others claimed that the human soul that had been good had been corrupted by the material world, or that it was still good but so deeply imprisoned in the material body (as "a divine spark") that it was unable to show its goodness. This latter was the view put forward by of one important school of thinkers who drew on Platonism, the Gnostics. The Gnostics were dualists in that they saw the world as evil, the creation of an evil creator, but the human soul as good and imprisoned in it. (The body, the evil gaoler of the good soul, was to be despised, and many Gnostics were aggressively ascetic.) The soul was, however, capable of enlightenment (*gnosis*), possibly through a teacher, and could be released to be reunited with God. Jesus was adopted as one of the teachers able to release the soul, but the relationship between the Gnostics and mainstream Christianity (in so far as this existed in the early Christian centuries) was complex, and Christians eventually separated themselves from Gnosticism. (Gnostics accepted the possibility of there being many Christs, and it was as a rejoinder to this that Christian creeds later spoke of "*one* [my emphasis] Lord Jesus Christ.")

The most sophisticated of the Platonic thinkers, and the one who conventionally marks the beginning of Neoplatonism, was Plotinus (204–70). Plotinus was from Egypt and had set off eastwards, to Persia and India, in search of wisdom, but when his travels were thwarted, he headed instead towards Rome. He can be seen as a mystic—for Plotinus, the supreme desire of the soul is to be reunited with "the One," and he describes the moment of reunion as one that could not be exchanged for anything else, even for the kingdom of all the heavens. Plotinus drew heavily on Plato (and, as scholars now recognize, on Aristotle) but developed an overtly spiritual philosophy. It was written up by his follower Porphyry and circulated as the *Enneads* in the early fourth century.

There is "a One," the Ultimate Being, who is supernatural, above all material being, self-caused and absolutely good. Plotinus preferred the term "the One" to "the Good" because it emphasized that "the One" was above all values. From this Being processes *nous,* or Mind. The procession is continual (and has existed through eternity), and *nous* appears in a whole range of manifestations in what might be called "thoughts" or, in Platonic terminology, the Forms. These in their turn project outwards to a "world soul," which exists as a composite of all animate beings in the world although appearing as an individual soul in each human being. Each of the three entities exists as "lower" than the one above, but "the One" does not lose anything of its goodness during the procession of *nous*—any more, said Plotinus, than the brightness of a lamp is diminished when it gives out light. "The One," the *nous* and the world soul share a single substance (*ousia*), but each maintains its distinct nature, its *hypostasis,* or personality. Plotinus went on to argue that the "lower" states would always be attracted back to the "higher." So the soul would be attracted to the *nous* and then back to "the One," in the final moment of mystical reunion achieved (as always in Platonic thought) by a very few. The material world has to exist in order for the soul to have something to live in, but as inanimate things cannot think, the material world represents the very furthest one can get from "the One." It is, in short, a state in which goodness is virtually nonexistent. While the soul's natural orientation is "upwards" to the *nous* and "the One," an individual soul can choose to turn "downwards" to the natural world. Thus, through its free choice, it can turn towards evil, a view shared by Christian theologians such as Origen, although it has to be stressed that Plotinus himself had no direct links with Christians and Porphyry actively opposed them.

It is also worth stressing that Plotinus, mystic though he might have been, was wary of attributing powers to supernatural sources. A record survives of a conversation he had as an old man in the 260s in which he discusses whether illnesses can be cured by casting out demons through special prayers. First, he says, there are no such things as demons, and, in any case, "real" gods would not respond to such mundane things as spells. There is a sense here, found in other pagan philosophers and arguably also in the Gospel of John, that a true god, secure in his own being, would not need to prove himself by effecting miracles. If one actually looks at cases of fever, he continues, one finds there are normally definable causes: exhaustion, overindulgence or the wrong kind of diet.

They should be cured through medicines and a disciplined way of life. Here Plotinus remains fully within the Greek tradition, in which reason and empirical evidence remain central and the material world operates according to its own ascertainable laws rather than in response to the interventions of the gods.[21] Miracles, in short, have no place in sophisticated thinking.

It is impossible to make any kind of assessment of how many adherents each of these movements and beliefs had. Most subjects of the Roman empire can hardly have had the time or the inclination to speculate about the nature of the spiritual world, and one can only assume that they continued with their traditional beliefs. Nevertheless, there clearly existed a wide range of spiritual possibilities, any of which could be followed without any sense of impropriety, and, even though there existed some degree of competition between the different movements for adherents, none excluded other beliefs. The traditional gods of the state might be offended by neglect, but they were not jealous of other cults. It is certainly too simplistic to argue, as many histories of Christianity have done, that spiritual life in the empire had reached some kind of dead end and that Christianity provided a solution all had been yearning for. In fact, studies of oracles in this period suggest that questioning, which had traditionally centred on personal affairs, was increasingly concerned with theological issues (such as what happens to the soul at death) that could be answered from within the very rich and varied pagan tradition and developed without inhibition.[22] As we shall see, Christianity did provide for important spiritual needs, but it was one of many movements that attempted to do so, and it was by no means the most sophisticated.

The Roman empire in the second century had reached the height of its maturity in that it was relatively peaceful, was able to defend itself and its elites flourished in an atmosphere of comparative intellectual and spiritual freedom. The empire had a sophisticated legal system, and the parameters within which justice was enforced, for instance, were clearly set out—although those who were actually Roman citizens (all subjects of the empire except slaves from A.D. 212) were better protected than others. "Good" emperors acted with reasonable benevolence, as did the more moderate governors. Those who were talented could rise far, particularly through service in the army.[23] Yet this is an idealized picture. There was a streak of cruelty in the Roman make-up that to us is nauseating. Criminals were deliberately humiliated by public execution, on the cross or in the amphitheatre. Even the most apparently benign of emperors watched such proceedings without flinching—in fact, they prided themselves on laying on a good show of slaughter. In religion there were limits to what the Romans would tolerate. They always distrusted fervour, *superstitio,* and indeed Christianity was mocked by one principal governor as "a degenerate *superstitio* carried to extravagant lengths."[24] Although Judaism was accorded some respect for its ancient roots, there are many accounts of open mockery of Jewish customs, and at times there was outright insensitivity: Hadrian, in his attempt to encourage Hellenism, tried to ban circumcision. The result was the outbreak of the Jewish revolt of 132, which was put down with great brutality and resulted in the reconstruction of Jerusalem as a Roman colony. Nor were things necessarily better at a local level. There were major riots between Jews and Greeks in Alexandria in A.D. 38 and 66. Then there was the problem of those who actively rejected the gods of the state and who expected to proselytize for converts. Such were the Christians, who referred in their sacred writings to Rome as "the whore of Babylon." Eventually a state-sponsored campaign of persecution was to be launched against them.

This was also a society which depended heavily on slaves and operated few effective controls over their treatment. Indeed, in the requirement that the evidence of slaves was admissible only after torture, the state participated in the cruellest of subjections. Although the Stoics preached the need for respect for slaves ("Remember, if you please, that the man you call slave springs from the same seed, enjoys the same daylight, breathes like you, lives like you, dies like you . . . ," wrote Seneca in one of his letters), and individual slaves were often released for good behaviour or on the death of their master, slavery was so deeply embedded in Roman society (as it was also in Greek) that even Christians did not challenge it.[25] At the same time there was continual low-level violence, banditry and the threat of overreaction by the authorities. *The Golden Ass* provides vivid descriptions of life in the less wealthy provincial towns, where the local youth ransack the town on an evening out and valuables have to be protected by servants in the very centre of the house. When suspects are arrested, torture is freely used. This is the wider context within which must be set the undoubted achievements of the Roman empire at its height.

# 7

# THE EMPIRE IN CRISIS, THE EMPIRE IN RECOVERY

## Political Transformations in the Third Century

The immortal gods in their providence have so designed things that good and true principles have been established by the wisdom and deliberation of eminent, wise and upright men. It is wrong to oppose these principles, or desert the ancient religion for some new one, for it is the height of criminality to try and revise doctrines that were settled once and for all by the ancients, and whose position is fixed and acknowledged.

THE EMPEROR DIOCLETIAN, A.D. 302[1]

Despite the energy of emperors in their role as protectors of its frontiers, the Roman empire was always vulnerable to attack. The distance from the mouth of the Rhine to that of the Danube was no less than 2,000 kilometres, while the shortest marching route between the Black Sea and the Red Sea was 3,000. The borders of the provinces of Africa ran for 4,000 kilometres, often across empty desert. While small raids could be dealt with by local troops, any efficient invader who could rely on overwhelming numbers or surprise could easily break through. Once inside the empire, its fine road network brought the raiders quickly within reach of opulent and undefended cities.

Often the peace could be kept through diplomacy. It was essential to keep the many German tribes who jostled with each other along the northern borders disunited. ("May the tribes ever retain, if not love for us, at least hatred for each other," as Tacitus put it.) Their leaders could be offered gifts of money, or special protection against their rivals. The sons of chieftains could be brought up within the imperial court and then sent back as "Romans" keen to maintain contact with the empire. "Germans" could serve in the Roman armies as mercenaries. There was thus a surprising amount of contact across the borders, as Roman merchants travelled among the neighbouring peoples and Roman money or support was used by local rulers to build their own prestige. However, a growing awareness of the riches of the empire was unsettling, especially as the population of the German tribes appears to have been growing in these centuries and their resources became increasingly stretched. Tensions between tribes caused shifting coalitions, some temporary, some forged by charismatic leaders into something more coherent and long-lasting. Peoples amalgamated. So there emerged on the central part of the German border in the early third century A.D. a loose confederation known as the Alamanni ("all the men"), and then to the north another people known as the Franks. On the Danube border a merging of migratory peoples with the local inhabitants of the Black Sea area produced the Goths. In their struggles with another tribe, the Sarmatians, a nomadic people from Asia, the latter were pushed towards the Roman border. None of these peoples could prevail in a direct confrontation with a Roman legion, but raids over the border caused considerable disruption. The problem for the Romans was that the barbarians could never be successfully and definitively defeated, as there was no way of controlling so many rival groups whose leaders depended on the prestige of war and the plunder of raids. The Romans tried everything—buying off tribes, stationing legions across the border so that raiders could be dealt with before they reached the frontier, using one tribe against another. None of these tactics brought lasting stability, and by the third century a new wave of raids began.[2]

It was unfortunate that these raids coincided with the emergence of a powerful new state in the east, that of the Sassanids. Its predecessor, the Parthian empire, had often been at war with Rome, but the campaigns of the 160s and the 190s had been successful. In 197, the emperor Septimius Severus had even sacked the Parthian capital, Ctesiphon, and extended the empire as far as the Tigris. The defeats were evidence of the decline of the Parthian empire after some 400 years of success, and in the

220s the Parthians finally succumbed to the Sassanids, a fiercely nation-
alistic people who claimed to be reviving the glories of the Achaemenids
(the Persian empire that had been overthrown by Alexander). Under
Shapur I (who ruled 239–70) the Sassanids claimed the ancient borders
of the Achaemenid empire, the western of which were, by now, deep in
Roman territory.

So began the so-called crisis of the third century, which saw a series
of attacks and border raids by both Sassanids and German tribes over a
period of some fifty years (234–84). On the German borders the raids
were small in scale; they were nevertheless often humiliating because of
both the distance the raiders were able to cover once the frontier had
been breached and the major cities that proved vulnerable to the raiders.
The Goths reached Ephesus in 253; in 260 the Alamanni assaulted
Milan. In 267 Athens was sacked by the Heruli (a people of whom there
is no other record), its celebrated Hellenistic stoas destroyed in the
onslaught. Some raiders even reached Spain. The Sassanids also had
their successes. In 253 or 254 they sacked Antioch, one of the great cities
of the eastern empire, and in 260 they inflicted the most profound
humiliation of all, the capture of the emperor Valerian, whom Shapur is
said to have used as a footstool from which to mount his horse. The triumph of the Sassanids over the Romans was celebrated throughout the
Sassanid empire on rock reliefs in which the humbled Roman generals
are shown pleading with Shapur for their release.

The defeats either caused or coincided with a rapid turnover of
emperors. Eighteen are known in these fifty years, with average reigns
of under three years. The emperor's authority was heavily dependent on
victory in battle; on several occasions defeated emperors were killed
by their own men. On the other hand, several victorious generals were to
be tempted to declare themselves emperor, turning the Roman armies
against each other just at a time when unity was most necessary. Not all
the emperors of this period were military failures. Gallienus (260–68)
and Claudius II (268–70) had great victories; Claudius' triumph over the
Goths was to become legendary (and was later to be exploited by Constantine for his own ends). Aurelian (270–75) defeated the Alamanni
and left a permanent mark on Rome by constructing a vast wall around
the city, much of which still stands. Unsurprisingly, the building of walls
now became a central preoccupation for cities, and other building projects faltered as a result. There is not a single dedicatory inscription at

Olympia dating from after 265. Some emperors proposed innovatory solutions to the crisis, suggesting that the empire's defence be shared among several emperors ruling concurrently, or the creation of cavalry forces that could respond to raids more rapidly than the infantry legions.

By the 280s, however, stability seemed no closer. Aurelian and his successor Probus were both killed by their own men. Their successor Carus launched a successful invasion of Persia but died while campaigning. His son Numerian, who was with him, was declared emperor of the east, but was found dead in his litter while the army was returning home. His supposed murderer, the praetorian prefect Aper, was himself killed in front of the army by Diocles, one of his senior officers. Diocles then defeated Carus' other son, Carinus, and in 284 declared himself sole emperor with the name Diocletian. Remarkably, he was still in power twenty years later, presiding over a settled and reinvigorated empire.[3]

Diocletian, like many of the most successful soldiers of the period, was from the Balkans. His background was humble; he may even have been a freed slave or the son of one, and his rise to power showed how much talent counted in these difficult times. Diocletian was tough, an effective general, but an even more remarkable organizer and statesman. He had both the vision to appreciate the necessity for a major reorganization of the empire and the skills to effect it. His achievement was staggering. To enable the empire to respond to attack more swiftly and buttress the stability of the imperial office, he appointed a deputy, Maximian, a fellow commander from the Balkans, as co-emperor with the title of Augustus. Then he appointed two junior "Caesars," Galerius and Constantius, the intention being that they should succeed the Augusti when either died (the system is known as the Tetrarchy, "a rule in four divisions"). Meanwhile, each of the four was to play an active role in defending the empire. Constantius was sent to the west, to Britain and Gaul; Maximian presided over Italy and the African provinces; Galerius was in charge of the Danube, while Diocletian remained in the east (although Galerius was later to assume command there). Under the Tetrarchy, Rome began to fight back, gradually consolidating its borders. In 297 Galerius' defeat of the Sassanids resulted in a decades-long peace on the eastern border.

These victories allowed resources to be released for long-term defence, and a programme of border fortification began. New forts were built, walls and barriers were strengthened and gateways narrowed, enabling them to be held more easily. The army, now some 400,000 strong, appears to have been divided into smaller units to allow it to respond more rapidly to attacks. To finance these developments Diocletian divided the empire into smaller provinces, depriving their governors of their traditional combined role of commander and tax collector. Henceforth in each province a civilian governor concentrated on collecting taxes while a military leader (*dux*) was responsible for defence. To increase the efficiency of the tax system, land was assessed according to its productivity and a fixed sum (reviewed every five years) was levied on it. For the first time it was possible for there to be an imperial budget and even some elementary long-term planning. Diocletian tackled the debilitating inflation (arising from the frequent debasing of the coinage) that had accompanied the crisis by introducing a standard gold coin, but when inflation continued (probably as a result of the large numbers of bronze coins still being minted) he attempted an empire-wide Edict of Prices (A.D. 301), which set out an approved price for every kind of produce and fixed rates for each kind of professional service. (A shipwright working on a seagoing ship was to be paid sixty denarii a day, teachers of Greek and geometry 200 denarii per pupil per month, a bathhouse attendant two denarii per bather.) It was far too ambitious an undertaking for a still undeveloped economy and, as socialist-planned economies showed 2,000 years later, only encouraged black-market activity. Despite severe penalties for evasion, the edict became moribund, but it remains a fascinating record of an assessment of comparative values of goods and activities in the empire and, of course, a symbol of Diocletian's determination.

The third century saw emperors increasingly distance themselves from their subjects. No longer could an emperor be accosted by an old woman, as Hadrian had been 150 years earlier. The figure of the emperor now emerged as a stage-managed presence, addressed not by name but by abstractions—Your Majesty, Your Serenity. Supplicants had to prostrate themselves and kiss the emperor's robes before making their petitions. These were frequently conveyed to the emperor and then relayed back through a series of officials so as to preserve his inaccessibility. Emperors dressed in purple, a dye so rare that 1,200 murex shells yielded only 1.6 grams of it. (The Edict of Prices valued purple-dyed wool as equal to its weight in gold, 50,000 denarii a pound.) The emperors displayed themselves in great audience halls; that used by Constantius in the northern border city of Trier still survives, though it has long been stripped of its mosaics and marble wall veneers.

The distancing saw the emperor linked ever more closely with the gods. The panegyrics, the speeches of praise offered to an emperor on formal occasions, proclaimed that the very fact that Diocletian had come to power confirmed that he was favoured by the gods, a much more explicit recognition of his semi-divine status than had been customary. (The term used to refer to the emperor's adoption by the gods was *consecratio*, "a making sacred.") Diocletian claimed a particular affinity with Zeus, while Maximian preferred Hercules, who had long been associated with commanders, including Alexander the Great. This was a significant development in the ideology of imperialism because it suggested that it was divine favour rather than either human support (of the army or Senate, for instance) or descent that provided the emperor with legitimacy. The emperor was divine by virtue of his successful accession. In the arch of Galerius in Thessalonika, built when Diocletian and Maximian were still alive, they are shown enthroned above the earth and sky.[4] Perhaps this marks the moment when the Hellenistic concept of kingship, initiated by Alexander, had been fully absorbed by imperial Rome. The monarch is removed and imbued with mystery— no longer would an emperor lower himself to engage in debate with philosophers. Imperial authority is clothed with a divine aura.[5]

In contrast to Alexander, this did not involve the neglect of administration. If there was a theme to Diocletian's programme it was to centralize the state so that it could function more coherently and effectively. He built on earlier developments. In 212, for instance, all subjects of the empire except slaves had been made Roman citizens so all could be taxed equally. Diocletian took this further by stressing that a common citizenship meant accepting common responsibility for the state, and so those whose allegiances were questionable suddenly found themselves more vulnerable. Prominent among these were the Christians, who, through their resolute rejection of paganism, found themselves in open defiance of the state, "the whore of Babylon," and its traditional gods, and thus were unable to take part in any public ceremonies or sacrifices. The Christians were well organized, with a clear structure of authority (the bishops); an evolving theology based on worship of the Christian God, drawn from the God of Judaism, and a "saviour," Jesus Christ, who was believed to have been some form of manifestation (exactly what kind of manifestation remained vigorously disputed) of God in human form; its own calendar, which evolved around its own feast days; initiation rites that distinguished believers from non-believers; and, like the schools of philosophy, its own ethical demands. In the unsettled conditions of the third century, Christians provided secure communities, and even army officers and state officials were now converting. Some of the eastern cities may have had a Christian majority by 300.

The state had always been uneasy about Christians. They posed the classic political dilemma: how far can one show tolerance to a group that itself condemns the tolerance of the state in allowing pagan worship to continue? Christians did not deny the existence of the pagan gods, but they saw them as demons and believed pagans would suffer eternal punishment after death. Up to the third century, persecution of Christians had been erratic, dependent on the whim of individual provincial governors; the crisis of the third century induced the first empire-wide persecution, under the emperor Decius in 250–51, during which bishops in particular were a target. (It has been argued, none the less, that Decius' objective, as outlined in his edict, was the restoration of traditional cults rather than the persecution of Christians *per se*.)[6] It remained possible for Christianity to survive; persecutions waxed and waned, and in practice the desperate need for talent in the army and the administration allowed Christians to remain in prominent positions. In many cases a senior official or soldier was dismissed or executed only after every possible means of making him offer a token sacrifice to the state had been tried. By the fourth century, however, Diocletian had to face up to the logic of his centralizing reforms: a large community that refused to show any allegiance to the gods of the empire could no longer be tolerated. Yet Diocletian was a shrewd politician. He was reluctant to become involved in a politically unwinnable campaign against a determined minority. Although in previous persecutions many Christians had capitulated, others had resisted to the point of martyrdom, willingly accepting their reward in heaven in preference to a life stuck in the misery of the material world. Jesus and several of his immediate followers, including Peter and Paul, had died at the hands of the state, so one might say that the readiness to suffer martyrdom was intrinsic to Christian commitment. While Galerius, who had much of the fanatic about him, wished to launch a devastating persecution, Diocletian was more cautious. He consulted widely and even sent to the oracle at Didyma on the coast of Asia Minor for advice.

When Diocletian finally decided to move against the Christians, his actions were marked by their restraint. His first edict (303) was directed at Christian property—buildings, texts, sacred vessels—rather than Christians themselves. Many bishops ordered their congregations to give up property, believing the faith would survive without it, but other congregations, notably in north Africa, refused to surrender anything and condemned those who had. So the persecutions led to a major and enduring schism. As tensions rose, any chance of compromise with the authorities receded. A fire in Diocletian's palace at Nicomedia was blamed on Christians, and uprisings in the east were also seen as Christian in inspiration. Diocletian might still have held back, but his own health was deteriorating and power was shifting towards Galerius (who was to become Augustus in the east when Diocletian abdicated in May 305). New decrees now demanded that all Christian clergy be imprisoned until they were prepared to sacrifice to the gods of the state and then, in April 304, that all Christians should be required to sacrifice on penalty of death.

Subsequent events depended on the vigour of the local emperors and their governors. In the west Constantius used persecution very sparingly, concentrating only on property belonging to Christians, while in the east Galerius was able to unleash his hatred for Christians. In some provinces the legal process broke down completely as Christians were rounded up, tortured and executed, although even in the east, other governors were able to deflect the legislation, claiming that all local Christians had sacrificed. One way of sidestepping the edicts was simply to ask Christians to affirm the existence of a supreme deity and not require any confirmation as to whether this was Zeus or the Christian God. There is evidence that in Alexandria many Christians were sheltered by pagans.

The impetus behind the orgy of bloodletting soon faltered, and by 310 persecution had become haphazard and without fervour. Galerius was desperately ill with bowel cancer. The Christian writer Lactantius revelled in describing the symptoms that God had sent him in punishment for the persecution he had instigated: "His bowels came out, his whole anus putrefied . . . the stench filled not just the palace but the whole city . . . his body, in intolerable tortures, dissolved into one mass of corruption." He died in 311.[7] Christianity survived. While the stress of persecution had divided Christian against Christian, the faith itself had proved highly resilient in the face of oppression.

Christianity and the new authoritarian empire of Diocletian were clearly incompatible, but there was an alternative to destructive and debilitating persecutions, and that was to absorb the religion within the authoritarian structure of the state, thus defusing it as a threat. Whatever his motives, personal or political, in first tolerating and then supporting Christianity, this was to be the achievement of Constantine. Before exploring his transformation of Christianity, however, we must make some attempt to understand how this religion, which had been a response to the execution of an apparent enemy of the empire by one of its provincial governors, had survived at all.[8]

# 8

## JESUS

The past thirty years have been especially fruitful for the study of early Christianity. This is partly because the churches appear more to be relaxed about the uncertainties of research findings but also because the available sources, particularly the range of Jewish texts, preeminent among them the Dead Sea Scrolls, have expanded enormously. We are better able to set Jesus within a historical context than at any time since the first century. If we can sum up the rich diversity of modern scholarship, it is distinguished both by the acceptance of the essential Jewishness of Jesus and by a fuller understanding of what it means to say that Jesus was Jewish in the first century of the Christian era. While traditional interpretations of Jesus have seen him as somehow apart from Judaism, his mission always focused on the outside world, it is now argued not only that he preached and taught within Judaism but even that he was advocating a return to traditional Jewish values. Nevertheless, the continuing lack of Jewish sources for Jesus' life means that any interpretation of his role and mission has to be made with caution.[1]

There are only a few historical references to Jesus outside the New Testament, and one of these, by the Jewish historian Josephus, may have been rewritten by Christians at a later date.[2] The earliest New Testament sources are Paul's letters, written in the 50s, not much more than twenty years after Jesus' crucifixion, but they say virtually nothing about Jesus' life. Later than Paul, but drawing on earlier material, are the four surviving Gospels, written for early Christian communities in the Gentile (Greco-Roman) world. As Luke reminds his readers in the opening verse of his Gospel, there were many other accounts of Jesus' activities (scholars suggest that there may have originally been some twenty Gospels), but these are now all lost apart from the odd fragment; the four we know were accepted as canonical (authoritative) during the second century. Other later non-canonical texts, such as the Gospel of St. Thomas, which does survive (in part) from the second century, and the mass of material from the Nag Hammadi library (a collection of papyrus codices of works from the third to fifth centuries discovered at Nag Hammadi in modern Egypt in 1945–46, some of which draw on second-century sources), are probably too late to be of much historical value. All four Gospels, as well as Paul's letters, were originally written in Greek, although on occasion they preserve Jesus' words in their original Aramaic. There is no account of Jesus' life written from a Jewish perspective, unless one interprets Matthew's Gospel in this light (see below). Also lost is a rich oral tradition—it is known that until about A.D. 135 many Christian communities preferred to pass on their knowledge of Jesus by word of mouth. Only a tiny proportion of what was originally recorded, whether orally or in writing, about Jesus has survived; some texts simply disappeared, others were suppressed as interpretations of Jesus evolved in the early Christian communities. The very fact that there are four different accounts of Jesus' mission and that these reached their final form some decades after his crucifixion suggests that a coherent historical (and, equally, a coherent spiritual or divine) Jesus will be difficult to recover.[3]

Most scholars now assume that Mark is the earliest of the surviving Gospels, perhaps written about A.D. 70, forty years after Jesus' death. It is the shortest of the canonical Gospels and begins with Jesus' baptism by John the Baptist and ends in its original version with the discovery of his empty tomb. (In other words, there are no birth stories and the resurrection accounts were added later.) It is believed to have been written for a Christian community in Rome and composed to be read aloud to them. Then follow Luke (after 70) and Matthew (between 80 and 90), drawing on a common (lost) source (known as "Q," from the German *Quelle,* or "source") as well as on Mark. There is no agreement among scholars as to where Luke's Gospel was written, but there is a degree of consensus in the belief that Matthew's was written for a community in Antioch in Syria. These three are known as the Synoptic Gospels (the word "synoptic," "with the same eye," reflecting their shared perspective on Jesus' life). The last of the canonical Gospels, that of John, dated from about A.D. 100, is very different from the earlier three and is a more considered theological interpretation of Jesus' life in which, for the first time, he is presented as divine. In one or two instances, the accounts of Jesus' trial, for example, John appears to draw on an independent witness and in some ways his Gospel, though the most removed from events, may in fact be the most historically accurate.

The Gospels are not written as a history or biography in the conventional sense. Events are shaped to provide a meaning for Jesus, partly through his teachings and partly through his trial and death (recounted in detail in all four Gospels) and resurrection. The earliest sources on which they draw appear to have been sayings of Jesus (assembled in collections known as "pericopes," from the original Greek word for "a cut-off section"), which were placed in contexts created by the Gospel writers themselves. (The same pericopes appear in different contexts in different Gospels, as one can see when comparing Luke's Sermon on the Mount, 6:17–49, with Matthew's much longer version, which incorporates material used elsewhere by Luke in his Gospel.) The selection, placing and development of the sayings vary from one Gospel to another, but one common theme, which is approached differently in each Gospel, is the question of how Jesus was to be related to his Jewish background at a time, some decades after the crucifixion, when the Christian communities were spreading into the Gentile world. The issue can be explored by taking Matthew's Gospel (highlighted here because it was the most influential of the three Synoptic Gospels in the early Christian centuries) as an example.

Matthew, as has been seen, shares a common source with Mark and also draws on "Q," but there are a number of emphases in his Gospel that are unique. One is the bringing together of Jesus' ethical teachings in the Sermon on the Mount, a version which is three times as long as the compilation by Luke, actually a "Sermon on the Plain" rather than "the Mount." Another involves the relating of Jesus' birth and life back to earlier Jewish prophecies; throughout his Gospel Matthew is concerned to place Jesus' teaching into the context of earlier scripture. Yet Matthew depicts Jesus himself as firmly, indeed violently, rejected by Jews—Pilate, for instance, is shown as reluctant to order the crucifixion until urged to do so by the Jewish crowds (27:22, "Let him be crucified!"). There is also in Matthew (but not in Mark or Luke) a powerful indictment of the scribes and Pharisees (23:13–33). So Matthew appears to be depicting a Jesus who is an important ethical teacher who can be seen as a fulfillment of Jewish prophecies, but who at the same time rejects Jewish sects and is rejected by the Jews themselves. Another central theme of Matthew is Jesus' warning of "a burning furnace" for those who have done evil and "eternal punishment" for those who neglect his demands to feed the hungry or clothe the naked (Matthew 13:36–43 and 25:31–46). Many Jews did not believe in an afterlife, but some talked of *sheol*, a shadowy "grave" or "pit," where departed spirits live, or Gehenna, a place of torment based on an actual valley in Judaea where human sacrifices had taken place. It is Gehenna to which Jesus refers in Matthew's telling of his indictment of the Pharisees.[4]

To establish how these emphases might relate to Matthew's own concerns, attempts have been made to establish the audience for whom Matthew was writing. One view is that Matthew led a community that was Jewish in origin and still saw itself as Jewish, despite the fact that its devotion to Christ had led to its ostracism by orthodox Jewish communities. It is usually suggested that this was in Antioch at a time when Judaism was narrowing its boundaries after the destruction of Jerusalem and the Temple by the Romans in A.D. 70. Determined that his community survive, Matthew, according to this interpretation, presented Jesus as the hoped-for Messiah, prophesied in the scriptures, but as a Messiah who has been rejected and betrayed by his own people. Such ideas of betrayal and renewal ran deep in Jewish history, and Matthew places Jesus within this tradition. Once again the Jews have betrayed the one who is sent from God, says Matthew, but this does not mean that Judaism in itself is at an end. Jesus had come "not to abolish but to *complete* [the Law]." It would remain in place "till heaven and earth disappear . . . until its purpose is achieved" (Matthew 5:17–18). Matthew thus presents Jesus as spearheading a *Jewish* renewal, even if it is one that has not been recognized by his own people. Matthew believes that his community has replaced the Jews as guardians of his Messiahship. One of the verses Matthew attributes to Jesus (21:43) is particularly telling here: "I tell you then, that the kingdom of God will be taken from you [i.e., those Jews who have rejected me] and given to a people who will produce its fruit," by implication Matthew's community. Matthew also lays greater stress than the other Synoptic Gospels on the church as an institution. Peter, whose Christianity, like Matthew's, was set within Judaism, is given a leadership role by Jesus, and there is specific mention of the community having disciplinary powers (18:15–20). This approach to Matthew's Gospel has been summed up as follows:

[Matthew's Jewish] community defines itself as the last sanctuary for the preservation of those fundamentals of Israel's faith. It tries desperately to live up to its true calling, as represented in these responsibilities to preserve true holiness. But it is also inclined to be bitter and vengeful; this typical, and entirely understandable, desire for vengeance (upon the Pharisees in particular) is expressed in the notion of eternal punishment and the principle of just requital.[5]

When Matthew's text was adopted as one of the four canonical texts by the emerging churches of the Gentile world, its origin as a Jewish text was glossed over, and Matthew's rejection of those Jews who had betrayed Jesus was transformed by later Christians into a justification for rejecting *all* Judaism—the cry of the crowd in Jerusalem, "His blood be on us and on our children!" (27:25), was to be frequently quoted in the diatribes that many of the Church Fathers launched against Judaism as a religion, something Matthew can hardly have intended. Again, the doctrine of eternal punishment in hell, which was further developed in the early church by interpreting Matthew's verse "Many are called but few are chosen" (22:14) to suggest that a majority of human beings would suffer eternal punishment, became an entrenched and highly influential part of Christian teaching. It is equally important, of course, to note the enormous influence of the Sermon on the Mount on Christian ethics. This is the challenge the Gospels pose for the historian—their own versions of Jesus were shaped to meet the needs of their immediate audience, yet when adopted into the canon they were interpreted to fit the needs of the emerging church. Is it possible to "decode" the Gospel texts so as to place Jesus back into his original background? Some scholars argue that it is now virtually impossible to find "the real Jesus" under the layers of later developments; others believe that something can be reconstructed from the material in the Gospels. This latter will be what is attempted here.

Jesus came to prominence only in the last years of his life, and the story essentially begins in Galilee in around A.D. 27 with his baptism by an itinerant preacher, John the Baptist, "a voice crying in the wilderness," who called on sinners to show repentance in view of the imminent approach of God's kingdom.[6] Throughout Jesus' life Galilee was ruled by client kings of the Romans, first Herod the Great (37–4 B.C.) and

then as tetrarch (a subordinate ruler) his son Herod Antipas (4 B.C.–
A.D. 39). (Contrary to popular belief, Jesus' ministry did not take place
within the "official" Roman empire, until he moved into Judaea, which,
as we have seen, had been a directly ruled province of the empire since
A.D. 6.) Galilee was a relatively prosperous area with fertile land and
good fishing in "the sea of Galilee," yet Galileans were remote from the
more sophisticated centres of Judaism and conscious that the peoples
surrounding them, largely Greek and Phoenician, were of very different
cultures. There is some evidence that there was an increasing Greek presence in Galilee in these years, but as the Greeks tended to consider themselves superior to local cultures and kept themselves distinct from them
(Greeks seldom bothered to learn native languages, for instance), this is
only likely to have exacerbated the feelings of exclusion among the native
Galileans. Furthermore, as has been persuasively argued by Richard
Horsley, the impact of taxation, a growing population and Herodian rule
was resulting in the fragmentation of peasant land holdings and placed
increasing pressure on traditional family structures.[7] Studies of Judaism
in Galilee and Judaea at the time suggest that there was relatively little
difference between the two areas in terms of religious belief and practice,
but, as Horsley again has argued, the pressures on peasant life may have
led to a more passionate defence of traditional religious values in Galilee
and an attraction to charismatic spiritual leaders who espoused them (in
this Galilee would have been typical of areas of peasant unrest through
the ages where social change or oppression result in resistance grounded
in traditional beliefs).[8]

Judaism was not a monolithic religion, and recent research has
served to stress the diversity of Jewish practice in the first century A.D.[9]
There were, of course, beliefs common to all Jews, above all belief in a
single providential God who had a special relationship with Israel exemplified by the covenant he had made with his people. Even if the
covenant were broken, which it often was in the troubled history of
Israel, God would always forgive (the point stressed by Matthew). The
requirements of the Law (central to Jewish life and ethical behaviour),
the sayings of the Prophets and the history of Israel were recorded in
scriptures that were studied by all educated Jews. Rituals shared by Jews
included circumcision, dietary restrictions (in practice tied to those
foods that most easily carried disease—pork, shellfish and carrion—
although the ban was held to be instituted by God) and a strict observance of the Sabbath. As laid down in the Ten Commandments, there

was an absolute prohibition on the worship of God through idols. A commitment to Jewish Law, which was believed to have been instituted directly by God (in the giving of the Ten Commandments to Moses, for instance), covered every aspect of life, with detailed prescriptions for living laid down in scriptures such as the Book of Leviticus. There was a strong emphasis on the value of family life and traditional family structures. Those who offended could redeem themselves through repentance, achieved through sacrifice.

The central focus for the worship of God was the great Temple at Jerusalem, and male Jews were required to visit the Temple three times a year, at the times of the major festivals, although in practice the diaspora of Jews throughout the ancient world had made this impossible for many. The Temple was staffed by a large class of priests, perhaps some 20,000 in total, if the assistant priests, the Levites, are included. The priesthood was an important and influential class—it was said that the Jewish revolt of A.D. 66 broke out at the moment when the priests refused to accept any more sacrifices on Rome's behalf. The priests alone had the right to sacrifice (on behalf of themselves and those who had come to the Temple as penitents). They took it in turns to officiate in the Temple, but all would be on duty there during the major festivals. The Temple had recently been rebuilt in magnificent style by Herod the Great, but in the eyes of many Jews the Temple elite had compromised itself in accepting the patronage of Herod and, after his death, through acquiescing in Roman imperial control.

Because the Law was so fully set out in the Hebrew scriptures, most Jews knew its requirements well. There were, however, groups such as the Pharisees, who had originated in the second century B.C. and who may have numbered some 6,000 in Herod's day, who had made their own interpretations of how the Law should be observed. They studied it intensively and insisted on its strict observance. One particular belief associated with the Pharisees, but not shared by all Jews, was that there was an afterlife and a final resurrection of the bodies of the dead. While the Pharisees had no political power (very few were actually priests) and did not proselytize, they were respected for their beliefs. Nevertheless, it was natural that they would feel threatened by groups or religious leaders who had a more relaxed attitude to the Law than they did or who claimed their own differing interpretation of the Law. Another group with distinctive beliefs, in this case that there was no afterlife, were the Sadducees, who were essentially conservative in their support of traditional priestly ritual and appear to have been well represented in the aristocratic priesthood. (This was one reason why they came into conflict with groups such as the Pharisees, who threatened to take the interpretation of the Law both outside the priesthood and also outside of Jerusalem.)

The majority of Jews, like all other peoples of the Mediterranean and the ancient Near East, were poor, susceptible to illness (much of it incurable), subject to taxation (whether from the Jewish authorities, a king or directly by the Romans), and vulnerable. In extreme cases these hardships could lead to agrarian unrest or even outright revolt, such as the disastrous uprisings against the Romans of A.D. 66 and A.D. 132. By contrast there was also the possibility of spiritual withdrawal. This was the path taken by the Essenes, a sect that seems to have formed in the second century B.C. Members of this sect, whose lifestyle and beliefs have been recovered from the Dead Sea Scrolls, were extreme in the strictness with which they observed the Law. They held property in common, encouraged celibacy (at least in the Qumran community, which produced the Dead Sea Scrolls) and believed that the soul, but not the body itself, would have an afterlife. They saw themselves as the only true believers, the "sons of light," while all others, including their fellow Jews, were "sons of darkness." One should "love all the children of light, each one according to his lot in the council of God, and abhor all the children of darkness, each one according to his guilt, which delivers him up to God's retribution." They had a deep-rooted distrust of outsiders, and newcomers were accepted into the group only after two or three years of spiritual instruction. The Essenes were millennarians, waiting for some form of liberation. As one of their texts put it: "The heavens and the earth will listen to His Messiah . . . He [the Lord] will glorify the pious on the throne of the eternal Kingdom, He who liberates the captives, restores sight to the blind, straightens the bent . . . For He will heal the wounded, and revive the dead and bring good news to the poor."[10] Although there is no evidence to connect Jesus with the Essenes, their teachings show that expectations of a Messiah with a special message for the poor who would introduce an eternal kingdom were active in the Jewish world of the first century. As we will see later, Paul appears to have been influenced by them.

The concept of Messiah (*Christos* in Greek, hence Christ) is so central to Judaism that it deserves to be explored here. The word was used in general of one who was anointed by God for some special purpose (it was even accorded to a Gentile, Cyrus of Persia, who liberated Israel from Babylonian rule), but it tended to be associated with King David and his royal line (God had promised the prophet Nathan that the throne of David's "seed" would be established "for ever" [2 Samuel 7:12–13]). The conviction that a descendant of David would come to power as a wise and secure ruler ran deep in Jewish thought. According to another tradition, the Messiah would be a priest, and it appears from one text that the Essene community in Qumran may have been waiting for two Messiahs, one a king and one a priest. In neither case was a Messiah seen as divine; rather, he was a human being who had been exalted by God.[11]

Many of the lives of Jesus that have appeared in recent years have tried to pin him down with a single epithet. Can he best be understood as a *hasid,* a Jewish holy man, or a prophet, "a magic man," a miracle worker, a teacher, a "marginal Jew," a peasant leader, even a revolutionary? Each has had its supporters, but Jesus does not fit neatly into any one category; perhaps he never did. Almost any statement of his views in one Gospel seems to be qualified or even contradicted by another, sometimes even from within the same Gospel. However, in an insight that does much to explain the continuing significance of Jesus to an enormous variety of Christian communities throughout the world, the theologian Frances Young notes: "Somehow he was all things to all men and broke down social, political and religious barriers . . . all manner of men found their salvation in him and were driven to search for categories to explain him, never finding any single one adequate."[12]

Some features of Jesus' personality can, however, be drawn unambiguously from the Gospel sources. He was highly charismatic; people were drawn to him by his personality and teaching, and herein lay much of his natural authority, but despite periods of withdrawal (and, according to the Synoptic Gospels, uneasy relationships with his mother and brothers [Mark 3:31–35]) he never distanced himself from his chosen followers or their modest way of life. He never, for instance, used his status so that he could avoid the discomforts of daily life on the road, and although there is some scholarly disagreement on this, he did not appear to give himself a privileged place above the Law. There is only one exception to this in the Gospels—when he required a man with a dead father to follow him rather than bury his father, as Jewish Law required (Matthew 8:21–22)—when he unambiguously put himself before the

Law. He chose twelve special companions, the disciples, all from humble backgrounds, with the possible exception of Matthew the tax collector. They shared his life closely and probably received confidences denied to others (twelve is the number of tribes of Israel and may echo the belief that at the final judgment Jews would be reassembled according to their tribe, each with a leader), but he was not fussy about whom he mixed with and shocked some by consorting with tax collectors and prostitutes. When he preached he showed a genius for making his points in parables that were rooted not in some abstract spiritual world but in the reality of the everyday life of the small agricultural communities around him. This was the environment in which he was most "at home." (Jesus appears to have some difficulty in spreading his message to the towns [Matthew 11:20].) His presence tended to have a beneficial effect on those who were ill, both mentally (inhabited by "demons") and physically, so that the masses were drawn to him as a healer, and word spread of him effecting miracle cures. Belief in "miraculous" interventions of this kind was common in the ancient world, and they were interpreted as a sign of holiness. Other Jewish "holy men" were associated with miracle working, but Jesus' effective use of miracles, especially exorcisms, was highlighted by his followers (notably Mark) and was to become one of the most common ways individual Christians later proclaimed their own distinct authenticity as those favoured by God.

Jesus had been brought up as a Jew and, like most Jews, knew the scriptures well. His immediate followers were almost without exception Jews, and his teaching made use of concepts that would have been recognizable to them. Much of his teaching took place in synagogues. He may not have foreseen his teaching spreading beyond the Jews—as he himself put it: "I was sent to the lost sheep of the house of Israel and to them alone" (Matthew 15:24), although this may reflect the particular perspective of Matthew described above, and the saying comes just before the disciples persuaded Jesus to heal the daughter of a Canaanite. It can, of course, be argued that if he had departed far from traditional Jewish teaching within the conservative agricultural communities in which he preached, he would not have survived as long as he did. On one occasion he stressed the continuing importance of the Law, which, he claimed, he had come "not to abolish but to complete." Paula Fredriksen establishes important guidelines for historians when she writes that "the prime goal of the historian is to find a first-century Jesus whose mission would make sense to his contemporary first-century [Jewish] hearers."[13] The question remains as to which "hearers" within the diversity of first-century Judaism Jesus was appealing. Those in the countryside suffering from encroachment on their land, taxation and pressures from Herod's administrators appear the most likely, yet an allegiance by any leader to one group within Judaism was likely to lead to opposition from others, as Jesus' difficulties with the conservative Pharisees and the elitist Temple authorities were to show.

Jesus' message echoed John the Baptist's in that he talked of the imminence of God's kingdom. It is not always clear from the Gospel sources what he meant by this. Some passages, such as Luke 17:21, suggest that the kingdom has already arrived with the coming of Jesus, others that it will come some day in the near future, perhaps after some cataclysmic event. Many assumed that it would involve the appearance of a king of the house of David as the Messianic tradition had predicted, and one cannot isolate Jesus from the long-held Jewish belief that a providential God will in the end redeem humankind. Much of Jesus' preaching about the coming of the kingdom is entirely positive in the sense that it talks of those who will be included rather than those who will not—but in some instances its arrival is set within the context of a "last judgment" at which the wicked will be punished at the same time as the good are rewarded. It seems impossible here to be sure of distinguishing Jesus' own words from traditional Jewish Messianic teachings on "the end," but it seems likely that the expectation of some major "happening" to come was among the forces which drew people to him. In this sense he can certainly be seen as a millennarian prophet.

The coming of the kingdom is set within the context of moral renewal. In Mark (10:13–27) Jesus teaches that at the coming of the kingdom worldly values will be overthrown; one would have to be without wealth and "like a little child" to be able to enter. This "social" message suggests that Jesus saw the coming of the kingdom as associated with the triumph of the outcast and perhaps with the restoration of traditional values that were under threat from outside forces (hence his stress on the importance of marriage and the honouring of parents—it has been noted that Jesus went further than traditional Jewish teaching in his strictures on divorce). Richard Horsley argues: "For the Jesus movement . . . the kingdom of God means the renewal of Israel, and the renewal of Israel means the revitalisation of families and village communities along the lines of restored Mosaic covenantal principles."[14] So,

Horsley suggests, Jesus' leadership role may have been rooted in and gained strength from the tensions within rural Galilean society.

As would be expected, Jesus drew heavily on Jewish ethical traditions. "Love thy neighbour as thyself," for instance, often seen as a quintessential "Christian" exhortation, comes originally from Leviticus (19:18). His teachings on ethics were brought together, as already mentioned, by Matthew, in the famous Sermon on the Mount, with its particular focus on those marginalized by society (Matthew 5–7). Although this focus is found elsewhere (in the Essene text quoted above, for instance), Jesus followed it through by practical example. There is a powerful sense, in Mark in particular, of his own compassion for those around him. He does not perform "miracles" to show off, but primarily to bring an end to suffering, whether mental or physical. Particularly striking are the parables, in which outcasts (Samaritans, prodigal sons, lost sheep) are used to show that anyone can be "good" and that those who repent will be welcomed even more warmly than those who have not strayed at all (Luke 15).

Inevitably, Jesus' followers also tried to pin labels on him. The "title" he used most often of himself was "Son of Man." The phrase appears to have been used in the Synoptic Gospels when Jesus wished to avoid direct reference to himself—Geza Vermes suggests the equivalent in English of the modest "yours truly." Yet in John's Gospel the title is associated with the Book of Daniel, where it is linked specifically to hopes of a Messiah and eternal life. At times of social stress it was perhaps natural to hope that any charismatic leader might be the promised Messiah, and word that Jesus was indeed the Messiah seems to have spread among his followers (and, understandably, given rise to stories that he was therefore "of the House of David"). It is not clear from the Gospel sources whether Jesus accepted Messiah status (suggestions that he did may well have been added by the Gospel writers at a time when the later Christian communities had come to believe that he was). After a long consideration of the evidence, two authorities on the Jewish roots of Christianity, E. P. Sanders and W. D. Davies, conclude: "It seems likely that the one who urged others to give up everything for the kingdom claimed for himself no title or position, except the position of one who bore a message from God, the acceptance or rejection of which would be crucial when the fullness of the kingdom arrived."[15] It has to be said that this remains a contentious area, and other commentators are convinced that Jesus proclaimed himself as Messiah while on earth.

Whatever he may have claimed to be, Jesus was bound to provoke reaction from the authorities. He was a highly popular leader, and although he never appears to have counselled any kind of active resistance to the governing group, crowds following charismatic men who appear to have miraculous powers are always a concern to authorities, especially at times of social unrest. Herod Antipas had already, after all, executed John the Baptist, whose teachings on the coming of the kingdom he appears to have seen as insurrectionary. There was also the underlying antagonism of local Pharisees, who were understandably wary of any teacher who claimed to have his own interpretation of the Law. In particular, Jesus' teaching that sinners would be welcomed in heaven even if they have not repented through the making of a sacrifice offended traditionalists.[16]

Clearly Jesus was vulnerable, and it may have been a growing sense of insecurity that drove him with his immediate followers from Galilee into the Roman province of Judaea, perhaps in A.D. 30 (although other dates between 29 and 33 have been proposed), and then to Jerusalem, where they arrived in time for the feast of the Passover. (John, however, suggests that Jesus had made several previous journeys to Jerusalem, as indeed would have been expected of a conventional Jew.) However, the journey to Jerusalem may also have been deliberately planned as the next step in his ministry, the culmination of his mission, even to the extent of bringing him into confrontation with the Temple authorities. Jesus' arrival was certainly greeted in the city as if it were about to inaugurate some kind of political or religious transformation in fulfillment of ancient prophecies. He rode in on a donkey as if to fulfill the prophecy that "a king" would enter Jerusalem on a donkey (Zechariah 9:9), and according to Mark (11:9) the crowd shouted, "Blessings on the coming kingdom of our father, David." In Matthew (21:9) the crowds actually call Jesus "Son of David."

As the great crowds of pilgrims in Jerusalem gathered for the Passover, the tension can only have been raised by the presence, with his troops, of the Roman governor Pontius Pilate, who had come inland from Caesarea, the seat of Roman government of the province, to make sure that order was maintained. This year there had already been trouble, some form of insurrection within the city, and one of its leaders, Barabbas, was in custody and facing almost certain execution. The official responsible to the Romans for good order was Caiaphas, the high priest. Now in his twelfth year of office, he was highly experienced and must have been a consummate political operator to have maintained the support of the Jews for so long while at the same time satisfying his Roman overlords. Pilate, who, as we have seen, had already shown himself to be erratic, cruel and insensitive to Jewish feeling, would have required very careful handling.

So then, among the mass of pilgrims, arrives an itinerant preacher from Galilee, an outsider who brings his followers, with their distinctive accents, with him. He enters on a donkey with the crowds shouting that he is perhaps the Messiah, or at least a member of "the House of David." In itself, his arrival might have been containable, but then comes the incident that tips the balance, Jesus' entry into the Temple, where he overthrows the tables of the money lenders and may have spoken of the later destruction of the Temple. There is no hint in the Gospel accounts that any of Jesus' followers were involved with him in this, understandably perhaps in view of the immense significance the Temple held for Jews. What Jesus meant to achieve by this provocative action has been endlessly debated. His gesture may have been a symbolic one, a recognition of the passing of the old order—and the Temple with it—at the coming of "the new kingdom," but he may also have had the more overtly political aim of expressing popular disquiet with the ruling elite. The intrusion was too threatening for the priests to overlook, and Caiaphas had little option but to take the initiative in dealing with it. There could have been many motives for his action—fear that disorder would spread if Jesus was not dealt with promptly, a need to be seen to be supporting his fellow priests in the Temple at one of the most sacred moments in the year when good order was essential, even a desire to show Pilate that he could act decisively if he needed to. John specifically notes that one of the fears of "the chief priests and Pharisees was that Jesus' teachings would bring Roman retaliation" (John 11:46–48), and if so Caiaphas had little alternative.[17] There may have been other motives. The crowds in Jerusalem were restless and might be more so if Barabbas was executed. It could be that Caiaphas decided to exploit the custom that a prisoner be set free at Passover to release Barabbas, thus avoiding the displeasure of the local crowds, while offering Jesus to the Roman authorities in his place as evidence that the Jewish authorities were committed to good order. "It was Caiaphas who had suggested to the Jews, 'It is better for one man to die for the people,' " notes John in his Gospel (18:14). So the chief priests and the elders "persuaded the crowd to demand the release of Barabbas and the execution of Jesus"

(Matthew 27:20). In short, Jesus the outsider was being used by the authorities in their quest for overall good order within the city.

Having decided to offer Jesus for execution, Caiaphas' problem was finding a reason for doing so; the varied debates outlined in the Gospels show that this was not easy. Attempts were made to make Jesus incriminate himself through admitting he was the Messiah or "the Son of God," and stress was laid on the disorder he was provoking. Eventually he was handed over to Pilate, who acquiesced in the accusation that Jesus had called himself "King of the Jews" and ordered the crucifixion. It seems likely that Pilate saw Jesus' mission primarily as a political issue—there is also evidence from John's account that he was influenced by threats of disorder from the crowd and fears that he would be denounced as disloyal to the emperor if he did not crucify Jesus (19:12–16). As we have seen, "good" emperors recognized that it made more sense to replace an unpopular governor than risk stirring up a major popular revolt. In the light of his unhappy experiences early in his rule, Pilate was probably acutely vulnerable to such threats. With such powerful considerations in mind, it is unlikely that a man so apparently insensitive would have hesitated long over ordering another crucifixion.

One remarkable thing about the trial and execution of Jesus is that neither the Jewish nor the Roman authorities followed it up with a move against Jesus' followers. There was no action on the suspicion that Peter was one of his adherents, and the disciples were left free to visit his tomb without hindrance. This tends to support the view that Caiaphas kept his response to Jesus to the minimum necessary (and also that it was Jesus' solitary intrusion into the Temple that was the catalyst for his arrest). Caiaphas presumably gauged, rightly as it turned out, that the Romans and the Temple officials would be satisfied with Jesus' crucifixion, and that he would not be faced with further disruption.

What Caiaphas could not have foreseen was the aftermath of the death for Jesus' followers. A charismatic leader who had made great promises of the coming of God's kingdom for the poor, who might even be the Messiah and thus royalty, come in triumph to Jerusalem to establish his rule, had been swept aside by the Roman administration backed by the Jewish hierarchy as if he had been no more than a minor political nuisance. One of his followers (Judas) had betrayed him, and the others had dispersed. One can only begin to imagine the psychological devastation of the disciples. Those close to him had spent months with him, sharing the dangers of the road and the tension of opposition, dealing with the crush of crowds and the emotional power of his teachings, a range of experiences unlike any they could have undergone before. His execution brought much more than the shock and emptiness of any sudden and unexpected death of a close companion. With the loss went the apparent destruction of all their hopes for the coming of the promised kingdom. The ritual humiliation inherent in crucifixion, the stripping naked and very public death agony, was particularly devastating. The point was underscored by the label on the cross, INRI, Jesus of Nazareth, King of the Jews. We are familiar with the image of the crucifixion now, but for nearly 400 years Christians could not bring themselves to represent Jesus nailed on the cross.[18]

The resurrection experiences reported in the Gospels and the letters of Paul have to be set within the context of this trauma and despair. As might be expected from the circumstances, the accounts of these experiences are confused and contradictory. Mark ends his original account with the empty tomb, and it seems that it was not until the second century that his version of Jesus' appearances was added. In his account Jesus appears first to Mary Magdalene, then to two of the disciples, then to all eleven "at table" before being taken up to heaven. (Mark does not make clear where these appearances take place.) Matthew reports one appearance near the tomb and then a single meeting with the eleven disciples at a mountain in Galilee, where Jesus had agreed to meet them. In Luke Jesus' appearances all occur in or near Jerusalem, but Jesus is not always immediately recognizable (24:16). John also credits Mary Magdalene with the first vision and reports two appearances to the gathered disciples in Jerusalem as well as one at the Sea of Galilee.

Separate from the Gospel accounts is that of the Apostle Paul. Paul had received a vision of Jesus as a blinding light on the road to Damascus, but he later returned to Jerusalem to meet Jesus' disciples. (According to Galatians 1:18, he was there with Peter for fifteen days.) The date, perhaps in the mid 30s, is not certain, but what is important is that Paul had direct contact with Peter only a few years after Jesus' crucifixion, and he records his own interpretation of the resurrection in the early 50s, at least twenty years before the Gospels or any other surviving sources. In his first letter to the Corinthians, Paul tells how it was Peter who experienced the first appearance, then the twelve disciples, then a meeting of 500, next James and then the Apostles and finally Paul himself, an appearance which Paul, doubtless wishing to reinforce his authority (hotly disputed as it was) with the Corinthians, equates with those earlier ones. Mary Magdalene is not mentioned, and one wonders whether this appearance to a "mere" woman was deliberately obliterated by either Peter or Paul. But what did Paul understand as having been seen? He goes on in his letter to stress the difference between the perishable human body and the body in which Jesus appeared, so it can be assumed that he believed that the resurrected Jesus was not a resuscitated corpse but some kind of spiritual being. In John's much later account, Jesus is able to pass through closed doors and to disappear into heaven. The first appearance of Jesus (by the tomb) and the last (the Ascension) take place in or near Jerusalem. Yet Jesus was also seen in Galilee. There is no record of any journey there or back. This suggests a series of distinct and unconnected apparitions and not Jesus living on earth as if his body had simply been restored to life.[19]

In Matthew, John (chapter 21), and possibly Mark's account, the disciples initially went home to Galilee, but they returned to Jerusalem, probably in the belief that the promised kingdom would still materialize there. From this time, when they strike out as independent preachers, one can call them Apostles, "those who are sent," and their activities are recorded in the Acts of the Apostles (whose author is, according to tradition, Luke, author of the third Gospel). It is certainly true that the imminent arrival of the kingdom dominated their thoughts, and under the leadership of Peter they began preaching their continued belief in Jesus and his promised return. As the followers of a man who had been condemned to death, they were under suspicion and experienced some harassment. However, they still saw themselves as part of Judaism, continued to frequent the Temple and observe Jewish rituals. As the second coming failed to materialize, they began to reflect on how Jesus could be interpreted within Jewish tradition. The idea that he might have been divine was too much for any Jew to grasp, as it was completely alien to any orthodox Jewish belief, but Jesus could be seen as one through whom God worked (as with the earlier Jewish prophets) and who had been exalted by God through his death. Peter put it as follows (Acts 2:22–24): "Jesus the Nazarene was a man [sic] commended to you by God by the miracles and portents and signs that God worked through him when he was among you . . . You killed him, but God raised him to life, freeing him from the pangs of Hades [Sheol, the underworld]." Jesus was still referred to as the Messiah, but how could he be accepted as a Messiah when his earthly life had ended not in the prophesied triumph but in tragedy? The only possible way to explain the crucifixion was to draw on different prophecies. The prophet Isaiah talks, for instance, of a servant of God who was "torn away from the land of the living, for our faults struck down in death. If he offers his life in atonement . . . he shall have a long life and through him what God wishes will be done" (53:8–10). Such texts were used by Christians to create the idea of a "suffering Messiah," who had died for the sins of mankind. This was very far from the most popular interpretation of Messiah as one coming in triumph, but it was enough for Jesus' followers to be able to call him *Christos,* the anointed one. The first recorded use of "Christians" to describe Jesus' followers comes not from Jerusalem but from Antioch in Syria (Acts 11:26).[20]

If we return to the question of whether the historical Jesus can be identified, the answer must be "only with the greatest difficulty." Although this chapter has tried to set out what appear to be the developments in his life and the elements of his teaching about which there is some consensus, virtually every point will still be challenged by one scholar or another. Jesus' charisma, the brutality of his death and stories of a resurrection had such an impact that they passed quickly into myth, and this myth was soon being used by those committed to his memory in a wide variety of ways. (The word "myth" is used here not pejoratively but as the expression of a living "truth" that can function, as it certainly has done in Jesus' case, at different levels for different audiences. Apart from Christianity itself, the impact of Jesus can be gauged from the number of spiritual movements outside Christianity—Gnosticism, followers of *theos hypsistos,* Manicheism and, later, Islam—that recognized him as a spiritual leader.) No one can be sure where the boundary between Matthew (and the other Gospel writers) and Jesus' original words should be drawn. This left and still leaves Jesus' life, death and teachings open to a wide variety of interpretations and uses by those who followed him. Nevertheless, the trend in recent scholarship towards relating Jesus to the tensions of first-century Galilee, in particular as a leader who appealed to the burdened peasant communities of the countryside and reinforced rather than threatened traditional Jewish values, has much to support it.

As Christian communities established themselves, it was perhaps inevitable that there would be tensions between those who remained traditional Jews, focusing on the Temple, and those who, perhaps drawing on Jesus' prophecy of the Temple's destruction, were more openly hostile to the Temple and all that it represented symbolically in terms of wealth and power. The Acts of the Apostles tell of one Stephen, a Hellenized Jew, who took the provocative line that the Temple should never have existed at all and that the God of Jesus stood independently of it (Acts 7). These assertions were treated by the Jews as blasphemy. Stephen was stoned to death and thus earned himself a revered place within the Christian tradition as the first martyr. Acts records that a man called Saul, or Paul as he was to become better known,[21] watched over the outer clothes of those who carried out the stoning.

# 9

# PAUL, "THE FOUNDER OF CHRISTIANITY"?

Paul occupies the dominant position in the early Gentile church, even to the extent of being called by some the founder of Christianity. It was he who formulated a meaning for Jesus' death and resurrection, one that he used creatively in the years in which the first troubled Christian communities were establishing themselves, and he was important too in planting these communities in Asia Minor and Greece and in devising ways for them to maintain themselves in a world they had come to see as hostile. Unlike Jesus he insisted on a dramatic break with traditional culture, not only his own, but also that of the Greco-Roman world, and so he brought new challenges and tensions to Christianity as it spread among Gentiles. While Peter and the Jerusalem Christians were, understandably, suffused with their memories of Jesus as a human being ("a man commended by God" as Peter had put it), Paul's Christ has relevance only through his death and resurrection, in a theology presented in his own words in letters whose eloquence has reverberated through the ages.

Yet any study of this highly emotional man is fraught with difficulties. Paul cares desperately about his fragile Christian communities and each letter records his frustrations and enthusiasms as they struggle to find their own identity. He is trying to formulate new conceptions of Christ, and Christ's meaning, in volatile situations. The demands he places on the recipient communities are heavy, and his own authority with them is often under threat. For Paul it is essential that each community flourish, and he is ready to adapt his theology of Christ to the needs of the moment. (As Paul's thoughts changed with the context in which they were expressed, often resulting in contradictions, it could even be argued that one should talk of his "theologies" of Christ, underlying which, of course, were some consistent themes.) Furthermore, while we are privileged to have Paul's own voice in his letters, they are responses to situations that can only be guessed at from their content. Hence the contradictions and obscurities that make the letters so difficult to interpret. This is not all. As the church subsequently became increasingly authoritarian, the Church Fathers (the term used to describe a loosely defined group of early Christian writers whose views on doctrinal matters carried special weight) were to attempt to press Paul's teachings into a coherent theology, bypassing or smoothing over the obvious contradictions. From the second century his letters had also become part of the New Testament canon and had been placed alongside the Gospels. So Paul's views on idols, sexuality and Greek philosophy, issues that had not featured strongly in Jesus' teachings and often sit uneasily with them, became embedded in the Christian tradition. When Paul composed responses to his communities in the turbulent and confused years after Jesus' death, years that Paul believed were a prelude to the imminent second coming, he could hardly have expected that they would be given the status of universal and authoritative truths and be used in contexts totally different from those in which he had written them. One consequence of Paul's elevation as a theologian was to shift the emphasis away from his personality, yet it is certainly arguable that his own psychological needs defined the distinctive teachings that he preached to his communities and should be central to any study of him.[1]

Paradoxically, "the Apostle to the Gentiles" was himself Jewish, and Judaism pervades his theology. Paul was a Pharisee, apparently from the Cilician city of Tarsus, and unusually for an easterner in this period he was also a Roman citizen.[2] He was one of those many thousands of Jews, far greater in number than those remaining in Judaea and Galilee, who had scattered in the Diaspora. By now many of these Jews spoke only Greek and used Greek translations of the Hebrew scriptures—the Septuagint, so called because some seventy scholars were supposed to be responsible for the translation, made in the third century B.C. The date of Paul's birth is unknown but is usually placed in the first decade A.D. He came from a very different world from that of Jesus' original followers; a tent-maker by profession, he knew city life, and he was at ease travelling the sea and land routes of the eastern Mediterranean. According to the

Acts of the Apostles, he had studied with Gamaliel, a well-known Pharisee teacher, in Jerusalem, and he certainly knew the scriptures in meticulous detail. He wrote in Greek ("fluent and competent Greek, although much of his vocabulary is coloured by Septuagint usage and he rarely achieves a really polished style"), and it is likely that he spoke Aramaic and knew Hebrew as well. Although no direct connection has been demonstrated between Paul and the Essenes, much of his terminology—"God's righteousness," "children of light," "sinful flesh"—is reminiscent of theirs, as is his eschatology (teaching on "the last things," such as the end of the world and rewards and punishment after death) with its strong emphasis on insiders and outsiders, the saved and unsaved.[3]

Paul's life is known from his letters (the Epistles) and from the Acts of the Apostles, about half of which is devoted to his activities. Not all the letters attributed to him are accepted as such by scholars—those usually recognized as his are Romans, both letters to the Corinthians, Galatians, Philippians, the first letter to the Thessalonians, possibly the second, and the letter to Philemon. Many would also add Colossians. Both the letters and Acts have limitations as biographical sources. As has already been suggested, the letters were written as responses to particular situations that confronted Paul and provide biographical information only by chance. It is also possible that when writing to Gentile Christian communities Paul played down his early missionary activity as a Christian among Jews. The author of Acts does mention this activity but appears to be concerned to stress reconciliation between Gentiles and Jews and may have provided a more harmonious account of Paul's relationships with the Jerusalem Apostles than was the case. Many scholars treat Acts with caution—some going so far as to doubt whether Acts is reliable in saying Paul had studied in Jerusalem. Even when both Acts and the letters are used together with the meagre information from other sources that correlates with them, much of Paul's life and the dates of his missions, particularly the early ones of the late 30s and 40s A.D., are difficult to reconstruct.[4]

In both the letters and Acts, Paul comes across as austere and, despite some physical ailment which he never specified (epilepsy has been suggested), extraordinarily tough and mentally resilient. After his conversion he maintained his commitment to Christ through every conceivable hardship, probably to the extent of martyrdom. He could also be abrasive and deeply sensitive to any threat to his assumed authority, which at the beginning of several of his letters (those to the Galatians and the Corinthians in particular) he proclaims to have come directly from God or Christ. He was, as he puts it in Galatians 1:2, "an apostle . . . who has been appointed by Jesus Christ and by God the Father who raised Jesus from the dead." He appears never to have married and to have been ill at ease with sexuality, above all homosexuality. It is difficult to know how much this was cultural, absorbed from his training as a Pharisee or perhaps from contacts with the Essenes, and how much inherent in his personality. He was certainly unusual in not being married, especially as mainstream Judaism was actively hostile to celibacy, though the Essenes were in favour of it. There are moments in his letters when he relaxes, writing with protective affection of his followers (see, for instance, 1 Thessalonians 2:7–9, and the tenderness with which he speaks of Onesimus in the letter to Philemon, even though in this case he was returning Onesimus, a slave, to his master), but no one could pretend that he was an easy man to work with. His life appears to have been one of constant conflict. Gamaliel is believed to have been tolerant to Christians (Acts 5:34–40), so Paul's early desire to persecute them must have come from elsewhere, perhaps from his own combative personality. He had violent confrontations with Barnabas, his companion who had put him in contact with the Apostles in Jerusalem (Acts 15:39), though he travelled extensively with him, and even with Peter, the undoubted early leader of the Jerusalem Christians (Galatians 2:11). In fact, he seems to have accepted that conflict with others was a normal part of life. As he puts it himself in writing to the Corinthians (2 Corinthians 12:20): "What I am afraid of is that when I come I may find you different from what I want you to be and you may find that I am not as you would like me to be; and then there will be wrangling, jealousy and tempers roused, intrigues and backbiting and gossip, obstinacies and disorder." This is certainly not a man who has any confidence in his ability to charm those he met. While Jesus drew people to him, Paul appears to have had the opposite effect; there was not one Christian community in which he can be said to have been fully at ease.

The result was that although Paul could write, and perhaps speak, with great eloquence, he often failed to win over audiences, and may even have provoked their opposition by his manner. In his final confrontation with the Sanhedrin, the supreme Jewish court at Jerusalem, he knew his speech on the resurrection of the dead would arouse the sensitivities of the Sadducees, who did not believe in an afterlife at all, and yet he went ahead. The ensuing confrontation between Sadducees and Pharisees was so heated that Roman soldiers had to intervene to haul Paul out of the council chamber (Acts 23:1–10). One senses also that he failed, as a Jew, to realize how difficult his theology would prove for a Gentile audience used to the polytheism and *mores* of the Greco-Roman world. On the other hand, without the turmoil and confusion that his preaching often created and his desperate need to maintain his authority, he would never have been impelled to define his beliefs in the depth he did.

According to Acts, it was while Paul was "on the road to Damascus" on a mission to persecute Christians there that he had a vision of Christ (Acts 9:1–9). Once in Damascus he began to preach that "Jesus is the Son of God." A date of about A.D. 33 is proposed by scholars. This sudden shift of perspective is difficult to explain (was it really a vision of Christ, or the culmination of a psychological crisis?), but it defined a new life for him. His first "Christian" mission, again according to Acts, was to Jews; in other words, like the Apostles in Jerusalem, he did not see himself as working outside Judaism. It seems, however, that he was unsuccessful, continually arousing opposition, and in his letters he makes no mention of this part of his life. He returned to Jerusalem but was accepted by the Apostles there only through the good offices of Barnabas, one of the earliest and most trusted of the Jerusalem Christians (middle to late 30s). Soon in trouble again, this time with the "Hellenists," the Greek-speaking Jewish community in Jerusalem (Acts 9:29), Paul returned home to Tarsus, and it was from there some years later that he was brought by Barnabas to Antioch, where the first community to call itself Christian was based. Perhaps because of his difficulty in preaching to the Jews, he began concentrating on those Gentiles, the *theosebeis,* or "god-fearers," who, while attracted to the fringes of Judaism, often through attendance at the synagogue, did not formally accept the Law and rituals such as circumcision. Many Jews accepted that there was a place for righteous Gentiles in God's kingdom (see, for instance, Isaiah 2:2, where it is said that all nations will eventually flow into God's house),[5] but Paul went further in developing a theology in which, through faith in the death and resurrection of Christ, the barrier between Gentile and Jew would be broken down, the Law superseded and rituals such as circumcision and dietary restrictions no longer be of importance. Some passages in his letter to the Romans (for example, 11:11–14) even suggest that the Gentiles are now God's preferred people because the Jews have broken his trust. Gradually Paul defined a role for himself as exclusively committed to the conversion of the Gentiles, though his Jewish background remained influential in his commitment to a single God, his hatred of idols and his adherence to the scriptures. As his role was clarified, his independence grew. His first missions to Galatia and Macedonia in the 40s may have been as an assistant to Barnabas, but he then returned to Jerusalem in around 50 and negotiated a role with the original Apostles as an Apostle working exclusively with the Gentiles. They would allow him to preach among the Gentiles without requiring converts to be circumcised; in return, he promised to collect money for the poor of Judaea (who were heavily burdened by the combined weight of Roman and priestly taxation).

In view of Paul's difficulties with other Christian leaders, this was probably the only role that was realistically sustainable, and he developed it to the full. Over the next few years, in the 50s, he travelled widely in Greece, to Philippi and Thessalonika in Macedonia and to Athens and Corinth. In Asia Minor he worked with the communities of Galatia, Colossae, and Ephesus, raising the collections he had promised the Jerusalem community. However, when he faithfully delivered the monies to Jerusalem around 57 he fell foul of the Jews and was taken into custody by the Roman authorities after creating mayhem in the Sanhedrin. Having successfully claimed that his Roman citizenship allowed him to appeal to the emperor, he was eventually transported to Rome and appears to have been martyred there in the 60s. As Paul reminded the Corinthians (2 Corinthians 11:22–29), there had not been much that he had not suffered on his missions. On no less than five occasions he had received the traditional punishment of thirty-nine lashes from Jewish opponents (his Roman citizenship apparently offering him no protection—one reason why some have doubted it).

Paul was always aware of his vulnerability as one who had not known Jesus personally—in one of his most attractive asides (1 Corinthians 15:8) he describes himself in this respect as like a child born late when no one expected it—and this may explain why he distanced himself from those who had known Jesus. This "distancing" is very evident. In Galatians (1:11) he goes so far as to emphasize that the "Good News" he preached was "not a human message given by men" but "a revelation of Jesus Christ"; in other words, his knowledge of Jesus has been received directly from revelation rather than through the disciples, a remarkable and telling assertion given that he had had every opportunity to learn directly from them. Moreover, Paul makes a point of stressing that faith in Christ does not involve any kind of identification with Jesus in his life on earth but has validity only in his death and resurrection. Why this particular emphasis? Could it be that as others can speak with much greater authority of Jesus' life, he feels he has to carve out a distinct area of expertise where he has scope to develop a theology that is not dependent on knowledge of Jesus' life on earth? Alternatively, he might, for motives of his own, have felt drawn to Jesus at his moment of greatest weakness, on the cross, seeing it as a prelude to the triumph of the resurrection, a transformation that reflected and symbolized the fulfillment of his own psychological needs. As he put it to the Romans (6:3–4): "when we were baptised in Christ Jesus we were baptised in his death; in other words, when we were baptised we went into the tomb and joined him in death, so that as Christ was raised from the dead by the Father's glory, we too might live a new life."

However, if Paul thought that a defined role outside Judaism and apart from the original Apostles would solve the problem of his authority, he was mistaken. There were Jewish Christians in the churches outside Jerusalem (perhaps including the community for which Matthew wrote his Gospel) who were outraged by his argument that the Law and ritual requirements such as circumcision for believers had been superseded (hence the beatings), and there were many Gentiles who found a theology that was rooted in Judaism yet not strictly part of it impossible to comprehend. Paul appears to have known little of the spiritual life of the Greco-Roman world outside Judaism and made little attempt in his letters to explain the Judaic concepts he used in a form that would have been comprehensible to those not brought up in that tradition. Others, such as the Alexandrian Jew Apollos, provided a more intellectual approach to Christianity. Buffeted by these conflicts, Paul seems at times to hardly know who he is. In particular, his identity as a Jew seems to fluctuate according to the pressures he encounters. "Paul's Judaism was no longer of his very being, but a guise he could adopt or discard at will," as one influential scholar, C. K. Barrett, has put it.[6] It is hardly surprising that on a personal level this highly insecure man became acutely sensitive to threats to his leadership. "Let me warn you," he tells the Galatians (1:8), "that if anyone preaches a version of the Good News different from the one we have already preached to you, whether it be ourselves or an angel from heaven [*sic*], he is to be condemned." He is desperately afraid of competition, and it is highly significant that in none of his letters does he ask his followers to evangelize themselves, as if by doing so they might undermine his own authority. In fact, his desperation as he hears of rival Christian preachers breaks through again and again in the letters. He boasts, cajoles, threatens, and pleads his case, claiming that because of his hard work and suffering for the cause he deserves to be seen as the foremost of the Apostles. In one passage of his letter to the Colossians (1:24), he even gives himself the role of completing what Christ has left unfinished. "It makes me happy to suffer for you, as I am suffering now, and in my own body to do what I can to make up all that has still to be undergone [sic] by Christ for the sake of his body, the Church."

And yet it was Paul's insecurities and abrasive personality that acted as a spur to his highly individual theologies. Paul was not an intellectual, certainly not when compared to his contemporary Philo of Alexandria, who wove Plato and other Greek influences into Judaism (and who was probably an influence on Apollos). There is virtually no evidence of the influence of Greek ways of thinking in his letters, though some have argued that he picked up elements of Stoicism from Tarsus, where there were a number of prominent Stoic thinkers. "It does not seem that he had more than a rudimentary knowledge of Greek literature or philosophy," his is "a rhetoric of the heart," and, as V. Gronbech has put it, "the attempt to understand the logic and argumentation of Paul must give a Greek a headache."[7] Although the account of his speech in Athens in Acts must be treated with a certain amount of caution, as probably re-created by the writer of Acts (traditionally Luke), his insistence that an "Unknown God" to whom an altar in the city was dedicated must be the Christian one, and that there would be a resurrection of the dead, clearly failed to convince his audience, and he was openly mocked by the sophisticated and sceptical thinkers of the city (Acts 17:23–34).[8] Even though Acts records that Paul attracted some new followers, a rejection by others in the public arena must have been unsettling and possibly underlies his powerful condemnation of Greek philosophy.

As has been suggested, Paul's theology developed in response to specific challenges—the nature of which is often unknown—that impelled him to provide varied and often inconsistent responses. It was not only the differing needs of the fledgling Christian communities which made coherence difficult; as John Barclay has suggested, there is a tension inherent in Paul's attempt to create a new spiritual world while remaining within a conceptual mould of Judaism from which he is unable to break free. As we have seen, "he interprets the Christ event in categories drawn largely from Jewish apocalyptic."[9] However, some broad themes can be established. Like all early Christians, Paul had come to terms with the horror of Jesus' crucifixion, and, as has already been suggested, an exploration of its meaning forms the core of his theology. The death and resurrection of Christ, proclaims Paul, bring a new era for mankind in which all who have faith in Christ (Greek and Jew, slave and free, male and female) will enter a new life. As is usual with Paul, those readers who rejoice in the equality of all enshrined in this proclamation are then brought down to earth with a text such as 1 Corinthians 14:34, which enjoins women to remain silent at meetings and, if they have questions to ask, to ask them of their husbands at home! Paul sets the coming of Christ in a historical context that can be reconstructed from different passages in the letters. The story starts with Adam. Adam sinned in the garden of Eden and with him sin entered the world. For Paul sin is a heavy, albeit abstract, entity that burdens the human race. Yet, and here Paul maintained his Judaism, there is a God who acts providentially for mankind. At times Paul even seems to go so far as to suggest that God introduced sin into the world deliberately so that he could exercise his saving compassion: "For God has consigned all people to disobedience, that he may have mercy upon all" (Romans 11:32). God is the opposite of the darkness of Sin, "the Spirit" that contrasts with "the Flesh." For Paul "the Spirit" is the power of God's love for humanity, the driving force of the Christian life. The term "Flesh" is used to sum up the state of humanity when in opposition to God. "Flesh" is backed by other dark forces. Paul saw the Greek gods as demons, and the letter to the Ephesians (probably not written by Paul but reflecting his theology) refers to "the Sovereignties and the powers which originate the darkness in this world, the spiritual army of evil in the heavens" (Ephesians 6:12). This concept of good and evil as two forces in opposition to each other can be traced back to Zoroastrianism, which spread from its native Persia into the Mediterranean world and can be found reflected in the Essene Judaism in the Dead Sea Scrolls and in Gnosticism. Paul presumably absorbed it from Jewish sources.

Until the coming of Christ, the conflict between Spirit and Flesh is unresolved. It is true that God has given the Law to one chosen people, the Jews. The Law gives Paul great problems. On the one hand it provides a code of behaviour, "Our guardian until the Christ came and we could be justified by faith" (Galatians 3:24); on the other it cannot be perfect as a standard because otherwise the salvation of Christ would not be necessary. Paul's attitude to the Law is ambivalent, as with much of his theology "he wrote different things about it according to the circumstances."[10] He praises the Law for its concept of loving one's neighbour as oneself, which he regards as its central message, yet he believes that those living under the Law remained enslaved and subject to Sin. An added difficulty is how to explain why the Jews alone had the Law and what would happen to them now that the Law is superseded. Paul's answer seems to be that they have to adapt to the new world where they too can share in the faith in the risen Lord (Romans 11:25 suggests this), but they will not be in a position of any privilege as their own relationship with God has not been perfect. In short, the Law has to be set in context as some kind of inadequate instrument available only to one people—the Jews—until Christ came for all, Jews and Gentiles alike, and the Law could be set aside as superseded. There is a sense, therefore, in which, for Paul, Christ replaces the Law. Jesus himself, as we have seen, may have intended only to fulfill the Law, not replace it.

It is not clear whether Paul believed that Jesus had been preexistent from the dawn of time. Many scholars think not, arguing that the "hymn" in Philippians (2:6–11) that suggests that Paul believed he was is a later addition.[11] Rather, Jesus appears on earth as a man, and it is through his death and resurrection that he is exalted by God as "a second Adam." Paul had, further, to explain why Christ had to die in such a horrific way; Geza Vermes suggests he may have drawn on Jewish myths (not contained in scripture) of an Isaac who was willing to be sacrificed for the Jews but never was. Isaac's readiness to be sacrificed was held in abeyance, as it were, until it was fulfilled by the death of Christ.[12] Paul also draws on the traditional Jewish idea that a sacrifice atones for past misdeeds, but he develops it to argue that Christ's is so significant that it does away with the need for any further sacrifices. As Hebrews (9:12–13), which develops Paul's ideas, puts it:

> The blood of his sacrifice is his own blood, not the blood of goats and calves, and thus he has entered the sanctuary once and for all and secured an eternal deliverance. For if the blood of goats and bulls and the sprinkled ashes of a heifer have power to hallow those who have been defiled and restore their external purity, how much greater is the power of the blood of Christ.

So Christians should not sacrifice; while Paul may have been thinking of sacrifice primarily in the Jewish context, the prohibition extends to pagan sacrifices as well.[13]

Exalted though Christ may have been, Paul does not go so far as to make him as part of the Godhead. He envisages him as subject to God. At the second coming, which Paul believes to be imminent, "When all things are subjected to Christ, then the Son himself will be subjected to the Father who put all things under him, that God may be everything to every one" (1 Corinthians 15:27–28). In other words, Christ is an intermediary between humanity and God. Paul casts himself in a comparable role. "Be imitators of me, as I am of Christ," he told the Corinthians (1 Corinthians 11:1). Although the particular instance of Jesus as intermediary between man and God was eclipsed by the later doctrine of the Trinity, stating that he was an intrinsic part of the Godhead, the concept of intermediaries—and these were to include the Virgin Mary, the martyrs and other saints—flourished in the early Christian centuries. Paradoxically, Paul's contribution in this respect was overlooked at the Reformation, when his writings were used to support the idea of direct faith in Christ without the mass of intermediaries, the saints and martyrs who had become part of Catholic Christianity over the centuries.

Paul's teachings on faith have proved difficult to interpret, but they are essential to his theology.[14] Having faith involves an opening of the heart to Christ, underpinned by a simple trust in God's goodness. It is essentially an emotional rather than rational state of being. "Faith," said the fourth-century ascetic Anthony, "arises from the disposition of the soul . . . those who are equipped with the faith have no need of verbal argument."[15] Yet, for Paul, the consequences of having faith in Christ's death and resurrection are dramatic. Through faith the believer is "rescued from the power of darkness and transferred to the kingdom of God's beloved son" (Colossians 1:13–24). Paul writes of the process by which the sinner who has faith dies with Christ (Romans 6:3–11), becomes part of a single body with Christ, even puts on Christ as if he were a piece of clothing, achieving a full identification with Christ through his death and then rising with him from the dead. This personal and highly emotional commitment to Christ is something new in antiquity (although again there are precedents in the writings of the Qumran community). Whereas in traditional Greco-Roman religion the public observation of rituals is primary, Paul presents something radically different, proposing that the orientation of the inner person to God and

Christ is essential. It is an idea that reaches its fruition in Augustine, who, in his *Confessions*, talks of God actually being inside a person's intimate being and in a continual and often, in Augustine's case, stormy relationship with him.

Many passages of Paul suggest that having faith is in itself sufficient to ensure salvation in Christ. This is the important concept of "justification" by which God accepts the believer as righteous simply because of his or her faith. In other passages, on the other hand, Paul stresses the importance of charity, as in the famous passage of 1 Corinthians 13, where it is the greatest of "faith, hope and charity," and in Galatians 5:6, where "what matters is faith that makes its power felt through love." This leaves open the question of whether "good works" are necessary for salvation. For Paul this may not have been a major issue because, like the Christian community in Jerusalem, he believed in the imminence of the second coming. There is an urgency in the need to adopt faith. So short is the time before Christ returns that there is not even a chance to make major changes in one's behaviour. However, as time elapsed, and the second coming failed to materialize, it became clear that this was not enough. Paul found himself in the difficult position of having to explain how the faithful should live when the death and resurrection of Christ had superseded the Law, which had hitherto provided a coherent basis for behaviour. Paul wrote of "living according to the Spirit" (Galatians 5:16–26), but what this would mean in practice was very vague. Perhaps without intending to do so Paul had raised a radical possibility, that through faith in Christ one might be free to live without the traditional restrictions of society. With the overthrow of old laws, the "liberated" could potentially grasp every kind of freedom. Many Christians had already begun to define their own lives—to Paul's horror, one Corinthian had even formed a sexual relationship with his stepmother! Paul's response to this was that "he is to be handed over to Satan so that his sensual body may be destroyed and his spirit saved on the day of the Lord" (1 Corinthians 5:5). There are echoes here of the banishment and perpetual exclusion ordered by the Essenes for those who transgressed their codes.

While the rewards for those with faith are great, the corollary dimension of Paul's teaching, the fate of those without faith, has had an equally powerful and enduring influence. Once again Paul's teaching is inconsistent: at times he suggests that the faithless will be condemned when Christ comes again, at others that all might be saved. So while

Paul tells the Corinthians that just as all died in Adam so all will be saved in Christ (1 Corinthians 15:22), the Philippians (3:19), in contrast, are told that the enemies of the cross of Christ are destined to be lost. In the first two chapters of Romans Paul seems to include not only the enemies of Christ among those who will be condemned. He implies (Romans 1:20–21) that the existence of God is so obvious those who "refuse to honour" him have no excuse.[16] They will be abandoned by him to their degrading (sexual) passions and worse. "Your stubborn refusal to repent is only adding to the anger God will have towards you on that day of anger when his just judgments will be known" (Romans 2:5). (It is significant that Paul refers to the day of judgment as one of "anger" rather than, say, "joy.") In the second letter to the Thessalonians it is made clear that those who refuse to accept "the Good News of our Lord Jesus Christ" will be punished for eternity (1:9). Perhaps the important point to be made is that Paul's teachings, or those assumed in the early Christian centuries to be his, read in conjunction with others in the New Testament, have allowed many Christians to conclude that punishment for evildoers is eternal, even for those who have not heard of Christ. Even as late as 1960, for instance, it was possible for the Chicago Congress of World Mission to declare that "in the years since World War II, more than one billion souls have passed into eternity and more than half of those went to the torment of hell fire without even hearing of Jesus Christ, who He was or why He died on the Cross of Calvary."[17]

The idea of being open to "faith" is a powerful one; the longing to surrender the self to another who can provide certainty is an enduring part of the human psyche. However, for those who believe in the importance of using reason to define the truth, this surrender must raise concerns. Plato, for instance, specifically condemned "faith" as a means of finding the truth; for him the only secure way of understanding the immaterial world was through the use of reason (note, however, the conceptual difficulties in Plato's "reasoning" explored in chapter 3). Although there is no evidence that Paul knew of Plato's thought, we can assume that he realized that his concept of "faith" was vulnerable when set against the mainstream of the Greek intellectual tradition. As we have seen, he may have been unsettled by his confrontation with the pagan philosophers in Athens. His response was to hit back with highly emotional rhetoric, the only weapon to hand. So for Paul it is not only the Law that has been superseded by the coming of Christ, it is the concept of rational argument, the core of the Greek intellectual achievement itself. "The more they [non-Christians] called themselves philosophers," he tells the Romans (1:21–22), "the more stupid they grew . . . they made nonsense out of logic and their empty minds were darkened." In his first letter to the Corinthians (1:25) he writes, "The wisdom of the world is foolishness to God." There is something of the mystic in Paul's disregard of logic (and a paradox in the way he uses his considerable rhetorical skills to attack the very intellectual tradition of which rhetoric was part).[18] This disregard had unfortunate consequences. As Paul's writings came to be seen as authoritative, it became a mark of the committed Christian to be able to reject rational thought, and even the evidence of empirical experience. Christians would often pride themselves on their lack of education, associating independent philosophical thinking with the sin of pride. Even educated Christians such as Gregory the Great (pope 590–604) followed Paul. Drawing directly on the Corinthians verse quoted above, Gregory commented, "The wisdom of this world is concealing the heart with strategems, veiling meaning with verbiage, proving false to be right, and true to be false,"[19] and, as we will see, the Greek intellectual tradition was to be increasingly stifled by the churches. So here are the roots of the conflict between religion and science that still pervades debates on Christianity to this day. By proposing that Christian faith (which exists in the world of *muthos*) might contain "truths" superior to those achieved by rational argument (*logoi*), it was Paul, perhaps unwittingly in that he appears to have known virtually nothing of the Greek philosophical tradition he condemned, who declared the war and prepared the battlefield.[20]

In elaborating his views on everyday conduct Paul had two particular preoccupations. Paul was true to his Jewish inheritance in deploring idols, and he denounced their worship. Here again he was challenging the deep-rooted spiritual traditions of the Greco-Roman world, which allowed the gods to be shown in human form and cult worship to be offered to statues. Now Paul insisted that Christians must remove statues of gods and goddesses from temples and public places. During Paul's lifetime Christians would have been unable to desecrate pagan temples without massive retaliation, but by the fourth century Paul's teachings, supported by Old Testament texts, were used to justify the wholesale destruction of pagan art and architecture. There were, nevertheless, tensions within Christianity itself over the issue. From early times Christians were scratching symbols and painting representations of Old and New Testament stories in their tombs; later Christians created reliefs and actual statues. As the adulation of relics developed, the boundary between simple representation of Christian stories and objects and the worship of idols became increasingly blurred. Eventually there were to be major reactions within Christianity (the iconoclast movement in Byzantium and the wholesale destruction of Catholic art during the Reformation are only two examples).[21]

Secondly, Paul appears preoccupied with the evils of sexuality. In Romans he fulminated against "filthy enjoyments and the practices with which they [non-Christians] dishonour their own bodies" and "degrading passions," which cause both sexes to commit homosexual acts (Romans 1:24–32). And in 1 Corinthians 6:9–11: "You know perfectly well that people who do wrong will not inherit the kingdom of God: people of immoral lives, idolaters, adulterers, catamites, sodomites, thieves, usurers, drunkards, slanderers and swindlers . . ." "Sex," he tells the Corinthians, "is always a danger." Paul stresses the value of celibacy, his own chosen path, but he accepts the importance of marriage, not least as a means of containing sexual desire; as his much quoted phrase puts it: "Better to marry than to burn." Although Judaism had always stressed the value of continence ("The Law recognises no sexual connections, except the natural union of man and wife, and that only for the procreation of children"),[22] Paul's strictures and the central place given to sexual "sins" in his theology suggest that the act of sex in itself troubled him deeply. (While Jesus went beyond conventional Jewish teaching in his prohibition of divorce, perhaps because family structures were under particular stress in first-century Galilee, he does not appear to have been preoccupied with sexuality in the way that Paul was.) Before Paul sex was not seen to raise major ethical problems, although sexual behaviour in the Greek world was constrained by deeply held conventions.[23] There were those Greeks who valued celibacy in so far as it allowed the mind to concentrate on philosophy, but a positive acceptance of celibacy was seldom accompanied by passionate rejection of the desires of the body. Most Greeks accepted sexual desire as a natural part of being human, which could be sublimated, temporarily or permanently, in the service of other values. The body as such was neutral. Paul introduced a very different view of sexuality (although one can see analogies in Plato's approach to sensual desire). As Peter Brown puts it, for Paul "the body was not a neutral thing, placed between nature and the city. Paul set it firmly in place as a temple of the Holy Spirit, subject to limits that it was sacrilegious to overstep."[24] The idea of the body as a "temple" that can be desecrated by sexual activity has been extraordinarily influential in Christianity, as can be seen in the enormous energy still devoted to debates on sexuality within the churches.

Central to Paul's teachings, therefore, is the condemnation of a variety of activities: idol worship, sexuality and—implicitly—the practice of philosophy. The roots of Paul's beliefs appear to be diverse. He drew on traditional Jewish teaching for his views on idols, possibly the Essenes and his own personality for his views on sexuality—while his condemnation of philosophy may have been evoked by his need to defend faith over reason. The punishment for following condemned practices is, for Paul, exclusion (here again there is a strong possibility of Essene influence), and although alternatives to permanent exclusion and/or punishment can be drawn from others of Paul's statements, these were not the ones that were to prevail. Guy Stroumsa has argued that the power of an insider/outsider dichotomy was intensified by the emphasis on the universality of the Christian message. "By right, the Christian community must include all mankind. A refusal to join the community of believers reflects a perverse and rather shocking vice."[25] The stress on perfection laid on Christians by Paul and other Christian leaders inevitably resulted in tensions that were projected onto those outsiders who refused to join the community, as can be seen in Paul's own letters, especially the first chapter of Romans. "Since they [the unbelievers] refused to see it was rational to acknowledge God, God left them to their own irrational ideas and to their monstrous behaviour" (Romans 1:28). This approach certainly does much to explain the reactions of Christians to "outsiders" both before and after the granting of toleration to Christianity in the fourth century.

No one reading Paul can ignore the powerful emotional force of this message: human beings live at the centre of a cosmic drama that reaches to the core of each personality as the forces of good and evil battle within the individual. Paul tells the Romans (7:14–20) that "I have been sold as a slave to sin. I fail to carry out the things I want to do, and I find myself doing the very things I hate . . . I know of nothing good living in me." The battle is not won until death, and the believer receives his reward with God. "The man who thinks he is safe must be careful that he does not fall" (1 Corinthians 10:12). It could be suggested that this stress on the fragmented personality that can never be at peace with itself until the final salvation through Christ is among the most enduring of Paul's legacies. It is certainly a feature that strikingly marks out the Christian thinkers discussed in this book from their pagan counterparts

(Stoics and Epicureans, for instance), who tended, although this must be a generalization, to deal with the challenges of life more calmly.[26]

Not least of Paul's legacies was his providing of an institutional framework for the church. By fixing on a comprehensible symbol, the death and resurrection of Christ, and by proclaiming the enormous and imminent rewards of Christian faith (and the awful consequences of rejection of "the cross of Christ"), Paul had created a focus for community worship. When the second coming failed to materialize, this had to be sustained in an institutional form. Paul cannot be given credit for founding every Christian community—the Christian churches in Antioch and Rome were founded without his direct influence or involvement, and there is no evidence of his having any contact with the church of Alexandria, soon to be one of the most important in the Mediterranean, or with the many communities of north Africa—but he did nevertheless provide a hugely significant impetus. However, it pays to be cautious here. While the letter to the Galatians is often seen to be one of Paul's finest, there is no material evidence of any surviving Galatian Christian community, nor of a Colossian one: the first archaeological evidence for Christianity in these areas comes centuries later. It is quite possible therefore that Paul's communities lapsed. He certainly seems to have been responsible for suggesting ways in which commitment to the Christian community could be expressed (through the rite of baptism) and sustained (through the Eucharist). His first letter to the Corinthians insists on the importance of all, whether rich or poor, sharing a communal meal at which bread is eaten and wine is drunk in commemoration of Christ's death (1 Corinthians 11:17–34). This letter dates from about A.D. 55, and some scholars suggest that it was Paul who, drawing on what he had heard from the Apostles of the Last Supper, established the Eucharist as a repeatable ritual. The Gospel writers, writing later than this, of course, may have recast their own descriptions of the Last Supper to accord with the existing practice of emerging Christian groups.[27]

In time, the Christian communities also needed some kind of administrative structure. Here again the influence of Judaism was profound. The earliest communities seem to have been led by presbyters who played a comparable role to the elders of a Jewish synagogue. Over time the need arose for a more senior figure, and again Judaism may have provided a model. The Essenes had acknowledged the need for a guardian who "shall instruct the Congregation in the works of God . . . he shall love them as a Father loves his children and shall carry them in his distress like a shepherd his sheep."[28] Such a role is echoed in descriptions of bishops in the letters to Timothy and Titus (neither by Paul and both written after his death). By the second century the bishop was accepted as the senior figure of a Christian community, with the presbyters (or priests as they in effect became) as his delegates. Increasingly, the priesthood became a distinct elite within a community, and only priests could administer the sacraments or offer interpretations of the scriptures. So began the evolution of institutional authority within the early church, a development that opened the way to conflict with rival sects such as the Montanists, who believed Christian revelation could come at any time to those who were open to it. The Greek word used for bishop, *episcopos,* traditionally referred to a secular administrative official, reflecting the fact that bishops had an administrative as well as pastoral role from early times.

Paul's influence has been immense—E. P. Sanders is surely right to call the Epistle to the Romans, which treats most of Paul's theological themes, "one of the most influential documents of western history."[29] It takes considerable imagination to conceive what form Christianity would have taken without his highly original and utterly distinctive formulations of Christian belief: institutionally, Christianity might have faltered without him. The richness and evocative power of his language still inspires. Paul's theology, however, is confined in that it is shaped by his personal isolation, his acute insecurity about his authority and his ambivalence about his Jewish roots. The difficult circumstances in which he wrote can explain much of the incoherence and contradiction in his letters, which have taxed theologians ever since. He seems to have failed to absorb, or at least express in his letters, any real awareness of Jesus as a human being, or to reflect his teachings, other than, significantly, the prohibition on divorce. It has always to be remembered that Paul is the only major Christian theologian never to have read the Gospels, and one cannot be sure that he interpreted Jesus' teachings, on the Law, for instance, with accuracy. Can one assume that Paul preached what Jesus would have wanted him to preach? It is worth reiterating that his theology was conditioned by his belief in the imminence of the second coming. Had Paul known that the second coming was to be delayed indefinitely, his theology may well have taken a different direction and would certainly have lost much of its sense of urgency (although a sense of urgency in general seems to have been an intrinsic part of Paul's personality). Furthermore, although his theology appears to be radically new, conceptually it is still rooted deeply in the Jewish (and perhaps to some extent the Essene) tradition. The paradox of Paul is that while he created a Christianity for the Greco-Roman world, he also confirmed or implanted within Christian theology elements that set it in conflict with Greco-Roman society and traditions, over sexuality, art and philosophy. Greeks were asked either to turn their backs on significant aspects of their traditional culture or to risk eternal condemnation. This aspect of Paul's teachings is often neglected in surveys of his theology, but the history of Christianity, in particular the relationship between Christians and the pagan world in the fourth century, a period when Paul's influence was very powerful, cannot be fully understood without it.

Paul cannot have expected his writings to have lasted—the second coming, the day of judgment, would have swept them into oblivion, their purpose in bringing some to salvation achieved. So it is again paradoxical that they not only survived but were placed alongside the Gospels and given, like them, canonical status as sacred texts. They were first collected by a fervent admirer, Marcion. Marcion, apparently the son of an early Christian bishop, was from Sinope on the Black Sea, but he moved to Rome, where he came deeply under the influence of Paul. He collected the texts of ten of Paul's letters, to which he added an edited version of Luke's Gospel to make the first canon of New Testament texts. Marcion went further. He believed that Paul had grasped the essential fact that Jesus was the instrument of a new God, one who was "placid, mild, and simply good and excellent," and thus entirely different from the God of the Old Testament, who was "lustful for war, inconstant in his attitudes and self-contradictory."[30] For Marcion, there was no way in which there could be a reconciliation between these two very different gods. Paul was, therefore, right to reject the Law of the Old Testament God, but, according to Marcion, the Hebrew scriptures should also be discarded by Christians on the grounds that Christ offered the world a totally new beginning. The idea that one god or set of gods could overthrow or otherwise replace another ran, of course, deep in Greek mythology. The Olympian gods had overthrown the Titans, and their power was demonstrated by their success in doing so. So, for Marcion, the Christian God too had demonstrated His power by overthrowing an old, untrustworthy and warlike God and his Law.

Marcion was excommunicated by the Roman church in 144, although his ideas continued to prove highly popular, and Marcionite communities flourished well into the third century.[31] In response, his opponents created their own canon of New Testament writings, including all the four canonical Gospels together with thirteen of Paul's letters. The "orthodox" Christians also reasserted their commitment to the Hebrew scriptures, so effectively that no challenge to their inclusion in the Christian canon has ever been raised subsequently. So began the formation of the Christian Bible as a set of disparate texts from Jewish history and the early Christian communities, which was, however, to share a common authority as the word of the Christian God. Within these texts, those of Paul were deeply embedded and his authority was assured.

Meanwhile, Paul's conflict with the Jerusalem Christians over the requirements for entry into a Christian community remained unresolved. According to the surviving sources (Galatians 2:11–14), the conflict reached its most personal and bitter moments when Paul and Peter confronted each other in Antioch. This conflict may have had important consequences. It has been argued that Matthew's community in its determination to maintain itself as a Christian community *within* Judaism, and thus faithful to the Law, had to define itself *against* the teachings of Paul with their insistence that the Law had been superseded.[32] This could explain why Matthew, in opposition to Paul, lays such powerful emphasis on the continuation of the Law (in statements of Jesus such as 15:24, where he says that he has come *only* to the "lost sheep of Israel," and 5:17: "I have come *not to abolish* [the Law and the Prophets] but to *complete* them" [my emphases]). In effect, Matthew is using Jesus to challenge Paul's claim to authority, and this raises again the question of whether Paul interpreted Jesus's teachings accurately. Furthermore, if Paul's leadership is rejected by Matthew, then where better for his community to look for inspiration than from Paul's rival, Peter, who would have been known to the Antioch Jewish Christians from his time (one tradition says some seven years) in the city and who would presumably have supported their continuing adherence to Jewish requirements?

Matthew stresses Peter's closeness to Jesus, perhaps again to distance his community from Paul. "You are Peter and upon this rock I will build my church," says Jesus in what has become, once it was used to justify the primacy of the bishops of Rome as successors to Peter, historically one of the most influential phrases of the New Testament. Evidence that supports the argument that Matthew's community was Jewish and rejected the attempts of Paul to supplant the Law can be found in the writings of Irenaeus, bishop of Lyons (died c. 200). Describing a Jewish sect, the Ebionites, he notes: "They use the Gospel according to Matthew only, and repudiate the apostle Paul, maintaining that he was an apostate from the law."[33]

With the destruction of the Temple at the hands of the Romans in A.D. 70, however, Jewish Christianity began to wither. Peter, Paul and James were all, if tradition is sound, martyred in the 60s, and in the intense passions raised by the Jewish revolt it appears that the loyalty of even those Christians who continued to follow Jewish Law and rituals was suspect. The future was to lie with the Gentile churches. While the earliest Jewish Christians had been able to make some, if uneasy, accommodation with the society in which they lived, Gentile Christianity, through Paul, had declared war on the Greco-Roman world, its gods, its idols and its *mores*. So we must see the early Christian communities as introspective and exclusive, even dysfunctional, in relation to their surroundings. Paul himself recognized their isolation (1 Corinthians 1:23): "While the Jews demand miracles and the Greeks look for wisdom here are we preaching a crucified Christ; to the Jews an obstacle that they cannot get over, to the pagans madness." The Greeks or Romans could not be expected to offer any support or particular tolerance for a movement that rejected such significant aspects of their culture. The isolation of the Christian communities was to be further deepened by their increasing rejection of their connection with Judaism. Christians desperately needed to find coherence in their beliefs and unity in their communities if they were to survive at all. This is the context within which the fledgling Christian churches developed; it does much to explain the search for authority which was to preoccupy them from the earliest times and help make Christianity so distinctive among rival spiritual movements.

## 10

## "A CROWD THAT LURKS IN CORNERS, SHUNNING THE LIGHT"
### The First Christian Communities

The author of the Acts of the Apostles may never have met Paul, but he knew the Greco-Roman world well and had no inhibitions about making Paul part of it. He describes how on one of their journeys among "the Galatians" Paul and Barnabas reached the city of Lystra, in the south of the Roman province of Galatia. Here they came across a man who had been crippled since birth. Paul cured him, and the man, for the first time in his life, began to walk. The crowds shouted out in amazement: "These people are gods who have come down to us disguised as men." Barnabas was assumed to be Zeus and Paul Hermes, the Greek messenger god.[1] The priests were bringing up garlanded oxen for sacrifice when Paul and Barnabas persuaded them that they believed in another "living God" (Acts 14). Many continued to believe that they were gods, but the fantasy was soon shattered when Jewish opponents of Paul appeared and drove him from the city, even leaving him for dead. The story survives as a reminder that in the Greco-Roman world, unlike the world of Judaism, human beings could appear to cross the boundary between human and divine. While Peter and Paul had implied that Jesus became someone "exalted" by God only on his death, it was now possible, in this very different spiritual setting, to assume that he might always have been divine. The interplay between the memories of Jesus and the spiritually fertile culture of the Greek world was to be an immensely creative one, and its legacy survives in interpretations of Jesus still held today.

It is within this new cultural context that we can view the Gospel of

John (which is usually dated to about A.D. 100). The background of its author is unknown and the subject of much speculation (the earliest tradition, which holds that it was written by John the Apostle, now has little scholarly support), including the suggestion that an original narrative was reworked over time by later contributors. The different emphases on the relationship between Christ and God, mentioned below, suggest two distinct conceptions of the divinity of Christ. Unlike in Matthew, there is little emphasis in the Gospel on the church as an institution, and it is assumed that John, who may well have been Jewish himself, was writing for a marginal Christian community, possibly Jewish in origin but now separate from and antagonistic to mainstream Judaism. It appears to have been uncertain of itself and riven by internal conflict. Yet it was these tensions that provided a springboard for John's creative theological thinking. John has to provide a clear image of Jesus that will unite and heal. He does this not by reproducing any specific ethical commands (there is no equivalent of the Sermon on the Mount, for instance) but by making general exhortations "to love one another." Jesus becomes divine (which, of course, effectively separates him from the world of Judaism) and strongly associated with symbols of unity and care, the vine and its branches, the shepherd and his flock.

John may have drawn on one of Jesus' own disciples as a witness ("the beloved disciple" who is mentioned in the Gospel but never identified), and so, despite its late date in comparison to the Synoptic Gospels, his Gospel may contain some historical detail—about Jesus' trial, for instance—not known from elsewhere. Some of the places around Jerusalem John mentions were completely unknown until recent excavations have shown they really did exist. It has even been suggested that John's community lived in Palestine, and another possibility is Ephesus. Yet while John may contain "new" details about Jesus' life that are historically accurate, his overall narrative is not. John writes for theological effect and adapts the sequence of events accordingly. Jesus' entry into the Temple, realistically placed in the Synoptic Gospels just before his arrest, comes, in John, at the beginning of Jesus' ministry (2:13–22) and may have been placed there to symbolize Jesus' transcendence over traditional Jewish religious practice. This rearrangement is typical of John's approach; his Gospel is structured to highlight a number of signs in Jesus' ministry that proclaim his status as the Son of God to those who can recognize them. The first, of seven, is the miracle at Cana, and the last, and perhaps best known, is the moving appearance to Thomas after the resurrection (20:24–29). Thomas doubts. Jesus appears and asks Thomas to place his hand in his wound. Thomas believes.[2]

In the famous prologue to the Gospel, "the Word [*logos*] was made flesh." It is not known how John absorbed Hellenistic philosophy, but he seems either to have been aware of assertions (of Philo, for instance) that God acted directly or indirectly through *logos,* the force of reason, or to have drawn on the concept of Wisdom as developed in Proverbs and other Jewish sources. According to John, "the Word" (the established English translation of *logos* but one which fails to bring out the complexity of the concept; the Latin *verbum* has the same problem) is described as being with God from the beginning but now is incarnated in Jesus. Platonic philosophy never countenanced the possibility of a Form becoming human, and the entry of *logos* into time and space as "flesh" was a bold innovation of John's—the Incarnation, later to be such a central concept in Christian doctrine, is mentioned nowhere else in the New Testament. It opened up a rich seam in speculative theology that was to be fully exploited by the more philosophical of the Church Fathers. *Logos,* as we have seen, was always associated with rational truth; by equating Jesus with *logos,* John was assuming that what could be said about him might have the force of certainty. This was to be one of the founding stones of church authority. Furthermore, if Jesus is the *logos* and the *logos* has been with God from the beginning, then Jesus must be in some way divine. What this actually means is not always clear. Some passages of the Gospel assume that Jesus is part of the Godhead ("To have seen me is to have seen the Father" [14:9]; "I and the Father are one" [10:27–30]), others that Jesus is subordinate (". . . for the Father is greater than I" [14:28]). At times the text comes close to asserting that Jesus even in his human form is above humanity, as in, for example, his foreknowledge of what is to happen to him. If we accept that John's Gospel was reworked by several authors with different conceptions of Jesus' relationship with God the Father, such inconsistencies are not surprising, but it should also be remembered that John was feeling his way into new theological territory and cannot be expected to address issues that arose only in later centuries. As in the case of Paul, John may never have imagined that his writings would be heard by anyone outside the community for which they were written.

Jesus has been sent by the Father as "the Son." This creation of Jesus as "the Son" with a particular mission through which God the Father is revealed is another of John's innovations, although it reflects Platonic philosophy in that it equates to a Form, here the *logos,* being generated by "the Good." There is a loving God who has sent his Son "so that everyone who believes in him may not be lost but have eternal life" (3:16).[3] In other words, Jesus as the Son/*logos* has the purpose of linking men back to God and offering them salvation. His role is a wholly positive one. "The Son is sent into the world not to condemn the world [*sic*] but so that through him the world might be saved" (3:17). So in John we have moved away from the "angry" day of judgment made so much of by Paul, and Jesus is presented as light, and as an essentially nourishing force, "the bread of life." John goes further in his theological innovations. While Jesus may have returned to the Father, his message lives on in the Holy Spirit. John elevates the power and importance of the Spirit, and in doing so creates the possibility of the concept of the Trinity, although it was to be a further 300 years before the doctrine was elaborated. John, late as he is in the sequence of Gospel writing, and writing, apparently, for a small group on the edges of institutional Christianity, provides fertile soil for the seedlings of Christian doctrine.

However, making Jesus divine or part of the Godhead, as John does, also fostered one of the less happy developments in Christian theology. If the Jews (as a whole, rather than one faction of them, the Temple elite, which appears to have been historically the case) were responsible for Jesus' death, then they were guilty of the murder not just of a holy man but of God himself, in other words, of deicide. John is clearly aware of this implication, as we can see when he introduces sayings of Jesus in which Jesus rejects the Jews and foresees their role as his killers: "I know that you are descended from Abraham but in spite of that you want to kill me because nothing I say has penetrated into you"; "The devil is your father and you prefer to do what your father wants" (chapter 8). Whether John himself is attempting to distance the community he is addressing from Judaism (by the time he was writing Christians themselves were increasingly excluded from Jewish synagogues) or whether he believed this is what his Jesus would have actually said, his Gospel is clear in its rejection of Judaism.

This trend was consolidated through another force that made hostility to Judaism an integral part of early Christianity, and that was its appropriation of the Hebrew scriptures. In the early years of Christianity, when the movement was an offshoot of Judaism, it was natural for Christians to use the Hebrew scriptures, as Jesus himself (from the original Hebrew) and Paul (from the Greek translation) had done, and they were now reinterpreted as foretelling the coming of Christ. Matthew had already done this in his Gospel, and the presentation of Jesus as "the suffering Messiah" drew heavily on the prophet Isaiah. However, as the Christian communities developed their own identity in the Greco-Roman world, they were forced to find further justification for their use of the texts of a religion from which they were now increasingly separate. It was perhaps inevitable that the argument would be made that the Jews had proved themselves not worthy of their own sacred texts. The fiery north African theologian Tertullian (c. 160–c. 240), the first Christian theologian to write in Latin (a reminder that for its first centuries the churches were overwhelmingly Greek-speaking), wove Paul's views on circumcision into the argument: God had shown that circumcision was unnecessary by creating an "intact" Adam. He wrote: "And so truly in Christ are all things recalled to their beginning, so that faith has turned away from circumcision back to the integrity of the flesh as it was in the beginning."

He wrote in another work: "Accordingly . . . we who were not the people of God previously, have been made [sic] His people, by accepting the new law, and the new circumcision before foretold." So, it followed, the Jews, by insisting on circumcision, were living in a state that was somehow spiritually and morally inferior to that of Christians, an idea that understandably outraged Jews, for whom circumcision was a mark of their commitment to God. The nature of the "inferiority" was elaborated by the Church Fathers. Justin Martyr (c. 100–c. 165) argued that God had had to provide the Law for the Jews "on account of their stubbornness and insubordination." They had shown their insubordination by openly rejecting the Messiah, even though his coming had been prophesied in the scriptures and he had lived among them. Cyprian, bishop of Carthage (d. 258), preached: "We Christians, when we pray, say Our Father; because He has begun to be ours, and has ceased to be the Father of the Jews who have forsaken him." No wonder, Christians argued, the Jews had suffered so badly at the hands of the Romans, their sacred city and Temple destroyed (A.D. 70) and a later revolt crushed by Hadrian (A.D. 132–35). Origen said: "They suffered because they were very ignoble people: and although they committed many sins they did not suffer from them any comparable calamities to those caused by what they had dared to commit against our Jesus."[4]

Almost all the early Church Fathers wrote a work entitled *Against the Jews* (the second quotation from Tertullian above comes from one of them). It seems to have become part of an assertion of Christian identity, almost a ritual which had to be gone through to claim credentials as a Christian theologian. This does not mean that in this early period Christians were able to make any impact on Jewish communities, other than in the negative sense of breaking off any contact with them. They were simply too isolated and vulnerable themselves. It was only much later, when Christianity achieved political power, that hostility to Jews was to become an openly destructive force. The turning point is usually seen as the moment in 388 when Ambrose of Milan persuaded the emperor not to rebuild a synagogue that had been burned down by a Christian mob.

The key to understanding the early Christian communities is their relative isolation and the desperate search for a distinct identity within a world whose gods and culture Paul had told them they must despise. To become a Christian was a conversion in the full sense of the word, a turning away from one belief system towards another, in this case one that was alien to and openly hostile to the Greco-Roman world. The consequence of the failure of the second coming was to leave Christians who followed Paul in a form of limbo. Jesus had rooted his teaching within his own religious tradition; in contrast, Gentile Christians withdrew from theirs. They focused on salvation in the next world rather than personal fulfillment or status in this one. We can assume that it was precisely this shared sense of knowing that they would be saved that provided the early Christian communities with their commitment and vigour.

Yet to survive within a culture they defined as evil, Christians had necessarily to be secretive. One Christian of c. A.D. 200 described his co-religionists as "a crowd that lurks in hiding places, shunning the light; they are speechless in public but gabble away in corners."[5] We have almost no evidence subsequent to the days of the Apostles of Christians preaching openly.[6] Celsus, one of their early critics, accused them instead of infiltrating private houses and spreading their beliefs particularly among women and children, trying in the process to break up the household's social structure.[7] Christian isolation and caution is suggested in a text possibly from mid-third-century Syria: "We should shun evil in all respects, lest we give away what is holy to the dogs or cast pearls before swine . . . When pagans are assembled we do not sing psalms nor read scriptures lest we appear like musical entertainers."[8]

This deliberate seclusion makes the understanding of early Christian history, particularly in its psychological and sociological dimensions, extremely difficult. The evidence is very limited. Documentary evidence does confirm that Christians met in the houses of their richer brethren and that Christians were able to construct their own underground burial places, the catacombs, in the lava rock around Rome. Nevertheless, only one Christian meeting place dating from before the fourth century has been found, at Dura-Europus in Syria. In contrast over 400 Mithraic meeting places have been discovered. One reason for the comparative lack of evidence may have been Christian teaching (Acts 17:24) that "the God who made the world and everything in it, being the Lord of heaven and earth, does not live in shrines made by man." This secretiveness also meant that what was known about Christians by contemporaries was both limited and vulnerable to distortion. The "eating of Christ's body" and "drinking of his blood" at the Eucharist could easily be presented as some kind of cannibalism, and the stress on Christian love could be mistaken for free sexual love, always a concern to traditionalists because it threatened the breakdown of social order.[9]

One of the many accusations made against Christians by their more sophisticated opponents was that they were of low social status. In the late second century Celsus, in the first survey of Christianity by an outsider to survive, complained that Christian communities were made up, among others, of wool-workers, cobblers and laundry workers, and that Christianity was suitable only for the most ignorant, slaves, women and children.[10] This seems to be as much a reflection of Celsus' snobbery as anything, since wealthier Christians are in fact known by name. An early example is one Lydia from Philippi, who was in the lucrative purple dye trade. Her conversion led to that of her whole household (Acts 16:13–16). Christianity drew converts from across the social spectrum, but specific groups were particularly welcomed. The ascetic element of early Christianity, with its particular distrust of sexuality, gave women who had renounced marriage or who were widows a haven often denied to them in traditional society. But there were disagreements over the roles that these women could play. The limited evidence suggests that while in Paul's communities women were known and mentioned by name, over the next 200 years they were to be relegated to more subordinate roles in the church, a relegation justified by the sexual threat they were seen to pose, but surely reflecting as well the power of traditional Greco-Roman social attitudes to women. There is the story of a group of girls from Tertullian's congregation in Carthage who renounced marriage and were then encouraged by the rest of the congregation to throw off their veils as they no longer needed to maintain their modesty. The conservative Tertullian disagreed. Sexual desire could not be overcome so easily—all women carry the stigma of Eve's sin with them and are by their very nature temptresses. It was only in the fourth century that women who proclaimed perpetual virginity were given a status of their own by their fellow Christians, greater, in fact, than they would have enjoyed in pagan society. (It helped if they renounced their wealth as well.)

Any institution that distances itself from mainstream society has to create its own support systems. As with the pagan "mystery religions," a ritual of initiation was important, and for this reason the earliest sacrament to receive a form still recognizable today was baptism, firmly in place by the end of the second century. Baptism, which effectively separated Christians from non-Christians, was normally effected after three years of preparation, though many delayed the sacrament much longer than that in the hope of shortening the period between the cleansing of sins and death. (Infant baptism was practised from the end of the second century, but in the third century theologians such as Origen could find no reason for it, as it implied that babies were sinners—which they could hardly be when only a few days old.) The Eucharist was celebrated by those baptized, although it only was much later in Christian history, in the Middle Ages, that the doctrine of transubstantiation was fully elaborated, to be rejected in its turn by the Protestant churches. Christians could only marry other Christians, and it is in fact probable that Christianity spread within kinship or household groups that already had links with each other. Within the communities Christians evolved a strong structure of social support for their members. "We Christians hold everything in common except our wives," wrote Tertullian in the late second century. It is known that the church in Rome was supporting some 1,500 poor in the middle of the third century, while the community in Antioch was providing food for around 3,000 destitute in the early fourth century. As Christianity grew, this pattern of providing care within the community, backed as it was by specific exhortations of Jesus recorded in the Gospels, was to be extended to the sick and destitute beyond the immediate community.

One of the legacies of Paul was the need for Christians to define the boundaries between themselves and the outside world they so vigorously rejected. (The Book of Revelation, whose author by tradition was the Apostle John of the Fourth Gospel, was vituperative in its condemnation of the Roman empire, symbolized in chapters 17 and 18 as "Babylon, the mother of all the prostitutes and all the filthy practices on the earth.") It could be argued, as Paul had done, that the coming of the kingdom was so imminent that a commitment to Christ was enough; the only question now was one of waiting until the coming. As late as the fourth century, Macrina, the sister of Basil of Caesarea, made a vow of perpetual virginity because the human race no longer needed perpetuation in view of the return of "her true promised love, Christ."[11] Some insisted, however, that Christian commitment required withdrawal from every kind of material and psychological comfort, even to the extent of leaving city life and social relationships to live in the desert, and facing martyrdom if required. Yet this was not practicable or attractive for the majority of Christians, who could hardly break completely with the pagan world. A compromise response was to create a Christian household, the conversion of the head leading to that of the family and their slaves. Tertullian believed that the traditional structure of the Roman household, with its wealth, slaves and customary obediences, of women to men, children to parents, was ideal for this, although the world was still to be treated as a potential source of contamination, particularly through the lure of sexuality. He worried endlessly as to how far a Christian should collaborate with a world full of idols.[12] It was a common and enduring problem, which appears to have caused tensions within Christian communities. One Christian of the late second century, for instance, complained that his fellow Christians were "absorbed in business affairs, wealth, friendship with pagans, and many other occupations of the world."[13] He, presumably, had rejected them.

It was as a result of the urgent need to define its boundaries and beliefs that Christianity developed sophisticated notions and structures of authority. Authority and Christianity are so intertwined that it is possible to forget how revolutionary a development this was for the Greco-Roman world, where allegiance to a number of different cults could be comfortably sustained. However, the psychological and emotional pressures on many of the early Christians must have been considerable. They had to live up to the demands made on them for moral perfection while isolating themselves from their traditional cultural backgrounds, whether in the Jewish or the Greek world. Jews were already distinguished by their own language, territory, dietary laws and practices such as circumcision, but Christians had no such distinguishing signs. Other religious groups were already adopting Jesus as a divine or semi-divine figure—the influential Gnostics saw him as a teacher able to give *gnosis*, "knowledge," to those souls trapped in an evil body, while the followers of *theos hypsistos* saw Jesus as "an angel of God," and the Jewish sect the Ebionites as a man who had been elected by God as "a Son" (the moment of election could be either his baptism or his resurrection). So Christians were losing control even of their ownership of Christ.

The development of Christian authority was a twofold process in which a canon of sacred texts, the Old and New Testaments, emerged alongside an institutional structure in which bishops held authority within their communities and also, eventually, claimed the absolute right to define and to interpret Christian doctrine through the scriptures and church councils. The concept of a text that contained spiritual "truths" was accepted in Judaism and in traditional Egyptian religion, but it was new to the Greco-Roman world (there are only a few examples of revered texts, such as the book of the prophecy of the Sibyl used by the Roman Senate at times of crisis). The idea that stories about God and his actions (*muthoi*) could be frozen in written form and interpreted to make statements of "truth" (*logoi*) was alien to the Greeks, and there was to be some resistance to it in early Christianity. It is not until about 135 that we find Christians accepting that written texts had greater authority than the oral traditions surrounding the life of Jesus that had been passed on from generation to generation and could therefore develop, like Greek myths, to meet changing needs.[14] Once the concept of a sacred text was generally accepted, the Old Testament based on the (Greek) Septuagint could be adopted more or less entire. The differences between the Septuagint and the original Hebrew version of the scriptures were eventually resolved by Jerome, who separated the so-called Apocrypha, the books found in the Septuagint but not in the Hebrew scriptures, from the rest. The adoption of the Old Testament had the added advantage of giving Christianity an ancient history, thus countering those who derided it as a religion without roots.

The Jews had a long tradition of scholarly interpretation of the scriptures, and their methods were adopted by Christians (the term used for such interpretation, "exegesis," comes from the Greek word "to explain"). Yet Christian exegetes started out with a very different purpose, seeing the Hebrew scriptures as prophecies of the coming of Christ: for this purpose they found the books of the prophets more fruitful than those of the Law, which were the main areas of study for Jewish scholars. Early Christian exegesis shows considerable ingenuity, but its findings are, to a modern mind, extraordinarily sweeping in scope.

Augustine, for instance, was to go so far as to claim that "you will rarely find phrases in the Psalms that do not refer to Christ and the Church." Christian theologians prided themselves on being able to find meanings in the scriptures that the Jews seemed unable to find and, in fact, saw the skills they possessed as exegetes as another justification for the superiority of Christianity over Judaism.[15]

It took much longer to complete a canon of early Christian texts (what came to be known as the New Testament), as it involved choosing between a large number of competing texts (including the twenty Gospels already mentioned), which were selected on the basis of their conformity with the evolution of doctrine. The need to define boundaries meant that the process was largely one of exclusion. "The canon was a deliberate attempt to exclude certain voices from the early period of Christianity; heretics, Marcionites, Gnosticism, Jewish Christians, perhaps also women," writes the Swiss theologian Helmut Koester. "It is the responsibility of the New Testament scholar," he continues, "to help these voices be heard again."[16] On the other hand, there still remained considerable diversity and a lack of doctrinal coherence between those Gospels, letters and "revelations" that were selected for the New Testament, and, as we shall see, there proved to be enormous difficulty in using them as an authoritative source for doctrine. Christians themselves had enough problems with interpretation, but non-Christians were also quick to point out inconsistencies, not only between Gospels but between the Old and New Testaments, as well as potentially embarrassing passages, such as the quarrel between Peter and Paul reported in Galatians. Critical analysis of the scriptures by non-Christians did not have to wait until the Enlightenment—it was there from the beginning of Christian history.

While almost all the texts of the New Testament were, as we have seen, written to and for specific, often small, communities faced with particular challenges, they were now assumed to have universal significance and to provide an unrivalled source for doctrine. One result was the gradual rejection of direct revelation. The Montanists, for instance, a Christian sect in Phrygia who claimed to receive messages directly from the Holy Spirit, were formally condemned by synods (local councils) of Asian bishops before A.D. 200. It is perhaps significant that the Montanists had an egalitarian rather than hierarchical leadership structure and that two of their three named leaders were women. The campaign against the Montanists made the bizarre Book of Revelation, reportedly the words of Jesus revealed to John the Apostle, vulnerable—but it was eventually included in the canon, with John given special status as the last of the prophets to be directly inspired by the Holy Spirit. This, in effect, gave the churches control over what was and was not to be accepted as revelation.[17]

With scripture to draw on and an evolving sense of tradition, the formulation of Christian doctrine gradually took shape. The affirmation of God the Father and Creator, Jesus the Son, whose death and resurrection had raised the possibility of salvation for all who repented, and a Holy Spirit who continued to act as a divine force in the world, formed the core of Christian belief. But the details of such doctrine were blurred, and there were many conflicting interpretations of the status, purpose and relationships between the three divine forces. There was not even a consensus on what salvation meant—the Church Fathers disagreed strongly on who was being saved, from what and for what purpose.[18] In short, the diversity of the early Christian experience cannot be overstressed: like spiritual movements in the Greco-Roman world, Christianity fragmented as it spread, and the fragmentation became more pronounced because of the variety of the scriptural and traditional sources on which doctrine could be based. Yet, and perhaps for this reason, the search for authority became more intense and with it came an increasing stress on an institutional hierarchy. An early statement of orthodoxy comes from Irenaeus, the bishop of Lyons from 178 to 200. The *Adversus Omnes Haereses* (to give it the Latin title by which it is normally known, although it was originally written in Greek) is one of the more important documents of the early church. Irenaeus was responding to critics who claimed that the diversity of the scriptures made it difficult to find a coherent message in them and that they should be open to interpretation by individuals. Not so, says Irenaeus. The Apostles knew what the truth was (he assumed that the Apostles were all of one mind), and they passed it down through their successors. Only those in direct succession from the Apostles "have received the sure gift of the truth according to the pleasure of the Father . . . the rest we must regard with suspicion, either as heretics or evil minded." He was echoed by Tertullian: "wherever it has become apparent that the truth of Christian teaching and faith exists, there will be the truth of the scriptures and of their interpretations and of all Christian traditions."[19] This truth exists only for those in true apostolic succession, in effect, the bishops.

It was Cyprian, bishop of Carthage from 248 until his martyrdom in

258, who made the firmest and most influential assertion of a bishop's authority. Cyprian was deeply humiliated in the persecution of 251, when the majority of his flock sacrificed to the pagan gods rather than face martyrdom, but he then found that his priests were readmitting the backsliders to the church. As the persecution waned, he called together his fellow north African bishops, who agreed that any readmission to the church could only take place publicly under the direct authority of the bishop through the rite of baptism, and then only after an admission of guilt. Only those who had stood firm could carry out the baptism: a baptism by anyone, even a bishop, who had buckled under persecution was invalid and would leave the "baptized" one "stained and polluted by the unholy water of heretics and schismatics." In reiterating, in his *De Unitate,* "On the Unity of the Church," that only bishops who had resisted persecution had the right to carry out the baptisms, Cyprian stressed the authority bishops had by virtue of their office. "Does anyone who acts against the bishops of Christ think that he is with Christ . . . he carries arms against the Church . . . he fights against the will of God . . . he is an enemy of the altar, a rebel against Christ's sacrifice."[20] Cyprian describes the bishop in similar terms to that of a provincial governor, having absolute authority in his province with his opponents described as rebels. This was a crucial stage in the evolution of church authority in that it adopted a powerful terminology of rebellion with which to describe heretics and was part of the process by which any avenues for the making of doctrine outside the institutional church were closed off. Cyprian assiduously built up support among his fellow bishops (some eighty-seven of them at one African synod he called in 256), even receiving support from as far afield as Cappadocia in Asia Minor.

Cyprian was adamant in his condemnation of any who promoted schism, but one was now in the making. On the issue as to whether those who had themselves lapsed could rebaptize Christians, Cyprian, who, as we have seen, believed they could not, embarked on a bitter conflict with the bishop of Rome, Stephen, who maintained that the lapsed clergy retained the power to baptize. The bishops of Rome, as successors of Peter, who, according to tradition, had been martyred in the city, had already tried to insist on their primacy over other bishops and had been supported by Irenaeus' assertion in his *Adversus Haereses* that Rome was the see "with which all must be in agreement." Yet Rome's efforts had not as yet met with much success: for example, an attempt in the 190s to tell the Asian bishops on what date they should celebrate Easter had been rebuffed. As a result of Cyprian's influence, Stephen was isolated. Firmilian, the bishop of Caesarea in Cappadocia, wrote to him: "Cut yourself off you most certainly have . . . since the genuine schismatic is the person who has made himself an apostate from the communion and the unity of the church. While imagining it was in your power to excommunicate everyone, you have in fact succeeded in excommunicating yourself alone, from everyone else!" While by the third century there is the concept of a single church ("He no longer has God for his Father who does not have the Church for his mother," wrote Cyprian), which through its bishops, its traditions and the scriptures defines orthodoxy, the reality seems to have been very different. The view put forward by Eusebius of Caesarea in the early fourth century, in what was the first detailed history of the church, that it had always been a monolithic institution with a unified faith, easily defensible from the heresies that pestered it, has little historical backing.[21]

While Christians looked back to the canon of scriptures and to tradition, they also accepted the continuing activity of God in the world in the form of miracles and portents that were effected through the power of the Holy Spirit. The Holy Spirit's earlier role as a revealer of divine truths was, after the suppression of the Montanists, somewhat in abeyance. The Acts of the Apostles are full of miracles (clearly attributed to the Holy Spirit), and in the early Christian centuries the effecting of miracles became a sign that an individual was favoured by God (who was responsible for the miracle itself). So at Ephesus, where Paul had so ignominiously been driven out for threatening the lucrative worship of the goddess Diana, the Apostle John succeeded where Paul had failed by praying in front of her temple, one of the Seven Wonders of the ancient world, as a result of which half the temple apparently fell down and a mass conversion followed (from the apocryphal Acts of John 38–45). Similarly, in Caesarea in the persecution of 305, when a Christian was executed by drowning, an earth tremor was felt and the body was washed ashore. The whole town was so overcome by this apparently unambiguous sign of the wrath of God that they converted en masse.

Stories of the exorcism of demons are particularly prevalent in early Christianity. Demons (who were believed to be the offspring of intercourse between fallen angels and earthly mothers—they had to have an origin later than the creation of the world as God could not have created anything evil) pervade the world of early Christianity. Far from disbelieving in the pagan gods, the Christians saw them as demons who were very much "alive." Ramsay MacMullen, in his survey of conversions before the toleration of 312, sees the "driving out of spirits and the laying of hands" on those possessed by demons as an essential part of the Christian drama as acted out for non-believers.[22] A story about the ascetic Anthony makes the point well, while also reinforcing Paul's claim that Christians outperformed the philosophers. A group of philosophers had visited Anthony, who proclaimed that the way to show the fruits of faith was to perform a miracle. He called up some local madmen.

> "Look now; here are some folk suffering from demons. Either cleanse these men by your logic chopping or by any other skill or magic you wish, or otherwise, if you can't, lay down your quarrel with us and witness the power of Christ's cross." And with these words he called on Christ, sealed the sufferers with the sign of the cross twice and a third time, and straightaway the men stood forth all healed.[23]

Inevitably a church that relied heavily on miracles as a means of securing status was vulnerable to criticism by intellectuals. One pagan response was that if a god had to resort to miracles to show his power, then he had surrendered his dignity. Celsus claimed that Christians were able "to convince only the foolish, dishonourable and stupid and only slaves, women and little children."[24] He was echoed by the physician Galen, who criticized Christians for their adherence to faith rather than reason and for relying on "undemonstrated laws."[25] There was some truth in these attacks. As we have seen, Paul had condemned the "philosophers," and his stress on "faith" rather than reason had shifted Christianity outside the world of traditional Greek philosophy with its stress on rational argument. This approach had now become a handicap. It was common for students in the Greek world to go from one school of philosophy to another, listening to debates and querying positions taken, and unless Christians were able to take part in such debates, Christianity was unlikely to achieve intellectual respectability. In a growing church, most Christians at any one time were converts, and there were many who had had a traditional training in philosophy either before encountering Christianity or while waiting for baptism. Some kind of accommodation had to be made with Greek philosophy. The Christian Justin Martyr (c. 100–c. 165), a Platonist by training, was among the first to argue that Christianity could draw on both scriptures and Greek philosophy and could even appropriate philosophy for its own ends. "Whatever good they [the philosophers] taught belongs to us Christians." He was echoed by Clement of Alexandria (c. 150–c. 215), who claimed that God had given philosophy to the Greeks as "a schoolmaster" until the coming of the Lord as ". . . a preparation which paved the way towards perfection in Christ." "If those who are called philosophers, and especially the Platonists, have aught that is true and in harmony with our faith, we are not only not to shrink from it, but to claim it for our own use from those who have unlawful [*sic*] use of it . . . ," added Augustine some 200 years later.[26] Whether the pagan philosophers were able to recognize the fact or not, their concept of *logos,* reasoning power, could be equated with the *logos* that was Christ. This strand of thought was developed so that Greek philosophers were even said to have absorbed "Christian" insights from the Old Testament, which they were assumed to have read. The theologian and historian Eusebius claimed that it was possible to find almost all of Plato's philosophy mirrored in the Old Testament. There was therefore no necessary contradiction between Greek philosophy and Christianity, but now that the *logos* had been incarnated as Jesus, the world had, Clement argued, moved into a new phase of history. The pagan philosophers should not be discarded, but their writings should be studied in such a way that their "Christian" teachings were disentangled from the rest. In the west, however, there continued to be a strong distrust of pagan philosophy, although Stoicism appears to have been an important influence for some, such as Tertullian.

Clement was in effect drawing on Middle Platonism, which stressed the power of "the Good" or "the One" to act in the world through the Platonic Forms. Platonism was ideally suited to providing the intellectual backbone of Christianity in that Platonists, particularly Middle Platonists, were dealing with the concept of an unseen, immaterial world in which "the Good," or God, could be described as absolute while at the same time being able to have a creative and loving role. Middle Platonists had developed the idea of the human soul from earlier Greek philosophy. They saw the soul as distinct from the human body and able to exist independently of it and to make its own relationship with a providential God, who, in his turn, might reach out to it lovingly and creatively through the Forms, or "thoughts of God," as they were now described by Christian theologians. The *logos* was one of these thoughts, but distinguished by becoming incarnate in Jesus Christ. It helped that Platonism had never compromised with the Greek gods and their mythology.

Platonism was to prove helpful in another sense. The Platonists argued that only a few could glimpse the reality of the immaterial world, including the true nature of "the Good"/God, but could prescribe what it consisted of for the rest. This was to be used to support the rationale for church authority, if the "few" were equated with the Christian hierarchy. The theologian Origen put the matter succinctly when he showed how the concept of faith could be used to keep the "multitude" in line: "As this matter of faith is so much talked of, I have to reply that we accept it as useful for the multitude, and that we admittedly teach those who cannot abandon everything and pursue a study of rational argument *to believe without thinking out their reasons*" (my emphasis).[27] Here the concept of faith has shifted, from being a state of openness to revelation (or directly to the teachings and personal charisma of Jesus as recorded in the Gospels) to one of being ready to accept what is authoritatively decreed by the church hierarchy. The readiness to do this without questioning becomes a virtue in itself. So reasoning, as an intellectual power open to every man in the sense proclaimed by Aristotle, is now reserved for the few. In effect, Platonism offered no threat to the evolving authority structure of the church—if anything it reinforced it. As is clear from the subsequent history of the churches, the idea that there are set dogmas laid down by church leaders that have to be believed by those entering the Christian communities and that cannot be challenged intellectually by either insiders or outsiders became part of the essence of Christianity. It should also be remembered that Plato had denigrated the natural world as inferior to the immaterial world of the Forms, and so the adoption of Platonism did nothing to undermine Paul's condemnation of any philosophy that concerned itself with finding truth in the material world.

So Platonism became entwined with Christianity. As Christopher Stead puts it: "The reality of God, his creation and providence, the heavenly powers, the human soul, its training, survival and judgment could all be upheld by the appropriate choice of Platonic texts."[28] With the scriptures and church tradition still providing the bedrock of Christian theology, this was a question of grafting Platonism onto Christianity rather than the creation of a new philosophy. One problem lay in reconciling the Hebrew concept of God with the single pure unity of "the Good" of Plato (a problem already addressed, as we have seen, by the Jewish philosopher Philo). The God of the Old Testament had "human" attributes; he was emotional, quick to anger but also loving and providential, and he could intervene directly in the world, winning battles for the Israelites or speaking through their prophets. The "God" of the Platonists was cooler, more austere, and both more consistent and more remote in his relationship with the world. He is essentially unchanging, "the rock of ages." For such a concept to display even a benevolent concern for individual human beings, let alone Old Testament emotions, was awkward. Imaginative thinking was needed. It proved possible, for instance, for "the divine Craftsman" introduced as a creator figure by Plato in his *Timaeus* to be assimilated with the creator God of Genesis, yet the tension between the concepts remained, as later disputes were to show. A further distinction between Platonists and Christians was that Platonists believed that matter had existed eternally alongside "God," while Christians believed that it would detract from the power of God if he had not existed before matter, which, of course, he had created.

One way of resolving the tension between scripture and philosophy was to draw a distinction between God as the ultimate supreme being (who could be equated with the Platonic God) and God as an outgoing power in the material world, able in this capacity to show some emotions, represented by the *logos,* itself incarnated in Jesus Christ. Most Christians agreed that there had to be a distinction between God and Jesus/the *logos,* in that God surely could not suffer, and so Jesus, who clearly did suffer on the cross, must be in some way a distinct creation who served as an intermediary between God and man. In the early fourth century, Eusebius provided a useful analogy when he said that if God had come down to earth himself, it would have been as if the sun itself had arrived on earth, and the result would have been devastation. God needed to reveal himself through some kind of intermediate force, and this is the *logos.* The *logos* is able to contain the power of God but then to transmit it to the earth in a milder form through the presence of Jesus in human form. In Platonic thought the relationship between "the Good," the Forms and the material world was conceptualized in many different ways, and the same was true for Christianity. The Sabellians, at one extreme, saw Jesus Christ/the *logos* simply as a manifestation of God, never fully distinct from him and with no separate personality or substance; the Adoptionists, at the other, saw the *logos* as a distinct entity, fully human and created separately by God like the Old Testament prophets.[29]

In contrast to Aristotle, who had talked of the soul as the essence of a human body, using the analogy that a body without a soul would be like an axe that cannot cut, Plato had stressed the independence of the soul from the body and its continuing existence from one body to another. Some early Christian theologians (Origen, for example) actually adopted this idea, arguing that the soul was preexistent to the body in which it came to live and could move on to others after the death of a body (transmigration), but gradually the belief was consolidated that each body had its individual soul given to it at conception and that soul continued to exist eternally after the death of that body, something Aristotle could never have imagined. It could enjoy the happiness of heaven or the suffering of punishment in hell for eternity. This left major conceptual problems. Did the soul enter the body with the semen—in other words, become associated with a purely material process—or was it created by God and placed there by him at the moment of conception? The second answer seemed more likely, but it became incompatible with the doctrine of original sin when that doctrine was elaborated by Augustine in the late fourth century. It seemed unlikely that God himself would place souls already tarnished with sin into the human foetus, and the question had to be left unresolved (or ignored).[30] Plato had always argued that there are echoes of the immaterial world of the Forms in the material world. The relationship works two ways. The Form of Beauty acts to create beautiful things on earth, while humans can create beautiful things themselves that give a hint of what the Form of Beauty itself might be. (This idea was later developed as part of the rationale through which Christians felt able to decorate their buildings so opulently—the opulence gives a glimpse of the reality of heaven.) In the same way, each soul has its own *logos* or reasoning power, which is an echo of the divine *logos* that reaches out to it and to which it is naturally attracted in return. This concept was to be creatively developed by the Alexandrian theologian Origen.

Origen (c. 185–c. 254), who was born a Christian in Alexandria, was a fervent believer. His father had been taken off to martyrdom, and he would have followed if his mother had not hidden his clothes. He may even, according to one report, have mutilated himself so he could not feel sexual desire, and he suffered so badly in the persecution of 251 that his health was permanently broken. He was a prodigious thinker, one of the most fertile writers of the ancient world, with possibly some 2,000 titles to his name (most have been lost or were destroyed when he was declared a heretic). He plunged himself into the scriptures, even mastering Hebrew, and is seen as the founder of biblical scholarship. He set texts from different versions of the scriptures alongside each other to explore the differences between them, and he wrote his own commentaries on the major books. Yet his approach was primarily allegorical. He claimed that much in the world was purely symbolic of something else and that the scriptures were no different. It was not necessary to adopt a literal interpretation of scripture but rather to search for the deeper truths concealed in the text. Such an approach had a respectable history in the Greek intellectual tradition. The epics of Homer, the closest the Greeks ever came to sacred texts, had long been interpreted allegorically. The reward in taking this approach was that it allowed Origen to think creatively about theological issues and to avoid the issues involved in reconciling a literal interpretation of the events of the Old Testament with his Platonic philosophy.[31]

Origen's greatest work, *De Principiis*, survives now only in an often obscure Latin translation made in the 390s, but its four books show the breadth and originality of his thinking. Origen's is a Platonic God, uncreated, transcendental, perfect in his unity and at the same time the source of all being. This God is given the supreme place in the powerful drama of human existence. Originally, argued Origen, all human souls were equal and attached to God, but all except one, Christ, fell away as a result of losing perfection, either through indifference or neglect of God. Origen described the unity of the *logos* and the soul of Christ as being like iron suffused by heat; the two are inseparable. Some remained as angels, but the more recalcitrant dropped down through the immaterial world towards the earth, where they became imprisoned in human bodies. This was the state in which most of those who neglected God existed, but a few, who were more violent in their rejection, became demons. Evil was not a separate force in the world (as some Christians believed: note "the Sovereignties and the powers which originate the darkness in this world, the spiritual army of evil in the heavens" of the letter to the Ephesians 6:12); it was rather a reflection of the degree to which an individual had rejected God.

However, human souls retained the memory of their previous state of being and experienced their separation from God as a loss; they also retained *logos*, the power of rational thought, even if this was now separated from the *logos* that remains fully in Christ, the only unfallen soul. It is this sense of loss that provides the impulse to return to God. Origen drew on the Platonic idea of a long, disciplined period of training before it was possible to achieve knowledge of the true reality—in this case God. The first step, the desire to commit oneself to the long path ahead, was the most important. This created the possibility of being "transformed," a key concept for Origen. Those who selected themselves for "transformation" were the equivalents of Plato's Guardians, and like the Guardians their selection distinguished them from those less committed to recovery. They would also, as the Middle Platonists had argued, be aided by the power of God's love, although Origen always emphasized the crucial importance of the individual will. The assistance of Christ was also essential. He was a reflection of God, with all the attributes of God, but he was somehow distinct from God. Origenist theology is not always clear about exactly how, although certainly it was in some form of subordinate role to God the Father—in one passage, for instance, as "the first born of all created, a thing created, wisdom." Christ's position as one close to God acted as a catalyst for those who wished to make the return. In so far as Origen had argued that all souls, including that of Christ, had started together, the ultimate aim was to become like Christ, in effect to reach divinity. Origen may have drawn on Paul's idea that we are co-heirs with Christ as "sons of God," as well as on Plato's assertion that we can become assimilated with "the Good." As it is human nature to try to reach God, and we have the freedom to do so, God will punish those who "have gone against the impulses of nature . . . And he threatens them through prophets and through the Saviour who came to visit the whole human race, in order that by means of the threat those who hear may be converted, while those who neglect the words aimed at their conversion pay penalties according to their deserts." However, whatever their just deserts, Origen believed that all would ultimately be saved. There would be an end point at which even the soul of Satan, the extreme case of one who had rejected God, would be reunited with him. If God is truly providential and powerful, argued Origen, there can be no other final state of being. "And providence will never abandon the universe. For even if some part of it becomes very bad because the rational beings sin, [God] arranges to purify it, and after a time to turn the universe back to himself."[32] Origen's followers also argued that

God's committing a soul to hell would be an admission that he had been thwarted by a mere human being, something inconceivable if God was truly all powerful. Ultimately God's concept of the world, one brought to order by his providence, must prevail, and so all must end subject to his care. Origen, like the traditional Platonists, also rejected the idea that there would be a bodily resurrection.

It was to prove impossible to achieve full philosophical coherence in Christian doctrine. Different sources for doctrine, a variety of scriptures, tradition and Platonism (which, as we have seen, had its own internal contradictions), conflicted with each other and were in themselves shaped by the internal needs of communities that until 312, the moment when Christianity was given toleration, had to define their identity within a hostile world. The future of Christian doctrine would depend on whether the church could open itself to these contradictions and see them as inevitable and containable or whether the desire to ensure conformity would lead to their suppression. In the end the combination of church and state authority was to prove too powerful. Origen was among those whose teachings were suppressed. After the formulation of the Nicene Creed in 325, he would be condemned for seeing Christ as a created—and thus subordinate—being rather than an eternal part of the Godhead. As Christianity became as much a political as a religious movement, the fear that without eternal punishment there would be insufficient incentive for being good predominated, and Origen was further condemned for his view that all would eventually be reunited with God. So by the end of the fourth century, the belief that God would ultimately be eternally unforgiving of some, perhaps even of most (a view found, of course, also in Paul and Matthew), with all the implications that raised about his fundamental goodness and the nature of the final state of the world, had become part of Christian doctrine. Augustine was to give his own formidable intellectual support to the idea of a hell for all eternity, pessimistically adding his doubts that humans had the freedom to overcome the burden of their sinfulness. The first condemnation of Origen, for providing a "hydra of heresies," came from Theophilus, the powerful patriarch of Alexandria, in 402. Theophilus (who was responsible for overseeing the destruction by Christians of the massive temple to Serapis in Alexandria and pillaging the great library there) insisted on the Hebrew concept of God, "with eyes, ears, hands and feet like men," and condemned Origen for preaching God was incorporeal. A final condemnation by the church as a whole came in 553 at the Second Council of Constantinople (although it is likely that this was on the basis of distorted interpretations of Origen's writings).

The adoption of the Platonic "Good" as God and its amalgamation, however unsatisfactorily, with the Hebrew God marked a major shift in the perception of the divine. Pindar, the great poet of the early fifth century whose odes celebrated the victors of the Greek games, had summed up the traditional Greek view:

> There is one race of men, one race of gods, both have breath of life from a single mother [Gaia, the earth, according to legend]. But sundered power holds us divided, so that the one is nothing, while for the other the brazen sky is established as their sure citadel for ever. Yet we have some likeness, in great intelligence and strength to the immortals, though we know not what the day may bring, what course after nightfall destiny has written that we must run to the end.[33]

Here there is a common mother for man and gods; despite the gulf between mankind on earth and the gods above, there is an overlap between them in strength and intelligence. Human beings are not entirely dissimilar to the divine. In Christian thinking, on the other hand, God, a transcendent and all-powerful force who had existed from before all time, had, at a distinct moment, created a material world totally dissimilar to him and subject to him. The gulf between God and the human race had become immense, in effect impassable, and the status of human beings had, in their own eyes, been diminished to that of sinners. This amounted to a dramatic overthrow of the traditional Greek world view, and once Christianity had been endorsed by the state as the only true religion, it became the paradigm within which debate about spiritual matters would be confined for centuries to come. There was an alternative view that drew on the verse in Genesis in which mankind was said to be created in God's image, yet this was incompatible with Christian Platonism, where the gulf between Creator and created was absolute. This second view fared better in the Aristotelian Christianity of Thomas Aquinas (see chapter 20 below).

The self-imposed isolation of Christians from the political and religious structure of Roman society was bound to evoke reaction. "These men all act against the edicts of Caesar, saying there is another king, Jesus," shouted the hostile crowds in Thessalonika in the first century (Acts 17:7). The Jews had earned grudging respect for the ancient origins of their religion and so were afforded some degree of toleration, but by breaking with Judaism Christians lost that respect and were derided (by the second-century historian Tacitus, for instance) for their creation of a religion without tradition. They also raised the challenging question of how far a society normally tolerant in religious affairs could contain a community that wished to overthrow the traditional gods. Their isolation made them easy to scapegoat as enemies. In the persecution of 64, Nero attempted to shift onto them responsibility for a great fire which devastated Rome, although it is interesting to note that this very persecution, clearly rooted in Nero's obsessional and vindictive character rather than in any activity of Christians, caused a backlash of sympathy for Christianity.

A more measured response to Christianity is detailed in the famous letters between the emperor Trajan and his governor Pliny in Bithynia from about 110, and it reflects the astuteness of the emperor. Pliny asked Trajan's advice about how he should deal with Christians. It was only those active Christians who refused to sacrifice who were of concern to the state, replied Trajan, but even then he was reluctant to order a witch hunt to search them out. The normal rules that accusers had to bring their case in person and be liable to a charge of malicious prosecution if their accusations proved unfounded were to be upheld. Those Christians who were no longer a member of a church community should normally be acquitted. In fact, in the second century persecution of Christians remained haphazard and dependent on the individual initiatives and responses of local governors. By the third century, however, the state was insisting on greater and more visible loyalty to the traditional gods. It was not so much the practice of Christians that offended as their refusal to sacrifice, a refusal which aroused ancient and deep-rooted fears that the protection of the gods would be lost. Persecution could be avoided by participating in an actual sacrifice witnessed by two officials, who would then issue a certificate. Many Christians complied, and then once the persecution had passed reapplied for membership of the church. As we have already seen, the conditions under which they should be readmitted caused major dissension.

Those who refused to sacrifice could face martyrdom, but this was a fate many Christians appeared to welcome, so intense seems to have been their belief in the glory of the life to come. While the numbers killed may have been small in comparison with, say, the casualties of the suppression of the Jewish revolt of 66–70, there developed a sophisticated presentation of martyrdom in which the martyr defied every attempt to make him (or her) renounce the faith and then faced appalling cruelties, often in the arena, unflinchingly. Accounts of the martyrs' deaths stress their own individual situations and all the gory details. Some of the most influential were women such as Perpetua, killed in the arena at Carthage in 203 with her faithful slave girl Felicity, or Agnes, who defied the advances of Roman soldiers and died rather than surrender her virginity. The impact of martyrdom was immense and even, according to Tertullian, acted as a seed-bed for Christianity. By the fourth century, when it was all over, the collective memory of the persecutions and the individuals who died in them became ever more powerful. The calendar of the church was dominated by their feast days, and their relics provided a focus for the creation of churches. Martyrdom became so closely intertwined with Christian commitment and status that every single early bishop of Rome had later (and in most cases clearly apocryphal) legends of martyrdom attached to him.[34]

It is virtually impossible to estimate the number of Christians in this period, although even in the third century they were a small minority within the empire. The evidence left by a group that was naturally reluctant to publicize its activities and which appeared unwilling to advertise its meeting places is sparse, and only estimates can be made. Those for the mid third century vary from as few as 2 percent of the population to as many as 10 percent.[35] Christianity was an urban phenomenon, eastern and Greek-speaking rather than western. Only twenty-five Christian communities, based, it seems, in apartment blocks in the city, are known from pre-Constantinian Rome, one reason why the bishops of Rome had to struggle so hard to make their voices heard among those of the bishops of the larger eastern communities. Many parts of the empire knew little of Christianity, and, as we have seen, one emperor of the west, Constantius, did not even find it necessary to implement the persecutions of Diocletian other than by destroying a few buildings allegedly belonging to Christians. Moreover, the boundaries between Christians and the rest of society were increasingly blurred. This was partly because, despite their rejection of all pagan cults, Christians borrowed from or shared many attributes with other religious movements. The pagan cult of *theos hypsistos,* for instance, had, like Christianity, both separated itself from Judaism and found a place for Jesus as "an angel." Economic pressures also played their part. Most Christians needed to work; by the third century Christians were to be found as state officials, soldiers and even members of the imperial household. A Spanish synod in the early fourth century allowed Christians to suspend their Christianity to become presidents of municipal councils—so long as they did not offer theatre or gladiatorial shows, they could be readmitted to their faith after two years. In 314, after toleration had been given to Christians, a synod in Arles allowed them to become governors of provinces as long as their bishop's approval had been sought. Tertullian may have been making a special plea for toleration when he wrote that his fellow Christians "live together with you in this world, including the forum, including the meat market, baths, shops, workrooms, inns, fairs, and the rest of commercial intercourse, and we sail along with you and serve in the army and are active in agriculture and trade," but by the third century this was very much the case.[36]

What is usually concealed in the histories of early Christianity is the tensions between different groups. This is partly because the earliest history of the church, Eusebius' fourth-century *Ecclesiastical History,* which was accepted as an authoritative account for centuries to come, glossed over these, presenting instead a church united in doctrine, hallowed by the blood of its martyrs and ready to take its rightful place in society with the ending of persecution. Yet in his *Life of Constantine,* as we shall see, Eusebius is forced to accept that there was often violent discord between Christian communities, particularly over rival interpretations of doctrine. This discord was only to be intensified as the emperors tried to integrate Christianity into the state. For Christianity was now to be transformed from a religion of outsiders to one of insiders, a transformation of incalculable importance for western history.

# 11

# CONSTANTINE AND THE COMING OF
# THE CHRISTIAN STATE

We have received from Divine Providence the supreme
favour of being relieved from all error.

THE EMPEROR CONSTANTINE IN A LETTER TO THE
CHURCH IN ALEXANDRIA[1]

In the fourth century Christianity became the "official" religion of the
Roman empire. The emperor responsible for ending Diocletian's persecution of Christians and bringing Christianity into the structure of the
state was his successor, Constantine. Constantine's story is often simply
told. He has a vision sent by God before a major battle (the battle of the
Milvian Bridge, outside Rome), wins the battle and then converts to
Christianity. It is often assumed that Constantine simply and wholly
accepted the authority of the church, which was now able to conduct its
business openly, consolidate its doctrine and proceed to convert the
masses. The main reason why this story has so often been accepted so
uncritically is that our major source for his exploits is the *Life of Constantine* by Eusebius, the bishop of Caesarea. Eusebius writes, as would
be expected, from a Christian perspective, and he shapes his evidence
accordingly—but he is also writing a new form of biography, that of the
Christian hero, and his *Life of Constantine* is openly panegyrical. His
account, for instance, equates Constantine with Moses, who received

evidence of God's support through divine signs. So too does God offer divine signs, visions and opportune military victories to Constantine.

Recent research, however, is emphasizing another Constantine. Outside Eusebius' *Life*, there is virtually no evidence that suggests that Constantine knew anything much about Christ or even of the requirements for Christian living. His main concern may rather have been to ensure that the growing Christian communities supported his imperial rule, but, shrewd political leader that he was, he also carefully maintained his relationship with paganism to a degree that Eusebius was unwilling to admit. In a recent assessment by H. A. Drake: "Constantine's goal was to create a neutral public space in which Christians and pagans could both function . . . [and] he was far more successful in creating a stable coalition of both Christians and non-Christians in support of this program of 'peaceful co-existence' than has generally been recognised."[2]

According to this interpretation, the battle of the Milvian Bridge, rather than being a conversion to Christianity in the traditional sense of the word, was a means by which Constantine could provide a rationale for his support for Christianity. Ironically (and here Constantine's lack of knowledge of Christianity becomes apparent), it meant creating a false link between Christianity and success in war that was subsequently integrated into the Christian tradition. The importance of this can hardly be exaggerated.

Constantine's family roots lay in the Balkans. His father, Constantius, came from Illyria and had served as governor of Dalmatia, the Roman province along the east of the Adriatic Sea, before being made one of the empire's two Caesars by Diocletian and given control in the west.[3] Constantine, born in 272 or 273, was by then twenty and old enough to start his own career. His first appointment was as a tribune, an officer of the imperial guard, at Diocletian's court. He was soon on active service against the Sassanids, in the east, and the Sarmatians, one of the many migratory tribes on the empire's northeastern frontiers. Then, released to join his father in the west, Constantine arrived in York in 306, just before Constantius died. Constantius' bereaved troops acclaimed his son as an Augustus, but Diocletian's successor as Augustus in the east, Galerius, would not accept such a dramatic promotion, and Constantine had to accept the more junior post of Caesar. He showed himself to be one of the finest commanders the empire had yet seen. He had a dominating personality, was a superb organizer (it was under Constantine that many of Diocletian's administrative and military reforms were finally implemented) and a decisive, if often brutal, general. He had soon brought the Rhine under control, as well as all of the western empire outside Italy and the African provinces that had been seized by Maxentius, the son of Diocletian's co-Augustus, Maximinian, in 307. By 307 Galerius had been forced to face political reality and acknowledge Constantine as co-Augustus of the empire. Even this was to prove too confining for Constantine, who could see the Tetrarchic system collapsing around him as rival Caesars and usurpers (Maxentius among them) struggled for power. By 310 he had broken free of the Tetrarchy and stressed his independent legitimacy as the son of his father. Panegyrics to Constantine that survive from the years immediately after Constantius' death assume that Constantius is among the gods and that Constantine, "similar to you [Constantius] in appearance, in spirit and in the power of empire,"[4] holds power on earth as a symbol of his father's immortality. Constantine also stressed his independence from Diocletian's Tetrarchy by stretching Constantius' own legitimacy back to an early-third-century emperor, Claudius Gothicus, emperor A.D. 268–70, whose major victory over the Goths at Naissus (Constantine's birthplace) in 269 blunted their strength for over a century. With a line of descent from an earlier emperor and divine support assumed through his father, Constantine had now established a firm claim to rule the western empire in his own right. It was an early indication of his political shrewdness and ambition.[5]

If Constantine's legitimacy depended on the support of the gods, then his own conception of the divine becomes crucial for understanding his reign. His early allegiances were entirely conventional. When in 307 he married, as a second wife, Fausta, the daughter of Maximinian, who had abdicated as Augustus in 305, he adopted Maximinian's favoured protecting god, Hercules. By 310, when he asserted his descent from Claudius Gothicus, he claimed that Apollo had appeared to him in a vision (clearly Constantine's favoured method of receiving divine messages), offering him a laurel wreath and promising that he would rule for thirty years. About the same time he became intrigued by the cult of *Sol Invictus,* the cult of "the unconquered sun." The sun, as the source of light and heat, had traditionally been integrated into an enormous variety of spiritual and philosophical contexts. Apollo had been associated with the sun since the fifth century B.C., while in the fourth century B.C. Plato had used the sun as a symbol of supreme truth, "the Good," the apex of the Forms. The cult of *Sol Invictus* had been imported from

Syria in the third century. It had proved popular among soldiers, and the emperor Aurelian (270–75) had built a massive temple to the cult in Rome. So when Constantine began using the sun as a mark of imperial power, often portraying himself on coins or statues with rays coming from his head, he was exploring a well-recognized symbol of both spirituality and power. Like many of his predecessors as emperor, he had a fine appreciation of the value of visual propaganda and he knew how to use a variety of symbols to enhance his image.

Then, in 312, Constantine moved against Maxentius. As he made his way through Italy, Maxentius sent three armies in succession to confront him. All were defeated. Finally, Maxentius himself marched north from Rome to where the Via Flaminia, the main road to the north, crossed the Tiber. Here he pulled down the Milvian Bridge, replacing it with a bridge of boats that could be broken up if Constantine tried to cross. It proved a disastrous strategy. Defeated on the far side of the bridge, Maxentius and his men fled back over it towards Rome. Under the weight of panicking soldiers, the "bridge" disintegrated and Maxentius was drowned with hundreds of his men. All Italy and then the provinces of north Africa were in Constantine's grasp.

Constantine announced that his victory was due to the support he had received from "the supreme deity," by which Christians such as Eusebius claimed he meant the God of the Christians. The earliest account we have is from two or three years after the battle. Lactantius, a convert to Christianity, reported that Constantine had had a dream the night before the battle in which he was commanded to place the "heavenly sign of god," the chi-rho sign, on his soldiers' shields, and he did so. Many years later Constantine, apparently under oath, told his biographer Eusebius a somewhat different version of the story. At some point before the battle, it is not clear when, a cross of light had appeared in the skies above the sun. (The placing of the cross by the sun in Constantine's memory seems significant.) It was inscribed "By this sign, conquer," and this command had been confirmed in a dream when Christ himself had appeared to Constantine and asked him to inscribe a cross on his standards as a safeguard against his enemies.[6] In another section of Eusebius' *Life* Constantine provides a wider perspective for his "conversion." He tells his biographer how he was struck by how his father, unlike all his immediate predecessors, had died while still emperor and had bequeathed his power to his son. This made him think that whichever god Constantius supported must be the most dependable. Yet who was this god? Constantine did not know (he had after all been separated from his father for a crucial thirteen years), but apparently on the basis that Constantius believed in "a supreme god" and had stood aside from the persecutions of the Christians in Diocletian's reign, Constantine had assumed that it was the God of the Christians.[7]

Within a few months of the battle Constantine had declared that Christianity should be tolerated, and within a year he had started an enormous building programme of churches, in a traditional (pagan) exercise of patronage that transformed the Christian communities. There is no doubt, therefore, that Constantine's victory was associated with a programme of active support for the Christian churches, but was Constantine's "conversion" quite as sudden and dramatic as the Christian commentators suggest? H. A. Drake argues that it was not.[8] Constantine was, as we have suggested, a shrewd political operator. As he had observed earlier attempts to eradicate Christianity, he must have realized that they they were fruitless. They were simply reinforcing the very precedent, that of martyrdom, with which the harassed Christians already identified. If there was to be harmony in the empire, something more imaginative was required, perhaps a political volte-face as a result of which Christianity could be integrated into the state. It was a mark of Constantine's political genius and flexibility that he realized it was better to utilize a religion that already had a well-established structure of authority as a prop to the imperial regime rather than exclude it as a hindrance. Drake argues that this idea of integrating rather than rejecting Christians may have grown in Constantine's mind as the failure of the persecutions became obvious, and that he used the victory at the Milvian Bridge as a platform from which to launch his new policy.

The adoption of Christianity was not, however, to prove entirely straightforward. Constantine knew so little about Christianity that he immediately ran into difficulties. First, Christ was not a god of war. The Old Testament frequently involved God in the slaughter of his enemies, but the New Testament did not. Constantine would have to create a totally new conception of Christianity if he was to sustain the link between the Christian God and victory in war. Second, it was crucial for Constantine's political survival that he did not break with the pagan cults that still claimed the allegiance of most of his subjects, yet Christianity emphatically rejected paganism; many Christian groups would never accept a relationship with a state still condoning paganism. Some very careful political manoeuvring was necessary if Constantine was to avoid offending either Christian or pagan. Finally, while Constantine might have hoped for a church that could be subservient to him, he found one racked with disputes and power struggles. This became even more apparent when he came to power in the east and confronted the maelstrom of conflict and rivalry among the Greek-speaking Christians.

Once he had announced his "conversion," Constantine's first task was formally to end the persecutions by ensuring toleration for Christians. Galerius' successor in the eastern empire, Licinius, anxious to strengthen his own precarious position, made an alliance with Constantine in 313, and they jointly issued a proclamation in Milan, usually known as the Edict of Milan, that henceforth Christianity, and all other cults, would be tolerated throughout the empire. Any buildings damaged as a result of the persecutions of Christians would be restored.

> With salutary and most upright reasoning, we resolved on adopting this policy, namely that we should consider that no one whatsoever should be denied freedom to devote himself either to the cult of the Christians or to such religion as he deems best suited for himself, so that the highest divinity, to whose worship we pay allegiance with free minds, may grant us in all things his wonted favour and benevolence.

So Constantine effectively brings the Christians back into the Roman community without jeopardizing the position of any other religious belief. A "highest divinity" is assumed, but the concept, as we have seen, could be as easily used in the pagan world as the Christian and offered no conflict with Constantine's desire for political harmony. This edict deserves an honoured place in European history as the first proclamation of the right to freedom of worship, an idea implicit in Roman government but never stated so clearly as here.[9]

Three years after his victory at the Milvian Bridge, Constantine was honoured by a grand triumphal arch in the centre of Rome (it still stands by the Colosseum), supposedly erected by a decision of the Senate of Rome but clearly a further statement of his new policy. The arch is conventional in form and is notable for its use of reliefs removed from monuments to earlier emperors, Trajan, Hadrian and Marcus Aurelius. This may have been the result of a desire to get the arch finished before the tenth anniversary of Constantine's accession to power, but it has also been suggested that Constantine wished to associate himself with "good" emperors, even though, of course, they had not been Christians. The imagery of the arch contains no suggestion of the influence of Christianity. There are, in fact, reliefs of Mars, Jupiter and Hercules, all traditional gods of war, and Constantine's victory at the Milvian Bridge is associated with the power of the sun and the goddess Victory. The depiction of the battle itself shows no sign of the Christian visions or Christian symbols on the soldiers' shields. Elsewhere on the arch Constantine is shown in traditional imperial roles, making a speech in the Roman Forum and handing out poor relief. On an inscription on the arch, Constantine's victory is credited to the "instigation of the Divinity," and bearing in mind that this was by now conventional pagan terminology, no one could have been offended by it.[10]

For committed Christians, the idea that their support might have been sought for purely political reasons would have been abhorrent. In so far as theirs was a religion requiring absolute dedication and the rejection of all other cults, conversion meant a complete change of lifestyle and the rejection of the conventional values and beliefs of Greco-Roman society. Constantine may not have been aware of this. As a traditional Roman, he had been brought up in a society where allegiance to several cults could be held simultaneously, as his own patronage of Hercules, Apollo and *Sol Invictus* shows. He seems to have assumed that Christianity would be the same and that any involvement he might have in Christian rituals would not be at the expense of earlier allegiances. This would explain why he continued to use the traditional imagery of the sun to support his authority. Constantine was still issuing coins bearing images of *Sol Invictus* as late as 320, and in the great bronze statue he later erected to himself in the Forum in Constantinople he was portrayed with the attributes of a sun-god, with rays emanating from his head.

One reason why this pagan association was so successful in maintaining the emperor's status was that the sun was also used in Christian worship and symbolism. The resurrection was believed to have taken place on the day of the sun, the most important day of the week for Christian worship (as the English word "Sunday" still suggests). A third-century fresco from the Vatican Hill in Rome even shows Christ dressed as the sun-god in a chariot on his way to heaven. The Christian writer Lactantius, who was writing at this time, urged Christians to observe the sun as if it were heaven and a symbol of "the perfect majesty and might and splendour" of God. "It is likely," concludes J. W. Liebeschuetz in his perceptive study of Constantine's proclamations, *Change and Continuity in Roman Religion,* "that in the minds of many fringe Christians, Jesus and the sun were closely associated."[11] In the fifth century Pope Leo was to rebuke Christians at St. Peter's for turning their backs on St. Peter's tomb and standing on the front steps of the basilica to worship the rising sun.[12] Remarkably, the main festival of *Sol Invictus* was the day of the winter solstice, December 25, adopted by Christians in the fourth century as the birthday of Christ. In short, the sun was a symbolic image through which Constantine could be presented effectively to both Christian and non-Christian audiences, thus maintaining his neutral position between opposing faiths. Constantine's balancing act continued. Liebeschuetz suggests that imperial panegyrics, or at least those written in Latin, are, after 321, "written in terms of a neutral monotheism which would be acceptable to Christians and pagans alike."[13] Later in his reign Constantine authorized the city of Hispellum on the Flaminian Way in Umbria to build a temple "in magnificent style" to the cult of his family, another indication of his reluctance to abandon traditional worship.

However, despite his balanced policy towards both pagan and Christian, nothing can obscure the scale of the commitment Constantine showed to Christianity. He started with the granting of special favours to Christian clergy, in particular exemption from the heavy burden of holding civic office and taxation. Earlier emperors had granted exemptions to specific groups (doctors, teachers, athletes are among those recorded) but never, outside the special circumstances of Egypt, to clergy. The exemption was, in Constantine's words, so that the clergy "shall not be drawn away by any deviation and sacrifice from the worship that is due to the divinity, but shall devote themselves without interference to their own laws . . . for it seems that, rendering the greatest possible service to the deity, they most benefit the state."[14] Here Constantine appears to be tying the Christian communities into the service of the state. He may have felt that only a powerful gesture such as tax exemption would succeed in allaying the distrust of Christians after so many decades of persecution by the state. However, he may not have foreseen the consequences. He appears to have been genuinely surprised at the number and diversity of communities calling themselves Christian, and soon after his victory he had to face the dilemma of whether to give patronage to all of these or to privilege some communities more than others. The issue arose first in north Africa. The provinces there, part of Maxentius' territory, had surrendered to Constantine, who had acknowledged the bishop of Carthage, Caecilian, with imperial patronage, granting the clergy of his diocese exemptions from civic duties and taxation. Rival African bishops protested, claiming that Caecilian had no right to hold office, and thus receive imperial support, because he had been consecrated by a bishop who, during Diocletian's first persecution, had surrendered the scriptures to the authorities to be burned—in other words, who had compromised with paganism. As Cyprian, the influential bishop of Carthage martyred in the previous century, had decreed, such a bishop had no legitimacy. The dissenting bishops went on to elect their own bishop of Carthage, Majorinus. Majorinus was succeeded by one Donatus in 313, and it is as the Donatists that the dissenters are remembered.

Writing to an official on the matter, Constantine expressed his fear that his own position as the ruler favoured by God would be jeopardized by these internal squabbles. He wrote: "I consider it absolutely contrary to the divine law that we should overlook such quarrels and contentions . . . whereby the Highest Divinity may perhaps be roused not only against the human race but also against myself, to whose care he has by his celestial will committed the government of all earthly things."[15] Reading between the lines, one might assume that Constantine's real concern was that his policy of using the Christian churches as a stabilizing force for his regime was unravelling as their dissensions became increasingly apparent. He referred the dispute to two successive councils of bishops, one in Rome, the other in Gaul. Neither supported the Donatists, and in 316 Constantine withdrew his patronage from them. The evidence suggests that at first he had no clear preference for either group but that with time he became increasingly irritated by the rigid stance of the Donatists, who were clearly reluctant to compromise with the state and accept its authority.[16] Constantine could hardly have foreseen the momentous consequences of his decision for the western empire. By isolating the Donatists, who made up the vast majority of Christians in north Africa, he helped to define in the western Christian communities that were left what was to become the Roman Catholic Church.

Whatever his religious concerns, Constantine's major preoccupations remained military ones. Between 313 and 315 he campaigned with further success along the northern borders of the empire, but he was also set on further expansion of his power within. He remained co-emperor with Licinius, his fellow signatory of the Edict of Milan. Licinius had married Constantine's half-sister, Constantia, and the two emperors appeared on coins together. However, both were ambitious men. In 316 they fell out, and Constantine forced Licinius to cede his European provinces, although he allowed him to remain as Augustus of his remaining eastern provinces. The final settlement came in 324 when Constantine won two major victories over Licinius and forced him to abdicate. Licinius was executed in 325 and his son Licinius II, who had been appointed a Caesar in 317, was killed a year later. Constantine was supreme within the empire.

The eastern empire with its long and rich cultural history was very different from the provinces of western Europe. It was also much more heavily Christianized, and a tradition of intense debate over doctrine was more deeply embedded than it had been, or ever became, in the west. The bishops of the great sees lived in continuous rivalry with each other. Constantine was shocked by what he found. Eusebius wrote: "The bishop of one city was attacking the bishop of another . . . populations were rising up against each other, and were all but coming to physical blows, so that desperate men, out of their minds, were committing sacrilegious acts, even daring to insult the images of the emperors." Addressing a group of bishops some years later, Constantine vented his own exasperation at their squabbles: "Even the barbarians now through me, the true servant of God [*sic*], know God and have learned to reverence him while you [the bishops] do nothing but that which encourages discord and hatred and, to speak frankly, which leads to the destruction of the human race."[17] In short, his political position was threatened by the endemic political and doctrinal disunity of the Christian Greeks. Almost immediately he was confronted by a major dispute between the bishop of the important see of Alexandria, Alexander, and a presbyter in the diocese called Arius. It concerned the central problem of Christian doctrine, the relationship between God the Father and Jesus Christ the Son. The dispute had erupted dramatically when Arius interrupted one of Alexander's sermons and Alexander, supported by other local bishops, had him excommunicated.

Few areas of church history have been so completely rewritten in the past twenty years as the "Arian controversy."[18] Traditionally church historians have suggested that an "orthodox" understanding, which accepted Jesus the Son as divine and fully part of the Godhead, was already in place by the 320s and that Arius challenged this "orthodoxy" with his claim that Jesus had been created as "Son," thus distinct from a pre-existing God and subordinate to him as Father. This tradition relied heavily on the main contemporary source for Arianism, the polemical anti-Arian writings of Athanasius, bishop of Alexandria from 328 to 373. In these Arius and all those who failed to accept the "orthodox" position were grouped together and excoriated. Later historians drew heavily on Athanasius. H. M. Gwatkin, for instance, writing in 1882, condemned the Arians with this trenchant judgment based on Athanasius' work: "On the one side their doctrine was a mass of presumptuous theorising, supported by alternate scraps of obsolete traditionalism and uncritical textmongering, on the other it was a lifeless system of unspiritual pride and hard unlovingness."[19] Recently, however, historians have begun to decode Arianism. They have found that the movement Athanasius dubbed "Arian" was much broader and more complex than Athanasius had suggested and had a great deal of scriptural and theological backing.

To see the strength of the Arian position and why Arianism proved so difficult to eradicate from the Christian tradition, we might begin with some excerpts from the Gospels.[20] Many passages suggest that Jesus himself saw God as somehow distinct from himself. Take, for instance, Mark 10:18, where Jesus says, "Why do you call me good? No one is good but God alone." Again, in his agony at Gethsemene (Matthew 26:39), Jesus calls on God. " 'My father,' he said, 'if it is possible, let this cup pass me by. Nevertheless, let it be as you, not I, would have it.' " In John 17:3 Jesus prayed, "And eternal life is this: to know you, the only True God and Jesus Christ whom you have sent" (that is, knowledge of God is distinguished by the "and" from knowledge of Jesus Christ). Similar passages are to be found in Paul's Epistles. The last verse of the Epistle to the Romans reads: ". . . it is all part of the way the eternal God wants things to be. He alone [sic] is wisdom; give glory therefore to him through [sic] Jesus Christ for ever and ever." The author of Hebrews (5:8), writing some time before A.D. 70, states, "Although he was the Son he learned to obey through suffering; but having been made perfect [the implication being that at some stage he was less than perfect], he became for all who obey him the source of eternal salvation and was acclaimed by God with the title of the High Priest of Melchizedek." Then there is the verse from Proverbs (8:22) in which Wisdom, often identified by Christian exegetes with Christ, proclaims that "Yahweh created me when his purpose first unfolded, before the oldest of his works," in other words, Christ, if identified with Wisdom, was a distinct creation. Drawing on such passages and ignoring those that were not so favourable to their interpretations, the Arians urged that Jesus was in some way distinct from and subordinate to God his Father, and perhaps essentially different in nature. Arian writings repeatedly return to the scriptures, in particular the Synoptic Gospels, for support.

In this the Arians drew on earlier Christian tradition. Many of the earlier Church Fathers, including Justin Martyr, Clement and Origen—the last two Alexandrians themselves—treated Jesus the Son as somehow derivative from the Father. Origen, perhaps the greatest of the early biblical scholars, used many of the texts cited above to make his point that the Son derives from the Father as the will derives from the mind. When Arius claimed to Alexander that he was following "our faith from our forefathers, which we have learnt from you,"[21] these were the formidable theologians whose work he could draw on. As Richard Hanson has written: "Indeed, until Athanasius began writing every single theologian, east and west, had postulated some form of Subordinationism . . . it could, about the year 300, have been described as a fixed part of catholic [the word being used here in the sense of universal] theology."[22]

The Arians also learned from those Platonists who had tried to link the eternal world of the Platonic Forms with the actual world of creation. As we have seen, the Platonists provided analogies that could be used to describe a supreme unchanging god, Plato's highest Form, and a subordinate entity, *logos,* the eternal principle of reason or Word that provided a link with the lower created world. This was all part of the much wider debate within paganism over the distinction between the divine power of a supreme deity and the manifestations of that power. Jesus could be equated with *logos,* as John had done in the famous opening verses of his Gospel as early as the end of the first century. The vital point, Arius seemed to be arguing, was that the *logos* required a separate act of creation by God, God Himself being indivisible and self-sufficient, and hence if Jesus was *logos* he was subordinate to the Father, although, of course, high in the Platonic hierarchy compared to the mass of humanity below. Arius appears to have believed that in fact the *logos* was created at the beginning of time with the supreme and distinct role of mediator of his Father's glory, a view that, if Christ was equated with Wisdom, received backing from the verse of Proverbs. In fact, it was this verse which became the centrepiece of the Arian argument and the most difficult for its opponents to refute. What clinched the matter for many

Arians was the suffering of Christ so vividly portrayed in the Gospels. The key verse here was the agonized cry of Jesus recorded by Mark (15:34): "My God, why hast thou forsaken me?" Surely God the Father as a supreme unmoving force above all things (note here again the influence of Platonism) was unable to suffer or "feel" anything. The fact that Christ could and did suffer, and called on God to rescue him from his suffering, was "proof" that he was a lesser divinity.[23]

So when Arius challenged Alexander, he believed he was representing a theological position that could be cogently justified, with philosophy and tradition backing the scriptures. Jesus was divine (that was the only possible interpretation of John's famous prologue, "And the Word was made flesh"—although some still argued that Jesus was merely human and had been "adopted" by God), but he was a distinct creation of God the Father, who became in fact "the Father" through the act of creation. There was no reason why God, as all-powerful, could not create a subordinate being, a "Son," to act out his purposes in the material world, but Jesus' exact status, in particular in his role as *logos*, the "Word" of John, and the ways in which he was similar to and different from his Father, were still disputed (which is why it is unwise to speak of a single coherent Arianism).[24] It was particularly difficult for those brought up on Platonism to accept a Platonic Form that had appeared as a human being.

This was the controversy facing Constantine, threatening his dream of political stability. Used to the more fluid spiritual allegiances of the Roman world, he could not believe that such "idle and trivial" speculations could cause so much unrest. As he complained in a letter to Arius and Alexander:

> The cause of your difference has not been any of the leadership doctrines or precepts of the Divine Law, nor has any new heresy respecting the worship of God arisen among you. You are in truth of one and the same judgement: you may therefore well join in communion and fellowship . . . the Divine commandment in all its parts enjoins on us all the duty of maintaining a spirit of concord.[25]

He went on to stress how much the squabbling Christians could learn from pagan philosophers about how to conduct their disputes. By this time, however, the controversy had spread as other bishops had associated themselves with one side or the other. Constantine had to act if he was to achieve any stable support from the Christians, and so he took the initiative in calling a council of bishops at which he could enforce an agreed definition of Christian doctrine to be backed by the state. So was initiated the process by which church doctrine was decided in councils of bishops called under the auspices of the emperor; all church councils up to the eighth century conformed to this model.

The bishops were to assemble at the imperial palace at Nicaea in Asia Minor. Constantine knew he had to create an impact, and he spared no effort in doing so. Eusebius, who was present, described the emperor as "like some heavenly angel of God, his bright mantle shedding lustre like beams of light, shining with the fiery radiance of a purple robe, and decorated with the dazzling brilliance of gold and precious stones." Those who beheld him were said by Eusebius to be "stunned and amazed at the sight—like children who have seen a frightening apparition."[26] The setting was designed to support the image, with the emperor sitting in a prominent place on a chair of gold. Constantine opened the council himself with a formal speech in Latin (reinforcing his distance from the Greek-speaking participants). Later Byzantine mosaics and frescoes (that from the monastery of the Great Lavra on Mount Athos, for instance) show Constantine as the central figure of the council, larger than the bishops assembled around him. Later tradition asserted that there were 318 bishops present, but the actual number was probably smaller; 318 was the number in the "domestic army" which Abraham gathered to rescue Lot (Genesis 14:14), an analogy used by later commentators on the Nicene Council as the number of bishops who rescued "orthodoxy" from the clutches of "heresy." With almost no exceptions they were easterners—such debates had largely bypassed the Latin-speaking Christians. The bishop of Rome was represented only by observers.

Accounts of the Council of Nicaea are fragmentary, but we can assume that Constantine's determination to establish a consensus, his dominating presence and the growing dependency of the church on him for patronage combined to give him an overpowering position. In his analysis of Constantine's opening speech, H. A. Drake shows how it was cleverly worded so as to stress the overriding need for harmony, fulsomely (if prematurely) praising the bishops for their own (assumed) desire to reach this end. If they settled this controversy, Constantine assured his listeners, they would be "at the same time acting in a manner most pleasing to the supreme God, and they would confer an exceeding favour" on their "fellow-servant" the emperor.[27] It was, after all, peace which was his aim.

The council began with the production of a creed drawn up by Eusebius, who was probably the most learned of the bishops present. It was conciliatory and cleverly avoided all the issues raised by Arius, stating belief first in God, then in Jesus Christ and then in the Holy Spirit. Jesus was "first born of all creation and begotten from the Father before all ages." This sidestepped the question of whether there was a time when Jesus was "not." The word "begotten" became crucial here, because it is possible to beget something of oneself without creating something new, and thus the word could be used to deny that Jesus was a separate creation. There was no mention of the relationship between Father and Son. Yet the creed which emerged from the conference was markedly different. First it included a statement that Jesus Christ "is of the substance (*ousia*) of the Father . . . true God of true God . . . consubstantial (*homoousios*) with the Father." It ended with a number of anathemas condemning specific Arian beliefs, notably that there was a time that Jesus had never existed and that Jesus was of a different substance from the Father. The creed even condemned the view that Jesus had a separate *hypostasis,* or personality, from the Father, taking the creed close to the extreme Sabellian position.

It is impossible to know from the surviving evidence how or why the word *homoousios,* "of identical substance," was introduced, although Eusebius later told his congregations that it was at the specific command of Constantine. It had no basis in scripture (as its opponents were repeatedly to stress in the years to come) and had seldom been used in theological discussions. In fact, at a council of bishops held in Antioch in 268, the word had been condemned as heretical, apparently on the grounds that a term implying a material entity was inappropriate to use for referring to God.[28] Plotinus had indeed used the word *ousia,* substance, to describe the common attributes of "the One," the *nous,* and world-soul, but it seems only to have been later in the century, in the writings of the Cappadocian Fathers (see below, pp. 188–89), that Plotinus' terminology entered Christian theology. One view is that the word may have been introduced at Nicaea because Arius himself had specifically condemned the use of *homoousios* as a term to describe the relationship between God and Jesus, and it was deliberately used to emphasize the rejection of Arius.[29]

It is also not known why the council rounded so emphatically on Arius. The most likely explanation, although this suggestion can only be tentative, is that an impatient Constantine simply forced the formula through in the hope of quelling the dispute. He may have sensed that a majority of the council opposed Arius and capitalized on its mood. There were also political advantages in having Christ within the God-head rather than, as in the Arian formulations, a distinct figure outside it. Christ, a figure of peace rather than war, a representative of opposition to the empire who had actually been executed by a Roman governor, fitted nowhere in Constantine's conception of Christianity—he may even have been an embarrassment. If he were kept apart as a distinct figure, what allegiances to the state might he not undermine? This may well explain why Christ plays such little part in Constantine's theology; Alistair Kee goes so far as to argue that "Christ had no part in the religion of Constantine."[30] The *homoousios* formula allowed Christ's identity to be subsumed in the Godhead. In doctrinal terms, of course, the formula had no precedent, and there is certainly some evidence that the bishops had to be pressured by Constantine into accepting it. In his *Life of Constantine* Eusebius has the emperor "urging all towards agreement, until he had brought them to be of one mind and one belief on all the matters in dispute." A letter also survives in which Eusebius tries to explain to his flock in Caesarea why he signed a creed that differed in important ways from the one he had presented to the council. He pretends that the word "substance" is really of little importance, but he is clearly very uneasy about the creed.[31] It was unlikely that the bishops, dependent as they were now on the patronage and support of Constantine, would have been able to resist him. The result was an enormous majority for the new creed, but Constantine used his own imperial powers to order the excommunication and exile from their sees of Arius and two of his closest supporters who refused to sign it. Nevertheless, wrote Eusebius, "the Faith prevailed in an unanimous form . . . ," and he concludes, "When these things were finished, the Emperor said that this was the second victory he [*sic*] had won over the enemies of the Church, and held a victory-feast to God." The churches had in fact succumbed to Constantine's own conception of their role.

The Council of Nicaea has a hallowed place in Christian history as the first ecumenical council and as the moment of the first expression of the Nicene Creed, still used as the essential expression of orthodox Christian faith today. Yet this status was acquired only much later, when the creed, in an expanded form, was endorsed by another emperor, Theodosius I, at the Council of Constantinople in 381. In the short term, no one seems to have taken the council or its creed seriously. As Jaroslav Pelikan puts it in his study of the making of Christian doctrine, "[Other than Arius and the exiled bishops] all the rest saluted the emperor, signed the formula and went on teaching as they always had." He continues: "In the case of most of them, this meant a doctrine of Christ somewhere between that of Arius and that of Alexander."[32]

It is significant that within ten years of the Council of Nicaea all the leading supporters of the Nicene Creed had been deposed, exiled from their sees, or otherwise disgraced. Traditionally this has been seen as the retaliation of frustrated Arians, but this is much too simplistic a judgment. There was a variety of reasons for the depositions, but they can certainly be read as suggesting that no bishop gained any lasting status as a result of supporting the creed, and that many of them felt uneasy about the defeat of subordinationism. In 343 Bishop Ossius of Cordoba, who had been a leading figure at Nicaea, felt free to suggest a different creed at a conference of western bishops at Serdica. It did not include the word *ousia* and contained no reference to either the Nicene Council or its creed.[33] The first mention of the council as ecumenical, and hence authoritative, comes only in the 350s, when Athanasius, Alexander's successor as bishop of Alexandria, who had attended Nicaea, revived *homoousios*.[34]

It seems that Constantine himself realized that his enforced creed did nothing to maintain the allegiance of the majority of the Greek-speaking Christian communities, who remained Arian. His agenda required that consensus be maintained and that Christians should be brought so far as possible under the umbrella of the state.[35] Freed from the immediate pressures of the council, Constantine actually began to move towards reconciliation with the Arians. The two exiled bishops were returned to their sees. Arius himself was welcomed personally by the emperor and his views (probably modified from those previously held) now declared to be orthodox. Bishop Alexander was ordered to reinstate Arius. He died without doing so, and his successor, Athanasius, also refused to carry out the order. Athanasius, who had shocked his fellow bishops by the violence with which he enforced his authority in Egypt, was the kind of hardline and intransigent bishop that Constantine knew would destroy his carefully balanced settlement, and he exiled him to Gaul, about as far from Alexandria as he could be sent.

Eventually, in 335, Constantine summoned Arius to Constantinople and ordered the bishop there to admit him to communion. However, there was a bizarre ending to the affair. The bishop, an opponent of Arius, apparently prayed that God should show who was right in the controversy by allowing only either himself or Arius to live to attend the service. The day before the service, Arius died, somewhat dramatically, of a haemorrhage in a public latrine in Constantinople. It was a convincing enough sign of God's will for some (the pro-Nicene Ambrose of Milan went so far as to claim that the fact that Arius' bowels spilled out showed that God equated him with the traitor Judas, who had suffered the same undignified end [Acts 1:18–19]), but the Arian tradition did not die with him. When Constantine himself was finally baptized it was at the hands of an Arian bishop, Eusebius of Nicomedia (not to be confused with the Eusebius who was Constantine's biographer). The Nicene Creed appeared to be dead—even, in terms of what Constantine had hoped to achieve, a failure. If the issues had not been revived in the 350s, the council might have occupied no more than a footnote in history.

Those impressed by Constantine's adoption of a Christian God might have hoped that he would have adopted Christian ethics. However, he appears to have shown no interest in the message of the Gospels. Rather, he attempts to use Christianity as a means of bringing order to society. In a letter issued to the peoples of the eastern empire in 324, Christianity is described as "the Law," the basis of a regulated way of life under the auspices of a single god.[36] Constantine did make divorce more difficult, requiring stated offences to be given as a reason, and he included infanticide in a law on murder. He banned crucifixion and public branding (and he may have banned sacrifices, although there is some scholarly dispute about this),[37] but in many other of his laws he maintained a traditional Roman brutality—he shows none of the studied saintliness of the more devout medieval kings of Europe, for example. If a free woman had a sexual relationship with a male slave, both were to die, the slave by being burnt alive. Slaves who were found to be an accessory to the seduction of a young girl were to have molten metal poured down their throats. Christians played very little part in Constantine's administration, and the army remained pagan. Nor did Constantine show any interest in creating a society of greater social equality, being concerned rather to maintain traditional distinctions. He enlarged, rather than diminished, the senatorial order, and at Constantinople, his "new Rome," he created a second Senate as well as according the city one of the empire's two consuls. Constantine's personal brutality was shown in a mysterious incident in which his second wife, Fausta, and Crispus, his son by his first wife, Minervina, were executed in Italy in 326. According to the pagan historian Zosimus (writing much later), Crispus was suspected of having an affair with Fausta, his stepmother. Crispus was disposed of, but Constantine's mother, Helena, took the death of her grandson so badly that to appease her Constantine had Fausta killed as well, drowned in an overheated bath. The event shocked non-Christians as much as it did Christians. One pagan source even suggests that it drew Constantine closer to Christianity because the Christians offered forgiveness for an offence no pagan would condone. It has also been suggested that Helena's famous expedition to the Holy Land was a penance demanded by the church for her part in the affair.[38]

The murders certainly overshadowed the visit to Rome that Constantine made in 326 as part of the celebrations to mark the completion of his first twenty years in power. Quite apart from the tensions caused by the death of his son and his wife, Constantine found it difficult to know which ceremonies to attend. He had retained the ancient title of *pontifex maximus,* the head of the priesthood, but, under pressure from Bishop Ossius of Cordoba, who appears to have acted as his ecclesiastical adviser, it is said that he refused to carry out the traditional sacrifices on behalf of the army on the Capitoline Hill and that many were offended. Inside the city his benefactions were conventional ones. He completed a great basilica begun by Maxentius on the edge of the Forum and graced it with an enormous statue of himself, the head of which survives in the Palazzo dei Conservatori on the Capitoline Hill in Rome. The impressive ruins of the basilica also stand. He also rebuilt parts of the Circus Maximus, the great hippodrome that ran alongside the Palatine Hill. His sensitivity to the pagan traditions of Rome was shown by the way in which he directed his patronage to the Christian communities of the city. The earliest Christian churches were confined to sites outside or on the edge of the city (the churches of St. John Lateran [originally dedicated to Christ the Redeemer] and St. Peter's on the Vatican Hill), and, although their interiors were extraordinarily opulent, their exteriors appear to have been kept deliberately plain so as to avoid offending pagans.

It is understandable, however, that with his personal position in Rome so insecure, Constantine would have looked elsewhere for a city in which to make his centre of government. Rome had, of course, the

additional disadvantage of being far from the empire's borders and use-
less as a base for defending the empire. Constantine might have
expanded one of the major cities of the north, Trier, Milan or Nicomedia, all suitable for the defence of the northern borders, but he wanted to
craft a new foundation to celebrate his own glory. He chose an ancient
Greek city, Byzantium, which occupied a stunning and well-defended
site overlooking the southern end of the Bosphorus and had an important strategic position on the main routes between east and west. Byzantium had been enlarged by the Roman emperor Septimius Severus in the
190s, but it remained small enough to be completely replanned.

As its name suggests, Constantinople was Constantine's city.[39] This is
an important point because there has been considerable debate over
whether Constantinople was founded as a Christian city or not. The issue
arose because of Eusebius' misleading claim, in his attempt to assert the
Christian commitment of Constantine, that Constantinople was always
wholly Christian and without a single pagan temple. For its founder this
was not relevant; this was the city of Constantine, not of Christ, and
Constantine may even have deliberately chosen a city without a Christian
history to stress the point. Many elements of the foundation were traditional. According to the fifth-century historian Philostorgios, Constantine traced the line of the future walls of the city with a spear just as a
Greek founder would have done. Pagan statues and monuments were
brought from all over the empire to grace the public spaces, and the hippodrome, where the finest were grouped, appears to have been modelled
on the Circus Maximus in Rome. Jerome tells of whole cities being
stripped of monuments—among those known to have been taken by
Constantine were the column commemorating the Greek victory over the
Persians in 479 B.C. from Delphi (the base survives today in Istanbul),
statues of Apollo, one of them possibly also from Delphi, and of the
Muses from Mount Helicon in Boeotia. Eusebius is deeply embarrassed
by these pagan imports, and he resorts to suggesting that Constantine
used them as "toys for the laughter and amusement of the spectators,"
but there is no evidence for this and, rather, ample evidence that many
pagan statues remained in place as respected monuments for centuries to
come. This was simply another example of Constantine using pagan
symbolism when it suited his purpose.[40]

In fact, Constantine recognized that Byzantium's protecting goddesses had to be respected. The most ancient of these was Rhea, the
mother of the Olympian gods. Another important deity was Tyche, the

personification of good fortune, who was believed to be able to protect and bring prosperity to cities. Constantine honoured them both with new temples. His most ambitious plans, however, were to create a central complex of forum, hippodrome and imperial palace as a setting for his own majesty. The hippodrome (enlarged from one built by Severus) had an imperial box placed halfway along its length that could be entered directly from the palace. The emperor and his successors were able to stage-manage their own imperial displays. In the circular forum, on one of the highest hills of the city, Constantine erected a great porphyry column twenty-five metres high and arranged for it to be crowned by a gold statue of himself; the column still stands, in battered form, today. Here the emperor was again associated with the sun, whose rays spread from the statue's head.[41] There was another forum built in honour of Constantine's mother, Helena (whose status appears to have been elevated after the death of Crispus and Fausta), and a major basilica in which the newly created Senate would meet.

All this was dedicated on a great day of celebration in May 330, as much a celebration of Constantine as of his city. A gold coin was struck to mark the occasion, and it showed Constantine gazing upwards in a pose made famous by Alexander the Great. Around his head ran an opulent diadem. The day's ceremonies began in the presence of Constantine with the lifting of the great gold statue of the emperor onto its column. Dressed in magnificent robes and wearing a diadem encrusted in jewels, Constantine then processed to the imperial box. Among the events that followed one stood out: the arrival in the hippodrome of a golden chariot carrying a gilded statue of the emperor. The statue held a smaller figure of Tyche. For the next 200 years, the ritual drawing of the statue and chariot through the hippodrome was to be re-enacted on the anniversary of the dedication. (The gilded horses, which stood with the chariot between ceremonies and said to be already ancient at the time of the ceremony, may well be the same ones which the Venetians plundered for St. Mark's when they sacked the city in 1204.)[42]

Where did Christianity fit into all this? In the original celebrations hardly at all. Space was, however, reserved in the centre of the city for churches, but their titles—*Hagia Sophia*, Holy Wisdom, *Hagia Eirene*, Holy Peace, and *Hagia Dynamis*, Holy Power—suggest that Constantine was once again deliberately using formulas that were as acceptable to the pagan world as to the Christian. According to Eusebius, statues of the Good Shepherd were erected on fountains in the city. "The Good

Shepherd," like the sun, was a symbol used by both pagans and Christians.[43] It was keeping the consensus which was important: the only saints honoured with churches were local martyrs, and it was not until the end of the century that Constantinople could be seen as a fully Christian city.

In April 337 Constantine realized he was dying. Only then did he allow himself to be baptized. In the last weeks of his life (he died on May 22) he discarded the imperial purple and dressed himself in the white of the newly baptized Christian. He had already built his final resting place within Constantinople, and it provided an apt testimonial to how he saw himself in relation to the Christian God. He was buried in a circular mausoleum, his tomb lying under the central dome. Placed around the tomb were twelve sepulchres—each the symbolic burial place of one of the original Apostles; Constantine was to be the thirteenth. To orthodox Christians this might seem blasphemous, but it is consistent with Constantine's perception of himself in relation to the "supreme deity." After all, as Constantine had once told a meeting of bishops: "You are bishops of those within the church, but I am perhaps a bishop appointed by God over those outside."[44] His position and his strategy required that he keep his distance from the institutional church. It is remarkable that there is no evidence that Constantine ever attended a church service. (The records suggest that bishops were summoned to attend him in his palaces.) After his death his sons issued a coin to commemorate their own *consecratio*. On one side it bore Constantine's veiled head and an inscription, "The deified Constantine, father of the Augusti"; on the other Constantine is seen ascending to heaven in a chariot with God's hand reaching out to welcome him, a portrayal similar to those of his pagan predecessors.[45] His links to the traditions of pagan Rome were preserved to the last.

Constantine's impact on the empire was dramatic, not least through his reassertion of the empire as a single political unity under one emperor. He had allowed Christianity to consolidate itself within his empire in a way that would not have seemed possible thirty years before, and he had achieved the remarkable feat of doing this without alienating those "pagans" drawn to monotheism, as many now were. However, by bringing Christianity so firmly under the control of the state, even to the extent of attempting to formulate its doctrine at Nicaea, Constantine was severing the traditional church from its roots. A host of new tensions—over the nature of Christian authority and where it lay, the appropriate use of material wealth for Christians now the subject of state patronage, the basis on which doctrine rested (the scriptures or imperially controlled councils)—had been created. Even today, 1,600 years later, many of them have not been resolved.

One of the most important of Constantine's legacies was the creation of a relationship between Christianity and war. Constantine was a brilliant and effective soldier, and he associated his continuing success with the support of the Christian God. Once he had used the victory at the Milvian Bridge as a platform for the granting of toleration to Christians, each new victory strengthened the link. Eusebius makes the point succinctly, describing him as

> the only Conqueror among the Emperors of all time to remain Irresistible and Unconquered, Ever-conquering and always brilliant with triumphs over enemies, so great an Emperor . . . so God beloved and Thrice blessed . . . that with utter ease he governed more nations than those before him, and kept his dominion unimpaired to the very end.[46]

In his *Ecclesiastical History*, Eusebius refers to Constantine as "God's Commander-in-Chief." So a new element enters the Christian tradition. When the papacy and the Roman Catholic Church came under sustained attack for the first time in the Reformation, the Medici pope Leo X (pope 1513–21) ordered a great room to be built in the Vatican. Known as the Sala di Constantino, it had an unashamedly propagandist purpose. Its frescoes, by Raphael, show the early popes from Peter onwards and then, in four great scenes, the achievement of Constantine. One fresco shows the vision of the cross, another the battle of the Milvian Bridge itself. Leo associated himself with the victory. The *palle* from the Medici coat of arms are on Constantine's tent, and lions, a reference to Leo's name, are also found on the tent, with another depicted on a standard. At a moment of crisis and confrontation, this was the event the pope chose to highlight. As late as 1956 Pope Pius XII refused the right of conscientious objection, acknowledging in effect the overriding power of the state. "A Catholic may not appeal to his conscience as grounds for refusing to serve and fulfill duties fixed by law."[47] Constantine would have approved.

However, the problem of how to present Jesus, the man of peace, in this new Christian world, persisted. The ultimate response was to transform him, quite explicitly, into a man of war. By the 370s Ambrose, bishop of Milan, is able to state in his *De Fide* that "the army is led not by military eagles or the flight of birds but by your name, Lord Jesus, and Your Worship."[48] In the Archiepiscopal Chapel in Ravenna (c. 500), Jesus is shown dressed as a Roman soldier trampling a lion and an adder beneath his feet. There is, of course, no New Testament source for the presentation of Christ as a soldier (other than one in the Book of Revelation, where a warrior for justice [often assumed to be Christ] appears from heaven on a white horse with "a sharp sword to strike the pagans with" [19:11–16]), and, as has already been suggested, a military image was particularly inappropriate when it is remembered that Jesus was crucified by Roman soldiers as an enemy of the empire. The mosaicist had to draw on the more appropriate models offered in abundance by the Old Testament, as in Psalm 91:13, where the supplicant is promised that with the help of God he will survive battle and "tread on lion and adder, trample on savage lions and dragons." This extraordinary transformation of Jesus' role is a mark of the extent to which Constantine forced Christianity into new channels. (A step further is taken when, on the eleventh-century bronze doors of San Zeno Maggiore in Verona, Christ is shown being nailed to the cross by Jews rather than by soldiers.)

This chapter has viewed Constantine as an emperor who in traditional Roman terms was one of the most successful the empire had yet seen. The achievements of Diocletian in rallying and refocusing the empire after the catastrophes of the third century were remarkable enough, but under Constantine Diocletian's reforms had been consolidated and the empire had been reunited under a single emperor who had survived in power longer than any since Augustus. Moreover, the empire's borders had been successfully defended and even, in Dacia, extended. None of this could have been achieved if Constantine had not been supremely self-confident, able and brutal when he needed to be. This was not a man who felt any need to compromise or be diverted from his primary commitment to the maintenance of his own position as emperor and to the defence of the empire. Yet, remarkably, Constantine also sustained religious toleration to a degree unknown before him. The question was whether the newly enriched and privileged Christian communities would settle happily under state power or whether they would unsettle it by continued dissension.

# 12

# "BUT WHAT I WISH, THAT MUST BE THE CANON"[1]

## Emperors and the Making of Christian Doctrine

On the death of Constantine I in 337, Constantine's three surviving sons, Constantine II, Constans and Constantius, eliminated other members of their family and divided the empire between them. Constantine II was killed in 340 when he tried to invade Constans' territory. Constans was assassinated in a palace coup in 350 led by one Magnentius, who was in his turn defeated by Constantius in a debilitating battle at Mursa in Gaul in 351. Constantius was now the sole ruler of the whole empire and remained so until his death in 361. He is known as Constantius II, with his grandfather becoming Constantius I.[2]

This was a particularly unsettled time for the church as it adapted itself to its new role as a religion sponsored by the empire. The immediate challenge for the new emperors, as it had been for Constantine, was to bring some form of order to the Christian communities, above all by establishing and, if necessary, imposing a doctrine that defined the natures of God and Jesus and the relationship between them. It was not only a matter of good order. Once Constantine had provided tax exemptions for Christian clergy, eventually including exemptions for church lands, it became imperative to tighten up the definition of "Christian." As Constantine had put it in a law of 326, "The benefits that have been granted in consideration of religion must benefit only the adherents of the Catholic [e.g., 'correct'] faith. It is our will, moreover, that heretics and schismatics shall not only be alien to those privileges but shall be bound and subjected to various compulsory public services." The definition of "Catholicism" and heresy took on a new urgency for the state.

This explains why the emperors came to play such a large part in the determining of doctrine, although their roles varied: some had personal convictions to impose, others were more concerned to find formulations of doctrine around which consensus could be built. By the end of the century emperors were imposing doctrinal solutions that were backed by imperial edicts.

The issue was a live one because Nicaea had solved nothing. The "startling innovations"[3] proclaimed by Constantine at the council, in particular the final declaration that Jesus was *homoousios* (of the same substance) as the Father, proved easy to attack on the grounds that they both offended the tradition of seeing Jesus in some way as subordinate to his Father and used terminology that was nowhere to be found in scripture. As we have seen, the council's formula was largely ignored. Yet how was an alternative to be found around which the churches could be gathered? Given the variety of sources and influences on the making of Christian doctrine—scripture, Greek philosophy, tradition, the Nicene Creed and the works of the Church Fathers—any coherent solutions seemed impossible, and the debates now entered a period of confusion. Personal rivalries became so hopelessly entangled with theological wranglings that it is hard to separate them. Accusations of heresy, deceit and fraud flew across the empire.

The Gospels, especially those of Matthew, Mark and Luke, seemed to support a subordinationist interpretation, but none of them treated the issue unambiguously (because no one perceived it as an issue when they were written), and in the Latin-speaking west there were as yet no reliable texts of the scriptures in any case. For the Old Testament, western theologians relied on weak Latin translations, themselves taken from the uneven Greek translations of the original Hebrew and Aramaic on which the eastern churches relied. (Very few Christians could read Hebrew, rendering the original scriptures beyond their grasp.) There were also immense problems in making use of Greek philosophy, the only language sophisticated enough for such debates, as the key terms— such as *ousia, homoousios, hypostasis* and *logos*—had all been developed in non-Christian contexts (and even in them had unstable meanings). They could not easily be reformulated to deal with specific Christian issues such as the precise nature of Jesus and his relationship with God the Father.[4] Formulating these concepts in two languages, Latin and Greek, when there was no strict equivalence between them further complicated the situation. Latin theologians translated the Greek *ousia* as *substantia,* but the Greeks translated *substantia* as *hypostasis,* "personality." So when the Latins talked of *una substantia,* in the sense of one divine substance (within which might be found the distinct personalities of the Trinity), it appeared in Greek as if they were affirming that there was only one *hypostasis* for the three persons of the Trinity, in effect preaching what was to become heresy.[5]

Constantius was nevertheless determined to find a workable formula; he appreciated that it would need to include some element of subordinationism and thus implicitly a rejection of Nicaea. A number of meetings of small groups of eastern bishops who were sympathetic to this approach hammered out some possible creeds (most originated in the imperial city of Sirmium in the Balkans and are known as the Sirmium Creeds—there are four in all). They were prepared to accept Jesus the Son as divine (as was Arius himself), but they all agreed that there could be no mention of the Nicene *homoousios*—given that the word was never found in scripture, it should be abandoned. One attack captures the flavour of the debate in describing the term *homoousios* as "hated and detestable, a distorted and perverse profession which is scorned and rejected as a diabolical instrument and doctrine of demons."[6] The word substituted for *homoousios* was much less charged, *homoios,* "like." The Son was thus declared to be "God from God; like [*homoios*] the Father who begat him" and "like the Father in all things," to which was later added "just as the Holy Scriptures say and teach," thus reaffirming the importance of the scriptures, seemingly bypassed by Constantine at Nicaea, to the debate. The vexed question of how the Son came into being was sidestepped by a declaration of ignorance. "The Father alone knows how he begot his Son, and the Son how he was begotten by the Father," as the First Creed of Sirmium tactfully put it.[7]

The breadth of these "Homoean" creeds offered the hope that a wider spectrum of opinion could accept them so that the Constantinian policy of consensus could be sustained. Yet for many this breadth was also their weakness. The use of the word "like" was to many simply blurring the issue. "The kingdom of God is 'like' a grain of mustard seed," one witty bishop who knew his parables remarked, "but not much."[8] "*Homoios,*" said another, "was a . . . figure seeming to look in the direction of all who passed by, a boot fitting either foot, a winnowing with every wind."[9] A wide variety of alternative formulas were championed in these years. In 358 Bishop Basil of Ancyra and a small group of bishops proposed the formula *homoiousios,* "of similar substance," rather than the Nicene *homoousios,* "of identical substance." These shifts in terminology and the intense debates which they provoked earned ridicule from Edward Gibbon in his *Decline and Fall of the Roman Empire,* who wrote sarcastically of "furious contests over a single diphthong." Others, following Arius, believed that the "unlikeness" of Father and Son should be stressed—the Son was a separate creation and totally distinct from the Father. Constantius eventually accepted the Fourth Creed of Sirmium, the so-called Dated Creed, of 359, as a rallying ground for consensus. The creed was awkwardly phrased. Jesus was declared

> one only begotten Son of God who before all ages and before all beginning and before all conceivable time and before all comprehensible substance was begotten impassibly from God, through whom the ages were set up and all things came into existence, begotten as only begotten, sole from the sole father, like to the Father who begot him, according to the Scriptures, whose generation nobody understands except the Father who begot him.

It ended:

> . . . the word *ousia* because it was naively inserted by the Fathers, though not familiar to the masses, caused disturbance, and because the Scriptures do not contain it, we have decided that it should be removed and there should be absolutely no mention of *ousia* for the future . . . but we declare that the Son is like (*homoios*) the Father, as also the Holy Scriptures declare and teach.[10]

Constantius' aim was to establish this cumbersome creed at two councils, one meeting in the western empire at Ariminum (modern Rimini) in the spring of 360 and the other planned for the autumn of the same year at Seleucia in the east.[11] Things did not go smoothly. The Ariminum council met and proved highly suspicious of this "eastern" creed. Even though there had been virtually no western representation at Nicaea, the western bishops seemed happier with the straightforward monotheism of the Nicene formula. It was close to the idea, always strong in the west even if not formulated with any precision, that Father and Son shared a divinity. Having revived the Nicene Creed, a delegation of ten bishops, together with a group representing the minority anti-Nicene view, set off to Thrace to put their views to Constantius. The emperor was away on campaign, but after discussions with eastern bishops the delegates changed their minds and persuaded a reconvened Ariminum council that they should accept the Dated Creed, possibly also arguing that they would be out of step with the eastern bishops if they did not.[12] There is some evidence that a consensus of the eastern bishops at Seleucia was then achieved by persuading them not to be out of step with what the western bishops had agreed!

The consensus that was achieved was hardly a stable one, but it was real enough for Constantius to call a joint council in 360 at Constantinople with delegations from each of the two earlier councils, at which he pushed through the Dated Creed (with additions that also proscribed the word *hypostasis* and declared all other earlier creeds heretical). It was promulgated through the empire in an imperial edict. Whatever the methods by which it had been achieved, the Dated Creed offered hope that the majority of Christian communities would accept it.

This was, however, to prove far from the end of the story. The acceptance of the Dated Creed clearly depended on consistent support from the emperors, but this could be achieved only if they were Christian and ready to enforce the Homoean formula that the Council of Constantinople had endorsed. Constantius' successor was his cousin Julian, the son of one of his father's half-brothers, who was not even Christian. Julian's survival to manhood was in itself remarkable, in that most of his family had been eliminated by Constantine's three sons. His father and seven immediate members of his family were executed in 337, when Julian was only six. His teenage years had been spent with his half-brother Gallus on a remote estate in Asia Minor, but Gallus himself was executed by Constantius in 354. Then Constantius, isolated and desperate to strengthen his legitimacy, appointed Julian as a Caesar with responsibility for the imperial troops in northern Gaul. Julian proved to be a fine general and had soon restored order to the borders. In 360 his troops acclaimed him as Augustus, to the fury of Constantius, who hurried back from the Persian border to confront him. When Constantius died unexpectedly in 361, Julian found himself sole emperor.[13]

Julian knew Christianity well—he had been brought up as a Christian and served as a lector—but he had been dismayed by the vicious infighting he saw around him. "Experience had taught him that no wild beasts are so dangerous to man as Christians are to one another," wrote Ammianus Marcellinus, who went on to suggest that Julian believed that the Christians left to themselves would simply tear each other apart.[14] The roots of Julian's distaste for Christianity may well lie in the brutal treatment of his close relations by Christian emperors. In any case, once he had buried Constantius with suitable Christian piety, Julian adopted "paganism," proclaiming that the very fact that he had come to power showed that the traditional gods were on his side.[15] Summoning the bishops, he ordered them "to allow every man to practise his belief boldly without hindrance." The clergy lost all their exemptions, and in 362 they were forbidden to teach rhetoric or grammar. It was absurd, declared Julian, for Christians to teach classical culture while at the same time pouring scorn on classical religion—if they wished to teach, they should confine themselves to teaching the Gospels in their churches.

Julian was a throwback, a philosopher emperor. For Julian, philosophy did not involve a withdrawal from the world (though he had spent most of the 350s as a student in Athens and other cities) but provided the underpinning for wise and moderate rule. His inspiration was the emperor Marcus Aurelius. However, although Julian left more writings than any other emperor, untangling his religious and philosophical beliefs from them has proved enormously difficult. Like many educated pagans, he drew on a variety of beliefs and movements (although Neoplatonism was probably the most significant) and combined mysticism with rationalism, particularly in his defence of traditional Greek secular learning.[16] In his *Contra Galilaeos* (*Against the Galileans*), written in 362–63, Julian challenges what he sees as the irrational nature of Christian belief. The work draws heavily on conventional pagan criticisms of Christianity, but it is enhanced by Julian's own knowledge of the scriptures, which enabled him to highlight their apparent contradictions. Only John among the Gospel writers accepts the divinity of Jesus; why did not all do so if he was truly a god? The so-called prophecies of Christ's coming in the Old Testament are based on misinterpretations of the texts—there is, for instance, no unequivocal prophecy of the virgin birth. Christian teachings about God, especially those which draw on the all-too-"human" Old Testament God with his sole commitment to the Jews, lack the sophistication of pagan conceptions of the divine.

Why did God create Eve if she was going to thwart his plans for creation? Why did he deprive Adam and Eve of the knowledge of good and evil? Turning to Paul, Julian questions why God neglected most of humanity for thousands of years but then arrived to preach to a small tribe in Galilee. Why were the Greeks not also favoured by his presence if he was, as Paul argues, a universal God? Do not the latest bitter arguments over Christian doctrine deprive Christians of their claim to have found the truth? In contrast, Julian argues, the Greeks have achieved superiority in every area of knowledge; in *Contra Galilaeos* he gives examples from law, mathematics, medicine, astronomy and philosophy as well as theology.

*Contra Galilaeos* also includes a sophisticated defence of the traditional deities. While Julian was happy to accept, along, as we have seen, with many pagans, that there was a supreme god, he saw no reason why that god should not preside over lesser deities. He proposed an argument, implicit in the nature of Roman government but rarely stated (note, however, Constantine's Edict of Toleration of 313), that an acceptance of different manifestations of God was essential to a flourishing empire.

> Since in the father all things are complete and all things are one, while in the separate deities one quality or another predominates, therefore Ares rules over the warlike nations, Athene over those that are wise as well as warlike, Hermes over those who are more shrewd than adventurous; and in short the nations over which the gods preside follow each the essential character of their proper god.[17]

Surely, Julian continues, a caring "supreme god" would want to encourage diversity and be happy to allow lesser gods to oversee a variety of nations and cultures. He even managed to find some biblical texts to support his argument. While Julian had no particular love of Judaism, being alienated by the exclusivity of its God, he accepted the logic of his position to put in hand the rebuilding of the Temple in Jerusalem. His motives, however, may primarily have been to reclaim Jerusalem from the Christians while contradicting Jesus' assertion that the destruction of the Temple would be permanent.

Julian's was a pointed challenge and is evidence of the extent to which Christians, despite their adoption of elements of Platonism, still failed to convince the pagan philosophers. However, Julian's own eclectic beliefs did not arouse enthusiasm either. In many ways he was traditional, a fervent believer in prophecy who regularly consulted oracles. He reintroduced blood sacrifices as part of his enthusiasm for the old gods but by doing so offended the more sophisticated pagans. He thus missed the opportunity to build an anti-Christian power base, although by this stage Christians had somehow to be accommodated. Naturally, the Christians themselves were furious with his policies, especially as these involved the withdrawal of their lucrative tax exemptions. There was great rejoicing when a fire brought the reconstruction of the Temple in Jerusalem to a halt ("proving" to Christians that Jesus had indeed been right in saying the destruction of the Temple would be permanent).[18] Nor did Julian's military success, so vital to the maintenance of imperial power, last. A campaign against Sassanid Persia ran into difficulties, and Julian himself was killed, by a spear throw by an unknown assailant, in 363. His reign had lasted only eighteen months.

With Julian's death the house of Constantine came to an end. The army in the east acclaimed a staff officer, Jovian, as emperor, but he died eight months later, shortly after ceding large areas of the eastern empire to the Sassanids. The next emperor, Valentinian (364–75), a tough if tempestuous army officer, was more successful.[19] Indeed, Valentinian has been seen as the last of the great Roman emperors; it was during his reign that the northern borders were effectively defended for the last time. He attempted to establish a dynasty. His brother Valens was appointed co-emperor in the east and his son Gratian, only eight at the time, became a co-emperor in 367. When Valentinian died in 375, Valens and Gratian remained as co-emperors, but the army also proclaimed Valentinian II, Valentinian's son by his second marriage, as Augustus.

Then, in 378, came disaster. The pressures on Rome's borders had been unremitting for decades, but following the reconstruction of the armies under Diocletian and Constantine they had been contained. Now a new people, the Huns, were on the move westwards. The Goths were driven before them, and in 378 a mass of refugees poured across the Danube. Valens hoped to recruit them as mercenaries for the overstretched Roman armies, but the situation was hopelessly mishandled by unscrupulous Roman officers, and the Goths began rampaging across Thrace.[20] Confronted by Valens and the elite of the Roman army at Adrianople in August, the Goths stunned the empire by achieving a crushing victory. Valens and some 10,000 of his men were killed. The battle of Adrianople has often been seen as the moment when the Roman empire finally lost the initiative against the "barbarians." Gratian hastily called on an experienced general, Theodosius, to become his fellow Augustus, but Theodosius was unable to avoid permitting the Goths to settle within the empire, ostensibly as allies to the Romans, but in reality, as it turned out, as a very substantial body of armed men with no real allegiance to Rome. In 383 the young Gratian was murdered by his own troops, forcing Valentinian II, aged twelve and still in the shadow of his formidable mother, Justina, to emerge as emperor in the west in his own right.

All these emperors were Christian, but their policies towards the churches differed. In the west Valentinian I chose to stand back from the debates. What mattered above all in a troubled empire was good order, and, following Constantine's lead, Valentinian was tolerant of diversity, both within Christianity and of paganism. "He took a neutral position between opposing faiths, and never troubled anyone by ordering him to adopt this or that mode of 'worship,' " according to Ammianus Marcellinus.[21] It was within this atmosphere of tolerance that the debate over Father and Son revived. As we have seen, the west had always been more sympathetic to a monotheistic formula in which they were of equal divinity, and there remained considerable resentment of Constantius' tactics at Ariminum. In the east, by contrast, there had been much less sympathy for Nicaea, but in the 350s for the first time an eastern bishop, Athanasius of Alexandria, attempted to provide a defence of the Nicene formula.

We have already met Athanasius as a determined anti-Arian. "He could," writes John Rist, "scent Arianism like a police dog sniffing out drugs."[22] His professional career was one of some turmoil. Appointed bishop in 428, he is known, from Egyptian papyri, to have enforced his authority with violence and to have been challenged on his right to hold his see.[23] On no less than five occasions, and for a total of fifteen of the forty-five years he was bishop, he was in exile, sent there by emperors (including, as we have seen, Constantine, who took exception to his anti-Arian intransigence) and his fellow bishops. It is impossible to establish the extent to which, in such troubled times, he was personally responsible, but the sources do suggest that his tendency towards violence and intimidation of opponents was partly to blame for his troubled career. On the other hand, it is hard to deny the courage and resolution with which he faced his ordeals.

It is as the champion of the shared and equal divinity of the Father and Son that Athanasius' theological reputation rests. In other words, he denied any separate creation of the Son: Jesus was part of the Godhead from all eternity. However, for many years Athanasius, like his fellow theologians, avoided using the charged word *homoousios* to describe the relationship, and it does not appear in his work until about 356 (in what appears to have been the first favourable use of the term for two decades).[24]

Given the term's association with Nicaea, its very use was enough to connect Athanasius with the Nicene Creed and thus to elevate his status into that of a revered theologian when the creed was eventually declared orthodox. (He also wrote the first full treatise on the Holy Spirit.) Christ as *logos* is incarnated because the human race is sunk in sin and cannot be left to suffer without redemption. So the *logos* becomes actively interventionist, appearing on earth as Jesus.[25] However, Athanasius got into enormous difficulties (as, it should be stressed, did most theologians) when he tried to make sense of a Jesus who is divine yet human. He created an elaborate distinction between the human body of Jesus, which appears to suffer, as when on the cross, and the divine *logos*, which is somehow inside the human body but does not suffer. So, for instance, the mind of Jesus, which he allocated to the *logos* rather than to his body, could not feel anything and was not even subject to moral dilemmas. "He was not subject to moral law, he did not weigh two choices, preferring one, rejecting another," as Athanasius put it. This goes as far as suggesting that Jesus lacked free will.[26]

Secure in his own beliefs, Athanasius let loose his invective on the Arians. His tactics were unscrupulous, and he brought a new level of intolerance into church politics. It is, Athanasius argued, the devil who inspires the "Arian" use of scripture in their cause, while any attempt by "Arians" to quote earlier theologians in their support is a slander on those theologians. Sometimes the Arians are described as no better than Jews; at others they are indistinguishable from pagans. This was clearly caricature, but unfortunately it was caricature that became embedded in the Christian tradition when the anti-Arian Nicene Creed became orthodox. Athanasius' elevation as a champion of orthodoxy had the unfortunate effect of legitimizing such intolerant invective.

Furthermore, in order to justify the incarnation, Athanasius provided a definition of man as inherently sinful. While a hundred years before Origen had looked optimistically at the human condition—"the universe is cared for by God in accordance with the conditions of the free will of each man, and . . . as far as possible it is always being led on to be better"; in other words, man is free to improve himself in a world which is itself getting "better," with, as we have seen, a final state of forgiveness of all—Athanasius was much more pessimistic. Men were inherently disobedient and "the cause of their own corruption in death." Things were not getting better but worse. Not satisfied with the sin of Adam, men "again filled themselves with other evils, progressing still further in shamefulness and outdoing themselves in impiety." These were important and enduring shifts in perspective, and they contrast strongly with the earlier optimism of Greek thinking.[27]

In the west the Nicene cause was furthered by a number of formidable protagonists, of whom Hilary of Poitiers was the most celebrated.[28] In 355 Hilary had been deprived of his see in Gaul by Constantius for his pro-Nicene views, but he had refused to be silenced and even demanded of Constantius that he be allowed to attend the Council of Constantinople in 360 to expound the Nicene cause. Rebuffed, he returned to Gaul and took advantage of the emergence of Julian to denounce Constantius as anti-Christ. He developed his ideas in De Trinitate, probably the first full defence in Latin (Athanasius wrote only in Greek) of the doctrine of God the Father, the Son and Holy Spirit as a single Godhead. Together with an Italian bishop, Eusebius of Vercelli, and with the support of the bishops of Rome, he recruited a large party of pro-Nicene bishops. Their cause was later to be energetically endorsed by the formidable Ambrose in Milan, whose own work (in Latin) in support of the Nicene Creed, De Fide, was written between 379 and 381.

So the struggle between the opposing factions raged on. The view that the Godhead was essentially unitary, that Jesus as the Son was simply a way in which God could show himself (during the Incarnation, for instance), a view associated with the Roman Sabellius in the early third century and endorsed in the fourth century by Marcellus of Ancyra, gained little support. The challenge for those who wished to revive the Nicene formula was to find a means of differentiating the Father and the Son that did not compromise their sharing of the same substance. It was the so-called Cappadocian Fathers, Basil of Caesarea (d. 379) and his brother Gregory of Nyssa (d. c. 395), together with another Gregory, of

Nazianzus (d. 390), who came up with a solution that eventually was to be accepted. There is one Godhead, of uniform substance, *ousia* (in other words, the Cappadocians accepted the *homoousios*), but the Godhead has three distinct *hypostaseis,* or personalities.[29]

The Cappadocian Fathers are an attractive trio. All were steeped in classical philosophy, Gregory of Nazianzus declaring that Athens, where he and Basil had studied, was "a city truly of gold and the patroness of all that is good."[30] Despite some disputes between themselves over doctrine, they had a mutual affection, and they drew into their circle Basil's sister Macrina, whom they revered for her saintliness and her own intellectual qualities. Basil, a fine administrator, is remembered for his monastic and charitable foundations, Gregory of Nazianzus for his impressive oratory (his funeral oration for Basil is often seen as one of the great speeches of late antiquity, fully equal to those of the fourth-century B.C. Athenian orator Demosthenes), and Gregory of Nyssa for his fertile mind. Their works, orations and letters present a fascinating example of the way in which classical philosophy could be yoked to Christian theology to formulate doctrine. In his important study *Christianity and Classical Culture,* Jaroslav Pelikan shows how they used a variety of arguments from both Christian and Greek culture to support and develop what was to become the Nicene orthodoxy.[31]

Although this remains a matter of scholarly dispute, Basil's inspiration for the terminology of the Trinity appears to have been the Neoplatonist philosopher Plotinus. As we have seen, Plotinus had proposed three entities in his metaphysical system: "the One"; *nous,* or Intellect, which presents the Platonic Forms to the material world; and the World-Soul. In his *Enneads,* published early in the fourth century, parts of which Basil of Caesarea is known to have studied in detail, Plotinus had argued that each one of these three entities had a distinct *hypostasis,* or personality, although they also shared a likeness, "as light is from the sun" ("the *ousia* of the divine extends to the [three] *hypostaseis,* [namely] the supreme god, the *nous,* the world soul"). As we have noted, Plotinus even used the word *homoousios* to describe the relationship of identity between the three. Here was "a vocabulary and a framework of ideas," as Henry Chadwick puts it, that was used by the Cappadocians to describe Jesus the Son as an integral part of a single Godhead but with a distinct personality, *hypostasis,* within it.[32]

The Cappadocians went further, incorporating the Holy Spirit as a third person of a Trinity, as part of the single Godhead but with a distinct *hypostasis*. The earliest treatise that presents the Spirit as a distinct personality is that by Athanasius dating from 350. The inclusion of the Holy Spirit satisfied those who wished to believe that God was, in some form, still actively involved in the world. The three are, it was argued, equal in status but differ in their origins. God always was, the Son was "begotten" from God the Father, and the Spirit "proceeded" in some way from the Father.[33]

Thus Greek philosophical terms, in themselves complex, were adapted and adopted to produce a solution that allowed the Nicene formula to be reasserted and the Holy Spirit integrated into the Trinity without reverting to Sabellianism. The doctrine of the Trinity is embedded so deeply in the Christian tradition that it is easy to forget how precarious was its birth. To the Cappadocians, in fact, it seems to have been a compromise formula. Within Christianity they had to find a middle path between the condemned Arianism and Sabellianism. In a wider world, the doctrine of the Trinity stood between the Jewish conception of a monotheistic God, in whose worship Jesus and the Holy Spirit had no place, and Greek polytheism that had no difficulty in accepting Jesus and the Spirit as lesser divinities. Gregory of Nyssa suggested: "It is as if the number of the Three were remedy in the case of those who are in error as to the One [i.e., the Jews], and the assertion of the unity for those whose belief are dispersed among a number of divinities [i.e., Greek polytheists]."[34]

One can understand why the concept of the Trinity was so difficult for many to accept. There is comparatively little in scripture that can be used to support the idea in its final form. The terminology of Father and Son used in the Synoptic Gospels, in fact, suggests a Jesus who saw himself as genuinely distinct from his "Father." This terminology could hardly be disregarded, and it needed some clever linguistic analysis by the Cappadocians to suggest that Father and Son could be equal and of the same substance as each other. It had, of course, to be accepted that Mary had carried the infant Jesus without providing any "substance" of her own. Although there was some scriptural backing for the concept of the Holy Spirit, it is not portrayed as enjoying a relationship with God the Father as powerful as that experienced by Jesus (as would have to be the case if the Spirit were to be accepted as an equal part of the Godhead). Basil had to fall back on "the unwritten tradition of the fathers" and "reason" to make his case. One particular challenge was that the only use in scripture of the term *hypostasis* in a context in which the Father was related to the

Son refers to the Son as "a perfect copy of his [God the Father's] *hyposta-sis*" (Hebrews 1:3), in other words *denying* the distinction between them which the Cappadocians had so painstakingly formulated.[35]

Then there was the issue of the eternal existence of the Son. The Nicenes had to deny that God could have "created" Jesus as his Son. Yet the only aspect of Jesus which gave him a distinct *hypostasis* from God the Father was the fact that he had been begotten as Son. Even if the terminology of "begetting" could be used instead of that of "creating," "begetting" still involved some kind of action that had to be fitted in without undermining the "eternal" status of the one begotten. As Gregory of Nyssa admitted, the concept of time could not be allowed to enter the process at all. So what did "begetting" mean in this context if there could not be a time when Jesus was not begotten? Athanasius too had got himself tangled up in this one. Then again, if the Spirit proceeded from the Father only, did that not assume some pre-eminence of the Father that the Son did not share with him? If so, could they then be said to be equal parts of the Godhead? In due course this problem was to lead Augustine to suggest that the Holy Spirit must process from both Father and Son, the so-called double procession, although this idea never travelled to the east. Further problems arose over reconciling the One of the Godhead with the Three of the Trinity. The Cappadocians drew on complex arguments based on the natural world. If there is one world made up of many different natures, fire, water, air and earth, as Basil put it, then the Trinity is the opposite, a oneness of nature but not of number.[36]

Was it acceptable, however, simply to manipulate pagan philosophical concepts in this way to create Christian truth?[37] Even Thomas Aquinas—himself highly ingenious in finding reasoned support for Christian doctrine—admitted that "it is impossible to arrive at a cognition of the Trinity of the Divine Persons by means of natural reason." It must, Thomas continues, be taken as a revelation from God.[38] When challenged themselves, the Cappadocians fell back on claims of the ultimate mystery of these things. As Gregory of Nazianzus retorted to one critic who had asked him to explain "proceeding": "You explain how it was impossible for the Father to be generated and I will give you a biological account of the Son's begetting and the Spirit's proceeding—and let us go mad the pair of us for prying into God's secrets!"[39] Basil argued that ultimately faith must be given primacy. Just because the *hypostaseis* could be counted singly, it did not mean that "an ignorant arithmetic could carry us away to the idea of a plurality of gods . . . Count if you must, but you must not by counting do damage to the faith!"[40] As Pelikan shrewdly remarks, the formulation of the doctrine of the Trinity did not lead to any greater knowledge of God. It just increased the extent to which he was unknowable![41]

The formulation of the doctrine of the Trinity did not mean, of course, that it was adopted as orthodoxy. Imperial support for the doctrine was essential, which made it necessary for the emperor to enforce the Nicene Creed. The Cappadocian Fathers developed their ideas in an imperial context that was still Homoean. Valens, emperor from 364 until his humiliating death at Adrianople in 378, was a keen supporter of Constantius' settlement of 360, and he actively promoted bishops in the Homoean cause. It was in this climate that large numbers of Goths were converted to Christianity. Although "a bishop of Gotha" had attended the Council of Nicaea, the first widespread conversion of the Goths came at the hands of the missionary Ulfila, a descendant of a Roman taken prisoner by the Goths. Ulfila was a remarkable man, fluent in Latin, Greek and Gothic and clearly an inspired missionary. He was consecrated bishop in 341 and worked with the Goths beyond the borders through the 340s. However, persecution drove him back into the empire with many of his flock, and Constantius gave him shelter. Ulfila supported the Homoean creed and in particular had great reverence for the scriptures, which he himself translated into Gothic (probably creating "the Gothic alphabet" in the process). The Goths' adherence to Homoean Christianity was consolidated when Valens insisted that Goths who entered the empire convert to his favoured formulation of Christianity; soon Homoean Christianity became inextricably associated with the ethnic identity of all the Gothic groups. They were to take it with them on their later migrations into the disintegrating empire.[42]

When Valens died, however, Homoean Christianity lost its main supporter. His successor, Theodosius, was pro-Nicene. Why is not clear. The traditional view is that his beliefs derived from his aristocratic Spanish background. In February 380, while in Thessalonika, which he was using as a base for his campaigns, he announced that the Nicene faith as supported by the bishops of Rome and Alexandria would be the orthodoxy and the alternatives would be punished as heresies. He was still not a baptized Christian, but his views and his determination to impose them appear to have been consolidated when he suffered a severe illness and was baptized by the staunchly pro-Nicene bishop of Thessalonika, Acholius.[43]

Theodosius then made for Constantinople. His arrival in late 380 was greeted with anger in a city where, in so far as tax exemption would be linked to the new orthodoxy, the majority of Christian communities stood to lose heavily through the imposition of a Nicene solution. Gregory of Nazianzus, who accompanied him, described his entry into Constantinople as being like that of a conqueror into a defeated city. In January 381 Theodosius issued an imperial decree declaring the doctrine of the Trinity orthodox and expelling Homoeans and Arians from their churches: "We now order that all churches are to be handed over to the bishops who profess Father, Son and Holy Spirit of a single majesty, of the same glory, of one splendour, who establish no difference by sacrilegious separation, but the order of the Trinity by recognizing the Persons and uniting the Godhead."[44] The Homoean bishop Demophilus was removed, and the emperor then called a council of pro-Nicene bishops (there were some 150 of them, "prelates of his own faith," as the fifth-century church historian Socrates put it, all of them from the east), whose first act was to install Gregory of Nazianzus as the new bishop of the city. The council appears to have been chaotic—at least according to Gregory, who spoke at one of its later sessions. However, it appears to have proceeded to affirm a creed based on Nicene principles. This affirmation remains one of the mysteries of the period. No record of it survives, and the first reference to a creed from this council comes only in 451, when it was read out twice at the Council of Chalcedon. It emerged then as an expanded form of the Nicene Creed, with the *homoousios* intact and the Holy Spirit referred to as "Lord and Life-giver who proceeds from the Father, who with the Father and Son is worshipped and glorified together." At Nicaea the Holy Spirit had been mentioned, but with no elaboration of "his" status. This is, of course, consistent with the Trinitarian formulation that had already been decreed by Theodosius in his edict, and in this sense the Council of Constantinople must have bowed to his influence, although the details of the wording suggest that earlier creeds were drawn on and that some parts of the creed were added at the council itself. At the end of the council a new imperial edict vigorously enforced the creed as orthodoxy.

> We authorise the followers of this law to assume the title
> of orthodox Christians; but as for the others, since in
> our judgment, they are foolish madmen, we decree that
> they shall be branded with the ignominious names of

heretics, and shall not presume to give to their conventi-
cles the names of churches. They will suffer in the first
place the chastisement of divine condemnation, and in
the second the punishment which our authority, in
accordance with the will of heaven, shall decide to
inflict.[45]

This council, together with the imperial edicts that accompanied it,
was the moment when the Nicene formula became part of the official
state religion (if only for the moment in the eastern empire). All those
Christians who differed from it—Homoeans, Homoiousians, Arians and
a host of other minor groups—were declared to be heretics facing not
only the vengeance of God but also that of the state. The decision of
Constantine to privilege one Christian community over another was
consolidated in that a "truth" was now defined and enforced by law,
with those declared heretical to be punished on earth as well as by God.
It was unclear on what basis this "truth" rested, certainly not one of
exclusively rational argument, so it either had to be presented as "the
revelation of God," as it was by Thomas Aquinas, or accepted that
"truth" was as defined by the emperor. Bearing in mind the degree to
which the emperors either handpicked councils in advance or manipulated them, one must hesitate in claiming that the church as a whole had
freely come to a consensus on the matter. The Nicenes spoke of their
beliefs as traditional but they were countered by Palladius, bishop of
Ratiaria, the most sophisticated of the Homoean bishops of the day,
who claimed that it was the Homoean view that was the tradition and
the Nicenes who were the innovators. After the edicts of February 380
and January 381, the council of 381 had been left with relatively little
room for theological manoeuvre.[46]

In effect, the edict finally confirmed the emperor as the definer and
enforcer of orthodoxy. In the future, when debates within the church
began to get out of hand and threaten the stability of the empire, it
would be the emperor who would intervene to establish the boundaries
between orthodoxy and heresy. This was not simply a theological issue.
"Orthodoxy" was now associated with tax exemptions for clergy as
well as access to wealth and patronage and the high status enjoyed by
the state church, while "heretics" lost all these. The commanding position exercised by the emperor in the definition of orthodox doctrine may
well have rested on the need to control the numbers of those able to

claim exemptions and patronage, but the language in which the heretics were condemned suggests that there was something more powerful behind the development. This was an empire under desperate threat from outside, and the activities of Theodosius in his first years as emperor were dominated by the need to regroup and inspire the Roman forces that had been so demoralized at Adrianople—it is certainly arguable that his religious policy should be seen in terms of the need to find symbols around which to define the unity of the empire and consolidate its counter-attack. Theodosius used orthodoxy as a focus for loyalty to the empire, so, for instance, the devastating defeat of Valens was reinterpreted as the judgment of God effected through the hand of those, the Goths, "whom he [Valens] had perfidiously led astray when they had sought the true faith, turning them aside from the flame of love into the fire of hell," that is, by initiating them into the Homoean Christianity they sustained after 381.[47] Every subsequent attack by the Goths on the empire could be characterized as the assault of evil on the true faith. It is possible to see the rise of Christian intolerance as essentially a defensive response to these threats.

In his fine study of these developments Richard Hanson concludes that "the religious policy of Theodosius on the whole succeeded, whereas that of Constantine, Constantius and Valens failed, because it was supported by a genuine widespread consensus of opinion in the church."[48] But there is little evidence to support this hypothesis—rather, as Hanson himself admits, it is clear that the expulsions of Homoean bishops were met with riots in many parts of the empire.[49] Moreover, Valentinian, emperor in the west 375–92, remained Homoean, even engaging in a power struggle with Ambrose of Milan over the issue. It is clear that the majority of the population in Constantinople were not Nicenes and were outraged when they lost their churches. A rare instance of popular gossip from Constantinople recorded by Gregory of Nyssa even suggests continuing sympathy for and from full-blown, traditional Arianism: "If you ask for change, the man launches into a theological discussion about begotten and unbegotten; if you enquire about the price of bread, the answer is given that the Father is greater and the Son subordinate; if you remark that the bath is nice, the attendant pronounces that the Son is from non-existence."[50]

Some Homoean communities, expelled from their churches, continued to hold services in the open air. Although gradually the record of their activity diminishes, there are reports of Homoean processions in the city at the time of John Chrysostom in the early fifth century. Stephen Mitchell, in his study of early Christianity in Anatolia, draws together evidence from a mass of inscriptions to show that an extraordinary diversity of Christian belief, much of it "heretical," flourished in the fourth century, and it was only gradually that orthodox bishops were able to impose their authority.[51] The speed of the process must not be overestimated. Christian literature may suggest a complete triumph of Christianity, but the discovery in the sixth century of large areas of coastal Asia Minor where Christianity had not yet penetrated speaks for caution. Common sense alone suggests that remote, largely illiterate communities, many of them beyond the effective control of imperial and church authorities, were not likely to be able to distinguish between orthodox and heretical doctrine (*pace* the bath attendants of Constantinople), particularly when the concepts around which the debates turned were themselves so hard to grasp.

The adoption of the Nicene formula had other consequences. As we have seen, it is clear that many Christians understood the Synoptic Gospels as giving the impression of a Son who sees his Father as greater than himself, even to the extent of pleading with his Father to be relieved of the agony of the cross. It was this evidence of Jesus' suffering that underpinned the belief of Arius and others that he must be a lesser being than God, who must by his nature be above all feeling. This impression of Jesus as a human being, eating, drinking, arguing, beset by emotion, undergoing the agonies of humiliation and crucifixion, tended to be eclipsed by his elevation into the Godhead. This problem underlay the entire Arian debate in that the adoption of *homoousios* threatened the primacy of the scriptures in the making of doctrine, not only because the term could not be found in the scriptures but because a Jesus "one in substance" with the Father seemed incompatible with the recognizably human Jesus of the Synoptic Gospels. The differences between the Arians, Homoeans and their supporters on one side and the Nicenes on the other were intensified by what seemed to be an abandonment of the scriptures by the Nicenes. They were accused by their opponents of ignoring crucial passages of the Gospels if they did not support their case or of interpreting them in ways that stretched credulity.

So when Ambrose of Milan produced his *De Fide,* a defence of Nicene doctrine, he was countered by Palladius, who wrote tellingly: "Search the divine Scriptures, which you have neglected, so that under their divine guidance you may avoid the Hell towards which you are heading on your own."[52] Hanson makes a full survey of the attempts by the Nicenes to fight the charge by making their own interpretations of scripture, but he does not rate them highly. He agrees with Palladius on the quality of Ambrose's efforts. "Generally speaking, throughout all his writings Ambrose tends to produce interpretations of the Bible whose undoubted poetic quality may charm the uncritical thinker but which in fact represent little more than fantastic nonsense woven into a purely delusive harmony." As we have seen, it required considerable ingenuity for the Cappadocians to equate the Father and Son of the Gospels with the Father and Son of the Trinity.[53]

The declaration of Nicene orthodoxy led over time to a gradual silencing of "Arians" and the suppression of their literature, but enough survives to show that the debate over the scriptures rumbled on. For example, the *Opus Imperfectum in Matthaeum,* a commentary on St. Matthew's Gospel, preserved among the papers of John Chrysostom and probably originating from a beleaguered Homoean community in early-fifth-century Illyria, claimed to represent "true" Christianity, now being persecuted by "false" (orthodox) Christians. The distinguishing mark of this community, the writer stresses, is its fidelity to scripture.[54] The Homoean Goths were noted for their reliance on the scriptures.[55] Maximinus, a bishop who claimed that his faith rested on the creed accepted in 360 at Constantinople, engaged in public debate with Augustine in Hippo in the 420s and put the Homoean (and the literalist) position well: "We believe in the Scriptures and we reverence those divine Scriptures; and we do not desire to pass over a single iota, for we dread the punishment which is to be found in the Scriptures themselves." Forcefully making the point that the pro-Nicenes distort scripture, he taunted Augustine: "The divine Scripture does not fare so badly in *our* [Homoean; my emphasis] teaching that it has to receive improvement."[56]

Maximinus' accusation against Augustine was that he was "improving" the scriptures to suit his orthodox case. Augustine would not have disagreed. He fully accepted that scripture should not be left open to individual interpretation but to the Church: "I would not believe the Gospel unless the authority of the Catholic Church moved me," he writes in one of his tracts against the Manicheans. This is, on the face of it, an astonishing assertion, but it is one which reflects the consolidation of Church authority. Now that the doctrine of the Trinity had been proclaimed, scripture had to be reinterpreted to defend it.[57] In his *De Doctrina Christiana* (completed in the 420s), Augustine considers the opening of John's Gospel. Different texts have different punctuations. One "heretical" punctuation "refused" to acknowledge that the Word was God, and Augustine says, "This is to be refuted, by the rule of faith, which lays down for us the equality of the members of the Trinity, and so we should say 'and the Word was God,' and then go on, 'This was in the beginning with God.' " In other words, it is now orthodox faith that shapes exegesis.[58] When considering a problem text, an occasion, for instance, when a holy person utters words appearing to be sinful, Augustine argues that these should not be taken literally but as allegorical of some other meaning. "Anything," writes Augustine in his *De Doctrina Christiana,* "in the divine discourse [the scriptures] that cannot be related to good morals or the true faith should be taken as allegorical."[59]

Such flexibility, which gave the interpreter enormous scope in dealing with awkward passages, echoed that of Origen. While the latter had used allegory to reconcile the scriptures with Platonism, Augustine used it to reconcile the scriptures to Nicene orthodoxy. Augustine's attitude to the scriptures can be said to have reached fruition in the profession of faith of the (Counter-Reformation) Council of Trent (1545–63), in which a Catholic is required to swear that "I accept Sacred Scripture in the sense in which it has been held, and is held, by Holy Mother Church, to whom it belongs to judge the true sense and interpretation of the Sacred Scripture, nor will I interpret it in any way other than in accordance with the unanimous [*sic*] agreement of the Fathers." It is certainly arguable that the declaration of the Nicene Creed forced the church into taking greater control over the interpretation of the scriptures and in doing so reinforced its authority over doctrine as already instituted by Theodosius. The effect, of course, was to make reasoned and open debate on theological matters increasingly difficult.

If Jesus was now fully part of the Godhead, how did the divinity of Christ and the common humanity of Jesus co-exist in one being when Jesus was on earth? The greater the divinity accorded to Christ, the more difficult it was to relate his divinity to his humanity. So was born what Jaroslav Pelikan has called "the almost insuperable task of attributing genuine birth, suffering and death to the Son of an impassible Deity."[60] Who or what actually suffered the agony of crucifixion, and was that agony in any way diminished or affected by the divine nature of Christ? Did Jesus suffer as much in his mind as he did in his body, or was his suffering alleviated by the knowledge that he was divine? Athanasius had encountered difficulties in tackling these problems (as we have seen, he

1, 2. Two details from "The Triumph of Faith" by Filippino Lippi, painted in the 1480s for the Dominican church of Santa Maria sopra Minerva in Rome. The great Dominican theologian Thomas Aquinas upholds the true faith, while below him the works of heretics lie discarded. The figures below Aquinas include the fourth-century combatants in the dispute, among them Arius and Sabellius, as well as contemporaries of the donor of the fresco, Cardinal Oliviero Carafa (1430–1511), the cardinal protector of the Dominicans.

Note Constantine's church of St. John Lateran in the view to the left of Aquinas (top) with the famous equestrian statue of Marcus Aurelius, then believed to be of Constantine, which is now on the Capitoline Hill. For further discussion of the fresco, see chapter 1. (Credit: Scala)

3, 4. "There is one race of men, one race of gods, both have breath of life from a single mother . . . so we have some likeness, in great intelligence and strength to the immortals." The poet Pindar, writing in the fifth century B.C., notes the contrasts and similarities between men and the gods in the Greek world. The Riace warrior (above), which forms part of an Athenian victory monument at Delphi (470s B.C.), represents man at his most heroic, almost a god in his own right, as the similarity to a portrayal of Zeus in a bronze of the same date (right) makes clear. This was the human world at its most confident, although the Greeks always warned of the impropriety of a mortal attempting to behave as if he were a god. (Credit: Ancient Art and Architecture Collection)

5, 6. By the fourth century A.D., such confidence has faded and human beings have become overwhelmed by forces over which they have little control. The gulf between God and man is now immense. On earth, the ascetic Anthony, here shown on the Isenheim Altar (above), painted for a monastery dedicated to St. Anthony in Alsace by Matthias Grünewald (1515), fights off a host of demons which threaten to overcome him (credit: Bridgeman Art Library). In the afterlife (left), devils drag unlucky souls down into hell from the ladder on which they are making the arduous ascent towards heaven (a twelfth-century icon from St. Catherine's Monastery in Sinai; credit: Ancient Art and Architecture Collection). It was perhaps inevitable in such a climate that creative thinking about the natural world would be stifled.

7. Marcus Aurelius (emperor A.D. 161–80) displays himself as one among his fellow humans. Here, in a contemporary panel (C. 176–80 A.D.) in Rome, he grants clemency to two kneeling barbarians (credit: Corbis). In his *Meditations*, much influenced by Stoicism, Marcus Aurelius stresses his optimism about the natural order of things. "Everything bears fruit: man, God, the whole universe, each in its proper season. Reason, too, yields fruit, both for itself and for the world; since from it comes a harvest of other good things, themselves all bearing the stamp of reason."

8, 9, 10. By the fourth century the emperor has become quasi-divine, as the monumental ide-alized head of Constantine (above left), from his basilica in Rome, suggests (credit: Scala). Recent studies of Constantine doubt that he was ever fully converted to Christianity, but aimed instead to bring Christianity, alongside paganism, into the service of the state. His Arch in Rome (315) (top) shows no Christian influence, but one can see in the third line of the inscrip-tion the words INSTINCTU DIVINITAS, "by divine inspiration," a use of terminology accept-able to both Christian and pagan (credit: Scala). In a coin of about 330 (above right), Constantine stands between two of his sons (credit: Kunsthistorisches Museum, Vienna). He receives a circlet directly from God, a symbol of divine approval of his rule, while Constantius is crowned by Virtus (virtue) and Constantine II by Victoria (victory). In Christian terms, Con-stantine sees himself as the "thirteenth apostle" and is buried as such.

11, 12, 13. By 390 Christ, here "in majesty" in the church of Santa Pudenziana in Rome (top), has been transformed from an outcast of the empire to one who is represented by its most traditional imperial images, fully frontal on a throne (credit: Scala). The setting echoes the portrayal of Constantine distributing largesse on his Arch (315) (above; credit: Alinari) and of the emperor Theodosius I on a silver commemorative dish of 388 (right; credit: Ancient Art and Architecture Collection). Note Christ's adoption of a halo, hitherto a symbol of monarchy (while his beard echoes representations of Jupiter). On Christ's left, Paul is introduced as an apostle, an indication of his growing status in the empire of the late fourth century.

14. According to the Gospels, Jesus was executed by Roman soldiers and offered no resistance to them. In imperial Christianity, by contrast, he himself has become a Roman soldier, "the leader of the legions," as Ambrose of Milan put it. With no supporting evidence for this role from the Gospels, the Old Testament Psalm 91, which portrays a protective God trampling on lion and adder, is drawn on to provide the imagery. (A mosaic from Ravenna, c. 500; credit: Scala)

15. Constantine's use of a military victory as the platform from which to announce his toleration of Christianity was a radical departure which defined the relationship between Christianity and war for centuries to come. The Sala di Constantino was commissioned from Raphael by the Medici pope Leo X (pope 1513–21). The early popes are shown alongside Constantine's vision. Leo associated himself with the victory by adding the *palle* (balls) from the Medici coat of arms to Constantine's tent; lions, a reference to Leo's name, are also found on the tent, with another depicted on a standard. (Credit: Scala)

16. "Alexamenos worships his god." Early Christians were ridiculed for their worship of a "god" who had suffered the humiliation of crucifixion. In this graffito of c. 200 from Rome, one Alexamenos is mocked for worshipping a donkey on a cross. (Credit: Scala)

17. Even in the fifth century, Christians themselves had inhibitions about representing Christ on the cross, as can be seen in this representation of Christ from the door of the Roman church of Santa Sabina (c. 420). (Credit: Scala)

concluded that the mind of Jesus was incapable of suffering), and his successors found it no easier. In the first half of the fifth century an entirely new set of debates on the issue, as bitter as any over Nicaea, consumed the church, and eventually, at the Council of Chalcedon in 451, the emperor, Marcian, would again have to intervene to settle them. This was another of the legacies of Nicaca—by "solving" one theological issue, it appeared to make another more difficult to solve. The assumption behind all these debates was, of course, the conviction that there could be coherent and unassailable solutions to them. This assumption is so deep-rooted in Christian theology that it is seldom questioned, but it was, in fact, a revolutionary development and reflects the successful integration of Platonism into Christian theology.

The transformation of Christ from the man of the Synoptic Gospels to the God of the Trinity was accompanied by a transformation in the way he was represented. A good place to see the result is in the church of S. Pudenziana on the Esquiline Hill in Rome. The apse mosaic of Christ in Majesty, the earliest known mosaic on this theme, dates from about 390, only a few years after the proclamation of Theodosius. It is not now at its best, botched restorations in the sixteenth century having led to the disciples losing their lower halves and two being cut out altogether. Their faces have been largely restored, and only Christ survives fully in his original form. He sits on a purple cushion on a throne facing down the basilica, wearing robes streaked with gold. He is shown bearded and with a halo, and in his left hand carries a scroll announcing his role as protector of the building. His right hand is stretched outwards in a gesture traditionally associated with teaching. Above Christ are a jewelled cross standing on Mount Zion and the symbols of the four evangelists. Below them is a representation of Jerusalem as a restored and ornate city. The representation may be drawn from Revelation 21:2, where "the Spirit carried me away to a great, high mountain and showed me the heavenly Jerusalem coming down out of heaven from God," or from chapter 4 of Paul's letter to the Galatians, which contrasts an enslaved Jerusalem on earth with a free one in heaven.[61]

What is striking about the mosaic is the degree to which Christ has been adopted into traditional Roman iconography. The fully frontal pose echoes the cult statues placed in pagan temples (it is comparable to the traditional representation of the robed and seated figure of Jupiter, the father of the gods, not least in the portrayal of both Jesus and Jupiter with beards), and this pose was frequently used in the representations of emperors. Only a few hundred yards from S. Pudenziana on the Arch of Constantine near the Colosseum (A.D. 315), the emperor is shown distributing largesse. He sits face on in authority, and the supplicants around him raise their arms in acclamation just as several of the disciples do in the mosaic. Another symbol of imperial power is the halo, representing the sun. It is not necessarily a mark of holiness—in the neighbouring church of S. Maria Maggiore, Herod himself is shown on a mosaic wearing one—so its appropriation in this early context suggests imperial rather than religious power. It has also been noted how close Christ's throne is to the seats of authority used by Roman magistrates.[62]

Another feature of the mosaic is the prominence of Paul. In its original form there were twelve disciples in the mosaic, with Paul being given the place left by Judas and seated immediately to the left of Christ. Thus he is given almost equal status to Peter, who sits in a similar position to the right of Christ, and they are distinguished from the other disciples in being accompanied by two female figures, one representing the Church of the Jews and the other the Church of the Heathen, offering wreaths to Christ. The elevation of Paul to equal status with Peter was a recent development. When Constantine built churches in Rome at the beginning of the fourth century, he honoured Christ the Redeemer (now St. John Lateran) and Peter (on the Vatican Hill). Paul's supposed burial place, on the road out from Rome to the port of Ostia, was marked only with a small shrine. In the late fourth century, in Rome in particular, Christianity was involved in a bitter struggle with the pagan aristocratic families who were well able to counter its teachings, especially, as we shall see, through appeals for intellectual tolerance. Rather than looking to Peter, the Apostle to the Jews, Christians increasingly focused on the "intellectual" Paul, whose authority rested on his conversion of the pagans. Between 384 and 392 Paul's modest shrine was transformed into a great new basilica, San Paolo Fuori le Mura, which rivalled St. Peter's in size and which appears to have been financed by the ruling emperors, Theodosius among them. It is symbolic of the revival of Paul's influence throughout the empire. So we find that the verse that converted Augustine to Christianity (in 386 in Milan) is from Paul's letters, not the Gospels, and that in his *Confessions* Augustine makes twice as many references to Paul's letters as he does to the four Gospels. In her fine study of the sermons preached by John Chrysostom on Paul, *The Heavenly Trumpet: John Chrysostom and the Art of Pauline Interpretation*, Margaret Mitchell notes that John's involvement with Paul borders on the obsessional.[63] Much further research is needed in this area, but it is arguable that the concentration on authority shown by Paul in his letters (a concentration, as has been argued, probably stemming from his own insecurities) met the needs of the imperial church more adequately than the Gospels, which show Jesus challenging the religious and imperial authorities of his day.

Paul's influence ran deep. In his letters he had inveighed against idols (by which he meant statues of the gods), Greek philosophy and sexuality, and attacks on these now became central to the Christian mission to eliminate paganism. So the S. Pudenziana mosaic reflects not only the reception of the criminal crucified by an imperial governor into the full majesty of imperial iconography (we might note also Ambrose's astonishing assertion that it is Christ who leads the legions) but also the strengthening of the attack on paganism. This transformation of the image of Jesus in both doctrine and art went hand in hand with the assertion of control by the emperors over the church hierarchy. As a result of the transfer of both power and massive economic resources to the church, European history was to be set in new directions.

# 13

# "ENRICHED BY THE GIFTS OF MATRONS"

## Bishops and Society in the Fourth Century

He [the emperor] does not bring you liberty by casting you in prison, but treats you with respect within his palace and thus makes you his slave.

HILARY, BISHOP OF POITIERS, ON THE NEW STATUS OF
BISHOPS, MID FOURTH CENTURY[1]

As the edicts of Diocletian, each one more punitive and wide-ranging than the last, were promulgated across the empire in the early fourth century, bishops lived in fear. And yet only a very few years later, in 325, the emperor Constantine, having concluded his business at Nicaea, welcomed the assembled bishops to a magnificent banquet where he celebrated what he termed "a great victory."[2] The emperor's desire to bring the bishops into the fabric of the state involved a dramatic reversal of their status. Enormous patronage became available to those bishops ready to accept the emperor's position on doctrine, and those who took advantage of it came to have access to vast wealth and social prestige. No less than a quarter of the income of the estates left to the Church in Rome was earmarked for the bishop's household,[3] so that by the end of the fourth century Ammianus Marcellinus was able to describe the extravagant lifestyle of the bishops of Rome: "Enriched by the gifts of matrons, they ride in carriages, dress splendidly and outdo kings in the lavishness of their table."[4] This was not the whole story, as Ammianus himself recognized. As we shall see, many Christians were sufficiently repelled by the new wealth of the Church to be drawn to asceticism; even if they did not make for the desert themselves, many bishops turned to austerity and gave their wealth to the poor to reinforce their Christian authority. Whether they succumbed to the financial temptations or not, however, bishops were now men with a stake in good order, and when the traditional city elites and, in the west, the structure of government itself collapsed, it was to be they who took control. One of the results of the fourth-century revolution (and it seems appropriate to call it this) was the association of the churches with wealth, conservatism and the traditional structures of society, an association that was to endure in European Christianity well into the twentieth century. By the time of the Domesday Book in 1086, a fifth of England's resources were under the control of the Church; in the sixteenth century Cranmer, the first Protestant Archbishop of Canterbury, had seven major palaces for his personal use, at least until the new Head of the Church, Henry VIII, appropriated the finest for himself.

The bishops had always been based in the cities. (The derogatory word "pagan" has the connotation of one who lives in the country.) After Constantine's reign the hierarchy of bishops began to mirror the political hierarchy. The capital city of each province, the seat of the provincial governor, became the seat of the metropolitan bishop, who exercised some authority over the other bishops of the province, calling synods, approving appointments and overseeing the activities of "his" bishops when they were outside their sees. The original idea of giving status to a bishopric because of its association with Jesus' ministry or the Apostles was eclipsed. If any one city deserved primacy in the Christian world, it was (as the Irish St. Columban was claiming as late as the seventh century) Jerusalem, the site of the crucifixion and resurrection. Yet the bishopric of Caesarea, where the governor lived (as he had done in Jesus' time), was given authority as metropolitan over the bishopric of Jerusalem, an authority underlined by the practice of calling Jerusalem by its Roman name (derived from the family name of its Roman founder, Hadrian), Aelia, a recognition that it was now formally a Roman colony. For many Christians the shame of the crucifixion appears to have tainted it as the city of Christ's killers. It was not until the Council of Chalcedon in 451 that Jerusalem was accorded a place of honour with its own patriarch.[5]

Other bishoprics were given special prominence. Rome claimed primacy over all others as the site of the martyrdom of Peter, who by tradition was its first bishop. As Rome's political significance waned, however, the influence of the city's bishops remained limited. Like all other bishops they were vulnerable to the whim or convictions of the emperor. So it was that Liberius, bishop from 352 to 366, was deposed by Constantius and restored only when he accepted a Homoean creed. After his death there was a particularly violent election in which the eventual victor, Damasus, called upon the *fossores,* the catacomb diggers, to defend his cause. Over a hundred are known to have died in the turmoil, and Damasus' authority was weakened for much of his reign. The bishops of Rome did not even attend the two councils at which the Nicene Creed was formulated. Whatever lip service was given to the primacy of the bishops of Rome, in practice they were too far from the main centres of the Christian church to have any substantive impact on the development of doctrine. In the city itself they were marginal figures so long as power lay in the hands of the pagan senatorial aristocracy, as it continued to do until the early fifth century.

In the east Antioch and Alexandria were the great Christian cities, and Alexandria maintained its prominence over the whole of Egypt, even after the country was divided into smaller provinces. However, just how closely the power of the church mirrored that of the state can be seen in the decision of the Council of Constantinople in 381 to elevate the bishop of the city "next after the bishop of Rome because Constantinople is the new Rome." Constantinople had no links to the early church at all—it was still only a minor bishopric when Constantine began rebuilding the city. Its new ecclesiastical prominence simply highlighted the extent to which the church had become a political institution. Both Damasus in Rome and the bishops of Alexandria were furious at the promotion—in retaliation Damasus claimed, apparently for the first time, that the primacy of the bishops of Rome rested on their status as successors of Peter—and a new rivalry entered the relationships of the eastern church. The bishops of Constantinople proved highly vulnerable to intrigues backed by Alexandria, in turn usually supported by Rome, as two of them, John Chrysostom, deposed in 403, and Nestorius, deposed in 431, were to find to their cost. The resentment was all the more intensely felt because of the added status and influence enjoyed by a bishop with direct access to the emperor.

The authority of the bishops within the state was consolidated by tying them into the structure of the legal system. Constantine had extended to bishops the longstanding right of all magistrates to free slaves. They could also hear civil cases if both sides agreed. Naturally, they also had power to uphold the laws, initiated by the state, supporting Nicene orthodoxy. This included establishing the suitability of those coming forward for ordination. In 407 the emperor Honorius gave bishops the specific right to ban pagan funeral rites, and in the same legislation their right to enforce the laws aimed at Jews, pagans and heretics was reaffirmed. In the following year bishops were given equal status to the praetorian prefects in that there was no appeal from their judgments. Sitting in the courts now became a major part of a bishop's life. Augustine would complain that he had so many cases he often had to sit through the whole morning and into the siesta. His time was filled with property disputes, cases of adultery, inheritance cases and the enforcement of laws against pagans and Donatists.

One indication of how tightly Christianity was now bound into the traditional structures of society can be seen in its attitude to slavery. While there are Christian exhortations (similar to those found among Stoics) to treat slaves well as fellow human beings, the concept of slavery itself was not challenged. In fact it has been argued, somewhat provocatively perhaps, that Christianity reinforced slavery by, from the earliest times, defining Christians as slaves of Christ and exhorting actual slaves to work hard because by doing so they will be fulfilling the will of God.[6] As the author of Ephesians, probably written about A.D. 90, puts it (6:5–7):

> Slaves, be obedient to the men who are called your masters in the world, with deep respect and sincere loyalty as you are obedient to Christ: not only when you are under their eye, as if you only had to please men, but because you are slaves of Christ and wholeheartedly do the will of God . . . Work hard and willingly . . . but do it for the sake of the Lord.

Examples from the Church Fathers and other sources show that Christians accepted slavery as part of normal life, and wealthier Christians owned slaves themselves. In the rules laid down by Basil of Caesarea for admission to monasteries, escaped slaves who craved admittance had to be returned to their masters unless the masters were exceptionally cruel; in the requirements laid down by Leo, bishop of Rome, slaves were ineligible for ordination. Augustine, who was always conservative in social affairs, took matters further in asserting that slavery is God's punishment for evil. He wrote: "The primary cause of slavery, then, is sin . . . and this can only be by a judgment of God, in whom there is no unrighteousness, and who knows how to assign divers punishments according to the deserts of the sinners."[7]

The aura of a bishopric in the empire's larger cities was enhanced by the buildings it had at its disposal. It was an ancient tradition that a city should glorify itself through its temples. Aristotle suggested in his *Politics* that a quarter of the revenues of a city's territory ought to be dedicated to the gods; others proposed as much as a third.[8] Since Hellenistic times kings and emperors had showered their patronage on favoured cities. Many temples were crammed with gold and silver statues, and imperial patronage was a means of raising support for the gods. A panegyric to Maximian makes the point: "You have heaped the gods with altars and statues, temples and offerings, which you dedicated with your own name and your own image whose sanctity is increased by the example you set, of veneration for the gods."[9] Constantine followed in this tradition and concentrated his patronage on the building and adornment of churches. As, unlike pagan temples, which were primarily designed to house cult statues, churches needed to house congregations, Constantine adopted the basilica as the most appropriate form. Yet as basilicas were now also used as the audience halls of the emperors (that surviving at Trier, although stripped of its original opulent decoration, gives some idea of the model), it is arguable that Constantine was stressing in yet another way the close links between the state and Christianity.

It is hard for us to grasp the sheer scale of this imperial patronage. It was so lavish that Constantine had to strip resources from temples to fund it. Some calculations of the monies involved have been from the *Liber Pontificalis,* an account of the early popes. One of Constantine's early foundations in Rome was a church to Christ the Redeemer, whose apse was to be coated in gold. This demanded some 500 pounds of it at a cost of some 36,000 *solidi.* This could have supported around 12,000 poor people for a year, and has been equated to around £60 million today.[10] This was for the decoration of the apse alone—another 22,200 *solidi* worth of silver (3,700 pounds) was required for light fittings and another 400 pounds of gold for fifty gold vessels. The costs of lighting were to be met by estates specifically granted for the purpose, which brought in 4,390 *solidi* a year. Everything in these new churches had to be of the highest quality. While early Christian decoration, in the catacombs or house churches, for instance, had consisted of painted walls, now nothing less than mosaic was appropriate. In order to make the effect more brilliant, the materials of the mosaic—gold, silver or precious stones—were set within glass. This was an enormously delicate and costly business. Studies of the original floor mosaics at the Church of the Nativity in Bethlehem, one of Constantine's foundations in the Holy Land, show the care lavished on decoration. While the high-quality mosaics in Palestine usually had about 150 tesserae per ten-centimetre square, those in the nave of the Church of the Nativity have 200, those of the Octagon at the end of the nave some 400.[11]

Adapting to this newfound opulence was a major challenge to the church. While Acts 17:24 said, "The God who made the world and everything in it, being the Lord of heaven and earth, does not live in shrines made by man," such "shrines" could hardly be avoided; instances where bishops refused the patronage of emperors were very rare, although Martin, bishop of Tours, did decline an offer from Valentinian I. There was little support from the Gospels for the display of wealth. Jesus had clearly disdained it (although commentators noted that the appropriate gifts for the baby Jesus had been gold, frankincense and myrrh), but in the Old Testament there were plenty of references to gold and silver and, in the Book of Revelation in the New Testament, to the heavenly city founded on precious stones. In Ezekiel the Lord is described as a mixture of gold and silver. In the Song of Solomon 5:11 the "beloved" (interpreted by Christians as Christ) has a head of the finest gold. So it could be argued that heaven was a place crammed with treasure, and that precious metals on earth, if used in the service of the church, became sacred by association. "What is meant by gold which surpasses all other metals, but surpassing holiness," as Gregory the Great put it.[12] If heaven is so rich in treasure, then a basilica can be seen as a symbol of heaven on earth and as worthy of similar decoration. "The solemn liturgy, the blaze of lights, the shimmering mosaics and the brightly coloured curtains of a Late Antique church were there to be appreciated in their entirety . . . Taken together they provided a glimpse of paradise."[13] Thus was a powerful visual rhetoric created. Once again Platonism was exploited to provide a philosophical rationale. For the Christian Platonist philosopher known as Pseudo-Dionysius, an image on earth could be the starting point for contemplation of immaterial things beyond. The gold of churches was necessary to give the believer a stepping stone to a full appreciation of the glories of heaven.[14]

Once a rationale had been created to divert the most precious of materials and the finest of buildings to Christian use, the old reservations were largely dissolved. In fact, the desire to create opulence came to condition the shape of architecture. The basilica was the most economical building type for a large congregation, but churches with central domes appeared with the dome reaching up to the sky, as if providing a representation of heaven itself. Domed churches provided no extra space for the congregation but were much more expensive to build; there was not only the construction and decoration of the dome itself to consider, but the walls also had to be strengthened to support its weight. The "Golden Octagon" of Antioch, consecrated in 341, was a magnificent early example; the dome of *Hagia Sophia* in Constantinople, described by the historian Procopius as appearing to be suspended from heaven, and still intact in its glory today, was perhaps the greatest. In Byzantine art the dome became ubiquitous, with God the Creator watching over the faithful from its centre. Byzantine services became a series of dramatic liturgical moments that the congregation, crammed in under the dome and separated from the sanctuary by the iconostasis, could experience rather than see.

If a church had now become a symbol of heaven, how were figures to be shown? The answer was to model them on the imperial court, the closest model for heaven on earth. An early example of the adoption of imperial themes for Christian iconography can be found on the sarcophagus of Junius Bassus, a Roman aristocrat who had served as city prefect and consul and had converted on his deathbed. His sarcophagus (of 359) was buried under the floor of St. Peter's (and is now in the Vatican Museum). On the central lower panel of its elaborately carved facade, Christ is shown entering Jerusalem as if he was an emperor entering a city, and above this image he is shown sitting in glory on an imperial throne set above a representation of heaven. Sabine MacCormack notes how once Christ was represented with such imperial imagery the emperors ceased to make use of it: "Once an image of majesty had been applied to Christ it was impossible to apply it again to the emperor." So the process by which Christ becomes integrated into the iconography of imperial government continued.[15]

In the mosaiced figures of the apses and walls of the churches of the subsequent centuries God, Christ, the Virgin Mary, the disciples and saints and martyrs are dressed as emperors or members of the imperial court. In the church of S. Apollinare Nuovo in Ravenna, Christ appears dressed in imperial purple, and the archangels Michael and Gabriel are depicted in court dress. The court itself (in the days of the Byzantine emperor Justinian and his wife, Theodora) is shown in the famous mosaics in San Vitale in Ravenna, and the Virgin Mary in the great basilica of Santa Maria Maggiore in Rome is dressed similarly to the attendants of the empress.[16] The martyr who challenged the Roman empire and was extinguished by it now appears in mosaic as if he were one of its own grand officials. The point could not have been made better than in the case of St. Agnes, martyred in Rome after she resisted the advances of a praetor's son. According to Prudentius, she trampled on all the vanities of the world, pomp, gold, silver garments, dwellings, anger, fear and paganism through the acceptance of her martyrdom. Her reward, in the depiction of her against a gold background in the apse of her basilica on the outskirts of Rome, is to become an empress draped with gems in heaven. Having rejected treasures on earth, she finds them with Christ.[17] Just as the martyrs are transformed through their sanctification, so are the symbols of Christianity. A cross is now presented encrusted with gold, as in the magnificent apse mosaic in S. Apollinare in Classe, Ravenna, or above the figure of Christ "the emperor" at S. Pudenziana. The Gospels are encased in jewelled covers as every aspect of church decoration is embellished with treasure.

While it was the emperors who initiated the massive patronage required to build these churches, it soon became a badge of faith for wealthy Christians to contribute. The most famous lay patron was Melania the Younger. Her annual income at the time of her marriage in 397 was said to be 120,000 *solidi,* perhaps equivalent to over £200 million. This was wealth on the scale of the most successful entrepreneurs of today (although it was, of course, income from land), yet Melania gave much of it away to the church, including a donation for the foundation of a monastery on the Mount of Olives in Jerusalem. In the same period in Constantinople, an aristocratic widow, Olympias, devoted immense riches to the church in Constantinople, while the empress Pulcheria gave a large jewelled chest to the church as a symbol of her commitment to virginity. In Rome it seems to have become the custom for each new bishop to make a foundation in his name that would be supported either by his own resources or those of a wealthy patron. So in the fifth century many of Rome's greatest churches, including S. Sabina, S. Maria Maggiore and SS. Giovanni e Paolo, were first established. One act of patronage encouraged another. Melania the Younger gave to the local church at Thagaste "revenues as well as offerings of gold and silver treasures, and valuable curtains, so that this church which formerly had been so poor, now stirred up envy on the part of other bishops of the provinces."[18] In Ravenna, the seat of government of the Goth, and hence Homoean, Theodoric the Ostrogoth, Homoeans and Nicenes struggled to outdo each other in the decoration of their churches. S. Apollinare Nuovo was one of Theodoric's foundations (c. 494–526) and shows that Goths could be no less lavish than "Roman" Christians. An exquisite "Homoean" Gospel book, the *Codex Argenteus,* survives from these years. It is clear too that church building was now also a matter of civic pride. "Other benefactions contribute to the decor of a city, while outlays on a church combine beauty with a city's renown for godliness . . . for wealth that flows out for holy purposes becomes an ever-running stream for its possessors," as one proud Christian put it.[19]

The allure of churches was further enhanced by the practice of bringing martyrs' bones and other relics to them, or, as in the case of St. Peter's in Rome, of building churches over their supposed burial places. As the age of martyrs slipped into the past, so the martyrs themselves tightened their hold on the Christian imagination. In facing death, the martyrs had reached perfection, and their very bones became sacred, able to perform miracles. There was a rush to the Holy Land to find relics of the life of Jesus himself. By the end of the fourth century, the legend of Helena's finding of the "True Cross" while on her pilgrimage to Jerusalem was fully established, and an improbably large number of churches around the Mediterranean claimed to have fragments of it. The opportune discovery of bones believed to be those of St. Stephen, Christianity's first martyr, near Jerusalem in 415 aroused enormous enthusiasm, and they were paraded through north Africa and the western empire. Even Augustine, who had been sceptical of the power of relics, was won over on their arrival at Hippo. It was reported that they proclaimed themselves genuine through emitting a sweet smell. Most martyrs, of course, were the local casualties of the third- and early-fourth-century persecutions, and they were buried in cemeteries outside the city walls. The translation of their bones to a church inside the city (thus breaking ancient taboos against burial within the walls) was a highly significant moment in the definition of a Christian community.

When the state condemned (in a law of 386, for instance) the unseemly practice of breaking up and distributing parts of dead bodies, Christians took no notice. It was argued that each part of a martyr's body, however small, retained the sacred potency of the whole. The major shrines, particularly those of early Christianity, now attracted worshippers from far afield, and so the great pilgrimage routes of the Mediterranean became established. An early record of pilgrimage survives by Egeria, a Spanish-born nun, who reached the Holy Land in 384, recording her trip in a diary.

The finest churches were those of the great cities, particularly those with links to the court or early Christianity. There were many dioceses beyond the reach of patronage where Christians had to make do with converted temples or bathhouses for churches, but within an empire under increasing financial stress the church held a privileged position. It enjoyed exemption from tax on any of its estates and property, and the growth of asceticism led, paradoxically perhaps, to a massive renunciation of private wealth in its favour, much of which went into further building projects. Inevitably the concerns of the bishops were enlarged. John Chrysostom complained that they were now more like merchants and shopkeepers than guardians of men's souls and protectors of the poor. Their estates, properties, churches and institutions transformed them into estate managers and financial overlords as well as major employers. The staff of one church alone, the great *Hagia Sophia* in Constantinople, numbered some 500 in the middle of the sixth century.[20] There are reports that bishoprics in Asia Minor could be bought.[21]

Although bishops exercised authority alongside the provincial governors, their status and influence made them major figures in their own right. They held office often for life (in comparison, a provincial governor may have stayed in post for only two or three years), and they had direct access to their congregation week by week in the pulpit. Inevitably, the more effective bishops absorbed the traditional responsibilities now increasingly evaded by the city elites. There are even cases of bishops— Synesius of Cyrene is a good example—securing the removal of an unpopular local governor. When riots broke out in Antioch in 387 and statues of the emperor were torn from their pedestals, the elderly Bishop Flavian interceded with the imperial commissioners who came to investigate the sacrilege and then hurried to Constantinople himself to plead, successfully as it turned out, with Theodosius for mercy on his city. Now that the church was free from all taxation, a key episcopal role was mediating with local government to extend the exemptions (not only from tax but also from military service) as widely as possible. Basil of Caesarea, for instance, fought against attempts by the imperial government to limit the number of clergy in a diocese who could claim tax exemption, arguing that the church should have an absolute right to decide for itself who should and should not be clergy. The largest group of his letters consists of pleas to local officials for relief from taxation or military service—in this he was exercising the traditional role of the city elite in which personal status depended heavily on the ability to create a network of satisfied clients through representing their cases with the imperial administration. Soon bishops were drawn into keeping law and order themselves. A later bishop of Antioch excused his late arrival at the Council of Ephesus in 431 on the grounds that he had been suppressing riots; another bishop wrote to a colleague, "It is the duty of bishops like you to cut short and to restrain any unregulated movements of the mob."[22] Synesius organized the defence of Cyrene and its surrounding estates from the incursions of desert nomads, and sometimes bishops even had to quell bands of enthusiastic monks who had come to desecrate pagan temples. As always in the empire, the desire for good order was more important than the condoning of Christian iconoclasm. There is vivid recognition of this in an edict preserved in the Theodosian Code of 438: "We especially command those persons who are truly Christians that they shall not abuse the authority of religion and dare to lay violent hands on Jews and pagans, who are living quietly and attempting nothing disorderly or contrary to the law. For if such Christians should be violent against people living in security or should plunder their goods they shall be compelled to restore triple or quadruple that amount which they robbed."

The men who could perform such roles were necessarily drawn from the traditional elites, and it was accepted that they would already be land-owning men of authority and education. "The cultural and social milieu which nurtured the urban upper classes of late antiquity did not distinguish future bishops from future bureaucrats," as one scholar puts it, a point that could equally be made of eighteenth-century French bishops and nineteenth-century English bishops, so enduring was the transformation of the bishop's status.[23] Even as early as 343 a council of western bishops meeting at Serdica agreed that bishops should be allowed time away from their sees if they needed to visit property they held as individuals outside them. Peter Brown has described how bishops acquired or absorbed *paideia*, "the exquisite condensation of hard won skills of social living . . . *Paideia* offered ancient almost proverbial guidance . . . on courtesy, on the prudent administration of friendship, on the control of anger, on poise and persuasive skill when faced by official violence."[24] Well might Gregory of Nyssa complain that the Church's leaders were consuls, generals and prefects, distinguished in rhetoric and philosophy, and no longer the ordinary men who had been Christ's disciples.[25]

As we have seen, the leaders of the second sophistic (see p. 62) had shown the uses of rhetoric in maintaining the status of the city elites. Most bishops were skilled speakers and knew how to play on emotions and rouse a crowd in their support. Ambrose of Milan was a master of oratory, and his most significant convert, Augustine, had first arrived in Milan from north Africa as the official city orator. A more subtle use of a congregation was to use it to pass a message to the imperial authorities. When the empress Eudoxia visited Jerusalem, she was met by a Christian congregation that had been coached by a local monk, Barsauma, to chant anti-Jewish slogans. " 'The cross conquered,' went the chant, and the voice of the people spread and roared for a long time like the great noise of the waves of the sea, so that the inhabitants of the city trembled because of the noise of the shouting . . . And the events were announced [presumably by Eudoxia and her retinue] to the emperor Theodosius [II]."[26]

The poor had always been of concern in large cities due to their propensity to riot at times of famine; the larger cities, such as Rome, had long made use of "bread and circuses" programmes in place to placate them. In offering help to the poor, a bishop was thus sustaining a traditional "pagan" role while at the same time acting as a pastor to his flock. This was recognized by Constantine, who distributed largesse for the poor of major cities through the bishops. Those entitled to help were entered on poor lists kept by the church and only through a licence given by the bishop could anyone beg. This was one of the ways that he used the bishops for state ends.[27] However, many bishops went far beyond any political needs in their active response to the poor. While in earlier centuries the giving of patronage had raised the status of the giver in this life, now the motivating force was redemption in the next. The contrast is vividly shown in an anecdote recounted by Ammianus Marcellinus of a Christian prefect of Rome, Lampadius, in 365.

> When this man during his praetorship gave magnificent
> games and very abundant largesse and yet could not
> endure the taunts of the common people continually
> shouting that a mass of gifts should be given to persons
> unworthy to receive them, to show his generosity and
> contempt for them he summoned some of the destitute
> from the Vatican and presented them with valuable gifts.

Lampadius was turning conventional notions of patronage on their
head; in this he was echoed by many bishops. Basil of Caesarea (in Cappadocia) urged his congregation, "As a great river flows by a thousand
channels through a fertile country, so let your wealth run through many
conduits to the houses of the poor. Wells that are drawn from flow better, left unused they go foul."[28] Basil is recorded as providing a great
complex of hospitals and a leper colony, appropriately called Basileia.
For the first time in classical literature, we see accurate descriptions of
the homeless poor, disfigured by disease, living as if they were animals,
huddled under the grand colonnades or corners of the agora. While we
have no means of knowing what proportion of the church's growing
wealth was diverted to the poor, it was already adopting its medieval
role as provider for the sick, one of its most effective and enduring func-
tions until the rise of modern medicine and state care.

In short, the bishops combined the roles of spiritual leader, patron,
estates manager, builder, overseer of law and order, city representative,
and protector of the poor among others. This variety can be seen in the
condolences sent by Basil of Caesarea to the people of Neocaesarea on
the death of their bishop, Musonius.

> Now withered is the bloom of your beauty; your church
> is dumb; your assemblies are full of mournful faces;
> your sacred synod craves its leader; your holy utterances
> wait for an expounder; your young men have a lost a
> father, your elders a brother; your nobles have lost a
> leader, your people their champion, and your poor their
> nurturer.[29]

However, the prestige of bishoprics was so high that they were often
fought over. Gregory of Nazianzus recounts of the bishopric of Sasima
in Cappadocia:

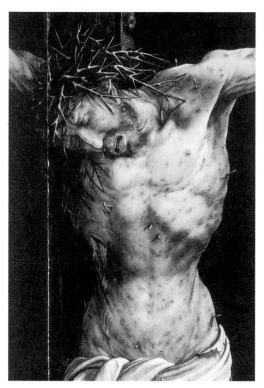

18. An increasing stress on the sinfulness of the human race led to graphic portrayals of the appalling agonies Christ had to go through to redeem humanity. ("The Crucifixion" from the Isenheim Altar, 1515; credit: Bridgeman Art Library)

19. A further development in the medieval iconography of Jesus was to differentiate him racially from his fellow Jews and to stress their responsibility for the crucifixion by caricaturing them. Note the same differentiation of Veronica, who has just wiped Christ's face with her veil. (*Christ Carrying the Cross* by Hieronymus Bosch, c. 1450–1516; credit: Bridgeman Art Library)

20. The motif of the Good Shepherd had been known in eastern and Greek art for over a thousand years before it was adopted for Christ, as here (c. 300; credit: Scala). Constantine is known to have erected emblems of the Good Shepherd on fountains in Constantinople, and in his *Life* Eusebius tells how his troops mourned him as their own "Good Shepherd." This is yet another example of how Constantine manipulated images to sustain consensus between pagan and Christian.

21. Traditional imperial iconography was also adopted as a setting for Christ's life. On the sarcophagus of Junius Bassus (359) in Rome, Christ is shown in the two central panels; in the upper panel, he appears in divine majesty ruling over the cosmos (in the same pose as an emperor is shown in a relief of 310), and, in the lower, entering Jerusalem, in a format also traditionally used for the arrival of emperors (credit: Scala). There were debates in this period over the relationship between the divine and human aspects of the emperor; here they appear to have been transferred into Christian theology, a forerunner of the great theological disputes over Christ's nature in the decades to come.

22. While Christian art often drew on pagan imagery, it also developed distinctive themes of its own. In this sixth-century ivory from Ravenna, the emphasis is on Christ as miracle worker. The four major miracles shown are (reading counter-clockwise from top left): the Cure of the Blind Man, the Cure of the Possessed Man, the Cure of the Paralytic Man and the Raising of Lazarus. Below Christ are the Three Young Men in the Burning Fiery Furnace from the Old Testament. By the fifth century miracles had become the primary way in which a Christian "holy man" could show authenticity as one favoured by God; stories of miracles pervade the lives of the saints. (Credit: Ancient Art and Architecture Collection)

23. We also find an increasing adulation of sacred objects, icons and the relics of saints. Here the bones of St. Stephen, the first Christian martyr, are borne into Constantinople by the patriarch of the city and welcomed by Senate, emperor, Theodosius II, and, probably, his pious sister Pulcheria, in 421. By now Constantinople is a Christian city. An icon of Christ appears at the gate into the imperial palace (upper left) and spectators in the top row of windows of the palace swing incense burners. (Credit: Bridgeman Art Library)

24, 25, 26. Goddesses had been prominent in Mediterranean religion, and the Egyptian Isis, here shown with her son Horus (above left; credit: Bridgeman Art Library) in a fourth-century A.D. limestone statue, was one of the most popular. As Christianity developed the role and status of Mary, she absorbed many of the attributes and iconographies of these goddesses. By the sixth century the Virgin and child, often accompanied by saints and angels, as in this example from St. Catherine's, Sinai (above right; credit: Staatliche Museen zu Berlin / Preussicher Kulturbesitz / Museum für Spatantlike und Byzantinische Kunst), is an integral part of Christianity. No one depicts the femininity, and motherhood, of Mary more exquisitely than Caravaggio (1571–1610), here in his *Rest on the Flight into Egypt* (detail, below; Ancient Art and Architecture Collection).

ANA ΤΡΟΦΗ NΥΜ ΦΑΙ ΑΜΒΡΟ ΓΙΑ ΕΡΜΗС ΝΕ ΚΤΑΡ

ΝΥСΑ ΤΡΟΦΕΥС ΔΙΟ ΝΥСΟС ΘΕΟ ΓΟΝΙΑ

27, 28. However rigid the theological definitions of the church, the boundaries between paganism and Christianity remained fluid. In this mosaic from Cyprus (first half of the fourth century), the god Dionysus is presented to onlooking nymphs as "a divine child" (above; credit: Scala). Perhaps more astonishing are the representations of the Virgin Mary produced by the medieval Italian confraternities. Here the confraternity of St. Francis in Perugia shows her protecting the people from the wrath of her son, who is shooting arrows of plague to earth (left; credit: Ancient Art and Architecture Collection). In Homer's *Iliad*, Apollo also spreads plague with his arrows, and the goddesses Hera and Athena intervene to calm his wrath.

29, 30. One of the major developments of fourth-century Christianity was the adoption of the pagan custom of celebrating God through magnificent buildings, many of them of great beauty, as the simple basilica of Santa Sabina (top) in Rome (c. 420) suggests (credit: Scala). In a lovely seventh-century mosaic in her church outside Rome (above), Saint Agnes has been transformed by her martyrdom into a Byzantine princess and set against a background of gold (credit: Scala). Two of the popes responsible for building her church (one of the most atmospheric in Rome) surround her.

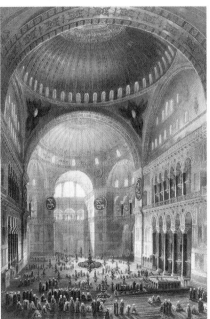

31, 32, 33. Among the most prominent church builders was the emperor Justinian (527–65), here shown with his entourage in the church of San Vitale in Ravenna (top; credit: Scala). His most majestic creation was Santa Sophia in Constantinople, here (above left) in a watercolour by Gaspard Fossati (1852, by which time it had become a mosque; credit: Scala). The massive transfer of resources into buildings was justified by Christians on the Platonic grounds that they provided an image on earth of the splendours of heaven. Any sacred object could be encased in gold and jewels, as this ninth-century gospel cover shows (above right; credit: Ancient Art and Architecture Collection). Well might Jerome complain that "parchments are dyed purple, gold is melted into lettering, manuscripts are dressed up in jewels, while Christ lies at the door naked and dying." These underlying tensions erupted, centuries later, during the Reformation, when vast quantities of Christian art were destroyed by the reformers.

34, 35. This diptych may well have been issued by the Symmachus and Nicomachus families as a memorial to the pagan senator Praetextatus, who died in 384. "He alone," it was said, "knew the secrets of the nature of the godhead, he alone had the intelligence to apprehend the divine and the ability to expound it." Here a wealth of traditional imagery suggests the resilience of paganism in the late fourth century. See chapter 15 for detailed discussion of the diptych. (Credit: Hirmer)

36. The death of Symmachus, the upholder of freedom of thought against Ambrose of Milan, is commemorated in traditional style in this depiction of his apotheosis (c. 402). He ascends in heroic nudity from the funeral pyre in a four-horse chariot and is then received into heaven. (Credit: Ancient Art and Architecture Collection)

> It was a no man's land between two rival bishops. A
> division of our native province gave occasion for the
> outbreak of a frightful brawl. The pretext was souls, but
> in fact it was desire for control, control, I hesitate to say
> it, of taxes and contributions which have the whole
> world in miserable confusion.[30]

This "desire for control . . . of taxes and contributions" was a corrosive feature of church politics. The linking of access to resources with orthodoxy was bound to lead to nasty rivalries when doctrine was so fluid. In Alexandria, Athanasius' chequered career meant that on three occasions one Christian faction was dislodged to be replaced by another, and the tax exemptions were transferred, to the fury of the dispossessed. There were many opportunities for the less scrupulous. The story is told of one bishop, Theodosius of Synnada in Phrygia, who was so angered by the heretics in his diocese that he set off to complain about them to the emperor in Constantinople. However, in his absence, the leading heretic, one Agapetus, declared that he had now become orthodox, seized control of the bishopric and was never to be dislodged.

Within a bishopric the different roles often came into conflict with each other. Cyril of Jerusalem was accused of selling off church treasures for poor relief at a time of famine (and this was a charge also brought against Ambrose by his Homoean opponents), while Theophilus of Alexandria, in contrast, was accused of diverting into his building programme money given to buy shirts for the poor. One of the complaints against Athanasius was that he had sold in the private markets grain specifically given to him by the emperor on behalf of the poor. For every Basil, ready to use his wealth for the poor, another diverted his to different ends. The case of Cyril of Alexandria, bishop from 412 to 444, illustrates the point well. His obsession was to discredit the rival bishop of Constantinople, Nestorius, through having the latter declared a heretic for his views on the two natures of Christ. Having manipulated a council held at Ephesus to uphold his view, he had to convince the emperor Theodosius II to support him. This involved, as a document sent secretly by Cyril to agents in Constantinople reveals, massive bribery at court. The sum of 77,760 gold pieces—enough, it has been estimated, to feed and clothe 19,000 poor people for a year—tapestries, carpets, even ostrich eggs were made available for distribution, with double handouts to those known to oppose Cyril. This strategy worked. Nestorius was deposed and forced into exile, and in 435 Theodosius ordered the burning of all his writings.[31]

The original message of Christianity, set in a framework in which power, wealth, even conventional social ties were renounced, and proclaimed as it was by a spiritual leader who had suffered the most humiliating punishments the empire could administer, could be seen as a threat to that empire. Yet now Christian leaders were firmly embedded within the social, political and legal establishment. By tying the bishops into the imperial administration and at the same time giving them access to wealth and status (which they could, of course, use in a variety of ways so long as these did not subvert the social order), the state had achieved a major political transformation from which there would be no turning back. One consequence was that the balance of power between church and state had shifted so that the more confident and determined bishops were even prepared to assert church authority over the state. The prime example of this is Ambrose of Milan.

# 14

## SIX EMPERORS AND A BISHOP
### Ambrose of Milan

Ambrose, bishop of Milan between 374 and 397, is perhaps the most fascinating example of how a bishop survived in the tricky and unsettled political climate of the late fourth century. His success meant that he is seen as one of the cornerstone figures of late-fourth-century Christianity, elevated together with his contemporaries Augustine and Jerome as one of the "Doctors of the Church." Much is known about him: his own words have come down to us in his carefully crafted letters, and an outline of his career survives in a panegyrical account of his life by Paulinus, his secretary, a "life" that has been memorably described as like "a tour of a grand cathedral conducted by a well-informed and helpful but rather overawed guide."[1] It presents Ambrose as a confident church leader, always able to control events. Recent research, however, is probing below the surface of this presentation, suggesting that behind the facade of imperturbability was a much less secure man, one whose career was characterized by "hectic improvisation."[2]

Milan was the linchpin of the western empire, well placed on the road network, its seventh city according to one ranking of 385. It was secure enough to serve as a court of the emperors but close enough to the northern borders to provide a base from which to launch campaigns against the barbarians. Understandably, it was a major priority of the emperors to maintain the city in good order. From 355 the bishop of Milan had been one Auxentius, a Homoean who had enjoyed the support of Constantius and Valentinian. On his death in 374, the peace of the city was threatened by unrest between the Homoeans and supporters of the Nicene Creed, and Ambrose, the local provincial governor, was summoned to keep order. To his surprise, he found himself acclaimed by the crowd and then accepted by the emperor Valentinian as the new bishop. He was not even a baptized Christian at the time, but within a week he had been baptized and installed. His sudden elevation is an example of just how far political needs, above all the need to keep good order, now predominated in church appointments.

Ambrose was at ease with the exercise of authority. He was the son of a praetorian prefect and had all the skills of the best of his class. To the outside world he maintained the impassive and impenetrable demeanour of a man born to dominate, and it was in vain that his most famous convert, Augustine, struggled to see behind the facade: "What hopes he nourished, what struggles he endured against the temptations that his very excellence brought or what solace he found in adversity, and what joys he felt upon the inner fact that were kept hidden in his heart when he tasted your [God's] bread: these I could neither guess nor discover."[3] He was highly able, an effective orator with impressive administrative skills and a flair for manipulating situations to his political advantage. He was not, however (again like most of the class he came from), an original thinker, and although he knew Greek, he never fully penetrated the intricacies of the theologies he now diligently set to absorbing. His most famous pastoral work, *On the Duties of Ministers,* was largely a reworking from a Christian perspective of Cicero's *On Duties,* and when he began plagiarizing Greek works he earned himself a stern rebuke from the scholarly Jerome for "decking himself out like an ugly crow with someone else's plumes."[4] Something of his natural austerity might be grasped from his preoccupation with virginity—he was one of the first theologians to preach the perpetual virginity of Mary, and he classified Christians according to their degree of sexual purity. His own chastity inspired others, notably Augustine, to make it a badge of Christian faith. Yet in his first years as bishop he seems to have achieved what Valentinian had hoped, good order between the rival Christian communities. Probably as a result of the close links he kept with Christians in Rome (Ambrose was known to see Damasus, bishop of Rome 366–84, as a father figure), he came to believe in the common divinity of God, Jesus and the Holy Spirit, and he emerged as a fervent support of the Nicene Creed.

After the catastrophic defeat of Valens in Thrace, the young co-emperor Valentinian and his mother, Justina, fled to Milan from Pannonia. The powerful Justina was a committed Homoean, and she demanded from the emperor Gratian, her stepson, a basilica in Milan to be the preserve of the Homoeans. Gratian, who was still only twenty, with no firm religious views of his own and somewhat out of his depth in the political turmoil of the time, assented. The basilica granted to the Homoeans was probably the Basilica Portiana, later known as San Lorenzo, just outside the city walls. Its closeness to the palace suggests it may have been built in the reign of Constantius specifically as a Homoean church, with an attached mausoleum for the bodies of emperors.[5] Ambrose found himself assailed by a Homoean community that not only was growing in confidence but also was swelled by refugees to the city. Doubtless complaints reached Gratian about Ambrose (Ambrose was charged with melting down plate donated to the churches by Homoeans, although Ambrose claimed that this was only to use the gold to ransom captives of the barbarians), and he finally asked Ambrose to give an account of his faith.

The result was the first two books of Ambrose's defence of the Nicene Creed, *De Fide*.[6] *De Fide* does little to develop the Nicene debate, simply adopting the belief, common in the west, that God, the Son and the Holy Spirit share a common divinity. Much of the work is a polemical attack on a range of beliefs which Ambrose brings together under the umbrella of Arianism. His method is to take a condemned figure or term and associate his opponents with it. This led to the creation of absurd alliances. So the Homoeans, who stressed the "likeness" of Father and Son, were grouped with those, closer to the original tradition of Arius, who stressed the *unlikeness* of the two. In sweeping condemnations reflecting Ambrose's background as a politician, the Homoeans were dubbed as enemies of the state, and Ambrose even claimed that God had sent the Goths as invaders of the empire as vengeance for its heresies. This was emotive stuff and aroused such great opposition from the Homoean community and in particular from Palladius, bishop of Ratiaria, the most sophisticated of the Homoeans, that Ambrose was impelled to expand his views in three more books of *De Fide*.

Whatever opposition *De Fide* aroused among the Homoeans, it impressed the uncertain Gratian, who seems to have been drawn to Ambrose as a father figure. In 380 or 381 Gratian moved his own court to Milan and announced that he himself would hold a council of bishops, from both east and west, which would meet at Aquileia, at the head of the Adriatic, in September 381. He was upstaged by Theodosius' own council of pro-Nicene bishops in Constantinople (the council described earlier), with the result that most of the bishops who attended at Aquileia were from northern Italy and were loyal adherents of Ambrose. Ambrose was an energetic networker and devoted a great deal of time to maintaining good relationships with his fellow bishops of northern Italy. Palladius arrived to defend the Homoean cause, to find to his horror that Ambrose had converted the "council" into a tribunal held in a side room to the basilica at Aquileia, with Ambrose installed on a special chair alongside the presiding pro-Nicene bishop. (The basilica has long since disappeared, but its magnificent fourth-century mosiac floor was rediscovered in the last century.) Palladius' account of the proceedings survives and, even if biased in the writer's cause, shows how Ambrose bullied his way through the proceedings by trying to associate Palladius with documents written by Arius that Palladius had neither seen nor was allowed to see. Ambrose also exerted his influence by insisting that every word be copied down by stenographers, a move which frightened Palladius, who knew the transcripts could be later used against him.[7] The end result of the "council" was not a creed but, predictably, a carefully stage-managed condemnation of the Homoean bishops. Ambrose's ascendancy over Gratian is suggested by the return, at about this time, of the Basilica Portiana to the Nicenes.[8]

Ambrose was not the only influence on the impressionable Gratian—there were other Christians in his court, many of them with links to Rome. When a group of senators travelled up from Rome with the traditional robes of the *pontifex maximus,* Gratian refused to accept them, the first emperor to make such a decisive break with the pagan world. (Ironically, the popes were later—in the fifteenth century—to adopt the title *pontifex maximus* as one of their own.) He also ended state subsidies to pagan ceremonies and ordered the Altar of Victory, on which sacrifices were made at the beginning of Senate meetings, to be removed from the Senate house in Rome. This was a much-resented intrusion and immediately a delegation of senators set out from Rome to protest. It was Ambrose, up to now apart from the debate, who persuaded Gratian that the senators should not be received.

Gratian never developed the toughness and tenacity needed to survive as emperor. In 383 he headed north at the head of his troops to confront German invaders, but his leadership was so unconfident that his men rose against him and executed him. Valentinian II, still in Milan, was now senior Augustus, but into the power vacuum in the north moved one Magnus Maximus, commander of the British legions, who had himself been acclaimed Augustus by his troops in the spring. Maximus hoped to lure the young Valentinian to Trier, where they could live, in Maximus' words, as "father and son." Ambrose knew how important it was to keep the young and malleable emperor in his own city, and he travelled himself to Trier to persuade Maximus, successfully, to defer the plan until winter had passed.

Next a new struggle broke out over the Basilica Portiana. While Gratian might have been able to stand up to Justina, her own son could not. Justina persuaded Valentinian to proclaim freedom of worship for those who were Homoeans and then attempted to reclaim the basilica for them. The first attempt to seize it, in 385, failed; in the second, the following year, imperial troops were sent to enforce Justina's demand and take over the more central Basilica Nova, then the cathedral as well. Ambrose was determined not to give in. He filled the Basilica Nova with his supporters and enthused them with passionate oratory.[9] The psalms were exploited for themes of persecution and a round of continuous hymn singing sustained morale. Historians of music note that the tense stand-off provides the first recorded instance in the west of a divided choir singing antiphonal hymns. The court was wise enough not to escalate the confrontation into violence, especially as its members became aware that Maximus, a staunch pro-Nicene who had possibly been alerted to the crisis by Ambrose himself, was considering taking the opportunity to enter Italy and depose Valentinian.[10] The troops were withdrawn, but it was a humiliating climb-down for the court.

Ambrose may have appeared to have won a victory, but he remained vulnerable to Valentinian's legislation, which allowed the execution of anyone interfering with Homoean worship. (It is important to remember that Theodosius' imposition of Nicene orthodoxy applied only in the east.) He needed a major propaganda coup to deflate the court's ambitions. Like most of the grander bishops of his day, Ambrose was an enthusiastic builder responsible for a number of large churches in Milan, among them the Basilica Ambrosiana, destined to be the city's new cathedral, outside the city walls, where he himself planned to be buried under the altar. His pretensions were criticized—the bones of martyrs, or Apostles if they could be found, were more appropriate founding relics for a church than those of the builder—although Constantine had set a precedent in Constantinople that some felt Ambrose was following. Ambrose took the point and went on the search for relics. Sometime after Easter of 386, Ambrose, as he tells the story in a letter to his sister,[11] had a presentiment that he knew where two local martyrs, Protasius and Gervasius, were buried. Sure enough, when the earth in the chosen spot was scraped away, two complete bodies were found. Their excellent preservation after perhaps some hundred years underground (there was even blood around their severed heads, Ambrose reported to his sister) might have cast doubt on the identification, but Ambrose hurriedly announced that this was the evidence that they were indeed the martyrs, miraculously preserved by God. As the bodies were carried off towards the Basilica Ambrosiana, the crowds surged round to touch them, and miracles were proclaimed, including the restoration of sight to a blind man who had wiped his sightless eyes with a handkerchief he had rubbed on the bones. Ambrose announced that this in itself proved that God supported the Nicene cause, and, in the mass hysteria of the moment, few disagreed.

Valentinian and Justina had been brilliantly out-manoeuvred, and in the volatile world of imperial politics it proved a massive blow to their credibility. Maximus, always alert to the weakness of the boy emperor, made his move in the summer of 387. He invaded Italy, and Valentinian and Justina had no alternative but to flee eastwards to Thessalonika and appeal to Theodosius for protection. Maximus arrived in Milan and appears to have attended Ambrose's services, although we have no other record of their relationship. However, Theodosius agreed to take revenge on Valentinian's behalf, and in 388 he himself marched into Italy, forced the surrender of Maximus at Aquileia and had him executed. Valentinian was restored as Augustus in the west and then set off to Gaul to regain the allegiance of his subjects there, while Theodosius remained in Milan.

Theodosius was the fifth emperor that Ambrose had served under and the first who was unequivocally supportive of the Nicene cause. (He soon repealed the Homoean laws of Valentinian, with the result that Nicene orthodoxy was now enforced across the whole empire.) However, it was difficult to find a context in which a relationship could be forged as, despite Ambrose's power and experience, the social and political gulf between a bishop and an emperor remained immense. Their first known encounter ended in mutual embarrassment. Theodosius attended mass in the Basilica Ambrosiana, now the city cathedral, and at the moment of communion he came up with the presbyters, as would have been expected for an emperor in the eastern church, but appears to have been rebuffed by Ambrose, who requested he come up with the ordinary faithful. Doubtless it was simply a misunderstanding, but it undermined Ambrose's chances of gaining a hold on the emperor, who, now nearly ten years in power, was a much more confident and inaccessible figure than his immediate predecessors.[12] Ambrose needed a cause that would enable him to develop a relationship with Theodosius. Predictably, he soon created one. In 388 a Christian mob, led by their own bishop, had destroyed a synagogue in Callinicum, a remote town on the Euphrates. Theodosius, who knew the importance of maintaining order on the borders and subjecting all equally to the laws, ordered the local governor to punish the criminals and compensate the victims. (Compare the edict from the Theodosian Code quoted earlier, p. 212.) Ambrose raised the issue directly in a letter to the emperor. Surely a Christian could not be responsible for re-creating a house "where Christ was denied"? And what if the bishop refused as a matter of conscience? Was Theodosius to make a martyr of him? Even more chillingly for the modern reader, Ambrose said that he himself would be happy to take responsibility for the burning: "I declare that I burned down the synagogue; at least that I gave the orders that there would be no building in which Christ was denied."[13] It is hard to know what was going on here. Ambrose shared with the Christians of his day an antipathy to Jews, and the destruction of a synagogue in itself clearly meant little to him. He was surely using the incident as a means of getting attention, and in his letter to Theodosius he elaborated what was perhaps the real issue, that the emperor should privilege Christians by actively supporting them against their enemies. When Theodosius next attended mass, Ambrose preached a sermon on the same theme. It was the duty of a Christian emperor to show solidarity with his fellow Christians. Theodosius then, in Ambrose's version of the encounter, appeared to capitulate over Callinicum and cancelled all his orders to the provincial governor.

In his influential study of the relationship between Christianity and Judaism, *Verus Israel,* Marcus Simon sees the Callinicum affair as marking a new departure, the moment when "the protection that the empire had granted to the persons and property of the Jews was relaxed."[14] Simon suggests that after Ambrose's "success" in Callinicum, references to Jews in imperial legislation become increasingly vituperative and the laws more discriminatory. That the climate of hostility towards Jews increased in these years is not in doubt, although other bishops were more openly vindictive towards the Jews than Ambrose was. (St. John Chrysostom and Jerome were profoundly anti-Jewish, with John Chrysostom at one point referring to the synagogue as a "dwelling place for demons . . . a hideout for thieves . . . a den of wild animals.") However, Simon may have drawn too readily on Ambrose's own triumphant account of the incident. It is known that when Ambrose prepared his letters for publication he added an extra paragraph to his original letter to the emperor to suggest that his victory over Theodosius was more resounding than it probably was.[15] In fact, Theodosius seems to have been unimpressed by Ambrose's manoeuvres. There is evidence that Ambrose was banned from the court,[16] and, far from being more openly Christian, Theodosius soon headed to Rome, where he vigorously courted the pagan senatorial aristocracy, whose political support he considered vital.

Up to this moment Theodosius had shown himself moderate and competent in his government (his response to anti-imperial riots in Antioch in 387 was comparatively restrained), but in 390 his reputation received a humiliating blow. Rioting in Thessalonika had resulted in the death of the garrison commander, one Butheric. Theodosius, far away in Milan, ordered retaliation, and the accounts suggest his temper got the best of him and he requested no quarter be given; thousands apparently died in the ensuing massacre. Surviving accounts may be oversimplified—the emperor's orders may not have been as harsh as was later reported, or the local troops may have been particularly ill disciplined—but Theodosius could not escape the ultimate responsibility for what was a public relations disaster. What happened next is difficult to unravel. Theodosius was clearly searching for some means of restoring his position, and he seems to have taken advantage of Ambrose's expressed horror at the incident (the bishop intimated that he could no longer give the emperor communion). In any event, Theodosius stage-managed a ceremony in the Basilica Ambrosiana, the largest public building in Milan, at which he asked for penance. Who was using whom is not easily established. In all the surviving historical accounts the massacre and Theodosius' penance are associated, suggesting that contemporaries saw the emperor as successfully redeeming himself. In other words, Theodosius extricated himself skillfully from a difficult situation. Ambrose, however, presented a completely different slant on the matter. Here was the emperor, deep in sin, coming to church to be purged of it—effectively an emperor was accepting the supremacy of the church over state matters.

In the long run it was Ambrose's interpretation (deepened as it was by medieval interpretations, possibly distorted, of Augustine's magisterial *City of God* and works such as Thomas Aquinas' *On Kingship*) that triumphed. While imperial rule in the west was to collapse in less than a hundred years, the church survived, and the event became part of its collective memory and the cornerstone of the Roman Catholic view of the Church-state relationship. When Pope Gregory VII excommunicated the emperor Henry IV in the 1070s, it was Ambrose's action against Theodosius that he called on to enforce his ultimate supremacy (successfully in that Henry came to seek penance). Ambrose's earlier ambition, to persuade the emperor to adopt a policy of direct support for Christianity against paganism, also met with success. Within a few weeks of his public penance, Theodosius had passed laws that in effect banned all expressions of cult worship at pagan shrines. Encouraged by the initiative, Christian mobs now began destroying the great shrines of the ancient world. Nearly twelve hundred years after their inauguration, the Olympic Games were held for the last time in 395.

In 392 Valentinian was found dead at Vienne in Gaul. One Eugenius declared himself Augustus, but his legitimacy was challenged by Theodosius, who declared his own son Honorius as his co-Augustus and successor in the western empire. Eugenius was defeated in September 394 at the battle of the river Frigidus. After his victory, Theodosius returned to Milan. However, at the games held to celebrate his arrival, he fell ill, and on January 17, 395, he died. In a masterly funeral oration, Theodosius was woven by Ambrose into the fabric of the Church and installed in glory in heaven:

> Relieved therefore of the doubt of conflicts, Theodosius
> of worshipful memory now enjoys everlasting light and
> eternal tranquillity, and for the deeds which he performed in this body, he is recompensed with fruits of
> divine reward. And it is because Theodosius of worshipful memory loved the Lord his God, that he deserved the
> company of saints.[17]

Maximus and Eugenius, Ambrose assured his listeners, had gone to hell. Ambrose then transferred the faith of Theodosius to his sons—Honorius, now emperor in the western provinces, and Arcadius, who was to rule in the Greek east. Not only Theodosius but the dynasty had been claimed for the church and Christ.

Ambrose died just two years later, at Easter 397. (He was indeed buried in his great basilica, near to Protasius and Gervasius, the first bishop known to have been buried in a church he had himself built.) His survival within the tangled political situation of late imperial politics was remarkable. His career may have been one of "hectic improvisation," but he proved astonishingly versatile in the range of tools he used. Whether composing letters to the emperor, using a small gathering to impose his views (Aquileia) or playing a crowd with the use of rhetoric, song and opportunely discovered martyrs' bodies, he knew how to create the effects he wanted. He did not always succeed—the Callinicum affair was almost certainly a failure—but he survived in office; by the end of his life the church, in the west if not in the east, had created a role for itself in state affairs from which it could not be easily dislodged.

This was not his only significance. Ambrose may not have been an intellectual, but he was determined to bring the ideology of Christianity into social and political life. He presented the orthodox (Nicene) church as battling against a world corrupted by paganism and heresies. It alone was the guardian of the great mysteries of God to which all, even emperors, were admitted on an equal basis. Ambrose was committed to imposing the dominance of the church on secular society, and he hammered home his message week by week through his powerfully delivered sermons. This was the redirection of rhetoric in the service of the church. Ivor Davidson writes:

> What mattered in the end was that Ambrose's intellectual showmanship worked for those he needed to sway most—the movers and shakers of his own city, and their social peers within a wider Italian radius (embracing Rome itself) who needed to be either convinced or reminded that the philosophy of the *saeculum* [the community outside the church] had been vanquished by a definitive revealed truth.[18]

It was the combination of this spiritual message with the use of personal authority and passionate rhetoric that made Ambrose so formidable and ensured his place among the founding figures of the Roman Catholic Church.

# 15

## INTERLUDE

## Quintus Aurelius Symmachus and the Defence of Paganism

Among the thousands of items on display in the collections of the Victoria and Albert Museum in London, it is easy to miss a small rectangular ivory plaque in a glass case in a gallery near the entrance hall. Carved as a relief, on its surface is a woman dressed as a respectable matron of ancient Greece, wearing a chiton, a long full tunic, covered by a mantle. An ivy garland is entwined in her hair. She is absorbed in some form of religious ritual—scattering incense over a fire set on a square altar— while on the other side of the altar a small girl holds out to her a small vase and a bowl filled with figs. An oak tree shadows them both.

An art historian would recognize the plaque as one leaf of a diptych, a double panel whose leaves fold together. In the ancient world diptychs were a means of communication, and originally they were made of wood with a wax surface set inside each panel. Messages would be inscribed on the wax, the two panels folded and sealed and sent off, secure, by messenger. By the late fourth century A.D. a diptych had acquired a more formal status as the format in which a major official, a consul, for instance, would announce his appointment to office to his friends. A surviving diptych of A.D. 406, in ivory, which had replaced wood as the favoured material, shows one Probus celebrating his appointment as consul in Rome. He is portrayed on one panel, and his emperor, Honorius, is on the other so that the recipients of the diptych could appreciate the glory of Probus' achievement and the favour he enjoyed within the imperial hierarchy.

Luckily, the other side of the Victoria and Albert panel survives, if in fragments, in the Musée de Cluny in Paris.[1] The Musée de Cluny panel also shows a priestess, although she is much less formally dressed than her sister in London, with one breast overflowing from her chiton and her mantle gathered round her hips. She is turning towards a small circular sacrificial altar on which a fire is burning and is shadowed by a pine tree from which hang a pair of cymbals (now damaged). In each hand she bears a flaming torch held downwards.

Clearly this diptych is not an official announcement. Something more private is being expressed, and fortunately the diptych provides its own clues. Each of the panels has a single word set below the top border: the London panel is inscribed SYMMACHORUM, "of the Symmachi," and the Parisian NICOMACHO[RU]M, of the Nicomachi." The Nicomachi and Symmachi were two of the leading Roman senatorial families in the late fourth century, and both heads of the families in these years, Virius Nicomachus (c. 340–94) and Quintus Aurelius Symmachus (340–402), enjoyed distinguished careers. The families were closely connected. Nicomachus' son married the daughter of Symmachus in the early 390s, and in 400 Symmachus' son married Nicomachus' granddaughter.[2] Many scholars have seen the diptych to be an announcement of one of these marriages. Yet the details of the reliefs do not suggest any celebration; in fact, the opposite—two lowered torches are traditionally a symbol of mourning or sorrow and are usually found in funerary contexts.

One of these contexts is the myth of Cybele and her lover Attis. The cult of Cybele, the mother goddess, had originated in Anatolia but had long been celebrated in both Greece and Rome. The myth tells of the castration and death of Attis followed by Cybele's desperate search for him; Cybele carries downturned torches on her quest, which will eventually end with his rebirth. A pine tree also figures in the myth. It was a symbol of Attis, and one was carried in procession each March to the temple of Cybele in Rome during Cybele's festival.[3] Cymbals hanging from a branch have also been found accompanying a representation of a high priest of Cybele from Ostia, the port of Rome. In 394, when Nicomachus was consul, he is known to have revived the festival, and so perhaps a specific connection between him and the iconography of "his" panel lies here.[4]

Reversed torches are found too in another context and in another part of the Roman empire, in the mysteries of Persephone, wife of Hades and goddess of the underworld, held annually at Eleusis near Athens. According to the myth, Persephone was compelled to spend part of the year in the underworld with her husband but was allowed to rejoin her mother, Demeter, each spring. Coins survive from about 80 B.C. showing Persephone bearing downturned torches, and the goddess is portrayed with similar torches on two altars, probably from the A.D. 380s, from Athens (now in the National Archaeological Museum there). Persephone, usually known as Kore in the Roman world, has also been found with her torches on an ossuary or child's stone coffin in Rome. It is believed that downturned torches were used in the preliminary ritual of purification before the initiation rites of the Eleusinian mysteries proper.[5] The altar on the Symmachi panel is typical of those found in rural areas, and an oak tree is often added to make a background in similar scenes. The sacrifice shown seems to be associated with the cult of Dionysus. Priestesses of Dionysus wore an ivy garland similar to the one carved on the panel, and it is known that children were given a role within Dionysiac ceremonies. There is, however, yet another allusion. A coin from the reign of Hadrian dated to A.D. 138 shows the traditional Roman virtue of *pietas,* normally associated with loyalty, comradeship and justice, both in public and private life, personified as a priestess standing by an altar with her right hand raised and the left carrying incense, a similar pose to that on the panel. A temple to *Pietas* as a goddess had been built in Rome as early as 191 B.C.[6]

The diptych thus includes several references to myths and images from the traditional "pagan" religions of the Greco-Roman world, and it shows the continuing spiritual vitality of the pagan tradition even late in the fourth century. It is remarkable how many sources are drawn on in these two images—Anatolian, Greek and Roman—while the reliefs echo the restrained style of Athenian gravestones of the fifth century B.C. What more can the diptych tell about the lives of two traditional and still pagan Roman families within the closing years of the fourth century A.D.?

Rome itself, though largely intact (it was sacked for the first time by the Goths in 410), was by now marginal to the government of the empire, whose administrative and strategic centres had, as we have seen, moved towards the northern and eastern borders. Despite this the senatorial families of the city had maintained their prestige and wealth, and many, though not all, had clung to the old gods of the empire as Christianity flourished. By the late fourth century there was increasing pressure from church and emperor to convert, which meant, of course, as Paul had preached, the rejection of all pagan symbols, including statues of the gods. As has already been mentioned, these were the years in which Paul's influence was particularly powerful, as the building of the basilica of S. Paulo Fuori le Mura on the outskirts of Rome in the 380s shows. It was in this context that the Altar of Victory had been removed from the Senate house. A delegation of senators sent to Milan in 382 had been refused admission to the emperor after Ambrose persuaded Gratian not to receive it. When Gratian died in 383 and was succeeded by the boy emperor Valentinian II, the senators tried again, and it was Symmachus himself, now prefect of the city, who wrote an eloquent and powerful letter to Valentinian. It was not just the removal of the altar that he deplored but the denigration of all that it symbolized, the diverse spiritual world of paganism and the freedom of thought it allowed. "What does it matter," he wrote, "by which wisdom each of us arrives at the truth? It is not possible that only one road leads to so sublime a mystery." Ambrose saw the letter and replied, "What you are ignorant of, we know from the word of God. And what you try to infer, we have established as truth from the very wisdom of God." Again, Ambrose prevailed and Valentinian refused Symmachus' request.[7]

This is one of the pivotal moments of our story. There could be no clearer expression of two wisdoms, one that of the Greek speculative tradition in which there are many ways to the truth, the other that of the Christian tradition in which wisdom rests with God alone. They represent totally different ways of approaching and interpreting the world, here directly in conflict. It is true that Symmachus gained a minor victory when Theodosius, the emperor of the east, visited Rome in 389 to woo the senatorial aristocracy and appointed him as consul for the year 391. Yet Theodosius did not permit the return of the Altar of Victory, and, in the 390s, under the influence of Ambrose, he passed the first comprehensive laws banning pagan worship.

There was to be one last defence of the old traditions. Valentinian, officially emperor in the western half of the empire, died in 392, and in his place an associate of Symmachus, Eugenius, a professor of rhetoric, was proclaimed emperor of the west. Eugenius was a flexible man, nominally a Christian, but tolerant of polytheism and ready to support its survival. The Victory Altar was triumphantly returned to the Senate house. This success, however, was short lived. Theodosius had earmarked the western empire for his own son, Honorius, and he marched westwards against the usurper. Symmachus did not join Eugenius' army, but Nicomachus did. As the two armies met at the river Frigidus (which flows into the north end of the Adriatic) in September 394, Eugenius set up a statue of Jupiter, the father of the gods, overlooking the battlefield, and his men went into battle behind statues of Hercules, the god/hero who for centuries had been adopted as a symbol of strength by Greek and Roman kings and commanders. In the heat of the battle a violent wind, the notorious *bora,* brought havoc to Eugenius' army, which was destroyed by Theodosius. Even though this was essentially a power struggle between imperial rivals, the storm was widely interpreted as a mark of the favour of the Christian God, and the battle came to be seen to mark the "triumph" of Christianity. It was after this defeat that Nicomachus committed suicide. His friend Symmachus died in 402.

So how does the diptych fit into the story? It is possible that it refers to the death of either Symmachus or Nicomachus, but it would be strange for the death of one of the two to have inspired a diptych in which both families are given equal treatment. There was, however, another notable death in these years that both families may have wished to commemorate, that of the prominent senator Vettius Agorius Praetextatus, who died in late 384. Praetextatus was typical of the pagans of his time in that he was linked to many different cults. His tomb in Rome has an inscription that describes him as priest and initiate to the Roman cult of Vesta, the Eleusinian mysteries in Greece, the cult of Hecate at Aegina (in the Aegean), the worship of the Egyptian god Serapis and the cults of Mithras, Cybele and Sol (the Sun), all from the east. He is known to have been initiated into the Eleusinian mysteries when he was proconsul in Greece between 362 and 364, and this may provide a link to the downturned torches of Persephone, although, like Nicomachus, he was also involved with Cybele. He was renowned for his knowledge of the gods. An account of one of his "discourses" survives:

> As Praetextatus ended his discourse [on the nature of the gods], the company regarded him in wide-eyed wonder and amazement. Then one of the guests began to praise his memory, another his learning, and all his knowledge of the observances of religion; for he alone, they declared, knew the secrets of the nature of the godhead, he alone had the intelligence to apprehend the divine and the ability to expound it.[8]

It is obvious, from Symmachus' letters, that he considered Praetextatus' death to be a devastating blow to the cause of paganism. The dead senator, Symmachus wrote to the emperors, was "the champion of every good thing, of old fashioned integrity"; his death had been such a shock to the people of Rome that many had stayed away from the theatres in mourning. Symmachus himself had been overwhelmed with grief. So it is possible that the diptych, composed to show the range of Praetextatus' spiritual allegiances, was sent out in later 384 or after to the sympathetic noble families of Rome not only to commemorate the dead senator but also to proclaim the survival of pagan cults. An allusion to *pietas* was particularly appropriate for a Roman senator, and there may have been good reason for it being highlighted here. The Christian ascetic and scholar Jerome, who was in Rome in these years, had written, in a highly publicized letter to a young girl, Julia Eustochium, in 384, just a few months before Praetextatus' death, that *pietas* in the home, in the sense of her loyalties to her father, should take second place to her own desires to preserve her virginity by not marrying.[9] This assault on traditional family values might (but we can only speculate) explain why Symmachus defiantly incorporated an image of *pietas* into "his" side of the diptych. The vituperative Jerome is also on record as saying that Praetextatus' zeal for his pagan religious duties was such that he had certainly gone straight to hell on his death.[10]

By the fifth century Christianity was dominant in Rome. Almost all the old families of Rome had converted and massive new churches were now built within the city walls—S. Maria Maggiore, completed in the 430s, and S. Sabina, 422–32, remain from this period. Their builders were the bishops of Rome and wealthy individuals who now had no fear of disturbing the ancient gods or their aristocratic supporters. The old temples, which, archaeological evidence suggests, were being restored as late as the 380s, were left to decay or were converted into churches. Jerome could now write, from Bethlehem, where he lived his last years, "The gilded Capitol falls into disrepair; dust and cobwebs cover all Rome's temples. The city shakes on its foundations, and a stream of people hurries, past half-fallen shrines, to the tombs of the martyrs."[11] The transition from the old wisdom to the new was irreversible. One final message from the oracle at Delphi runs:

> Go tell the king
> Apollo's lovely hall
> Is fallen to the ground. No longer has the god
> His house, his bay-leaf oracle, his singing stream.
> The waters that spoke are stilled.[12]

# 16

## THE ASCETIC ODYSSEY

A clean body and clean clothes betoken an unclean
mind.

THE ASCETIC PAULA, A ROMAN ARISTOCRAT,

TO HER NUNS[1]

As should already be clear, the spread of Christianity was a much more
complex and tortuous affair than conventional histories of Christianity
allow. Not least of the complexities was the contrast between the new
wealth of the church, exemplified by one of the greatest and most costly
building programmes in European history, and the complete renunciation of wealth by the many individual Christians who sought refuge in
asceticism.

The idea of disciplined training, *askesis,* was intrinsic to the ancient
world, from the preparation for games or practice as a rhetor to the
clearing of the mind for profound philosophical study. In a sense the victory odes of Pindar, the great poet of the fifth century B.C., which suggest
that a winning athlete comes close to the gods through his success, celebrate the same attributes required by the Christian hermit who tortures
his body so as to come close to his God. In both cases, discipline eventually brings the possibility of a spiritual transformation. Paul in
1 Corinthians 9:24 actually makes the comparison between training for

the games and for the Christian life, in the latter case for "a wreath which will never wither."

Asceticism is a complex phenomenon, and there are many issues raised by the adoption of an ascetic life. First there is the implication that the mind or soul has a relationship with the body (and that they are indeed separate entities), and that this relationship can be manipulated for some higher end, normally through the mind or soul "subjugating" the "desires" of the body. From the philosophical point of view Plato offers one of the clearest rationales for asceticism. The soul and body are distinct. The soul is made up of three parts, reason, spirit (emotion) and sensuality (desire), and when the "sensual" part of the soul aligns itself with the body the individual is prevented from reaching any kind of "higher" state. In the *Phaedo* Plato complains that the body "fills us up with lusts and desires, with fears and fantasies of every kind and with any amount of trash, so that really and truly we are never able to think of anything at all because of it." So the body must somehow be subjected to the reasoning part of the soul, if there is to be any kind of philosophical progress. The association of renunciation and the achievement of a higher state of being is at the heart of the ascetic experience.[2]

Plato's approach cannot be separated from other contexts in which asceticism appears in the ancient world. Continence and emotional restraint were widely valued, especially among the Roman elite, and they covered any form of excess passion, any behaviour which demeaned a man in front of his peers. This is why Stoicism proved so popular; it provided a philosophical framework that supported the traditional instincts of the elite, and there are many instances of upper-class Romans facing pain or death in service of a higher cause. A connection was made between a settled family life and good government, so that Augustus was able to make use of traditional "family values" in his stabilization of the empire after the civil wars. Sexual desire was, of course, one of the passions to be restrained, not least because the legitimacy of offspring was seen as crucial. Augustus tapped into older traditions of both the Greek and Roman world stressing the importance of sexual restraint. One pseudo-scientific theory, for instance, taught that a man had only a limited amount of semen and that its preservation helped preserve the body's strength until it was needed to produce heirs. (Traditionally, men in both the Roman and Greek worlds married late.) Abstinence from sex and physical strength went hand in hand. "As long as he remained a virgin, his athletic career was brilliant and distinguished. But once he began to have sexual intercourse, he ended his career ingloriously," one reads of an athlete.[3]

So when Christians turned towards asceticism they were taking a path that was not in itself remarkable, but there were nevertheless elements of Christian asceticism that took it well beyond mere conventional restraint, often into a realm of obsessive intensity. We should remember, however, that there were other groups, such as the Jewish Essenes, the Gnostics and the Manicheans, who also preached extreme asceticism. Jesus himself had enjoined poverty, and his death, as well as those of the Christian martyrs, enshrined a tradition of suffering at the heart of Christian history. Christians of the fourth century were haunted by the agonies of martyrs of the previous generation. "We have seen no executioners, we have not known swords drawn against us, yet we set up altars of divinity. No bloody enemy assails us today, yet we are enriched by the Passions of the saints. No torture has stretched us on the rack, yet we bear the Martyrs' trophies . . . ," as one bishop of Rouen put it as he welcomed the relics of martyrs to his church.[4] For many fourth-century Christians, it was as if suffering had to be undergone as a mark of one's faith, even to the extent of deliberately inflicting it on oneself.

This sense of guilt could only have been reinforced by the new wealth of the church and what the historian Eusebius was to call the "hypocrisy of those who crept into the church" in order to enjoy its benefits. Jerome confessed himself appalled at how "parchments are dyed purple, gold is melted into lettering, manuscripts are dressed up in jewels, while Christ lies at the door naked and dying."[5] Cassian, who brought monasticism from east to west, and who, unlike (as we shall see) Jerome, had a relatively balanced and perceptive view of asceticism, put it more prosaically:

> As their [the early Christians'] fervour cooled, many combined their confession of Christ with wealth; but those who kept the fervour of the apostles, recalling that former perfection, withdrew from the cities and from the society of those who thought this laxness of living permissible for themselves and for the church, to spots on the edges of towns, or more remote places and there practised privately and in their own groups the things they remembered the apostles had instituted for the whole body of the church.[6]

All this was set against the infinite rewards if the soul could be purified for heaven. Once the possibility of an afterlife was accepted, powerful images of it could be developed. Christianity's heaven of eternal bliss and a hell of perpetual torment had a powerful impact. In his Letter XXII to Eustochium, Jerome waxes on the great glory of the virgin as she reaches heaven, while, in the same letter, he describes his own fears of hell. To be confident of salvation, one could not take the risk of anything less than total commitment. Sexual renunciation was a central issue. Augustine took it for granted that his conversion would involve the adoption of a celibate lifestyle, and one young Alexandrian from the 320s was equally clear about what Christianity would mean for him: "If the Lord leads me on the way that I may become Christian, then I will also become a monk, and will keep my body without stain until the day when the Lord will come for me."[7]

So there were many impulses towards an ascetic way of life for Christians, and in the fourth century such a life was increasingly presented as drama. Written accounts of martyrdom had dwelt in prurient detail on the dismemberings, flayings, burnings and bone breaking involved, and the body now became the stage on which a different kind of performance was played out. Simply because the body has desires, for food, water, sex or human companionship, does not mean that they are necessarily difficult to control; many pagan philosophers appear to have seen an ascetic approach as requiring no more than a shift in perspective, a reorienting of the personality or soul (or, in many cases, simply living within the conventions of one's class). As the Stoic philosopher Epictetus put it, "there is nothing easier than to manage a human soul. What is needed is to will; and the deed is done, success is achieved," and the practice of philosophy can continue. Christians, on the other hand, tended to dramatize desires, particularly those of sexual desire (and here they followed Paul), as if they were cosmic forces, inspired by demons with whom deadly battles had to be fought. Jerome is an excellent example. Always a restless man, wracked by guilt and desire, he had come to the desert as a young man, and he later recalled the experience.

> O how often, when I was living in the desert, in the
> lonely waste, scorched by the burning sun, that affords
> to hermits that primitive dwelling place, how often did I
> fancy myself surrounded by the pleasures of Rome . . .
> though *in my fear of Hell* [my emphasis], I had con-

demned myself to this prison house, where my only
companions were scorpions and wild beasts, I often
found myself surrounded by bands of dancing girls. My
face was pale with fasting; but though my limbs were
cold as ice, my mind was burning with desire, and the
fires of lust kept bubbling up before me while my flesh
was as good as dead.

He was echoed by St. John Chrysostom, another preacher consumed by
the rage of sexuality and profoundly influenced by Paul. "How shall we
tie down this wild beast? How shall we put a bridle on it? I know none,
save only the restraint of hell fire."[8] Augustine's *Confessions* has an
extended dramatization of its author's struggles with his sexual feelings,
while for Anthony (see below) the devil appears in the shape of a woman
when his other ploys fail.

There is an important point to be made here. The aim was not to
torment the flesh itself in asceticism but, as Paul reminded his readers,
the sins of the flesh. After all, Christ himself had taken on flesh, and, at
the last judgment, the individual's flesh would be returned to his soul. So
flesh could not be evil in itself, otherwise it would come to a final end at
death and would never have been adopted by Christ. It was the demons
who took advantage of the flesh who were the problem. Paul laid down
one of the foundational statements of Christian asceticism as essentially
a battle between the unworthy self and sin/demons when he wrote in
Romans 7:18–20, "The fact is I know of nothing good living in me—
living, that is, in my unspiritual self—for though the will to do what is
good is in me, the performance is not . . . when I act against my will,
then, it is not my true self doing it, but sin which lives in me." Asceticism
is necessary to strengthen the will against the onslaught of demons (or
"sin"), and the battle is better prepared for if the body, and the will, are
trained.[9]

As Jerome's account suggests, the place in which the battle took
place became as important as the struggle itself. In retreating to the
desert, the body is tested to its physical limit by submitting it to unremitting heat, dehydration and isolation and thus strengthening it for its task
of overcoming sin. The desert was also removed from the city, the setting
for any form of "civilized" living, and was outside the rhythms of the
seasons so fundamental to preindustrial society. Life in the desert is constant, unchanging, in these senses very much, in fact, like the Platonic

God on whom many ascetics meditated. In so far as the aim of asceticism was to bring the individual close to God, the very peace of the desert, its lack of distraction, the chances it offered to conquer the demons that held back the soul from union with the divine, was ideal.

The Egyptian desert was the first setting for the ascetics' struggles. In Egypt there was a clear demarcation between the fertile Nile valley, watered each year by the floods, and the desert beyond, and the abrupt contrast between the two worlds provided a vivid backdrop for the ascetic drama. From the beginnings of Egyptian history the desert had been feared as the home of demons. If these spirits were now appropriated by Christians as "their" demons, entering the desert was taking the battle to the source of evil. So Egypt became the most prestigious ascetic destination—Cassian, who had spent several years in the Egyptian desert before moving west, told his audience of Gauls that they were unlikely ever to reach the perfection of the Egyptian ascetics. This did not prevent those who never travelled there from making use of its image. Martin of Tours in Gaul, for instance, discarded plain wool, the usual clothing of the ascetic, for a shirt of real camel hair, and another Gallic ascetic insisted on living on imported Egyptian herbs.[10] Special desert tours to see the ascetics *in situ* and ask their guidance became a favourite of aristocratic women. A particularly apt story is told of one Arsenius, a Roman of senatorial rank, who had taken to the Egyptian desert. A "rich and god fearing virgin from Rome" had come all the way to see him, expecting to be received with enthusiasm by her social equal, yet Arsenius rejected her, taunting her with coming only so that she could boast to her aristocratic friends in Rome that she had seen him. The last thing he wants, he tells her, is a host of women "making the sea a thoroughfare" on their way to disturb him.[11] His fears were justified. Eventually so many took to the desert that it was said to be as busy as a city. While the Egyptian ascetics were the most celebrated, those of the Syrian desert ran them close. Here the custom was for ascetics to ascend pillars (hence their name, Stylites, from *stulos,* a pillar) in the hope of coming to heaven. Some would stay up there for decades, with their lower limbs festering through inactivity. The faithful would be hauled up in baskets for consultations.

The archetype of the desert ascetic was Anthony. Anthony was an Egyptian Christian and spoke Coptic rather than Greek. It is said that he did not bother to learn to read or write, the point being made by his biographer that academic achievement was not important for a "man of

God" and could even be despised. After both his parents had died, Anthony became inspired by the Gospel text that those who would be perfect should give away all that they owned and commit themselves to God. His qualms that his unmarried sister would miss his support were soothed by a revelation that he should not care about the morrow, and he sent her off to a nunnery. He then, in about 269, embarked on a long retreat (he may have lived until he was over a hundred, dying in 356) in which he settled first on the fringes of the Egyptian desert, then moved to an abandoned fort across the Nile and eventually even further, into places where only nomadic Arab tribes wandered. Thus was established the idea in which an ever-deeper journey into physical remoteness corresponded to a pilgrimage to the innermost depths of being. Anthony's life was written up either by Athanasius or someone close to him, in about 357, and this "vibrant ascetic odyssey," as Peter Brown has described it, caught the imagination of Christians throughout the empire. Anthony, wrote its author, "possessed in a very high degree *apatheia*—perfect self-control, freedom from passion—the ideal of every monk and ascetic striving for perfection. Christ, who was free from every emotional weakness and fault, is his model."[12]

Augustine gives an account in his *Confessions* of two of his friends coming across the text and being inspired to give up their careers in the imperial service to follow in Anthony's footsteps instead. So began a new genre of literature in which the ascetic acquired the status of a celebrity. Famous collections of holy lives blended historical facts with amazing tales of miracles, and manuals allowed the reader to plot an ascetic path for her- or himself. Other works, more philosophical in tone, explored the language of asceticism, such as the state beyond all passion, the moment of absolute quietude when the end of the ascetic path has been reached, *apatheia*. Popular lives spread quickly. A life of one Paul of Thebes by Jerome is known to have been translated into Latin, Greek, Syriac, Coptic and Ethiopian almost immediately. With this substantial body of manuals available to those able to acquire copies, many ordinary Christians took up asceticism in their homes. Women refused to marry; some married couples stayed together but gave up sex. Others renounced their property and built monasteries for others or even ran their own. Some parents vowed to consecrate their baby daughters to perpetual virginity. Jerome grudgingly acknowledged that marriage had its purpose as a means of producing more virgins.

Yet while asceticism was appealing to some, it was also repugnant to many. It involved a reversal of the values of society, a rejection of traditional statuses and even a threat, some feared, through mass virginity, to the survival of humanity itself. Paula, the companion of Jerome, who founded a nunnery alongside him in Bethlehem, expressed the reversal of values in telling her nuns that "a clean body and clean clothes betoken an unclean mind." An account by Eunapius, a devout Neoplatonist, illustrates the shock effect of those ascetic monks who took to direct action against paganism, invading sanctuaries that had always been held sacred.

> At that time they brought into the holy places [the pagan temples] so-called monks: men by all appearances, though they lived like pigs; and they openly tolerated, and indeed executed, evil deeds past number or description. Yet it was seen as a work of piety to despise the divine: for any man at that time dressed in black and ready to demean himself in public, possessed a tyrannical power. Such was the depth to which human virtue had declined.[13]

Asceticism has always had an impact. In the modern world we need no reminding of the guru who preaches asceticism and yet who ends up a multi-millionaire fawned over by credulous celebrities; in contrast, we have the example of Gandhi, who used his asceticism with great sincerity but also shrewdness in the fight for India's freedom; he makes a fascinating case study of how asceticism disturbs those who have to deal with its political fallout. Perhaps the most profound transformation brought about by asceticism in the fourth and fifth centuries was in women who adopted a view of perpetual virginity. Renouncing sex involved a rejection of women's primary purpose in ancient society, to produce and care for the next generation, as well as the subversion of the view, found, for instance, in the Greek world, that women's sexual feelings were so powerful that women could not be allowed outside the home. Completely different patterns of life were now possible. In his letter to Eustochium, who had consecrated herself to virginity while remaining in her family home in Rome, Jerome explores the major reorientation needed in her life if she is to break her bonds to traditional Roman society. Eventually she came to live alongside him in Bethlehem. It proved so difficult to know how to deal with these "new women" that they were often referred to as if they were honorary men. "The manly deeds of this blessed woman" was how the (male) biographer of Melania the Younger referred to her renunciation of her wealth and all sexual contact with her husband. A story is told of a bishop who was discussing Olympias, who gave so freely to the church in Carthage. "Do not say 'woman'; say 'what a remarkable human being,' for she is a man despite her outward appearance," he told his listener.[14]

The extraordinary result of this resolute rejection of old roles was to create new ones of much greater power and influence, especially for those women who took the chance to read the scriptures and other sacred writings and even in some cases to learn Hebrew. "Generous in giving . . . outstanding in nobility, fertile in writing, worthy of the esteem of the whole world," was how one was described, while another man related how "in the land of Sicily I found a woman, most distinguished in the eyes of the world, but even more outstanding in the things of God. She showed me the way of truth in all things . . . convincing me how [best to live the Christian life] by reason and out of the scriptures."[15] Macrina, the sister of the Cappadocian Basil of Caesarea and Gregory of Nyssa, and a scholar in her own right, is given enormous respect by her brothers and their colleagues. One has to go a long way back in classical literature—to the days of Homer, for instance, where women of the noble class such as Odysseus' wife, Penelope, and Arete, wife of king Alcinous of Phaeacia, treated by all with honour because "she is full of unprompted wisdom," enjoy similar admiration.

Hand in hand with the elevation of virginity in these years came the development of the cult of the Virgin Mary. She was now placed on a pedestal as the ideal of virgin womanhood, "alone of all her sex she pleased the Lord," as Caelius Sedulius put it.[16] The references to Mary in the Gospels are relatively few; John does not even mention her by name. A particular emphasis on her virginity first arose when a verse in Isaiah, "Behold a virgin will conceive," was interpreted as prophesying the birth of Christ and hence inspired or corroborated the Gospel accounts of the virgin birth. This interpretation, however, was drawn from the Septuagint (Greek) version, which had used the word *parthenos* to render the Hebrew for *almah,* which meant no more than a young girl, so the scriptural base of Mary's virginity was shaky, especially as the Gospels specifically mention that Jesus had brothers and sisters—this was a point made by Julian in his *Contra Galilaeos.* The earliest references by the Church Fathers (Tertullian and Irenaeus, for instance) concentrate on contrasting Mary with the fallen Eve, and it is only the fourth century that sees the development of a cult of Mary as perpetually virgin—Athanasius was among the first to use the term "ever virgin."[17] The cult took its strength from the need for a symbol of female virginity, and its power is evident in the way the interpretation of the scriptures was distorted to support it. Jerome, in his commentary on Isaiah, even went so far as to argue that here if nowhere else the Septuagint version was superior to the original Hebrew,[18] and Jesus' brothers and sisters were now recast as "cousins," "brethren" or even children of Joseph by an earlier marriage. Once the doctrine of Mary's perpetual virginity was accepted as unassailable, it was possible for Augustine, for instance, to develop the argument that Jesus had been born of a virgin so as to escape the taint of sin which would have been absorbed if the sexual act was involved—an approach which only served to reinforce Augustine's view that those conceived in the normal way were corrupted by sin. This concern with the physical elements of Mary's virginity became so intense that it was even argued that she gave birth without losing her virginity. Once again Jerome produced an appropriate verse in support, in the prophet Ezekiel: "This gate will be kept shut. No one will open it to go through it, since Yahweh the God of Israel has been through it, and so it must be kept shut" (44:2). Doctrinally, the cult reached its climax with the declaration that Mary was Theotokos, Mother of God (still her preferred title in the eastern church), which was proclaimed at the Council of Ephesus in 431.

The cult of Mary was not confined to ascetic intellectuals. The need for a goddess figure was profound in a religion founded by Jesus and shaped by Paul, two unmarried men, and at the popular level there are numerous apocryphal stories about Mary's parents, childhood and upbringing and her assumption into heaven. The idea that she might have died and her body become corrupted became unimaginable, hence her "assumption" into heaven, noted in apocryphal sources for the first time in the late fourth century. In the east the emphasis was on "a dormition" (a falling asleep). Mary came to absorb the attributes of pagan goddesses. Vasiliki Limberis shows how the goddesses Rhea and Tyche, to whom temples had been built by Constantine in Constantinople, gradually became transformed into Mary, the Virgin Mother of God, as Christianity ousted the remnants of paganism in the city in the fourth century. It helped that Rhea, like many other goddesses, was herself associated with "virgin birth" stories.[19] A particularly fruitful source was the Egyptian goddess Isis, who had become a universal mother goddess in her own right. Isis had developed the role of protector of sailors just at the time when her cult was transferred from Egypt to the Aegean by merchants. Mary too becomes a protector of sailors, the "star of the sea." Isis' emblem was the rose, and this too is appropriated by Mary, while representations of Isis with her baby son Horus on her knee seem to provide the iconic background for those of Mary and the baby Jesus. These representations, richly developed in Christian art, suggest a yearning for tenderness that had not previously been satisfied.[20]

So the cult of the Virgin Mary developed much deeper populist roots than many others and was strengthened by support at the highest levels of the church (as it still is in Roman Catholic Christianity). A good example of how the apocryphal stories about Mary were adopted by the church hierarchy can be seen in the fifth-century mosaics of S. Maria Maggiore in Rome. The basilica was built by Sixtus III in the 430s in celebration of the declaration of the Council of Ephesus that Mary was the Mother of God. In the Annunciation scene, which presents Mary in great splendour arrayed as a Byzantine princess, she is shown to have been spinning—drawing on an apocryphal story that she was in service in the Temple where she wove a veil for the Holy of Holies. Here Sixtus has appropriated a story with no scriptural support at all in order to make contact with popular devotion.

One of the results of the elevation of virginity was to transform women who did not espouse it into temptresses, the "dancing girls" of Jerome's vision. While Mary was contrasted with Eve, women as a whole were equated with Eve, perpetuating her guilt through the temptation they offer to men. "Do you not realise that Eve is you?" inveighed the tempestuous Tertullian. "The curse God pronounced on your sex weighs still on the world . . . You are the devil's gateway, you desecrated the fatal tree, you first betrayed the law of God, you who softened up with your cajoling words the man against whom the devil could not prevail by force . . ."[21] So arises the dichotomy between virgin and whore, allowing no acceptable expression of female sexuality in between.

This approach to sexuality became so deeply ingrained in the later Christian tradition (and influences it still) that it is important to note that there were committed Christians who refused to endorse it. One such was Jovinian, a monk from Rome who became an ascetic himself but subsequently renounced asceticism as spiritually meaningless. Its rationale seems to have simply dissolved for him. Why should a virgin be given prominence in the eyes of God over a married person? he asked. Why should not one eat and drink freely so long as one offered thanks to God for one's good fortune? What was important was baptism followed by a life committed to faith and true repentance after sin. Jovinian argued his case well, with strong support from scripture. Right at the beginning of the Bible, for instance (Genesis 1:28), God had ordered Adam and Eve to be fruitful and multiply. There was no rejection of sex here (and, as we have seen, Judaism was actively hostile to celibacy). Jovinian also ridiculed the idea that Mary could possibly have given birth without losing her physical virginity. His was a down-to-earth, balanced and realistic approach, and his views appealed to many. Naturally Jerome, now in Bethlehem, was outraged and was impelled to write one of his most vicious counter-attacks—he described Jovinian's book as "vomit which he has thrown up" and its writer as a debauchee who gambolled in mixed baths (a particular place of iniquity for the ascetic) while true Christians fasted. Jovinian was declared a heretic, ordered to be flogged with leaden whips and forced to leave Rome for Milan. There he found himself again in the line of fire, this time from Ambrose, another fervent defender of the superiority of virginity over marriage. Jovinian's counter-attack failed, and sex and sin remained inextricably linked in the Christian tradition. "Marriage and fornication are different only because laws appear to make them so; they are not intrinsically different, but only in the degree of their illegitimacy," was Tertullian's bleak view.[22]

Christian asceticism could easily appear to be self-serving, in essence a turning one's back on one's fellow men in search of salvation for oneself. There was an inevitable tension between the Judaeo-Christian ethical tradition which stressed one's care for one's fellow human beings and the ascetic response which involved withdrawal from human society. Many saw the rejection of human contact as a spiritual liberation. "With no human company to hold him back, his union with God would be all the easier," as Cassian wrote of one of his ascetic acquaintances,[23] and Jerome approved of the response of Melania when her husband and two sons died in quick succession: "Now I shall serve you, Lord, all the more readily, since You have freed me from this burden [sic]."[24] But was there a purpose to asceticism beyond the search for an individual's internal peace and—until Augustine rejected the idea that a "good" life guaranteed a place in heaven—personal salvation?

One notable and recurrent theme was that the ascetic acted as an intermediary between God and man. There is an account of an ascetic being asked about the merits of two brothers—he retreats "to receive some revelation from God" and then returns to say that he has been shown both in paradise. Pachomius, by tradition the first ascetic to found a monastery, saw this as the essential mark of the ascetic. "When the Lord ceases to reveal himself, we are but men, like every man."[25] Another skill, long known in Christianity but now honed to even greater sensitivity by the committed ascetic, was the recognition of demons, false prophets and harbingers for Antichrist. The continual shifting of the boundaries between what was heretical and what was not, what was a Christian revelation and what was not, with the awful consequences of being wrong, resulted in major anxieties that ascetics were expected to calm. Martin of Tours was particularly adept at spotting devils even when they were disguised as professing Christians. Presented with a vision of Christ in majesty, Martin proclaimed that the true Christ would have appeared as a sufferer and this must be Antichrist in disguise.[26] Other ascetics claimed that in their struggles with the flesh they were drawing the demons to themselves and so diverting them from other Christians: they were, as one put it, "defending the walls of the fortress."[27]

Increasingly, however, the more stable and less tortured of those drawn to asceticism began to realize that peace of mind did not come easily. There was a growing recognition of both the immense loneliness of the ascetic journey and the presence of gnawing doubt as to whether one had done enough to be saved.[28] Cassian, who had originally seen the solitary life as an ideal, began to realize its drawbacks, not least in that personalities which were already deranged could become far worse in solitude. "The more it [a vice] is hidden [as when an ascetic goes off on his own], the more deeply will that serpent foment in the sickening man an incurable disease," he shrewdly noted.[29] Others pointed out the illusion that solitude necessarily brought peace. "Wherever you may go, you will find that which you flee from goes before you . . . If you do not first set yourself to rights in the company of men, you will never be able to do so on your own."[30]

By the fourth century there was a growing impulse to come together to share an ascetic life in community. Pachomius (c. 295–346), an Egyptian inspired by a vision to set up a monastery on the Upper Nile, is credited with the first rule for communal living. It proved so popular that by his death in 346 he is said to have presided over nine monasteries and two nunneries. In these early days solitude was still regarded as the aim of the true ascetic, and Pachomius' monasteries were seen as a sort of halfway house, providing, as it were, an initial training where the believer could learn to live in silence and good order before retreating into a more remote setting. Eventually, however, to live in a monastery became an end in itself (although as William Dalrymple points out in his fine study of eastern monasticism, *From the Holy Mountain,* the ideal remains to this day that a monk is free to leave a monastery of his own accord in order to continue his spiritual journey elsewhere), and the concept of communal living spread quickly throughout the east. By 355, Basil of Caesarea, one of the celebrated Cappadocian Fathers, was able to tour monasteries in Egypt, Palestine, Syria and Mesopotamia. Back on his family estate in Cappadocia, he decided himself to withdraw from the world "to break all the links that bind the soul to the body, that is, to be without city, without house, without personal property, without particular friendships, without possessions, without means of livelihood," and so he set out to found the earliest known monastery in Asia Minor. He appears to have been joined by or have joined others in a remote corner of his estate, and soon he was laying down rules for their communal living. There was to be a rota of prayer, the reading of scriptures, silence and the maintenance "of a profound sense of humility and self abasement."[31] One of the most important features of his monastic houses was their insistence on an authoritarian structure. For Basil the monks had to be divided into "those who are entrusted with leadership and those whose duty it is to follow and obey."[32] This is ordered living with individual self-expression now firmly discouraged.

In the east it remained the custom for monasteries to be established in remote places. So even today Greek monks segregate themselves on Mount Athos, restricting visitors to men and not even allowing female animals to live on the mountain. There remains in the Egyptian desert a monastery built on the site of Anthony's furthest withdrawal. It is 300 miles southeast of Cairo and 50 from the shores of the Red Sea; until forty years ago, when a road was built, it took three weeks to reach. In the west, in contrast, monasticism developed closer to cities. This was largely the result of the teachings of Cassian, a Scythian who had had personal experience of monasticism in Bethlehem and the Egyptian desert. He then travelled westwards, was in Rome by 405 and Marseilles by 415, and it was here that he founded two monastic houses, one for each sex (although these were not the first in Europe).

Cassian is important because he appreciated the benefits of ascetic life without being a fanatic. In his *Institutes* and *Conferences,* two surviving works which explore the nature of asceticism and its relationship to life in a monastic community, he meditates on the meaning of spirituality, assessing the vices that have to be overcome and the virtues that have to be cultivated to arrive at the true end of the ascetic journey, which he terms "purity of heart." Life in the monastery must be a combination of ceaseless prayer, reading of the scriptures and active meditation. There had also to be a well-defined structure to ascetic life, a disciplined pattern of living under authority. Cassian was well aware of the dangers of following a charismatic ascetic leader. It was too easy to become confused or misled. Instead the ascetic path had to be set within "the royal road built upon the Apostles and prophets, and worn smooth by the footsteps of all the saints, and of the Lord himself." Knowledge of this path could be achieved by constant reading of the scriptures and prayer but also by the acceptance of the authority of those who had trodden the way before, in the case of a monastery that of its elders. As Cassian put it, echoing Basil, "the first proof that you possess humility is this; that you submit to the judgment of the elders, not only what you are to do, but also what you are to think [*sic*]."[33] It is in the very discipline of living that the monk comes close to God. Order brings its own reward. The exhortation on the walls of one monastery provides an effective summary: "Examine thyself, be contented, control thyself alone, obey, be humble, judge not, condemn not, forgive that you may be forgiven and that you may live in God."

Cassian also urged his readers to be sensitive to the needs of the immediate community of fellow monks, so as to make oneself "loved by the brethren who share one's task." Extreme asceticism is not encouraged. If there is food available, the monk should not necessarily reject it—it is when the desire for food (or wealth or property) predominates that one wanders off the path. There is a wider community too, outside the walls of the monastery but not without its own needs. Cassian recognized that this community might have legitimate demands on the monks. Monks are an elite who provide a model for those who wish to come close to God, but through understanding God's will they are also able to show his love to others. "So we cannot assure ourselves of a deeply rooted charity unless, easing a little the proper demands of a rigorous and perfect life, we show a ready willingness to adapt ourselves to the needs of others."[34] No longer should believers rejoice at freeing themselves from the demands of their fellow humans; monasteries could adopt new roles as havens for the poor, hospitals or schools. So Cassian advocated a stable community in which the primary purpose remained the search for "purity of heart" for its members, but which was at the same time sensitive to the needs of others.[35] Once Cassian had shown that asceticism did not necessarily mean withdrawal from the local community, it became clear that those working within the community might also benefit from asceticism themselves. In Gaul the example had already been set by Martin of Tours (d. 397). Martin founded the first monastery north of the Alps at Liguge, in 360, and then, some ten years later, became a bishop, but he did not renounce his ascetic background. As his biographer Sulpicius put it, after he became a bishop,

> Martin concentrated rigorously on maintaining his for-
> mer character and attitude. His heart was blessed with
> the same humility, his clothing with the same coarse-
> ness. In this way, with a totally commanding but gener-
> ous bearing, he did justice to his rank as bishop without
> abandoning the tasks and virtues of a monk.[36]

So in the west asceticism becomes part of the mainstream of Christianity. Robert Markus sums up the process well:

> The boundary between Desert and City was being
> blurred, and the distance between the monastic life and
> life of the parishes diminished. The image of the monas-
> tic community was becoming adapted to serve as a
> model for the Christian community in the world, while
> the ascetic model it proposed to its members was
> becoming adapted to serve as the model for bishops and
> clergymen.[37]

Jerome, when out in the desert in his early life, had been asked to take sides in a dispute between two bishops. He replied, "Why should we bandy opinions about bishops, while clothed in sackcloth and ashes? . . . Chains, dirt, disordered hair: these are not the symbols of a ruler, but of one who weeps. Let them allow me my silence, I beg you."[38] So the ascetic rejects political involvement. While asceticism might have offered a potential challenge to the new wealth and political status of the fourth-century church, in practice it proved politically quiescent, and the state expected it to be so. Those who indulged in ascetic free enterprise were now reined in. As we will see, the emperor Marcian (450–57) used the Council of Chalcedon (451) to strengthen imperial control over the church, and Canon Four of the council deals specifically with the monks. "Since certain persons under the guise of monks disturb church and civil matters, travelling about various towns and presuming to establish monasteries for themselves," let them be aware that they should "embrace peace and occupy themselves only with their fasting and prayer, and remain in the place assigned them, and involve themselves in none of the business of the church [sic] nor of the secular world."[39] The authority of church and state was not to be challenged by those offended by its wealth and power. In practice, through enjoying the protection of the state and by remaining clear of politics, many monasteries were eventually to become among the wealthiest institutions in the community.

Yet, and this is important, asceticism reflected and reinforced an intense preoccupation with the individual self that was to become central to the Christian experience. Plato talked of the essential struggle between the soul and the desires of the body, but he does not involve himself personally in it. It is one of the marks of his greatness as a philosopher that he distances himself from the debate through the medium of dialogues, often using Socrates as a representative of his views. So it is possible to engage with Platonism intellectually rather than emotionally; there can be no sense of guilt, certainly no fear of eternal punishment, deriving from disagreement with Plato. The Stoics similarly made no heavy emotional demands on their audiences, because they did not see the achievement of "goodness" as a major challenge. Seneca put it in terms similar to Epictetus (p. 236 above): "The body requires many things for health, the soul nourishes itself [sic] . . . Whatever can make you good is in your power. What do you need in order to be good? To will it."[40] Paul, by contrast, both dramatizes the struggle and entangles it in the complexities of his own personality. "What a wretched man I am. Who will rescue me from this body doomed to death?" (Romans 7:24). While the answer lies in the death and resurrection of Christ, this did not appear to release committed Christians from a continuing process of struggle. Ambrose echoes him: "Greater danger lies not in attacks from outside, but from within ourselves. Inside us is the adversary, inside is the author of error, inside us I say, closed up within our very selves . . . it proceeds not from nature but from our own wills."[41]

It is hard to find a Christian of the period who has found serenity, and the most committed, Jerome and Augustine, for instance, appear to be the most tortured. It seems that once the body has been alerted to the dangers that lie within it, it can never rest. Tertullian warns his flock that they are as defendants perpetually in the dock, with the punishment for those who lose their case an eternal one. There is no more revealing account of the struggle within than Augustine's *Confessions,* where he battles to come to peace with a God who pries into his innermost thoughts. One can never know whether one is truly saved. There is no way to judge objectively just how guilty one is in the eyes of God. The only true way to secure a rest from tension on earth is to escape completely from the exercise of moral responsibility; here the "virtue" of obedience becomes crucial. William James, in his celebrated study *The Varieties of Religious Experience,* makes the point, quoting the response of a Jesuit:

> One of the great consolations of the monastic life is the assurance that we have that in obeying we can commit no fault. The Superior may commit a fault in commanding you to do this or that, but you are certain that you commit no fault so long as you obey, because God will only ask you if you have duly performed what orders you received, and if you can furnish a clear account in that respect, you are absolved entirely . . . The moment what you did was done obediently, God wipes it out of your account and charges it to the Superior [*sic!*] . . . So that Saint Jerome well exclaimed, "Oh, holy and blessed security by which one becomes almost impeccable."[42]

Here the abdication of the power to think for oneself is complete.

# 17

# EASTERN CHRISTIANITY AND THE EMERGENCE OF THE BYZANTINE EMPIRE, 395–600

In 395 the Roman empire was formally divided into two parts, each under a son of Theodosius: Arcadius in the east and Honorius, still only aged ten, in the west. The boundary was drawn so that the west was predominantly Latin speaking and the east Greek. The two parts were never reunited and were to have very different fates. While the east managed to consolidate its territory around Constantinople and so develop into the Byzantine empire, which lasted until its final overthrow by the Ottoman Turks in 1453, the western empire disintegrated. This had profound implications for Christianity, which from now on would develop within two different linguistic cultures, each with its own political context. Whatever doctrinal differences are proposed to mark the eventual divorce of the Roman Catholic and Orthodox Churches, the split was rooted in the political and linguistic division of 395. While in the Byzantine empire state and church were closely bound, so that the emperor represented God on earth and the church remained ultimately subservient to him, in the west the bishops, above all the bishop of Rome, eventually regained their independence and were able to negotiate new roles within society. Christianity was to be humbled by successful Islamic invasions in the seventh and eighth centuries, as a result of which both parts of the empire lost extensive territories, including the Holy Land, the great Christian cities of Antioch and Alexandria and the vigorous north African Christian communities.

During the fourth century the emperor had consolidated his position as absolute ruler; intrinsic to this had been an elaboration of his quasi-divine status. Diocletian had perfected the process of the elevation of the emperor above his subjects, linking himself to a favoured pagan god, Jupiter. For Constantine that god was Christian; in his *Life of Constantine* Eusebius describes the ideal of the Christian monarch, the mirror of God on earth (there are again shades of Platonism here). When Eusebius described the great banquet given by Constantine after the Council of Nicaea, for instance, it was as "an imaginary representation of the kingdom of Christ."[1] Eusebius gave the emperors the role of upholding Christian law and worship even if in Constantine's specific case Eusebius seems to distort history to make his case (as with his assertion, for instance, that Constantinople was founded as a Christian city).[2] Some forty years later the Roman Ambrosiaster (whose name derives from the mistaken belief that his commentary on Paul was written by Ambrose) commented that "the King [emperor] bears the image of God, just as the bishop bears the image of Christ,"[3] while the orator Themistius proclaimed that "the emperor is an emanation of that divine nature; he is providence nearer the earth; he looks toward God from all directions, aiming at imitation of Him in every way."[4] In Theodosius II's Law Code of 438, the imperial palace, even its stables, were declared to be "sacred," as if they were the precincts of a temple.[5] As we have already seen, representations of heaven in Christian mosaics were modelled on the imperial court, and when John Chrysostom searched for imagery to describe the second coming he chose to describe Christ as like an emperor arriving in the full glory of his office, weighted with gold and precious stones. While the theologians argued that there was an impassable gulf between the Creator and the created, in practice images of the world of God and that of the emperor blurred.[6]

The image of the emperor was matched by his power. The office had always been formidable, but under Diocletian its powers had been centralized and made more coherent. As leader of the armies, controller of all foreign relations and with absolute powers of life and death, an emperor had enormous destructive force at his disposal. During the riots in Antioch in 387 over tax demands, images of the emperor Theodosius I were defaced (an awesome offence in that statues of the emperor were to be honoured as if they were the emperor in person). As the mood calmed in the city, the terrible realization struck the citizens of just how mighty the wrath of the emperor could be, and rumours even spread that Antioch might be razed to the ground. Many fled to the hills. The bishop of the city, Flavian, set out to plead with the emperor, and John Chrysostom, the city's most popular preacher, told his congregations that they now had to throw themselves on the mercy not only of the emperor but of God. This was how the last judgment would be.[7] In the event the city was treated relatively leniently, although, as we have seen, three years later in Thessalonika Theodosius was not to be so restrained. A hundred and fifty years later Constantinople suffered an even worse fate. The emperor Justinian, faced by similar riots, the Nika revolt of 532, was encouraged by his wife, Theodora, to send in troops. Between 30,000 and 50,000 citizens are believed to have been massacred. It was the arbitrary exercise of this absolute power which was most unsettling; the fact that Justinian supposed himself to be a quintessentially Christian monarch made no difference. It was, after all, fully accepted that God might act punitively, and there were dozens of Old Testament texts to back the point, so why should his representative on earth be different? In any case, as the contemporary historian Procopius put it in another context, "Justinian did not see it as murder if the victims did not share his own beliefs."[8]

The Byzantine empire had always to be preoccupied with survival. This meant raising resources, in men and taxes, for defence while maintaining some sort of order among the burdened subjects of the empire. Christianity was increasingly interwoven with the authority of the state in that both church and state defined themselves as embattled by numerous enemies, and so, despite the very different contexts in which their fears of the outside world had evolved, they were natural allies. In legislation, the laws against Jews ("the madness of the Jewish impiety") reached a new coherence and severity, as did those against polytheists ("the error and insanity of stupid paganism") and non-orthodox Christians ("all heresies, all perfidies and schisms"). A law of Theodosius II of 438 speaks of "the thousand terrors" of the laws "that defend the boundless claim to honour" of the Church.[9] Punishments were harsh, including, for example, capital punishment for the making of a sacrifice. For the first time in the history of the Roman empire, correct religious adherence became a requirement for the full enjoyment of the benefits of Roman society. There remained, however, an immense gap between the legislations and its implementation. The empire was vast, many of its territories were outside effective imperial control and local elites jealously maintained their independence. There is little evidence, for instance, that the penalties for sacrifice were imposed, and Judaism, far from being eradicated, seems to have enjoyed fresh vigour in Palestine in the fifth century.[10] An edict from the same code quoted earlier (p. 212) suggests Jews and pagans were not to be molested by Christians if they remained law-abiding.

For the leaders of Christianity life was still seen as it had always been since the days of Paul, predominantly as a battle between the Christian way of life and a corrupt world. The mentality of Christian "weakness" persisted even when the church had in truth achieved strength. Through the life of John Chrysostom, John of "the Golden Mouth," we can build up a picture of the tensions that beset the church in the late fourth and early fifth century, not least in the conflict between the roles of bishop as Christian leader and as imperial servant.[11]

John Chrysostom, born c. 347, the son of a civil servant from Antioch, one of the great cities of the eastern empire, was another of those Christians who had been educated traditionally in rhetoric (under the influential pagan teacher Libanius), and he seemed set for a career in the courts until he converted to Christianity as a young man. Like so many others in this period, he spent several years as an ascetic, and he always retained his abhorrence of sex. His treatise *Virginity* relied heavily on Paul but interpreted the Apostle's writings in the most gloomy and grudging way. The original intention of God, John claimed, was to create Adam and Eve as an asexual couple—it was their fall which corrupted them and released the "dangers" of sex on the world. Like his contemporary Augustine, John was to take Paul as his mentor.

> Whenever I hear the epistles of Paul read out in the liturgy, I am filled with joy ... If I'm regarded as a learned man, it's not because I'm brainy. It's simply because I have such a love for Paul that I have never left off reading him. He has taught me all I know. And I want you to listen to what he has to teach you. You don't need to do anything else [*sic*].[12]

John's ascetic experience permanently damaged his health, but he was eventually ordained a priest and threw himself into pastoral life in his native city. The clarity of his language, the emotional power of his rhetoric and his concentration on the everyday challenges of life quickly made him the most popular and influential preacher in Antioch. His sermons are full of vivid denunciations, of the wealthy women, even those consecrated to virginity, who come to church flaunting their pearls and luxurious dresses, and men, obsessed with chariot races, pantomimes and banquet delicacies, who recline on ornate couches while dancers and flautists (the flute, as opposed to the lyre, was always a traditional symbol of abandonment) cavort round them. In contrast are the beggars, freezing in the winter cold, who even blind their own children to earn more money, and the city's prisoners lying in rags and chains, the open wounds of their latest scourgings still oozing blood. "Do you pay such honour to your excrements," one congregation was told, "as to receive them in a silver chamber pot when another man made in the image of God is perishing of cold?"[13]

Less happily, John also employed his considerable powers of invective against the Jews. It is possible from his eight surviving sermons *Against the Jews* to reconstruct a Jewish community in Antioch which, far from being abashed by the rise of Christianity, still celebrated its festivals openly and attracted Christians to them. John was furious, and his fury perhaps reflects Christian frustration at the obstinacy of the Jews in maintaining their ancestral religion when so many pagans were rejecting theirs for Christianity. How, he queried, could a Christian consort with those who had shed the blood of Christ and then come to a church and partake of that same blood at the Eucharist? Much worse was to follow. John was never restrained in his language, and he now resorted to scurrilous invective. The status of Jews was that of dogs. Their festivals were full of sensuality, their processions made up of "perverts and tarts," their synagogues the equivalent of brothels. They should be shunned as if they were a plague threatening the whole world. Quite unabashed in doing so, John employed Old Testament verses taken out of context, as well as those New Testament texts (such as Matthew's "His blood be upon us and our children") that had expressed early Christian anti-Judaism, to consolidate his argument. In later sermons he becomes more directly theological—the supreme proof that Christ was truly God lay in his prediction, fulfilled in A.D. 70, that Jerusalem would be captured and the Temple destroyed. As a result of their rhetorical power, these sermons were translated into Latin and became as much part of the western Christian tradition as of the eastern. Their influence persisted long after their composition.[14]

In 398, unexpectedly, John was asked to become bishop of Constantinople. For the right man this would have been an important promotion. Constantinople was an imperial city, wealthy and confident of its new status, and a sociable and politically astute bishop had the chance of enjoying considerable influence within the court and thus the empire. It was important to cultivate this influence, as the bishop was vulnerable to the intrigues of the bishops of Alexandria, who remained embittered at their demotion within the church hierarchy after the elevation of Constantinople in 381. In no other bishopric was *paideia*, the ancient art of courtesy, more essential. John was hopelessly unsuited for the post. He failed to grasp that in Constantinople more than anywhere else the church was subservient to the state—his own view that "the one appointed to the priesthood is a more responsible guardian of the earth and what transpires on it than one who wears the purple" was incompatible with his new position. Moreover, he preferred eating alone, was made uneasy by the luxury of the court (at one point referring to the empress Eudoxia as a Jezebel) and unceasing in his criticism of his clergy for their supposed laxities. He aroused enormous resentment when he inveighed against clergy who shared their homes with professed virgins in what he termed "the pretence of living together as brothers and sisters," and monks who ventured out of their monasteries onto the streets. He also weakened his position in the wider church by taking a tour of Asia Minor, where, probably overreaching his powers of jurisdiction, he deposed several bishops.[15] His only power base lay with the people, many of whom relished his populist sermons.

So when the bishop of Alexandria, Theophilus, set out to challenge John's position, John was vulnerable. Theophilus, in order to strengthen his own position in Egypt, had condemned Origen for preaching that God was without human attributes. As a result of the subsequent witch hunt against Origenists, a group of some fifty monastic refugees, known as the Tall Brothers after their four tall leaders, arrived in Constantinople (probably in the autumn of 401) and sought the assistance of its bishop. The "correct" stance for John would have been to support Theophilus' ban; John did not allow them to attend communion but he did offer them hospitality. They then appealed to the emperor, and the young and still inexperienced Arcadius, concerned at their ill-treatment, summoned Theophilus to explain the situation. Theophilus knew he would be undermined if the emperor supported John and the Tall Brothers, and he set out for Constantinople with some foreboding. As his luck would have it, a sermon preached by John on the vanities of women, a favourite subject of his, had been interpreted as a veiled attack on the empress Eudoxia, and she was outraged. Rather than being judged for his mistreatment of the Tall Brothers, Theophilus was able to install himself near Constantinople with several supportive bishops from Egypt and gather charges against John. Most were trivial, dredged up by two deacons whom John had dismissed, but when John refused to come and answer them (at what is known as the Synod of the Oak), he was deposed by Theophilus, a deposition at first supported by the court (403). John was arrested and exiled. Hardly had he left, however, than some misfortune "in the imperial bedchamber," possibly a miscarriage, was taken by Eudoxia to be a sign of God's wrath for the expulsion, and he was ordered to return. At this a group of monks, hostile to John after his harsh and insensitive treatment of them, rioted, and order had to be restored by the imperial troops aided by the civilian population who still supported John.

John did not last long after his return. There was never any likelihood that he could forge a stable relationship with the court, and Eudoxia was soon furious with him again over another sermon she, and most of John's congregation, assumed to be an attack on her. John's status remained unclear. The decree of the Synod of the Oak was declared invalid, but this did not lead to a formal reinstatement of John as bishop. He was acutely vulnerable, he had too many enemies around and near the court, few friends among the clergy and his primary supporters, in the crowd, were too volatile to help his cause. When he was finally expelled from the city in June 404, a popular revolt led to the great church of *Hagia Sophia* being burnt down (Justinian was to rebuild it in its present magnificence in the next century), along with Constantinople's Senate house. John died in exile, in 407 in Pontus (in Asia Minor).[16]

It is instructive to contrast John's unhappy term of office with that of his contemporary Ambrose in Milan. Ambrose had the immense advantage that he knew the intricacies of imperial administration, but he also realized the importance of keeping local bishops and clergy (so long as they supported the Nicene Creed) on his side. As a result, he was never as isolated as John. When Ambrose used crowds it was in an organized way and with clear objectives—it is even possible that he was sufficiently in control to manipulate them. In John's case the masses were ready to riot in his support, but unrestrained disorder did nothing to help his cause. John had the added problem of the rivalry of Theophilus (in contrast, the bishops of Rome, who might have resented Ambrose's dominance, were no match for him), but here, in allowing himself to be outmanoeuvred, he threw away the advantage he had as the man closest to the imperial court.

The rivalry between Constantinople and Alexandria erupted again in the debate that dominated the first half of the fifth century over the true nature of Jesus while he was on earth. By incorporating Jesus fully into the Godhead, the Nicene Creed had created a new Christological controversy.[17] In the traditional, pre-Nicene, formulations, the *logos* as Christ was something less than the Godhead; as there was no precedent for an incarnated *logos* (the idea was inconceivable to Platonists, who also made the point that if the *logos* could be incarnated in one man, then why not more than one?), it was possible simply to take the Gospel depictions of Jesus as they were. The *logos* was not God, and while incarnated in Jesus did not have to show the attributes of an impassible God; so, for instance, there was no difficulty in accepting a Jesus/*logos* suffering on the cross. However, the Nicene formulation, in which Jesus was always part of the Godhead and remained so while on earth, raised new difficulties as to how he could be human at the same time. The gulf between man and God was so wide that any form of unity seemed conceptually impossible. Then there remained the old problem that if the *logos* really *was* part of the Godhead, consubstantial with it, then the *logos* could not suffer any more than God could. Yet Jesus in the Gospel accounts did appear to suffer. So in what ways could he be classified as human while at the same time being fully God?

Once again the diversity of sources and the tendency of the Greek mind to speculate had spawned a range of different solutions. Despite Nicaea, there could still be found those, the Adoptionists, who insisted that Jesus was fully human and only "adopted" by God as his Son. Augustine himself has heard Jesus described as "a man [*sic*] of extraordinary wisdom, whom none could equal."[18] At the other extreme was Docetism, which taught that Jesus only gave the appearance of being human (*dokeo*, "I seem") but was, in fact, completely divine and unable to suffer. Other groups, such as the Apollinarians, named after Apollinarius, bishop of Laodicea (c. 310–90), argued that Christ had a human body but that his soul and his mind remained divine. Apollinarius was declared a heretic for these views, but his followers kept his memory alive by the ingenious device of pretending his writings were by the highly orthodox Athanasius. Some, such as Cyril of Alexandria, were completely caught out by this ruse. Then there was Theodore, bishop of Mopsuestia in Asia Minor, who argued that Jesus had been conceived twice, once in a divine form and once in a human form, the so-called Two Sons formula. In contrast to Apollinarius, however, Theodore did not believe these natures were divided between body and soul but some-how united in one person. Each attempted resolution simply raised more issues. If Jesus was fully man when he suffered, was he still man when he worked a miracle, or was he then acting in his divine role? What form of humanity did he take—man as before the fall, man as now lost in sin or man as he would be when redeemed? If Jesus was created as a perfect man, what did Luke mean when he wrote (2:52) that "Jesus increased in wisdom, stature and in favour with God and men"? Surely an "increase" implied that he was at some point an undeveloped human being, but was this possible? It could be assumed that he was not man in any way before the Incarnation, but after his resurrection did he revert to being only God, or did he retain some of his humanity? (Hilary of Poitiers argued that he remained both perfect man, fully human but without sin, and perfect God.) Connected to these debates was the status of the Virgin Mary. She was now the object of growing personal devo-tion, and her status rested on her role as the mother of Jesus. Yet was she the bearer of God (*Theotokos*) or of a man (*Anthropotokos*)?

The person around whom the debate was to crystallize was Nesto-rius, appointed bishop of Constantinople in 428. Nestorius had shown concern at the use of the title of *Theotokos* for Mary. He felt that this title denied the human nature of Jesus altogether and would have pre-ferred to see Mary as *Anthropotokos*, though he was prepared to com-promise on *Christotokos*, "bearer of Christ." After all, Mary had given birth as a human being to a man who was capable of suffering and dying, although he was, of course, the divine *logos* as well. Calling Mary *Theotokos* risked falling into the heresy of denying Jesus' humanity. Where Nestorius, like everyone else, experienced difficulty was in find-ing a formula which could explain how Jesus' two natures, human and divine, could co-exist. He favoured the term "conjunction" rather than "union," but his theological fumblings made him vulnerable to the new bishop of Alexandria, Theophilus' nephew Cyril. Cyril championed the *Theotokos* formula, and he saw the issue as one through which he could undermine Nestorius and humble the see of Constantinople. He pre-pared his ground carefully. He circulated a pastoral letter to his local bishops explaining that since the promulgation of the Nicene Creed as orthodoxy the only possible title for Mary was "bearer of God," and he then persuaded the bishop of Rome, Celestine, a natural supporter of Alexandria against Constantinople, to agree to this formulation. Next he won over Pulcheria, the powerful elder sister of the young emperor

Theodosius (who had succeeded Arcadius in 408). Pulcheria, who ruled as Theodosius' regent, had a personal devotion to Mary, and Nestorius had offended her by refusing to allow her to take communion alongside the clergy in the sanctuary of his church. (A similar standoff took place between Theodosius and Ambrose in Milan.) Having thus isolated Nestorius, Cyril began writing provocative letters to him, accusing him of undermining orthodoxy and causing dissension. Nestorius at first replied with reasoned defences of his position, relying on the scriptural accounts of Jesus' humanity, but Cyril's letters became increasingly virulent, demanding complete submission. Eventually he issued twelve devastating anathemas containing a full denunciation of Nestorianism, although in the process Cyril himself came close to denying Jesus' human nature altogether. If Christ as *logos* was now, as the Nicene Creed insisted, fully part of the Godhead, then he was beyond all suffering, yet Cyril claimed in the Twelfth Anathema that the *logos* itself could indeed suffer "in the flesh." This formulation made it difficult to see why Jesus needed to take on a human nature at all! The anathemas simply inflamed the debate. In fact, Cyril was no more able than Nestorius to explain with any clarity how the two natures could co-exist. A divine Jesus, he put it in one formulation, "inconceivably and in a way that is inexpressible, united to himself a body ensouled with a rational soul." Much of the attack on Nestorius depended on distorting Nestorius' views to the point of caricature by overemphasizing his stress on the humanity of Jesus, even to the extent of accusing him of Adoptionism.

Muddled by these vague formulas and distortions, the debate degenerated into a power struggle, and it was here that the determined Cyril triumphed over the less politically adept Nestorius. At the Council of Ephesus, called in 431 by the emperor Theodosius II to settle the matter, Cyril arrived early with a large group of strong men (they were euphemistically referred to as "hospital attendants"), overawed the imperial commissioner sent by Theodosius to preside, completed the business before the supporters of Nestorius had even assembled and then used massive bribery to keep Theodosius and his court on his side. Nestorius was condemned as a heretic. Theodosius was stunned by the controversy and bargained with the Alexandrians that the divisive anathemas be withdrawn from the debate in return for his condemnation of Nestorius, whose works were ordered by imperial decree to be burned in 435. The council left much bitterness in its wake. Cyril was applauded by his supporters and condemned by those he had outmanoeuvred. When he died in 444, one opponent suggested that a heavy stone be placed on his grave to prevent his soul from returning to the world when the inmates of hell threw it out as too evil even for there!

In 449 another attempt at solving the controversy aroused even greater anger. A second council at Ephesus was dominated by Cyril's successor as bishop of Alexandria, Dioscorus. Dioscorus drew on those aspects of Cyril's theology that implied that the human nature of Jesus was subordinate to the divine. He had imperial support and even used armed guards to bully his way ferociously into control of the council and push through sweeping condemnations of any bishops who could be associated with Nestorianism. The condemnations included charges of usury, sorcery, blasphemy and sodomy and were passed with the help of massive intimidation. Bishops were forced to sign their names to blank pieces of paper and one of the casualties was another bishop of Constantinople, Flavian, who suffered so harshly either at the council or in its aftermath that he died of his injuries. Dioscorus even excommunicated Leo, the bishop of Rome, whose *Tome,* a statement setting out a formula for the two natures of Christ in one person, was condemned. Leo, in retaliation, gave the council the name by which it is still known to historians, "the robber council."[19]

The emperors had learned their lesson. Doctrine could not be settled when personal and institutional rivalries were allowed to swamp debate. Once again imperial control, so crucial in establishing the Nicene orthodoxy, had to be reasserted. Theodosius had died in 450, and Pulcheria had maintained her position in the court by marrying an elderly soldier, Marcian (emperor in the east 450–57). A new council had been scheduled to meet at Nicaea, but it was now relocated to Chalcedon, close to Constantinople and therefore to imperial supervision. Marcian and Pulcheria were even to attend one session, to acclamations as "the new Constantine and the new Helena." As the council assembled the local governor was ordered to expel "riotous clergy" from the surrounding territory. A large group of imperial administrators was assembled to run the proceedings, and they insisted that the issues be presented in writing and debated as if they were legal documents. Even after all these preparations, many of the council's sessions were chaotic. "Popular acclamations are not suitable for bishops," the harassed organizers announced after one tumultuous session. Much of the business of the council was concerned with bringing the church to order. It was now that the canon banning monks from church business was passed (see p. 249), and the opportunity was taken to further enhance the prestige of Constantinople by giving the see greater authority in the surrounding territories. The furious response of Rome (in an angry letter sent by Leo to Pulcheria) went unheeded. Doctrinally Leo fared better. A sensible solution to the debilitating debate over the nature of Christ was eventually reached in that Leo's *Tome* was accepted (a significant moment in church history as "the first time Rome took a determining role in the definition of Christian dogma"), and Cyril's writings were ingeniously interpreted so that they did not conflict with Leo's formula. It was a stage-managed compromise that Marcian hoped, as he expressed it in an imperial edict issued after the council, would bring division to an end. It was declared that after the Incarnation Christ was "at all times fully God and fully human, with two natures, without confusion, without change, without division, without separation." The council was followed by an imperial law that made any discussion disagreeing with the council's conclusions punishable.[20]

As far as the east was concerned, Marcian's hopes for peace were misplaced. The debate had gone on for so long and had spawned so many different solutions that it could not so easily be subdued. Nestorius, now about seventy, had read Leo's *Tome* and felt that it represented his position fairly, although he died soon afterwards, and it is not known whether he heard that it had been accepted, and his own approach vindicated, at Chalcedon. However, what Nestorius had actually said was no longer as important as what his opponents had said that he had said. Nestorianism was now the name of a heresy that emphasized Christ's human nature much more than Nestorius had ever done; it was, in fact, closer to the teachings of Theodore of Mopsuestia, and as such it enjoyed considerable success in the far east of the empire and Persia.

On the other side of the debate, the Monophysites (who believed that Christ had a single nature, albeit one in which there were both divine and human elements) acclaimed Dioscorus as their inspiration even though he had been condemned at Chalcedon for his disgraceful behaviour at Ephesus—"Cast out Dioscorus the murderer" had been the cry of one group of bishops at the council. The Monophysites drew comfort from the fact that Dioscorus had not actually been declared a heretic, and they too set up independent churches (the Coptic Church in Egypt and the Jacobite Church in Syria among them), but even between the Monophysites there was acute dissension. Many felt that the declaration of Jesus' separate human nature compromised the concept of the

Trinity. Once again the masses developed a sophisticated understanding of every nuance in the debate. In the 490s there were riots in Constantinople when the news spread that a phrase suggesting Monophysitism had been added to the liturgy of the church of *Hagia Sophia.* The emperors shifted their ground in an attempt to find a consensus. A new declaration by the emperor Zeno in 482 stressed that "the Trinity remains the Trinity even after one of the Trinity, God the *logos,* becomes flesh." Christ, it was ingeniously suggested, was "*homoousios* with the Father according to his divinity and *homoousios* with us according to his humanity" while remaining one Son. The emperor Justinian made a further condemnation of the Nestorian position at a council of Constantinople in 553. In truth, it was probably impossible to make any satisfactory reconciliation between the doctrine of the Trinity and the doctrine of a Christ with two natures, and once again the state had to declare a compromise formula that was then enforced by law.

Because the writings of John Chrysostom, Ambrose, Jerome and Augustine were preserved and given such status, and because the church and its teachings became so deeply embedded in the legal and political system, it is easy to regard Christianity as much more powerful at this stage than it really was. Yet the fulminations of the preachers against the wickedness of the world arose partly because the mass of citizens continued to live within their traditional cultures. While in the legislation of the period one sees an intensification of the Christian state, this did not necessarily mean that the subjects of the empire became orthodox Christians—or even Christians at all. Recent studies have probed behind the triumphalist writings of church leaders to suggest that there was a much more fluid pattern of relationships between Christian and non-Christian, and there was certainly no clear demarcation between an advancing Christian wave and an ever-diminishing and engulfed pagan minority. The sheer breadth of the empire, the need for the remaining pagan elites to be wooed rather than alienated by the embattled emperors and the diversity and remoteness of many of its communities meant that much remained untouched. The traditional approach to the late empire by Christian historians, which suggests that paganism had somehow lost its force and "deserved" to succumb, underestimates its depth and resilience.

If we turn from the intense debates between theologians over doctrine to Christianity as it appeared "on the ground," we find that the boundaries between orthodox and heretic and even between Christian and non-Christian remained indistinct. The true commitment of Christians to their faith came with baptism, but many lingered for years as catechumens, in effect living in a no-man's-land in which they would continue to attend pagan festivals. In north Africa Augustine worked hard to quell the wine drinking and dancing that had always been part of traditional festivals, but when he rebuked a crowd of catechumens who were enjoying a local celebration in Bulla Regia in 411, he received the reply that they, as mere catechumens, did not have to avoid such festivities, unlike the bishops and clergy! Even if, after 381, Christ and the Holy Spirit were fully incorporated into the Godhead, Christianity could provide a mass of figures who had some form of "divine" status in the afterlife as companions of God, such as the Virgin Mary, the saints and the martyrs. Then there were the angels and demons whose combined presence filled the Christian world with as many supernatural presences as there had been in earlier times. It needs to be remembered that Christians continued to believe in the existence of the pagan gods—as demons. None of this would have been alien to pagans. G. W. Bowersock describes a number of instances, from Syria and Mesopotamia in particular, of gods being worshipped in groups of three.[21]

So a conversion to Christianity need not have been abrupt. Often pagans compromised with Christianity by linking a particular martyr with an existing pagan festival so that celebrations and rituals could continue as before. Paulinus, bishop of Nola in Campania, whose poetry and correspondence are a major source for local customs in the early fifth century, recorded how he offered the first shaving of his beard to the shrine of the Christian saint Felix and how the peasants in his diocese would bring pigs to the shrine to be slaughtered as if making a sacrifice of old. He mentions that good weather, fertility, safe childbirth and escape from enemies have become the concerns of local martyrs.[22] As Ramsay MacMullen has put it, "The principal business of the martyrs by far [by the late fourth century], as for a thousand years to come, was to restore fertility, straighten limbs, clear the sight, or untwist the mind." In other words, the same roles that the pagan gods such as Asclepius had fulfilled for centuries.[23] The authorities helped the process either by acquiescence or direct initiative. Jerome was rebuked by one earnest Christian for allowing a martyr's tomb to be surrounded by a mountain of candles even in daylight, as the tomb of a pagan deity might be. Jerome replied lamely that the candles were to provide light for all-night vigils, but "what used to be done for idols, and is therefore detestable, is

[now] done for martyrs, and on that account is acceptable."[24] Candles are still, of course, to be found before the images of saints in both Catholic and Orthodox churches. Cyril of Alexandria, aware that many locals were still attending a shrine of Isis at a nearby town and recognizing that "these districts were in need of medical services from God," promoted two local martyrs, John and Cyrus, to fulfill the role, creating a new shrine in their honour for the sick to attend. Gregory the Great showed the same shrewdness during the conversion of the Angles. He ordered the idols to be taken from the existing British temples, holy water sprinkled over the shrines to purify them, then altars built and relics put in place "so that the Angles have to change from the worship of the demons to that of the true God" without having to change their places of worship.[25] When Augustine was confronted by a inquirer who said that while he was happy to accept the Christian God as a bringer of eternal life, he wished to keep with the everyday gods for day to day living, Augustine promised that God cared about everything and would even "see to the salvation of your hen."[26]

From the other side of the divide one finds pagans actually treating Christian shrines as another manifestation of the divine, not necessarily of greater or less significance than any other spiritual site. There is a story of a pagan lady from Seleucia who broke her leg and travelled first to Jewish magical healers, then to the supposed tomb of Sarpedon, a mythical hero from the Trojan war, and then to the shrine of the Christian saint Thecla in search of a cure. Bowersock shows how pagan cults, far from being curtailed or overwhelmed by Christianity, even adopted Christian images. In a series of mosaics found in the 1980s in New Paphos in Cyprus, Dionysus presides in tableaux that start with him as a baby sitting "very much like the child on the lap of the Virgin" on the lap of Hermes and ending with him portrayed in triumph.[27] Often, of course, pagans simply adapted their activities so as to avoid breaking the law. The pagan rhetorician Libanius talks of pagans sending out invitations for feasts in the name of a presiding deity, meeting together outside rather than inside a temple sanctuary, killing beasts and then eating and singing hymns to the deity together as if nothing had changed. Libanius cannot see how this can be against the law, although more wide-ranging laws passed in the early fifth century aimed at "any solemn ceremony" may have made it so.[28]

Yet, however much assimilation and sharing took place, the church was bound to fit awkwardly with the surrounding cultures. Its very theology was deeply rooted in, and shaped by, rejections of Judaism, of paganism and, since the emperor had imposed an orthodox creed on the empire that was backed by law, of other "heretical" Christian groups. Now, with its new status as representative of the state in religious affairs, the church could take the initiative against its enemies. What strikes the modern reader is the passion and conviction with which Christians laid into their adversaries. Powerful imagery of heaven and hell, a range of supportive texts from the Bible and the urgings of church leaders gave intensity to their onslaughts. Much of this must have been rooted in the tensions of the age, the insecurities of continual warfare, high taxation and the brutality of the regime expressed in a religious formulation, but it probably reflects tensions with the increasingly authoritarian churches as well. Attacks against Jews, especially their synagogues, were now tolerated, or even, in extreme circumstances, seen as a badge of Christian commitment. In one instance recounted in the *Letter of Severus* (written by the bishop of Mahon in Minorca in 415), the bishop describes how he overawed the local Jewish community by bringing in Christians from neighbouring communities and demanding a public meeting with the Jews on their Sabbath. When they refused and began barricading their synagogue in self-defence, Severus ordered that the interior should be burnt out. As Severus triumphantly records, the Jews were forced into making their peace.[29] Violence and intimidation at this level and anti-Jewish legislation at state level cold-shouldered the Jews into, in the words of Nicholas de Lange, "a long period of desolation."[30]

However, Judaism survived. It was not, in this period at least, subject to a coherent campaign of elimination, unlike the Christian Donatists in north Africa, who were made subject to laws as wide ranging in scope as those used in the persecutions of Diocletian. Nor were synagogues subject to quite the same level of destruction as many pagan shrines. The Old Testament (and, of course, Paul) gave support for the overthrow of idolatrous worship. "Ye shall destroy their altars, break down their images, and cut down their groves . . . for the Lord, whose name is Jealous, is a Jealous God" (Exodus 34:13). Destruction was now urged with some vigour. "Abolish, abolish in confidence the ornaments of temples," the emperors were petitioned by one enthusiast in 346. "Upon, you most holy emperors, necessity enjoins the avenging and punishing of this evil . . . so that your Severities [*sic*] persecute root and branch the crime of idol worship."[31] The impetus was maintained by arguing that the pagan gods' failure to retaliate would show that they had no power: the more statues and temples were destroyed, the more strongly the point would be made to pagans. Of course, this could backfire as it did in Rome, where, after the sack of 410, pagans argued that the disaster was the revenge of the gods on those who had destroyed them. In the early fifth century laws were passed transferring the income from properties owned by temples to the church, which thereby consolidated its economic position. By the end of the century gifts or bequests to temples were forbidden altogether, resulting in a natural atrophy as buildings fell into disrepair. The process was hastened by deliberate destruction. The archaeologist finds signs of Christian iconoclasm everywhere: the cutting out of phalluses of Amun on Egyptian temples, the carving of crosses on pagan statues, the erasure of the inscriptions of gods' names, bathhouses that have lost their function (bathing naked was condemned) and have a cross at the door or have been converted into churches, the breaking up or melting down of statues. The quality of what was destroyed can sometimes be gauged only by what little has survived—the magnificent bronze statue of Marcus Aurelius on horseback (which long stood on the Capitoline Hill in Rome until it was removed to the neighbouring Capitoline Museum to escape pollution), for instance, which remained intact only because it was mistakenly believed to be of Constantine. (Note its presence in the fresco of Thomas Aquinas with which this book opened.)

The process of destruction was revolutionary in that the very fabric of city life, its rituals, its very sense of community, had grown around the sacred precincts over centuries. It was the equivalent of razing to the ground the medieval parish churches of England; the impact of the destruction would have resonated far beyond their congregations. This impact was recognized at the time. As the pagan orator Libanius wrote to Theodosius I: "temples are the soul of the countryside; and the property that suffers thus [through their destruction] is destroyed along with the zeal of their peasantry, for they believe that their labours will be in vain, being deprived of the gods that direct those labours towards their needs."[32] The elimination of paganism was accompanied by a dampening-down of emotions, dance and song so effective that we still lower our voices when we enter a church. Plato would have approved. The voices of the dispossessed, like most losers in history, have seldom survived, but in a rare text of pagan feeling from the early sixth century an Athenian philosopher describes Christians as "a race dissolved in every passion, destroyed by controlled self-indulgence, cringing and womanish in its thinking, close to cowardice, wallowing in all swinishness, debased, content with servitude in security."[33]

Others would suffer as a result of conflicts between the religious and secular authorities. When Cyril became bishop of Alexandria in 412, he asserted himself with some energy. His "shock troops," the *parabalani*, were viewed with such terror that the emperor himself had to ask that their numbers be limited to 500. Virtually every tension in the city was exacerbated by Cyril's intrusions. The city prefect Orestes, who was attempting to resist the encroachment on his secular powers, was injured by a mob of monks, Jewish synagogues were seized, but most shocking of all was the murder by a Christian mob of Hypatia, a philosopher and mathematician (who had written commentaries, now lost, on Diophantus and Apollonius). She was attacked on the streets and her body pulled to pieces. This was more than the death of a respected intellectual: for the historian of mathematics Morris Kline, "the fate of Hypatia symbolises the end of the era of Greek mathematics," and Edward Gibbon makes her death a set piece in his *Decline and Fall of the Roman Empire*.[34]

It was, however, only under Justinian, emperor 527–65, that the full weight of the law was enforced against paganism. One of his laws of the 530s signals the end of the imperial toleration extended to all religions by Constantine in 313:

> All those who have not yet been baptised must come forward, whether they reside in the capital or in the provinces, and go to the very holy churches with their wives, their children, and their households, to be instructed in the true faith of Christianity. And once thus instructed and having sincerely renounced their former error, let them be judged worthy of redemptive baptism. Should they disobey, let them know that they will be excluded from the state and will no longer have any rights of possession, neither goods nor property; stripped of everything, they will be reduced to penury, without prejudice to the appropriate punishments that will be imposed on them.[35]

The death penalty was decreed for those who practised pagan cults. Pagan teachers (who included, of course, philosophers) were banned and their licence, *parrhesia,* to instruct others was withdrawn. The term *parrhesia* had been used for a thousand years to denote "freedom of speech." Justinian was not content with empire-wide bans, which could easily be evaded by local elites, but aimed at specific centres of paganism. So it was now that after 900 years of teaching Plato's Academy was closed in Athens in 529 (the displaced philosophers sought refuge in Persia), and the last of the functioning Egyptian temples, that to Isis on the island of Philae in southern Egypt, was shut down in 526.

Yet even then paganism continued to flourish. There is a vivid account from John, bishop of Ephesus, that records how in 542 he went inland into the mountains and found thousands of pagans still worshipping at traditional temples with pagan sacrifices. The main temple near the town of Thralles claimed that it had jurisdiction over 1,500 other shrines. This testimony, which was discovered only by chance in a manuscript found in an Egyptian monastery in the nineteenth century and now in the British Museum, shows that we should be very hesitant in talking of "the triumph" of Christianity. Even among Christians, archaeological evidence (in the shape of inscriptions) from Anatolia suggests that in many parts of Asia Minor groups known to be heretics and schismatics were in the majority.[36] While eventually the Byzantine empire does present itself as Christian in its very essence, in vast areas of the former eastern empire spiritual allegiances were to change with the ebb and flow of history. So it is that in 515 at Zoara, south of the Dead Sea, a local god, Theandrites, was replaced by St. George and his temple reconstituted as a church with the inscription "God has his dwelling where there was once a hostel of demons; redeeming light now shines where once darkness spread its veil; where once sacrifices were made to idols, angels now dance."[37] (Note the presence of either demons or angels.) Yet just over 100 years later another spiritual transition took place as the Arabs swept through the Holy Land, Syria, Egypt and beyond. Now at the Dome of the Rock in Jerusalem a different faith proclaims itself:

> O you people of the Book, overstep not bounds in your religion, and of God speak only the truth. The Messiah, Jesus, son of Mary, is only an apostle of God, and his Word which he conveyed unto Mary, and a Spirit proceeding from him. Believe therefore in God and the apostles, and say not Three. It will be better for you.

God is only one God. Far be it from his glory that he
should have a son.[38]

It is worth remembering in this context the statement made by the
sophist Maximus in A.D. 390 that nobody denies that "the supreme
God" is "without offspring." So, while Byzantium survived as a Christian theocratic state, around it other pieces of the puzzle that still define
world politics in the twenty-first century were being put in place.

# 18

## THE EMERGENCE OF CATHOLIC CHRISTIANITY
## IN THE WEST, 395–640

Traditional Catholic histories of Christianity present Peter in his later years as a man who brims with conviction, energy and vision. His ambivalence about his mission to the Gentiles (as seen in the dispute with Paul at Antioch) had been resolved after God commanded him to extend his mission to the Gentiles (Acts of the Apostles 10). He set off to Rome because it was the capital of the empire, and he knew that it was the ideal place to establish the Church.[1] A later tradition even suggests that he was bishop of Rome for no less than twenty-five years before his martyrdom. Yet, while there is no reason to doubt Peter's convictions, he was actually heading to the far edges of the Christian world. The early church was predominantly Greek and flourished far more vigorously in the eastern than in the western empire, and from an eastern perspective the city of Rome was the "wrong" side of Italy. In Acts Paul tells of his great difficulties in travelling from Judaea to Rome (though admittedly his voyage was at a time of year when the weather had broken). Some six centuries later Pope Gregory the Great summed up the remoteness of Rome from the traditional Greek centres of Christianity. "Separated from you by great stretches of land and the sea," he wrote to his brother bishops in Antioch and Alexandria, "yet I am bound to you in my heart." The geographical separation was intensified by the linguistic gulf between the two parts of the empire, which grew as the Roman community became Latin—rather than Greek-speaking as it had been originally. The works of many of the Greek Church Fathers never reached the Latin west in translation. There were even difficulties in getting hold of Latin texts of the ecumenical councils.[2]

Even within Rome the Christian community was marginal in a city where the pagan senatorial aristocracy remained powerful to the end of the fourth century. In the dispute over the Altar of Victory in the Senate house in the 380s, it was Ambrose in Milan, where he had direct access to the emperor, a vital consideration so far as ecclesiastical power was concerned, who masterminded its removal, rather than Damasus, the bishop of Rome. Although lip service was paid to the concept of Roman primacy, particularly in the western empire where Rome had no rivals, attempts by the bishops of Rome to enforce this primacy had not been successful. In particular, as the conflict between Stephen and Cyprian of Carthage in the third century had shown, the Christians of north Africa were vigorous, independent-minded and reluctant to submit to anyone. Rome's political position within the empire atrophied over the centuries and received a further blow when the first Christian emperor himself set up his new capital at Constantinople. Then, at the Council of Constantinople of 381, Constantinople was made second in honour only to Rome as a bishopric. What hurt Rome in particular was that this move implied that a bishopric's authority was based as much on its political importance as on its Christian origins. This was the situation when the empire was split in 395.

Part of the problem was, of course, the difficulty of translating a movement deeply rooted in the Greek cultural and philosophical world into the Latin one. The first significant theologian to write in Latin was Tertullian, the son of a centurion, born in the north African trading city of Carthage. He has to be seen as much as a representative of the ebullient north African Christians as of western Christianity as a whole. Centurions were highly respected members of the Roman state, and Tertullian was well educated, able to speak both Greek and Latin. He may have trained and served as a lawyer until his conversion to Christianity, probably in the 190s when he was in his thirties, and, if so, he conforms to the stereotypes of his profession in his conservatism, his rigid approach to social issues and his ability to use uncompromising rhetoric with great emotional effect. There is something of Paul in the way that Tertullian castigates intellectuals and glories in paradox. How could one have answered his most famous statement, "The Son of God died; it must needs be believed because it is absurd. He was buried and rose again; it is certain because it is impossible"? Like many Latin Christians, he taunted the Greek philosophers: "Wretched Aristotle who taught them [the heretics and philosophers] dialectic, that art of building up and demolishing . . . self-stultifying since it is ever handling questions but never settling them . . . what is there in common between Athens and Jerusalem?"

He was, writes one scholar, "pre-eminently a theologian of revelation and an opponent of all *curiositas* beyond the church's rule of faith."[3] He had much more of the Stoic in him than the Platonist. So Tertullian helped to keep the western church outside the great debates over theology raging in the eastern empire. In general, western theologians were wary of the more sophisticated easterners' readiness to accept that "Christian" insights might be embedded in Greek philosophy. On the other hand, his attempt to formulate his own theology led him to devise specific Latin terms for Greek concepts. One of these was the word *Trinitas*. (In "his" Trinity the divine *logos* exists in the mind of God from the beginning of time but is "shot out" at the moment when the cosmos begins.) Here are the first stirrings of a specifically western theology expressed in its own language rather than in translation from the Greek.

Although Tertullian was to argue that Christians posed no threat to the state, in his ethical writings he portrayed the world as essentially hostile to Christians. As a Christian one was unable ever to relax one's guard. The threat of sexual temptation, in particular, was ever present, and Tertullian does not seem to have believed that sexual urges could be fully tamed until old age had exhausted them. (He argued that a church community should be run by the elderly as only they might have gone beyond temptation.) Tertullian contributed an abiding fear of woman as temptress to the western tradition, and his views became more rigid with age. Beset with the continuing "immorality" of those around him, he came to believe that God would have to continually update his message to mankind, and in his last years he joined the Montanists, who claimed to be in direct contact with God. He passes from the scene (his last known writings date from A.D. 212) and the date of his death is unknown but perhaps as late as 240.

One westerner deeply influenced by Tertullian was Jerome; in fact, much of what is known about Tertullian's life comes from Jerome himself.[4] As has already become clear, Jerome (c. 345–420) seems to have been an isolated and troubled individual, tormented by his sexuality, vulnerable to any hint of personal betrayal (and vituperative in response) and obsessive about the necessity for asceticism. So he is hardly an attractive figure; yet his mastery of Latin (his native language, in which he wrote with great elegance), Greek and Hebrew and his meticulous knowledge of the scriptures gave him the reputation as the leading scholar of his day. His monument remains the Latin translation of the Old and New Testaments, the Vulgate, which reigned as the official Latin translation of the Bible for the Roman Catholic Church until the 1960s. (Although the whole of the Vulgate is traditionally attributed to Jerome, it is probable that of the New Testament only the Gospels are his.)

Jerome was born, probably about 345, on the border of Dalmatia but was educated in Rome and baptized as a Christian there. Then he set out to the east, first staying in Antioch, where he was ordained a priest, and next retreating to the Syrian desert, where he was to spend several years. Here he was tortured by his sexual desire, but he also later recorded a terrible dream in which he was flogged for preferring Cicero to the scriptures. He was warned that if he ever read non-Christian writers again he would suffer worse torments. He seems to have resolved his guilt and continued his reading (or at least he continued to fill his writings with classical allusions). Naturally, while in the east he perfected his Greek, but, more unusually, he learned Hebrew (apparently, so he said, to be able to fight the Jews on their own ground). No Christian other than Origen had studied it in such depth, and Jerome's knowledge served to distinguish him from his fellow theologians.

When he returned to Rome in the 380s, Jerome's breadth of learning recommended him to Damasus, bishop of Rome, as a personal secretary, and it was Damasus who first suggested that he provide a proper translation into Latin of the Bible. The "Old Latin" versions, as they were known, dated from the second century; they were poorly translated and varied from one copy to the next. They urgently needed revision and correction. The task gave Jerome the purpose in life that he seems to have craved, and these next three years in Rome were the most emotionally settled of his life. He reached out to a group of ascetic women, who adopted him as a sort of father confessor. Emboldened by their respect, Jerome produced some of his most weighty letters, notable among them the somewhat oppressive but highly revealing Letter XXII to the young Eustochium on virginity. Yet Jerome could never be fully at peace with his fellow men. His aggressive asceticism and apparently baleful influence on so many leading women of the city created resentment among their class, and he compounded this by accusing his fellow priests of laxness and hypocrisy. His relationship with a wealthy ascetic, Paula, mother of Eustochium, aroused particular scorn, and so on Damasus' death he was in effect driven from the city, the scandal intensifying when Paula left with him. Jerome was never to forgive the Roman clergy, that "senate of Pharisees," for the rejection. For Jerome, Rome itself was indeed "the whore of Babylon" of the Book of Revelation.

Jerome and Paula eventually settled in Bethlehem, where Paula's wealth was used to found two monasteries to support them and their followers. The new Latin version of the Gospels had now been completed and for the next twenty years Jerome worked on his translation of the Hebrew scriptures. At first this work aroused deep suspicion. The Greek Septuagint version had achieved a canonical status, and there was much unease over a rival version that might threaten its dominance. Augustine prophesied that there would be a break between east and west if the west abandoned the Septuagint, which Greek-speaking Christians believed to have been divinely inspired, for the Jewish original. It was only in the ninth century, in the great Bibles produced by Charlemagne, that Jerome's version was fully accepted (and by that time the breach was in any case complete).

Translation seems to have been Jerome's forte; he was notably less at ease with original and creative work. Many of his commentaries on the Old Testament are drawn almost entirely from earlier commentators (despite his abuse of Ambrose for doing the same). He was thoroughly caught out as late as 1941 when the discovery in the Egyptian desert of a voluminous five-book commentary on the prophet Zachariah by Didymus the Blind showed how heavily Jerome had relied on Didymus in his own commentary on the prophet. It has to be remembered that before the invention of printing there were very few copies of most works available and the opportunities for successful plagiarism were widespread. Also, to be fair to Jerome, there are many occasions in these commentaries when he does record his sources. Perhaps Jerome's greatest inspiration came from Origen, whose works were available in manuscript in nearby Caesarea, where Origen had spent his last years. Origen had been the first Christian to compare systematically Hebrew versions of the scriptures with the Septuagint and was a model for Jerome on those grounds alone, but he had also written major commentaries on many of the books of the Old and New Testaments, adaptations of which appear in Jerome's own work. It has been shown, for instance, that in his Commentary on the Epistle to the Ephesians, which can be compared to parts of Origen's own commentary, Jerome passed off Origen's ideas as his own, even to the extent of unwittingly repeating under his own name some of Origen's errors!

Yet it was also the legacy of Origen which exposed Jerome at his weakest. The sheer creativity and originality of Origen had left him vulnerable to critics, and by the end of the fourth century these were gathering. Epiphanius, the ardently orthodox bishop of Salamis in Cyprus, included Origen as one of a long list of heretics he had compiled, on the grounds that Origen had been an inspiration for Arius. An intransigent and forceful man, Epiphanius then began to approach scholars such as Jerome to win them over to his rigid brand of orthodoxy. He sent a group of monks to Bethlehem, and, for reasons that have never fully been understood, they were able to persuade Jerome to abandon his mentor. Perhaps the reason lies in Jerome's fundamental lack of self-confidence, which made him particularly vulnerable to pressures of this kind. Others, however, were not to be so easily bullied, among them the bishop of nearby Jerusalem, John, and Rufinus, a friend of Jerome's from his school days who had settled in a monastery on the slopes of the Mount of Olives in Jerusalem and had been responsible for the Latin translation of works of several of the great Greek theologians, among them the Cappadocian Fathers. Rufinus now set about a translation of Origen's major work, *On the First Principles* (*De Principiis* in Rufinus' Latin version, which is the only one to survive). He was aware that in Rome, where the Latin version would be read, Origen was already being treated with suspicion, so he prefaced his translation with the comment that he believed that Origen had been unfairly represented by his critics. He also proclaimed that he was only following in the footsteps of a far greater scholar then himself, Jerome, the well-known enthusiast for Origen! Jerome was outraged, as he had some right to be (Rufinus knew of his change of heart), but his response, dispatched to Rome in a letter intended to be made public, was vituperative. Rufinus was branded as a heretic who had covered himself with infamy through translating such a heretical work as *De Principiis*. Jerome went on to create distorted versions of the translation so as to associate Rufinus with extreme views he had never expressed. Although Jerome later wrote a more moderate personal letter to Rufinus, it never reached him, and the damage was done—an old friendship had been rudely shattered. Rufinus retaliated by quoting passages of Jerome's where he had borrowed from Origen without any acknowledgement. While things moved Jerome's way when, as we have seen, in 400, Theophilus, bishop of Alexandria, also branded Origen a heretic, Jerome's inability to control his vindictiveness and his unashamed readiness to distort the writings of an opponent has lingered across the centuries.

Among Jerome's many correspondents was a younger and brilliant theologian from north Africa, Augustine. Augustine's first letter, in 394 or 395, actually asked Jerome to make more Latin translations of Greek theologians for those in north Africa, such as himself, whose Greek was weak ("especially," one reads with some unease "that Origen you mention in your writings with particular pleasure").[5] However, the main purpose of the letter was to comment on Jerome's suggestion that the famous/notorious row between Peter and Paul recounted in Galatians was a deliberate simulation, with both Apostles acting a part in collusion with each other. Augustine argued that Galatians was describing the event as it actually took place and that once one began to suggest things may have been otherwise, the authenticity of any other part of the scriptures might be challenged. A sermon of Augustine's only recently discovered in Mainz shows that he believed that Peter's humble acceptance of rebuke by Paul actually enhanced the former's authority as a moral leader. This correspondence was interrupted for some years by postal problems, but the very hint of criticism was enough to launch Jerome into another of his vindictive letters. This time he had met his match: Augustine replied with a letter of conciliation and magnanimity.[6] Although he tried to shift the blame for the controversy onto others (including Rufinus), Jerome appears to have been genuinely moved by the care Augustine had taken. At heart Jerome was a lonely man, and his last years, during which Paula and Eustochium, who had herself come out to Bethlehem, died, and even his monastery was sacked by a mob, were unhappy ones. Nevertheless, his last surviving letter to one Donatus (of whom nothing else is known, the name being a common one in north Africa) inveighs against the Pelagian heretics and expresses the hope that the new bishop of Rome, Boniface, will "cut them to pieces with Christ's sword, for neither plasters nor soothing medicaments can enable them to recover sound health."[7] Combative to the last, Jerome died in 419 or 420.

So we come to Augustine. Through his sheer intellectual power, probing curiosity, originality, extraordinary range of concerns and enormous output of work (it has been said that anyone who claims to have read all of Augustine's works must be lying), Augustine has come to be seen as the cornerstone of the western Christian tradition.[8] There is no other Christian theologian (Origen possibly excepted) who shows such uninhibited philosophical curiosity. It is truly through Augustine that we pass from the classical world to the medieval, in that Augustine brought to fruition much of earlier Christian theology and gave it powerful expression, vigour and coherence. Thomas Aquinas cites Augustine in his works nearly ten times as often as he cites Jerome. When printing was invented, Augustine's works were the earliest to be printed after the Bible; a complete edition of his massive *City of God* was published at Subiaco in Italy as early as 1467. Martin Luther was deeply influenced by Augustine, often using Augustine's theology as a starting point for his own.[9] He remains a deeply controversial figure, his reputation burdened with the responsibility of integrating sinfulness into human nature (at least in the western Christian tradition if not elsewhere): "the man who fused Christianity together with hatred of sex and pleasure into a sys-tematic unity," as the German theologian Uta Ranke-Heinemann has put it.[10] The truth is necessarily more complex, and Augustine, while undeniably pessimistic by temperament and increasingly so with age, is certainly a more remarkable man than he is often portrayed by his crit-ics. Nevertheless, his legacy, developed as it was by his successors, remains an awkward one. In particular, his gradual subjection of reason to faith and authority did much to undermine the classical tradition of rational thought.

Like Tertullian, Augustine came from northern Africa; he was born in the inland city of Thagaste in 354. It is impossible to discuss Augustine without assessing the impact on his character of his mother, Monnica, a Christian. His preoccupation with her still pervades the *Confessions,* which he wrote in his forties, ten years after her death. In comparison to Monnica, his father, Patricius, a civil servant, who was not baptized until the end of his life, is a shadowy figure hardly mentioned by Augustine. Monnica appears to have been stifling in her love for her son; any lapse on his part brought out agonies in her as crippling, her son commented, as the pains of labour. However, determined that he should succeed, she, supported by her husband and the help of a patron, insisted on the best education for him, and by the age of seventeen he was at university in Carthage, the ancient port on the north African coast, specializing in law. His curriculum, in the traditional Latin authors, may have been restricted (he never properly mastered Greek, for instance), but he received a firm grounding in rhetoric, and this was to be the skill which gave him hope of advancement in the imperial service. However, a reading at the age of eighteen of Cicero's *Hortensius,* a now-lost "exhortation to philosophy," convinced Augustine that a life of philosophy was the true one, especially when he compared the sophistication of Cicero's prose with the clumsy and incoherent scriptures that he was also reading for the first time. This in itself was a form of conversion, a dedication to the path of knowledge rather than to an imperial career, and one senses that Augustine had also achieved a precarious form of psychological independence from his mother. He lived with a woman (whose name has not been recorded). Far from being debauched (a legend propagated by himself and indicative of his own deep sense of guilt about even minor peccadilloes), his life appears to have been stable. The relationship lasted some fifteen years, and he had a son, Adeodatus, who survived until his late teens. Apart from a brief visit home in 375, Augustine remained based in Carthage as a teacher of literature until 383.

Augustine desperately needed a spiritual home, and he was prepared to leave the mainstream to find it. For nine years he was attached to the Manicheans, an isolated and somewhat elitist sect whose beliefs centred on the teachings of Mani, an influential Persian prophet of the previous century. With Persia so often at war with Rome, emperors distrusted the Manicheans' Persian origins and the sect was often persecuted, giving its members even more of a sense of exclusiveness. The Manicheans drew heavily on Christianity and accepted the authenticity of Jesus as an important spiritual leader, but their main teachings centred on the nature of evil. Evil, symbolized by darkness, and to be found in all matter, was involved in an endless struggle against Good, the forces of light that it often defeated and fragmented. However, uncontaminated light remained in the sun and the moon, and these acted as rallying points for the forces of light themselves, with God as the ultimate force of life. The human body, like all matter, was evil, and had been deliberately designed by the forces of evil as a mechanism for keeping the soul, a potential source of light, imprisoned. The soul had to be set free, and this was the role of Christ, but, in contrast to orthodox Christians, the Manicheans believed that he could never have entered a human body, as thereby he would have lost his power. The Manicheans, in fact, saw themselves as teachers of a pure "scientific" Christianity closer to the truth than that of the church. They derided the scriptures for their contradictions and the Old Testament prophets for the immorality of their lives. The more committed Manicheans were profoundly ascetic and attempted to remove themselves as far as they could from matter, even going so far to employ "hearers" who served them by handling their food and other needs. Augustine was a "hearer," in other words outside the elite, and as such he was allowed to have sexual relationships, although having children (in other words, producing more evil matter) was frowned on.

Augustine appears to have valued the comradeship of the Manichean group and the apparent coherence of their teachings, but he gradually came to be disillusioned with them. Not all Manicheans lived up to the high standards they set themselves, and Augustine's wider readings in philosophy showed him that far from being "scientific" they disregarded the findings of Greek science. He found the definition of all matter as evil too crude, especially in the implication that the forces of Good could be defeated by it. His instinct was to find "a Good" that was unassailable, and it was this search that was to lead him to Platonism.

Augustine had by this time left Africa. First in 383 he had gone to Rome, in the hope, he tells us, of finding a better living as a teacher with more disciplined students than the unruly ones he found in Carthage. His mother continued to dominate him—his father had died when he was about eighteen. She had already been deeply upset by his Manicheism but made matters worse by turning up on the quayside in Africa, apparently hoping either to drag him back home or go with him to Rome. When he gave her the slip and boarded the ship alone, she was distraught at his betrayal. The matter troubled Augustine deeply, and it is possible the illness which struck him while he was in Rome was some form of breakdown associated with the break with his mother. (In the *Confessions* Augustine dwells on the terrible blow it would have dealt to his mother if he had died of his illness, still mired in evil and assuredly on his way to hell.) Rome was not a success, but then he had the break he needed. The prefect of the city, Symmachus, the Symmachus of the diptych discussed earlier, had been asked to find an imperial orator for Milan, and having heard Augustine speak, recommended him to the emperor. The post was granted, and Augustine set off north. One of his first encounters in his new home was with none other than Symmachus' adversary in the dispute over the Altar of Victory, Ambrose, bishop of the city.

Augustine came to Milan not as a Christian but as a man still searching for truth. It was the Platonists who first impressed him there. Platonism was popular among both Christians and non-Christians, although those Platonists whom Augustine met appear to have been

Christians who had drawn their Platonism from Plotinus and Porphyry (even though the latter was strongly anti-Christian). It is not known exactly what authors Augustine read (although it appears that they did include Plotinus and Porphyry), but Platonism now gave him much of what he was looking for: the sense of an ultimate incorporeal reality, eternal, unassailable and all powerful, the source of creation, good and happiness, which a human soul, if committed to the task, was able to grasp. Evil, far from being the powerful and destructive force preached by the Manicheans, could be seen in Platonism as a departure from goodness. This was a foundation on which Augustine could build. Yet Platonism was not fully satisfying. The traditional Platonic view had been that, while it might take many years, the ultimate reality could be grasped by reason. Augustine wanted to avoid, perhaps needed to avoid, this long journey. His stay in Milan was marked by another emotional crisis, and he suffered asthmatic attacks so debilitating that he had to give up his post as orator. He yearned for a more immediate means of bridging the gap between the human soul and the incorporeal God. Into the void came Christianity.

Augustine was deeply impressed by Ambrose's preaching and personality. Here was a man brought up in the classical world who was true to his background yet who had espoused Christianity. When Augustine, still under the influence of the Manicheans, expressed his concern with the "grossness" of the Old Testament, the urbane Ambrose said that he should see the "gross" passages as allegories, as Origen had done. As his doubts dissolved, Augustine now began to believe that Christ was the intermediary he searched for, and that through accepting the authority of the church, its tradition and the scriptures he could gain a direct relationship with God. While Platonism might represent the highest intellectual and spiritual point of the pagan world, Christianity went beyond it and provided an everlasting haven. As Augustine later put it in the *City of God,* Christianity "is the religion that embodies a universal path to the liberation of the soul, since the soul can be liberated no other way but this. For this is the royal road that alone leads to the kingdom, a kingdom not doomed to sway uneasily upon a pinnacle of time but solidly founded on eternity."[11] His actual conversion, as he described it in the *Confessions,* was sudden. While in emotional torment in a garden he heard the voice of a child in a nearby house saying over and over, "Take it and read, take it and read." He took up Paul's Epistles and came across a verse from Romans (13:13–14), "Not in revelling and drunkenness, not in lust and wantonness, not in quarrels and rivalries. Rather arm yourselves with the Lord Jesus Christ; spend no more thought on nature and nature's appetites." This was for him the final piece of the puzzle. He had found a spiritual home and was now ready to embrace celibacy.[12]

A major psychological benefit of conversion was that Augustine could now make his peace with his mother. She had appeared in Milan, arranged a suitable marriage for him (now that he appeared to be well established in the imperial administration) and was probably responsible for sending his lover of so many years back to Carthage. (Augustine was distraught and sought comfort in another relationship.) In his new state he felt that marriage was impossible, although reconciliation with Monnica was not. One of the most moving parts of the *Confessions* describes Augustine and Monnica together leaning from a window in Ostia, the port of Rome, shortly before Monnica's death.

> And while we spoke of the eternal Wisdom, longing for
> it and straining for it with all the strength of our hearts,
> for one fleeting instant we reached out and touched it.
> Then with a sigh, leaving our spiritual harvest bound to
> it, we returned to the sound of our own speech, in which
> each word has a beginning and an ending—far, far dif-
> ferent from your Word, our Lord, who abides in himself
> for ever, yet never grows old and gives life to all things.[13]

It is a significant passage, partly for its spiritual beauty, but also because it shows that an intellectual can share with a devout and less-educated believer a recognition of the divine.

Augustine returned to north Africa in 388, at a time when orthodox Christianity was on the defensive there. Christians were outnumbered by the Donatists and (as studies of inscriptions show) still surrounded by pagans. A man of Augustine's learning and personal qualities was desperately needed by the orthodox Christian communities, not least to act as a mediator with the civil authorities. So he was persuaded to become a priest (391) and then a bishop, of Hippo on the coast (395–96). Here Augustine was to remain until his death in 430. His hopes that he would live a life of intellectual discussion in semi-monastic seclusion with a chosen group of friends were disappointed, while his busy life as pastor was made more onerous by the mass of legal work that now came any conscientious bishop's way. The challenges were many, from the Donatists, the Manicheans and his own flock, most of whom were illiterate. Yet for the thirty-five years during which he was bishop, Augustine appears to have been an excellent pastor, and he was particularly concerned with bridging the gap between himself, as a highly educated man, and the mass of his congregation. In this he seems to have been exceptional for his time, above all in the way he thought deeply on how to present the complexities of theology to uneducated minds. In such a busy and committed life, the scale and breadth of his writings were remarkable, but as the years went by they were marked increasingly by Augustine's cultural isolation. He was gregarious by nature and perhaps he needed the intellectual vitality of a Rome or a Milan. Hippo was a backwater in comparison, and the African tradition of theology bleakly authoritarian. The combination of increasing age (Augustine was over forty when he became bishop) and remoteness from any centre of debate narrowed his perspectives as the years passed. His debates were no longer set among friendly equals with whom there was a genuine attempt to explore issues but became polarized confrontations conducted on an imperial stage. They did not always show his subtle mind at its best. The use of reason in his writings diminishes as his reliance on faith increases, and the results were not happy. As far as his intellectual development goes, moving back to Africa seems to have been a mistake.

None the less, it was in these early years as bishop that Augustine wrote his most famous and accessible work, the *Confessions,* which reviews his early life and his path to conversion. The word "confessions" carried connotations of testimony or witness as much as "confession" as such, although the work is certainly infused with Augustine's revelation of his past "sins." It is not a coherent work. While the first nine chapters deal with Augustine's past life and chapter ten with his present one, the last three chapters are unrelated reflections on the Book of Genesis. One can, however, bind the three parts together as the story of a soul coming to accept God and the implications of reaching the end of the search. Even so, many scholars feel that when the suddenness of his conversion is put alongside his writings from the mid-380s, he represented the process as much more coherent and final than perhaps it was. It has been suggested, for instance, that, for his readers, he deliberately modelled his own dramatically sudden conversion on Paul's own.[14]

What is remarkable about the *Confessions* is that for the first time in western literature the world of the interior mind—with, in this case, all its guilt and uncertainty—is explored in detail in what is essentially a dialogue with God. Augustine knows he is breaking new ground. "Men go out and gaze in astonishment at high mountains, the huge waves of the sea, the broad reaches of rivers, the ocean that encircles the world, or the stars in their courses. But they pay no attention to themselves." He will pay attention to himself, and in the breach of convention required in doing so one senses just how deeply inward his creative mind had been driven by his upbringing. One cannot read the *Confessions* without being aware of Augustine's preoccupation with his own sinfulness. He is deeply overcome, for instance, by what seems a fairly harmless prank of shaking down the ripe pears from a tree and stealing them. His sexual feelings and experiences, even if in reality they were relatively limited, disturb him continuously. Augustine talks in the *Confessions,* as throughout his writings, of the supreme importance of the love of God, but the dominant picture he gives in the *Confessions* is of a God who is angry and punitive.

> I broke all your lawful bounds and did not escape your lash. For what man can escape it? You were always present, angry and merciful at once, strewing the pangs of bitterness over all my lawless pleasures to look for others unallied by pain. You meant me to find them nowhere but in yourself, O Lord, for you teach us by inflicting pain, you smite so that you may heal and you kill us so that we may not die away from you.[15]

Far from being a Platonic God—above earthly things and free of emotion—this is a God who actively punishes as a form of showing love (as, Augustine was often to remark, a schoolmaster would). It is a confused and unsettling picture and becomes even more disturbing as Augustine elaborates his doctrine of original sin. God's punishment even extends to life on earth, so that the slave is a slave because God wishes him punished. The contrast with Origen's loving God who welcomes all souls, even that of Satan, back to him is obvious.

Yet Augustine had found his home, and from within its confines he set about sweeping floors clean, exploring the nooks and crannies, transforming the decor, even if with the most sombre of hangings, while preserving and strengthening the foundations. However, the house had walls outside of which he did not venture. It was also under continual attack. Much of Augustine's work is developed in responses to challenges from the Manicheans, the Donatists and later the Pelagians. Against all these he worked within the orthodox tradition. One sees this in his major study on the Trinity, *De Trinitate,* which he worked on over many years (it was completed only in 427). It is largely a defence of the Trinitarian creed developed at Nicaea, though with the western bias towards emphasizing the common divinity of Father, Son, and Holy Spirit, somewhat at the expense of their individual "personalities." (There is no evidence that Augustine knew of the creed's endorsement at Constantinople in 381.) Augustine reviews the Arian and Homoean positions and interprets the scriptures so as to discredit them. Any saying of Jesus that seems to suggest he is subordinate to the Father is attributed to his human nature and, Augustine argues, does not detract from his divinity. There is nothing here that contradicts the new orthodoxy, but where there are loose ends Augustine ties them up. He sorts out some of the philosophical confusions caused by the use of Latin terminology, preferring to use *essentia* instead of *substantia,* which had caused difficulty when translated into Greek, for the "substance" of which God was made. He worried, too, that describing the Holy Spirit as "processing" from the Father but making no mention of a procession from the Son might give the impression that the Son was lesser than the Father. So he added "procession" from the Son (the so-called "double procession"). While this became dogma in the west, the east regarded it as no more than a private idea of Augustine's, and it has never been accepted there. It was later to become one of the doctrines on which the schism between east and west was consolidated. Also within *De Trinitate* is an imaginative and original development of human psychology. Augustine suggests that when creating the soul, God endowed it with self-awareness, understanding and will. Will is an essential element of Augustine's thought—intelligent life is always lived with energy and purpose and the will is the embodiment of this. It has been suggested that "the notion of will, as used in many philosophical doctrines from the early Scholastics through to Schopenhauer and Nietzsche, was invented by St. Augustine."[16] These qualities are linked to each other within the soul but also have their distinctive roles, and so provide a mirror, as it were, of the Trinity. If God chooses to give an individual his grace, the human soul, because of its "trinitarian" make-up, will be better able to respond: through knowing God, Augustine suggests, one knows oneself. For Augustine, therefore, the soul is naturally Christian, with the implication that a rejection of Christianity is a rejection of one's human nature. *De Trinitate* is typical of Augustine's work in so far as it is rooted in orthodoxy, but uses that orthodoxy as a springboard for further highly original speculation. This work was so much more sophisticated than that produced by any other western theologian on the Trinity (Augustine went far beyond his mentor Ambrose in originality, perceptiveness and depth) that Augustine's dominance in western Christianity was assured.

The springs of Augustine's theology soon came to lie in faith rather than reason. In his earliest writings from the 380s Augustine appears to have accepted the importance of reason in finding truth. In his *On Order,* written about 386, for instance, he outlines a rational ascent towards the incorporeal through the academic disciplines in much the same way as plotted by Plato. However, there are now signs of an intellectual struggle in which Augustine explores whether one can ever know anything fully. He concludes that some things have to be taken on trust and this involves the acceptance of the authority of others. This acceptance of authority in itself requires humility, and here the humility of Christ in becoming human provides the model for one's own humility. Augustine follows Paul's example in deriding "the philosophers" as arrogant in the belief that they can find truth for themselves. "For Augustine the root of sin lies in pride, and this includes pride in one's own intelligence."[17]

From here Augustine moves to the authority of the church and thence to the authority of the scriptures. "I would not have believed the Gospels, except on the authority of the Catholic Church." The problem remains that while it is true that in many situations one has to rely on the authority of others, there is no reason why that authority should be accepted blindly or uncritically; perhaps Augustine's own psychological need for certainty was the most important factor here. One of the benefits of making the leap to faith, Augustine argues, is that in doing so one breaks through a barrier and reaches a higher level of understanding. "Unless you believe you will not understand," as the prophet Isaiah had put it. By 396 Augustine had progressed to saying belief in God, faith, is a gift of God. Reason now plays only a supporting role as the means through which one learns that authority must be accepted. "The main use of reason by the mature Augustine," writes Adrian Hastings, "is unquestionably to understand what is already believed."[18] Augustine's later stress on the debilitating effects of the Fall provided him with further support for his beliefs—man, now corrupted, is incapable of using reason to grasp the incorporeal and can only rely on God to reveal himself.

Parallel to these developments is Augustine's growing acceptance of miracles. In the 380s Augustine was sceptical and distanced himself from those who were "daunted by the hollow claims of the miraculous." Later, in about 390, in *True Religion,* he argues that "miracles would not have been allowed to stretch into our time, or the soul would always be looking for sensations, and the human race would go jaded with their continual occurrence."[19] By the end of his life, however, Augustine is reporting miracles as everyday occurrences and using them to encourage faith. He regaled his congregations with a long list of cures that had been effected at the shrine to St. Stephen in Hippo, including those of a number of people who had been raised from the dead. A local landowner had brought back some earth and baptismal water from a pilgrimage to Jerusalem. These brought about so many cures that Augustine advised him to place them in a special shrine so that they could be available to the public at large.[20] In Augustine's own development, we can see in microcosm a crucial shift away from the Greek tradition of rational thought.

From the 390s Augustine studied the scriptures intensively, writing commentaries on them, among which those on the Psalms and the Gospel of John are the best known. The basis for interpretation of scripture, he argued, was the love of God and love of one's neighbour (drawing on Matthew 22:37–40), and ultimately the scriptures had to be used to play a full role in the daily life of the church, in service, in fact, of its pastoral activity. This approach enabled Augustine to relate the scriptures to the real world around him. As a biblical scholar, however, Augustine was severely handicapped. He could not read Hebrew and had relatively little Greek (and in any case there is no evidence that he ever saw any original Greek version of the Gospels). The Latin versions of the scriptures he used were often so badly translated as to be near to incomprehensible. (When he came across passages he could not understand, far from blaming the translation, Augustine argued that God had deliberately made them difficult so as to humble those who thought interpretation would be easy.) Yet he was not to be deterred. He followed conventional thinking in being convinced that all scripture had an inner coherence and that passages could not contradict each other. Similarly, as the truth according to the doctrines of the Catholic Church is already known, exegesis is mainly a matter of interpreting texts, allegorically and thus imaginatively if necessary, to fit orthodoxy (as in the opening of John's Gospel described earlier) or the life of the contemporary church. So a verse of the Song of Songs in which the bridegroom addresses his bride with the compliment "Thy teeth are like a flock of sheep that are shorn" (4:2) is interpreted by Augustine to refer not only to the saints ("the teeth of the church, tearing men away from their errors and bringing them into the church's body, with all their hardness softened down, just as if they had been torn down and masticated by the teeth") but also to the newly baptized, who are like shorn sheep in that they have laid down their fleeces, a metaphor for the burdens of the world.[21] With imagination allowed such a free rein, difficulties in finding scriptural sources for church doctrine are easily dissolved.

Augustine believed that every other form of learning had to be subordinated to the scriptures, so in *De Doctrina Christiana,* his major work on the exegesis of scripture, worked on throughout his later life, secular knowledge, whether provided by mathematicians, scientists or philosophers, is said to be valid only in so far as it leads to an understanding of scripture. However, in this respect Augustine was more broad-minded than those scholars who would have nothing to do with secular learning at all; witness John Chrysostom's exhortations to Christians to empty their minds of secular knowledge. The result was that Augustine thought less critically about the scriptures, believing that they could be interpreted only in such a way as supported orthodoxy. Augustine's uncritical reliance on the inadequate Latin translations of the original Greek and Hebrew versions made things worse. For instance, he interpreted the Latin of verse 12 of chapter 5 of Paul's Epistle to the Romans to mean that all individuals sinned through Adam, hence to support the doctrine of an original sin, whereas if he had gone back to the original Greek he would have found that sin, which entered the world as a result of Adam's transgression, was a "cosmic" force burdening all humanity in general rather than being born uniquely in each individual. No wonder the concept of original sin never travelled to the Greek world.

In so far as he came to take refuge in scriptures, Augustine was particularly influenced by Paul, and, as noted above, it was from a misreading of Paul that Augustine developed his doctrine of original sin.[22] He was tackling a major theological and philosophical problem, perhaps the most profound and challenging of all, the cause of evil. There are various ways of approaching the problem of evil. Clearly human beings can act, knowingly or unknowingly, so as to produce evil consequences for those around them. In the Platonic tradition evil was the result of the withdrawal of the soul from God/the Good and its increasing subjection to the material body with its emotions, passions and desires. The focus here was on the individual soul, which in the interpretation offered by Origen could move "upwards" or "downwards" of its own free will, closer to God, or away from him, away from the demands of the body, or more deeply into its snares—even to the point of becoming a demon. However, all was not lost if one could posit that God was benevolent and ready to reach out to the soul, which might have its own innate desire to reach back. Here was the basis of a coherent theology incorporating free will, giving God a role that was providential and offering the hope and possibility of reward for all. It also accepted the reality of human evil, making it the responsibility of its perpetrators. There remained unresolved issues. In so far as there were those souls that refused or failed to begin the return to God and sank themselves into the lower reaches of the material world and thus into commission of evil, there was the implication either that God lacked the power to prevent them from doing so or that he was willing to allow the continuation of evil in the world. One response has been to argue that free will is God's gift and that he considers that it is better to be used even for evil purposes than to be constrained; in other words, he condones evil.[23]

In Augustine's writings in the 380s there are indications that he accepts the existence of free will. In the opening of *On Free Will*, begun in 388, he argues that "what each one chooses to pursue and embrace is within the power of his will to determine." Man must take responsibility for the evil he commits. This was in line with established thinking on the issue. Earlier Christian commentators had stressed how Jesus' exhortations to his followers (in the Sermon on the Mount, for instance) seem to take for granted that they could act freely in making the choice to care or not to care for those around them. The essence of Jesus' message appears to be that human beings have choice, and he, in his teachings, is pointing out the way in which that choice should be exercised.[24] As he continued to write *On Free Will* over the next eight or nine years, however, Augustine's position changed. The later parts of the book accept only one true instance of the exercise of free will: Adam's decision to eat the forbidden fruit. (There remains a significant issue. If Adam was the perfect man, created as such by God, why did he give in to temptation so easily?) As a result of the Fall, Adam becomes imbued with sin, "original sin," as it came to be known, which he then passed down to the human race. The power of this sin is so debilitating that it even limits the extent to which human beings can enjoy free will. Mankind is now, Augustine writes in his *Letter to Simplicianus* (397), no more than "a lump," infused with the guilt of Adam. As a result of this corruption all are deprived of the power to save themselves. Here Augustine follows in the tradition of human sinfulness stressed by Athanasius, although it is possible that he may still have been influenced by Manicheism, with its own stress on the power of evil. The effect of being burdened by sin is profound; it not only makes our lives on earth ones of certain wrongdoing that our own efforts can do little to avoid, it makes damnation (which Augustine, drawing on Jesus' words in Matthew, believes to be eternal) very likely.

While Augustine retained the idea that human beings had a sense of the truth of God and yearned for it—in *De Trinitate* he argued that God had provided the soul with the means of recognizing him when grace was offered—the truth could not be gained except through God's grace. Grace was possible through the sacraments, but even baptism did not necessarily relieve (fallen) man of sin, nor could good works. Augustine rejected the idea that those who are in the church are more likely to be saved than those who are not. "Many who seemed to be without are within, many who seem to be within are without." Good and bad, saved and unsaved, are mingled together on earth, until the last judgment divides them. God alone knows who will be saved; as one of Augustine's critics remarked, "God does not desire all men to be saved, but only the fixed number of the predestined." Sin is passed on through sexual intercourse; so once again sexual desire is woven into evil, this time through its very transmission.[25]

This is the doctrine of a deeply pessimistic, isolated and guilt-ridden mind, although there were precedents for Augustine in the north African theological tradition. Augustine had moved far from an optimistic assessment of human nature. "The consoling, confidence-inspiring certainties of a rationally ordered universe, controlled and subject to man's free will, which Augustine had enjoyed in his earlier works, were now taken from under his feet," as Carol Harrison puts it. By the late 390s Augustine's rejection of reason and the wider philosophical tradition of the classical world had led him to a philosophical dead end. The scriptural backing for original sin was flimsy; only five texts from the whole of scripture can be claimed to support it, and it has been argued that three of those, including the crucial verse from Romans, rest on mistranslations into Latin from the original Greek. To accept original sin is to accept that one generation can be held responsible for the guilt of another, an assumption alien to most ethical systems. As guilt is independent of any action, good or bad, by the individual, even a baby can be damned to eternal fire. Augustine's God, for all his apparent "love," is credited with little in the way of compassion. Later Augustine even argued that we should be grateful that God is prepared to save even a minority, so terrible was the sinfulness of mankind as a result of the Fall.[26] Augustine expects human beings to fail.

Augustine's theology was, of course, challenged. His first major opponent was Pelagius. Pelagius, who originally came from Britain, is first recorded as living in Rome in the 390s and subsequently in Jerusalem. He knew Jovinian and Rufinus and was sympathetic to their views, hence giving Jerome the opportunity to condemn him—in his usual robust way—as "that fathead bloated with Scotch porridge." Pelagius stressed the possibility that human beings might conduct their own salvation through the power of reason and the exercise of free will. "By our reason, we are superior to those who live by their senses." The Fall had had no effect on the natural abilities of human beings. "It is on this choice between two ways, on this freedom to choose either alternative, that the glory [*sic*] of the rational mind is based."[27] Given free will, the individual was not dependent for salvation on the grace of God, although Pelagius argued that those who had set out to find God would be helped to do so. He provided the analogy of a man who sets out of his own accord to row across a lake but who is helped by God, symbolised as a following wind. For Pelagius the sacrament of baptism was crucial in that it ensured forgiveness of prior sins and released the power of reason, enabling the individual to turn to God. Essentially he offered optimism as a contrast to the pessimism of his adversary. The path Pelagius offered was not, however, an easy one. Despite his connections with Jovinian, Pelagius was profoundly ascetic, critical of corruption and social injustice, and he expected his followers to be as well. According to him, we have free will to be perfect and therefore perfection is obligatory. The weakness of Pelagianism was that it was designed for an ascetic elite who, in the tradition of Christian asceticism, declared themselves in opposition to contemporary society. It was always an unsettling

movement, and it has been noted that Pelagianism attracted more supporters in areas where invasion and social breakdown had been prevalent than it did in the more settled areas of the empire.

In 415 the debate over free will and original sin burst into open conflict. It seems that Pelagius cited Augustine to defend his own position,
thus demanding a response from Augustine and his supporters. It was
soon apparent that the church was divided. One synod, at Jerusalem,
condemned Pelagius; another endorsed his views. Two councils in north
Africa (where both the tradition of original sin and Augustine's own
influence were strongest) condemned the Pelagians in 416. They were
supported by the bishop of Rome, Innocent, after Augustine wrote to
him suggesting that too great a stress on the free will of an individual
threatened to undermine the authority of the bishops. However, Innocent's successor, Zosimus, a Greek with no loyalties to Augustine or the
African tradition, proved sympathetic to Pelagius, who had come to
Rome to plead his case personally. The emperor Honorius, apparently
disturbed by news of rioting in Rome that was blamed on Pelagius' supporters, but that the Pelagians themselves attributed to the supporters of
Augustine, condemned the Pelagians in an imperial edict of April 418
and ordered them to leave Rome. Honorius' motives are unclear, but it
appears that he took exception to Pelagius' forceful condemnation of
corruption. It was also said that a colleague of Augustine's, the bishop of
his home town, Thagaste, employed bribery at the court in his cause.
The imperial condemnation was then endorsed by a synod of north
African bishops held in Carthage. At this juncture Zosimus changed
sides and himself condemned Pelagianism; there was further disarray
when eighteen of the Italian bishops refused to support him. Few issues
of doctrine have been settled less satisfactorily. Pelagius, forbidding
though his strictures were, was entirely sincere in his commitment to
Christianity. He was certainly no heretic. Once again it was the emperor,
whose primary concern was good order, who settled the issue.

One of the eighteen dissenting Italian bishops, Julian of Eclanum,
who was forced into exile by the debate, set out the clearest and most
powerful objection to Augustine's position in a letter addressed to
Augustine himself.

> Babies, you say, carry the burden of another's sin, not
> any of their own . . . Explain to me, then, who this per-
> son is who sends the innocent to punishment. You

answer, God . . . God, you say, the very one who com-
mends his love to us, who has loved us and not spared
his son but handed him over to us, he judges us in this
way; he persecutes new born children; he hands over
babies to eternal flames because of their bad wills, when
he knows that they have not so much formed a will,
good or bad . . . It would show a just and reasonable
sense of propriety to treat you as beneath argument: you
have come so far from religious feeling, from civilized
standards, so far indeed from common sense, that you
think your Lord capable of committing kinds of crime
which are hardly found among barbarian tribes.[28]

Augustine's confusing concept of God, a loving but punitive deity, was
exposed with great clarity. Augustine nevertheless stood firm and was
preaching to worried and perplexed enquirers on the issue until his
death.

Running alongside Augustine's battles with the Pelagians were disagreements with the Donatists, the largest Christian community in north
Africa; Augustine's orthodox Christian church was much smaller. The
battles arose, of course, because the state had decreed that there could
only be one orthodox church, which would have undisputed access to
state patronage. It was a particularly difficult issue in that, quite apart
from their size, the Donatists had a compelling case for representing the
Christian church in north Africa. Their bishops were the leaders of those
communities who had refused to bow to persecution and surrender their
scriptures. Their pedigree was unchallengeable. Their bishops and clergy
held their offices in direct descent from the original Apostles, and they
argued that they drew on a purer tradition than the orthodox church in
that they had never compromised with the Roman state, the state that
had, after all, been responsible for the execution of Jesus. They had
adopted orthodox doctrine and so could not be classed as heretics (who
by now were beyond the law), and they preached austerity in the tradition of Tertullian. They would welcome back those whose faith had
lapsed under persecution so long as a rebaptism took place (any orthodox Christian converting to Donatism needed to be baptized because the
original baptism was not valid). Here again they represented tradition,
in that rebaptism had been required by Cyprian, the bishop of Carthage
martyred in the third century, whose own prestige and authority was

immense. While Cyprian had stressed the need for unity in the church, the Donatists argued that unity had been undermined by those Christians who surrendered the sacred scriptures to the authorities. Crucial to the Donatists was their sense of being a national African church, representing African traditions against those of the more cosmopolitan orthodox church, with its ties to the imperial government. Although many Donatist bishops were sophisticated men, presiding over wealthy city sees, Donatism reached far into the rural areas in a way orthodox Christianity did not. Yet Donatism should not be idealized. The Donatists were also prone to internal dissensions and schism, and outside the cities Donatists, perhaps as much imbued with anti-imperialist as with anti-orthodox feeling, often used violence against orthodox Christians, even though their bishops tried to discourage them. Constantine had isolated the Donatists by refusing them state patronage. Now, ninety years on, it was increasingly difficult for a state that had taken the radical and unprecedented step of insisting on religious uniformity to allow them to persist, yet one could hardly deny that they were committed Christians. Any attempt to persecute them would only confirm their belief in themselves as the true church, that of the martyrs. It was a matter of some embarrassment to orthodox Christians that the Donatists could claim the backing of the influential Cyprian, whom the orthodox themselves wanted to use as champion of episcopal authority. Augustine found himself in the difficult position of having to distinguish the Donatists from the minority orthodox church in such a way as to allow the former to be condemned. And yet this could be done only by declaring them to be heretics, which they were clearly not. Augustine was reduced to inadequate statements such as "Anyone separated from the church would end by saying false things" and "A characteristic of heretical sects is to be incapable of seeing what is obvious to everyone else."[29]

Once again the state had come to the rescue of the orthodox church. In 405 Honorius issued an edict ordering the unity of both churches, branding the Donatists as heretics, partly on the grounds of their insistence on rebaptism, thus making them subject to the rigour of the law. Their property was to be confiscated, their services forbidden and their clergy exiled. Augustine ejected the Donatists from Hippo and, taking over their bare churches—they did not believe in decoration and whitewashed their church walls—he posted his own anti-Donatist texts on the walls. When persecution was relaxed, Augustine petitioned the emperor to summon a conference, and this, presided over as it was by an orthodox Christian, Marcellinus, could only end in a further condemnation of the Donatists, who were represented by nearly 300 bishops. Donatism in itself became a criminal offence (only just over a hundred years previously, of course, the last edicts of Diocletian treated Christianity as a whole in a similar way), and Donatists were now actively compelled to join the orthodox church.[30]

In his earlier works Augustine was reluctant to condone the compelling of outsiders into the church. "Words should be our instruments, arguments our weapons, reason our means of conquest [*sic*] and we should avoid making enforced Catholics out of those whom we had known as open heretics." There was no support from New Testament texts for persecution (in fact, the Donatists were to taunt Augustine with Jesus' words from the Sermon on the Mount, "Blessed are they who are persecuted for righteousness' sake . . ."), and Christianity itself had its own recent memories of how destructive persecution could be. The saintly and highly orthodox Gregory of Nazianzus had specifically condemned coercion: "Whatever is done against one's will, under the threat of force, is like an arrow artificially tied back, or a river dammed in on every side of its channel. Given the opportunity it rejects the restraining force. What is done willingly, on the other hand, is steadfast for all time. It is made fast by the unbreakable bonds of love."[31] However, the works of Athanasius and the edicts of 380 and 381 enforcing Trinitarian orthodoxy were loaded with condemnation of "heretics." It was Augustine who developed a rationale of persecution.

Augustine's earlier, more tolerant, views were to change in the early fifth century. He began with the argument that Donatism intimidated many ordinary Christians and it was the duty of the "true" church to release them from such coercion. Furthermore, his experience of ordinary former Donatists was that most became excellent Christians when forced to do so. Therefore, compulsion was permissible. Just as God could punish in the exercise of his love, so too could the church, knowing as it did so that it was saving sinners from everlasting hell fire. "What then does brotherly love do? Does it, because it fears the short-lived fires of the furnace for the few, abandon all to the eternal fires of hell? And does it leave so many . . . to perish everlastingly . . . whom 'others' [i.e. the Donatists] will not permit to live in accordance with the teaching of Christ?"[32] Not for the last time in Christian history, fantasies about hell fire were being used as a means of manipulating Christian behaviour on earth. As for coercion, God himself had shown the way.

The conversion of Paul had been effected by God throwing him to the ground; Augustine finds comparable examples of forced conversions in the Old Testament. Yet Augustine's views on the sinfulness of every individual left him with a problem. Since even orthodox Christians were still burdened with sin, how was it possible to be sure that persecution was not an exercise of sinfulness? Augustine fell back on assertions that the church was divinely inspired and that any action undertaken in "love" must have God's support. While Augustine pleaded for restraint (he never condoned the death penalty, for instance, on the grounds that it deprived the sinner of the possibility of repentance), he had nevertheless provided a rationale for persecution, however circumscribed, which was to be exploited in the centuries to come. By the thirteenth century a papal legate reported on the extermination of the Cathars, a sect which preached a return to the ascetic ideals of early Christianity: "Nearly twenty thousand of the citizens were put to the sword regardless of age and sex. The workings of divine vengeance have been wondrous."[33]

The Donatist dispute challenged Augustine to develop another line of thinking. The Donatists, drawing on the teachings of Cyprian, argued that baptism at the hands of a priest or bishop who had apostatized could not be valid. Those who ministered the sacraments must be worthy men, in fact the church itself must be a community of saints. So long as the orthodox church, whose bishops had their succession from those who had lapsed, was, so far as the Donatists were concerned, in schism, their ministers could not be worthy. Augustine was forced to argue in reply that the quality of the minister was not essential to the sacrament. It was a direct expression of the grace of God and passed from God to the recipient without losing its purity (as water passed down a stone channel). So long as the sacrament was administered in the name of Christ and the correct form was used, it was valid (although as already seen, baptism did not necessarily free the recipient of original sin, so that Augustine raised the possibility of a "valid" sacrament that brought no benefit to its recipient!). The church could be made up of sinners without losing its unique role as the conduit of God's grace. However badly its members, even those in the hierarchy, behave, the church can never lose its true role as guardian of orthodoxy. The role of the church was further elaborated in Augustine's last and perhaps greatest work, *The City of God,* finally completed just four years before he died, in 426.

Augustine lived in a disintegrating world; the first sack of Rome by (Homoean Christian) Gothic invaders in 410 sent a shock wave through the empire. Refugees scattered even as far as Africa. Many Christians had claimed that the empire had been instituted by God so that Christianity could flourish; now, in the west at least, it was collapsing around them. Other Christians saw the fall of Rome as the beginning of the last times so vividly forecast in the Book of Revelation. Pagans claimed that it was precisely because their gods had been abandoned through the coming of Christianity that the city had fallen. Augustine's position, by contrast, was detached, as if such disasters meant little in God's great scheme of things; this was the attitude that he spelled out at length in *The City of God*. His elaboration of two cities, one of the world and one of God, drew on earlier ideas of his own as well as echoing the opening chapters of Paul's letter to the Romans (and later theologians who talked in terms of the "saved" versus the "unsaved"). But *The City of God* set these ideas into a specific historical context, spending many pages on the failure of the pagan gods to support Rome in its past history.[34] Augustine rejected Eusebius' claim that Constantine had inaugurated a Christian state. The state, however Christian it may appear, can only be a community in which saints and sinners are mingled. The work of a providential God can be discerned in human history through studying the Bible and enters a new, final stage with the coming of Christ, but the true "City of God" can only be in heaven after death, when the unsaved have been segregated and sent to hell. We cannot identify those who will be saved in advance; while they are on earth they are like pilgrims, wandering in exile in the hope of finding their promised land in heaven. So "the city of the world" must be by definition flawed; in *The City of God* Augustine dwelled on the imperfections of human societies with their continual wars and corruption, so far from "the peace of the Heavenly City . . . a perfectly ordered and perfectly harmonious fellowship in the enjoyment of God, and a mutual fellowship in God."[35] Here Augustine consciously rejected the classical ideal, espoused by both Plato and Aristotle, that it was within the city that an individual reaches his higher state. As J. S. McClelland puts it, Augustine "signals the definitive end of the ancient idea that the state is the school of the virtues and the stage on which the virtues are to be seen at their best advantage."[36] However, Augustine also discussed the nature of the ideal state on earth. It is worth working towards good order, he argued, because although absolute peace and justice cannot be reached on earth, a state that works towards them can relieve the burdens of earthly life. Nor can the church survive except in conditions of good order.

The Christian can, and should, participate in the state's activities, as a soldier or administrator, and Augustine expected the Christian to uphold the authority of the state and play an active part in supporting its values. ("What is more horrible than the public executioner? Yet he has a necessary place in the legal system, and he is part of the order of a well governed society.") War was to be avoided if possible, but Augustine accepted it as part of life: Christians should not shrink from it if their state was threatened or if it would secure peace and safety for human society. Once Christians were in the army, it was not wrong to kill in the obedience of orders, even if they were unjust. Hierarchy, where those below have the duty to obey those above them, is the natural way of things, whether in church, state or family. Even at its best, however, the state can only be an echo of the "City of God." The greatest happiness on earth is as utter misery compared to the joys of heaven. Augustine had little faith in the possibility of progress. As we have seen, he accepted slavery, claiming that it was God's punishment of the slave. In short, Augustine was a social conservative: he saw human beings as inevitably flawed, reforms as bringing illusory benefits and the maintenance of good order as a priority. The Christian could only act within the world as it existed, never change it for the better. *The City of God* proved to be the foundation document of Christian political thought, though it presents a view of society which seems radically different from that of the Gospels.

Even the briefest familiarity with Augustine's writings convinces one that he is an intellectual giant in the range of issues he tackles, in the creative way in which he approaches each one and in his sensitivity to human psychology; he has, *pace* Freud, been credited with the discovery of the unconscious. He deals with issues independently and often creatively so long as established orthodoxy is not challenged. When one compares the obsessively vindictive attitude to the Jews of Ambrose or John Chrysostom, for instance, with the more thoughtful, even tolerant, attitude of Augustine, the latter's greater intellectual and personal maturity is clear. Augustine recognized that Jews and Christians have a common father in Abraham and share in man's fallen nature, and that the Jews (even if they proved blind to Christ's presence among them) had been given a providential role by God as witness to the prophecies of his coming. They should not be totally cast out. The Catholic Church, anxious to reject charges of anti-Semitism in the twentieth century, has felt able to use Augustine's writings in its cause.[37] In Book 2 of *De Doctrina*

*Christiana,* he considers the value of secular learning with some objectivity, even if only as an aid to understanding the scriptures more profoundly. Yet Augustine's achievements are flawed by the underlying pessimism and guilt that permeate his theology. His personal tragedy was that he could never bring himself to trust that his "loving" God would save all those who committed themselves freely to him in the hope of receiving his love—becoming Christian, in other words, did not bring with it the assurance of salvation. Perhaps somewhere deep in his psyche there was irreparable damage that distorted his perspective so that, at least in the second half of his life, he could see human existence on earth only at its very bleakest, without even any certain hope of divine rescue. Whatever its sources, the theology that emerged was to Augustine the truth for all time; as his role in the Pelagian controversy showed, he expected his views to prevail in the church as a whole. "One of Augustine's failings," writes Christopher Stead, "was that he was apt to read off lessons from his own experiences and erect them into principles equally applicable to all mankind." Unlike Paul, who, as we have seen, had no reason to expect his writings to last, Augustine expected his to become the orthodoxy.[38] In the words of John Rist:

> Part of the tragic side of Augustinianism is that his work
> was received uncritically for so long . . . He would be
> the authority; his views would be canonized as authoritative proof-texts rather than as starting points for more
> impartial investigations. A nearly inevitable side effect
> of such reverence . . . was the likelihood that Augustine
> himself would be misread, even tendentiously, so that he
> might be harmonised with someone else's convictions.[39]

Augustine's intellectual stature has earned him an unassailable place in Christian theology. But while his writings had an understandable relevance to the troubled times within which he lived, and in other contexts in which mankind needs to be reminded of the evil of which it is capable, they give little room for hope or optimism. For Augustine the reality of life on earth cannot be transformed by human effort as it will always be mired in sin. Augustine's rationale for persecution was to be used to justify slaughter (as of the Cathars or the native people of America). In the seventeenth century the French saint John Eudes could even argue that "it is a subject of humiliation of all the mothers of the children of Adam to know that while they are with child they carry within them an infant . . . who is the enemy of God, the object of his hatred and malediction and the shrine of the demon."[40]

In 430 the Vandals, one of the Gothic tribes, swept across north Africa. Hippo itself was besieged, but Augustine died on August 28, before the city fell. Even though Hippo was partially burnt, Augustine's library miraculously survived. Both orthodox and Donatist Christians were overwhelmed by that old heresy, Homoean Christianity, which the Goths had adopted with some fervour before it had been outlawed by Theodosius.

It was, however, in this context, with imperial authority crumbling in the west, that the role of the bishops of Rome gradually expanded. One by one the ancient senatorial families of Rome had converted to Christianity; in the city we can see the shift in patronage from the old and now decaying ceremonial centre to the great new basilicas which were being built around it.[41] If there is one figure who symbolizes the growing power and influence of Rome, it is Leo, one of only two popes to be termed "the Great." Leo, who became bishop of Rome in 440 and reigned until his death in 461, is an outstanding figure, not only by virtue of his forceful personality but also for his determination to enforce his authority as heir of Peter over the other bishops of the west. He interpreted the Roman law of succession to suggest that he had even assumed the legal personality of Peter by virtue of the unbroken line of bishops of Rome since Peter's time, an interpretation reflected in his confident dealings with bishops in Africa, Italy, Spain and Gaul. His sermons, like the man himself, are direct and lacking in rhetorical flourish, and they are supplemented by a growing number of decrees, on church government, the authority of bishops and the ordination of clergy. Heretics were dealt with firmly, a council of bishops in northern Italy issuing a further condemnation of Pelagianism. Shrewdly, Leo also tied his authority to the state by acting through Valentinian III (emperor of the west 425–55) in civil affairs. He asserted his own authority in the secular sphere in 452, when he personally led a delegation from Rome to confront Attila the Hun, whose armies were ravaging northern Italy. When Attila withdrew, possibly because of a lack of resources, Leo successfully took the credit. Three years later he had another coup when he persuaded the Vandal leader Gaiseric, who entered Rome unopposed, to deal leniently with the city.

As we have seen, Leo was also the first bishop of Rome to play a decisive part in the making of Christian doctrine. His *Tome,* a formulation of the two natures of Christ in one person, was adopted by the Council of Chalcedon in 451. While Leo saw this as an acceptance of his primacy over the whole church, the eastern bishops claimed that they had accepted it because it represented what had already been agreed at earlier councils. The disagreement was but one stage in the long and complicated process by which east and west were separating from each other.

Leo's ascendancy, however, was as much a reflection of his determination and personality as it was of Rome's rise to preeminence. A century later, by contrast, Vigilius, bishop of Rome 537–55, was unable to resist the forceful Justinian. While the Chalcedonian formula had been accepted in the west, as it still is, controversy over the nature of Christ continued in the east. In order to gain support from Monophysites, Justinian decided to condemn their opponents, the Nestorians, by declaring the *Three Chapters,* texts in which Nestorian views had been expressed by Theodore of Mopsuestia and others, to be heretical. Justinian needed to have the support of the bishop of Rome. Vigilius had apparently promised the empress Theodora that he would favour Monophysitism in return for help in gaining the bishopric. Called on to honour his promise, Vigilius became aware that there was intense opposition in the west to any imperial attempt to revise or reverse the decisions of Chalcedon. He hesitated and in 545 was kidnapped on the orders of Justinian and eventually taken to Constantinople. Here, worn down by the emperor's demands, he was persuaded to condemn the *Three Chapters*—to the outrage of the clergy in the west. Feelings ran so high that he was excommunicated by the African bishops. Eight years later, Vigilius refused to attend the sessions of the council of 553 in Constantinople, where the *Three Chapters* were formally condemned, on the grounds that there was no proper representation from the west, but a year later he came out in support of the rulings of the council. Further embarrassment resulted from the publication of his secret correspondence with Justinian over the issues. Finally released from Constantinople, Vigilius died on his return to Italy but was so unpopular in Rome that he was refused burial in St. Peter's. Justinian's own army in Italy then imposed a new bishop, Pelagius, on the city, creating such resentment that at first no other bishop could be found willing to consecrate him.[42]

It was in these years, perhaps inevitably given the developments described above, that the relationship between east and west began to disintegrate. There had been virtually no western representation at the Council of Constantinople—in fact the bishops of the Balkans had met in a synod of their own to condemn it. As a result of the weakness of Rome, the bishops of Milan declared themselves out of communion with the city and remained so for twenty years: in Aquileia the bishop set up a separate patriarchy. All this at a time when the cultural unity of the empire was breaking down, classical learning was fading, the main diet of scholars was made up of Christian rather than secular texts, and east and west were forgetting each other's languages. Greek was virtually unknown in the west after 700, just at the point when Latin was being eclipsed by Greek in the court at Constantinople.[43]

The new world that was emerging in the west was symbolised by Gregory the Great, bishop of Rome 590–604, "the harbinger," as Judith Herrin puts it, "of a purely Latin and clerical culture of the medieval west."[44] Gregory was the son of a Roman senator and had served as prefect of the city before he sold his vast properties and diverted the proceeds to the relief of the poor and the founding of monasteries. He himself spent several years as a monk, the vocation to which he always felt most drawn. Later he was sent by the bishop of Rome as an emissary to Constantinople, but, unlike Vigilius, he successfully avoided becoming caught up in the intrigues of the imperial court, and when he returned to Rome, as abbot of his monastery, he was uncompromised by his experience in the east (he had even managed to avoid learning Greek). He became pope (the term was now in use with specific reference to the bishop of Rome) in 590, but his was a decaying city. The great aqueducts that had supplied the city with water for centuries had been cut, many of the old senatorial families had left and large parts of the city were now deserted. Northern Italy was held by the Lombards. So while Gregory is remembered for his careful and charitable management of the papal estates around Rome (their produce being passed on to the poor), his temporal power did not extend much further. In the event, the mission he sent to effect a conversion of the Angles in Britain was a triumph. Despite his lack of power, Gregory showed no inhibitions in standing up to the emperors in Constantinople and insisting on the ancient privileges of his position.

Gregory was not an original thinker; he relied heavily on his forerunners in the western theological tradition—Augustine (and hence Paul), Ambrose and, in monastic affairs, Cassian. He distrusted secular learning, and for him the deadliest of the seven deadly sins was pride, by which he meant intellectual independence. "The wise," he said, "should be advised to cease from their knowledge," to be "wise in ignorance, wisely untaught." The philosophers, he went on, were so concerned with finding the immediate causes of things that they were blind to the ultimate "cause," which was the will of God.[45]

Gregory celebrated miracles, even telling how the bishop of Placentia had been able to quell a flood in the river Po by dropping a letter of command into its waters. By this time, however, when traditional philosophy had been long suppressed and with it the stabilizing force of reason, Gregory was expressing the conventional wisdoms of his time. These views should not overshadow his major achievements as a moral teacher. His writings are free of the obsession with heresy that make those of many of his predecessors so dispiriting—he preferred instead to stress good example—and he thought deeply and with much sensitivity about how bishops and pastors could exercise their authority. The ideal priest, said Gregory, must be "intimately close to each person through compassion, and yet to hover above all through contemplation." He was a champion of the rule of St. Benedict (c. 540), that balance of austerity and humanity that in itself drew on the works of Cassian and the rule of Basil of Caesarea, and he extolled those church leaders, such as Benedict, whom he felt provided a model for Christian living. He resisted extremes. When a fellow bishop threw out all the statues in his church on the grounds that they encouraged idolatry, Gregory reproached him with the shrewd advice that "to adore images is one thing; to teach with their help what should be adored is another."[46] (A story that he threw the surviving pagan statues in Rome into the Tiber appears to have been a later fabrication.) His method of converting the Angles was also sensitive when compared with the more robust methods of many of his fellow Christians. Despite being a devotee of Augustine, Gregory moved to moderate the more extreme consequences of Augustinian theology. He refused to believe that God was so harsh that a sinner who died by accident before he could complete a penance set for his sins would necessarily end up in hell, and it is in Gregory that one finds an early definition of purgatory, a halfway house where sins are purified before the sinner progresses to heaven. Those left on earth are given the role of interceding with God to speed the process, and, unlike Augustine, Gregory accepts that their good works and pious practices are of value to God. He stressed the importance of music in worship, and he is the Gregory of the Gregorian chant (although a direct link to plainsong has never been proved). He put aside the problem of evil as an unfathomable mystery, although he argued that suffering does act to test the faith of believers. Nor was he as obsessed with sexuality as many others. If clergy found it difficult to remain celibate, then they should be free to marry. It was just this kind of leadership, humane but unquestioned in its moral authority, which was needed to establish the papacy's independence of the east, and Gregory is usually seen as the founder of the medieval papacy. His legacy endured and the office gained in stature. In 800 the emperor Charlemagne travelled to Rome to receive coronation at the hands of a successor of Gregory's, Pope Leo III.

The provinces of north Africa had been reconquered by Justinian in the 530s and restored to orthodox Christianity, but in the seventh century they were overrun by the Arabs. For good or ill, Rome lost those provinces of the west that had provided the most effective challenge to her authority, with the result that, in the words of Robert Markus, "Rome's world became radically simplified; and the Roman see emerged as the single, isolated, religious centre of the barbarian west."[47] The history of western Christianity was rewritten so successfully to reflect this fact that many western Christians are hardly aware of the predominently Greek nature of the early church. In fact, it is still possible to read of the eastern churches "breaking away" from Catholicism. Though the story is necessarily complicated, it seems rather to have been one of "the final detachment of the papacy from Byzantine political allegiance and the creation of a new western empire" in the eighth century.[48]

A story survives of one Fursey, an Irish ascetic of the seventh century, who dreamed that he had died and was facing the last judgment. He was assailed by a mass of demons, who pointed out that many of his deeds, apparently good in themselves, were tainted because they had not sprung from love alone. There would be no justice, the demons told him, if God was to accept him in paradise. They even doubted, they told him, that God was as fully aware of his shortcomings as they were! To remind him of his peril, as he passed through the flames of hell, the required route to reach heaven, the body of a burning sinner, to whom on earth he had given a light penance in return for a gift of clothing, brushed against him, leaving a scar on his face. Although with the help of protecting angels Fursey did make it to heaven, the scar remained on his cheek when he awoke from his dream, and every time he recounted his terrifying experience he was seen to break out into sweat.[49]

Ever since Paul described the last judgment as "a day of anger," anxiety had formed a significant part of the Christian experience; reading the writings of the western Church Fathers, it is easy to see why this was so sustained. They expressed intense anxiety over authority, over sex, over the punitive powers of their God. No one who follows Augustine can be sure of salvation. What has been particularly important has been the conceptualisation, following Plato, of the human *psyche* as at continual war with itself. We are caught as individuals in a cosmic drama, and one can never relax in case the demons take hold. (There is an interesting analogy here with Freud, who saw the unconscious ready to ambush our rational behaviour at any moment.) It deserves repeating that this is only one possible way of conceptualising the *psyche;* others, following Aristotle, would prefer to stress its potential for harmonious *eudaimonia*. However, in medieval Christianity preoccupation with internal battles and the inherent sinfulness of humankind took an ever more powerful hold. As so often, art reflects the process. As Neil MacGregor has put it in his thoughtful study of Christian art, *Seeing Salvation,* "as the number and scale of our wrong doings grow, so, necessarily do his [Christ's] sufferings."[50] The rare depictions of crucifixion in the fifth century show no sign of Christ's humiliation and suffering—perhaps Christians still found it difficult to accept the degradation of crucifixion. The words "who was crucified for us" were added to the litany for the first time in the 470s in Antioch.[51] By 1300 his suffering is shown in prurient detail. Christ's agony on the cross makes sense only in the context of man's sinfulness; if Christ brings salvation, then it follows that humanity is in need of it and the nature of man is defined accordingly. Thus the profound rupture with the classical world's conceptions of "man." And the rupture was firmly associated with the attack on rationalism, as can be seen in Augustine's assertion that man's power to think rationally had been corrupted forever by Adam's sin.

Yet at the same time, what was now the Roman Catholic Church was assuming responsibility for the poor and unloved. The tradition of learning was narrow, particularly by comparison with the classical world, but in so far as education was preserved it was through the Church, as was a system of health care. These centuries were also a time when imperial authority had disappeared and the Church in the west began to fill the vacuum. The Church preserved Roman law and the bishops a structure of institutional authority. The different cultures of western Europe may have adopted different kinds of Christianity as they fused their local cultural and spiritual traditions with those of the church, but there was a sense of a common language, even if it was a restricted one, with which communities could communicate with each other across Europe. If imperial Christianity—the Christianity of the empire in its death throes, in which even Jesus emerges as a warrior—was far removed from the Christianity of the Gospels, Christianity now takes on a new role as an agent of social cohesion in a world built out of the ruins of the empire. What remained was a tension between the obedience demanded by institutional Christianity and the original Gospel message of ambivalence to authority. (Paul provided a much more effective model than the Gospels for those who wished to stress the importance of authority, one reason, perhaps, why he became so prominent in the fourth century.) It is a tension which has persisted throughout Christian history and remains alive today, as reformers, in most cases drawing directly on the words of Jesus, have challenged the power, wealth and social conservatism of the established churches.

# 19

# "WE HONOUR THE PRIVILEGE OF SILENCE WHICH IS WITHOUT PERIL"

## The Death of the Greek Empirical Tradition

In a famous passage in Dostoyevsky's *Brothers Karamazov,* Jesus returns to earth, is recognized by the Grand Inquisitor and is thrown into prison for threatening to subvert the Church. His message of universal freedom had proved impossible to follow. As the Inquisitor taunts Jesus:

> Did you forget that a tranquil mind and even death is dearer to man than a free choice in the knowledge of good and evil? ... Instead of the strict ancient law, [when you came] man had in future to decide for himself with a free heart what is good and what is evil ... But did it never occur to you that he would at last reject and call in question even your image and your truth, if he were weighed down by so fearful a burden as freedom of choice?

You hoped, the Inquisitor tells Jesus, that people would worship you out of free will and without the need for miracles, but what they really yearn for is good order. Otherwise they tear themselves apart.

> Freedom, a free mind and science will lead them into such a jungle and bring them face to face with such marvels and insoluble mysteries that some of them will destroy themselves, others will destroy one another, and the rest, weak and unhappy, will come crawling to our

> [the church's] feet and cry aloud: "Yes, you were right,
> you alone possessed his mystery and we come back to
> you—save us from ourselves."

The Church, the Inquisitor concludes, had, through the use of "mystery, magic and authority," soothed the anxieties that Jesus had aroused. Hence the threat posed by his return.[1]

"Mystery, magic and authority" are particularly relevant words in attempting to define Christianity as it had developed by the end of the fourth century. The century had been characterized by destructive conflicts over doctrine in which personal animosities had often prevailed over reasoned debate. Within Christian tradition, of course, the debate has been seen in terms of a "truth" (finally consolidated in the Nicene Creed in the version of 381) assailed by a host of heresies that had to be defeated. Epiphanius, the intensely orthodox bishop of Salamis in the late fourth century, was able to list no less than eighty heresies extending back over history (he was assured his total was correct when he discovered exactly the same number of concubines in the Song of Songs!), and Augustine in his old age came up with eighty-three. The heretics, said their opponents, were demons in disguise who "employed sophistry and insolence. Through the former they won over the less intelligent by specious argument; through the latter they attacked the weaker, terrified them with fear of their effrontery, and tried to make them submit to their heresies."[2] From a modern perspective, however, it would appear that the real problem was not that evil men or demons were trying to subvert doctrine but that the diversity of sources for Christian doctrine—the scriptures, "tradition," the writings of the Church Fathers, the decrees of councils and synods—and the pervasive influence of Greek philosophy made any kind of coherent "truth" difficult to sustain, even by such sophisticated thinkers as the Cappadocian Fathers. Both church and state wanted secure definitions of orthodoxy, but there were no agreed axioms or first principles that could be used as foundations for the debate. As soon as the essentials of Christianity were explored, a mass of underlying philosophical problems emerged—witness the many different ways of conceiving the supreme deity. As we have seen, the scriptures were so diverse that texts, none of which had been written with the theological issues of the fourth and fifth centuries in mind, could be produced to support a wide variety of doctrines. The very fact that Augustine and Epiphanius could each list over eighty different interpretations of Christian doctrine ("heresies") makes the point. A desperation to establish doctrinal certainty, a desperation made more intense by the fear of eternal punishment in an area where certainty was, in rational terms, so hard to achieve, helps explain why the level of bitterness in Christian debate was so high, much higher than it was in the more open world of pagan philosophy. It is hard to imagine a situation more conducive to frustration. It was not that Christians were any less able or forgiving than their pagan fellows. It was rather that they had become trapped in a philosophical cul-de-sac. The resulting tension explains why the emperors, concerned with maintaining good order in times of stress, would eventually be forced to intervene to declare one or other position in the debate "orthodox" and its rivals "heretical." This in its turn led to the heretical groups being deprived of imperial patronage. Hence the widespread rioting reported in the east when Arianism was finally condemned in the 380s.

One way of calming the theological turmoil was to declare that ultimately God was unknowable and that therefore speculation about his nature was futile, even blasphemous. We see such an approach in the preaching of Gregory of Nazianzus (c. 329–90), already encountered as one of the Cappadocian Fathers and as a thinker very much at home with Greek philosophy.[3] Gregory's enthusiasm for public speaking conflicted with a fundamentally shy nature, and throughout his life he was torn between the demands of public life and the attractions of asceticism and personal study. The conflict was crystallized by his arrival in 379 in Constantinople, where he was asked to become preacher to the small Nicene community in the city (at a time when Homoeanism and Arianism were still the most popular forms of Christianity there). With the arrival of the emperor Theodosius and his declaration of Trinitarian orthodoxy he found himself thrust into unexpected prominence. As leader of a minority position now declared by the emperor to be the "truth," he was confronted by a maelstrom of debate, as much in the streets as elsewhere.[4] His reaction was to try to find a rationale to defuse it. In his *Theological Orations,* delivered in Constantinople in 380, he drew on a tradition established by his fellow Cappadocian Basil that ultimately the nature of God is a mystery and that the proper response to questions about his nature should be silence. Basil had argued:

> It should be enough for you to know that there is a good
> shepherd who gave his soul for his sheep. The knowl-

edge of God is comprised within these limits. How big God is, what His limits are, and of what essence He is, such questions are dangerous on the part of the interrogator; they are as unanswerable on the part of the interrogated. Consequently they should be taken care of with silence.[5]

In his *Orations* Gregory follows Basil's lead. Unlike many of his contemporaries he avoids attacking specific heresies but instead confronts the tradition of questioning itself. So much speculation, he claims, is purely for effect, reminiscent of the promoters of wrestling bouts who stage-manage contests "to give the uncritical spectators visual sensations and compel their applause." The questioners are manipulating others' minds, trying to mould men into holiness, but they produce instead "ready-made councils of ignorant intellectuals." Only those who are pure in heart, by which he appears to mean ascetics, and have theological grounding, in effect priests and bishops, should contemplate the mystery of the divine and even then "to tell of God is not possible."[6]

Whether Gregory was right even to include bishops as worthy participants in the debates was brought into question when he was asked to preside over the Council of Constantinople, which passed the final formulation of the Nicene Creed. The experience appalled him. He records of one meeting of the bishops:

> I finished my speech, but they squawked in every direction, a flock of jackdaws combining together, a rabble of adolescents, a gang of youths, a whirlwind raising dust under the pressure of air currents, people whom nobody who was mature either in the fear of God or in years would pay any attention, they splutter confused stuff or like wasps rush directly at what is in front of their faces.[7]

He was challenged over whether he should be bishop at all (a challenge rooted in the struggle for primacy between Alexandria and Constantinople), and in 381, complaining of ill health, real or imagined, he left Constantinople for good, dying in Nazianzus some nine years later. "We are quiet here without strife and disputes," he wrote before his death, "since above all else we honour the privilege of silence which is without peril."[8]

It is telling that after Gregory of Nazianzus was deposed as bishop, his replacement was the urban prefect Nectarius, like Ambrose of Milan an unbaptized layman when he was appointed. Clearly the priority was the maintenance of good order in an unsettled city, and one assumes that another "Nicene" appointment would have threatened this.

Gregory's views were echoed by his much more outspoken and confident contemporary John Chrysostom. In a series of sermons preached in his native Antioch between 386 and 387 John inveighed against those who speculated on God. It is faith that matters, says John; it provides the limits within which one can know about God, but "they [the speculators] invent and meddle in everything so that faith is excluded from the understanding of their listeners . . . Whenever God reveals something, it is necessary to accept what is said in faith, not to pry impetuously." John compares the subservience of the angels in heaven to the irreverent prattle of those on earth: "Did you see how great the holy dread in heaven and how great the arrogant presumption here below? The angels in heaven give God glory; these on earth carry on meddlesome investigations." In fact, God was beyond human understanding, and human language was unable to capture his true nature.[9] A century later the mystical theologian known as Pseudo-Dionysius (who probably wrote in Syria c. 500–520) summarized the essence of the debate: "It is most fitting to the mysterious passages of scripture that the saved and hidden truth about the celestial intelligences be concealed through the inexpressible and the sacred and be inaccessible to the *hoi polloi*." Dionysius, who has proved a highly influential figure in Christian mysticism, partly because for many centuries his writings were believed to be those of a first-century Dionysius, a convert of Paul, until modern textual analysis showed the extent to which they were influenced by Neoplatonism, argued that the soul should progress beyond the senses and reason, entering "a darkness beyond understanding" in which God cannot be conceptualized at all. "God is in no way like the things that have being and we have no knowledge at all of His incomprehensible and ineffable transcendence and invisibility."[10] Perhaps consciously Dionysius echoed Paul, who famously noted (1 Corinthians 13:12): "We are seeing a dim reflection in a mirror; but then we shall be seeing face to face. The knowledge I have now is imperfect; but then I shall know as fully as I am known."

There were, of course, conceptual issues raised by the idea of an unknowable God. Could a creed which consisted overwhelmingly of positive assertions about the nature of God, Jesus and the Holy Spirit (the only negative assertion in the Nicene Creed is the phrase "not made" in "begotten, not made") co-exist with the belief that God is unknowable? Conversely, how was it possible to say we have "no knowledge" of a God who has frequently revealed himself in the Old Testament, and, through Christ, in the New? Gregory of Nyssa was forced to admit that this might indeed be the case: "Whoever searches the whole of revelation will find there no doctrine of divine nature at all, nor indeed a doctrine of anything else that has a substantial existence, so that we pass our lives in ignorance of much, being ignorant first of all of ourselves as human beings and then of all other things besides."[11] There was surely a fundamental conceptual incoherence here. If God is essentially unknowable, what implications does this have for the authority of the Church so far as doctrine is concerned? Could Christian doctrine be divided into some areas where certainty is possible and others where it is accepted that it is not; if so, where is the boundary between the two to be drawn and the distinction justified in any coherent way? Essentially, the problem was that the Christian concept of God had evolved in too many different and conflicting contexts. As we saw earlier, this did not trouble a pagan like the orator Themistius, who revelled in the 300 ways of describing God, but Christians were forced to narrow their definitions of God to a few fundamental attributes. It could not be done in any philosophically coherent way, and claiming that God was unknowable can perhaps be seen a pragmatic response to the difficulties.

By the end of the fourth century this theological development (or it might equally be described as the extinction of theology in that the freedom to explore the nature of God was becoming restricted to the point of extinction) suited the political needs of the emperors. They too wished to defuse the acrimony of Christian debate in a world that seemed increasingly beyond their control politically as well as spiritually. Theodosius II was particularly anxious to bring order into government and religion. His Code of Laws, an accumulation of some 2,500 imperial laws since the time of Constantine, promulgated in 438, brought together an extensive range of edicts defending Christianity and condemning its rivals. When preparations were under way for the Council of Ephesus of 431, Theodosius II tried to settle the Nestorian debate without engendering the chaos and acrimony of earlier councils. Recognizing how easily debates could degenerate into personalized abuse, he pleaded with Cyril of Alexandria that "true doctrine with respect to religion" should be sought "by means of research rather than by arrogant disputations concerning words."[12] He planned that the council should be presided over by an imperial commissioner who would guide the assembled bishops towards consensus. As we have seen, Theodosius was outmanoeuvred by Cyril, who pushed through a doctrine for which he then attempted to gain the support of the imperial authorities through massive bribery. However, in 451 at Chalcedon, the imperial authorities were, as we have seen, better prepared. A compromise formula on the nature of Christ was prepared and imposed and an attempt (unsuccessful in this instance) made to silence further debate through an imperial decree.

In the west, however, which after the fall of the Latin empire in the 470s was increasingly free of imperial control, it became possible to construct alternative structures of authority. Gregory the Great consolidated a rationale of papal supremacy that once again stressed the bishop of Rome's precedence in both west and east. Inevitably much tidying up of Christianity's turbulent past needed to be done to give it ideological coherence. The doctrines of orthodox Christianity, it was now said, had been known throughout the ages. Even the patriarchs, who had lived before the time of Moses, "knew that one Almighty God is the Holy Trinity," though Gregory admitted that "they did not preach very much publicly about the Trinity whom they knew." Now that it was claimed that the scriptures, of both the Old and New Testaments, spoke with one voice, the Church Fathers' impassioned and bitter disagreements over the interpretation of contradictory passages could be expunged from the record; in fact, they were now said to have spoken with unanimity. What the scriptures taught, Gregory argued, had been upheld by the four councils that could be associated with orthodoxy—Nicaea, 325; Constantinople, 381; Ephesus, 431; Chalcedon, 451—and these were given status as ecumenical councils at which the genuine voice of the Church had been heard. "In like manner," wrote Gregory, "all the four holy synods of the holy universal church we receive as we do the four books of the Holy Gospels." Orthodoxy is seamless and given unanimous and consistent backing from scriptures, Apostles, Church Fathers and ecumenical councils. The role of the emperors in calling the councils and pressuring them into consensus was, perhaps understandably, passed over, as was the lack of significant western participation. As orthodox doctrine was now presented as though it had been settled and accepted from the beginning of time, heretics were consequently accused of "bringing forth as something new which is not contained in the old books of the ancient fathers." So, whatever inspection of the historical record might suggest, it became impossible to see Christian doctrine as the product of a process of evolution. A "heresy" could not have "matured" into "orthodoxy." Isolated in the west and free of the imperial presence, Gregory was free to proclaim papal supremacy. When new disputes arose, it was to be the pope, as successor of Peter, who would have the final say, even if a council had made its own decisions: "Without the authority and consent of the apostolic see [Rome]," said Gregory, "none of the matters transacted [by a council] have any binding force." The supremacy of the pope in all matters of doctrine was now fully asserted.[13]

Confronted by the terrible animosities of Christian debate in the fourth century, one has reason to be relieved that silence fell in the churches (even if this silence did not extend to Nestorians and Monophysites). One can sympathize with the words of Gregory of Nazianzus, "It is better to remain silent, than to speak with malice." Yet there is a difference between accepting that ultimately the nature of God (or any spiritual force) cannot be known (a view which mainstream Greek philosophy would have accepted as perfectly valid)[14] and proscribing speculation about it altogether. The ancient Greek tradition that one should be free to speculate without fear and be encouraged to take individual moral responsibility for one's views was rejected. This was especially clear in rhetoric. Previously (in the writings of Isocrates and Quintilian, for instance) good rhetoric had been inseparable from the speaker who composed it. The words said could not be isolated from the character of the one who said them; this is why both Isocrates and Quintilian laid such stress on the moral goodness of the speaker. In the Christian tradition, on the other hand, it was God who spoke through his preachers, who were merely the conductors of his words. Here again it was Paul who initiated the new approach, turning his back on traditional philosophy in the process. From 1 Corinthians 2:4–5: "In my speeches and sermons that I gave, there were none of the arguments that belong to philosophy; only a demonstration of the power of the Spirit. And I did this so that your faith should not depend on human philosophy but on the power of God." In other words, it is the Spirit rather than the individual who speaks, and "human philosophy" is specifically rejected as a means of finding truth. With the integration of aspects of the Greek philosophical tradition into Christianity, pagan rhetoric came again to be valued; in his funeral oration to Basil, Gregory of Nazianzus is still able to present rhetoric as an art dependent on the skill of the speaker. Yet it was Paul's view that the speaker is only an intermediary that came to predominate. As Gregory of Nyssa put it: "The human voice was fashioned for one reason alone—to be the threshold through which the sentiments of the heart, inspired by the Holy Spirit, might be translated clearly into the Word itself."[15] No longer is coherence of argument valued. Augustine follows Tertullian in arguing that it is the very irrationality of the Christian message that is its strength: "If by calling yourself wise, you become a fool, call yourself a fool, and you will become wise," he says, echoing Paul's observation to the Corinthians, "The foolishness of God is wiser than men, and the weakness of God is stronger than men."[16] In his *De Doctrina Christiana* Augustine argued that the moral quality of the speaker was not relevant so long as the doctrine he preached was orthodox. "It is possible," he wrote, "for a person who is eloquent but evil actually to compose a sermon proclaiming the truth for another, who is not eloquent but who is good to deliver."[17] So much for the tradition of Isocrates and Quintilian. Here again the influence of Platonism was strong. Truth exists eternally and totally independently of the one who speaks it, and there is evidence that priests increasingly used approved sermons, such as those by Augustine or other recognized orthodox thinkers, rather than their own.[18] So the art of rhetoric declined as was inevitable with the devaluation of reasoned argument and individual creativity. Richard Lim has noted how councils were now dominated by texts prepared for the occasion rather than by spontaneous speeches.[19]

Aristotle was another casuality of this. Attacks were focused on his work the *Categories*. The *Categories* sets out ten questions that needed to be asked about any entity, such as its size, its qualities, its relationship to other entities and its place in time. In the debates of the fourth century, some participants, such as Aetius the Syrian, had used the *Categories* as a framework for speculating about the divine and had taught that dialectical questioning on the Aristotelian model was the way to progress in theological matters. By the mid fifth century, however, it was no longer possible to enjoy open-ended discussion as to the nature of God, and the *Categories* became "a prime villain." In the seventh century Anastasius, abbot of the monastery of St. Catherine in Sinai, was to argue that the ten horns of the dragon in the Book of Revelation (12:4) were none other than the ten categories ("heresies" as he termed them) of Aristotle.[20] With the exception of two works of logic, Aristotle vanishes from the western world; his work only reappears in the thirteenth century thanks to its preservation by Arab interpreters.

It was perhaps particularly unfortunate that the silencing of debate extended beyond the spiritual and across the whole Greek intellectual tradition. The effects of Paul's condemnation of "the philosophers" could not have been put more clearly than by John Chrysostom, an enthusiastic follower of Paul. "Restrain our own reasoning, and empty our mind of secular learning, in order to provide a mind swept clear for the reception of divine words."[21] Basil echoes him: "Let us Christians prefer the simplicity of our faith to the demonstrations of human reason . . . For to spend much time on research about the essence of things would not serve the edification of the church." This represented no less than a total abdication of independent intellectual thought, and it resulted in a turning away from any speculation about the natural world as well as the divine. "What purpose does knowledge serve—for as to knowledge of natural causes, what blessing is there for me if I should know where the Nile rises, or whatever else under the heavens the 'scientists' rave about?" wrote Lactantius in the early fourth century. One Philastrius of Brescia implicitly declared that the search for empirical knowledge was in itself a heresy.

> There is a certain heresy concerning earthquakes that they come not from God's command, but, it is thought, from the very nature of the elements . . . Paying no attention to God's power, they [the heretics] presume to attribute the motions of force to the elements of nature . . . like certain foolish philosophers who, ascribing this to nature, know not the power of God.[22]

(There is an intriguing echo here of Plato's "We shall approach astronomy, as we do geometry, by way of problems, and ignore what's in the sky, if we intend to get a real grasp of astronomy.")

The impact of this fundamental change in approach on intellectual life was profound. One effect, noted by Averil Cameron, was the decline of book learning. "Books ceased to be readily available and learning became an increasingly ecclesiastical preserve; even those who were not ecclesiastics were likely to get their education from the scriptures or from Christian texts."[23] And one contemporary observer, questioned on the state of philosophy in that former great centre of intellectual life, Alexandria, replied that "philosophy and culture are now at a point of a most horrible desolation."[24] Edward Gibbon notes the story that Bishop Theophilus of the city allowed the celebrated library to be pillaged "and nearly twenty years afterwards, the appearance of the empty shelves excited the regret and indignation of every spectator whose mind was not totally darkened by religious prejudice."[25] No less a figure than Basil of Caesarea lamented the atrophy of debate in his home city. "Now we have no more meetings, no more debates, no more gatherings of wise men in the agora, nothing more of all that made our city famous." The change of atmosphere can be seen in a letter written by the metropolitan bishop of Melitene in Armenia in 457. One of a group of bishops asked by the emperor Leo I whether they wished to reopen the declaration of Chalcedon, he replied, "We uphold the Nicene creed but avoid difficult questions beyond human grasp. Clever theologians soon become heretics." It was a shrewd appreciation of the limitations of intellectual debate. There was no longer any joy to be had in the cut and thrust of discussion—the penalties for transgressing the boundaries, in this world and the next, were too great. [26] The diminution of learning appears to have been greater in the east than in the west, where, in the middle of the sixth century, Cassiodorus was still stressing the importance of an education in secular matters—the seven liberal arts—even if it must take second place to theology. However, when Isidore of Seville began compiling his collection of *Etymologies,* an ambitious summary of sacred and secular knowledge, at the end of the same century he was already finding it difficult to locate the texts of classical authors. The authors stood, he said, like blue hills on the far distant horizon and now it was hard to place them even chronologically. A hundred years on we have details of the library of the Venerable Bede, the Northumbrian scholar (672–73 to 735). The library consisted overwhelmingly of commentaries on scripture, the patristic treatises of the Latin Fathers (the Greek Fathers were not represented) and secular works like Pliny's *Natural History,* which would be of value in biblical exegesis. This was already a much more limited range of books than that enjoyed by Cassiodorus— books on the liberal arts had now disappeared, and there may not even have been a copy of Virgil's *Aeneid* in Bede's library. Bede's most famous work, the *Ecclesiastical History,* could be seen to be modelled on Eusebius' own history of the church, and like his life of St. Cuthbert it resounds with the miraculous. The scholar Gerald Bonner sees Bede as working within the parameters established by Augustine in his *De Doc-trina Christiana,* in which secular knowledge is of use only in so far as it helps biblical exegesis. Fine writer though he is, Bede can hardly be called an original thinker, and this reflects an age when learning had become circumscribed and available sources limited compared to what they had been.[27]

In the east, there came to be increasing emphasis on learning by rote from a select list of texts and a shift from written material to the visual. The rise of a fixed repertoire of images, icons, especially of the Virgin and Child, was another means by which the church defined what it was acceptable to believe, or in this case, to see. Icons not only played their part in defining correctness but acquired their own prestige, as "not made by human hands," together with the power to effect miracles, in the case of one icon of the Virgin even to the point of saving Constantinople from defeat when it was stormed by the Persians in 626.[28]

If the Greek intellectual tradition was to be so comprehensively rejected, what was to be done with its great thinkers? Should the Christian simply ignore Aristotle, Galen and Ptolemy? Plato could become an honorary Christian—there is a statue of him on the twelfth-century facade of the Siena cathedral and his dialogue *Timaeus* was used to support the idea of an orderly universe created by God, the "Master-Craftsman." However, by the twelfth century the *Timaeus* was the only one of his many works known in the west, and even then only in an incomplete translation. Two more of his dialogues, the *Phaedo* (on the soul) and the *Meno,* were to be rediscovered in the thirteenth.[29] The approach to the others was the same: either simply to ignore them as thinkers or to transform them into authorities whose views were integrated into a "Christian" view of the world. The sheer breadth and originality of much of Ptolemy's work, both in astronomy and geography, suggest that he was always open to the possibility of new understandings based on fresh empirical evidence; by contrast, his cosmology, including his view that the universe had the earth at its centre, was frozen into Christian Platonism, becoming itself a matter of doctrinal orthodoxy. In his late work *Planetary Hypotheses,* Ptolemy had suggested that the planets could be arranged into a unified system in which each planet occupied its distinct orbit and did not intrude on the orbits of the others as they moved around the earth. (In other words, the earth was surrounded by a series of layers each occupied by a single planet.) Now a Platonist gloss was added in which the earth was seen as not only the centre point of creation but also its "lowest" part, where all was change, decay and fragility. Moving away from the earth, from the moon to the planets and then to the apparently fixed stars, each sphere was closer to "the unchanging," with heaven, the ultimate immutable sphere, lying beyond the stars. Then Genesis was integrated into this model so that "the firmament" was identified with the eighth layer of Ptolemy's universe and "the waters above the firmament" (Genesis 1:7) with the ninth. The outermost layer of all consisted of the heavens created by God on the first day. Ptolemy's works were thus absorbed into a Christian cosmology.[30]

A comparable process took place in medicine. Galen, the great physician of the second century A.D., had argued that a supreme god (here he was within the mainstream pagan monotheistic tradition, as most pagan intellectuals were) had created the body with a purpose to which all its parts tended. This fitted nicely with Christianity, and so the pagan Galen (who had in his time criticized Christians for their failure to think rationally) also became absorbed into Christian tradition, in effect, "frozen" into it in so far as some of his writings were collected into sixteen volumes of canonical medical texts around 500 and then remained unquestioned for another thousand years. While Greek physicians had certainly made little progress in finding actual cures, they had nevertheless instituted a rational method of approaching and attempting to understand the workings of the human body. This vanished. In effect, we see the preservation of the "magic" of traditional Greek medicine, which had never been eclipsed by the rise of the Hippocratic tradition, and the abandonment of later "scientific" approaches. The sacred springs of the pagan world came to be associated with saints offering the possibility of miraculous cures. In the early fifth century the Asclepion (a temple dedicated to Asclepius, the god of medicine) in Athens was adopted by Christians, and the stoa of incubation (where the sick slept in the hope of receiving an advisory dream from the god), the sacred spring and the adjoining hostel were all incorporated into the church built on the site. Accounts of healing experiences at Christian shrines, the saint appearing, offering a cure and then being thanked with hymns and offerings, mirror those at shrines dedicated to Asclepius. While in Homer's world, before the rise of Greek philosophy, it is Apollo who is responsible for visiting plague on the Greeks at Troy to punish them for their misdeeds, now it is the Christian God who sends plagues as punishment. In medieval Italy, paintings still depicted plague as being transmitted by

God through arrows, as it had been by Apollo, and in some remarkable cases, the Virgin Mary shields the populace with her cloak against the Lord's wrath.[31] When a crowd of pagans who had crammed into a theatre at Neocaesarea in Asia Minor for a local festival desperately needed more space and called on Zeus to provide it, the local Christian "wonderworker" Gregory, who had previously brought plagues to an end, successfully petitioned God that disease should spread among those who had unwisely called on a pagan god.[32]

Despite these continuities with the past, however, sickness is now understood within a specifically Christian perspective. The rejection of a scientific approach to medicine is underlined by the belief (again rooted in Platonism) that the soul is of greater value than the body and that suffering is part of the Christian condition, even to be welcomed as a test of faith. A sick man in danger of death urgently needed, it was said, a priest for his soul rather than a doctor for his body. It is undoubtedly true that Christians cared for the sick "as if Christ were being directly served by waiting on them," and that hospitals attached to the ordered life of the monastery achieved much good, but there was a risk of caring becoming an end in itself, a means of salvation for the carer, rather than being primarily focused on curing the diseased. There is a story told, for instance, by St. Bonaventura (1221–74) of St. Francis of Assisi, who

> rendered humble service to the lepers with humane concern in order that he might *completely despise himself* [my italics], because of Christ crucified, who according to the prophet Isaiah was despised as a leper. He visited their homes frequently, generously distributed alms to them, and with great compassion kissed their hands and their mouths.[33]

The sick risk being used here to fulfill the spiritual needs of their carer. The causes of sickness were seen within a religious perspective. So leprosy, which we now understand to be spread by any kind of physical contact, was said to be a punishment sent by God for lust. Meanwhile saints become associated with specific diseases, often ones related to their own life experiences. Two martyrs from Asia Minor, Damian and Cosmas, who went through a particularly brutal martyrdom in which their bodies were cut up, re-emerge as patron saints of surgery. Similarly, St. Apollonia, whose teeth were knocked out during her martyrdom, is the patron saint of toothache. St. Margaret of Antioch had been swallowed by a dragon. Making the sign of the cross while inside its belly, she was miraculously delivered and subsequently became a patron saint of childbirth.

The relics of martyrs, sacred texts and icons became mechanisms through which miracles are effected. John Chrysostom noted that children in Antioch were given a small codex of the Gospels to hang round their necks to protect them from harm. Epilepsy, which Hippocrates described as a natural illness, is now placed under the care of St. Christopher; the English physician John of Gaddesden (1280–1349) recommended a composite cure—the reading of the Gospel over the epileptic while simultaneously placing on him the hair of a white dog. The relics of Thomas à Becket at Canterbury were believed to cure blindness, insanity, leprosy and deafness.

So a different and increasingly "magic" Christian world emerges. Demons are to be found everywhere. One Byzantine source lists them as to be found in seas, rivers, wells, cliffs, ponds, marshes, forests, trees, and pagan tombs and describes the need for them to be driven from such places into the wilderness.[34] The world becomes suffused with miraculous happenings, and they become part of the repertoire of any successful holy man. (Even today no saint can be declared by the Catholic Church without evidence of at least two miracles effected by him or her.) Accounts of miracles were repeated and elaborated so extensively that miracle literature becomes a genre in its own right, the founding texts being, of course, the Gospels themselves. A sick man visits a monk, he is healed, he converts. On the other hand holy men promise to effect a miraculous cure, or disperse demons who have brought a crop failure, if the suppliant will convert in advance. Miracles become so commonplace in the records that Edward Gibbon was led to remark sarcastically that "we may surely be allowed to observe that a miracle, in that age of superstition and credulity, lost its name and merit, since it could scarcely be considered as a deviation from the ordinary and established laws of nature."[35] While the miraculous had long been part of everyday life, in the Christian world it was further highlighted as a mark of status. In short, the subversion of the natural order of things by miracles becomes one of the distinguishing features of Christianity and, necessarily, goes hand in hand with the waning of scientific thought.

There is increasing scientific evidence that reason and emotion need to live side by side in the healthy mind. It appears that some degree of irrationality acts as a healthy corrective to the aridity of narrowly logical thought.[36] So when Christians talked in apparent paradoxes, claiming that the ignorant was closer to the truth than the educated, or that the foolishness of God was greater than the wisdom of the wise, there was much that was healthy in their approach. There are areas of the human psyche which reason cannot reach and they may provide "truths" of their own—one is reminded of the paradox attributed to the physicist Niels Bohr, "The opposite of one profound truth is often another profound truth." Jesus' insistence that the poor, the rejected and the unloved may have something to contribute was a major development in the western ethical tradition. However, Christian thought that emerged in the early centuries often gave irrationality the status of a universal "truth" to the exclusion of those truths to be found through reason. So the uneducated was preferred to the educated and the miracle to the operation of natural laws.[37] After the defeat of Pelagius, the possibility that man was free to manage his own destiny was diminished. This reversal of traditional values became embedded in the Christian tradition and was, among other things, used to sustain the authority of the church. Intellectual self-confidence and curiosity, which lay at the heart of the Greek achievement, were recast as the dreaded sin of pride. Faith and obedience to the institutional authority of the church were more highly rated than the use of reasoned thought. The inevitable result was intellectual stagnation. It is hard to see how mathematics, science or associated disciplines that depended on empirical observation could have made any progress in this atmosphere. The last recorded astronomical observation in the ancient Greek world was one by the Athenian philosopher Proclus in A.D. 475, nearly 1,100 years after the prediction of an eclipse by Thales in 585 B.C., which traditionally marks the beginning of Greek science. It would be over 1,000 years—with the publication of Copernicus' *De revolutionibus* in 1543—before these studies began to move forward again.[38]

# THOMAS AQUINAS AND THE
# RESTORATION OF REASON

Among the many martyrs of the persecutions of the early years of the
fourth century was Sergius, a high-ranking army officer and a friend of
the emperor (probably Maximinus, Augustus in the east from 310 to
313). He was also a Christian. His Christianity had never interfered with
his military duties, but when he was denounced by rivals the emperor
insisted that he sacrifice to the Roman gods. He refused, but the
emperor, reluctant to lose him, sent him away to the east to Antiochus,
one of Sergius' former protégés who had become the governor of a
remote frontier province. Antiochus also did his best to persuade Sergius
to sacrifice—unsuccessfully—and finally Antiochus ordered Sergius'
execution by the sword. The site of the martyrdom was the fortress city
of Rusafa on the Syrian steppes, thirty miles from the Euphrates. It was a
remote area, constantly disputed between the Romans and the Persians
and known to the Greeks as "the Barbarian Plain."

In the middle of the fifth century a local bishop gave 300 pounds of
gold so that a basilica could be erected over Sergius' remains. Rusafa
became a place of pilgrimage and the city grew wealthy. Then, in the seventh century, Arabs overran the area. Rusafa was now no longer a frontier town but lay well within the territories of the Ummayads, Syria's
rulers between 661 and 750; one of these rulers, the caliph Hisham,
made Rusafa the site of his summer palace. The basilica still stood, but
Hisham did nothing to disturb it directly. Rather, in the courtyard of the
building he erected a mosque, and there is evidence that Sergius was
adopted as an Islamic holy man. ("An old Christian saint at Damascus,

now of Islam," as the Victorian traveller Charles Doughty was to put it.)
The presence of Islam was affirmed, but so was the continuation of
Christian worship. As the patriarch of the Nestorian Christians, who
had themselves been cast out as heretics by their fellow Christians, put it
in 649, "These Arabs fight not against our Christian religion; nay, rather
they defend our faith, they revere our priests and saints, and they make
gifts to our churches and monasteries." In 1150 an Arab source referred
to the inhabitants of Rusafa as "mostly Christians," occupied in the caravan trade. In 1982 some silver vessels, two of them chalices dating from
the mid thirteenth century, were found. The chalices came from northern
Europe, perhaps even from England, and appear to have been buried
just before the Mongol invasions. Rusafa continued as a centre of Christian pilgrimage for 600 years after the Arab conquest.[1]

The story of the basilica at Rusafa shows that it was possible for a
monotheistic faith to assert its identity without necessitating the destruction of other faiths. They could even be shown continuing respect and "a
holy man" might be honoured for his piety rather than his specific religious allegiance. Arab toleration extended also to the Greek intellectual
tradition, which the Arabs had encountered in the course of their conquests and which they both preserved and built on. The ninth-century
scholar Abu al-Hasan Tabith paid fulsome tribute to the achievements of
"the heathen," by whom he meant the Greeks.

> And we are the heirs and transmitters to our heirs, of
> heathenism, which is honoured gloriously in this
> world . . . Who made the world to be inhabited and
> flooded it with cities except the good men and kings of
> heathenism? Who has constructed harbours and con-
> served the rivers? Who has made manifest the hidden
> sciences . . . and it is they who have also made to arise
> the medicine for bodies. And they have filled the world
> with the correctness of modes of life and with the wis-
> dom which is the head of excellence. Without these
> products of heathenism the world would be an empty
> and a needy place and it would have been enveloped in
> sheer want and misery.[2]

Reflecting this readiness to accept the best of Greek thought, not
only were Plato's "the Good," Aristotle's "unmoved mover" and Ploti-

nus' "the One" appropriated to provide insights into the nature of Allah, but also in the ninth and tenth centuries most of the great Greek thinkers—Aristotle, Plato, Hippocrates, Galen, Euclid and Ptolemy among them—were carefully translated by teams of scholars into Arabic.

What proved crucial for its survival in this new context was the fact that Greek thought did not have to be doctored for the Islamic world. As the philosopher Averroës argued, religion and philosophy reached the same truths but by different routes and thus could exist alongside each other. Nor was original thinking stifled by the adoption of Greek thought. Avicenna, for instance, compiled a major textbook of medicine based on Greek sources but added to it the results and conclusions of his own researches and observations. Al-Razi, a Persian who studied at Baghdad before returning to Persia, deliberately set out, in the best tradition of Greek thinking, to expose his forebears to rational criticism, in Al-Razi's case even including Aristotle. Reason should come first; it is "the ultimate authority which should govern and not be governed; should control and be not controlled; should lead and not be led." While Al-Razi declared that he was a disciple of Galen, he also wrote books criticizing some of Galen's precepts; he was the first to distinguish between smallpox and measles. Ibn al-Nafis also directly criticized Galen, noting how the blood passed through the lungs, not between the cavities of the heart as Galen had claimed. By contrast, Galen's works were at this time being treated as sacred texts in Christian Europe and no attempt was being made to progress from them. In short, the Arabs sustained the Greek tradition by valuing the intellectual achievements of the past without being overawed by them and in using empirical evidence and reason to carry the understanding further. All this was possible without threatening Islam itself.[3]

So the classical tradition survived and in time it was once again to filter through to Europe. While fifth-century Christianity defined itself, in a defensive tradition inherited from Paul, largely in terms of its enemies—Judaism, paganism and other heretical Christians (as Augustine was to put it: "heretics, Jews and pagans; they have formed a unity against our Unity")[4]—even by the time of Gregory there is a sense of a lessening of insecurity and a relaxation of tension. As Christianity spread inexorably through western Europe, it gained confidence in itself, though this confidence was for some time expressed solely in spiritual rather than intellectual terms.[5] One of the results of the massive shifts of perspective consequent on the "triumph" of Christianity was an intense concentration on the other world at the expense of this one. For centuries there was virtually no sign of any renaissance of independent thought, and most scholarly work focused on analysing, summarizing and commenting on the canon of authoritative texts.

The only western Christian philosopher of note in the 500 years between Boethius (whose *Consolation of Philosophy* of c. 524 became a medieval best-seller) and Anselm in the eleventh century was the ninth-century Irishman Erigena, who was remarkable for his time in knowing Greek. It was through him that the works of Pseudo-Dionysius entered the west, and so he played an important role in founding western mysticism. Erigena is intriguing in that he seems to come from nowhere; he has no links to an existing tradition or centre of learning. In his *Division of Nature,* he explores "nature," by which he means the totality of all that exists or does not exist, from a Neoplatonist perspective. *The Division* was, in fact, too original for the church, which disapproved of his views on the identity of God (and presumably his endorsement of Origen's view that ultimately everyone would be saved), and all Erigena's works were declared heretical in the thirteenth century. He was removed so effectively from the western tradition that he still does not appear in many standard introductions to medieval thought, and it is only recently that his importance has been recognized.

In the eleventh century, Anselm of Canterbury (1033–1109) raised the possibility that reason could again play a part in orthodox Christian thought. He argued that certain tenets of faith—for instance, the impossibility of salvation without divine assistance in the shape of an incarnated Jesus—could be proved by reason. However, it was not until the twelfth century that a newly emerging investigative spirit in the west (usually referred to as Scholasticism) began to rediscover the classical tradition as it had been preserved in the writings of the Islamic east. Early stirrings of this spirit can be seen in the work of the Augustinian canon Hugh of Saint-Victor in Paris early in the century. Hugh asserts that accumulating knowledge about the world does not necessarily threaten the supremacy of either God or the Church. So begin the compilations of *summae,* encyclopaedic works synthesizing what was known to the medieval world, and also the foundation of the first universities (Paris, for instance, in 1170, Oxford at about the same time), in which secular learning could be taught so long as it was not seen to subvert the authority of the Church. Instruction in scientific method was inevitably sought in the works of Aristotle, which, along with the massive commentaries of the Arab philosophers, now began to be translated into Latin. With them came a fuller knowledge of the work of Ptolemy—his great astronomical treatise is still known by its Arab name, the *Almagest,* the "greatest."[6]

Yet Aristotle offered an obvious challenge to Christianity: he was a pagan philosopher (whose "unmoved mover" did not even relate to the created world), and he extolled reason not only through the use of formal logic (the syllogism), but also as a means of understanding the natural world through the analysis of empirical evidence. As we have seen, his works had long since been discredited; suspicions still lingered. In 1215 the Faculty of Arts of the University of Paris forbade the use of his works as a basis for discussion. For Christians to accept Aristotle, his work had somehow to be made compatible with Christian doctrine, which in turn made it necessary for Christianity to allow reason and the study of the natural world a new role. A German Dominican, Albert the Great (c. 1200–1280), was the first to present Aristotle in full to Christian Europe. To Albert the scientific exploration of the world was of value in itself, and he claimed that its findings could never conflict with those arrived at through faith. Aristotle was not to be feared, and, as the philosophers of Islam had already argued, reason and faith would eventually reach a harmony in the knowledge of God. His was a major endorsement of the significance of reason and empiricism (and eventually, in the twentieth century, earned Albert the title of "patron saint" of the natural sciences). Yet this was just a beginning; in 1248, Albert acquired a new student, a young Dominican who already shared his enthusiasm for "the Philosopher," as Aristotle was known, called Thomas Aquinas. Aquinas was to incorporate Aristotle into the Christian, above all Roman Catholic, tradition with such intellectual power and coherence that in some areas of thought Aristotelianism and Catholicism became virtually indistinguishable. As one commentator has put it, Aquinas converted Aristotle to Christianity and carried out the baptism himself! In view of Aquinas's heavy dependence on Aristotle, it might rather be said that Aquinas was converted to Aristotelianism.

A prodigious worker, Aquinas wrote several million words of lucid, albeit technical, medieval Latin prose. He avoids rhetoric and exposes little of his personality in the relentless logic and thoroughness with which his great works unfold. Unlike Augustine, he does not offer insights into his own character—there is none of Augustine's struggle with sexual temptation and a difficult mother to appeal to the modern reader. Adopted into the Catholic tradition as the great teacher, above all

in the nineteenth and early twentieth centuries, he remains a major figure in Catholic theology. Outside Catholicism, philosophers of religion
still have to tackle his five "proofs" of the existence of God. He is little
read today, but it is arguable that Thomas Aquinas revived the Aristotelian approach to knowing things so successfully that he unwittingly
laid the foundations of the scientific revolution that was to transform
western thought.[7]

Aquinas was born near Naples in southern Italy almost certainly in
1225.[8] His background was aristocratic, but as a seventh son he was
expected to join a religious order, probably the Benedictines—at the age
of five he was sent off to the celebrated Benedictine abbey of Monte
Cassino. His university studies were in Naples, where he was introduced
to secular learning and the works of both Jewish and Arab philosophers;
it was here he had his first acquaintance with Aristotle. He was also
drawn to the Dominican order, in some ways a surprising choice for one
of his background. Compared to the wealthier and more established religious orders, the Dominicans were new (Dominic, their founder, had
died only five years before Aquinas' birth) and relied on begging as a
means of support. However, they had already established a reputation
for learning and teaching, and this may have attracted the somewhat
reserved Aquinas. Shocked by Thomas' choice of this low-status order,
his brothers kidnapped him and removed him to a family estate. He
escaped to the Dominicans' teaching house at Paris, where his extraordinary intellect was soon recognized, and he was then sent to Cologne to
study with Albert, the academic star of the order, before returning to
Paris, the most celebrated of Europe's universities, for seven intensive
years of study. He was already writing, and even at this early stage the
contours of his philosophy, with its emphasis on the use of reason to
explore all that can be explored within a creation that was wholly God's,
were established.

Having been licensed to teach theology, Aquinas spent the next ten
years in Italy, moving from one Dominican house to another, and even
spending time at the papal court at Orvieto. Here he caught up with his
old mentor, Albert, but also met another Dominican, William of Moer-
beke, who was able to translate Aristotle for him directly from the original Greek. Some previous versions of Aristotle's works had made their
way from Greek to Syriac to Arabic to Spanish to Latin, losing much of
their original meaning in the process. It was in these years that he pro-

duced his first great work, *Summa contra gentiles,* a defence of Christianity against unbelievers, and began the most celebrated of all his works, the *Summa theologiae,* a comprehensive synthesis of theology aimed at Dominican students. The second part of the *Summa theologiae* was written during Aquinas' most productive period, as professor of theology in Paris between 1269 and 1272. Alongside the vast *Summa* (the second part alone comprises a million words) he wrote commentaries on most of Aristotle's surviving works. He subsequently returned to Italy, to his old university, Naples, where he became head of a Dominican teaching house and continued work on the *Summa.*

Here, in December 1273, Aquinas appears to have had some form of breakdown. This has been variously explained in terms of a mystical experience, complete exhaustion or as a possible moment of realization that reason was breaking the bounds of orthodoxy. He had always had his enemies, among traditionalists who resented the Dominicans and Aquinas in particular for his stress on rationalism, and among enthusiastic Aristotelians who disapproved of his integration of Aristotle and Christianity. In the year of his breakdown he was strongly criticized in Paris for his insistence on a natural underlying order of things (which appeared to deny God's power of miraculous intervention) and his respect for the body as the sustainer of the soul. In 1274 Aquinas was summoned by the pope to a council at Lyons, where it is possible that he would have been confronted with these criticisms, but he fell ill on the way, in unknown circumstances, and died. Three years later, several of his theses were formally condemned, first in Paris and then in Oxford; the Paris condemnation lasted fifty years, and there is no record that the Oxford condemnation has ever been revoked.

Aquinas avoided the abusive and aggressive language of the more combative theologians, believing that reason could convince on its merits. In his *Summa contra gentiles,* a missionary tract for those working with Muslims and pagans, he even avoids drawing on the scriptures on the grounds that his readers did not know them. "Hence we must have recourse to natural reason, to which all men are forced to assent." (Aquinas has here reached a point where Christianity seems to have become largely divorced from the scriptures.) It is not until the fourth and final book of the *Summa* that he introduces those Christian doctrines sustainable only by faith, among which he includes the doctrine of the Trinity, the Incarnation and the creation of the world by God *ex nihilo*, "out of nothing" (the alternative view, held by both Aristotle and Plato, which Aquinas accepted he could not disprove, being that matter had existed eternally alongside God).

While Aquinas accepted the articles of faith which had been revealed by God, he did not denigrate reason in the way many of his fellow Christians had done. Challenging the pessimism of Augustine and his followers, he presents reason as a gift of God, not a means of subverting God. A deeper understanding of the natural world leads only to greater conviction of the greatness of its creator. Rather than ignore what is to be seen in the sky, as Plato had argued, we should observe it in the confidence that it would help explain God's natural order. God wants man to reach towards Him and has given him the means, his rational mind, to do so; in return God will reveal, as articles of faith, those things that remain impossible for the human mind to grasp. To denigrate humanity as corrupted by sin is to make nonsense of God's creation. "To take something away from the perfection of the creature is to abstract from the perfection of the creative power [i.e. God] itself," as Thomas himself put it. Furthermore, man's possession of a rational mind with, inherent in its rationality, the possibility of choice ensures free will: "that man acts from free judgement follows necessarily from the fact that he is rational." The contrast with Augustine's view of man as trapped in self-loathing and engulfed in his sinfulness is striking. It is a contrast as much of temperament as of theology (arguably, one fed into the other). Augustine expects human beings to fail; inspired by Aristotle, Aquinas is naturally optimistic that they will use their God-given reason to find spiritual and personal fulfillment.[9]

If we are to value empirical knowledge, we must also value the means by which it is obtained, the senses. In contrast to the Platonic Christian view that envisaged the human body as pulling the soul away from God, Aquinas argues, following Aristotle, that the soul and body are inexorably joined. "Plato said that the soul is in the body 'as a sailor in a ship.' Thus the union of soul and body would only be by contact of power. But this doctrine seems not to fit the facts," as Aquinas boldly writes in the *Summa contra gentiles*. The essence of being human lies in having an ensouled body, and it is no more possible to distinguish between body and soul than between a piece of wax and the impression a stamp has made on it. Since the rational mind can only act on what it learns from the senses, the body itself should not be despised.[10]

Aristotle's contribution in every respect was immense: one scholar has gone so far as to say, "In so far as Thomas 'had' a philosophy it was simply Aristotle's . . . in so far as he thought philosophically, his thought moved in Aristotelian grooves."[11] Aristotle's insistence on the importance of rational thought and the accumulation of empirical evidence was, of course, crucial, but even more so was his work on the nature of man. In the second part of the *Summa theologiae* Aquinas virtually takes over the *Nicomachean Ethics,* even modelling the *Summa* on the structure of Aristotle's work. It is the natural instinct of man, Aristotle had argued, to develop into his final and most complete form, that of a flourishing human being capable of using rational thought at the highest level; it was this optimistic approach that Aquinas absorbed into Christianity. The end result, for Aquinas, would be a full appreciation of the nature and love of God. He also derives from the *Nicomachean Ethics* a belief in the importance of using reason to make moral choices; in so doing he argues, as had Aristotle, for the necessity for achieving control over the emotions without, however, denying their importance. Temperance and prudence, fortitude and justice are important virtues and should be deliberately cultivated. This realistic approach comes as somewhat of a relief after the tortured struggles that Paul, Jerome and Augustine believed intrinsic to man's time on earth. (Aquinas' writings may be dull, but in contrast to those of some of the more excitable Church Fathers they radiate good sense, optimism and down-to-earth practicality.)

Aristotle had argued that it was the natural impulse of human beings to desire "the good." Aquinas goes further. The combination of this impulse towards "the good" with the power of rational thought allows human beings to reach an understanding of what is morally right.

> There is in people an appetite for the good of their nature as rational, and this is proper to them, that they should know truths about God and about living in society. Correspondingly whatever this involves is a matter of natural law, for instance that people should shun ignorance, not offend others with whom they ought to live in civility, and other such related requirements.[12]

The concept of natural law was one of Aquinas' most influential contributions to western thought (although there are precedents in Plato, Aristotle and in Roman law). God's law is eternal, made up of absolute precepts, and it is possible to grasp it by means of reason. Here, ironically for someone so steeped in Aristotle, Aquinas drew on Platonism; the concept of natural law, or moral law—as it is sometimes termed— has raised the same philosophical challenges that Platonism did. Is it possible to be sure of the moral absolutes or to define with any clarity the ways in which they should determine our behaviour? Though Aquinas made a distinction between universal and absolute values and those that are relative to time, place and cultures, where is the line to be drawn? Aquinas' concept of natural law remains influential: the 1968 papal encyclical *Humanae Vitae* forbade artificial contraception for Catholics partly on the grounds that it was against "natural law," here as defined by Pope Paul VI on behalf of the Catholic Church.[13] Less con- troversially, natural law has been used as a means of defining inviolable human rights and crimes against humanity. Aquinas' formulation of the concept of "the just war" remains crucial to modern debates.[14]

Aquinas restored the relationship between reason and faith; to him, the one sustained the other. Thus Thomas could argue that articles of faith, which were by definition true as the revealed word of God, could act as the axioms from which rational thought could progress. Aquinas had, of course, no reason to foresee how much they would come into conflict after his death. To him "faith" included belief in the teachings of the Church and of scripture. So it was an article of faith to believe that "the earth was fixed on its foundation, not to be moved for ever" (Psalm 103), yet by the sixteenth century observation and reason (by Coperni- cus and then Galileo) suggested that it moved around the sun. The famous clash between Galileo and the Catholic Church was the result. This was the inherent flaw in Aquinas' legacy. Empirical evidence could challenge the authority of the scriptures, but, more than this, Aquinas, perhaps unwittingly, had exposed the potential clash between reason and faith. It was impossible to allow orthodox Christian doctrine, much of which depended on faith or revelation, to be undermined by reason, and this meant that the uses of reason in the Christian tradition had to be circumscribed so as not to subvert orthodoxy. This was certainly alien to the Aristotelian tradition, where, as we have seen, empirical evidence was seen as superior to "theory." In the event the power of orthodox theology was such that Aristotle became integrated into Christianity as Plato, Ptolemy and Galen had been, and the sheer innovatory power of Aquinas' achievement was forgotten. It is ironic to find the seventeenth- century rationalists using "reason" as a weapon with which to attack the Christianized version of Aristotle![15]

The contrasting approaches of Aquinas and Augustine to the nature of man and the use of reason reflect the earlier contrast between Aristotle and Plato. It is perhaps a measure of the Greek achievement that both were eventually absorbed into Christianity. If there are arguably two historical Christianities, that of the early church (and even here the Gospel evidence needs to be distinguished from the theologies of Paul) and that of the imperial church, there are also two philosophical Christianities, one resting on the Platonic tradition and the other on the Aristotelian. Any study of Christianity needs to recognize these different strands of thought and aim to disentangle them from the specific historical circumstances that shaped them. In short, while traditionally theologians have presented Christian doctrine as having an inner philosophical coherence independent of events, historians, both Christian and non-Christian, are increasingly coming to recognise that it is impossible to divorce the making of doctrine from the society in which it evolved.

Despite the condemnations of his work soon after his death, Thomas' brilliance was soon recognized; by 1316, when his works were still banned in Paris, the process of canonization began. Normally two miracles were required as evidence of God's power working through a potential saint. Those produced for Thomas were scarcely convincing. On his deathbed it was said he had asked for herrings, unknown in the Italian seas, and sure enough in the next load of fish produced by the local fishmonger there were indeed herrings. As it transpired that the witnesses had never seen herrings before and could not be sure what they had seen, the case faltered. It was left to the pope, John XXII, to break the impasse: "There are as many miracles as there are articles of the *Summa.*" Thomas was duly acknowledged as a saint in July 1323. Thus the power of words and independent thinking were once again given a status that they had almost lost.

# Epilogue

It has never been part of the argument of this book that Christians did not attempt to use rational means of discovering theological truths.[1] The problem was rather that reason is only of limited use in finding such truths. Any rational argument must begin with axioms, foundations from which an argument can progress, and proceed to conclusions on which all concur. Pythagoras' theorem starts from a right-angled triangle—the important point being that any conceivable right-angle triangle can serve as the "axiom" from which the theorem is proved—and ends with a proof which is logically irrefutable at any time or in any place. This is the essence of mathematical logic. Similarly, empirical evidence serves as axioms from which inductive proofs are made, although the empirical evidence which exists will always be provisional.

So where are the axioms from which theology can progress? Attempts by Thomas Aquinas and others to provide self-evident principles from which logical argument about the nature of God could progress collapsed as soon as it became clear (in the Enlightenment, for example) that there was no agreement about what these principles might be (as there had to be if they were "self-evident"!). One can talk of the revelation of God, but, as the Montanists showed, anyone can claim to have received a revelation from God, and there is virtually no way of assessing what is a valid or invalid revelation. In practice, revelation does not prove susceptible to reason because there is no way through which it can be assessed by reasoning minds. The result is that in the churches there was soon a battle for control over what counted as revelation, and the Montanists were among the casualties. The scriptures are often cited by theologians as the primary source of "axioms." However, when one puts together the Gospels, the letters of Paul, the Book of Revelation and the Old Testament, there is no sense of a coherent "axiomatic" basis on which to build theological truths. As any study of, say, the Arian dispute shows, the different sides to the conflict drew on different texts to "support" their argument. Again the churches had eventually to assume control of how scripture was to be interpreted, in effect so that interpretations never conflicted with what became established as orthodoxy. Even Thomas Aquinas, one of Europe's most outstanding champions of rational thought, had to suspend reason when it conflicted with orthodoxy.

So the point being made here is not that the Christians did not attempt to use reason but they could never reach agreed truths, any more than there could be, in practice, an agreed formulation of what is meant by Plato's "the Good." The evidence of Christian disputes shows conclusively that reason failed in achieving any kind of consensus, and, in fact, like other spiritual movements in the ancient world, Christianity splintered as it settled into different cultural and philosophical niches across the empire. The important question to answer is why Christianity was different from other spiritual movements in the ancient world in insisting that Christians throughout the empire should adhere to a common authority. This was the aspect of Christianity which was truly revolutionary, even if the fact is often overlooked in histories of the church. The common adherence to the message of Christ, both in his teachings and in his death and resurrection (and the need to control Christ in face of the many other spiritual movements which appropriated him), provides much of the answer, but it also seems to have been important to define the boundaries of what it meant to be Christian in a society many of whose values Paul had told Christians they must reject. Christians did not have the distinguishing physical and cultural marks of Judaism; they had to create these marks and enforce them in the highly fluid spiritual world of the Greco-Roman empire. Crucial to the establishment of authority in the early church was the emergence of the bishop and the consolidation of his position within a hierarchy of bishoprics based on the doctrine of apostolic succession. Ultimately this, and not reasoned argument, was where authority rested. Even though the hierarchy remained a loose one, authority rested here and not on the fruits of reasoned argument.

Increasingly, the history of the early church is being written in terms of diversity rather than unity of belief. Most communities were remote from each other. The varied cultural and religious traditions which shaped local theologies—now more fully recognized with the ever growing number of early Christian inscriptions being found and published—coalesced with the lack of axiomatic foundations to make doctrinal certainty impossible. When the bishops of Rome adopted Latin rather than Greek for the western church in the fourth century, they distanced themselves from the ancient centres of Christianity and destroyed any chance of asserting their primacy over the Greek world. As we have seen, orthodoxy eventually had to be imposed from above.

What seems to have marked the turning point is Constantine's appreciation that the authority of the bishops could be used in support of the empire. However, he failed to appreciate how intractable the doctrinal disputes between the bishops had become, and his hope of having the church as a united body brought into the structure of the state by patronage, tax exemptions and toleration soon proved to be a fantasy. "You [the bishops] do nothing but that which encourages discord and hatred and, to speak frankly, which leads to the destruction of the human race," he fumed. Hence his initiative in calling the Council of Nicaea to define and enforce a common doctrine. The theological history of the fourth century is largely one of the emperors, under immense pressure from invaders, attempting to achieve a foundation of orthodoxy so that they could preserve a united society. The embattled Theodosius eventually enforced Nicene orthodoxy by imperial decree and then, unlike his predecessors, moved vigorously to crush those Christians and others who continued to oppose it. Here politics won over theology.

In short, the argument is first that despite attempts by Christians to use reason, it was not an appropriate way of finding theological truths. The frustrations which followed led to arguments becoming personal and bitter. The texts of a Jerome or an Athanasius are marked by invective at the expense of reasoned argument. This was not only deeply unfortunate for Christianity but became a major hindrance to a state which was hoping to use a docile church to support its authority. Hence the imposition of authority, an imposition which, backed by Christian suspicions of scientific argument, crushed all forms of reasoned thinking.

Why was the suppression of reasoned argument so important? Reason is a means of finding truths through deductive and inductive logic. These truths may be valuable in themselves in helping us understand who we are (the theory of evolution), but they have also, through medicine, for instance, transformed human life. We are free to apply the fruits of reasoned thought to some of our greatest needs, in many areas with enormous success. Yet built into a tradition of rational thought is the necessity for tolerance. It is the only way in which it can progress. Reason also provides external standards of truth, often, for instance, from empirical evidence. This helps take personal animosity out of debates in that disputes over the interpretation of external evidence are normally less abrasive than those between human beings struggling to assert or maintain their personal authority. History suggests that conflicts between religions tend to be more destructive than those between scientists! In this sense, the price to pay for the assumption that there can be doctrinal certainty has been a heavy one.

Philosophically, therefore, it becomes crucial to define the areas where certainty is possible and those where it is not. This was another of the intellectual achievements of the Greeks. *Pace* Plato, they understood that the nature of the divine, if such spiritual force exists, cannot be grasped when there is no external evidence for it. The troubles described in this book come not from the teachings of Jesus or from the nature of Christians themselves (though arguably one can trace them to Paul), but from the determination to make "certain" statements about God. Tragically, the pressures to do so, many of them politcal and economic, were intensified by the introduction of the concept of an afterlife, in which most would be punished eternally for failure to adhere to what was eventually decided to be orthodox. If there is no external standard by which one can define God, then figures who have the authority to define him for others have to be created and this authority given ideological support. This invariably means the suppression of freedom of independent thought. It was unfortunate that Christianity became embroiled in historical circumstances which made this such a dominant issue.

One important theme which has run through this book is the linking of belief in rational thought with a belief in free will. Because rationalism has in so many fields enriched humanity's understanding of itself and improved human life, rationalists have every right to believe in further progress. Those who have decried the possibility of rational thought or denigrated it do seem to have a much more pessimistic view of human existence. That was why I preferred to end this book with Aquinas rather than Augustine! Yet at the same time we do have a spiritual and emotional nature, and without it rational thought in itself would be arid. It is a healthy balance between the two which seems the goal.[2]

In conclusion, it is worth asking why the political dimension to the making of Christian doctrine has been so successfully expunged from the history of the western churches. It is virtually ignored in most histories of Christianity. (The important role of the emperors and their successors has been more readily accepted by the Orthodox churches.) It is understandable, of course, that the churches wished to claim control over their own history, but the disappearance is also a symbol of Plato's greatest triumph, the successful integration of his thought into Christian theology. Plato argued that his Forms were realities which existed eternally and independently of whether or not they were grasped by the reasoning mind at any historical moment. The context, the time or place or particular historical circumstances, in which orthodox doctrine (if it was given the same status as a Platonic Form) was formulated was immaterial. As we have seen, Eusebius assumes that doctrinal truth was known from the beginning of time and had to be protected from novelties introduced by heretics. The church councils were simply markers in the process of protecting the truth. So one could disregard the role of the emperor in calling or influencing the outcome of councils.

History still has to be rewritten in the west, but the process is complete by the time of Gregory the Great. His immediate concern was to establish his own authority over the remains of an empire in which traditional imperial authority had disintegrated. There was no one to prevent him from rewriting the history of Christian doctrine as if the emperors had never played a part in it, and so he did. Drawing on the precedents set by Ambrose, the popes were now assumed to have control over emperors, a reversal of the political realities of the fourth century. It is only recently that scholars have begun to appreciate the extent to which the emperors actually made, in the words of Hilary of Poitiers, the bishops their slaves. It is simplistic to talk of the Greek tradition of rational thought being suppressed by Christians. It makes more sense to argue that the suppression took place at the hands of a state supported by a church which it had itself politicized (and, in the process, removed from its roots in the Gospel teachings).

The history of Christianity is often presented as if it had a natural coherence. The evidence suggests that this is not true. The church of Constantine and his successors, embedded as it was in the stressed environment of the late empire, was radically different from that of earlier times. It was in this context that the suppression of rational thought took place, for reasons which I hope this book has made clear. Likewise, after the collapse of the empire, the medieval church in western Europe developed new roles and strategies to cope with a society in which a number of weaker political authorities (the early states of Europe) were emerging in competition with each other. The battle to defeat the classical intellectual tradition was, for the moment, a thing of the past, and the church could turn itself to new and different challenges. Gregory is the linchpin. There is no doubt that he is one of the greatest spiritual leaders the west has ever produced, not least in terms of his restoration of moderation and moral integrity to the Christian tradition after the obsessional ascetic narcissism and destructive invective of the fourth and fifth centuries.

I would reiterate the central theme of this book: that the Greek intellectual tradition was suppressed rather than simply faded away. My own feeling is that this is an important moment in European cultural history which has for all too long been neglected. Whether the explanations put forward in this book for the suppression are accepted or not, the reasons for the extinction of serious mathematical and scientific thinking in Europe for a thousand years surely deserve more attention than they have received.

# Notes

I

1. It is now known to be of the emperor Marcus Aurelius, but the mistaken belief that it was of Constantine led to it being spared when pagan statues were being destroyed by Christians. It was later moved to the Capitoline Hill and can now be seen under cover there in the Palazzo Nuovo.

2. The information used in this chapter comes from the fine study of the fresco by G. Geiger, *Filippino Lippi's Carafa Chapel: Renaissance Art in Rome* (Kirksville, Mo., 1986), chap. 5, on which my own text is based.

3. The text itself is from Paul's first letter to the Corinthians, 1:19, where it is related back to earlier scripture. In the subsequent verses Paul goes on to place God's wisdom above human wisdom. The consequences of this condemnation of pagan philosophy are a major theme of this book, although, as will be argued later, Paul appears to have known very little of the philosophical tradition which he was attacking.

4. Filippino Lippi was the son of the Florentine Fra Filippo Lippi, an important painter of narrative scenes, and, between 1488 and 1493, a student of Botticelli. The chapel—the only commission known to have been undertaken by Filippino in Rome—was undertaken at the behest of Cardinal Oliviero Carafa (1430–1511), cardinal protector of the Dominicans and a staunch upholder of papal authority. Carafa was a man of action who led a crusade against the Turks in the 1470s. (The Porta Ripa Grande is probably included in the fresco because it was from here that he embarked for the crusade.)

5. The concept of "faith" will be explored in different contexts in this book. For some of the philosophical problems involved see chap. 9, note 14. The words "all will be well" come from the writings of the Christian mystic Julian of Norwich and refer directly to the peace and serenity brought by Jesus.

2

1. Aristotle, *Metaphysics* II. 1 993a30–34, trans. W. D. Ross.

2. The story is told in book 5 of the *Odyssey*. A recommended translation is that by R. Fagles (London and New York, 1996). Examples of "heroes" consciously using rational thought to decide on a course of action can also be found in Homer's

*Iliad.* In book 17, lines 101–21 (trans. R. Fagles, Harmondsworth, 1991), Menelaus, "deeply torn, as he probed his own great heart," weighs up whether to fight Hector in single combat or to withdraw from battle. In an important article, "The Epic Cycle and the Uniqueness of Homer" (*Journal of Hellenic Studies,* vol. 97 [1977], pp. 39–53), Jasper Griffin compares Homer's epics, the *Odyssey* and the *Iliad,* with an epic cycle that survives from the same period. In the epic cycle heroes are immortal and there are monsters and miracles, while Homer's is a cosmos where even heroes cannot escape death and the natural world is presented as it really is. (Animals cannot change shape or form, for instance.) In Homer's world, of course, the gods still hold some power, as in the passage here, but over the next centuries the development of rational thought was to diminish their role in the natural world. Homer can thus be seen to have made an important contribution to the transition from a world of magic and miracles to one of reason.

3. The evolution of the city state can be traced in O. Murray, *Early Greece,* 2nd ed. (London, 1993), and R. Osborne, *Greece in the Making, 1200–479 B.C.* (London, 1996).

4. For an introduction to Greek religion see S. Price, *Religions of the Ancient Greeks* (Cambridge, 1999).

5. Quoted ibid., p. 79.

6. Thucydides, *The Peloponnesian War* 3:82, trans. R. Warner, Penguin Classics.

7. Homer's epics already include some appreciation of an underlying natural order. In this extract, the gods themselves act to impose it. Poseidon, the god of earthquakes, helped, significantly, by Apollo, the god of reason among other things, gets rid of the intrusive settlement made by the Greeks along the coastline outside Troy.

> The earth-shaker himself, trident locked in his grip,
> led the way, rocking loose, sweeping up in his breakers
> all the bastions, strong supports of logs and stones . . .
> He made all smooth along the rip of the Hellespont
> and piled the endless beaches deep in sand again
> and once he had levelled the Argives' mighty wall
> he turned the rivers flowing back in their beds again
> where their fresh clear tides had run since time began.
> So in the years to come Poseidon and the god Apollo
> would set all things to rights once more.

Trans. R. Fagles, *The Iliad,* Penguin Classics. The "Argives" are the Greeks.

8. Translation by O. Murray.

9. As an overview of the "scientific revolution," see C. Kahn, "The Origins of Greek Science and Philosophy," in A. Bowen, ed., *Science and Philosophy in Ancient Greece* (New York and London, 1993). *The Cambridge Companion to Early Greek Philosophy,* ed. A. A. Long (Cambridge, 1999), has articles on the main pre-Socratic (that is, those practising before Socrates, late fifth century) philosophers. For a broad survey of Greek thinking in general, see J. Brunschwig and G. E. R. Lloyd, eds., *Greek Thought: A Guide to Classical Knowledge* (Cambridge, Mass., and London, 2000), and the chapter "Philosophy" by B. Williams, in M. I. Finley, ed., *The Legacy of Greece: A New Appraisal* (Oxford, 1984).

10. Lloyd's case for the relationship between politics and philosophy is argued most strongly in his *Magic, Reason and Experience* (Cambridge, 1979). See especially chap. 4, "Greek Science and Greek Society."

11. M. West, "Early Greek Philosophy," in J. Boardman, J. Griffin and O. Murray, eds., *The Oxford History of the Classical World* (Oxford, 1986).

12. For Aristotle a particularly good introduction is J. Barnes, *Aristotle* (Oxford, 1982). Chap. 7, "Logic," deals with syllogisms. A more advanced survey is J. Lear, *Aristotle: The Desire to Understand* (Cambridge, 1988).

13. Quoted in P. Hoffman, *The Man Who Loved Only Numbers* (London, 1999), p. 113. A good introduction to Greek mathematics is to be found in M. Kline, *Mathematical Thought from Ancient to Modern Times,* vol. 1 (New York and Oxford, 1972). Euclid and Apollonius are given full treatment in chap. 4.

14. Herodotus used to be derided by commentators for his continuing use of myth and uncritical use of oral evidence, in contrast, it is argued, with the more "scientific" Thucydides. Recently, however, R. Thomas, in her *Herodotus in Context: Ethnography, Science and the Art of Persuasion* (Cambridge, 2000), has argued that Herodotus deserves to be placed in the forefront of intellectual developments of the fifth century.

15. From *Sacred Disease,* attributed to Hippocrates, VI 352, 1–9L; 364, 9–15; 366, 5–6L. Trans. J. Longrigg; quoted in his *Greek Medicine: From the Heroic to the Hellenistic Age. A Source Book* (London, 1998), p. 21. *Sacred Disease* is considered at some length by G. E. R. Lloyd, in his *Magic, Reason and Experience* (Cambridge, 1979), pp. 15–29.

16. The Ionian physician Alcmaeon (Ionian, fifth century B.C.) transfers the concept of stability being achieved through the union of opposites, surely a concept taken from notions of "the ideal city," to the human body.

> Alcmaeon holds that what preserves health is the equality of the powers, moist and dry, cold and hot, bitter and sweet, and the rest—and the supremacy of any one of them causes disease, for the supremacy of either is destructive. The cause of disease is an excess of heat or cold, the occasion of it surfeit or deficiency of nourishment: the location of it, marrow or the brain. Disease may come about from external causes, from the quality of water, local environment or toil or torture. Health, on the other hand, is a harmonious blending of the qualities.

Longrigg, *Greek Medicine,* p. 31. For Galen's attempts to find a mathematical base for scientific demonstration, see G. E. R. Lloyd, "Demonstration in Galen," in M. Frede and G. Striker, eds., *Rationality in Greek Thought* (Oxford, 1996), pp. 255–78.

17. This is how Aristotle defended the spherical nature of the earth:

> (i) If the earth were not spherical, eclipses of the moon would not exhibit segments of the shape they do . . . (ii) Observation of the stars also shows not only that the earth is spherical but that it is of no great size . . . we do not see the same stars as we move to the North or South . . . For this reason those who imagine that the region around the Pillars of Heracles [Straits of Gibraltar] joins on to the regions of India, and that in this way the ocean is one, are not, it would seem, suggesting anything incredible.

From *On the Heavens,* trans. W. Guthrie, Loeb Classical Library, 1939, 297b25–298a10.

18. For introductions to Greek science, see T. E. Rihill, *Greek Science* (Oxford, 1999), and G. E. R. Lloyd, *Early Greek Science: Thales to Aristotle* (London, 1974),

and *Greek Science After Aristotle* (London, 1973). For astronomy there is Michael Hoskin, ed., *The Cambridge Concise History of Astronomy* (Cambridge, 1999).

19. Barnes, *Aristotle,* is excellent on all this.

20. These examples are taken from Aristotle's *Historia Animalium* and *De Partibus Animalium,* which are discussed in G. E. R. Lloyd, *Aristotelian Explorations* (Cambridge, 1996), chap. 3. When Aristotle was absorbed into Christianity (see chap. 20 of this book), his readiness to question was played down, and it was only fully recognized again in the twentieth century.

21. G. E. R. Lloyd, *The Revolutions of Wisdom* (Berkeley and London, 1957), p. 153.

22. Ibid., p. 57.

23. It is easy to pick up, from Paul's letters and from Christian thought in general, the idea that rational thinking is somehow an arrogant enterprise, trespassing on what belongs to God. However, in so far as rational argument is subject to public scrutiny at every stage, the opposite is the case. A mathematician or scientist can be humiliated by his peers when his arguments are shown to be invalid. As E. R. Dodds put in in his well-known study *The Greeks and the Irrational* (Berkeley and London, 1951): "That honest distinction between what is knowable and what is not appears again and again in fifth-century thought, and is surely one of its chief glories; it is the foundation of scientific humility [*sic*]" (p. 181). The real problem, as Dodds suggests, lies in taking rational thought in directions where it cannot go—in cases where there are no firm axioms from which the argument can begin. This is, arguably, the problem with Plato. Plato believed that the ultimate truth about everything from "the Good" to beauty and justice could be solved by the use of rational thought. The difficulties this led to will be discussed in the next chapter and at other points in this book. There was an important strand in Greek thought—known usually as Pyrrhonist Skepticism, after its supposed founder, Pyrrhon (c. 365–275 B.C.)—that used rational argument to delineate the problems in making rational argument. The Greeks were also aware of how the value of materials or concepts may be relative to their context. Heraclitus, inventive as ever, noted, "Sea: purest and most polluted water, for fish drinkable and life-sustaining, for people undrinkable and death-bringing," suggesting in other words that what may appear to have value in one context may lack it in another. See the article "Skepticism" by J. Brunschwig and G. E. R. Lloyd, eds., *Greek Thought: A Guide to Classical Knowledge* (Cambridge, Mass., and London, 2000), and R. Mortley, *From Word to Silence: The Rise and Fall of Logos* (Bonn, 1986).

24. How a language which can deal with abstract things and states of being emerged has been a subject of great controversy centring around the work of Eric Havelock. See C. L. Johnstone's introductory essay in *Theory, Text, Context: Issues in Greek Rhetoric and Oratory* (New York, 1994), and the essays by Havelock, J. Margolis and others in K. Robb, ed., *Language and Thought in Early Greek Philosophy* (La Salle, Ill., 1983). For the foundations of the term *logos,* see Mortley, *From Word to Silence,* chap. 1, "*Logos* Identified."

25. The Athenians, for instance, believed that their founding king, Erectheus, had sprung from semen placed directly in the earth of Attica, the plain surrounding the city, by the god Hephaestus and so they alone among Greeks could be said to be truly native to Greece and thus superior to other Greeks. Most of their rivals had foundation myths in which the founder came from elsewhere. Having a "better" foundation myth than anyone else was typical of Athenian arrogance.

26. The use of myth in tragic drama was such a sophisticated way of dealing with apparently resolvable ethical issues that a digression seems justified here. The

play *Antigone* by Sophocles (performed in 468 B.C.) offers an excellent example of how a moral dilemma is presented in drama. The brother of Antigone, Polyneices, has been killed attacking the city of Thebes. Creon, the king of Thebes, declares him polluted and thus not worthy of burial. Antigone is determined that he should be buried according to the "unwritten and unfailing conventions of the gods" and goes ahead to scatter earth on his body. Which should take precedence, the authority of the city ruler or the conventions of the gods? This had become an issue of crucial importance as city authority grew in the sixth and fifth centuries. Sophocles makes the dilemma more complex through his portrayal of the characters. Creon is hard, emotionally clumsy and inflexible. Antigone is also inflexible (in comparison to her more pliant sister Ismene, for instance) but expresses herself more nobly. The play ends tragically. Antigone commits suicide, as does Creon's son who has been in love with her, and his wife, but Sophocles allows other characters in the play to consider the need for living flexibly within the world without losing one's sense of overall purpose. An analogy is made with a ship. It has its purpose, to sail towards a destination, but it would never arrive if it tried to sail directly there in the face of the wind. It has to learn how to exploit the winds for its own ends. Sophocles is suggesting that inflexibility in support of absolute values may not be the best way of living. The play is discussed in detail by M. Nussbaum, *The Fragility of Goodness* (Cambridge, 1986), chap. 3.

*The Suppliants* by Aeschylus (performed in 463 B.C.) deals with a problem facing any city state (and many states today), how to deal with those seeking refuge from tyranny. The "Suppliants," fifty daughters of Danaus, arrive in the city of Argos fleeing from the fifty sons of the king Aegyptus (of Egypt) who wish to marry them; their objections to the marriages are not explored but the king was a usurper of the Egyptian throne. The king of Argos is reluctant to shelter them—it could lead to war with Egypt. Yet the popular assembly of the city overrules him. Zeus is the protector of the suppliant and he must not be offended, so the welcome must be given. There are two issues here, that of acceptance of refugees and that of who should make decisions within a city. The Athenian audience must have watched with fascination as they heard of an assembly actually voting and carrying the day, and it was only two years later, in 461, that a revolution in the city led to the Athenian assembly of all its male citizens taking full control of Athens. So *The Suppliants* can be seen as a consideration of the issue, which must have been very much alive in the city when the play was acted.

The strength and importance of drama lay in its use of myth to take an issue out of contemporary politics or society and so defuse it. The audience could see the dilemma as an issue to be meditated on, and their reflections can be fed back, in a measured way, to the debates of everyday life. It is the sheer courage of the dramatists which most impresses. In his *Helen* (412), for instance, Euripides suggests that it was not really Helen but a phantom of her that was taken to Troy, and therefore the Trojan war was futile. All this when the Athenians had just learned of the appalling losses of their own Sicilian expedition, during which some 40,000 may have died. It is hard to imagine any twentieth-century state allowing its participation in war to be questioned in such an open way before the whole community.

27. The quotation on the "unmoved mover" comes from Aristotle's *Physics* 259a. Aristotle provides the concept of a supreme "God" who may have initiated motion but who does not necessarily have any active relationship with the world thereafter. For Aristotle and monotheism, see M. Frede, "Monotheism and Pagan Philosophy," in P. Athanassiadi and M. Frede, *Pagan Monotheism in Late Antiquity* (Oxford, 1999), pp. 44–50.

For introductions to the debates on the nature and powers of the gods see G. Kerferd, *The Sophistic Movement* (Cambridge, 1981), especially chap. 13, "Religion and the Gods," and A. A. Long, ed., *The Cambridge Companion to Early Greek Philosophy* (Cambridge, 1999), especially chap. 10 by S. Broadie, "Rational Theology." See also S. Price, *Religions of the Ancient Greeks* (Cambridge, 1999), especially here chap. 7, "Greek Thinkers." While it was believed by conservatives that the gods could intervene when outraged, the attitude of the Greeks in general was optimistic rather than pessimistic. "For they say that foolish decisions are typical of this city, but the gods turn up for the best whatever mistakes you make," as the chorus in Aristophanes' play *Clouds* put it. It is worth stressing that even centuries later when Augustine in the Latin west argued for the existence of original sin burdening humankind so heavily that even the power to reason had been corrupted, the idea never caught on in the Greek east.

28. Helen King's study was published in London and New York, 1998.

29. Trans. A. Oksenberg Rorty.

3

1. There is a mass of new work on rhetoric, but a good place to start is G. Kennedy, *A New History of Classical Rhetoric* (Princeton, 1994); see chap. 1, "Introduction: The Nature of Rhetoric." See also Robert Wardy, "Rhetoric," in J. Brunschwig and G. E. R. Lloyd, eds., *Greek Thought: A Guide to Classical Knowledge* (Cambridge, Mass., and London, 2000), and Wardy's longer consideration of the issues, *The Birth of Rhetoric* (London, 1996). There are also essays in I. Worthington, ed., *Persuasion: Greek Rhetoric in Action* (London and New York, 1994).

2. The speech which swayed the argument back towards leniency was made by one Diodotus. Part of the speech, as reported by Thucydides, is worth quoting in this context and as a paean to free speech and rational argument.

> Haste and anger are, to my mind, the two greatest obstacles to wise counsel—haste, that usually goes with folly, anger, that is the mark of primitive and narrow minds. And anyone who maintains that words cannot be a guide to action must be either a fool or one with some personal interest at stake: he is a fool if he imagines that it is possible to deal with the uncertainties of the future by any other medium, and he is personally interested if his aim is to persuade you on into some disgraceful action, and knowing that he cannot make a good speech in a bad cause, he tries to frighten his opponents and his hearers by some good-sized pieces of misrepresentation . . . the good citizen, instead of trying to terrify the opposition, ought to prove his case in fair argument; and a wise state, without giving special honours to its best counsellors, will certainly not deprive them of the honour they already enjoy; and when a man's advice is not taken, he should not even be disgraced, far less penalised.

Thucydides, *The Peloponnesian War* 3:42–3 (trans. R. Warner).

3. Quoted in Wardy, "Rhetoric," p. 467.

4. The quotation is from Kennedy, *A New History of Classical Rhetoric*, p. 47. Kennedy discusses Quintilian on pp. 177–86. An excellent analysis of Isocrates'

views is to be found in chap. 5 of J. Ober, *Political Dissent in Democratic Athens: Intellectual Critics of Popular Rule* (Princeton and Chichester, Eng., 1998).

5. Quoted in Wardy, "Rhetoric," p. 483. The original is to be found in Aristotle's *Rhetoric* I:2:3 1335b.

6. For the issues surrounding Socrates' death, see R. Parker, *Athenian Religion: A History* (Oxford, 1996), pp. 199–207.

7. On Plato, see R. M. Hare, *Plato* (Oxford, 1982), as an introduction. The essay on Plato by G. Press in R. Popkin, ed., *The Pimlico History of Western Philosophy* (New York, 1998; London, 1999), is also recommended.

8. Quoted in C. Stead, *Philosophy in Christian Antiquity* (Cambridge, 1994), p. 19. This work is particularly useful because it sets Christian theology within its Greek philosophical background.

9. A full account of Plato's doctrine of the soul is to be found in J. Cooper, "Plato's Theory of Human Motivation," in *History of Philosophy Quarterly* 1, no. 1 (January 1984). I am grateful to my son Barney for bringing this article to my attention.

10. Plato, *The Republic* 7.530 B–C. One should contrast Plato's approach with Aristotle's privileging of empirical observation over theory. As Aristotle puts it when discussing the reproduction of bees:

> This then seems to be what happens with regard to the generation of bees, judging from theory (*logos*) and from what are thought to be the facts about them. But the facts have not been sufficiently ascertained, and if they ever are ascertained, then we must trust perception rather than theories, and theories too, so long as what they show agrees with what appears to be the case.

*De Generatione Animalium* 760 b. 27ff., quoted in G. E. R. Lloyd, *Magic, Reason and Experience* (Cambridge, 1979), p. 138.

11. If Plato had been right there would surely have been someone who would have left record of the Form of, say, Justice that others, using no more than the power of reason, would have agreed with totally. There is little evidence for this, although some Christian theologians would claim that there is. The problem lies in finding a relationship between a mathematical proof and the concept of, for example, "justice." Plato would have argued that both could be found in the same way using deductive logic, although he accepted that the task of finding "justice" would be much more intellectually demanding. A mathematical proof starts from an agreed symbolic representation (for instance a drawing of a square divided into quarters) and a proof can be developed from there. All are agreed on the first principles (as set out in the drawing), and each step follows logically from the one before to the satisfaction of all. The proof fails as soon as one person can find a valid reason for disagreeing. While individuals can come up with instances of what they, as individuals, consider to be beautiful, it is hard to see how an agreed symbolic representation could ever be set out from which to start the process of deductive reasoning towards a Form of Beauty that has the same degree of truth as a mathematical proof. What has happened more often is that one figure or ruling elite has claimed to have found the Forms and then imposed them on others. The French revolutionary leader Robespierre, for instance, who, like his colleagues, was deeply influenced by his classical education, stated his political aims in absolutely Platonic terms: "the peaceful enjoyment of liberty and equality; the reign of eternal justice, whose laws are engraved, not in marble or stone, but in the hearts of all men, even in

that of the slave who forgets them [compare Meno] and of the tyrant who rejects them." When others disagreed with his interpretation of "Virtue" they were, in the manner recommended by Plato in his *Laws,* eliminated in the Terror. The classic book on all this is K. Popper's *The Open Society and Its Enemies* (reprint, London, 1995). Of course, for many the sheer sparkle of Plato, and his method of using dialogues to explore all possible points of view, lead to all this being forgiven. The point is also made later in this book that Plato attempts to convince through reason (even though we may have doubts about the way he uses it) rather than by the power of emotion.

12. Aristotle, *Nicomachean Ethics* 1155a3. As an introduction to Aristotle's ethics, see chap. 5, "Ethics and the Organisation of Desire," in J. Lear, *Aristotle: The Desire to Understand* (Cambridge, 1988).

13. *Nicomachean Ethics* 1144b3.

14. The contrast is developed in the conclusion of the first part of *The Passion of the Western Mind* (London, 1996) by R. Tarnas.

## 4

1. The term "Hellenistic," coined in the nineteenth century to describe the fusion of Greek and non-Greek, is given to the period between the death of Alexander (323) and the conquest of Egypt by Rome (30 B.C.). For a recent and comprehensive introduction to the period, see G. Shipley, *The Greek World After Alexander, 323–30 B.C.* (London, 2000).

2. See W. G. Runciman, "Doomed to Extinction: The *Polis* as an Evolutionary Dead-End," in O. Murray and S. Price, eds., *The Greek City from Homer to Alexander* (Oxford, 1990). For a survey of the Greek world in the fourth century, see the later chapters of J. K. Davies, *Democracy and Classical Greece,* 2nd ed. (London, 1993).

3. For Alexander, a judicious life which avoids over-romanticization is by A. B. Bosworth, *Conquest and Empire: The Reign of Alexander the Great* (Cambridge, 1988).

4. See A. B. Bosworth, *Alexander and the East: The Tragedy of Triumph* (Oxford, 1996), for a study of the sources behind Alexander's campaigns there.

5. See R. R. R. Smith, *Hellenistic Sculpture* (London, 1991), chap. 1, pp. 19–33.

6. On ruler cults in this period, see Shipley, *The Greek World After Alexander,* pp. 156–63. There is a good exposition of the theory of divine kingship in a (? third century A.D.) tract attributed to the Egyptian god Thoth in his Hellenistic guise of Hermes Trismegistus. (Hermes Trismegistus is credited with some forty-two books of spiritual wisdom.)

> There are in the universe four regions . . . namely, heaven, the aether, the air, and the earth. Above, my son, in heaven dwell gods, over whom, as over all else likewise, rules the maker of the universe . . . and upon earth dwell men, over whom rules he who is king for the time being; for the gods, my son, cause to be born at the right time a man that is worthy to govern upon earth . . . he who is king on earth is the last of the four rulers, but the first of men. As long as he is on earth, he has no part in true deity; but as compared with other men, he has something exceptional, which is like to God.

Quoted in H. A. Drake, *Constantine and the Bishops: The Politics of Intolerance* (Baltimore and London, 2000), p. 128. Echoes of such statements survived to justify the Byzantine emperors' role as representatives of God on earth.

7. The careful and critical work of A. B. Bosworth has done much to produce a balanced assessment of Alexander. One reason why Alexander's reputation has remained high is the influence of the main surviving source for his life, Arrian's, written in the second century A.D. In fact, Arrian based his life on one of Alexander's commanders, Ptolemy, whose eulogistic account of Alexander's campaigns was developed to boost his own claim to succession to Alexander in Egypt. (See A. B. Bosworth, *From Arrian to Alexander: Studies in Historical Interpretation* [Oxford, 1988], and A. B. Bosworth and E. J. Baynham, eds., *Alexander the Great in Fact and Fiction* [Oxford, 2000].)

See A. B. Bosworth, *Conquest and Empire: The Reign of Alexander the Great* (Cambridge, 1988), pp. 285–86 for Callisthenes' opposition to *proskynesis* and pp. 118–19 for his death. For a sober assessment of Plutarch's view that Alexander tried to create some form of unity between Greeks, see R. Baldry, *The Greeks and the Unity of Mankind* (Cambridge, 1965), chap. 4, esp. pp. 113–34. For an assessment of Plutarch's eulogy, see also J. R. Hamilton, *Plutarch's Alexander: A Commentary* (Bristol, 1999), pp. xxiv–xxxiii. Hamilton shows how it was a rhetorical display piece in which the speaker, here a young Plutarch, was expected to make the very best case possible, even at the risk, as here, of gross distortion of the reality. Adulation of Alexander was boosted in the nineteenth century by the Prussian historian Droysen's claim that without Alexander the Greek world would have remained confined to the Aegean, and Christianity would have been unable to spread across the Mediterranean and Asia. The implication is that the pagan Alexander was sent by God to pave the way. Droysen's view reached its apogée in the work of William Tarn. In his *Alexander* (Cambridge, 1948), Tarn makes the suggestion that

> Alexander lifted the civilized world out of one groove and set in in another . . . In so far as the modern world derives its civilization from Greece, it largely owes it to Alexander that it had the oppor-tunity . . . when at last Christianity showed the way to that spiritual unity after which men were feeling, there was ready to hand a medium for the new religion to spread in the common Hellenistic civilization of the "inhabited world."

Even today, when we are much more sensitive to imperialist propaganda, there are those who see Alexander's immediate legacy as positive, but on the whole the brutality of his conquests and the lack of vision beyond them is now being recognized. It was his successors who provided the stability within which Greek civilization could spread, and there is much evidence that it was not until the long Roman centuries that Greek culture penetrated below the surface of the native cultures of Asia. The Romans never swallowed the Alexander legend uncritically. In a bitter attack on Alexander in his *History of Rome,* Livy suggests that it was one thing for Alexander to conquer barbarians—if he had met the Romans the outcome would have been very different! (Livy, *History of Rome* 9, xviii) Cicero in his *De Republica* tells the story of a pirate captured by Alexander.

> Alexander asked the fellow, "What is your idea in infesting the sea?" And the pirate answered, with uninhibited insolence, "The same as

yours, in infesting the earth! But because I do it in a tiny craft, I'm called a pirate: because you have a mighty navy, you are called an emperor."

*De Republica* 3.14.24.

8. Translation by P. Green from Apollonios Rhodios, *The Argonautika* (Berkeley and London, 1997), book 3, lines 760–65.

9. An introduction to Archimedes can be found in M. Bragg, *On Giants' Shoulders* (London, 1998), chap. 1, a discussion of Archimedes' achievements that includes a contribution by Geoffrey Lloyd. See also M. Kline, *Mathematical Thought from Ancient to Modern Times*, vol. 1 (New York and Oxford, 1972), chap. 5, which, besides discussing Archimedes, considers the work of Alexandrian mathematicians in general.

10. See, as an introduction to Epicureanism and Stoicism, A. A. Long, "Hellenistic Philosophy," in R. Popkin, ed., *The Pimlico History of Western Philosophy* (New York, 1998; London, 1999), and C. Stead, *Philosophy in Christian Antiquity* (Cambridge, 1995), chap. 5. Another excellent, and lively, survey of Stoicism is to be found in "Stoicism" by J. Brunschwig, in J. Brunschwig and G. E. R. Lloyd, eds., *Greek Thought: A Guide to Classical Knowledge* (Cambridge, Mass., and London, 2000), pp. 977–96. A much fuller and demanding study is M. Nussbaum, *The Therapy of Desire: Theory and Practice in Hellenistic Ethics* (Princeton, 1994). A recent, well-received book on the difficult but important subject of Stoicism and free will is S. Bobzien, *Determinism and Freedom in Stoic Philosophy* (Oxford, 2000), while there is much on the relationship between the Stoics and emotion in R. Sorabji, *Emotion and Peace of Mind: From Stoic Agitation to Christian Temptation* (Oxford, 2000).

11. Much of the old way of life remained undisturbed, and it was only in the stable Roman centuries that followed that Greek culture penetrated "to the most remote of rural contexts." See F. Millar, *The Roman Near East 31 B.C.–A.D. 337* (Cambridge, Mass., and London, 1993), especially the summing-up, pp. 523–32.

## 5

1. For the origins of Rome, see T. J. Cornell, *The Beginnings of Rome* (London, 1995), which takes the story up to 264 B.C. Essential for an understanding of Rome's expansion is W. Harris, *War and Imperialism in Republican Rome* (Oxford, 1979).

2. In one early layer of the Roman forum, dating from the second quarter of the sixth century B.C., a sanctuary to the god Volcanus, an ancient Roman god of destructive, devouring fire (as, for instance, in volcanoes), has been uncovered. Among the votive deposits found in the sanctuary was a black-figure vase from Athens with a representation of the Greek god of fire and blacksmiths, Hephaestus. This shows at how early a date Greek and Roman mythology interacted. In later Roman mythology Volcanus and Hephaestus were merged. See M. Beard, J. North and S. Price, *Religions of Rome* (Cambridge, 1998), p. 12.

3. E. Gruen, *Culture and National Identity in Republican Rome* (Ithaca, 1992), is the essential introduction to the relationship between the Romans and Greek culture.

4. On Cicero, E. Rawson, *Cicero: A Portrait* (London, 1995), is a good starting point. There has been renewed interest in Cicero's philosophy in recent years. See J. G. F. Powell, ed., *Cicero the Philosopher* (Oxford, 1995). The introductory essay by the editor covers the main issues.

5. A concise overview of these years can be found in D. Shotter, *The Fall of the Roman Republic* (London and New York, 1994).

6. C. Meier, *Caesar* (London, 1995), is a thorough and thoughtful biography of Julius Caesar.

7. The Philippics were called after the famous speeches made in fourth-century Athens by the orator Demosthenes in response to the growing power of Philip of Macedon.

8. For a general survey of these years see M. Goodman, *The Roman World, 44 B.C.–A.D. 180* (London, 1997).

9. Among the manifestations of Augustus' *pietas* was a return to a sterner sexual morality after the undoubted decadence of the late republic. While Greek sculptures of the god Priapus show him as phallic and randy, the Augustan equivalent is decently clothed and his energies are diverted towards a mass of children clambering over him. See K. Galinsky, *Augustan Culture: An Interpretive Introduction* (Princeton, 1996), p. 345. This is an essential book for those who wish to study the cultural effects of Augustus' rule, as is P. Zanker's *The Power of Images in the Age of Augustus* (Ann Arbor, 1988).

10. Galinsky, *Augustan Culture*, p. 197 with plan.

11. Paraphrase of the original by D. Ross, quoted ibid., p. 354. Sappho (seventh century B.C.) is, of course, the great Greek lyric poet from Lesbos; Alcaeus, her contemporary, another lyric poet from Lesbos. Callimachus was the highly erudite Hellenistic poet from Alexandria, probably the most influential of his period.

12. The translation is by Robert Fitzgerald.

13. Tacitus, the most astute of the Roman historians, had no illusions about the process that he describes in his account of his father-in-law Agricola's period as governor in Britain.

> Agricola had to deal with people living in isolation and ignorance, and therefore prone to fight: and his object was to accustom them to a life of peace and quiet by the provision of amenities. He therefore gave private encouragement and official assistance to the building of temples, public squares and good houses. He praised the energetic and scolded the slack; and competition for honour proved as effective as compulsion. Furthermore he educated the sons of the chiefs in the liberal arts . . . The result was that instead of loathing the Latin language they became eager to speak it effectively. In the same way, our national dress came into favour and the toga was everywhere to be seen. And so the population was led into the demoralising temptations of arcades, baths and sumptuous banquets. The unsuspecting Britons spoke of such novelties as "civilization," when in fact they were only a feature of their enslavement.

Translation from *Agricola*, S. A. Handford, Penguin Classics.

14. These themes can be followed up in Janet Huskinson, ed., *Experiencing Rome: Culture, Identity and Power in the Roman Empire* (London, 2000). The process by which a particular family could be integrated into the administration of the empire can be seen through the descendants of a Gallic aristocrat, Epotsorovidius. After Caesar's conquest of Gaul in the 50s B.C., Epotsorovidius' son appears as a Roman citizen with the name Gaius Julius Agedomopas, an indication that his citizenship was granted by Caesar himself. Two generations later the family has become completely Romanized, and Latin may have become their first language.

Gaius Julius Rufus, of the fourth generation, was a priest of the cult of Rome and Augustus at Lyons and a *praefectus fabrorum,* an army official concerned with building works. His wealth was such that he was able to choose from among the traditional repertoire of Roman buildings to donate an amphitheatre to Lyons and a triumphal arch to his native town, Mediolanum Santomum (the modern Saintes). Over time the conquered had become the patrons of the regime that had conquered them, and herein lay the reasons for the empire's success.

15. The relatively detached approach taken by the Romans to Judaism can be sensed from this assessment by the historian Dio Cassius writing in the early third century A.D.:

> They [the Jews] are distinguished from the rest of mankind in practically every detail of their lives, and especially in that they honour none of the other gods, but show extreme reverence for one particular deity. They have never had a statue of him even in Jerusalem itself, but believing him to be so unnameable and invisible, they worship him in the most extravagant way among humans. They built him a large and splendid temple . . . and dedicated to him the day of Saturn, on which, among other peculiar observances, they undertake no serious occupation.

Dio Cassius's *History* 39, xvii. Compare this assessment with the frenzied outbursts of John Chrysostom quoted in chap. 17.

16. Censuses and assessments for tax were made when a province was first incorporated into the empire. There is no record of any empire-wide census. The assessment was made on land and property so taxpayers were assessed in the area where they held land, not in the town in which they or their forebears originated. At the time of Jesus' birth (before the death of Herod the Great and therefore c. 4 B.C.), Nazareth in Galilee was not under direct Roman control and so was not subject to Roman taxation. There was certainly a census by Quirinius in Judaea in A.D. 6, and doubtless Luke had heard of this. However, whether Jesus was born in Bethlehem or not—and Matthew relates separately (without any mention of the census) that he was born there—it would not have been a census that required Mary and Joseph to travel there.

17. Compared to the wealthy provinces of Asia Minor to the north and Egypt to the south, Judaea was not a major contributor of taxes. In fact, it has even been suggested that it failed to provide enough taxes to cover the costs of its own administration. The main objective of the Romans was stability in the region, and they knew that this came from supporting local elites, not provoking them. Nevertheless, in Judaea, as elsewhere, the imposition of a new tax system when Rome took control in A.D. 6 was met with opposition. What really offended the Jews, however, was religious provocation, above all any intrusion in the sacred areas of Jerusalem. For the interaction of Judaism and Rome, *The Cambridge History of Judaism,* vol. 3, ed. W. Horbury, W. D. Davies and J. Sturdy (Cambridge, 1999), provides the essential background.

18. Philo, *Embassy to Gaius,* trans. F. A. Colson (Loeb Classical Library), 302.

19. The Romans were so disillusioned by the problems of governing Judaea that in 41 they even handed back the province to a grandson of Herod, Agrippa. Agrippa was popular, but he died in 44 and direct Roman rule was restored. By now heavy taxation (Jews had to pay both Roman and Jewish taxes) and tensions between the rich, who benefited from the wealth coming into Jerusalem for the Temple, and the poor were fuelling resentments that could not be contained. In A.D.

66 a massive if uncoordinated revolt broke out. Roman retaliation was thorough and brutal. Perhaps a million died in the repression, and the Temple itself was sacked by Titus, the son of the emperor Vespasian. Some of his plunder can be seen on reliefs on the triumphal arch in the Forum in Rome erected to celebrate the victory. Another revolt in 132–35 (under the emperor Hadrian) led to Jews being excluded from Jerusalem and the refounding of the city as a Roman colony. Judaea then remained a subdued province of the empire, its priests turning inwards to intensive study of sacred texts of the Torah (the Law), until the Arab invasion of A.D. 640 that brought the loss of the province to the empire.

6

1. From Plutarch, "On the Face of the Orb of the Moon," translated in the Loeb edition of the *Moralia*, vol. 12, by H. Cherniss. Discussed in T. Rihill, *Greek Science* (Oxford, 1999), pp. 76–80.

2. Edward Gibbon, *The Decline and Fall of the Roman Empire*, chap. 2, Penguin Classics.

3. See S. Swain, *Hellenism and Empire: Language, Classicism and Power in the Greek World*, A.D. 50–250 (Oxford, 1996), for a full survey of the movement and its main practitioners. Plutarch is covered in chap. 5. For the second sophistic from an art historian's point of view, see J. Elsner, *Imperial Rome and Christian Triumph: The Art of the Roman Empire*, A.D. 100–450 (Oxford, 1998), chap. 7.

4. See G. Kennedy, *A New History of Classical Rhetoric* (Princeton, 1994), pp. 233–37, for Dio Chrysostom and this speech, which is translated in the Loeb edition of his works.

5. On Nero, a fine biography is M. Griffin, *Nero: The End of a Dynasty* (London, 1984).

6. Hadrian had certainly been very close to the emperor Trajan, his predecessor, serving as a governor in two provinces, including Syria, and on the imperial staff as a speech writer, but his proclamation as emperor immediately after Trajan's death smacked of opportunism, and many believed that he had usurped the post. When he surrendered some of Trajan's conquests, there was even more antagonism, and four former consuls had to be executed for plotting to overthrow him. Many among the Roman elite refused to forgive him for the executions. Hadrian was never at ease in Rome, the centre of hostility to him, but in any case he was a wanderer by nature. Twelve of his twenty-one years of rule were spent in the provinces.

Hadrian's surrender of territory was, in fact, a brave move. He grasped the important fact that expansion for its own sake was self-defeating. Trajan had become preoccupied with the ambition of emulating Alexander—shortly before he died he had broken down in tears at the mouth of the Euphrates when it became clear that an unsettled empire behind him forced him to give up a campaign to the east. Hadrian not only surrendered the newly conquered provinces, he also put in place a policy of consolidating the frontiers of the existing empire. Along the northern borders, always vulnerable to raiding Germanic tribes, he strengthened the *limes,* a military road overlooked by watchtowers joined by palisades. In Britain he created an even more formidable barrier between Roman and barbarian, Hadrian's Wall, somewhat south of what is now the border between England and Scotland. As if this was not enough, he appreciated that legionaries stationed behind defensible frontiers would soon become unfit and demoralized. He visited the legions regularly, and insisted that they keep up their training. A hundred years after his death he was still remembered for his "training and disciplining of the whole army." Anthony Birley, *Hadrian, the Restless Emperor* (London and New York, 1997), p. 303, quoting Cassius Dio.

7. Quoted, along with other assessments, ibid.

8. For Hadrian's villa, see W. MacDonald and J. Pinto, *Hadrian's Villa and Its Legacy* (New Haven and London, 1995). For Hadrian and the cities, see M. T. Boatwright, *Hadrian and the Cities of the Roman Empire* (Princeton and Chichester, Eng., 2000).

9. For the Antonine Altar, see S. Price, *Rituals and Power: The Roman Imperial Cult in Asia Minor* (Cambridge, 1984), pp. 158–59 (complete with illustration of a reconstruction). Most of the remaining fragments are now in the Kunsthistorische Museum in Vienna.

10. The gratitude that members of the Greek elite felt toward the Romans was memorably expressed by one of the leaders of the second sophistic, Aelius Aristides, in his famous panegyric to Rome delivered in the city in A.D. 150. Aristides talks of the cities of the empire relaxing in contentment now that all their ancient quarrels with each other are over.

> You continue to care for the Greeks as for foster parents. You protect them; you raise them up as though prostrate . . . Their energies are now focused in a frenzy of rebuilding. While all other competition between cities has ceased, but a single rivalry obsesses every one of them—to appear as beautiful and attractive as possible. Every place is full of *gymnasia,* fountains, gateways, temples, shops and schools . . . All the monuments, works of art and adornments in them mean glory for you . . .

A long quotation from this speech, from which this extract is taken, can be found in N. Lewis and M. Reinhold, *Roman Civilization, Sourcebook II: The Empire* (New York, 1995), pp. 135–38.

11. For a mathematician's assessment of Diophantus' achievement, see M. Kline, *Mathematical Thought from Ancient to Modern Times,* vol. 1 (New York and Oxford, 1972), pp. 138–44.

12. For Galen, see Roy Porter, *The Greatest Benefit to Mankind: A Medical History of Humanity from Antiquity to the Present* (London, 1997), pp. 73–77; G. E. R. Lloyd, *Greek Science After Aristotle* (London, 1973), and chap. 6 of Rihill, *Greek Science.* The quotation on Galen as both logician and physician comes from G. E. R. Lloyd, "Demonstration in Galen," in M. Frede and G. Striker, eds., *Rationality in Greek Thought* (Oxford, 1996), p. 256.

13. The translation is by Peter Green. Compare Einstein's words from his *Ideas and Opinions:* "The most beautiful experience we can have is the mysterious. It is the fundamental emotion which stands at the cradle of true science." For Ptolemy, see Lloyd, *Greek Science After Aristotle,* the source of his comment, as well as an introductory history of astronomy such as M. Hoskin, ed., *The Cambridge Concise History of Astronomy* (Cambridge, 1999). The major contribution that Ptolemy made to geography is also being recognized. The review quoted here of *Ptolemy's Geography: An Annotated Translation of the Theoretical Chapters,* ed. and trans. J. Lennert Berggren and Alexander Jones (Princeton, 2002), is by Peter Green, from *London Review of Books,* Feb. 21, 2002, vol. 24, no. 4, p. 35.

14. An essential book on Roman religion is M. Beard, J. North and S. Price, *Religions of Rome* (Cambridge, 1998). For a briefer introduction, see James Rives,

"Religion in the Roman Empire," in Janet Huskinson, ed., *Experiencing Rome: Culture, Identity and Power in the Roman Empire* (London, 2000).

15. Available in Penguin Classics, trans. E. J. Kenny.

16. For *theos hypsistos,* see Stephen Mitchell, "The Cult of *Theos Hypsistos,*" in P. Athanassiadi and M. Frede, eds., *Pagan Monotheism in Late Antiquity* (Oxford, 1999), pp. 81–148. There is an early-fourth-century gravestone from Laodicea Catacecaumena which reads, "First I shall sing a hymn of praise for God, the one who sees all, second I shall sing a hymn for the first angel, Jesus Christ." Stephen Mitchell, *Anatolia: Land, Men and Gods in Asia Minor,* vol. 2 (Oxford, 1993), p. 46.

17. The quotation, which comes from Origen's *Contra Celsum* 5:41, is to be found in the introduction to Athanassiadi and Frede, eds., *Pagan Monotheism,* p. 8. See also the quotation from the so-called *Theosophy of Tubingen* in Mitchell, *Anatolia,* vol. 2, p. 44:

> There is one god in the whole universe, who has set boundaries to the wheels of heavenly rotation with divine ordinances, who has distributed measures of equal weight to the hours and the moments, and has set bonds which link and balance the turnings of the heavens with one another, whom we call Zeus, from whom comes the living eternity, and Zeus bearer of all things, life-providing steward of breath, himself, proceeding from the one into the one.

18. Athanassiadi and Frede, eds., *Pagan Monotheism,* pp. 185–86 for the quote of Maximus and p. 20 for the quotation from the editors' introduction. See further chap. 11 of this book for how the concept of the supreme deity was used by Constantine.

19. For Mithraism, see chap. 6 of Beard, North and Price, *Religions of Rome.*

20. "Middle Platonism" and "Neoplatonism" are terms that were developed in the nineteenth century. Their practitioners would have simply seen themselves as Platonists. Introduction can be found in R. Popkin, ed., *The Pimlico History of Western Philosophy* (New York, 1998; London, 1999), "Middle Platonism" by H. Tarrant and "Plotinus and Neoplatonism" by L. Gerson. There is a wealth of useful material in C. Stead, *Philosophy in Christian Antiquity* (Cambridge, 1994). An important passage for Middle Platonists was the following from *The Republic* 509 B.

> The sun . . . not only makes the things we see visible, but causes the processes of generation, growth and nourishment, without itself being such a process . . . The Good therefore may be said to be the source not only of the intelligibility of the objects of knowledge, but also of their existence and reality; yet it is not itself identical with reality, but is beyond reality, and superior to it in dignity and power.

Translation H. D. P. Lee. Note the analogy between the sun and "the Good," the definition of the sun/Good as an active, nurturing force, which is, however, independent from the process of nurturing, and the definition of "the Good" as "beyond reality." These were all important concepts in Middle Platonism.

21. The point is made by Ramsay MacMullen, *Christianity and Paganism in the Fourth to Eight Centuries* (New Haven and London, 1997), p. 78. Looking at oracles from the third century, Stephen Mitchell (*Anatolia,* vol. 2, p. 44) stresses:

> One notion that these oracles should dispel at once is that there was any dichotomy in the middle and later empire between rational thinkers, who based their religious and philosophical ideas on the exercise of a logical critique, and devotees of the god or of the gods, who relied for their religious intuitions on a form of divine inspiration which was denied to others . . . There is no evidence for any conflict between those who adhered to intellectual reasoning and those who simply turned to the god for instruction.

The tradition of trying to reconcile Neoplatonist principles with empirical evidence was carried on in the works of Proclus, the fifth-century Athenian philosopher, the last of the "great" Greek thinkers. See L. Siorvanes, *Proclus: Neo-Platonic Philosophy and Science* (Edinburgh, 1996), especially chaps. 4 and 5.

22. See Athanassiadi and Frede, eds., *Pagan Monotheism,* p. 15, for examples.

23. For instance, one can trace the career of one Quintus Lollius Urbicus, son of a Berber landowner in the province of Africa. He served first in Asia, then in Judaea, where he was involved in putting down the revolt of 132–35, then along the Rhine and Danube before being made governor in Britain. He ended his career as prefect of the city of Rome. Many of these themes can be traced in M. Goodman, *The Roman World,* 44 B.C.–A.D. 180 (London, 1997), and J. Huskinson, ed., *Experiencing Rome* (London, 2000).

24. Beard, North and Price, *Religions of Rome,* p. 225.

25. It is interesting in this context that one of the most important Stoic philosophers of the early second century A.D., Epictetus, was a freed slave, yet he may have been consulted by one emperor, Hadrian, and was certainly an influence on another, Marcus Aurelius.

## 7

1. In instructions to Julianus, proconsul of Africa, concerning the Manicheans. Quoted in S. Williams, *Diocletian and the Roman Recovery* (London, 1985), p. 153.

2. The third-century crisis tends to get neglected in accounts of the Roman empire as it is too late for many general books on the empire and too early for those on late antiquity. The *Cambridge Ancient History* volume on the period is still unpublished. See my *Egypt, Greece and Rome: Civilizations of the Ancient Mediterranean* (Oxford, 1996), chap. 26, for a short overview (which draws, with his permission, on the chapter by John Drinkwater which will eventually appear in the *Cambridge Ancient History*).

3. Williams, *Diocletian,* is a thorough treatment of Diocletian and is drawn on heavily for this chapter. See also Averil Cameron, *The Later Roman Empire* (London, 1993).

4. See S. MacCormack, *Art and Ceremony in Late Antiquity* (Berkeley and London, 1981), p. 107 and plate 10. This is an essential book for the study of the imperial ceremonies and creation of the emperor as a semi-divine figure.

5. The point is made by J. W. Liebeschuetz, *Continuity and Change in Roman Religion* (Oxford, 1979), p. 243.

6. M. Beard, J. North, S. Price, *Religions of Rome,* vol. 1 (Cambridge, 1998), p. 243. See also J. Rives, *Religion and Authority in Roman Carthage from Augustus to Constantine* (Oxford, 1995), in which he states (p. 259) that

[Decius'] motive seems to have been a desire to join together, by force if necessary, all the inhabitants of the empire in one religious act. This was no doubt on one level an attempt to win back the favour of the gods in a time of crisis, but on another to establish among the inhabitants of the empire some sense of a shared religious identity.

7. Quoted in Williams, *Diocletian,* p. 198.

8. Without anticipating the argument, the following quotation from Rives, *Religion and Authority,* p. 251, is helpful.

The fact that the great persecution of the Tetrarchs and the conversion of Constantine took place within a decade of each other was no coincidence, but a reflection of the ambivalence of the imperial elite. For their part, the leaders of the Christian community were increasingly ambivalent in their own attitudes towards the imperial government. To a large extent they viewed it as a source of oppression, but as their own concern with authority grew, they began to appreciate its exercise of a sort of authority that they lacked. As a result, Constantine discovered after his conversion that he shared many concerns with the leaders of the church.

## 8

1. There have been many scholars involved in reconstructing the life and teachings of Jesus within his Jewish heritage. The three I have drawn on here are Geza Vermes, W. D. Davies and E. P. Sanders. See, for instance, E. P. Sanders and W. D. Davies, "Jesus; From the Jewish Point of View," in William Horbury, W. D. Davies and John Sturdy, *The Cambridge History of Judaism,* vol. 3 (Cambridge, 1999). One result of a deeper understanding of the Jewish roots of Christianity has been to defuse the anti-Semitism that has scarred the Christian experience so deeply. In 1999 the Catholic Church recognized "the weaknesses" shown "by so many of her sons and daughters" in this respect (*Memory and Reconciliation: The Church and the Faults of the Past,* issued by the Congregation for the Doctrine of the Faith, Vatican, December 1999), although the Church fell short of assuming any responsibility as an institution for teaching anti-Semitism. Jews themselves increasingly feel able to reclaim Jesus as part of their own inheritance. (It is always instructive, however, to read the entry "Jesus" in a dictionary of Judaism.) Here is a rare example where long years of patient academic study of ancient documents have proved able to dissolve deep-rooted prejudices (although no one, Christian or not, with a knowledge of European history can have failed to reflect on the underlying long-term causes of the Holocaust, which took part deep in a predominantly Christian Europe).

2. G. Vermes, *The Changing Faces of Jesus* (London, 2000), p. 258.

3. There is, of course, a mass of material on the Gospels. A useful starting point for contemporary thinking is the relevant entries in F. L. Cross and E. A. Livingstone, eds., *The Oxford Dictionary of the Christian Church,* 3rd ed. (Oxford, 1997), and M. Coogan and B. Metzger, eds., *The Oxford Companion to the Bible* (Oxford and New York, 1993). See also, for an overview, J. Court and K. Court, *The New Testament World* (Cambridge, 1999).

4. For a summary of Jewish views on the afterlife, see L. Grabbe, *Judaic Religion in the Second Temple Period* (London and New York, 2000), chap. 12, "Eschatologies and Ideas of Salvation." See also the entry "Gehenna" in *The Oxford Dictionary of the Christian Church*. Adrian Hastings, writing on "hell" in A. Hastings, ed., *The Oxford Companion to Christian Thought* (Oxford and New York, 2000), notes: "It is especially the judgement scene as described in Matthew 25:31–46, one of the most influential of biblical passages, which has established the doctrine of hell, both theologically and for public imagination." In particular, Augustine, who reinforced the concept of eternal punishment for western Christianity, used this text as backing.

5. The quotation is taken from Court and Court, *The New Testament World,* p. 207. See this book for a discussion of all the Gospels and the contexts in which they were written. The fullest exposition of the essential Judaism of Matthew's community is to be found in D. C. Sim, *The Gospel of Matthew and Christian Judaism* (Edinburgh, 1998). Sim agrees with the traditional placing of Matthew's community in Antioch and argues strongly that it should be seen as a sect within Judaism.

6. E. P. Sanders, *The Historical Figure of Jesus* (Harmondsworth, 1993), is a good starting point. A very well illustrated recent survey is J. R. Porter, *Jesus Christ: The Jesus of History, the Christ of Faith* (London, 1999). *The Cambridge Companion to Jesus,* ed. Markus Bockmuehl (Cambridge, 2001), has a series of essays on the quest for the historical Jesus. There is broad agreement in the Gospels over the "baptism" of Jesus by John the Baptist, although some scholars believe that Jesus was originally a follower of John's and it was only later that the account of the baptism was developed to give him a higher status than John. The birth stories associated with Jesus are full of contradictions, and it is difficult to find any scholarly agreement, even over whether he was born in Bethlehem.

7. See R. Horsley, "Jesus and Galilee: The Contingencies of a Renewal Movement," in E. Mayes, ed., *Galilee Through the Centuries: Confluence of Cultures* (Winona Lake, Ind., 1999). In his earlier work on Galilee, *Bandits, Prophets and Messiahs: Popular Movements at the Time of Jesus* (New York, 1985), Horsley explored the social tensions in Galilee in Jesus' time and related his teachings to them. There is a mass of background material on first-century Galilee in E. W. Stegemann and W. Stegemann, *The Jesus Movement: A Social History of Its First Century* (Edinburgh, 1999). There was certainly a tradition of unrest in Galilee— Galileans were seen as making good fighters and providing revolutionary leaders, and many of the leaders of the Jewish revolt of A.D. 66 were from that area.

8. For the relationship between Galilean and Judaean Judaism, see the detailed study by M. Goodman, "Galilean Judaism and Judaean Judaism," chap. 19 in Horbury, Davies and Sturdy, eds., *The Cambridge History of Judaism,* vol. 3. The issue is also discussed by Vermes, *The Changing Faces of Jesus,* pp. 225–26.

9. A useful introduction is to be found in the entry "Judaism of the First Century A.D.," in Coogan and Metzger, eds., *The Oxford Companion to the Bible,* Fuller treatments of particular groups are to be found in Horbury, Davies and Sturdy, eds., *The Cambridge History of Judaism.*

10. The quotation on "children of light" and "darkness" comes from Dead Sea Scroll texts I QS I 3f 9f and is quoted in Otto Betz, "The Essenes," chap. 15 in Horbury, Davies and Sturdy, eds., *The Cambridge History of Judaism.* The quotation on liberation comes from the same texts, 94Q521, and is from Vermes, *The Changing Faces of Jesus,* p. 17.

11. As an introduction to the concept, see the entries for "Messiah" in F. L. Cross and E. A. Livingstone, eds., *The Oxford History of the Christian Church,* and

Coogan and Metzger, eds., *The Oxford Companion to the Bible*. A much fuller analysis from a Jewish perspective is to be found in chap. 13, "Messiahs," in Grabbe, *Judaic Religion*. See also S. Freyne, *Galilee and Gospel* (Tubingen, 2000), chap. 11, "Messiah and Galilee," where Freyne considers Messianism in a specifically Galilean context.

12. M. Allen Powell, *The Jesus Debate* (Oxford, 1999), reviews the various historical interpretations of Jesus' life and shows just how diverse the approaches are. Frances Young's point is made in "A Cloud of Witnesses," in J. Hick, ed., *The Myth of God Incarnate*, 2nd ed. (London, 1993), p. 22. It is interesting to find that the theological presentations of Jesus have not obscured his essential humanity. "They seem to say he was a goodish kind of man," says a Victorian costermonger interviewed by Henry Mayhew in his *London Labour and the London Poor* (London, 1861–62), "but if he says as how a cove's to forgive a feller who hits you, I should say he know'd nothing about it" (vol. 1, pp. 21, 40).

13. Fredriksen's point comes from her *Jesus of Nazareth, King of the Jews* (London, 2000), p. 268.

14. On "the kingdom," see the exhaustive discussion in E. P. Sanders and W. D. Davies, "Jesus; From the Jewish Point of View," in Horbury, Davies and Sturdy, eds., *The Cambridge History of Judaism*, pp. 636–49. Richard Horsley's comment is to be found in "Jesus and Galilee: The Contingencies of a Renewal Movement," in Mayes, ed., *Galilee Through the Centuries*, p. 68.

15. Sanders and Davies, "Jesus; From the Jewish Point of View," p. 676. Geza Vermes' views on the "Son of Man" title, of which he has made a particular study, are summarized in his *The Changing Faces of Jesus*, pp. 38–41 and 175–77.

16. The subject is well covered by E. P. Sanders in his "Contention and Opposition in Galilee," chap. 14 in *The Historical Figure of Jesus* (Harmondworth, 1993). The reasons for John's execution are also discussed, pp. 93–95.

17. The responsibility for arresting Jesus has been placed by scholars on virtually every group including Jews outside the priesthood, the priesthood, and the Romans (see Sanders and Davies, "Jesus; From the Jewish Point of View," p. 668, for the range of interpretations), but the central role of Caiaphas, who was responsible for keeping order in the city, seems likely. Richard Horsley makes the following point:

> Jesus' agenda of renewing Israel required what must be seen as a challenge to illegitimate rulers and/or as an attempt to reach out to the rest of Israel from the capital. Israelite tradition was rich with prophetic precedents of challenge to and condemnation of—or simply laments over—the ruling institutions and their families.

"Jesus and Galilee: The Contingencies of a Renewal Movement" in Mayes, *Galilee Through the Centuries*, p. 73.

18. The earliest representation is actually an anti-Christian taunt from a third-century graffito in Rome mocking a Christian called Alexamenos, who is shown worshipping a donkey hanging from a cross. One of the earliest "public" Christian representations, on the fifth-century wooden door of Santa Sabina in Rome, shows Christ with his arms outstretched and nail marks in them but no actual cross behind him. The elaboration of Christ's suffering on the cross was a much later development in Christian iconography. The issue is well dealt with in Robin Margaret Jensen, *Understanding Early Christian Art* (London and New York, 2000), chap. 5, "Images of the Suffering Redeemer."

19. See chap. 17, "Epilogue: The Resurrection" in E. P. Sanders, *The Historical Figure of Jesus* (Harmondsworth, 1993). For a traditional perspective, see Markus Bockmuehl, "Resurrection," chap. 7 in Bockmuehl, ed., *The Cambridge Companion to Jesus*. In her book *The Gnostic Gospels* (London, 1980), chap. 1, E. Pagels suggests a battle for control over the resurrection experience, one in which Peter attempts to claim the earliest experience of the resurrection in order to justify his leadership of the church. This explains why Paul, who reports Peter's claim that he was the first, is also so keen to equate his own experience on the road to Damascus with those of the disciples. Pagels suggests that the Catholic Church was to insist on the primacy of Peter's experience of the resurrection, followed by that of the remaining Apostles, in order to sustain the idea of apostolic succession, so crucial to upholding church hierarchy and tradition.

From earliest times concerns have been raised over the credibility of the resurrection accounts. They were dismissed by pagans as "a fable or the report of a hysterical woman." The theologian Origen (who will be discussed in detail in chap. 10) made a Platonic distinction between the few who could grasp the allegorical meaning of the resurrection, "that in the body there lies a certain principle which is not corrupted from which the body is raised in corruption"—not the same body that died but a body appropriate to the new and immortal life—and the many who could only grasp a literal explanation (that Jesus' actual body was raised) "preached in the churches for the simpleminded and for the ears of the common crowd who are led on to lead better lives by their belief." (See Jaroslav Pelikan, *The Christian Tradition*, vol. 1: *The Emergence of the Catholic Tradition* (100–600) [Chicago and London, 1971], pp. 30 and 48.)

Powell, *The Jesus Debate*, p. 191, notes that the Jesus Seminar, a group of theologians and historians who vote on contentious issues in Jesus' life, decided by "a large majority" that Jesus' resurrection did not involve the resuscitation of a corpse. (Note, however, that the Jesus Seminar is regarded as radical by traditionalists.) This is in line with Paul's view. However, if the risen Jesus was not his own corpse resuscitated, where did this go? The earliest account (Mark 16:1–8, the last verses of the original Gospel) suggests that when the disciples came across the opened tomb, there was a man in white robes inside telling them they would see the risen Jesus in Galilee. There is a possible explanation in terms of Caiaphas' own desperate need to deal with Jesus' followers without further trouble. So long as they believed his actual body was in the tomb, they could be expected to congregate there and keep the movement alive. There is increasing evidence, archaeological and otherwise, of "cults of the dead" in Palestine during this period, which would explain why Jesus' tomb might become a centre of cult worship. See L. Grabbe, *Priests, Prophets, Divines, Sages: A Socio-Historical Study of Religious Specialists in Ancient Israel* (Valley Forge, Pa., 1995), pp. 141–45. Taking the body out (and making it clear that it had gone by leaving the tomb open) would dissolve this possibility, but Caiaphas, anxious to settle things down while Pilate was still in Jerusalem, needed to go further. He had to find a way of persuading the disciples to return home to Galilee, out of his jurisdiction and back into that of Herod Antipas. So a messenger is left telling them that the body is gone but Jesus would rise in Galilee if they would return there. If there is any truth in this account it was, of course, essential that Jesus' body was *not* produced by Caiaphas or his associates, as it would undermine any reason for the disciples returning to Galilee. One assumes that there would be no incentive for preserving it anyway. Matthew suggests that Caiaphas used Roman guards on the tomb so that the disciples would not take Jesus' body away, but when the body was discovered missing, these were bribed by the chief priests to tell Pilate that the body had been taken by the disciples. There could be hidden in this story an attempt by the chief priests to cover up the fact that they had arranged the body's removal.

Matthew's account is repeated with elaboration in the so-called Gospel of Peter, a fragment of which was found in the nineteenth century. It probably dates from the second century A.D. Here the author talks of the elders approaching Pilate for a guard, as Matthew does (in other words, the Gospel appears to draw on an early source), but adds the detail that there were crowds around the tomb on the Sabbath following the crucifixion. The guards seal up the tomb, but that night the stone is rolled away, and three men, two of them supporting another (the body of Jesus?), are seen to emerge. As in Matthew's Gospel, the centurion and the soldiers are commanded not to repeat what they have seen. The text of the Gospel of Peter is to be found in R. E. Brown, *The Death of the Messiah* (London, 1994), vol. 2, pp. 1318–21.

A fuller historical study of the resurrection would need to examine the many other accounts of charismatic leaders who had been "seen" by their followers after their deaths.

20. Jewish scholars have not shared this perspective. For a Jewish view on the concept of the "suffering Messiah," see L. Grabbe, *Judaic Religion in the Second Temple Period* (London and New York, 2000), who concludes his analysis of the texts (p. 291), including the Dead Sea Scrolls: "As far as can be determined from present textual evidence, the New Testament view of Jesus as both a messiah and one who suffered and died for the sins of his people was developed from the experience of the early church and has no precedent as such in Judaism." He notes (p. 290) that the "servant of Isaiah 40–55 was not a messianic figure in its original context."

21. It has been suggested that Saul adopted the name Paul, essentially a Roman name, after his conversion of Sergius Paulus, the proconsul of Cyprus, Acts 13:4–12. See S. Mitchell, *Anatolia: Land, Men and Gods in Asia Minor,* vol. 2 (Oxford, 1993), pp. 6–8. Mitchell suggests that Sergius Paulus, who came from Pisidian Antioch in the south of the Roman province of Galatia, was the impetus for Paul's missionary journeys to the Galatians in that after his conversion he would have been able to provide Paul with contacts, letters of introduction and other assistance.

## 9

1. I have drawn heavily on E. P. Sanders, *Paul* (Oxford, 1991), for this chapter, and this short biography provides an excellent starting point. Further sources are cited in the following notes. Paula Fredriksen sums up the problem of Paul's enduring authority as follows: "The problem of history did not resolve itself as Paul so fervently believed it would. What arrived was not the kingdom but the Church, and Paul came to serve as the foundation for something he certainly never envisioned: orthodox ecclesiastical tradition." From "Paul and Augustine: Conversion Narratives, Orthodox Traditions, and the Retrospective Self," *Journal of Theological Studies* 37 (1986): 31. For a recent and comprehensive introduction to Paul's theology, see J. Dunn, *The Theology of Paul the Apostle* (Edinburgh, 1998).

2. Many scholars doubt that Paul was born a Roman citizen. For discussion as to how Paul might have become one, see R. Wallace and W. Williams, *The Three Worlds of Paul of Tarsus* (London, 1998), pp. 137–46. See also the important article by J. Barclay, "Paul Among Diaspora Jews: Anomaly or Apostate," *Journal of the Study of the New Testament* 60 (1995): 89–120.

3. Barclay, "Paul Among Diaspora Jews," p. 105, for the quotation on Paul's Greek. On Paul's links to the Essenes, M. Hengel puts it as follows:

Paul is akin to the Qumran writings in his basic eschatological dualist attitude, his sense of an imminent end and of the concealed presence of salvation, the eschatological gift of the spirit, which makes it possible to interpret scriptures in terms of the eschatological present, the predestination bound up with God's election and the inability of human beings to secure salvation by themselves—a feature which was controversial in contemporary Judaism.

From "The Pre-Christian Paul" in J. Lieu, J. North and T. Rajak, eds., *The Jews Among Pagans and Christians in the Roman Empire* (London and New York, 1992), pp. 40–41. Paul was one of those people who was desperate to belong and to express his commitment. The similarities to the Essenes in his eschatology, his language, his commitment to celibacy and his attitudes to those who offend (see the Corinthian who lived with his stepmother, below) make it possible that he was a member of this sect before "conversion," in much the same way as Augustine found a temporary resting place in Manicheism. It has to be stressed that there is no evidence for Paul's involvement with the Essenes and most commentators do not even raise the issue.

4. See, for instance, the alternative chronologies in J. Becker, *Paul: Apostle to the Gentiles,* trans. O. C. Dean, Jr. (Louisville, 1993), chap. 2, and Jerome Murphy O'Connor, *Paul, a Critical Life* (Oxford, 1996), chap. 1.

5. The issue of the righteous Gentiles and Judaism is discussed in depth by Alan Segal, "Universalism in Judaism and Christianity," in Troels Engbury-Pedersen, ed., *Paul in His Hellenistic Context* (Edinburgh, 1994). On an inscription found at the city of Aphrodisias, possibly third century A.D., which records a list of benefactors from the Jewish community in the city, ninety Jews are named and alongside them sixty-five "god-fearers" (*theosebeis*). Nine of the "god-fearers" were members of the city council. This suggests, alongside material given in Acts, that "god-fearers" were not only numerous in the Jewish communities but also often influential members of the community. One might even argue that the "god-fearers" were a means through which the Jews mediated and sustained their position within the local community. See S. Mitchell, *Anatolia: Land, Men and Gods in Asia Minor,* vol. 2 (Oxford, 1993), p. 32, for details of the Aphrodisias inscription.

6. On Apollos, see O'Connor, *Paul,* pp. 276 and 281. The quotation from Barrett is taken from his *A Commentary on the First Epistle to the Corinthians* (London, 1971), p. 211.

7. Gronbech is quoted in J. D. Moores, *Westling with Rationality in Paul* (Cambridge, 1995), p. 1. "A rhetoric of the heart" is the view of E. Norden, quoted in Barclay, "Paul Among Diaspora Jews," p. 105, where the quotation about Paul's "rudimentary knowledge of Greek literature or philosophy" comes from.

8. S. Mitchell suggests that the "Unknown God" was *theos hypsistos,* who was described as the god "not admitting of a name, known by many names." See Mitchell's "The Cult of *Theos Hypsistos,*" in P. Athanassiadi and M. Frede, eds., *Pagan Monotheism in Late Antiquity* (Oxford, 1999), p. 122.

9. See Barclay, "Paul Among Diaspora Jews," p. 108. The quotation is also by Barclay (p. 114), drawing on the view of Richard Hays from the latter's *Echoes of Scripture in the Letters of Paul* (New Haven and London, 1989). A wide-ranging study of the relationship of Paul and Jewish apocalyptic teachings is to be found in M. C. de Boer, "Paul and Apocalyptic Eschatology," in John J. Collins, ed., *The Encyclopaedia of Apocalypticism,* vol. 1 (New York, 1998).

10. Sanders, *Paul,* p. 84. An excellent introduction to Paul's relationship with

Judaism is provided by W. D. Davies, "Paul from a Jewish Point of View," in W. Horbury, W. D. Davies and J. Sturdy, eds., *The Cambridge History of Judaism,* vol. 3 (Cambridge, 1999), chap. 21. The section on Paul and the Law (pp. 702–14) is especially good on Paul's complex and ambiguous attitude to the Law.

11. See J. Macquarrie, *Jesus Christ in Modern Thought* (London and Philadelphia, 1990), pp. 55–68, for the debate in relation to Paul's writings, and G. Vermes, chap. 4, "The Christ of Paul: Son of God and Universal Redeemer of Mankind," in *The Changing Faces of Jesus* (London, 2000). See also the discussion in Frances Young, "A Cloud of Witnesses," in J. Hick, ed., *The Myth of God Incarnate,* 2nd ed. (London, 1993), pp. 20–22.

12. See Vermes, *The Changing Faces of Jesus,* p. 85, for this idea. In the later second century, Melito, bishop of Sardis, followed up the idea, writing, "He [Jesus] carried the wood upon his shoulders and he was led up to be slain like Isaac by his father. But Christ suffered, whereas Isaac did not suffer; for he was the model of the Christ who was going to suffer." Quoted in Robin Margaret Jensen, *Understanding Early Christian Art* (London and New York, 2000), p. 146.

13. See Sanders, *Paul,* pp. 78–79, for the background to this idea. It has to be remembered that sacrifices were important social rituals that probably served to legitimize the killing of domestic animals. To see them as unnecessary acts of cruelty, as implied in many Christian critiques of sacrifice, is wrong. Animals had to be killed somehow if the community was to survive, and it can certainly be argued that Greek attitudes to domesticated animals were more sensitive than Christian ones. Richard Sorabji, in an essay titled "Rationality" in M. Frede and G. Striker, eds., *Rationality in Greek Thought* (Oxford, 1996), pp. 328–30, cites the pagan philosopher Porphyry's taunt that Christ was not much of a saviour as he was quite happy to transfer demons into the Gadarene swine, which then galloped over a cliff to their deaths. This was not the issue, replied Augustine (*The City of God* 1:20): animals "did not belong within the community of just dealing"; and Christ was making the point that it was superstitious to refrain from killing animals. Augustine later went on to draw on Stoicism in order to argue that as animals lack a rational mind they have no rights and are subordinate to the needs of man. Augustine is cited by Thomas Aquinas in his own defence of the killing of animals. For the development of these ideas in a later historical context, see K. Thomas, *Man and the Natural World: Changing Attitudes in England, 1500–1800* (London, 1983). It was the Enlightenment that introduced the idea that animals have a "right" not to feel pain. (Some relevant quotes relating to this new approach, including one from Jeremy Bentham, are in Thomas, *Man and the Natural World,* pp. 179–80, while the works of Peter Singer should be addressed for a deeper understanding of the philosophical issues.)

14. Chaps. 6 and 7 of Sanders, *Paul,* provide a full discussion. The original Greek word for faith (*pistis*) can be translated as meaning both "firm assurance" and "that which gives firm assurance." Hebrews 11:1 gives a definition of faith which was to be particularly influential: "the assurance of things hoped for and the evidence of things unseen." A discussion of the various nuances of the word "faith" can be found in C. Stead, *Philosophy in Christian Antiquity* (Cambridge, 1994), pp. 110–13, and the complexities of the word are also explored by N. Wolterstorff in his article "Faith" in the *Routledge Encyclopaedia of Philosophy* (London and New York, 2000). Wolterstorff writes:

> Of what genus is faith a species? Is it a species of believing propositions on say-so? Is it a species of loyalty to some person or cause? Is it a species of trusting someone? Is it a species of believing what someone

has promised? Is it a species of "concern"? Is it a virtue of a certain sort? Is it a species of knowledge?

Enough has been said here to show that it will have different meanings in different contexts and therefore needs to be used with some caution.

15. Quoted in A. Cameron, *Christianity and the Rhetoric of Empire* (Berkeley and London, 1991), p. 28.

16. This is a passage used by those who argue that Paul did have some knowledge of Stoicism—the Stoics had put forward proofs for the existence of God and Paul appears to be assuming that they are valid ones; C. Stead, *Philosophy in Christian Antiquity*, pp. 115–16. Compare, for instance, Paul in Romans 1:19–20: "What can be known about God is plain to men for God has shown it to them. Ever since the creation of the world his invisible nature, namely his eternal power and deity, has been clearly perceived in the things that have been made," with the Stoic philosopher Lucillus quoted by Cicero in his *On the Nature of the Gods* 2, iii, c. 45 B.C.: "The point seems scarcely to need affirming. What can be so obvious and clear, as we gaze up at the sky and observe the heavenly bodies, as that there is some divine power of surpassing intelligence by which they are ordered?"

17. This statement is quoted in John Hick, "Interpretation and Reinterpretation in Religion," in S. Coakley and D. Pailin, eds., *The Making and Remaking of Christian Doctrine: Essays in Honour of Maurice Wiles* (Oxford, 1993). "The majority of human beings, most theologians agreed, do end up in hell, including, the Council of Florence (1439–45) insisted, all Jews, heretics, and schismatics unless they become Catholic before they die." This is from the entry on "hell" in A. Hastings, ed., *The Oxford Companion to Christian Thought* (New York and Oxford, 2000). This problem of inclusion versus exclusion is well dealt with in G. Stroumsa, *Barbarian Philosophy: The Religious Revolution of Early Christianity* (Tubingen, 1999), chap. 1, "Early Christianity as Radical Religion." On the debate over whether in Paul's letters all will be saved, see the section "Does Paul Believe All Human Beings Will Be Saved in the End?" in de Boer's article "Paul and Apocalyptic Eschatology," p. 371.

18. As J. D. Moores puts it, *Wrestling with Rationality*, p. 31, Paul's logic is "so wayward that we may wonder whether Paul is not just ironically exposing the irrelevance of logical argument."

19. Quoted in Robert Markus, *Gregory the Great and His World* (Cambridge, 1997), p. 38.

20. This may seem a sweeping statement, but it is hard to know where else the famous conflict originated. It is perhaps possible to take it back to Plato, but Paul's condemnation of logic and philosophy is so violent, his statements came to have such authority and the rejection of traditional philosophy, including science, is so marked in the Christian tradition that Paul is the obvious starting point. While Paul's concept of faith implies openness to God's revelation, the concept shifted and expanded as the institutional church and its hierarchy developed, so that having "faith" meant accepting "specific articles of faith" that had been "communicated to Christ and mediated through the church" (see the article on "faith" by Avery Dulles in Hastings, ed., *The Oxford Companion to Christian Thought*), an interpretation that consolidated the faithful as acceptors who were not required to question articles of faith for themselves. In fact, it was seen as a virtue that they did not. This shift, which is related to the growth of authority in the church, will be discussed further in the next chapter.

21. See Hans Belting, *Likeness and Presence: A History of the Image Before the*

*Era of Art,* trans. E. Jephcott (Chicago and London, 1994). This is a penetrating study of the art of icons and the contexts in which images were appreciated or abhorred. While early Christianity put a great deal of energy into distancing itself from Judaism, the Jewish rejection of idols continued to give Judaism some value among Christians. The theologian Origen, for instance, wrote in his *Contra Celsum* (V, 43): "The Jews do possess some deeper wisdom, not only more than the multitude, but also than those who seem to be philosophers, because the philosophers in spite of their impressive philosophical teachings fall down to idols and daemons, while even the lowest Jews look only to the supreme God."

22. The summary of the Jewish writer Josephus, quoted in chap. 10, "Behaviour," in Sanders, *Paul.*

23. One needs to get away from the idea that there was a sexual free-for-all in the Greek and Roman world before the coming of Christianity. See, as an introduction to this issue, M. Nussbaum, "Platonic Love and Colorado Love: The Relevance of Ancient Greek Norms to Modern Sexual Controversies," in R. B. Louden and P. Schollmeier, eds., *The Greeks and Us: Essays in Honor of Arthur W. H. Adkins* (Chicago and London, 1999), pp. 168–223. However, it is also clear that there was widespread sexual exploitation of women, particularly slaves by their owners and others. See also chap. 18, "Sex, Love and Marriage in Pagan Philosophy and the Use of Catharsis," in R. Sorabji, *Emotion and Peace of Mind: From Stoic Agitation to Christian Temptation* (Oxford, 2000).

24. For Paul's contribution to Christian views on sexuality, see P. Brown, *The Body and Society: Men, Women and Sexual Renunciation in Early Christianity* (New York, 1988; London, 1989), pp. 44–57.

25. G. Stroumsa, *Barbarian Philosophy,* especially chap. 1, "Early Christianity as Radical Religion"; the quotation comes from p. 25.

26. Few questions can be more complex than that of the relationship between emotion and will and the question of whether the self is divided (as Plato believed), which is why I hesitate in making too many generalizations here. (In *The Republic* 444 B, Plato talks of "the injustice, indiscipline . . . and vice of all kinds" that are the result of "internal quarrels" between the three parts of the soul.) It is a mark of the intellectual sophistication of ancient thought that the question was tackled in the depth it was, particularly by the Stoics. See, as a starter, chap. 20, "Emotional Conflict and the Divided Self" in Sorabji's important *Emotion and Peace of Mind.* In his chapters on Christianity (22 onwards), Sorabji shows how in a Christian context "bad thoughts" came to be seen as the intrusion of the devil. The question then became how one dealt with the thought—did one linger over it or enjoy it? If so, one had already committed sin. Compare Matthew 5:27: "if a man looks at a woman lustfully, he has already committed adultery with her in his heart." The possibility of committing evil when no outward sign of any evil action is apparent is an important component of the Christian conception of sin.

27. See Vermes, *The Changing Faces of Jesus,* pp. 68–69, for the view that Paul founded the Eucharist as a feature of Christian communal life, and Wayne Meeks, *The First Urban Christians* (New Haven and London, 1983), especially chap. 5, for the early practice of the Eucharist. For archaeological evidence for the early Christian communities in Anatolia, see Mitchell, *Anatolia,* vol. 2, chap. 16, part iv. As Mitchell states, p. 38, there is only one Christian inscription from Celtic Galatia (possibly not the main focus of Paul's activity) from before the fourth century. He sums up (p. 41): "It is interesting that the Asian communities with which Paul himself had been involved, for instance the churches in south Galatia, and at Laodicea and Colossae, by no means always prospered."

28. Quoted in Vermes, *The Changing Faces of Jesus,* p. 105.

29. Sanders, *Paul,* p. 2.

30. Quoted in K. Armstrong, *A History of God* (London, 1993), p. 115.

31. For an analysis of Marcion's thought, see Jaroslav Pelikan, *The Christian Tradition* (Chicago and London, 1971), vol. 1, pp. 71–81. It is important to stress the resilience of the Marcionites, as Marcion has been largely obliterated from the Christian tradition. If his approach to Christianity had been adopted, as it might well have been, and the "Old Testament" discarded, European culture would have been severely impoverished—but on the other hand, Christianity might have avoided the debilitating conflict with Judaism over "ownership" of the scriptures (see chap. 10) and been deprived, as Marcion hoped they would, of the model of a warlike and vengeful God that has been particularly influential at specific periods of Christian history. There would also not have been such backing for the destruction of idols, which was to include both pagan and, in the Reformation, Christian art. It was the Greek Septuagint, rather than the Hebrew Bible known to Jesus, which was adopted by Christians.

32. The argument has to be a complex one (one can as easily find statements in Matthew supporting the Gentiles), but it is the central thesis of D. Sim in his *The Gospel of Matthew and Christian Judaism* (Edinburgh, 1998), one he argues convincingly.

33. Quoted in Pelikan, *The Christian Tradition,* vol. 1, p. 24. Sim, in *The Gospel of Matthew,* leaves himself, of course, with the problem of fitting Matthew's community back into mainstream Christianity, as Christian Judaism withered and Gentile Christianity prevailed; see his chap. 7: "The Fate of the Matthean Community." Peter, too, has somehow to be transferred to the Gentile world. Luke achieves this through a message from God in which Peter is commanded to accept the Gentile Cornelius as a Christian and then persuades the other Apostles that the Church should be open to Gentiles (see Acts of the Apostles 10).

10

1. There is evidence from Lystra itself that these two gods were, in fact, worshipped together in the city, so the story is plausible. S. Mitchell gives a number of cases of the association between Zeus and Hermes in this very area. At Kavak in the territory of Lystra, a relief has been found showing Hermes accompanied by the eagle of Zeus, while in Lystra itself a stone has been found showing Hermes with a second god, arguably Zeus. A number of other examples have been found in Asia Minor, but, as Mitchell suggests, the concentration in the Lystra area is "highly suggestive and confirms the historical precision" of the episode. It is also interesting that Paul and Barnabas are acclaimed in the local language, Lycaonian (Acts 14:11), as Greek gods, an indication of the superficial adoption of Greek culture by the native peoples of the area. Mitchell goes on to suggest that Paul is referring to this same incident when, in Galatians 4:14, he reminds the Galatians that they welcomed him as "angel of God." S. Mitchell, *Anatolia: Land, Men, and Gods in Asia Minor,* vol. 2 (Oxford, 1993), p. 24.

2. See the article on the Gospel in B. Metzger and M. Coogan, eds., *The Oxford Companion to the Bible* (Oxford and New York, 1993), and J. Court and K. Court, *The New Testament World* (Cambridge, 1999), especially chap. 5, "John and the Community Apart." There has been much argument over whether John drew on the Synoptic Gospels or wrote independently of them. The scholarly consensus (in so

far as such a thing is possible in this area) at present seems to be that he did know of them. The other "signs" are Jesus' healing of an official at Capernaum, his cure of a cripple at the pool, the feeding of the five thousand, the walking on water, the giving of sight to the blind man and the raising of Lazarus.

3. The concept of a son from God the Father means something very different in a Greco-Roman context from what it means in a Jewish one. As G. Vermes puts it:

> In Hebrew or Aramaic "son of God" is always employed figuratively as a metaphor for a child of God, whereas in Greek addressed to Gentile Christians, grown up in a religious culture filled with gods, sons of gods and demigods, the New Testament expression tended to be understood literally as "Son of God," spelled as it were with a capital letter: that is to say, as someone as the same nature as God.

*The Changing Faces of Jesus* (London, 2000), p. 3. See also, from Vermes' book, pp. 32–34 on John's concept of "the Son" and pp. 183–85 on the Synoptic Gospels' approach to the concept. It is important to be aware of these conceptual shifts that took place as Jesus came to be seen through Greek rather than Jewish eyes. The relationship between Christ and the *logos* was, of course, a complex one, as *logos* had so many different meanings. On the other hand, as Jaroslav Pelikan has noted, the diversity of meanings could allow the word to be used creatively as a principle of creation, rationality, of speech ("the Word") and of revelation. It could also be used to give philosophical respectability to the Son of God, whom pagans such as Celsus were to deride as degraded by his crucifixion. In some instances the *logos* was even described as an angel, that is, taking on a "Christian" role totally independent of the Platonic tradition. See J. Pelikan, *The Christian Tradition,* vol. 1 (Chicago and London, 1971), pp. 188–89 and pp. 197–98, for the relationship between the *logos* and angels. The great issue of later centuries was that of how the divine *logos* could suffer on the cross.

4. I have deliberately not used the term "anti-Semitism," as it was coined in the nineteenth century in a specific racist context. Opposition to Judaism was in this period rooted in theology, not race. The whole question of anti-Judaism/anti-Semitism and Christianity is enormously contentious, particularly in light of the Holocaust. With Christianity's roots so deeply embedded in Judaism and Jesus himself a Jew, the development of Christianity as a religious movement separate from Judaism was bound to be difficult. It was inevitable that Christians would draw and defend boundaries between themselves and orthodox Jews, and that Jews would do the same to a religion which rejected their Law: witness the many lashings administered to Paul. The process of disentangling Christianity from this past has been a tortuous one and continues to this day. I have drawn heavily here on M. Taylor, *Anti-Judaism and Early Christian Identity* (Leiden and New York, 1995); the quotations all come from chap. 4, "Symbolic Anti-Judaism." Taylor in her turn pays respect to R. Ruether's *Faith and Fratricide: The Theological Roots of Anti-Semitism* (New York, 1974). For an excellent overview of the issues involved, see G. Stroumsa, *Barbarian Philosophy: The Religious Revolution of Early Christianity* (Tubingen, 1999), chap. 8, "From Anti-Judaism to Anti-Semitism in Early Christianity?"

5. Quoted in M. Beard, J. North and S. Price, *Religions of Rome* (Cambridge, 1998), vol. 1, p. 267.

6. R. MacMullen, *Christianising the Roman Empire* (A.D. *100–400*) (New Haven and London, 1984), p. 34.

7. Ibid., p. 37.

8. Ibid., p. 111.

9. Stephen Mitchell in his study of Asia Minor, *Anatolia*, pp. 37–38, notes only a handful of Christian inscriptions from Pontus and Bithynia (an area described by Pliny in A.D. 110 as having many Christians) from before Constantine's toleration and, interestingly in view of Paul's mission, only one in Galatia. There are rather more from Phrygia, the home of the Montanists, for whom see further below. A good example of the kind of story told about Christians by outsiders is to be found in the *Octavius* of Minucius Felix (third century). Christians

> come from the lowest ranks of the people . . . ignorant and gullible women who indeed, just because of the weakness of their sex, are easily persuaded . . . [These] bands of conspirators [*sic*] . . . fraternise in nocturnal assemblies and at solemn fasts and barbarous feasts, not through a holy ceremony, but through an unatonable crime . . .
> Everywhere they also practise among themselves, so to speak, a kind of cult of sensuality; without distinction they call each other brother and sister, and through this holy name even the usual immorality becomes incest . . . In a darkness that is favourable to shamelessness they are consumed by unspeakable passion, as determined by chance . . .

Quoted in E. W. Stegemann and W. Stegemann, *The Jesus Movement: A Social History of the First Century* (Edinburgh, 1999), pp. 405–6.

10. A full extract from Celsus is provided by MacMullen, *Christianising the Roman Empire*, p. 37. As an introduction to women in the early church, see the chapter "Women in Urban Christian Communities" in Stegemann and Stegemann, *The Jesus Movement*. The authors see the originally extensive involvement of women in the early Christian communities as having been eclipsed as traditional Greco-Roman attitudes reasserted themselves.

11. P. Brown, "Asceticism: Pagan and Christian," chap. 20 in A. Cameron and P. Garnsey, eds., *The Cambridge Ancient History*, vol. XIII (Cambridge, 1998), p. 610. The idea of the bride of Christ proves a strong one, and in his Letter XXII Jerome goes so far as to say that one of the benefits of virginity for Eustochium will be that Christ will put his hand through an opening in the wall of her bedchamber and "caress her belly." Note too the famous sculpture of Teresa of Avila by Bernini in the church of Santa Maria della Vittoria in Rome, where the saint is shown in marble in the act of surrendering herself, some would say sexually, to Christ (the moment draws on extracts from her diary).

12. P. Brown, *The Body and Society: Men, Women and Sexual Renunciation in Early Christianity* (New York, 1988; London, 1989), pp. 78–79. See also G. Stroumsa, *Barbarian Philosophy*, chap. 6, "Tertullian on Idolatry and the Limits of Tolerance."

13. Beard, North and Price, *Religions of Rome*, pp. 295–96.

14. This preference for oral tradition and debate appears strange to the modern world. Plato, however, had made the point that a written word is static. "If you ask them [written words] anything about what they say, from a wish to know more, they go on telling you the same thing over and over again forever." In other words, an intellectual *debate* cannot be carried on with the written word. This is perhaps the point to be recognized here. In *The Tyrant's Writ* (Princeton, 1993), Deborah Steiner stresses how the written word often stood for authority in the ancient world,

perhaps a point of interest in this context. One of the early Christian Platonists, Clement of Alexandria, appears to have been heavily influenced by this aspect of Plato's ideas and to have shown "considerable reluctance" to write anything down. In the opinion of Raoul Mortley, his decision to write down his thoughts "marks the beginning of the Christian commitment to documentary history" (Mortley, *From Word to Silence* [Bonn, 1986], vol. 2, p. 39). The shift from debating Christian doctrine orally to a consideration of it through the comparison of written statements is discussed by R. Lim, *Public Disputation, Power, and Social Order in Late Antiquity* (Berkeley and London, 1995). See also Robin Lane Fox, "Literacy and Power in Early Christianity," chap. 9 in A. Bowman and G. Woolf, eds., *Literacy and Power in the Ancient World* (Cambridge, 1994).

A reminder of how many oral traditions about Jesus and his family must have disappeared can be found through the art that survives. See D. Cartlidge and J. K. Elliott, *Art and the Christian Apocrypha* (London and New York, 2001).

15. Augustine, *Ennarrationes in Psalmos*, 59:1. The methods used to interpret the Bible form an enormous subject. See, however, as an introduction, the relevant chapters in J. Rogerson, ed., *The Oxford Illustrated History of the Bible* (Oxford, 2001), and in P. R. Ackroyd and C. F. Evans, eds., *The Cambridge History of the Bible*, vol. 1 (Cambridge, 1979); the article "Interpretation, History of," in Metzger and Coogan, eds., *The Oxford Companion to the Bible*; and Stroumsa, *The Barbarian Philosophy*, chap. 2, "The Christian Hermeneutical Revolution and Its Double Helix." It was assumed by the Christian exegetes that the mind of God remained unchanged and that he knew from the earliest book in the Bible that Christ would appear on the earth. It was also assumed that the Bible, despite the variety of texts, had an inner consistency. Once this was accepted, it was "only" a matter of spotting the relevant references. One method is termed "typology," which consists of making a direct link between a happening or symbol in the Old Testament and an equivalent in the New. So the story of Noah's ark is seen as a "type" for baptism, and any wood as a "type" for the cross. More sweeping is allegory, used extensively by Origen and Augustine. It involves what often appears to be quite arbitrary linking of any person, event or object in the Old Testament to objects in the New and the use of imagination to find symbolic meaning within almost any verse of the Bible.

16. In the "Epilogue" to B. Pearson, ed., *The Future of Early Christianity: Essays in Honor of Helmut Koester* (Minneapolis, 1991), p. 472. See H. Koester, *Ancient Christian Gospels: Their History and Development* (London, 1999), for his views on the importance of integrating what survives of the "apocryphal" Gospels with the canonical Gospels.

17. See Metzger and Coogan, eds., *The Oxford Companion to the Bible*, p. 103. The Montanists are covered in Pelikan, *The Christian Tradition*, vol. 1, pp. 97–108. It was Hippolytus of Rome, a contemporary of Tertullian, who put forward the idea that direct prophecy had ceased with John. The Book of Revelation was and remains part of the New Testament to this day. D. H. Lawrence, however, saw it as "the Judias Iscariot of the New Testament," and it remains an uneasy amalgam of extravagant terminology and wild imagery. It has had its uses within the church, however. Its description of the heavenly Jerusalem as a city of precious stones allowed it to be used to support the opulence of church building in the fourth century; see further p. 207. More positively, Richard Bauckham has commented that, despite modern readers finding it "baffling and impenetrable . . . yet this is a book that in all centuries has inspired the martyrs, nourished the imagination of visionaries, artists, and hymn writers, resourced prophetic critiques of oppression

and corruption in state and church, sustained hope and resistance in the most hopeless situations." From the introduction to "Revelation" in J. Barton and J. Muddiman, eds., *The Oxford Bible Commentary* (Oxford, 2001), p. 1287.

Direct revelations, especially through the Virgin Mary, continue to be reported and, in some cases (Lourdes and Fatima), accepted as valid by the Catholic Church. Pope John Paul announced in 2000 that the famous third secret of Fatima, for long known only to the popes, had in fact contained a warning from the Virgin Mary of his attempted assassination. The problem here is how to recognize the continuing activities of the Holy Spirit. Is it conceptually possible for the Holy Spirit to make a revelation that conflicts with Christian orthodoxy, or is the validity of any revelation to be recognized because it reinforces orthodoxy?

18. Jaroslav Pelikan, one of the shrewdest commentators on the evolution of Christian doctrine, surveys the different meanings of salvation in early Christianity in *The Christian Tradition*, vol. 1, pp. 141–55.

19. The quotation from Irenaeus is taken from H. Bettenson, ed., *Documents of the Christian Church* (Oxford, 1943), p. 99. That of Tertullian, from his *Praescriptio Haereticorum* 19:2, is quoted in J. Rives, *Religion and Authority in Roman Carthage from Augustus to Constantine* (Oxford, 1995), p. 278. Rives has much of importance to say about church authority in that chapter. The notion of apostolic succession was crucial for the church as it gave a means by which the authority of the church could be passed on from bishop to bishop. For a full discussion, see Pelikan, *The Christian Tradition*, vol. 1, pp. 108–20.

20. Cyprian, *De Unitate* 17.428. An excellent discussion of Cyprian's views on authority can be found in Rives, *Religion and Authority,* pp. 285–307, from which the quotation and material for the next paragraph is drawn. It is interesting to note that the need to impose authority in terms comprehensible to north African Christians threatened to eclipse the reality of a Jesus executed as a rebel *against* Roman authority.

21. Jaroslav Pelikan sums up the approach of Eusebius as follows: "According to the Ecclesiastical History of Eusebius, orthodox Christian doctrine did not really have a history, having been true eternally and taught primitively; only heresy has a history, having arisen at particular times and through the innovation of particular teachers" (in *The Christian Tradition,* vol. 1, pp. 7–8). Eusebius' view that orthodoxy was established early in church history and simply had to defend itself against the onslaughts of heretics has been particularly influential in the Roman Catholic tradition and still conditions many histories of the Church. However, as Pelikan shows throughout his study, it was diversity rather than uniformity that marked the early development of Christian doctrine.

22. MacMullen, *Christianising the Roman Empire,* deals with conversion and John's prayers at Ephesus; see p. 40 for his discussion of the demons.

23. Ibid., p. 112. Exorcism has not wholly died out within Christianity in that both the Catholic and the Anglican Churches still have rites of exorcism and even specially appointed exorcists to drive out "demons."

24. Quoted ibid., p. 37. Celsus contrasted pagans, who could be accepted into their mysteries if they had "pure hands and wise tongues," with Christians, for whom sinfulness seemed to be a prerequisite for entry to theirs.

25. See L. Alexander, "Paul and the Hellenistic Schools: The Evidence of Galen," in Troels Engbury-Pedersen, ed., *Paul in His Hellenistic Context* (Edinburgh, 1994). The third-century theologian Origen taught that the "simpleminded" Christians should be told that the resurrection was a literal resurrection of Jesus'

body (while he and other more sophisticated Christians could see it in a more symbolic sense); see chap. 8, note 19 above.

26. Bettenson, *Documents of the Christian Church,* p. 9, for the quote from Clement. The quote from Augustine comes from *De Doctrina Christiana* 2:144.

27. MacMullen, *Christianising the Roman Empire,* p. 32.

28. C. Stead, *Philosophy in Christian Antiquity* (Cambridge, 1994), p. 14. There is a vast amount of material on the relationship between Platonism and Christianity. Did Platonism corrupt an original "pure" Christianity or was it the "nurse" without which it would not have survived as a respectable participant in a highly competitive intellectual world? No easy answers are to be found in what has been a celebrated debate. A useful overview, with reading list, can be found in A. Le Boullec, "Hellenism and Christianity," in J. Brunschwig and G. E. R. Lloyd, eds., *Greek Thought: A Guide to Classical Knowledge* (Cambridge, Mass., and London, 2000).

29. Definitions of these "heresies" and alternative interpretations can be found in F. L. Cross and E. A. Livingstone, eds., *The Oxford Dictionary of the Christian Church,* 3rd ed. (Oxford, 1997). The Sabellians used the sun as an analogy. God the Father, the Son and the Holy Spirit are the equivalent of the heat, light and what Sabellius called "the astrological energy" of the sun, in other words different manifestations of the same essence.

30. See the article "Soul" in A. D. Fitzgerald, ed., *Augustine Through the Ages* (Grand Rapids, Mich., and Cambridge, 1999), and Kallistos Ware, "The Soul in Greek Christianity," in M. James and C. Crabbe, eds., *From Soul to Self* (London and New York, 1999), p. 53. Thomas Aquinas was to talk of the "ensouled body," deliberately turning his back on Plato's conception (see chap. 20 of this book). The mind/body debate so beloved of philosophers is tied in with all this.

31. An interesting example is the Song of Solomon, which most would read at face value and without qualms as a mildly erotic love poem. However, the Church Fathers were deeply troubled by any hint of sexuality, and Origen interpreted the Song as an allegory of God's relations with the individual soul, an approach that removed the sexual "danger" implicit in a straightforward reading of it. The "allegorical" approach to biblical interpretation taken by Origen was followed by Jerome and Augustine.

32. The first quotation is taken from Origen's *Contra Celsum* 4:99. The second is from J. Clark Smith, *The Ancient Wisdom of Origen* (London and Toronto, 1992), p. 52. There is an echo here of Homer's depiction of the gods returning all to how it used to be; see chap. 2, note 7 above.

33. From Pindar, *Nemean Ode 6,* trans. R. Buxton.

34. See the individual entries for the early popes in J. Kelly, *The Oxford Dictionary of the Popes* (Oxford, 1986). A good study of the psychology and impact of martyrdom is to be found in R. Lane Fox, *Pagans and Christians* (London, 1986), chap. 9. I wonder whether an analogy might be made between the memory of martyrdoms and the memory of the Holocaust, both of which seem to have intensified rather than diminished through time.

35. R. Stark, in his *The Rise of Christianity* (Princeton, 1996), makes some calculations in chap. 1. His estimate of the Christian population for A.D. 274 is 4.2 percent for the whole empire, and he compares this with evidence from Egypt, a more heavily Christianized part of the empire, that suggests that just over 10 percent of the population there were Christian by this date. Whether these figures mean anything is open to doubt. There was no clear definition of what it meant to be a

Christian in the third century, and, as has been seen, many religious movements included Christ among their spiritual leaders, so it is hard to see how any valid calculations could be made. Again, one has only to read of the mass rejection of their faith by Christians at times of persecution in north Africa to realize how fluid a conception "being a Christian" was. See also K. Hopkins, "Christian Number and Its Implication," *Journal of Early Christian Studies* 6 (1998): 185–226.

36. MacMullen, *Christianising the Roman Empire,* p. 40. A useful account of the growth of Christianity in Asia Minor in this period is to be found in Mitchell's study *Anatolia,* vol. 2, chaps. 16 (pp. 37–42) and 17. Mitchell suggests that Phrygia was perhaps the most highly Christianized part of the empire by 300, but he emphasizes that while some communities in the province were heavily Christian, others were still largely pagan. As he puts it, a map of cities highlighting those that were Christian would "resemble an irregular patchwork quilt, not a simple monochrome blanket" (p. 63).

<h1 style="text-align:center">11</h1>

1. Quoted in R. MacMullen, *Christianity and Paganism in the Fourth to Eighth Centuries* (New Haven and London, 1997), p. 130. See the new edition of *Eusebius: Life of Constantine,* trans. with introduction and commentary by A. Cameron and S. Hall (Oxford, 1999), and pp. 27–48 of the editors' introduction in particular for an assessment of the work in literary terms.

2. H. A. Drake, "Constantine and Consensus," *Church History* 64 (1995): 7. Drake has now expanded his argument in *Constantine and the Bishops: The Politics of Intolerance* (Baltimore and London, 2000).

3. For a survey of Constantine's life, see H. Pohlsander, *Constantine the Emperor* (London, 1997); the chapters on Constantine in A. Cameron, *The Later Roman Empire* (London, 1993); and D. Bowder, *The Age of Constantine and Julian* (London, 1978).

4. S. MacCormack, *Art and Ceremony in Late Antiquity* (Berkeley and London, 1981), p. 108.

5. Ibid., pp. 106–15, for Constantine's definition of his own legitimacy.

6. Cameron and Hall, eds., *Life of Constantine,* 1:28–32.

7. Ibid., 1:27. See J. W. Liebeschuetz, *Continuity and Change in Roman Religion* (Oxford, 1979), pp. 278–80, for comment.

8. H. A. Drake, *Constantine and the Bishops: The Politics of Intolerance* (Baltimore and London, 2000).

9. The decree is given in full in N. Lewis and M. Reinhold, *Roman Civilization, Sourcebook II: The Empire* (New York, 1995), pp. 602–4, from which this translation is taken. Drake, *Constantine and the Bishops,* p. 195, stresses the importance of the edict in proclaiming freedom of worship, and on p. 249 he quotes the pagan orator Themistius (second half of the fourth century) addressing the emperor Valens as follows:

> The law of God and your law remains unchanged for ever—that the mind of each and every man should be free to follow the way of worship which it thinks [to be best]. This is a law against which no confiscation, no crucifixion, no death at the stake has ever availed; you may hale and kill the body, if so be that this comes to pass; but the mind will escape

you, taking with it freedom of thought and the right of the law as it goes, even if it is subject to force in the language used by the tongue.

10. For the arch, see Bowder, *The Age of Constantine and Julian,* pp. 24–28, and A. Claridge, *Rome: An Oxford Archaeological Guide* (Oxford and New York, 1998), pp. 272–76.

11. Liebeschuetz, *Continuity and Change,* pp. 283–84.

12. P. Chuvin, *A Chronicle of the Last Pagans* (Cambridge, Mass., and London, 1990), p. 125. There is also the prayer of St. Francis: "Praise be to you, oh God my Lord, and to all your creatures, and above all to their great brother the sun, who brings the day and illumines with his light; and he is beautiful and brilliantly radiant; he is the symbol of you, oh Lord."

13. Liebeschuetz, *Continuity and Change,* p. 300. In *Life of Constantine* 2:48, Eusebius quotes a decree that Constantine sent out to the eastern provinces which, in its insistence on the natural order of things, suggests a Stoic influence. It begins:

> Everything embraced by the sovereign laws of nature provides everybody with sufficient evidence of the providence and thoughtfulness of the divine ordering; nor is there any doubt among those whose intellect approaches that topic by a correct scientific method, that accurate apprehension by a healthy mind and by sight itself rise in a single impulse of true virtue to the true knowledge of God.

Compare chap. 9, note 16, above.

14. Quoted in M. Beard, J. North and S. Price, *Religions of Rome* (Cambridge, 1998), vol. 1, p. 367.

15. Ibid., p. 370.

16. Drake, *Constantine and the Bishops,* p. 230, makes this important point. For the elimination of the Donatists, see chap. 18.

17. Cameron and Hall, eds., *Life of Constantine* 3:4. The quotation from Constantine's address is from Drake, *Constantine and the Bishops,* p. 4. One dispute between rival bishops in Ancyra in Galatia was described (to a synod of bishops meeting in Africa in 343) as follows:

> Houses were burned down and all manner of fighting broke out. Priests were dragged naked to the forum by the bishop himself . . . he profaned the sacred Host of the Lord by hanging it openly and in public from the necks of priests, and with horrendous barbarity tore the vestments from holy virgins dedicated to God and Christ, and displayed them naked before the public in the forum, in the middle of the city.

18. See R. Hanson, *The Search for the Christian Doctrine of God* (Edinburgh, 1988); M. Wiles, *Archetypal Heresy: Arianism Through the Centuries* (Oxford, 1996); and D. Williams, *Ambrose of Milan and the End of Nicene-Arian Conflicts* (Oxford, 1995), for recent surveys of the issues and of traditional historiography. There is also an excellent survey of the controversy as it took place over the fourth century in R. Vaggione, *Eunomius of Cyzicus and the Nicene Revolution* (Oxford, 2000). Eunomius was the most articulate defender of the extreme Arian position that the Father and the Son are to be seen as dissimilar to each other.

19. Quotation from Wiles, *Archetypal Heresy,* p. 9.

20. The examples come from ibid., chap. 1.

21. Ibid., p. 17.

22. R. Hanson, "The Achievement of the Orthodoxy in the Fourth Century A.D.," in R. Williams, ed., *The Making of Orthodoxy: Essays in Honour of Henry Chadwick* (Cambridge, 1989), p. 153. J. Pelikan notes four different approaches to the Christ as God debate, all of which could draw on scriptural backing: (1) Christ was born a man but became divine either at his baptism or at his resurrection. (2) Christ was fully God from eternity and to be equated with the Yahweh of the Old Testament. (3) There were two distinct "Lords," God and Jesus. (4) There was a Father who had a son, who is referred to in the scriptures as variously Son, Spirit, the *logos,* even an angel, but always in a context that suggested he was subordinate to the Father. (See Pelikan's *The Christian Tradition,* vol. 1: *The Emergence of the Catholic Tradition (100–600)* [Chicago and London, 1971], p. 175.) This simply underlines one of the major problems in Christian doctrine. Everyone felt that scriptural backing was important, but the sheer diversity of texts meant that almost any formulation of doctrine could find support from one text or another. It is hardly surprising that the church had eventually to assume absolute authority over the interpretation of scripture, a development that had the effect, of course, of stifling debate.

23. See the article on Arianism by R. Williams in E. Ferguson, ed., *Encyclopaedia of Early Christianity* (Chicago and London, 1990), p. 85.

24. Again see ibid. for some of the variations of Arianism.

25. Quoted in Drake, *Constantine and the Bishops,* p. 240.

26. Cameron and Hall, eds., *Life of Constantine* 3:10. See also Bowder, *The Age of Constantine and Julian,* p. 70, and R. Hanson, *The Search for the Christian Doctrine of God* (Edinburgh, 1988), chap. 6.

27. Drake, *Constantine and the Bishops,* p. 253, note 2.

28. Hanson, *The Search for the Christian Doctrine of God,* looks at the evidence on pp. 190–202. There is also an excellent account in C. Stead, *Philosophy in Christian Antiquity* (Cambridge, 1994), chap. 14, "Unity of Substance."

29. See Stead, *Philosophy in Christian Antiquity,* p. 169, for this idea. As H. Chadwick notes in his "Orthodoxy and Heresy," in A. Cameron and P. Garnsey, eds., *The Cambridge Ancient History,* vol. XIII (Cambridge, 1998), p. 573, "the epithet *homoousios* was an ordinary term in Plotinus' vocabulary." The response of the Cappadocian Fathers to *homoousios* as a term is discussed by J. Pelikan, *Christianity and Classical Culture* (New Haven and London, 1993), p. 43.

30. Kee, *Constantine Versus Christ* (London, 1982), p. 15.

31. Hanson, *The Search for Christian Doctrine of God,* deals with Eusebius' letter on pp. 163–66. Hanson's analysis of the terminology is invaluable.

32. Pelikan, *The Christian Tradition,* vol. 1, p. 203.

33. Once again Hanson's analysis of the twists and turns in the attempt to accommodate the council's creed (*The Search for Christian Doctrine of God,* chap. 10) is masterly. See D. Williams, *Ambrose of Milan,* p. 16, for Ossius and Serdica. The full text of the western bishops' statement at Serdica is given in Hanson at pp. 301–2. As Hanson makes clear (p. 303), Ossius was not at home with Greek philosophy and the statement is "confused."

34. D. Williams, *Ambrose of Milan,* p. 15. Vaggione, *Eunomius of Cyzicus,* notes on p. 151: "Over the next fifteen years [from the death of Constantine in 337] the Creed of Nicaea was more ignored than opposed, even by those who were later considered 'Nicene.' During this period, public ecclesiastical loyalty tended to be expressed in terms of political and theological loyalty to specific bishops." Vaggione goes on to argue that accounts of the controversy written from hindsight in the

following century, by which time the Nicene Creed was enshrined as orthodoxy, tended to describe the leading figures of the period in terms of their allegiance, or otherwise, to the Nicene Creed even though no defined parties emerged until the 350s.

35. See Drake, *Constantine and the Bishops,* chap. 8, "Controlling the Message." Drake shows how Constantine used texts from the Bible to isolate the more intransigent of the Christians from the majority, whom he wished to keep on his side.

36. Liebeschuetz, *Continuity and Change,* p. 281.

37. In Cameron and Hall, eds., *Eusebius,* the editors state that the sources for the assertion that he did "are tendentious: the extent to which Constantine did attempt to suppress pagan worship [including sacrifice] is therefore disputed." They go on to provide references to recent articles on the issue (pp. 319–20). If Drake's thesis is accepted, it is unlikely that Constantine felt strongly about the issue, but it should be noted that by now many sophisticated pagans had themselves rejected sacrifices.

38. D. Bowder, *The Age of Constantine and Julian,* p. 33. For Constantine's legislation see A. Cameron, *The Later Roman Empire* (London, 1993), p. 58. The influential legend that Helena found "the True Cross" in the Holy Land appears only much later, for the first time in 395, when it was mentioned in an oration by Ambrose, bishop of Milan. It is not mentioned in Eusebius' biography, an omission which suggests that it is a later development in Christian mythology. Despite this later date, Helena's "finding of the True Cross" has proved to be one of the most influential of Christian legends, and even recently it has been argued that the *titulus,* the board bearing the inscription "Jesus of Nazareth, King of the Jews," from the cross survives in the church of Santa Croce in Gerusalemme in Rome (Matthew D'Ancona and Carsten Peter Thiede, *The Quest for the True Cross* [London, 2000]). In view of the embarrassment and shame Christ's crucifixion caused to his followers, it seems highly unlikely that they would have preserved the cross. It is also worth mentioning that another complete "True Cross" is recorded in Jerusalem in the seventh century. It was looted from there by the Persians but returned to the city by the Byzantine emperor Heraclius in 630.

39. For Constantinople, see the relevant chapters in R. Krautheimer, *Three Christian Capitals* (Berkeley, 1983), and Christopher Kelly, "Empire Building," in G. W. Bowersock, P. Brown and O. Grabar, eds., *Late Antiquity: A Guide to the Postclassical World* (Cambridge, Mass., and London, 1999).

40. Cameron and Hall, eds., *Life of Constantine* 3:48 for Constantinople as a Christian capital. For the pagan statues, see ibid., 3:54, and the comments on the passage made by the editors on pp. 301–3. Later (tolerant) attitudes to pagan art in Constantinople are discussed in C. Mango, "Antique Statuary and the Byzantine Beholder," *Dumbarton Oaks Papers,* no. 17 (1963): 55–75. The same point could be made of Constantine's activities in Rome, as it was by the anti-clerical Italian aristocrat Count Leopoldo Cicognera in his history of sculpture (Venice, 1813–18):

> The same hand that raised so many basilicas to the true God was also generous in beautifying and restoring the temples of the gods in Rome; and the medals that were issued in his imperial mint carried the images and attributes of Jupiter, Apollo, Mars and Hercules, while through the apotheosis of his father Constantius he added a new deity to Mount Olympus.

41. See C. Kelly, in Bowersock, Brown and Grabar, eds., *Late Antiquity,* for details of the ceremony of dedication and the building of the city. A story was told by

later Byzantine writers that hidden underneath the column was an ancient statue of Pallas Athene, which had been taken to Rome by Aeneas after the sack of Troy and then secretly brought on by Constantine for his new city.

42. See my *The Horses of St. Mark's in European History* (forthcoming, London, 2004), where it is argued that it was the set of horses associated in later sources with Constantine's golden chariot that were the ones selected by the Venetian Doge Enrico Dandolo for Venice after the sack of Constantinople by the Venetians in 1204.

43. Cameron and Hall, eds., *Life of Constantine* 3:49. In her book *Divine Heiress: The Virgin Mary and the Creation of Christian Constantinople* (London and New York, 1994), Vasiliki Limberis argues that Constantine was deliberately setting out "to make Christianity a Greco-Roman civic religion" (p. 27). He could do this because his new foundation had no pre-existing Christian community with which he had to compromise, so he was able to create his own ceremonies without opposition.

44. Cameron and Hall, eds., *Life of Constantine* 4:24.

45. MacCormack, *Art and Ceremony,* p. 122, with her illustrations nos. 33 and 34.

46. Cameron and Hall, eds., *Life of Constantine* 1:6.

47. *New Catholic Encyclopaedia* (Washington D.C., 1967), entry on "Conscientious Objection." The comparison with the pre-Constantine period makes the point. There were those such as Marcellus the Centurion who refused to fight for the state. He threw off his arms and proclaimed to his superiors that "a Christian who is in the service of the Lord Christ should not serve the affairs of this world." As a result he was made a saint (see entry for Marcellus in D. Farmer, *The Oxford Dictionary of the Saints,* 4th ed. [Oxford, 1997]). The adoption of Christianity by the state made this approach impossible. For the Sala di Constantino, see the description in Loren Partridge, *The Renaissance in Rome* (London, 1996), p. 152.

48. The quotation comes from *De Fide* 2:16. It appears to have been written about the time of the devastating Roman defeat at Adrianople in 378. A common Christian symbol from the fourth century onward was a chi-ro placed above a cross, a composition adapted from a Roman cavalry standard. In later centuries, there was a relative lack of inhibition as regards Christians fighting wars (despite a doctrine of the conditions for "a just war" elaborated by Thomas Aquinas). Augustine had argued that a soldier who killed in war was not guilty of sin so long as he acted under the orders of a recognized authority, even if that authority or the war itself was unjust (see C. Harrison, *Augustine: Christian Truth and Fractured Humanity* [Oxford, 2000], p. 291), and in practice the doctrine of "a just war" proved elastic as the number of cases where both Christian sides to a conflict have relied on it shows. As an example of the lack of inhibition, one can take the outspoken remarks of A. F. Winnington-Ingram, bishop of London, during the First World War, a war fought between Christian nations. The war was, he proclaimed, "a great crusade to kill Germans, to kill them not for the sake of killing but to save the world; to kill the good as well as the bad, to kill the young as well as the old . . . ," and on a later occasion he called the war ". . . a war for purity, for freedom, for international honour and for the principles of Christianity . . . everyone who dies in it is a martyr." Quoted in N. Ferguson, *The Pity of War* (London, 1998), pp. 208–9. There is, of course, a deep-rooted Christian pacifist tradition, but the point made here can be underlined by realizing how impossible it would be for an Anglican bishop of the period to have argued, for instance, for a less rigorous approach to the ethics of sexuality. There is much to reflect on here, but a knowledge of why Christianity and

war became so closely linked in Constantine's reign and those of his successors does help clarify matters. Christianity is not easily separated from the specific historical circumstances in which it developed, but at least these circumstances can be recognized.

12

1. Statement to a church council of 355 attributed to Constantius II, quoted in R. Hanson, *The Search for the Christian Doctrine of God* (Edinburgh, 1988), p. 849.

2. For the background to the politics of this period, see D. Hunt, "The Successors of Constantine," chap. 1 in Averil Cameron and Peter Garnsey, eds., *The Cambridge Ancient History,* vol. XIII (Cambridge, 1998).

3. See Hanson, *The Search for the Christian Doctrine of God,* p. 166. I have drawn heavily on Hanson's book for this chapter, as it provides the fullest account of the tortuous process by which an orthodoxy was eventually established. This again is an area where there has been some major rethinking in recent years. The traditional account is, as already mentioned in the previous chapter, that Nicaea affirmed traditional teaching, then "evil-minded" Arians (the term was often extended to include the Homoeans, who were termed "semi-Arians") attempted to subvert orthodoxy until Theodosius triumphantly saw off the "heretics" at the end of the century. Discovering what really happened is particularly difficult for two reasons: (a) Christian history was effectively rewritten from the Nicene point of view, so that many texts supporting the alternative positions have been lost, and (b) there is very little evidence to show how the western view of the single Godhead evolved. See D. Williams, *Ambrose of Milan and the End of Nicene–Arian Conflicts* (Oxford, 1995), for the problems. As Williams suggests, it is very difficult to trace the revival or adoption of Nicene thought in the west, especially as there was virtually no western representation at Nicaea itself. Certainly the fight over the issue was as much a political as a theological one, and, in different circumstances, the question might have been left open or an alternative formulation adopted.

4. See H. Chadwick, chap. 19, "Orthodoxy and Heresy from the Death of Constantine to the Eve of the First Council of Ephesus," in Cameron and Garnsey, eds., *The Cambridge Ancient History,* vol. XIII, and generally Hanson, *The Search for the Christian Doctrine of God.*

5. C. Stead, *Philosophy in Christian Antiquity* (Cambridge, 1994), p. 160.

6. Williams, *Ambrose of Milan,* p. 136.

7. Ibid., p. 19.

8. Chadwick, "Orthodoxy and Heresy," p. 572.

9. M. Wiles, *Archetypal Heresy: Arianism Through the Centuries* (Oxford, 1996), p. 28.

10. Quoted in Hanson, *The Search for the Christian Doctrine of God,* pp. 363–64.

11. See ibid., chap. 12, and Williams, *Ambrose of Milan,* chap. 1. The two councils between them attracted some 600 bishops, twice as many as Nicaea and four times as many as the Council of Constantinople of 381. The pagan historian Ammianus Marcellinus (*The Later Roman Empire* xxi, 16) memorably described the process by which the bishops gathered: "Public transport hurried throngs of bishops hither and thither to attend what they call synods, and by his attempts to impose conformity, Constantius only succeeded in hamstringing the postal service."

12. See Williams, *Ambrose of Milan,* p. 27. Why they changed their minds is

not clear. One report (by a pro-Nicene) suggested it was because they were "of weak character" but also "because of weariness of being threatened with expulsion into foreign lands." In other words, the message from the east must have been that they would lose their sees if they did not accept the Dated Creed.

13. For short introductions to Julian, see D. Hunt, "Julian," chap. 2 in Cameron and Garnsey, eds., *The Cambridge Ancient History*, vol. XIII, and the chapter "Julian the Apostate," by M. B. Simmons, in P. Esler, ed., *The Early Christian World*, vol. 2 (New York and London, 2000). Julian is one of the most complex of the Roman emperors, and he has aroused approval and hostility in equal measure ever since his reign. R. Smith, *Julian's Gods: Religion and Philosophy in the Thought and Action of Julian the Apostate* (London and New York, 1995), is a useful survey of the difficulties in coming to a fair assessment of him.

14. Ammianus Marcellinus, *The Later Roman Empire* xxii, 5.

15. "He turned to paganism with the zeal of the convert," as G. W. Bowersock puts it in his *Hellenism in Late Antiquity* (Ann Arbor, 1990), p. 6.

16. See Smith, *Julian's Gods*, for a full and balanced discussion of Julian's ideas. Smith (p. 183) quotes the pagan orator Libanius on Julian's "conversion."

> And upon your arrival in Ionia you encountered a wise man, you heard of those who fashioned and maintained the universe, you gazed upon the beauty of philosophy and tasted its sweetest springs. Then you quickly threw aside your error [Christianity], released yourself from darkness and grasped truth instead of ignorance, reality in place of falsehood, our old gods in place of that wicked one and his rites.

*Contra Galilaeos* is available in the Loeb Classics (*Works of Julian,* vol. 3).

17. Julian, *Contra Galilaeos* 115 D–E, trans. W. C. Wright.

18. The destruction of the Temple was so deeply engrained in Christian thought as a symbol of God's rejection of the Jews that its rebuilding aroused deep emotional reaction, and the fire was later used by Christians as convincing evidence of God's continuing hostility to the Jews. It was "a fire from heaven," as Ambrose of Milan was to put it. Ambrose's *Letters,* trans. S. Mary Melchior Beyenka (New York, 1954), letter no. 2 in this collection, no. 40 according to the traditional Benedictine enumeration.

19. For the reigns of Jovian through to Theodosius, see J. Curran, chap. 3 in Cameron and Garnsey, eds., *The Cambridge Ancient History,* vol. XIII.

20. The most lively account of this disaster is to be found in Ammianus Marcellinus' history, *The Later Roman Empire* xxxi.

21. Ibid., xxx, 9.

22. J. Rist in "Plotinus and Christian Philosophy," in Lloyd P. Gerson, ed., *The Cambridge Companion to Plotinus* (Cambridge, 1996), p. 396. For Athanasius' writings and a critical discussion of his theology, see Hanson, *The Search for the Christian Doctrine of God,* chap. 14. There is also a good chapter on Athanasius by David Brakke in Esler, *The Early Christian World,* vol. 2, chap. 44.

23. Hanson, *The Search for the Christian Doctrine of God,* pp. 239–62.

24. Ibid., p. 436.

25. Ibid., p. 446, for the text of Athanasius' analysis of the Incarnation followed by Hanson's own assessment of it.

26. Quotation from ibid., p. 449.

27. The quotations from Origen and Athanasius come from J. Pelikan, *The*

*Christian Tradition,* vol. 1 (Chicago and London, 1971), pp. 282 and 285. Pelikan's section on "The State of Christian Anthropology," from which these quotations are drawn, is helpful in exploring the development of Christian ideas on the nature of sin and free will. Some idea of Athanasius' polemical style can be gauged from the following quotation from *Against the Arians,* discourse II, para. 58.

> A heretic is a wicked thing in truth and in every respect his heart is depraved and irreligious. For behold, though convicted on all points and shown to be utterly bereft of understanding, they show no shame, but as the hydra of Gentile fable, when its former serpents were destroyed, gave birth to fresh ones, contending against the slayer of the old by the production of the new, so also they are hostile and hateful to God, as hydras losing their life in their objections which they advance, invent for themselves other questions, Judaic [*sic*] and foolish, and new expedients, as if Truth were their enemy, thereby to show that they are Christ's enemies in all things.

For the rhetorical devices used by Athanasius, see the article by C. Stead, "Rhetorical Method in Athanasius," *Vigiliae Christianae* 30 (1976): 121–37. As suggested in the main text, this kind of polemic helped undermine the tradition of rational argument, and it was deeply unfortunate that it became such a prominent part of Christian discourse. Not least, it undermined the concept of a loving God who could accept diversity among his creatures. As will be seen, Jerome and John Chrysostom, and, to a lesser extent perhaps, Ambrose, sustained this tradition so that the more measured works of Augustine, despite their underlying pessimism, come as something of a relief.

28. See Williams, *Ambrose of Milan,* chap. 2, and Hanson, *The Search for the Christian Doctrine of God,* chap. 15. As Williams points out, one must be cautious in the use of "Nicene" for the beliefs of the bishops of the west. Speaking of the 340s, he suggests that "outside Rome, the Nicene creed appears to have been known but not relevant to the confessional needs of western bishops" (*Ambrose of Milan,* pp. 16–17). There is no evidence that Hilary of Poitiers even knew of the creed before the 350s. One cannot stress too strongly the lack of any immediate impact on the church from the Nicene Council, which really deserves to be called an imperial council rather than a church one.

29. See Hanson, *The Search for the Christian Doctrine of God,* chap. 21. For a good résumé of the Cappadocians' case, see T. Hopko, "The Trinity in the Cappadocians," part 1 of chap. 11 in B. McGinn and J. Meyendorff, eds., *Christian Spirituality: Origins to the Twelfth Century* (London, 1986).

30. Jaroslav Pelikan, *Christianity and Classical Culture* (New Haven and London, 1993), p. 175.

31. Ibid. Pelikan shows how "natural theology," based on classical philosophy, was woven into the Cappadocians' work so that they would use reason, "the natural apprehensions of humanity," analogies from the physical world and so on in the search for support for Christian orthodoxy. The difficulty was how to distinguish between those aspects of pagan philosophy that they could use to support Christianity from those they had to condemn as pagan. Then they had to reconcile the parts of pagan philosophy they used with the teaching of the scriptures. No one can doubt the quality and ingenuity of the minds of the Cappadocian Fathers, but, as Pelikan shows, they often had to indulge in special pleading to achieve results that coincided with Nicene orthodoxy. A more supportive view is that of Hopko:

> Their glory . . . lay in their ability to overcome those elements of this [Greek philosophical] tradition that were incompatible with Christianity, particularly in regard to the vision of God, and to coin new terms and formulate new explanations to protect and preserve the authentic experience and proper understanding of Christians.

Hopko, "The Trinity in the Cappadocians," p. 261.

32. H. Chadwick, in "Orthodoxy and Heresy," chap. 19 in Cameron and Garnsey, eds., *The Cambridge Ancient History,* vol. XIII, p. 573, does suggest the connection between the Cappadocians and Plotinus, but J. Rist, in "Plotinus and Christian Philosophy," in Gerson, ed., *The Cambridge Companion to Plotinus,* argues against it, pp. 397–401. Rist's view is in its turn rejected by Hanson, *The Search for the Christian Doctrine of God,* who concludes (p. 866): "It seems impossible to deny that Basil knew something of the work of Plotinus and consciously employed both his ideas and vocabulary when he thought them applicable." For an overview of the whole problem from a philosophical point of view, see Stead, *Philosophy in Christian Antiquity,* chap. 15, "Substance and Persons." The Cappadocians were certainly not blind followers of Plotinus, because the latter made it quite clear that his three *hypostaseis* were in a hierarchy, while the Trinitarian formulation insists that they are equal to each other.

33. Gregory of Nazianzus illustrates how fluid the concept of the Holy Spirit was at this stage: "Of the wise men among ourselves, some have conceived of the Holy Spirit as an activity, some as a creature, some as God; and some have been uncertain which to call him . . . And therefore they neither worship him nor treat him with dishonour, but take up a neutral position." *Orations* 21.33, quoted in Pelikan, *The Christian Tradition,* vol. 1, p. 213. Pages 211–25 give a full account of the difficulties involved in defining the Holy Spirit as God.

34. Pelikan, *Christianity and Classical Culture,* p. 245.

35. Ibid., pp. 237–38 for the problems with the terminology of Father and Son and pp. 195–96 for Basil's views on the Holy Spirit. The key passage from the New Testament is Matthew 28:19 where Jesus calls upon the disciples to baptize "all nations . . . in the name of the Father, and of the Son, and of the Holy Spirit." However, this says nothing about the relationship between them, which is so crucial a part of Trinitarian orthodoxy, and according to Pelikan, *The Christian Tradition,* vol. 1, p. 212, the lack of any direct reference to the Spirit as God in the scriptures was "a source of considerable embarrassment" to Gregory of Nazianzus. In his letter to his flock after the Council of Nicaea, Eusebius of Caesarea assured them that the use of *homoousios* was consistent with Matthew 28:19 being interpreted in terms of a *"hierarchy"* of Father, Son and Holy Spirit (see R. Vaggione, *Eunomius of Cyzicus and the Nicene Revolution* [Oxford, 2000], p. 60). The point about Hebrews 1:3 is made by Pelikan, *The Christian Tradition,* vol. 1, pp. 219–20.

36. These points are taken from chap. 15 of Pelikan, *Christianity and Classical Culture,* "The One and the Three."

37. "If your own Scriptures are sufficient for you, why do you nibble at the learning of the Greeks?" Julian had asked in his *Contra Galilaeos* (quoted in Smith, *Julian's Gods,* p. 198). For the philosophical problems created by the Trinity, see the entry "Trinity" in Edward Craig, ed., *The Routledge Encyclopaedia of Philosophy* (London and New York, 1998).

38. Thomas Aquinas, *Summa theologiae* 1a 3c.1c.

39. Pelikan, *Christianity and Classical Culture,* p. 241.

40. Ibid., pp. 246–47.

41. Ibid., p. 233:

> The Nicene dogma did not abolish the need for *apophasis* [assertions about God expressed in a negative form], as a shallow interpretation of orthodox doctrine might have led someone to suppose. If anything, orthodox trinitarianism intensified that need, for any increase in knowledge about God (above all the revelation of the knowledge of God as Father, Son, and Holy Spirit) ultimately consisted in an increase in the knowledge that God was and remained incomprehensible and transcendent.

42. See, for this, Wiles, *Archetypal Heresy*, pp. 40–51.

43. N. McLynn, *Ambrose of Milan: Church and Court in a Christian Capital* (Berkeley, 1994), p. 106.

44. Quoted in Hanson, *The Search for the Christian Doctrine of God*, p. 821. Hanson has full details of the Council of Constantinople, but I have also drawn on Deno John Geanakoplos, "The Second Ecumenical Council at Constantinople (381): Proceedings and Theology of the Holy Spirit," in his *Constantinople and the West* (Madison, Wis., and London, 1989).

45. Hanson *The Search for the Christian Doctrine*, p. 828. There is one theory that the final form of the Nicene Creed (that is, with the Holy Spirit fully part of the Godhead) dates from the 370s, although another says it was originally a baptismal creed from Constantinople that was developed. The first known recitations of the creed in a service date from much later, from Antioch at the end of the fifth century. Rome did not adopt the creed officially until 1014 (and so it is hardly surprising that Augustine does not seem to have heard of it). See entry "Nicene Creed" in F. Cross and E. A. Livingstone, eds., *The Oxford Dictionary of the Christian Church*, 3rd ed. (Oxford, 1997). The links between Theodosius, the council and the Cappodocian Fathers still needs further research, particularly concerning the degree to which the council drew directly on the writings of the Cappadocian Fathers. For divine condemnation, note the words of the theologian Ambrosiaster from these same years: "Those people who have discordant opinions, their thoughts being different from the Catholic faith about Christ . . . their exchange of thoughts will accuse them on the day of judgement." Quoted in Peter Garnsey and Caroline Humfress, *The Evolution of the Late Antique World* (Cambridge, 2001), p. 137.

46. Gregory of Nazianzus is worth quoting in this context:

> If the truth be told my attitude towards all gatherings of bishops is to avoid them. I have never seen a good outcome to any synod, or a synod which produced deliverance from evils rather than the addition to them . . . rivalries and manoeuvres always prevail over reason [*sic*] . . . and in trying to decide between others it is easier to get accused of wickedness itself than to deal with their wickedness. Consequently I have withdrawn to myself. I consider retirement to be the only means of saving my soul.

Epistle 130, quoted in Rosemary Radford Ruether, *Gregory of Nazianzus, Rhetor and Philosopher* (Oxford, 1969), p. 48.

47. Wiles, *Archetypal Heresy*, p. 44.

48. Hanson, *The Search for the Christian Doctrine of God,* p. 855.

49. Ibid., p. 852. In his *Ecclesiastical History* (V, 8), the early-fifth-century Socrates notes: "Great disturbances occurred in other cities as the Arians were ejected from their churches." Williams, *Ambrose of Milan,* suggests that Ambrose's attempt to impose Nicene orthodoxy in Milan at the Council of Aquileia in 381 actually led to an increase in support for the Homoean alternative. See his chap. 7, "A Homoian Revival in Milan."

50. Quoted in Kallistos Ware, "Eastern Christendom," chap. 4, in John McManners, ed., *The Oxford Illustrated History of Christianity* (Oxford, 1990), p. 137. It is certainly arguable that historians and theologians have underestimated the hostility to Theodosius' imposition of "his" faith—the widespread opposition to the imposition of Nicene orthodoxy in Constantinople provides a plausible explanation as to why the creed formulated by the council of 381 was given so little publicity. One could go on to suggest that it was not until 451, when Homoean Christianity had largely disappeared, that it was possible to proclaim the creed openly in the east. As mentioned above there is no record of its public use in the east before the late fifth century. This is an area of history that needs further research.

51. S. Mitchell, *Anatolia: Land, Men and Gods in Asia Minor* (Oxford, 1993), vol. 2, ch. 17, section X, "The Epigraphy of the Anatolian Heresies."

52. For Palladius' attack on *De Fide,* see Williams, *Ambrose of Milan,* pp. 148–53.

53. Hanson, *The Search for the Christian Doctrine of God,* pp. 672–73.

54. Wiles, *Archetypal Heresy,* p. 39.

55. See comment ibid., p. 50. One scholar quoted by Wiles describes the Homoean Goths as having "a ponderous and earthbound reliance on the text of the Bible" (E. A. Thompson, *The Visigoths in the Time of Ulfila* [Oxford, 1966]). There is perhaps a hint of condescension here reflecting the traditional attitude to Arians by a conventional scholar, but the point is made—they clung to the scriptures.

56. Hanson, *The Search for the Christian Doctrine of God,* p. 831. For the debate, in which Maximinus was considered the winner, see A. D. Fitzgerald, ed., *Augustine Through the Ages* (Grand Rapids, Mich., and Cambridge, 1999), p. 550. The full text of the debate is given in *Arianism and Other Heresies,* vol. 18 of *The Works of Saint Augustine,* Augustinian Heritage Institute, J. Rutelle, ed. (New York, 1995), pp. 175–230.

57. Fitzgerald, ed., *Augustine Through the Ages,* p. 80. The article on "authority" in this excellent survey of Augustine and his time gives a number of quotations from Augustine illustrating his adherence to orthodoxy when interpreting the scriptures. His insistence that the scriptures be interpreted to support the doctrine of the Trinity comes from his *De Trinitate* 1.11.22. One prominent Italian scholar has summed it up as follows: "The whole development of Catholic doctrine is based on the interpretation of a certain number of passages in Scripture in the light of particular needs" (M. Simonetti, *Profilo storico dell'esegesi patristica* [Rome, 1980], quoted in D. Janes, *God and Gold in Late Antiquity* [Cambridge, 1998]).

58. Augustine, *De Doctrina Christiana* 3:5. The translation is from the Oxford World's Classics edition (Oxford, 1999) by R. P. H. Green. Pelikan explores the same issue from the perspective of the Cappadocian Fathers in *Christianity and Classical Culture;* see pp. 225–26 especially.

59. Augustine, *De Doctrina Christiana* 3:33.

60. Pelikan, *The Christian Tradition,* vol. 1, p. 76.

61. The most common interpretation of the S. Pudenziana mosaic, adopted

here, is of Christ as emperor, with reference being made back to the frontal image of Constantine on his arch as a model. However, a strong critique of this interpretation has been made by T. Mathews in his *The Clash of Gods: A Reinterpretation of Early Christian Art,* rev. paperback ed. (Princeton, 1999), chap. 4. Mathews sees the Christ of the mosaic essentially as a teaching figure, with his Apostles as "co-philosophers," and as representative of a bishop rather than an emperor. He concludes his assessment (p. 114): "The mosaic is propaganda not for the imperial aspirations of Christ, but for the divine origins of ecclesiastical authority." A full study of the iconography is to be found in G. Hellemo, *Adventus Domini* (Leiden, 1989), pp. 41–64, and it is this I have drawn on here. There is also much relevant material in A. Grabar, *Christian Iconography: A Study of Its Origins* (London, 1968), esp. pp. 60–86, which has a wealth of illustrations relating the mosaic to contemporary pagan art.

62. Mathews, *The Clash of the Gods,* p. 104.

63. R. Krautheimer, *Rome: Profile of a City, 312–1308* (Princeton, 2000), pp. 12–13. Margaret Mitchell's study was published in Tübingen in 2000.

<h2 style="text-align:center">13</h2>

1. Quoted in Philip Rousseau, *Ascetics, Authority and the Church in the Age of Jerome and Cassian* (Oxford, 1978), p. 84.

2. *Eusebius: Life of Constantine,* ed. A. Cameron and S. Hall (Oxford, 1999), 3:14.

3. R. Krautheimer, *Three Christian Capitals* (Berkeley, 1983), p. 100.

4. Ammianus Marcellinus, *The Later Roman Empire* xxvii. 3.14.

5. D. Hunt, "The Church as a Public Institution," chap. 8 in A. Cameron and P. Garnsey, eds., *The Cambridge Ancient History,* vol. XIII (Cambridge, 1998), is my main source for these points. Guy Stroumsa notes on p. 112 of his *Barbarian Philosophy: The Religious Revolution of Early Christianity* (Tübingen, 1999): "in pre-Nicene Christian writings the birthplace of the new religion was first and foremost identified as the city of Christ's killers." Chap. 18 in Stroumsa's book, "Mystical Jerusalems," is also of interest.

6. See K. Bradley, *Slavery and Society at Rome* (Cambridge, 1994), pp. 145–53, for this argument.

7. Augustine, *The City of God* 19:15. No effective Christian opposition to slavery was shown until the eighteenth century, and, as debates over the issue during the American Civil War showed, there was no consensus that it was against the teachings of the Bible even a century later. For Augustine's thoughts on slavery, see Peter Garnsey, *Ideas of Slavery from Aristotle to Augustine* (Cambridge, 1996), chap. 13. Garnsey also discusses the views of Paul (chap. 11) and Ambrose (chap. 12) in addition to those of earlier classical authors.

8. Aristotle, *Politics* 1330 a 8–160.

9. Quoted in S. Williams, *Diocletian and the Roman Recovery* (London, 1985), p. 162.

10. These calculations come from D. Janes, *God and Gold in Late Antiquity* (Cambridge, 1998), pp. 55–57. Janes' study is essential for an understanding of the rationales that lay behind accepting opulence in building.

11. The relationship between Christianity and art remained an ambivalent one. There is no indication that Jesus wished resources to be spent on opulent decoration (if anything the opposite, Luke 21:5–6). The spending of so much money on material

possession was in essence a pagan custom transferred by the state into Christianity. It is remarkable how many traditional histories of church architecture fail to mention the enormous resources involved and the shifts in perspective needed to justify the building of churches. A common approach in such histories is to say the large churches were built simply because Christianity was now free to operate openly and was attracting larger congregations.

Such offerings were always vulnerable to alternative interpretations of the Christian message, as witnessed by the massive destruction of Christian art by the iconoclasts of eighth-century Byzantium and by Protestant Christians in Reformation Europe. One must also remember that vast quantities of pagan art and architecture were destroyed by Christians.

12. Janes, *God and Gold*, p. 78.

13. P. Brown, "Art and Society in Late Antiquity," in K. Weitzmann, ed., *Age of Spirituality: A Symposium* (New York, 1980).

14. Janes, *God and Gold*, p. 145.

15. S. MacCormack, *Art and Ceremony in Late Antiquity* (Berkeley and London, 1981), p. 130.

16. Janes, *God and Gold*, p. 119.

17. Ibid., p. 169.

18. Ibid., p. 137. Specifically on renunciation of property, see D. Trout, *Paulinus of Nola* (Berkeley and London, 1999), chap. 6, "Salvation Economics: The Theory and Practice of Property Renunciation."

19. Quoted in P. Brown, *Power and Persuasion in Late Antiquity* (Madison, Wis., and London, 1992), p. 121.

20. Hunt, "The Church as a Public Institution," p. 263.

21. R. MacMullen, *Christianising the Roman Empire* (A.D. *100–400*) (New Haven and London, 1984), p. 115.

22. Brown, *Power and Persuasion*, p. 148. For Synesius, see J. W. Liebeschuetz, *Barbarians and Bishops: Army, Church and State in the Age of Arcadius and Chrysostom* (Oxford, 1990), chap. 23, "The Bishop and Public Life in the Cyrenaica of Synesius."

23. Quoted in Hunt, "The Church as a Public Institution," p. 265. An anonymous Catholic priest writing in the April 2000 edition of the magazine *Prospect* (London) tells the story of how a Vatican representative sent to Britain after the Second Vatican Council (1962–65) brought the message that English Catholic bishops should be of the appropriate class, public school and Oxbridge educated, so that they would be socially fitted to develop ecumenical links with the Anglican bishops!

24. Brown, *Power and Persuasion*, p. 122. See also chap. 2 of his study.

25. Hunt, "The Church as a Public Institution," p. 266.

26. Brown, *Power and Persuasion*, p. 150.

27. Ibid., p. 98. The issue is fully discussed by Peter Brown in his *Poverty and Leadership in the Later Roman Empire* (Hanover and London, 2002). Brown argues that the bishops' acceptance of their responsibility for the poor was in part a recognition of the privileges they had been granted (p. 32).

28. The quotation from Ammianus Marcellinus (xxvii.3.5) comes from S. Mitchell, *Anatolia: Land, Men and Gods in Asia Minor* (Oxford, 1993), vol. 2, p. 82. The quotation from Basil is in the same book, p. 83.

29. Letters of Basil 28, quoted ibid., vol. 2, p. 84.

30. Ibid., vol. 2, p. 77.

31. Brown, *Power and Persuasion*, p. 16.

## 14

1. N. McLynn, *Ambrose of Milan: Church and Court in a Christian Capital* (Berkeley and London, 1994), p. 371, which I have drawn on heavily for this chapter. See also D. Williams, *Ambrose of Milan and the End of the Nicene–Arian Conflicts* (Oxford, 1995). A short and balanced account of Ambrose's career is that by Ivor Davidson, chap. 47 in P. Esler, ed., *The Early Christian World,* vol. 2 (New York and London, 2000).

2. McLynn, *Ambrose of Milan,* p. 376.

3. Augustine, *Confessions* 6.3.3.

4. J. Kelly, *Jerome* (London, 1975), p. 143. For an alternative view on Ambrose and *On Duties,* see M. L. Colish, "Cicero, Ambrose and Stoic Ethics: Transmission or Transformation?" in A. S. Bernardo and S. Levin, eds., *The Classics in the Middle Ages* (New York, 1990).

5. For discussion of this basilica, see R. Krautheimer, *Three Christian Capitals* (Berkeley, 1983), pp. 81–86, and McLynn, *Ambrose of Milan,* pp. 174–79.

6. Williams, *Ambrose of Milan,* chap. 5; R. Hanson, *The Search for the Christian Doctrine of God* (Edinburgh, 1988), pp. 667–75.

7. R. Lim, *Public Disputation, Power and Social Order in Late Antiquity* (Berkeley and London, 1995), explores the way in which written texts presented as the basis for discussion came to displace oral debate during these years.

8. Williams, *Ambrose of Milan,* pp. 154–55.

9. McLynn, *Ambrose of Milan,* pp. 181–95.

10. Williams, *Ambrose of Milan,* p. 216.

11. Ambrose, *Letters,* trans. Sr. Melchior Beyenka (New York, 1954). Letter number 61 in this collection, number 22 in the older Benedictine enumeration.

12. McLynn covers these points in *Ambrose of Milan,* chap. 7.

13. Ambrose, *Letters;* letter number 2 in this collection, number 40 in the Benedictine enumeration.

14. M. Simon, *Verus Israel* (Oxford, 1986), pp. 227–28.

15. McLynn, *Ambrose of Milan,* p. 308.

16. Ibid., p. 315.

17. Ibid., pp. 358–60. The quotation is taken from S. MacCormack, *Art and Ceremony in Late Antiquity* (Berkeley and London, 1981), pp. 145–50.

18. Davidson, in Esler, ed., *The Early Christian World,* vol. 2, p. 1197.

## 15

1. The diptych had apparently been brought from Rome in the seventh century by one Bercharius and lodged in an abbey he founded in France at Montier-en-Der (Haut Marne). There the panels had been adapted to serve as the door leaves of a thirteenth-century reliquary casket. The abbey had suffered badly in the French Revolution, and the panels had been burned and apparently lost. The Musée de Cluny panel was recovered in a well in 1860 and acquired by the Musée soon afterwards. The Victoria and Albert panel was found by a local collector in France who sold it in 1862 to a Mr. Webb, who in his turn sold it to the Victoria and Albert Museum in 1865. I found it a moving experience to visit an exhibition in Rome in the spring of 2001 at which the two sides of the diptych had been reunited, presumably for the first time in the city since the seventh century. Here I have drawn on two major articles on the diptych: B. Kiilerich, "A Different Interpretation of the

Nicomachorum-Symmachorum Diptych," *Jahrbuch für Antike und Christentum* 34 (1991): 115, and D. Kinney, "The Iconography of the Ivory Diptych Nicomachorum-Symmachorum," *Jahrbuch für Antike und Christentum* 37 (1994): 64.

2. Kiilerich, "A Different Interpretation," pp. 118–19.

3. Ibid., p. 123.

4. Ibid., p. 122.

5. See Kinney, "The Iconography of the Ivory Diptych," pp. 74–82, for the wide variety of contexts in which such torches have been found.

6. Ibid., pp. 67–73, for the contexts in which representations of *pietas* have been found.

7. For the full text of the letters and background details, see B. Croke and J. Harries, *Religious Conflict in Fourth-Century Rome* (Sydney, 1982), chap. 2, "The Debate on the Altar of Victory, A.D. 384." Earlier the pagan orator Themistius had used a similar argument in an *Appealing Oration* to the emperor Valens (364–78), who had tried to uphold Homoean Christianity against its rivals. Themistius told Valens

> that he ought not to be surprised at the difference of judgement in religious questions among Christians; inasmuch as that the discrepancy was trifling when compared to the multitude of conflicting opinions current among the heathen; for these amount to above three hundred, that dissensions occurred was an inevitable consequence of this disagreement, but that God would be more glorified by a diversity of sentiment, and the greatness of his majesty be more venerated from the fact of its not being easy to have knowledge of him.

The oration is quoted in Socrates, *Ecclesiastical History,* 4, 32.

8. For the argument that Praetextatus is the man commemorated, see Kiilerich, "A Different Interpretation," pp. 126–27, from which the quotation in the next paragraph has been taken. The quotation about Praetextatus' intellectual qualities, which was recorded by one Macrobius, can be found in W. Liebeschuetz, "The Significance of the Speech of Praetextatus," in P. Athanassiadi and M. Frede, eds., *Pagan Monotheism in Late Antiquity* (Oxford, 1999), p. 196. Praetextatus' funerary monument has survived (in the Capitoline Museum in Rome). It includes details of the many cults with which he was associated. The dedication on it to his wife, Paulina, is worth quoting to give a flavour of pagan marriage in late antiquity.

> Paulina, partner of my heart, nurse of modesty, bond of chastity, pure love and loyalty produced in heaven, to whom I have entrusted the deep secrets of my heart, gift of the gods who bind our marriage couch with friendly and modest ties; by the devotion of a mother, the bond of a sister, the modesty of a daughter, and by all the loyalty friends show, we are united by the custom of age, the pact of consecration, by the yoke of the marriage vow and perfect harmony, helpmate of your husband, loving, adoring, devoted.

Paulina's own tribute to her husband is inscribed on the back of the monument. Quoted in Croke and Harries, *Religious Conflict,* pp. 106–7.

9. See Jerome's Letter XXII in *Select Letters of St. Jerome,* trans. F. A. Wright (London, 1933).

10. See J. Kelly, *Jerome* (London, 1975), p. 96. Jerome makes the point in his Letter XXIV.

11. Quoted in P. Rousseau, *Ascetics, Authority and the Church in the Age of Jerome and Cassian* (Oxford, 1978), p. 119.

12. Quoted in R. Smith, *Julian's Gods: Religion and Philosophy in the Thought and Action of Julian the Apostate* (London and New York, 1995), p. 224. There is some dispute over the origin and date of this anonymous poem, but it is possibly an authentic plea to the emperor Julian.

16

1. Quoted in J. Kelly, *Jerome* (London, 1975), p. 132.

2. *Phaedo* 66 C; quoted in J. Dillon, "Rejecting the Body, Redefining the Body: Some Remarks on the Development of Platonist Asceticism," in V. Wimbush and R. Valantasis, eds., *Asceticism* (New York and Oxford, 1995).

3. The quotation is from P. Brown, *The Body and Society: Men, Women and Sexual Renunciation in Early Christianity* (New York, 1988; London, 1989), p. 19.

4. Quoted in G. Clark, "Women and Asceticism in Late Antiquity: The Reversal of Status and Gender," in Wimbush and Valantasis, eds., *Asceticism*, p. 43.

5. Quotations from his Letter XXII.

6. R. A. Markus, *The End of Ancient Christianity* (Cambridge, 1990), p. 166.

7. P. Brown, "Asceticism: Pagan and Christian," in A. Cameron and P. Garnsey, eds., *The Cambridge Ancient History*, vol. XIII (Cambridge, 1998), p. 618.

8. The quotation from Epictetus is from his *Discourses* 4.10.16. The other two quotations are taken from Brown, *The Body and Society*, pp. 375 and 309. Aristotle's views on moderation between two extremes are also important here. See his *Nicomachean Ethics* II. 6–7 and comments on the theme in R. Sorabji, *Emotion and Peace of Mind: From Stoic Agitation to Christian Temptation* (Oxford, 2000), chap. 14, "The Traditions of Moderation and Eradication."

9. See G. Stroumsa, *Barbarian Philosophy: The Religious Revolution of Early Christianity* (Tubingen, 1999), chap. 10, "*Caro Salutis Cardo*: Shaping the Person in Early Christian Thought," especially pp. 177–81. There are immense philosophical problems about what is meant by "will" here. See, as an introduction, C. Kahn, "Discovering the Will: From Aristotle to Augustine," in J. M. Dillon and A. A. Long, eds., *The Question of Eclecticism: Studies in Later Greek Philosophy* (Berkeley and London, 1988).

10. P. Brown, "Asceticism: Pagan and Christian," in Cameron and Garnsey, eds., *The Cambridge Ancient History*, vol. XIII, p. 616.

11. See A. Cameron, *Christianity and the Rhetoric of Empire* (Berkeley and London, 1991), p. 153.

12. Brown, "Asceticism," p. 607. The quotation comes from section 67 of the *Life of Anthony*.

13. Eunapius of Sardis, *Vitae Sophistarium* vi.11 (c. 395); quoted in P. Rousseau, *Ascetics, Authority and the Church in the Age of Jerome and Cassian* (Oxford, 1978), p. 9.

14. Quoted in Clark, "Women and Asceticism," pp. 34 and 43.

15. Brown, *The Body and Society*, p. 370.

16. Quoted on p. xix of M. Warner, *Alone of All Her Sex* (London, 1985).

17. See H. Bettenson, *The Early Christian Fathers* (Oxford, 1956), pp. 82–83 for Irenaeus' views and pp. 126–27 for Tertullian's.

18. Kelly, *Jerome*, p. 301.

19. Vasiliki Limberis, *Divine Heiress: The Virgin Mary and the Creation of Christian Constantinople* (London and New York, 1994). As Limberis shows, in the great hymn to Mary, the Akathistos Hymn, Mary absorbed many of the epithets used of both Rhea and another ancient goddess, Hecate. For instance, Hecate is virgin but also a protecting mother (one of her most common roles was as a carer for orphans), and the Virgin Mary is acclaimed in the same role in the hymn. Hecate is also seen as an initiator into divine knowledge, and Mary is hailed as "O knowledge, superseding the wise," the one "who enlightens the minds of believers" and "who extricates us from the depths of ignorance."

20. For further examples of the adoption of Isis' attributes by Mary, see R. Witt, *Isis in the Greco-Roman World* (London, 1971), pp. 272–73.

21. Warner, *Alone of All Her Sex,* p. 58.

22. Kelly, *Jerome,* pp. 180–87, for Jerome's views on Jovinian. P. Brown, "Christianisation and Religious Conflict," in Cameron and Garnsey, eds., *The Cambridge Ancient History,* vol. XIII, p. 638, for Jovinian's flogging in Rome. Tertullian's view is quoted in Jaroslav Pelikan, *The Christian Tradition,* vol. 1 (Chicago and London, 1971), p. 288.

23. Rousseau, *Ascetics, Authority and the Church,* p. 179.

24. Kelly, *Jerome,* p. 99.

25. Rousseau, *Ascetics, Authority and the Church,* p. 29.

26. Ibid., p. 152.

27. Kallistos Ware "The Way of the Ascetics, Negative or Affirmative?" in Wimbush and Valantasis, *Asceticism,* p. 7. See also the account of the life of St. Theodore of Sykeon, pp. 122–50 in vol. 2 of S. Mitchell, *Anatolia: Land, Men and Gods in Asia Minor* (Oxford, 1993). Theodore specialized in cures and exorcisms.

28. The French sociologist Emile Durkheim spotted the problem.

> Imagine a society of saints, a perfect cloister of exemplary individuals. Crimes, properly so called, will be there unknown; but faults which appear venial to the layman will create the same scandal there that the ordinary offence does in ordinary consciousness. If, then, this society has the power to judge and punish, it will define these acts as criminal and judge them as such.

From Emile Durkheim, *Rules of Sociological Method,* Eng. trans. (Glencoe, Ill., 1950).

29. Rousseau, *Ascetics, Authority and the Church,* p. 187.

30. Ibid., p. 49.

31. S. Elm, *Virgins of God* (Oxford, 1994), p. 63.

32. Ibid., p. 69.

33. Rousseau, *Ascetics, Authority and the Church,* pp. 195–96.

34. Ibid., p. 55.

35. Ibid., p. 220.

36. Ibid., p. 151, and one might mention the modern example of the late Cardinal Basil Hume, who followed the same path.

37. Markus, *The End of Ancient Christianity,* p. 197.

38. Quoted in Rousseau, *Ascetics, Authority and the Church,* p. 105.

39. Quoted in R. MacMullen, *Christianity and Paganism in the Fourth to Eighth Centuries* (New Haven and London, 1997), p. 16.

40. Seneca, Letter LXXX, 3–4.

41. Ambrose, *Expositio in Psalmum 118,* 4.22; quoted in R. F. Newbould,

"Personality Structure and Response to Adversity in Early Christian Hagiography," *Numen* XXXI (1984): 199.

42. William James' book originated as the Gifford Lectures delivered in Edinburgh in 1901–2 and was published for the first time in 1902. The quotation comes from lecture 13.

17

1. *Eusebius: Life of Constantine,* ed. A. Cameron and S. Hall (Oxford, 1999), 3:15.

2. See the introduction ibid., especially pp. 34–39.

3. Quoted in E. M. Pickman, *The Mind of Latin Christendom* (New York, 1937), p. 545.

4. See C. Kelly, "Emperors, Government and Bureaucracy," in *The Cambridge Ancient History,* vol. XIII, ed. A. Cameron and P. Garnsey (Cambridge, 1998), p. 141.

5. Ibid., p. 143.

6. Ibid., p. 142.

7. For a full account of the affair, see J. Kelly, *Golden Mouth: The Story of John Chrysostom* (London, 1995), chap. 6.

8. Quoted in R. MacMullen, *Christianity and Paganism in the Fourth to Eighth Centuries* (New Haven and London, 1997), p. 27.

9. As in *The Cambridge Ancient History,* vol. XIII, pp. 638–39.

10. Ibid., p. 642.

11. I have relied heavily on J. Kelly, *Golden Mouth,* for my account of John Chrysostom's life, but see also J. Liebeschuetz, *Barbarians and Bishops: Army, Church and State in the Age of Arcadius and Chrysostom* (Oxford, 1990), part 3 in particular.

12. J. Kelly, *Golden Mouth,* pp. 45–46, for Jerome's views on Paul and virginity. The quotation comes from Hubart Richards, *St. Paul and His Epistles: A New Introduction* (London, 1979). See now Margaret Mitchell, *The Heavenly Trumpet: John Chrysostom and the Art of Pauline Interpretation* (Tubingen, 2000), for an analysis of John's attitude toward Paul.

13. J. Kelly, *Golden Mouth,* pp. 97–98. The "silver chamber pot" quotation comes from Liebeschuetz, *Barbarians and Bishops,* p. 176.

14. J. Kelly, *Golden Mouth,* pp. 62–66, for a survey of the sermons. The fullest analysis is to be found in R. L. Wilken, *John Chrysostom and the Jews: Rhetoric and Reality in the Late Fourth Century* (Berkeley and London, 1983). There is useful background information (relating John's sermons to earlier anti-Judaism) in chap. 8 of G. Stroumsa, *Barbarian Philosophy: The Religious Revolution of Early Christianity* (Tubingen, 1999).

15. For the conflict between John Chrysostom and the emperor's views of the church, see Vasiliki Limberis, *Divine Heiress: The Virgin Mary and the Creation of Christian Constantinople* (London and New York, 1994), pp. 37–40. Limberis sees the conflict as one not just of personalities but of irreconcilable differences over the degree to which the church should submit to the state. Kelly considers the issues surrounding the intervention in Asia Minor in *Golden Mouth,* pp. 178–80.

16. Despite their unruliness, the loyalty of the crowds was eventually rewarded. In 438, the emperor Theodosius II, anxious to calm tensions within the church, ordered the return of John's body to Constantinople. It was received with great

ceremony, although whether John would have approved of his resting place, in the church of the Holy Apostles close to the bodies of Arcadius and Eudoxia, is another matter. Even this was not his final grave—his body was one of the many relics stolen by the Venetians and the Crusaders after their sack of the city in 1204 and is reputedly now in St. Peter's in Rome.

17. For the controversy and its main protagonists I have drawn on the excellent accounts given by F. Young in her *From Nicaea to Chalcedon* (London, 1993), chap. 5, and J. Pelikan, *The Christian Tradition*, vol. 1 (Chicago and London, 1971), chap. 5, "The Person of the God-Man." The complex philosophical problems involved are also dissected by C. Stead in chap. 17, "Two Natures United," of his *Philosophy in Christian Antiquity* (Cambridge, 1994). There is much in this chapter about the ingenuity of the theologians. How could two natures, divine and mortal, which were opposites, possibly be combined? What physical analogy might be used? Were they like a pile of beans and peas, materially separate from each other even when mingled, or two coexisting entities that maintain their identities like heat in a piece of iron, or did they lost their identity in each other, like tin and copper in bronze (an analogy drawn from Stoic physics)?

18. Augustine, *Confessions* 7:19. Adoptionism had an important revival in Spain as late as the eighth century.

19. There are short historical accounts of the Council of Ephesus and that at Chalcedon in the encyclopaedia section of G. W. Bowersock, P. Brown and O. Grabar, eds., *Late Antiquity: A Guide to the Postclassical World* (Cambridge, Mass., and London, 1999). See also the comments on Chalcedon by R. Lim in his *Public Disputation, Power, and Social Order in Late Antiquity* (Berkeley and London, 1995), pp. 224–26.

20. The quotation on Leo's role comes from J. Herrin, *The Formation of Christendom* (Oxford, 1987), p. 103. While the council provided a formulation of co-existence of the two natures, it did not, perhaps wisely, try to suggest *how* they co-existed, and the debate over the two natures of Christ was "acted out" when Christ had to be portrayed on the cross. H. Belting, *Likeness and Presence: A History of the Image Before the Era of Art,* trans. E. Jephcott (Chicago and London, 1994), poses the question (p. 102): "Who was it who hung on the Cross? The man Jesus or only God or both in one. And who, if anyone, died on the Cross? If Jesus is shown dead does this not risk falling into the heresy of suggesting that God died? If he is shown alive to what extent is it right to show his suffering?" There were clearly inhibitions about showing Christ as dead. The earliest known depiction is believed to be one from the ninth century in the monastery of St. Catherine in the Sinai desert.

Stead, *Philosophy in Christian Antiquity,* pp. 193–94, sums up the Council of Chalcedon as follows:

> I take the view that the Chalcedonian definition was a fairly limited definition; it was a statement of the conditions that needed to be met, within a given horizon of thought, for a satisfactory doctrine of Christ; it did not amount to a positive solution . . . My case is that the problem could not then be solved because too many issues were simultaneously in question, some of them matters of open controversy, some of them undetected assumptions and inconsistencies.

He then goes on to try to sort some of these out. This is, of course, the essential difficulty in Christian theology, finding firm foundations on which to build coherent doctrine.

21. G. W. Bowersock, *Hellenism in Late Antiquity* (Ann Arbor, 1990), pp. 17–19.

22. P. Brown, "Christianisation and Religious Conflict," in Cameron and Garnsey, eds., *The Cambridge Ancient History*, vol. XIII, p. 660. On Paulinus there is now an outstanding biography, which ranges far wider than just the life of its subject: D. Trout, *Paulinus of Nola: Life, Letters, and Poems* (Berkeley and London, 1999). The sacrifice of two hogs and a heifer at St. Felix's shrine is recounted in a poem of Paulinus written in 406 and described by Trout, p. 179.

23. MacMullen, *Christianity and Paganism*, p. 121.

24. Ibid., p. 116.

25. Ibid., p. 124.

26. Ibid., p. 121.

27. Bowersock, *Hellenism in Late Antiquity*, pp. 49–52, with illustrations.

28. MacMullen, *Christianity and Paganism*, pp. 43–45.

29. Story recounted in Brown, "Christianisation and Religious Conflict," pp. 648 49.

30. N. de Lange, *Atlas of the Jewish World* (Oxford, 1984), p. 34.

31. MacMullen, *Christianity and Paganism*, pp. 13–14.

32. Ibid., p. 66.

33. Ibid., p. 60.

34. M. Kline, *Mathematical Thought from Ancient to Modern Times*, vol. 1 (Oxford and New York, 1990), p. 181. Gibbon writes as follows (chap. 47):

> Hypatia, the daughter of Theon the mathematician, was initiated in her father's studies: her learned comments have elucidated the geometry of Apollonius and Diophantus; and she publicly taught, both at Athens and Alexandria, the philosophy of Plato and Aristotle. In the bloom of beauty, and in the maturity of wisdom, the modest maid refused her lovers and instructed her disciples; the persons most illustrious for their rank and merit were impatient to visit the female philosopher; and Cyril beheld with a jealous eye the gorgeous train of horses and slaves who crowded the door of her academy. A rumour was spread among the Christians that the daughter of Theon was the only obstacle to the reconciliation of the prefect and the archbishop; and that obstacle was speedily removed. On a fatal day, in the holy season of Lent, Hypatia was torn from her chariot, stripped naked, dragged to the church, and inhumanly butchered by the hands of Peter the reader and a troop of savage and inhuman fanatics: her flesh was scraped from her bones with sharp oyster shells, and her quivering limbs were delivered to the flames. The just progress of inquiry and punishment was stopped by seasonable gifts: but the murder of Hypatia has imprinted an indelible stain on the character and religion of Cyril of Alexandria.

The story of Hypatia lived on. The novelist Charles Kingsley used Gibbon's account for his own novel, *Hypatia*, a best-seller in Britain in 1853.

35. Quoted in P. Chuvin, *A Chronicle of the Last of the Pagans* (Cambridge, Mass., and London, 1990), p. 133.

36. Bowersock, *Hellenism in Late Antiquity*, pp. 1–3. For evidence of the Christian groups see S. Mitchell, *Anatolia: Land, Men and Gods in Asia Minor*, vol. 2, chap. 17, part X, "The Epigraphy of the Anatolian Heresies."

37. Chuvin, *A Chronicle of the Last of the Pagans*, p. 141.

38. Quoted in Jerome Murphy-O'Connor, *The Holy Land: An Oxford Archaeological Guide,* 4th ed. (Oxford, 1998), p. 86.

## 18

1. The evidence for Peter's presence in Rome is flimsy, but no other city (outside Antioch, where by tradition he was the first bishop, and, of course, Jerusalem) lays claim to his presence, and so most scholars are prepared to accept that he did travel to Rome. How and why is difficult to guess. It is known that Jewish groups from the city made pilgrimages to Jerusalem, so Peter, perhaps at a time when his own authority among Christian Jews in Jerusalem was coming under threat from James, "the brother of Jesus," may have decided to return with them in the hope of regaining his status elsewhere. The legend that he was bishop of Rome (if that was the position he held when in the city) for twenty-five years seems to have been a third-century invention.

2. Gregory is quoted in R. Markus, *Gregory the Great and His World* (Cambridge, 1997), p. 7. For the linguistic separation of east and west, see J. Herrin, *The Formation of Christendom* (Oxford, 1987), pp. 104–5.

3. From *De praescriptione haereticorum* (c. 200), quoted in H. Bettenson, *Documents of the Christian Church* (Oxford, 1943), p. 8. For Tertullian, see the entries in general reference books such as *The Oxford Dictionary of the Christian Church,* 3rd ed., ed. F. Cross and E. Livingstone (Oxford, 1997), and P. Esler, ed., *The Early Christian World* (London and New York, 2000), vol. 2, chap. 40, by David Wright. The quotation about Tertullian's lack of *curiositas* comes from Wright, p. 1033, although Wright warns his readers not to dismiss Tertullian's lack of interest in Greek philosophy too readily. He had read widely in the classics although he kept them subordinate to the Christian faith that he preached so vigorously. One can find, for instance, elements of Stoicism in his thinking as when he argued that through God "we find this whole fabric of the universe to be once for all disposed, equipped, ordered as it stands, and supplied with the complete guidance of reason." (The Stoics argued that the supreme divine principle, call it what you will, suffused the cosmos and provided it with an underlying order.) Also see chap. 3 in P. Brown, *The Body and Society: Men, Women, and Sexual Renunciation in Early Christianity* (New York, 1988; London, 1989), for views on Tertullian and his abiding concern, human sexuality. A full selection of Tertullian's writings is to be found in H. Bettenson, *The Early Christian Fathers* (Oxford, 1956), pp. 104–67.

4. For this account of Jerome I have drawn on the full and readable life by J. Kelly, *Jerome* (London, 1975).

5. Ibid., p. 218. Taken from Letter LVI in Jerome's collected correspondence.

6. Letter CX in Jerome's collected correspondence.

7. Quoted in Kelly, *Jerome,* p. 331.

8. There is a mass of work on Augustine. The standard life is still P. Brown, *Augustine of Hippo* (London, 1977; rev. ed., Berkeley and London, 2000). It is very vivid and insightful, and certainly one of the finest biographies of any figure from the ancient world. A shorter life is by H. Chadwick, *Augustine* (Oxford, 1986). The massive encyclopaedic study *Augustine Through the Ages,* ed. A. Fitzgerald (Grand Rapids, Mich., and Cambridge, 1999), is an essential companion to further study. Highly recommended are C. Harrison, *Augustine: Christian Truth and Fractured Humanity* (Oxford, 2000); J. Rist, *Augustine: Ancient Thought Baptised* (Cambridge, 1994); and a more critical study by a philosopher, C. Kirwan, *Augustine* (London and

New York, 1989). Harrison contains an overview of the main works analysed in the text and is perhaps the best starting point. Recent issues in Augustinian studies are covered in R. Dodaro and G. Lawless, eds., *Augustine and His Critics* (London and New York, 2000).

9. See the entry on Luther in Fitzgerald, ed., *Augustine Through the Ages,* p. 515. One of the themes of the Council of Trent (1545–63) was a reassertion of Catholic interpretations of Augustine against those of Luther.

10. Uta Ranke-Heinemann, *Eunuchs for the Kingdom of Heaven: Women, Sexuality and the Catholic Church,* trans. P. Heinegg (New York, 1990), p. 75.

11. *The City of God* 10:32.

12. *Confessions* 8:12. I have used the translation by R. S. Pine Coffin in the Penguin Classics edition, first published in 1961. It is interesting that Augustine was converted by a verse of Paul's, not one of Jesus'. Scholars have noted that he seemed relatively uninterested in the person of Christ.

13. *Confessions* 9:10.

14. See P. Fredriksen, "Paul and Augustine: Conversion Narratives, Orthodox Traditions and the Retrospective Self," *Journal of Theological Studies* 37 (1986): 3–35.

15. These two quotations are taken from the *Confessions,* 10:8 and 2:2. The introspective nature of Augustine is well illustrated by the following quotation: "We do not consult a speaker who utters sounds to the outside, but a truth that resides within . . . Christ, who is said to dwell in the inner man—he it is who teaches." The influence of Platonism, in the idea that one is recollecting what is already inside oneself, can also be seen here. From Augustine's *De Magistro,* "On the Teacher," paragraph 38, quoted in J. Pelikan, *The Christian Tradition,* vol. 1 (Chicago and London, 1971), p. 295.

16. G. Wills, *Saint Augustine* (London and New York, 1999), p. 93, quoting Albrecht Dihle.

17. C. Stead, *Philosophy in Christian Antiquity* (Cambridge, 1994), p. 223. Stead goes on (p. 227) to consider the problems of isolating oneself from empirical evidence.

> One cannot explain human knowledge as a purely active process; it always involves attention to data which are not of our own making, apart from the exceptional case where we attend to our own creative thoughts and fantasies. Augustine often seems to see this clearly enough; but he does not take the decisive step of abandoning the will-o'-the-wisp of a purely active intellect, and the artificial theories to which it leads.

There is much wisdom in this statement, and it is of relevance to the theme in this book as a whole.

18. From the article "Reason" in A. Hastings, ed., *The Oxford Companion to Christian Thought* (Oxford and New York, 2000), p. 596. Compare the words of Joan of Arc in George Bernard Shaw's *St. Joan,* scene 5, when she is asked by Dunois, the Bastard of Orleans, why she provides him with reasons for her belief in her voices. "Well, I have to find reasons for you, because you do not believe in my voices. But the voices come first; and I find the reasons after . . ."

19. Quotations taken from Wills, *Saint Augustine,* p. 44.

20. R. MacMullen, *Christianity and Paganism in the Fourth to Eighth Centuries* (London and New Haven, 1997), p. 94.

21. See G. Bonner, "Augustine as Biblical Scholar," in P. R. Ackroyd and C. F.

Evans, eds., *The Cambridge History of the Bible,* vol 1 (Cambridge, 1970), pp. 541–63. In order to show how lively Augustine's imagination could be, I summarize (from this article) Augustine's analysis of the 153 fish caught in the miraculous draught (John 21:11). The sum of the integers 1 to 17 is 153. Taking 17, this is the sum of 10 (the Ten Commandments) and 7 (the number of the Holy Spirit, who enables the elect to fulfill the law). Thus 153 fishes comes to represent the whole number of the elect, as regenerated by the Holy Spirit. It is also three times 50 plus 3, the persons of the Trinity. The number 50 represents the square of 7 (the number of the Spirit) with one added to show the unity of the Spirit, whose operations are sevenfold and who was sent on the fiftieth day to the disciples! Note the mildly sarcastic comment of R. Mortley in his *From Word to Silence,* vol. 2, *The Way of Negation, Christian and Greek* (Bonn, 1986), p. 246: "At times it appears as if Augustine's pursuit of meaning in the pages of Scripture is somewhat like that of the modern literary critic [note Mortley is writing in the mid 1980s], who by multiplying a series of references and subjective connections, finds a meaning which is far removed from the text itself and any possible authorial intention."

22. See Kirwan, *Augustine,* p. 131, for Augustine on original sin. Paul's influence on Augustine was profound, so much so that one scholar has gone so far as to claim that "much of western Christian thought can be seen as one long response to Augustine's Paul" (P. Fredriksen in the entry on Paul in Fitzgerald, ed., *Augustine Through the Ages*).

23. The old question of how a god who is conceptualized as omnipotent and omniscient can allow evil seems impossible to answer. The pagan philosopher Sextus Empiricus (probably end of the second century A.D.) put the issue well in his *Outlines of Pyrrhonism,* 3:12: "For in claiming that he [God] is provident in all things, they will be saying that he is the cause of evil, but if they claim that he is provident only about some things or nothing, they will be forced to say either that God lacks good will or is weak; yet obviously only people who are impious will say this." Quoted in M. Frede, "Monotheism and Pagan Philosophy" in P. Athanassiadi and M. Frede, eds., *Pagan Monotheism in Late Antiquity* (Oxford, 1999), p. 56. In the mid second century, Marcion (the champion of Paul) attempted to solve the problem by arguing that there were two Gods, the powerful Creator God of the Old Testament, whose behaviour as related in the Old Testament was quite clearly wicked, and a good, all-knowing God who was the father of Christ. See Pelikan, *The Christian Tradition,* vol. 1, pp. 71ff. An introduction to the problems can be found in any study of the philosophy of religion, for instance, that edited by B. Davies, *Philosophy of Religion: A Guide and Anthology* (Oxford, 2000). There is a short overview in the article "Evil, the Problem of" by Thomas P. Flint in Hastings, ed., *The Oxford Companion to Christian Thought.* I have always been unhappy with the argument that evil should be seen as the inevitable consequence of God's gift to humanity of free will. Should one attempt to persuade those whose lives have been irretrievably ruined by the evil actions of others that this is because of the exercise of a free will given to the perpetrator of the evil by a God whom they should believe to be fully loving?

24. See Harrison, *Augustine,* p. 87, for the quotation from Augustine. The earlier history of Christian thinking on free will (as well as Augustine's views) is covered by Pelikan, *The Christian Tradition,* vol. 1, chap. 6, "Nature and Grace."

25. Pelikan's chapter on "Nature and Grace" is outstanding on Augustine's views. The problem remained of why anyone should behave well if it was already predestined who should be saved and who condemned. At the same time, if God can grant or withhold grace at will, then the responsibility of "allowing" human beings

to go to hell is his. Augustine argued in return that God created men whose damnation he could foresee as a means of manifesting his anger and demonstrating his power. The contradictions involved in sorting out predestination can be seen in the following quotation from Augustine cited by Pelikan (p. 297): "As the one who is supremely good, he made good use of evil deeds [*sic!*], for the damnation of those whom he had justly predestined to punishment and for the salvation of those whom he had kindly predestined to grace." One hardly needs to go further to explain the profound sense of insecurity that Augustine and his followers brought into the Christian tradition.

26. Harrison's quotation comes from her *Augustine*, p. 28. Kirwan, *Augustine*, lists the "original sin" texts on p. 131. They are also discussed by Pelikan in *The Christian Tradition*, vol. 1, pp. 299–300. Pelikan notes how Augustine was misled by a Latin mistranslation of Romans 5:12 in which "death spread to all men, through one man, in whom all men sinned," whereas the Greek original reads, "Death spread to all men, through one man, because all men sinned." See Stead, *Philosophy in Christian Antiquity*, pp. 232–33, for Augustine's views that the number of saved equalled the number of angels. In his *City of God* (22:24), Augustine leaves only the smallest scope for reasoned thought in "fallen man." "There is still the spark, as it were, of that reason in virtue of which he was made in the image of God: that spark has not been fully put out" (trans. H. Bettenson).

27. Pelikan, *The Christian Tradition*, vol. 1, p. 315, for the first of Pelagius' quotations; Harrison, *Augustine*, p. 103, for the second. Gerald Bonner has useful essays on Augustine and Pelagianism in his *Church and Faith in the Patristic Tradition* (Aldershot, U.K., and Brookfield, Vt., 1996).

28. Quoted in Kirwan, *Augustine*, p. 134. Richard Sorabji in his *Emotion and Peace of Mind: From Stoic Agitation to Christian Temptation* (Oxford, 2000), concludes that Julian (and Pelagius) won the philosophical argument but that the political argument (which was what now mattered) was won by Augustine. Sorabji concludes his chapter "Augustine on Lust and the Will" as follows (p. 417):

> To many, myself included, the Pelagian view that lust is a good thing, which may be put to bad use, is far more attractive than Augustine's view that lust is a bad thing which may, in marriage, be put to a good use. If Pelagius had prevailed on this and more generally on original sin, a British theologian would have been at the centre of western theology, and western attitudes to sexuality, and to much else besides, might have been very different.

The question of how an "evil" thing (sexual incontinence as Augustine conceived it) can be made good simply through the circumstances in which it is undertaken is another example of Augustine tying himself up in knots (and defying his own mentor Paul, who had condemned the idea of doing evil that good may come of it, Romans 3:8). The contradictions here are dissected by J. Mahoney on "Augustinism and Sexual Morality" in his *The Making of Moral Theology: A Study of the Roman Catholic Tradition* (Oxford, 1987), pp. 58–68.

29. The quotations are taken from the article by H. Chadwick, "Orthodoxy and Heresy," in A. Cameron and P. Garnsey, eds., *The Cambridge Ancient History*, vol. XIII (Cambridge, 1998), p. 583.

30. The conference of 411 is well covered by M. Tilley in "Dilatory Donatists or Procrastinating Catholics: The Trial at the Conference of Carthage," in E. Ferguson, ed., *Doctrinal Diversity: Varieties of Early Christianity* (New York and London,

1999). Tilley argues that the Donatists assumed that this conference would be a proper chance to discuss theology, but in fact it turned out to be no more than "an imperial administrative process" through which to condemn them. The Donatists attempted to argue that the issue was one of the goodness of individuals and mocked Augustine's view that good and bad individuals could co-exist within the same institution without defiling that institution.

31. The quotation from Augustine is from Kirwan, *Augustine*, p. 212, and that from Gregory from H. Drake, *Constantine and the Bishops: The Politics of Intolerance* (Baltimore and London, 2000), p. 407. See C. Kirwan, *Augustine*, pp. 212–18, for Augustine's shifting views on persecution. See also Rist, *Augustine*, "Towards a Theory of Persecution," pp. 239–45.

32. Rist, *Augustine*, p. 215. Like the Homoeans, the Donatists were casualities of the new principle that there should be only one state church based on one interpretation of Christianity. As rivals to the ownership of Christian "truth," the Donatists were treated far more harshly than Jews or pagans.

33. The quotation, itself quoted from a review, comes from Stephen O'Shea's *The Perfect Heresy: Life and Death of the Cathars* (London, 2000).

34. A point made by Harrison, *Augustine*, p. 197, who elaborates, on pp. 200–202, the sources for the idea of "the two cities." The rigid dichotomy between polarized extremes, good and bad, saved and unsaved, not only draws, like so much of Augustine's thought, on Paul but is typical of Augustine's polemical rhetoric. As such, it has created a great deal of unnecessary anxiety among Christians (if one does not agree totally with what has been defined as orthodoxy, one is condemned), and it has hindered the exploration of unresolved theological issues.

35. *The City of God* 19:13, quoted ibid., p. 207.

36. J. S. McClelland, *A History of Western Political Thought* (London, 1996), p. 108.

37. The point is made in Michael Signer's article "Jews and Judaism," in Fitzgerald, ed., *Augustine Through the Ages*, pp. 470–73. See also Harrison's sympathetic assessment in *Augustine*, pp. 142–44.

38. Stead, *Philosophy in Christian Antiquity*, p. 235.

39. Rist, *Augustine*, pp. 291–92. Note St. Jerome's comment in his Letter CVC: "You are renowned throughout the world. Catholics venerate you, and look upon you as a second founder of the old faith. And, surely what is a sign of greater glory [*sic*], all the heretics detest you." Mahoney, "Augustinism and Sexual Morality," p. 69, notes that Augustine's use of polarized language "can lead to violent and extreme language and entrenched positions, in which words become weapons with which to crush an adversary rather than inadequate counters of that humble exploration of divine reality which should be characteristic of theological discourse."

40. Quoted by M. Warner, *Alone of All Her Sex* (London, 1985), p. 57. As she notes, the idea "is an extension of Augustine's argument about original sin."

41. For this period, see chap. 5, "A Divided City: The Christian Church, 300–460," especially the section "The Primacy of Peter," in R. Collins, *Early Medieval Europe, 300–1000*, 2nd ed. (London, 1999). On Rome, R. Krautheimer's *Rome: Profile of a City, 312–1208* (Princeton, 2000), is an excellent starting point.

42. A good starting point for the tortuous career of Vigilius is his entry in J. Kelly, *The Oxford Dictionary of the Popes* (Oxford, 1986).

43. Herrin, *The Formation of Christendom*, pp. 125–27. Her chap. 3, "The Churches in the Sixth Century: The Council of 553," is essential for more detailed study of this period.

44. Ibid., p. 182. On Gregory, Herrin has good points to make—see her chap. 4, "The Achievement of Gregory the Great." For a fuller study, see R. Markus, *Gregory the Great and His World* (Cambridge, 1997), and for Gregory's thought, C. Straw, *Gregory the Great: Perfection in Imperfection* (Berkeley and London, 1988). There is also a sensitive introduction to Gregory by M. Colish in her *Medieval Foundations of the Western Intellectual Tradition* (New Haven and London, 1997), pp. 37–41.

45. Quoted in MacMullen, *Christianity and Paganism,* p. 97. R. A. Markus considers Gregory's approach to secular learning in *Gregory the Great,* pp. 34–40.

46. Herrin, *The Formation of Christendom,* p. 177. The longer extract from this reproach that Herrin gives has much to say about Gregory's view of the ministry, in particular that the need for unity in the church requires that bishops should be prepared to cooperate and compromise with each other when necessary. The quotation on "compassion" and "contemplation" comes from Gregory's *Regula Pastoralis,* his great work on the exercise of spiritual power.

47. Markus, *Gregory the Great,* p. 204.

48. Collins in *Early Medieval Europe,* p. 233. Chap. 13, "The Sundering of East and West," provides a good overview of the process.

49. The story of Fursey is told by P. Brown in "*Gloriosus Obitus:* The End of the Ancient Other World," in W. Klingshirn and M. Vessey, eds., *The Limits of Ancient Christianity: Essays on Later Antique Thought and Culture in Honor of R. A. Markus* (Ann Arbor, 1999), pp. 294–95. The problem of why Christianity laid such heavy stress on punishment in the afterlife is, of course, a major subject in itself and has only been partially addressed in this book. The words of Jesus in Matthew (25:31–46) have been fundamental, and Matthew 22:14, "Many are called but few are chosen," was used "generation after generation as proof that only a minority ever reached heaven" with the majority consigned everlastingly to hell. See the article on "hell" by A. Hastings, ed., in *The Oxford Companion to Christian Thought.*

50. N. MacGregor, *Seeing Salvation: Images of Christ in Art* (London, 2000), p. 127. See also M. Merback, *The Thief, the Cross and the Wheel: Pain and Punishment in Medieval and Renaissance Europe* (London, 1999), although this book concentrates primarily on the crucifixion of the good and bad thieves. The chapter "Images of the Suffering Redeemer" in R. M. Jensen, *Understanding Early Christian Art* (London and New York, 2000), provides an excellent exploration of the issues involved.

51. See Peter Brown, *The Rise of Western Christendom,* 2nd ed. (Malden, Oxford, Melbourne, and Berlin, 2003), p. 119. This magnificent survey of western Christendom takes the story up to 1000.

## 19

1. Book 5, chap. 5. The extracts are from the Penguin edition, translated by D. Magarshack.

2. Tenth-century *Ecomium* of Gregory of Nazianzus, quoted in R. Lim, *Public Disputation, Power and Social Order in Late Antiquity* (Berkeley and London, 1995), p. 158. A survey of how these heresies interacted on the ground can be found in S. Mitchell, *Anatolia: Land, Men and Gods in Asia Minor* (Oxford, 1993), vol. 2, pp. 91–108. Mitchell's survey shows that in fourth-century Phrygia and Lycaonia, orthodox Christianity was virtually unknown in an area that was, however, heavily Christian.

3. J. Pelikan, *Christianity and Classical Culture* (New Haven and London, 1993), is especially helpful here. See in particular chap. 3, "The Language of Negation."

4. As reported by his fellow Cappadocian Gregory of Nyssa, above, p. 195.

5. Lim, *Public Disputation,* p. 168.

6. See ibid., pp. 158–71, for a full analysis of these orations.

7. R. Hanson, *The Search for the Christian Doctrine of God* (Edinburgh, 1988), p. 809. Edward Gibbon made the point that if one wanted to know just how vicious debates were in these councils, one turned not to opponents of Christianity but to "one of the most pious and eloquent bishops of the age, a saint and a doctor of the church," Gregory of Nazianzus. A member of the Anglican commission on liturgy, the late Michael Vesey, is said to have compared preparing liturgical texts for the Anglican Synod with "trying to do embroidery with a bunch of football hooligans." Quoted in a letter to the *Independent* newspaper (London), November 29, 2000.

8. Lim, *Public Disputation,* p. 171.

9. Ibid., pp. 171–81.

10. The first quotation is from Pseudo-Dionysius, *The Celestial Hierarchy,* quoted in A. Cameron, *Christianity and the Rhetoric of Empire* (Berkeley and London, 1991), p. 219. Pseudo-Dionysius claimed that his works had been written by Dionysius the Areopagite, a convert of Paul's. The claim was so successful that it was not until 1895 that his writings were recognized as coming from the fifth century. See Paul Rorem, "The Uplifting Spirituality of Pseudo-Dionysius," in Bernard McGinn and John Meyendorff, eds., *Christian Spirituality: Origins to the Twelfth Century* (London, 1986); the quotation about "God being in no way like the things that have being" is taken from p. 135.

11. Quoted in Pelikan, *Christianity and Classical Culture,* p. 234.

12. Quoted in Lim, *Public Disputation,* p. 221.

13. I have taken these points from chap. 7, "The Orthodox Consensus," in J. Pelikan's *The Christian Tradition,* vol. 1 (Chicago and London, 1971). They remain recognizable in contemporary Roman Catholicism. Standard histories of Christian doctrine still tend to exclude mention of the historical context within which doctrine developed. This is one area of Christianity where the influence of Platonism remains strong. Correct doctrine is like the Platonic Forms, eternal, unchanging and available for an elite to grasp. This elite alone (the church hierarchies) has the right to interpret it for others. In such a context ideas cannot be relative to the society in which they are formed, and it is hardly surprising therefore that standard histories of Christian doctrine tend to ignore the wider historical context in which doctrine developed. Richard Hanson was one of the first theologians to declare, in *The Search for the Christian Doctrine of God* (Edinburgh, 1988), that it was the emperors who were the main force in establishing orthodoxy. Even then, his view, which was supported by a mass of historical evidence, was described in one review as "provocative."

14. There is Protagoras' famous saying from the fifth century B.C.: "About the gods I am not able to know whether they exist or do not exist, nor what they are like in form; for the factors preventing knowledge are many: the obscurity of the subject, and the shortness of human life." There is no indication here that Protagoras believed no one should have a go at defining the nature of the gods, in fact there is a record that he wrote just such a work himself and recited it in the home of the playwright Euripides.

15. Quoted in Cameron, *Christianity and the Rhetoric of Empire,* p. 15.

16. Ibid., p. 67. See also chap. 13, "Madness and Divinization: Symeon the

Holy Fool," in Guy Stroumsa, *Barbarian Philosophy: The Religious Revolution of Early Christianity* (Tubingen, 1999).

17. Augustine, *De Doctrina Christiana* 4:163 (translation: Green). A little earlier (section 161) Augustine suggests that God's words are like a possession that can be stolen. The fact that such a possession is held by a thief does not diminish its value. The point remains that the link stressed by Isocrates and Quintilian between the moral character of the speaker and the words he spoke has been broken.

18. G. Kennedy, *A New History of Classical Rhetoric* (Princeton, 1994), pp. 269–70.

19. Lim, *Public Disputation*, p. 233 and elsewhere in his book.

20. Ibid., pp. 231–32. Earlier attacks on Aristotle are to be found, as in the works of Tertullian. Arius was even referred to at one point as "the new Aristotle" on the grounds that he employed dialectic, in other words examined issues critically, rather than relying on faith. See R. Vaggione, *Eunomius of Cyzicus and the Nicene Revolution* (Oxford, 2000), p. 95.

21. Lim, *Public Disputation*, pp. 174–75.

22. These quotations are taken from R. MacMullen, *Christianity and Paganism in the Fourth to Eighth Centuries* (New Haven and London, 1997), pp. 86–89.

23. Cameron, *Christianity and the Rhetoric of Empire*, p. 206.

24. MacMullen, *Christianity and Paganism*, p. 90.

25. Edward Gibbon, *The Decline and Fall of the Roman Empire*, chap. 28.

26. Basil is quoted in Pelikan, *Christianity and Classical Culture*, p. 177. For the bishop of Melitene, see Henry Chadwick, *The Church in Ancient Society* (Oxford, 2001), p. 591.

27. "Bede and Medieval Civilization" and "Bede and His Legacy," reprinted as items XI and XIV in Gerald Bonner, *Church and Faith in Patristic Tradition* (Aldershot, U.K., and Brookfield, Vt., 1996). As Bonner puts it, "Bede's outlook is a narrow one, not merely in the sense that any specialist, theologian or otherwise is professionally narrow, but in the sense of deliberatly seeking to exclude a whole department of human experience—the non-Christian—from his considerations. . . . Bede did not seek to be original, but to stand in the tradition of the Fathers of the Church" (p. 10).

28. H. Belting, *Likeness and Presence: A History of the Image Before the Era of Art,* trans. E. Jephcott (Chicago and London, 1994). There is a wealth of material in this book on icons and the theological dimensions within which they were set. See also A. Cameron, "The Language of Images: The Rise of Icons and Christian Representation," in D. Wood, ed., *The Church and the Arts* (Oxford, 1992), pp. 1–42. An atmospheric account of these changes is to be found in P. Brown, *The World of Late Antiquity* (London, 1971), chap. 14, "The Death of the Classical World: Culture and Religion in the Early Middle Ages."

29. R. McInerny, *Saint Thomas Aquinas* (Boston, 1977), p. 18.

30. M. Hoskin and O. Gingerich, "Medieval Latin Astronomy," chap. 4 in M. Hoskin, ed., *The Cambridge Concise History of Astronomy* (Cambridge, 1999).

31. See the essay by Louise Marshall, "Confraternity and Community," in B. Wisch, ed., *Confraternities and the Visual Arts in Renaissance Italy: Ritual, Spectacle, Image* (Cambridge, 2000), above all the illustrations on pp. 22 and 23 (examples from Genoa and Siena). The examples are all the more remarkable in that when Apollo sends his plague on the Greeks at Troy (through arrows), it is the goddesses Hera and Athena who intervene to find a solution by which the plague is withdrawn.

32. Examples of shrines which maintain their continuity from pagan to

Christian are taken from MacMullen, *Christianity and Paganism*, pp. 126–27, but most of the examples quoted here and in the following paragraph come from R. Porter, *The Greatest Benefit to Mankind: A Medical History of Humanity from Antiquity to the Present* (London, 1997), chap. 4, "Medicine and Faith," and chap. 5, "The Medieval West." Miracles were, of course, known in the pagan world as well. One can learn a great deal from studying the contexts in which miracles take place and the range of miracles, some harming God's apparent enemies, others healing, others used as a means of effecting conversions. See W. Cotter, *Miracles in Greco-Roman Antiquity: A Sourcebook* (London, 1999).

33. *The Life of Saint Francis of Assisi,* trans. Ewart Cousins, 1:5–6, in Bonaventura, *The Soul's Journey unto God and Other Writings* (Paulist Press, 1978), pp. 34–35.

34. The *Euchologion,* quoted by P. Horden and N. Purcell, *The Corrupting Sea* (Oxford, 2000), p. 411.

35. Gibbon, *The Decline and Fall of the Roman Empire,* chap. 28.

36. See Antonio Damasio, *Descartes' Error: Emotion, Reason, and the Human Brain* (New York, 1994; London, 1995).

37. An excellent exploration of this aspect of Christianity is to be found in Averil Cameron, *Christianity and the Rhetoric of Empire* (Berkeley and London, 1995), especially chap. 5, "The Rhetoric of Paradox."

38. As Morris Kline, the historian of mathematics, puts it: "It is doubtful whether medieval Europe, if permitted to pursue an unchanging course, would ever have developed any real science or mathematics." M. Kline, *Mathematical Thought from Ancient to Modern Times,* vol. 1 (Oxford and New York, 1972), p. 214. For Copernicus' achievement within the context of medieval astronomy, see Hoskin and Gingerich, "Medieval Latin Astronomy."

## 20

1. This example is drawn from Elizabeth Fowden's study *The Barbarian Plain* (Berkeley and London, 1999). The quote from the Nestorian patriarch comes from an article, "Two Civilizations Entwined in History," by William Dalrymple in the *Independent* (London), October 12, 2001. I was intrigued to read in Jan Morris' *Trieste and the Meaning of Nowhere* (London, 2001) that Sergius had, in legend, been converted to Christianity while serving as a soldier in Trieste, and that at the moment of his martyrdom on the Barbarian Plain his halberd fell miraculously from the sky into the main piazza of the city. It is still preserved and is the main feature of an annual procession on his feast day.

2. Quoted in R. MacMullen, *Christianity and Paganism in the Fourth to Eighth Centuries* (New Haven and London, 1997), p. 19.

3. I have drawn material for this section from R. R. Bolgar, "The Greek Legacy," in M. Finley, ed., *The Legacy of Greece: A New Appraisal* (Oxford, 1984), and chap. 4 of R. Porter's *The Greatest Benefit to Mankind: A Medical History of Humanity from Antiquity to the Present* (London, 1997). For fuller coverage of Islamic philosophy, whose contribution to western thought is increasingly being recognized, see R. Popkin, ed., *The Pimlico History of Western Philosophy* (New York, 1998; London, 1999), sect. 2, "Medieval Islamic and Jewish Philosophy." The works of Jewish philosophers such as Moses Maimonides were also an important influence on western philosophy.

4. Quoted in P. Brown, "Christianisation and Religious Conflict," in A.

Cameron and P. Garnsey, eds., *The Cambridge Ancient History*, vol. XIII (Cambridge, 1998), p. 639. Compare the statement made at the Council of Florence (1439–45): "No one who is outside the Catholic Church, not just pagans, but Jews, heretics, and schismatics, can share in eternal life."

5. See R. Fletcher, *The Conversion of Europe* (London, 1997), for an overview. The consolidation of a rationale for church authority in both east and west is well covered by J. Pelikan, *The Christian Tradition,* vol. 1 (Chicago and London, 1971), chap. 7, "The Orthodox Consensus."

6. See R. Tarnas, *The Passion of the Western Mind* (London, 1996), part IV, "The Transformation of the Medieval Era," and M. Colish, *Medieval Foundations of the Western Intellectual Tradition* (New Haven and London, 1997), especially chap. 20, "Scholasticism and the Rise of Universities."

7. This view is argued with impressive power by Tarnas, *The Passion of the Western Mind*, "The Quest of Thomas Aquinas," pp. 179–90.

8. For Thomas Aquinas, a good short introduction is A. Kenny, *Aquinas* (Oxford, 1980). For more extended treatment, see R. McInerny, *Saint Thomas Aquinas* (Boston, 1977), and B. Davies, *The Thought of Thomas Aquinas* (Oxford, 1992). While one can applaud Thomas Aquinas for his courage and independence in bringing back rational thought into the Christian tradition, he remained a man of his time in many of his attitudes, especially to women, whom he would consciously avoid, and sexuality in general.

9. McInerny provides a typical statement of Aquinas' defence of free will, in which free will is seen as intrinsic to man's status as a rational being. The extract also gives an idea of Aquinas' method of exposition.

> For the sheep seeing the wolf judges that she should flee by a natural judgment which is not free since it does not involve pondering but she judges by natural instinct. So it is with every judgment of the brute animal. Now man acts by means of judgment, because through a knowing power he judges that something should be pursued or avoided, yet this instinct is not by a natural instinct toward a particular action but from a rational pondering. Thus he acts by free judgment since he is capable of directing himself in diverse ways . . . For this reason, that man acts from free judgement follows necessarily from the fact that he is rational.

McInerny, *Saint Thomas Aquinas,* p. 54. One less happy result of the argument presented above was that Aquinas followed Augustine in seeing animals as non-rational beings who were thus entirely at the service of man. He also followed Aristotle in believing that women are "by nature subordinate to man, because the power of rational discernment is by nature stronger in man."

There has been a tendency in Catholic theology to smooth over the difference between the major theologians. However, surely the contrast between Aquinas and Augustine is profound. Aquinas could never have written as Augustine did: "To approve falsehood instead of truth so as to err in spite of himself, and not to be able to refrain from the works of lust because of the pain involved in breaking away from fleshly bonds: these do not belong to the nature of man as he was created [before the Fall]. They are the penalty of man as [now] condemned [by original sin]." From *On Free Will* 3:18:52, quoted in C. Harrison, *Augustine, Christian Truth and Fractured Humanity* (Oxford, 2000), p. 86. Compare too the words of Athanasius, "We are not permitted to ask presumptuous questions about the begetting of the Son of God *nor to make our nature and our limitations the measure of God and his wisdom"* (my emphasis). This is the exact opposite of Aquinas' "To take something away from the perfection of the creature is to abstract from the perfection of the creative power [i.e. God] itself."

10. Aquinas left himself, of course, with the problem of defining what happened to the soul after death. He had to admit that it was no longer the person who had lived, but what was it? "A disembodied soul does not feel joy and sadness due to bodily desire, but due to intellectual desire, as with the angels." For these issues, see the excellent chapter "Being Human" in Davies, *The Thought of Thomas Aquinas*.

11. R. Markus, "Aquinas and Aristotle," *Blackfriars,* March 1961. Compare Pelikan's view that Aquinas' treatise *On the Soul* was "determined more by philosophical than by biblical language about the soul" (Pelikan, *The Christian Tradition,* vol. 1, p. 89). It perhaps needs to be stressed how fascinated by science Aquinas was. He did, after all, write commentaries on Aristotle's physics, cosmology and meteorology, and he is known to have secured a copy of Heron of Alexandria's work on the mechanics of steam engines before anyone else at the University of Paris.

12. Quoted in Davies, *The Thought of Thomas Aquinas,* p. 246.

13. See J. Mahoney, *The Making of Moral Theology: A Study of the Roman Catholic Tradition* (Oxford, 1987), chap. 7, "The Impact of *Humanae Vitae*." For the relationship between Aristotle, Plato and Aquinas in the formulation of the concept of natural law, see J. Finnis, *Natural Law and Natural Rights* (Oxford, 1980), chap. 13, "Nature, Reason, God." Finnis sees Plato's late work *The Laws* as one of the foundation texts of the concept. Aquinas asserts that natural law cannot conflict with the teachings of the scriptures, but this gives rise to further conceptual problems (for example, is each one of the Ten Commandments to be regarded an expression of natural law?). In the *Catechism of the Catholic Church* (London, 1994), the sections on "Natural Moral Law," numbers 1954–60, are supported, rather surprisingly, by a quotation from Cicero but otherwise by none other earlier than Augustine.

14. An excellent survey of Aquinas' political views can be found in J. S. McClelland, *A History of Western Political Thought* (London and New York, 1996), chap. 7, "Christendom and Its Law." McClelland not only compares and contrasts Aquinas with Augustine but discusses the implications of natural law for medieval political thought. The philosopher Alisdair MacIntyre claims that Aristotelianism as developed by Thomas Aquinas represents the high point of western thought on ethical issues.

15. The tendency was to use Aristotle as an authority figure in support of Christian theology rather than as a means of invigorating it. Aristotle's view (supported by Greek thinkers in general) that the male provides the essential element of life at conception, with the woman providing a stable fluid in which it can grow, fitted well with traditional ideas of the virgin birth, and may actually have influenced the development of these views; see M. Warner, *Alone of All Her Sex* (London, 1985), chap. 3, "Virgin Birth." If the modern scientific view that Mary's genetic contribution to Jesus would be equal to God's is taken at face value, the theological problems are daunting. Aristotle's ideas were also used to support the doctrine of transubstantiation (the doctrine that the bread and wine are changed totally into the body and blood of Christ at the moment of consecration). By the seventeenth century the English philosopher Thomas Hobbes was to write that in the universities philosophy "hath no other place than as the handmaiden to the Roman religion; and

since the authority of Aristotle is only current there, that study is not properly philosophy but Aristotelity." Louis XIV was to make the astonishing assertion that *"notre religion et Aristote sont tellement liez qu'on ne puisse renverser l'un sans ébranler l'autre"*—"our religion and Aristotle are so closely linked that one cannot overthrow one without undermining the other" (quoted in J. Israel, *Radical Enlightenment: Philosophy and the Making of Modernity 1650–1750* [Oxford and New York, 2001]; this brilliant book shows just how tightly a sterile Aristotelianism dominated conservative thinking in the seventeenth century).

As already stressed in this book, the essence of Greek intellectual life lay in its stress on the provisional nature of knowledge and the acceptance that all "authorities" were there to be challenged, and one can assume that Aristotle would not have approved of the "fixed" status given to his works by theologians, any more than Ptolemy or Galen would have approved of the way that their work was frozen. It was not until the twentieth century that Aristotle's extraordinary intellectual achievement was once again fully recognized.

## EPILOGUE

1. See Jonathan Barnes, "Galen, Christians, Logic," in T. P. Wiseman, ed., *Classics in Progress* (Oxford, 2002), for fuller discussion.

2. On the relationship between reason and emotion in the healthy mind, see Antonio Damasio, *Descartes' Error: Emotion, Reason and the Human Brain* (New York, 1994; London, 1995). On free will and optimism, see the works of Raymond Tallis, especially *Enemies of Hope: A Critique of Contemporary Pessimism* (London, 1997).

# Modern Works Cited in the Text and Notes

References to ancient texts can be followed up in the Loeb Classical Library, although many of the major works can be found in the Penguin Classics series. The Penguin Classics also include the works of the more prominent Christian thinkers, such as Augustine. Note also the compilations by Henry Bettenson cited below. Otherwise, the original works of the Church Fathers are not always easy to track down, and often the easiest way to find translations is through the Internet. For early Christianity in general I can recommend www.christianorigins.org, through which can be reached www.newadvent.org/fathers/, which has translations of most of the key works of the Church Fathers.

Ackroyd, P. R., and C. F. Evans, eds. *The Cambridge History of the Bible.* vol. 1. Cambridge, 1970.

Alexander, L. "Paul and the Hellenistic Schools: The Evidence of Galen." In Troels Engbury-Pedersen, ed., *Paul in His Hellenistic Context.* Edinburgh, 1994.

Alison, James. *Faith Beyond Resentment: Fragments Catholic and Gay.* London, 2001.

Armstrong, Karen. *A History of God.* London, 1993.

Athanassiadi, P., and M. Frede. *Pagan Monotheism in Late Antiquity.* Oxford, 1999.

Baldry, R. *The Greeks and the Unity of Mankind.* Cambridge, 1965.

Barclay, John. "Paul Among Diaspora Jews: Anomaly or Apostate." *Journal of the Study of the New Testament* 60 (1995): 89–120.

Barnes, Jonathan. *Aristotle.* Oxford, 1982.

———. "Galen, Christians, Logic." In T. P. Wiseman, ed., *Classics in Progress.* Oxford, 2002.

Barrett, C. K. *A Commentary on the First Epistle to the Corinthians.* London, 1971.

Barton, John, and John Muddiman, eds. *The Oxford Bible Commentary.* Oxford, 2001.

Beard, M., J. North, and S. Price. *Religions of Rome.* Cambridge, 1998.

Becker, J. *Paul: Apostle to the Gentiles.* Trans. O. C. Dean, Jr. Louisville, Ky., 1993.

Belting, Hans. *Likeness and Presence: A History of the Image Before the Era of Art.* Trans. E. Jephcott. Chicago and London, 1994.

Berggren, J. Lennert, and Alexander Jones, eds. and trans. *Ptolemy's Geography: An Annotated Translation of the Theoretical Chapters*. Princeton, 2002.

Bernado, A. S., and S. Levin, eds. *The Classics in the Middle Ages*. New York, 1990.

Bettenson, Henry, ed. *Documents of the Christian Church*. Oxford, 1943.

———. *The Early Christian Fathers*. Oxford, 1956.

Birley, Anthony. *Hadrian, the Restless Emperor*. London and New York, 1997.

Boardman, John, Jasper Griffin, and Oswyn Murray, eds. *The Oxford History of the Classical World*. Oxford, 1986.

Boatwright, M. T. *Hadrian and the Cities of the Roman Empire*. Princeton and Chichester, Eng., 2000.

Bobzien, Suzanne. *Determinism and Freedom in Stoic Philosophy*. Oxford, 2000.

Bockmuehl, Markus, ed. *The Cambridge Companion to Jesus*. Cambridge, 2001.

Bolgar, R. R. "The Greek Legacy." In M. Finley, ed., *The Legacy of Greece: A New Appraisal*. Oxford, 1984.

Bonner, G. "Augustine as Biblical Scholar." In P. R. Ackroyd and C. F. Evans, eds. *The Cambridge History of the Bible*, vol. 1: *From the Beginning to Jerome*. Cambridge, 1970.

———. *Church and Faith in Patristic Tradition*. Aldershot, U.K., and Brookfield, Vt., 1996.

Bosworth, A. B. *Alexander and the East: The Tragedy of Triumph*. Oxford, 1996.

———. *Conquest and Empire: The Reign of Alexander the Great*. Cambridge, 1988.

———. *From Arrian to Alexander: Studies in Historical Interpretation*. Oxford, 1988.

Bosworth, A. B., and E. J. Baynham, eds. *Alexander the Great in Fact and Fiction*. Oxford, 2000.

Bowder, Diana. *The Age of Constantine and Julian*. London, 1978.

Bowen, Alan, ed. *Science and Philosophy in Ancient Greece*. New York and London, 1993.

Bowersock, G. W. *Hellenism in Late Antiquity*. Ann Arbor, 1990.

Bowersock, G. W., Peter Brown, and Oleg Grabar. *Late Antiquity: A Guide to the Postclassical World*. Cambridge, Mass., and London, 1999.

Bowman, A., and G. Woolf, eds. *Literacy and Power in the Ancient World*. Cambridge, 1994.

Bradley, Keith. *Slavery and Society at Rome*. Cambridge, 1994.

Bragg, M. *On Giants' Shoulders*. London, 1998.

Brakke, David. "Athanasius." In P. Esler, ed., *The Early Christian World*, 2 vols. New York and London, 2000.

Brown, Peter. "Art and Society in Late Antiquity." In K. Weitzmann, ed., *Age of Spirituality: A Symposium*. New York, 1980.

———. "Asceticism: Pagan and Christian," and "Christianisation and Religious Conflict." In Averil Cameron and Peter Garnsey, eds., *The Cambridge Ancient History*, vol. XIII: *The Late Empire, A.D. 337–425*. Cambridge, 1998.

———. *Augustine of Hippo*. London, 1977; 2nd rev. ed., Berkeley and London, 2000.

———. *The Body and Society: Men, Women and Sexual Renunciation in Early Christianity*. New York, 1988; London, 1989.

———. "*Gloriosus Obitus*: The End of the Ancient Other World." In W. Klingshirn and M. Vessey, eds., *The Limits of Ancient Christianity: Essays on Later Antique Thought and Culture in Honor of R. A. Markus*. Ann Arbor, 1999.

———. *Poverty and Leadership in the Later Roman Empire*. Hanover and London, 2002.

———. *Power and Persuasion in Late Antiquity*. Madison, Wis., and London, 1992.

———. *The Rise of Western Christendom*. 2nd ed. Malden, Oxford, Melbourne, and Berlin, 2003.

———. *The World of Late Antiquity*. London, 1971.

Brown, R. E. *The Death of the Messiah*. London, 1994.

Brunschwig, Jacques. "Skepticism." In J. Brunschwig and G. E. R. Lloyd, eds., *Greek Thought: A Guide to Classical Knowledge,* pp. 937–56. Cambridge, Mass., and London, 2000.

———. "Stoicism." In J. Brunschwig and G. E. R. Lloyd, eds., *Greek Thought: A Guide to Classical Knowledge,* pp. 977–96. Cambridge, Mass., and London, 2000.

Brunschwig, Jacques, and G. E. R. Lloyd, eds. *Greek Thought: A Guide to Classical Knowledge*. Cambridge, Mass., and London, 2000.

Cameron, Averil. *Christianity and the Rhetoric of Empire*. Berkeley and London, 1991.

———. "The Language of Images: The Rise of Icons and Christian Representation." In D. Wood, ed., *The Church and the Arts,* pp. 1–42. Oxford, 1992.

———. *The Later Roman Empire*. London, 1993.

———. *The Mediterranean World in Late Antiquity*. London and New York, 1993.

Cameron, Averil, and Peter Garnsey, eds. *The Cambridge Ancient History*. Vol. XIII: *The Late Empire,* A.D. *337–425*. Cambridge, 1998.

Cameron, Averil, and Stuart Hall, eds. and trans. *Eusebius: Life of Constantine*. Oxford, 1999.

Cartlidge, D., and J. K. Elliott. *Art and the Christian Apocrypha*. London and New York, 2001.

Chadwick, Henry. *Augustine*. Oxford, 1986.

———. *The Church in Ancient Society*. Oxford, 2001.

———. "Orthodoxy and Heresy." In Averil Cameron and Peter Garnsey, eds., *The Cambridge Ancient History,* vol. XIII. Cambridge, 1998.

Chuvin, Pierre. *A Chronicle of the Last Pagans*. Cambridge, Mass., and London, 1990.

Claridge, Amanda. *Rome: An Oxford Archaeological Guide*. Oxford and New York, 1998.

Clark, Gillian. "Women and Asceticism in Late Antiquity: The Reversal of Status and Gender." In V. Wimbush and R. Valantasis, eds., *Asceticism*. New York and Oxford, 1995.

Clark Smith, John. *The Ancient Wisdom of Origen*. London and Toronto, 1992.

Coakley, S., and D. Pailin, eds. *The Making and Remaking of Christian Doctrine: Essays in Honor of Maurice Wiles*. Oxford, 1993.

Colish, Marcia. "Cicero, Ambrose and Stoic Ethics: Transmission or Transformation?" In A. S. Barnardo and S. Levin, eds., *The Classics in the Middle Ages*. New York, 1990.

———. *Medieval Foundations of the Western Intellectual Tradition*. New Haven and London, 1997.

Collins, John J. *The Encyclopaedia of Apocalypticism*. Vol. 1: *The Origins of Apocalypticism in Judaism and Christianity*. New York, 1998.

Collins, Roger. *Early Medieval Europe, 300–1000*. 2nd ed., London, 1999.

Coogan, M., and B. Metzger, eds. *The Oxford Companion to the Bible*. Oxford and New York, 1993.

Cooper, John. "Plato's Theory of Human Motivation." *History of Philosophy Quarterly* 1, no. 1 (January 1984).

Cornell, T. J. *The Beginnings of Rome*. London, 1995.

Cotter, Wendy. *Miracles in Greco-Roman Antiquity: A Sourcebook.* London, 1999.

Court, John, and Kathleen Court. *The New Testament World.* Cambridge, 1990.

Crabbe, C., and M. James, eds. *From Soul to Self.* London and New York, 1999.

Craig, Edward, ed. *The Routledge Encyclopaedia of Philosophy.* London and New York, 1998.

Croke, B., and J. Harries. *Religious Conflict in Fourth Century Rome.* Sydney, 1982.

Cross, F. L., and E. A. Livingstone, eds. *The Oxford Dictionary of the Christian Church.* 3rd ed. Oxford, 1997.

Dalrymple, William. *From the Holy Mountain.* London, 1997.

———. "Two Civilizations Entwined in History." *Independent* (London), October 12, 2001.

Damasio, Antonio. *Descartes' Error: Emotion, Reason and the Human Brain.* New York, 1994; London, 1995.

D'Ancona, Matthew, and Carsten Peter Theide. *The Quest for the True Cross.* London, 2000.

Davidson, Ivor. "Ambrose." In P. Esler, ed., *The Early Christian World,* vol. 2. New York and London, 2000.

Davies, Brian. *Philosophy of Religion: A Guide and Anthology.* Oxford, 2000.

———. *The Thought of Thomas Aquinas.* Oxford, 1992.

Davies, J. K. *Democracy and Classical Greece.* 2nd ed. London, 1993.

Davies, W. D. "Paul from a Jewish Point of View." In William Horbury, W. D. Davies and John Sturdy, eds., *The Cambridge History of Judaism,* vol. 3, chap. 21. Cambridge, 1999.

Davies, W. D., and E. P. Sanders. "Jesus: From the Jewish Point of View." In William Horbury, W. D. Davies and John Sturdy, eds., *The Cambridge History of Judaism,* vol. 3. Cambridge 1999.

de Boer, M. C. "Paul and Apocalyptic Eschatology." In John J. Collins, *The Encyclopaedia of Apocalypticism,* vol. 1: *The Origins of Apocalypticism in Judaism and Christianity.* New York, 1998.

de Lange, Nicholas. *Atlas of the Jewish World.* Oxford, 1984.

Dillon, J. M. "Rejecting the Body, Redefining the Body: Some Remarks on the Development of Platonist Asceticism." In V. Wimbush and R. Valantasis, eds., *Asceticism.* New York and Oxford, 1995.

Dillon, J. M., and A. A. Long, eds. *The Question of Eclecticism: Studies in Later Greek Philosophy.* Berkeley and London, 1988.

Dodaro, R., and G. Lawless, eds. *Augustine and His Critics.* London and New York, 2000.

Dodds, E. R. *The Greeks and the Irrational.* Berkeley and London, 1951.

Drake, H. A. "Constantine and Consensus." *Church History* 64 (1995).

———. *Constantine and the Bishops: The Politics of Intolerance.* Baltimore and London, 2000.

Dunn, J. *The Theology of Paul the Apostle.* Edinburgh, 1998.

Durkheim, Emile. *Rules of Sociological Method.* Eng. trans. Glencoe, Ill., 1950.

Elm, S. *Virgins of God.* Oxford, 1994.

Elsner, Jas. *Imperial Rome and Christian Triumph: The Art of the Roman Empire, A.D. 100–450.* Oxford, 1998.

Engbury-Pedersen, Troels, ed. *Paul in His Hellenistic Context.* Edinburgh, 1994.

Esler, P., ed. *The Early Christian World.* 2 vols. New York and London, 2000.

Farmer, D. *The Oxford Dictionary of the Saints.* 4th ed. Oxford, 1997.

Ferguson, Everett, ed. *Doctrinal Diversity: Varieties of Early Christianity.* New York and London, 1999.

————. *Encyclopaedia of Early Christianity.* Chicago and London, 1990.

Ferguson, N. *The Pity of War.* London, 1998.

Finley, M. I., ed. *The Legacy of Greece: A New Appraisal.* Oxford, 1984.

Finnis, John. *Natural Law and Natural Rights.* Oxford, 1980.

Fitzgerald, A. D., ed. *Augustine Through the Ages.* Grand Rapids, Mich., and Cambridge, 1999.

Fletcher, Richard. *The Conversion of Europe.* London, 1997.

Flint, Thomas P. "Evil, the Problem of." In A. Hastings, ed., *The Oxford Companion to Christian Thought.* Oxford and New York, 2000.

Fowden, Elizabeth. *The Barbarian Plain.* Berkeley and London, 1999.

Frede, M. "Monotheism and Pagan Philosophy." In P. Athanassiadi and M. Frede, *Pagan Monotheism in Late Antiquity.* Oxford, 1999.

Frede, M., and Gisela Striker, eds. *Rationality in Greek Thought.* Oxford, 1996.

Fredriksen, Paula. *From Jesus to Christ.* 2nd ed. New Haven and London, 2000.

————. *Jesus of Nazareth, King of the Jews.* London, 2000.

————. "Paul and Augustine: Conversion Narratives, Orthodox Traditions, and the Retrospective Self." *Journal of Theological Studies* 37 (1986).

Freeman, Charles. *Egypt, Greece and Rome: Civilizations of the Ancient Mediterranean.* Oxford, 1996.

————. *The Greek Achievement: The Foundation of the Western World.* London, and New York, 1999.

Freyne, Sean. *Galilee and Gospel.* Tubingen, 2000.

Galinsky, K. *Augustine Culture: An Interpretative Introduction.* Princeton, 1996.

Garnsey, Peter. *Ideas of Slavery from Aristotle to Augustine.* Cambridge, 1996.

Garnsey, Peter, and Caroline Humfress. *The Evolution of the Late Antique World.* Cambridge, 2001.

Geanakoplos, Deno John. "The Second Ecumenical Council at Constantinople (381): Proceedings and Theology of the Holy Spirit." In Deno John Geanakoplos, *Constantinople and the West.* Madison, Wis., and London, 1989.

Geiger, Gail. *Filippino Lippi's Carafa Chapel: Renaissance Art in Rome.* Kirksville, Mo., 1986.

Gerson, Lloyd P. "Plotinus and Neoplatonism." In Richard Popkin, *The Pimlico History of Western Philosophy.* New York and London, 1999.

————, ed. *The Cambridge Companion to Plotinus.* Cambridge, 1996.

Goodman, Martin. "Galilean Judaism and Judaean Judaism." In W. Horbury, W. D. Davies and John Sturdy, eds., *The Cambridge History of Judaism,* vol. 3. Cambridge, 1999.

————. *The Roman World, 44 B.C.–A.D. 180.* London, 1997.

Grabar, A. *Christian Iconography: A Study of Its Origins.* London, 1968.

Grabbe, L. *Judaic Religion in the Second Temple Period.* London and New York, 2000.

————. *Priests, Prophets, Diviners, Sages: A Socio-Historical Study of Religious Specialists in Ancient Israel.* Valley Forge, Pa., 1995.

Green, Peter. *Alexander to Actium.* London, 1990.

————. Review of J. Lennert Berggren and Alexander Jones, eds. and trans., *Ptolemy's Geography: An Annotated Translation of the Theoretical Chapters,* Princeton, 2002. In the *London Review of Books,* vol. 24. no. 4, February 21, 2002, p. 35.

————, ed. and trans. *The Argonautika.* Berkeley and London, 1997.

Griffin, Jasper. "The Epic Cycle and the Uniqueness of Homer." *Journal of Hellenic Studies* 97 (1977): 39–53.

Griffin, Miriam. *Nero: The End of a Dynasty*. London, 1984.

Gruen, E. *Culture and National Identity in Republican Rome*. Ithaca, 1992.

Hamilton, J. R. *Plutarch's Alexander: A Commentary*. 2nd ed. Bristol, 1999.

Hanson, Richard. "The Achievement of Orthodoxy in the Fourth Century A.D." In Rowan Williams, ed., *The Making of Orthodoxy: Essays in Honour of Henry Chadwick*. Cambridge, 1989.

———. *The Search for the Christian Doctrine of God*. Edinburgh, 1988.

Hare, R. M. *Plato*. Oxford, 1982.

Harris, W. *War and Imperialism in Republican Rome*. Oxford, 1979.

Harrison, Carol. *Augustine, Christian Truth and Fractured Humanity*. Oxford, 2000.

Hastings, Adrian, ed. *The Oxford Companion to Christian Thought*. Oxford and New York, 2000.

Hays, Richard. *Echoes of Scripture in the Letters of Paul*. New Haven and London, 1989.

Hellemo, G. *Adventus Domini*. Leiden, 1989.

Hengel, M. "The Pre-Christian Paul." In J. Lieu, J. North and T. Rajak, *The Jews Among Pagans and Christians in the Roman Empire*. London and New York, 1992.

Herrin, Judith. *The Formation of Christendom*. Oxford, 1987 (Fontana ed., London, 1989).

Hick, John. "Interpretation and Reinterpretation in Religion." In S. Coakley and D. Pailin, eds., *The Making and Remaking of Christian Doctrine: Essays in Honour of Maurice Wiles*. Oxford, 1993.

———, ed. *The Myth of God Incarnate*. 2nd ed. London, 1993.

Hoffman, Paul. *The Man Who Loved Only Numbers*. London, 1999.

Hopkins, Keith. "Christian Number and Its Implication." *Journal of Early Christian Studies* 6 (1998): 185–226.

Hopko, Thomas. "The Trinity in the Cappadocians." In Bernard McGinn and John Meyendorff, eds., *Christian Spirituality: Origins to the Twelfth Century*. London, 1986.

Horbury, William, W. D. Davies, and John Sturdy, eds. *The Cambridge History of Judaism*. Vol. 3. Cambridge, 1999.

Horden, P., and N. Purcell. *The Corrupting Sea*. Oxford, 2000.

Horsley, Richard. *Bandits, Prophets and Messiahs: Popular Movements at the Time of Jesus*. New York, 1985.

———. "Jesus and Galilee: The Contingencies of a Renewal Movement." In E. Mayes, ed., *Galilee Through the Centuries: Confluence of Cultures*. Winona Lake, Ind., 1999.

Hoskin, Michael, ed. *The Cambridge Concise History of Astronomy*. Cambridge, 1999.

Hunt, David. "The Successors of Constantine," "Julian," and "The Church as a Public Institution." In Averil Cameron and Peter Garnsey, eds., *The Cambridge Ancient History*, vol. XIII: *The Late Empire, A.D. 337–425*. Cambridge, 1998.

Huskinson, Janet, ed., *Experiencing Rome: Culture, Identity and Power in the Roman Empire*. London, 2000.

Israel, Jonathan. *Radical Enlightenment: Philosophy and the Making of Modernity 1650–1750*. Oxford and New York, 2001.

James, William. *The Varieties of Religious Experience*. Edinburgh, 1902, and many later editions.

Janes, Dominic. *God and Gold in Late Antiquity*. Cambridge, 1998.

Jensen, Robin Margaret. *Understanding Early Christian Art*. London and New York, 2000.

Johnstone, C. L. *Theory, Text, Context: Issues in Greek Rhetoric and Oratory*. New York, 1994.

Kahn, Charles. "Discovering the Will: From Aristotle to Augustine." In J. M. Dillon and A. A. Long, eds., *The Question of Eclecticism: Studies in Later Greek Philosophy*. Berkeley and London, 1988.

———. "The Origins of Greek Science and Philosophy." In Alan Bowen, ed., *Science and Philosophy in Ancient Greece*. New York and London, 1993.

Kee, Alistair. *Constantine Versus Christ*. London, 1982.

Kelly, Christopher. "Emperors, Government and Bureaucracy." In Averil Cameron and Peter Garnsey, eds., *The Cambridge Ancient History*, vol. XIII. Cambridge, 1988.

———. "Empire Building." In G. W. Bowersock, Peter Brown and Oleg Grabar, eds., *Late Antiquity: A Guide to the Postclassical World*. Cambridge, Mass., and London, 1999.

Kelly, J. *Golden Mouth: The Story of John Chrysostom*. London, 1995.

———. *Jerome*. London, 1975.

———. *The Oxford Dictionary of the Popes*. Oxford, 1986.

Kennedy, George. *A New History of Classical Rhetoric*. Princeton, 1994.

Kenny, Anthony. *Aquinas*. Oxford, 1980.

Kerferd, G. *The Sophistic Movement*. Cambridge, 1981.

Kiilerich, B. "A Different Interpretation of the Nicomachorum-Symmachorum Diptych." *Jahrbuch für Antike und Christentum* 34 (1991).

King, Helen. *Hippocrates' Women: Reading the Female Body in Ancient Greece*. London and New York, 1998.

Kinney, D. "The Iconography of the Ivory Diptych Nicomachorum-Symmachorum." *Jahrbuch für Antike und Christentum* 37 (1994).

Kirwan, Christopher. *Augustine*. London and New York, 1989.

Kline, Morris. *Mathematical Thought from Ancient to Modern Times*. Vol. 1. New York and Oxford, 1972.

Klingshirn, W., and M. Vessey, eds. *The Limits of Ancient Christianity: Essays on Later Antique Thought and Culture in Honor of R. A. Markus*. Ann Arbor, 1999.

Koester, Helmut. *Ancient Christian Gospels: Their History and Development*. London, 1990.

Krautheimer, R. *Rome: Profile of a City, 312–1308*. Princeton, 2000.

———. *Three Christian Capitals*. Berkeley, 1983.

Lane Fox, Robin. "Literacy and Power in Early Christianity." In A. Bowman and G. Woolf, eds., *Literacy and Power in the Ancient World*. Cambridge, 1994.

———. *Pagans and Christians*. London, 1986.

Lear, Jonathan. *Aristotle: The Desire to Understand*. Cambridge, 1988.

Le Boullec, Alain. "Hellenism and Christianity." In J. Brunschwig and G. E. R. Lloyd, eds., *Greek Thought: A Guide to Classical Knowledge*. Cambridge, Mass., and London, 2000.

Liebeschuetz, J. W. *Barbarians and Bishops: Army, Church and State in the Age of Arcadius and Chrysostom*. Oxford, 1990.

———. *Continuity and Change in Roman Religion*. Oxford, 1979.

———. "The Significance of the Speech of Praetextatus." In P. Athanassiadi and M. Frede, eds., *Pagan Monotheism in Late Antiquity*. Oxford 1999.

Lieu, J., J. North, and T. Rajak, eds. *The Jews Among Pagans and Christians in the Roman Empire*. London and New York, 1992.

Lim, Richard. *Public Disputation: Power and Social Order in Late Antiquity.* Berkeley and London, 1995.

Limberis, Vasiliki. *Divine Heiress: The Virgin Mary and the Creation of Christian Constantinople.* London and New York, 1994.

Lloyd, G. E. R. *Aristotelian Explorations.* Cambridge, 1996.

———. "Demonstration in Galen." In M. Frede and G. Striker, eds., *Rationality in Greek Thought.* Oxford, 1996.

———. *Early Greek Science: Thales to Aristotle.* London, 1974.

———. *Greek Science After Aristotle.* London, 1973.

———. *Magic, Reason and Experience.* Cambridge, 1979.

———. *The Revolutions of Wisdom.* Berkeley and London, 1957.

Long, A. A. "Hellenistic Philosophy." In Richard Popkin, *The Pimlico History of Western Philosophy.* New York, 1998; London, 1999.

———, ed. *The Cambridge Companion to Early Greek Philosophy.* Cambridge, 1999.

Longrigg, James. *Greek Medicine: From the Heroic to the Hellenistic Age: A Source Book.* London, 1998.

Louden, R. B., and P. Schollmeier, eds. *The Greeks and Us: Essays in Honor of Arthur W. H. Adkins.* Chicago and London, 1999.

Maas, Michael. *Readings in Late Antiquity: A Sourcebook.* London and New York, 2000.

MacCormack, Sabine. *Art and Ceremony in Late Antiquity.* Berkeley and London, 1981.

MacDonald, William, and John Pinto. *Hadrian's Villa and Its Legacy.* New Haven and London, 1995.

MacGregor, Neil. *Seeing Salvation: Images of Christ in Art.* London, 2000.

MacMullen, Ramsay. *Christianising the Roman Empire* (A.D. *100–400*). New Haven and London, 1984.

———. *Christianity and Paganism in the Fourth to Eighth Centuries.* New Haven and London, 1997.

Macquarrie, John. *Jesus Christ in Modern Thought.* London and Philadelphia, 1990.

Mahoney, John. *The Making of Moral Theology: A Study of the Roman Catholic Tradition.* Oxford, 1987.

Mango, C. "Antique Statuary and the Byzantine Beholder." *Dumbarton Oaks Papers,* no. 17 (1963): 55–75.

———, ed. *The Oxford History of Byzantium.* Oxford, 2002.

Markus, Robert. "Aquinas and Aristotle." *Blackfriars,* March 1961.

———. *The End of Ancient Christianity.* Cambridge, 1990.

———. *Gregory the Great and His World.* Cambridge, 1997.

Marshall, Louise. "Confraternity and Community." In B. Wisch, ed., *Confraternities and the Visual Arts in Renaissance Italy: Ritual, Spectacle, Image.* Cambridge, 2000.

Matthews, Thomas. *The Clash of Gods: A Reinterpretation of Early Christian Art.* Rev. paperback ed. Princeton, 1999.

Mayes, E., ed. *Galilee Through the Centuries: Confluence of Cultures.* Winona Lake, Ind., 1999.

Mayhew, Henry. *London Labour and the London Poor.* London, 1861–62.

McClelland, J. S. *A History of Western Political Thought.* London and New York, 1996.

McGinn, Bernard, and John Meyendorff, eds. *Christian Spirituality: Origins to the Twelfth Century.* London, 1986.

McInerny, R. *Saint Thomas Aquinas*. Boston, 1977.

McLynn, N. *Ambrose of Milan: Church and Court in a Christian Capital*. Berkeley, 1994.

McManners, John, ed. *The Oxford Illustrated History of Christianity*. Oxford, 1990.

Meeks, Wayne. *The First Urban Christians*. New Haven and London, 1983.

Meier, Christian. *Caesar*. London, 1995.

*Memory and Reconciliation: The Church and the Faults of the Past*. Vatican City, 1999.

Merback, M. *The Thief, the Cross and the Wheel: Pain and Punishment in Medieval and Renaissance Europe*. London, 1999.

Millar, Fergus. *The Roman Near East 31 B.C.–A.D. 337*. Cambridge, Mass., and London, 1993.

Mitchell, Margaret. *The Heavenly Trumpet: John Chrysostom and the Art of Pauline Interpretation*. Tubingen, 2000.

Mitchell, Stephen. *Anatolia: Land, Men and Gods in Asia Minor*. 2 vols. Oxford, 1993.

———. "The Cult of *Theos Hypsistos*." In P. Athanassiadi and M. Frede, *Pagan Monotheism in Late Antiquity*. Oxford, 1999.

Morris, Jan. *Trieste and the Meaning of Nowhere*. London, 2001.

Moores, J. D. *Wrestling with Rationality in Paul*. Cambridge, 1995.

Mortley, Raoul. *From Word to Silence*. Vol. 1: *The Rise and Fall of* Logos. Vol. 2: *The Way of Negation, Christian and Greek*. Bonn, 1986.

Murphy-O'Connor, Jerome. *The Holy Land: An Oxford Archaeological Guide*. 4th ed. Oxford, 1998.

———. *Paul: A Critical Life*. Oxford, 1996.

Murray, Oswyn. *Early Greece*. 2nd ed. London, 1993.

Murray, Oswyn, and Simon Price, eds. *The Greek City from Homer to Alexander*. Oxford 1990.

Newbould, R. F. "Personality Structure and Response to Adversity in Early Christian Hagiography." *Numen* 31 (1984).

*New Catholic Encyclopedia*. Washington, D.C., 1967.

Nussbaum, Martha. *The Fragility of Goodness*. Cambridge, 1986.

———. "Platonic Love and Colorado Love: The Relevance of Ancient Greek Norms to Modern Sexual Controversies." In R. B. Louden and P. Schollmeier, eds., *The Greeks and Us: Essays in Honor of Arthur W. H. Adkins*. Chicago and London, 1999.

———. *The Therapy of Desire: Theory and Practice in Hellenistic Ethics*. Princeton, 1994.

Ober, Josiah. *Political Dissent in Democratic Athens: Intellectual Critics of Popular Rule*. Princeton and Chichester, Eng., 1998.

Osborne, Robin. *Greece in the Making, 1200–479 B.C.* London, 1996.

O'Shea, Stephen. *The Perfect Heresy: Life and Death of the Cathars*. London, 2000.

Pagels, Elaine. *The Gnostic Gospels*. London 1980.

Parker, Robert. *Athenian Religion: A History*. Oxford, 1996.

Partridge, Loren. *The Renaissance in Rome*. London, 1996.

Pearson, B., ed. *The Future of Early Christianity: Essays in Honor of Helmut Koester*. Minneapolis, 1991.

Pelikan, Jaroslav. *Christianity and Classical Culture*. New Haven and London, 1993.

———. *The Christian Tradition*. Vol. 1: *The Emergence of the Catholic Tradition (100–600)*. Chicago and London, 1971.

Pickman, E. M. *The Mind of Latin Christendom*. New York, 1937.

Pohlsander, H. *Constantine the Emperor*. London, 1997.

Popkin, Richard, ed. *The Pimlico History of Western Philosophy*. New York, 1998; London, 1999.

Popper, Karl. *The Open Society and Its Enemies*. 1945; republ. London, 1995.

Porter, J. R. *Jesus Christ: The Jesus of History, the Christ of Faith*. London, 1999.

Porter, Roy. *The Greatest Benefit to Mankind: A Medical History of Humanity from Antiquity to the Present*. London, 1997.

Powell, J. G. F., ed. *Cicero the Philosopher*. Oxford, 1995.

Powell, Mark Allen. *The Jesus Debate*. Oxford, 1999.

Price, Simon. *Religions of the Ancient Greeks*. Cambridge, 1999.

———. *Rituals and Power: The Roman Imperial Cult in Asia Minor*. Cambridge, 1984.

Ranke-Heinemann, Uta. *Eunuchs for the Kingdom of Heaven: Women, Sexuality and the Catholic Church*. Trans. P. Heinegg. New York, 1990.

Rawson, Elizabeth. *Cicero: A Portrait*. London, 1995.

Reinhold, M., and N. Lewis. *Roman Civilization, Sourcebook II: The Empire*. New York, 1995.

Richards, Hubert. *St Paul and His Epistles: A New Introduction*. London, 1979.

Rihill, T. E. *Greek Science*. Oxford, 1999.

Rist, John. *Augustine: Ancient Thought Baptised*. Cambridge, 1994.

———. "Plotinus and Christian Philosophy." In Lloyd P. Gerson, ed., *The Cambridge Companion to Plotinus*. Cambridge, 1996.

Rives, J. *Religion and Authority in Roman Carthage from Augustus to Constantine*. Oxford, 1995.

Robb, Kevin, ed. *Language and Thought in Early Greek Philosophy*. La Salle, Ill., 1983.

Rogerson, John, ed. *The Oxford Illustrated History of the Bible*. Oxford, 2001.

Rorem, Paul. "The Uplifting Spirituality of Pseudo-Dionysius." In Bernard McGinn and John Meyendorff, eds., *Christian Spirituality: Origins to the Twelfth Century*. London, 1986.

Rousseau, Philip. *Ascetics, Authority and the Church in the Age of Jerome and Cassian*. Oxford, 1978.

Ruether, Rosemary. *Faith and Fratricide: The Theological Roots of Anti-Semitism*. New York, 1974.

———. *Gregory of Nazianzus: Rhetor and Philosopher*. Oxford, 1969.

Runciman, W. G. "Doomed to Extinction: The *Polis* as an Evolutionary Dead-End." In Oswyn Murray and Simon Price, eds., *The Greek City from Homer to Alexander*. Oxford, 1990.

Sanders, E. P. *The Historical Figure of Jesus*. Harmondsworth, 1993.

———. *Paul*. Oxford, 1991.

Segal, Alan. "Universalism in Judaism and Christianity." In Troels Engbury-Pedersen, ed., *Paul in His Hellenistic Context*. Edinburgh, 1994.

Shipley, Graham. *The Greek World After Alexander, 323–30 B.C.* London, 2000.

Shotter, David. *The Fall of the Roman Republic*. London and New York, 1994.

Sim, David C. *The Gospel of Matthew and Christian Judaism*. Edinburgh, 1998.

Simmons, M. B. "Julian the Apostate." In P. Esler, ed., *The Early Christian World*, vol. 2. New York and London, 2000.

Simon, Marcus. *Verus Israel*. Oxford, 1986.

Simonetti, M. *Profilo storico dell'esegesi patristica*. Rome, 1980.

Singer, Peter. *Animal Liberation*. 2nd ed. London, 1990.

Siorvanes, Lucas. *Proclus: Neo-Platonic Philosophy and Science*. Edinburgh, 1996.

Smith, R. R. R. *Hellenistic Sculpture*. London, 1991.

Smith, Rowland. *Julian's Gods: Religion and Philosophy in the Thought and Action of Julian the Apostate*. London and New York, 1995.

Sorabji, Richard. *Emotion and Peace of Mind: From Stoic Agitation to Christian Temptation*. Oxford, 2000.

———. "Rationality." In Michael Frede and Gisela Striker, eds., *Rationality in Greek Thought*. Oxford, 1996.

Stark, Rodney. *The Rise of Christianity*. Princeton, 1996.

Stead, Christopher. *Philosophy in Christian Antiquity*. Cambridge, 1994.

———. "Rhetorical Method in Athanasius." *Vigiliae Christianae* 30 (1976): 121–37.

Stegemann, E. W., and W. Stegemann. *The Jesus Movement: A Social History of Its First Century*. Edinburgh, 1999.

Steiner, Deborah. *The Tyrant's Writ*. Princeton, 1993.

Straw, Carole. *Gregory the Great: Perfection in Imperfection*. Berkeley and London, 1988.

Stroumsa, Guy. *Barbarian Philosophy: The Religious Revolution of Early Christianity*. Tubingen, 1999.

Swain, S. *Hellenism and Empire: Language, Classicism and Power in the Greek World, A.D. 50–250*. Oxford, 1996.

Tallis, Raymond. *Enemies of Hope: A Critique of Contemporary Pessimism*. London, 1997.

Tarn, William. *Alexander*. Cambridge, 1948.

Tarnas, Richard. *The Passion of the Western Mind*. London, 1996.

Tarrant, Harold. "Middle Platonism." In Richard Popkin, ed., *The Pimlico History of Western Philosophy*. New York, 1998; London, 1999.

Taylor, Miriam. *Anti-Judaism and Early Christian Identity*. Leiden and New York, 1995.

Thomas, Keith. *Man and the Natural World: Changing Attitudes in England, 1500–1800*. London, 1983.

Thomas, Rosalind. *Herodotus in Context: Ethnography, Science and the Art of Persuasion*. Cambridge, 2000.

Thompson, E. A. *The Visigoths in the Time of Ulfila*. Oxford, 1966.

Tilley, Maureen. "Dilatory Donatists or Procrastinating Catholics: The Trial at the Conference of Carthage." In Everett Ferguson, ed., *Doctrinal Diversity: Varieties of Early Christianity*. New York and London, 1999.

Trout, Dennis. *Paulinus of Nola: Life, Letters and Poems*. Berkeley and London, 1999.

Vaggione, Richard. *Eunomius of Cyzicus and the Nicene Revolution*. Oxford, 2000.

Vermes, G. *The Changing Faces of Jesus*. London, 2000.

Wallace, R., and W. Williams. *The Three Worlds of Paul of Tarsus*. London, 1998.

Wardy, Robert. *The Birth of Rhetoric*. London, 1996.

———. "Rhetoric." In J. Brunschwig and G. E. R. Lloyd, eds., *Greek Thought: A Guide to Classical Knowledge*. Cambridge, Mass., and London, 2000.

Ware, Kallistos. "The Soul in Greek Christianity." In C. Crabbe and M. James, eds., *From Soul to Self*. London, and New York, 1999.

———. "The Way of the Ascetics, Negative or Affirmative?" In V. Wimbush and R. Valantasis, eds., *Asceticism*. New York and Oxford, 1995.

Warner, Marina. *Alone of All Her Sex*. London, 1985.

Weitzmann, K., ed. *Age of Spirituality: A Symposium*. New York, 1980.

West, Martin. "Early Greek Philosophy." In John Boardman, Jasper Griffin and Oswyn Murray, eds., *The Oxford History of the Classical World.* Oxford, 1986.

Wiles, Maurice. *Archetypal Heresy: Arianism Through the Centuries.* Oxford, 1996.

Wilken, R. L. *John Chrysostom and the Jews: Rhetoric and Reality in the Late Fourth Century.* Berkeley and London, 1983.

Williams, Bernard. "Philosophy." In M. J. Finley, ed., *The Legacy of Greece: A New Appraisal.* Oxford, 1984.

Williams, Daniel. *Ambrose of Milan and the End of Nicene–Arian Conflicts.* Oxford, 1995.

Williams, Rowan. "Arianism." In E. Ferguson, ed., *Encyclopaedia of Early Christianity.* Chicago and London, 1990.

———, ed. *The Making of Orthodoxy: Essays in Honour of Henry Chadwick.* Cambridge, 1989.

Williams, Stephen. *Diocletian and the Roman Recovery.* London, 1985.

Wills, Gary. *Saint Augustine.* London and New York, 1999.

Wimbush, V., and R. Valantasis, eds. *Asceticism.* New York and Oxford, 1995.

Wisch, B., ed. *Confraternities and the Visual Arts in Renaissance Italy: Ritual, Spectacle, Image.* Cambridge, 2000.

Witt, R. *Isis in the Greco-Roman World.* London, 1971.

Wolterstorff, Nicholas. "Faith." In *Routledge Encyclopedia of Philosophy.* London and New York, 2000.

Worthington, Ian, ed. *Persuasion: Greek Rhetoric in Action.* London and New York, 1994.

Wood, D., ed. *The Church and the Arts.* Oxford, 1992.

Young, Frances. "A Cloud of Witnesses." In John Hick, ed., *The Myth of God Incarnate,* 2nd ed. London, 1993.

———. *From Nicaea to Chalcedon.* London, 1993.

Zanker, Paul. *The Power of Images in the Age of Augustus.* Ann Arbor, 1988.

# Index

Abu al-Hasan Tabith, 324
Acholius, bishop of Thessalonika, 192
Adeodatus, 279
Adoptionism, 146, 258, 260
Adrianople, battle of, 186
*Adversus Omnes Haereses* (Irenaeus),
   139, 140
*Aeneid* (Virgil), 56
Aeschylus, 345n26
Aetius the Syrian, 315
afterlife, 338, 358n4, 397n49;
   asceticism and, 236; eternal
   damnation in Christian doctrine, 91,
   92, 149; Judaism and, 94, 95;
   Pauline theology and, 118–19;
   Platonism and, 32
*Against the Arians* (Athanasius),
   379n27
*Against the Jews* (John Chrysostom),
   255
Agapetus, bishop of Synnada, 215
Agnes, St., 209
Agricola, 351n13
Alamanni confederation, 80, 81
Albert the Great, 327, 328
Alcmaeon, 343n16
Alexander, bishop of Alexandria, 163,
   166, 170
Alexander (son of Alexander the
   Great), 39
*Alexander* (Tarn), 349n7

Alexander the Great, 20, 36, 37–9, 40,
   41–2, 349n7
allegorical interpretation of scripture,
   147, 198, 288, 369n15, 371n31
*Almagest* (Ptolemy), 67, 327
Ambrose, bishop of Milan, 133, 171,
   177, 188, 195, 196, 197, 201, 213,
   215, 216, 230, 244, 249, 260, 272,
   298, 302, 339, 375n38; Augustine
   and, 218, 280, 281; authority
   exercised over state, 216, 220–6;
   John Chrysostom, comparison with,
   257; life and work, 217–20, 226
Ambrosiaster, 252, 381n45
Ammianus Marcellinus, 183, 186,
   202–3, 213–14, 377n11
Anastasius, 315–16
Anaximander, 12
Anaximenes, 12
Angles, 265, 302, 303
Annas, 58
Anselm of Canterbury, 326
Anthony the ascetic, 117, 142, 237,
   238–9
*Antigone* (Sophocles), 25, 345n26
Antigonids, 39, 52
Antinous, 63–4
Antiochus, 323
Antonine Altar at Ephesus, 65
Antoninus Pius, Emperor, 65
Antony, Mark, 51, 52, 53

## A NOTE ABOUT THE AUTHOR

Charles Freeman is the author of *The Greek Achievement* and *Egypt, Greece, and Rome.* He lives in Suffolk, England.

A NOTE ON THE TYPE

The text of this book was set in Sabon, a typeface designed by Jan Tschichold (1902–1974), the well-known German typographer. Based loosely on the original designs by Claude Garamond (c. 1480–1561), Sabon is unique in that it was explicitly designed for hot-metal composition on both the Monotype and Linotype machines as well as for filmsetting. Designed in 1966 in Frankfurt, Sabon was named for the famous Lyons punch cutter Jacques Sabon, who is thought to have brought some of Garamond's matrices to Frankfurt.

Composed by
North Market Street Graphics
Lancaster, Pennsylvania

Printed and bound by
Berryville Graphics
Berryville, Virginia

Designed by
Soonyoung Kwon